Woman's Body, Woman's Right

Woman's Body, Woman's Right

A Social History of Birth Control in America

Linda Gordon

Grossman Publishers
A Division of The Viking Press   New York   1976

First published in 1976 by Grossman Publishers
625 Madison Avenue, New York, N.Y. 10022
Published simultaneously in Canada by
The Macmillan Company of Canada Limited

Library of Congress Cataloging in Publication Data
Gordon, Linda.
  Woman's body, woman's right.
  Includes bibliographical references and index.
  1.   Birth control—United States—History.
I.   Title.
HQ766.5.U5G67   301.32'1   76-22691
ISBN 0-670-77817-6

ACKNOWLEDGMENT: Baywood Publishing Company, Inc.: "The Politics of Birth
Control, 1920–1940: The Impact of Professionals," Linda Gordon,
International Journal of Health Services, Volume 5, Number 2, 1975.
Copyright Baywood Publishing Company, Inc., 1975.

Acknowledgments

THE INTERPRETATIONS offered in this book depend on virtually everything I have learned about sexual politics. It is difficult for me to know where this book began. While the immediate labor on it is mine, congealed in it, invisible to most readers, is the labor of many others. I can mention only those to whom my debt is quite specific.

Parts of the manuscript were read and criticized by Ros Baxandall, Frank Brodhead, Mari Jo and Paul Buhle, Nancy Chodorow, Michele Clark, Ellen DuBois, Elinor Langer, Charles Rosenberg, Sheila Rowbotham, Kathryn Kish Sklar, Carroll Smith-Rosenberg, Marilyn Webb, and Peter Weiler, and their comments and suggestions were very helpful. Ellen DuBois, Elinor Langer, Martin Legassick, and Rabbi Saul Spiro generously contributed useful source materials. Susan Siens typed a great deal of this manuscript beautifully. My editor, Ellen Posner, and copy-editor, Caroline Lalire, helped me to clarify my thoughts.

The discussions I have had for several years with many feminists enabled me to offer whatever analysis of women's sexual situation I have been able to contribute. Particularly I would like to thank my Bread and Roses women's collective; my students at the University of Massachusetts, Boston; my sisters in the Marxist-Feminist conference group; the Radical America editorial board; the Marxist Institute for a New History; Ros Baxandall, Elizabeth Ewen, Stuart Ewen, Susan Reverby, and Meredith Schwarz. My comrade Allen Hunter read virtually the entire manuscript, demanding clarity, proof, and precision in many places; although I was not always able to meet his demands, their existence as goals greatly improved what I was able to accomplish.

Many years ago I spent a great deal of time with Dr. Lena Levine, and I remember her warmth and intelligence vividly. Had she been alive today, I suspect that my interpretation of her sex-counseling work would have been greatly strengthened through discussion with her.

This book took me years to write, and during that time I was always working full time and participating in various political activities. I could never have done this without the support and confidence I got from many friends, especially Wini Breines, Michele Clark, Margery Davies, Ann Froines, David Hunt, and Allen Hunter. Danny Schechter's solidarity remained with me throughout some very hard times, and I could not have written this without it.

October 1975

For my parents, and
for all our children

Contents

Introduction

THERE has never been a general history of the birth-control movement in the United States. What historical work has been done on it falls into two categories: technological and medical histories of contraception, and profiles of prominent personalities in the birth-control cause. Neither of these approaches has stressed the importance of birth control as a social movement.

This book is intended to fill that void in our knowledge of the history of sex and reproduction, to trace the influence of birth control as a social issue and a social movement. The acceptability of birth control has always depended on a morality that separates sex from reproduction. In the nineteenth century, when the birth-control movement began, such a separation was considered extremely immoral. The eventual widespread public acceptance of birth control required a major reorientation of sexual values. This book tells that story from the point of view of those at the center of the conflict—women seeking sexual and reproductive self-determination.

Woman's Body, Woman's Right surveys this movement in its largest sense—its ideas, its constituency, the motivations and needs of its advocates and its opponents. It is a movement with a continuous history from the mid-nineteenth century, when feminists attacked unwanted pregnancies in the name of sacred female chastity, to the twentieth century, when contraception has been blamed for a breakdown of traditional standards of chastity. It began in the 1870s as a campaign for "voluntary motherhood," a view that disapproved of contraception and proposed long periods of sexual abstinence for married couples as the remedy for unwanted children. It has culminated in a campaign for the legalization of abortion in the 1970s, with contraception supported on a mass scale by governments all around the world. Clearly, such an enormous change both reflects and has nurtured parallel changes in sexual attitudes and practices. This book argues that birth control has always been primarily an issue of politics, not of technology. Effective forms of birth control were used in nearly all ancient societies; in the modern world restrictive sexual standards forced birth control underground. The re-emergence of birth control as a respectable practice in the last century was a process of changing sexual standards, largely produced by women's struggle for freedom.

Since this is both a historical and a political work, it seems necessary to explain several definitions and some of the methods I have used in finding information and in explaining it. As a piece of history, this book rests within two new fields—women's history and the history of sexuality. In comparison with work done in historical fields where there are strong, tested methodologies, a study about women and/or about sex will necessarily be naïve.

The weakness and newness of these fields are related. The lack of adequate history about sexual behavior and attitudes is a result of the inattention to women in history, because sex itself cannot be comprehended except as a facet of the relations between the two sexes. (This is because sex has been primarily, though not exclusively, defined in terms of relations between men and women.) The relations between the sexes cannot, in turn, be analyzed correctly except from an understanding of the subordination of women and their resistance and accommodation to it. Not having incorporated an analysis of this subordination, no historical tradition can yet produce sophisticated work on human sexual behavior.

It seemed to me, thinking that we must start somewhere, that a major factor in the development of women's sexuality was birth control. My premise was that birth control represented the single most important factor in the material basis of women's emancipation in the course of the last century—that contraception promised the final elimination of women's only significant biological disadvantage. (The capacity to reproduce is not a disadvantage, but lack of control over it is.) So I began to study birth control, and rather quickly had to question my original premise. It is true that the technology of contraception provided women with a valuable tool, but why did the technology develop when it did? And why did some women seize upon it more eagerly than others? I discovered that there is a complex, mutual, causal relationship between birth control and women's overall power. Birth control was as much a symptom as a cause of larger social changes in the relations between sexes.

My mistake in seeing birth control as only causal was characteristic both of my academic training and of the early phases of women's liberation analysis. Although always sympathetic to the people on the bottom, wanting to see history from below, I had been accustomed to view the fate of the poor as determined by the power of the rich. The working class, for example, appeared solely as the creation of the capitalist class. So in our frustration at our women's roles, many feminists of my generation at first saw ourselves as the victims of male supremacy, battling an ideology of femininity created by men for their benefit. The complexities of the birth-control question were merely one illustration of the inadequacy of that whole approach. The suppression of birth control in class society was partly a means of enforcing male supremacy but partly, too, a self-protection for women, a means of enforcing men's responsibility for their sexual behavior. Indeed, all the cultural aspects of womanhood were created and re-created jointly, though not usually amicably, by men and their female subjects, resisting and accommodating to their subjection. Even while unable to overthrow their rulers, women could and did change the terms of their labor and limit the privileges of their masters. In no area of life have women ever accepted unchallenged the terms of service offered by men. Sexuality and reproduction were no exception. The major institutions of sex and reproduction, such as the family and codes of morality, were established as much by women's struggle to protect themselves as by men's struggle to protect their property.

Both the suppression and then the legalization of birth control were developments in the struggle between the sexes and the changing economic organization of society. Since I could not describe these processes by looking at birth control alone, I had to broaden this book and make it more complex. It is about birth control, sexuality, and women. But it is about women as subjects, women trying to create the conditions of their lives in their own interest. So the book is about a social movement: birth control, sexuality, and *feminism.*

There is a definitional problem in the word "feminism," since it originally referred to a specific tendency and period within the women's rights movement.* I have had to use it more generally, however, since there is no all-encompassing word to describe women's struggles. The definition of "feminist" in this book is: sharing in an impulse to increase the power and autonomy of women in their families, communities and/or society.

There is also a definitional problem about the phrase "birth control." † By birth control I mean efforts to increase individual

---

* "Feminism" was originally a French word describing what in the United States in the nineteenth century was called the woman movement: a collection of groups and single-issue political campaigns all aimed at, to use nineteenth-century language again, "advancing" the position of woman. When the word "feminist" first appeared in the United States in the early twentieth century, it referred to a particular strain of thought among women's rights advocates, one that asserted the uniqueness of women, the special joys and even mystical experience of motherhood, as opposed to another strain that tended to emphasize the basic similarity between women and men. Today the word has been stretched to refer to any advocate of increased rights for women. More specific definitions are not broad enough to include the varied "feminist" points of view and their historical changes. For example, most nineteenth-century women's rights advocates did not endorse sexual equality or the abolition of all legal distinctions between the sexes. It is significant that the nineteenth-century movement did not feel the need for an "ism" word to describe their common ideology. Their phrase, the "woman movement," correctly expressed the multiplicity of groups whose participants, including men, nevertheless perceived themselves as part of a fundamentally coherent movement. But "woman movement" offers us no convenient adjective. I use the term "feminist," therefore, in a deliberately ahistorical manner, referring to the whole range of views contained in the movement for the advancement of women.
† Modern uses of the phrase "birth control" reflect contemporary political conflict. Birth control has often come to poor, working-class, minority and Third World people, in the United States and abroad, in the form of prescriptive, even coercive, programs urging birth-rate reduction. (See Chapter 13.) Class-conscious people have seen in these programs attempts to weaken the oppressed, to pacify their discontent without requiring fundamental changes in the distribution of wealth and power and the organization of production. Such programs are properly called population control, and historically they have had a distinct, separate history from that of birth control. Once called neo-Malthusianism, its chief strategic principle is that population growth tends to prevent economic development. Politically, population control has almost nothing in

control over reproduction. Wanting to focus on birth control as a struggle for self-determination by women, I found I had to trace briefly the influence of population control—which was a separate movement—on the modern birth-control struggle.

Still another tricky question is identifying at what point the use and advocacy of birth control became a social movement. The fact that its advocates at times had no other purpose than controlling their own childbearing did not prevent them, in my understanding, from creating a movement. Workers often strike "only" for higher wages yet form a social movement when they struggle collectively. It was the collectivity of birth-control advocacy, not an ideological consciousness, that transformed it into a movement. When the women who argued for birth control developed an ideology, it was an analysis of needs and motives that had already created a movement. It was an articulation of what was already objectively present in their actions.

The birth-control movement passed through three distinct stages. Each stage was identified with a different term for reproductive control. The first was "voluntary motherhood," a slogan advanced by feminists in the second half of the nineteenth century. It expressed very exactly the emphasis on choice, freedom, and autonomy for women around which the "woman movement" was unified. Voluntary motherhood was a basic plank in the feminist platform, much more universally endorsed than woman suffrage and reaching further to describe and change the total plight of women than any other single issue. Stage two, approximately 1910–1920, produced the term "birth control." It represented not only a new concept but a new organizational phase, with separate birth-control leagues created mainly by feminists in the large socialist movement. It stood not only for women's autonomy but for a revolutionizing of the society and the empowering of the powerless—the working class and the female sex primarily.

---

common with birth control. The former applies norms of ideal family size without respect for cultural, social, or political self-determination. The latter has been precisely a campaign for self-determination. The fact that both rely on contraception as a tool, although population controllers tend to favor sterilization as well, has led to an understandable popular association of the two. But the main reason for their association has been the capitulation of the birth-control organizations to population-control theory and objectives (a phenomenon we shall examine in the last chapters of this book), with the result that in popular usage in the last few decades "population control" and "birth control" have been virtually synonymous. One of the contributions I hope this book can make is to separate the two concepts as two political struggles.

(Unfortunately, although "birth control" was originally associated with this specific, radical movement, it has since become the accepted generic term for reproductive control, so that I have no choice but to use it in both senses in this book.) From 1920 on, the movement evolved away from the radicalism of its second stage into a liberal reform movement. This stage three finally produced a new slogan, "planned parenthood," in the 1940s, though the new content had been developed in the 1930s.

From one perspective, these three stages were part of a continuous process away from a solely woman-centered, feminist use of birth control. From another point of view, however, the three stages delineated the rise and fall of a broad social analysis of the contribution that reproductive self-determination could make to over-all human liberation. The second phase included men among the beneficiaries of birth control because it was concerned with the over-all power structure in the society. Birth controllers of the 1910–1920 period considered men as well as women damaged by the subjection of women, and especially lamented the weakening of the whole working class by the inequalities within it. They wished to use birth control not just to help women win equality with the men of their own class, but to strengthen the whole working class for the struggle to democratize the whole society. Planned parenthood, in the 1940s, had shed not only a feminist orientation but also eschewed any organizational interest in restructuring power in the society.

In each of these three stages the birth-control movement expressed the interests of different classes of women. Class analysis of feminism has been obscured by a number of factors: the long-dominant consensus among historians that there were no distinct classes in the United States; the tendency to apply the term "middle class" to everyone neither a factory operative nor a capitalist; and the resulting meaningless commonplace that feminism was a middle-class movement. The class structure of the United States has been transformed radically and rapidly in the period covered by this book, so that the categories we must use are both complex and dynamic. Generally the voluntary-motherhood advocates of the nineteenth century came from independent farm, artisanal, commercial, and professional families, who clung to a preindustrial, largely rural vision of economic independence, cultural and religious unity in a "Wasp" mold, and strong family units. The birth-control movement of the second decade of the twentieth century expressed the interests of a growing working class, largely immigrants, who recognized the evaporation of America's promise of upward mobility. Working-class women in particular faced the loss of control over children and housework and living style itself, whether in the hideous slums of the industrial cities or the more isolated poverty of smaller towns. A unified socialist movement brought them together with educated radicals and professional organizers, and the participation of women workers in massive strikes gave them models of militancy and confidence. Planned parenthood, in the 1940s, by contrast, represented the interests of the professional and managerial classes whose social and cultural values influenced largely the upper strata of the working class, effectively setting models for the urban and suburban majority of the country. In all these descriptions we must bear in mind that the economic roles of women in capitalist society cannot always be fitted into class categories based on men's work. Working-class and middle-class housewives often do the same work and have the same relationship to production; working-class clerical workers share many experiences with lower professionals—such as school teachers, librarians, and social workers—often categorized as middle class. If birth-control demands appear to cross class lines, or not to represent the wives of industrial workers, we must not simply deny the class content of the movement or brand it as middle-class; we must continue to reshape our categories until they correctly describe reality.

As I write, in 1975, further changes in class and sex relations have produced a revived feminist movement, and it has produced a fourth stage in the birth-control movement. It is hard for me to write about this new movement because I am part of it. This revived women's movement has already won important victories for birth control—better sex-education materials, legal abortion—and it has placed birth control in the context of attacks on rape, demands for equal pay and equal work, criticisms of sexist education, and many other campaigns that chip away at male privilege and capitalism's exploitation of women and sexual division of the working class. Because it has been placed in this context birth control has again become a political issue.

These achievements are flawed and partial. The women's movement is divided; its range is from revolutionaries to Republicans. Its influential sectors are dominated by professional-class white women, and their program largely ignores the predicament of most working-class and poor women, whose problems require structural change in the society. Smaller groups struggle to demonstrate that women's liberation, as opposed to women's equality with the men of their own class, requires the abolition of class society.

Still, this divided, clumsy, contradictory, often pernicious mass women's movement made me write this book. I wrote this book, in fact, to argue for my own view of the direction that feminism should take, and my understanding of its history underscores my certainty that I am right. The poses of neutrality or relativism are available only to those who already have power; few women can afford them. I hope to have written something that will be useful to those who are grappling with the political problems of creating a liberated human sexuality.

Woman's Body, Woman's Right

Part I
The Politics of Reproduction

1

The Prohibition on Birth Control

ALTHOUGH BIRTH CONTROL is very old, the birth-control movement is young, with less than two centuries behind it. In the nineteenth century, when the movement began, birth control had become immoral and illegal with legal dangers so great that propaganda on the subject was written and distributed anonymously. Birth-control advocates were sentenced to jail terms for violation of obscenity laws. A campaign for freedom of speech and freedom of the press, therefore, became part of the modern birth-control movement. To understand these struggles we must first understand something about the nature and sources of the censoring ideology.

Birth control has always been socially regulated in some way. This is because birth control has consequences for two social issues crucial to overall societal development: sexual activity and population size. Birth control bears, too, on a third social phenomenon: the role of women. Women's status cannot be correlated on a one-to-one basis with any particular system of sexual regulation. But if the connections between social patterns of sexual activity and female activity are complex, they are nonetheless close. Systems of sexual control change as women's status changes; they both reflect and affect each other. There has been an especially strong causal connection between the subjection of women and the prohibition on birth control: the latter has been a means of enforcing the former. The prohibition on birth control can be traced not only back into history but into prehistory as well—that is, into an era before the existence of written records that could provide evidence about birth-control use and legality.*

Birth control itself was generally not controversial in preagricultural and nomadic societies. But the question of who controlled birth-control technology has always been at issue. Biologically, it would be "natural" for women to control reproduction. But once men discovered their role in conception, they assumed control by exercising their general control over when, how often, and with whom women could have sexual intercourse. Men's control over sexual activity was well established in most preagricultural societies. In many cases men extended their control over population beyond sexual regulation to regulation of infanticide and abortion.

The development of agriculture produced an important change in the optimum population size. A sedentary life ended the burden of carrying children during travels, and the capacity of agriculture to absorb labor made large families an asset. Especially among the poor, children usually contributed more to the family economy than they cost. The economic utility of large families, in combination with continuing high infant-mortality rates, made birth control by individuals an economic threat to the family and community. Thus agricultural societies produced the first ideologies that entirely banned birth control.

The prohibition on birth control required constant reinforcement because some women have always wished to limit and space their pregnancies, a motive at times overwhelming their understanding of

---

* The study of prehistory is difficult, for anthropological evidence tells us about simple societies only as they persist in the modern world, all of them affected by modern influences. The anthropological evidence can be used to support only surmises, therefore, about what actually happened in ancient times. The discussion that follows of the origins of the prohibition on birth control is not a history but a schematic hypothesis. It does not purport to describe what actually happened but offers a theoretical model of the way it might have happened. It seems a reasonable hypothesis because it can explain the historical developments that followed.

the need for large families. Legal prohibitions and sanctions could suppress birth-control propaganda but could not stop birth-control use. Private practices could more effectively be altered by convincing the individuals themselves that birth control was immoral, and in this task religious ideologies played the major role. The religious tradition dominant in the United States has been the Judeo-Christian tradition, and is thus our focus here.

The ancient Jews had a somewhat mixed attitude toward birth control, which reflected, no doubt, their nomadic origins. One method—*coitus interruptus,* or withdrawal—was condemned by the Talmud on the basis of a passage from Genesis:

> And Er, Judah's first-born, was wicked in the sight of the Lord; and the Lord slew him. And Judah said unto Onan: "Go in unto thy brother's wife, and perform the duty of a husband's brother unto her, and raise up seed to thy brother!" And Onan knew that the seed would not be his; and it came to pass, whenever he went in unto his brother's wife, that he used to spill it on the ground, lest he should give seed to his brother. And the thing which he did was evil in the sight of the Lord; and He slew him also.[1] *

From the sin of Onan came the word "onanism," later applied by Christian theologians to both masturbation and all nonprocreative intercourse. The Talmudic tradition, however, interpreted it much more narrowly. Some scholars argue for a literal reading of the passage, in which Onan's crime consists specifically in refusing to perform the required levirate marriage† and impregnate his brother's wife. Most Talmudists hold that the passage forbade any form of "unnatural intercourse," their descriptions of that process mostly referring to ejaculation outside the vagina.[2] Contraception that did not interfere with "correct" heterosexual intercourse was, however, permitted in some cases in ancient Jewish law, and the Talmud itself prescribed two methods—a potion called the Cup of Roots‡ and a vaginal sponge.[3] Drinking the Cup of Roots was permitted to women and forbidden to men, because the responsibility for propagation was laid on men but not on women.[4] Thus ironically, in male supremacist

---

* Reference notes begin on page 419.
† Custom by which the brother or next of kin to a deceased man was bound to marry the widow.
‡ According to the Talmud, the Cup of Roots was made of Alexandrian gum, liquid alum, and garden crocus, pulverized together.

law, women because of their very insignificance became free to practice birth control.

The permissibility of contraception in ancient Jewish law is part of a relatively relaxed attitude toward sexuality. For the ancient Jews, sexual abstinence was never a virtue. Marriage was not a necessary evil, but a *mitzvah*, a religious duty; and within marriage the husband had the duty not only to procreate but also to give his wife sexual satisfaction. At times when conception would be either impossible (as with a sterile woman) or dangerous, the Jewish husband nevertheless had the obligation to continue having sexual relations with his wife.[5] Indeed, the Talmud is somewhat egalitarian on sexual matters, treating men and women as having equal sexual needs, in contrast to its male-supremacist assumptions in most other areas. This may be connected to the fact that population expansion was neither a religious priority nor an economic necessity for the ancient Jews, since the sexual suppression of women had been partly a means of enforcing frequent motherhood upon them.

In contrast to the Jews, the Christians gradually evolved a total condemnation of birth control, a condemnation integral to the over-all Catholic attitude toward sexuality and women. The general hostility to women, sex, and birth control did not appear immediately, however. The Christianity of Jesus, in terms of the status of women in his historical period, was, to a revolutionary extent, pro-woman. Never before had a religion argued the universal equality of human beings. Jesus' respectful behavior toward women was often astonishing to contemporary observers. Even the notorious antiwoman declarations of the Pauline tradition ("Let a woman learn in silence with all submissiveness. I permit no woman to teach . . .", "and Adam was not deceived, but the woman was deceived . . . ," and so forth) are much worse as they have been used, out of context, by misogynistic churchmen; Paul himself was preoccupied with order and the good image of his new religion, and his pronouncements against women were conventional at worst.[6]

The early Christians developed an ascetic ideal that rejected sexual pleasure as the most evil of many evil pleasures, but at first it was not exclusively directed at the suppression of women. The Christian ascetics sought righteousness through mortifying themselves, not

women. St. Paul's ideal was celibacy. When this was impracticable—
"It is better to marry than to burn," * after all—there was no
condemnation of sexual enjoyment within marriage.

> Let the husband render to his wife what is due her, and likewise the
> wife to her husband. . . . You must not refuse each other, except
> perhaps by consent, for a time, that you may give yourselves to
> prayer, and return together again lest Satan tempt you because you
> lack self-control. But this I say by way of concession, not command-
> ment.[7]

The Church Fathers developed these antisexual attitudes in new
directions. In the first place, they had to be concerned with reproduction and with increasing the number of Christians. Paul had been able
to recommend celibacy freely, since he expected the second coming
imminently; Augustine, four centuries later, was more skeptical about
the Messiah's imminent arrival and wanted to strengthen his religion.
He distinguished for the first time in the Christian tradition between
lust and procreation in order to condemn the former entirely, for
married and unmarried people alike. Sexual intercourse, according to
Augustinian thought, was inherently evil and could be justified only if
procreation was its intent. The sexual drive itself was evil, laid as a
burden upon man as a result of the Fall. Augustine's image of hell was
"the burning of lust." [8] The pleasure of sex created a constant temptation to indulge in it for the wrong reasons. Best, perhaps, would have
been to try to make the necessary procreative intercourse as pleasureless as possible. Couples that used an "evil appliance" to prevent
propagation were not worthy of the name man and wife, were no
longer covered by the license of matrimony, so to speak; they were in
mortal sin. Augustine specifically condemned the "rhythm method" to
avoid conception.[9]

In the thirteenth century Thomas Aquinas dogmatized and cod-
ified the idea that even within marriage sexual intercourse was
justifiable only for procreation. Every act of intercourse was a sin
unless performed with a reproductive intent.[10] That point of view was
reaffirmed by Pope Pius XI in 1930 in the encyclical *Casti connubii:* the
goods of marriage, it said, are offspring, fidelity, and sacrament, and
offspring is the primary one.[11]

* That is, to burn with passion.

With the decline of Christian asceticism, the aspect of sexual repression that was directed against women became dominant. The chaste ideal was not imposed equally on men and women. In Christian society chastity became the ideal for all women, not freely chosen as a form of dedication to God, as in monasticism, but imposed on women by their masters. The ideal of human equality was systematically distorted to exclude women. The Christians, soon after Jesus' death, claimed the Jewish tradition of excluding women entirely from the religious community. The Council of Carthage in 391 prohibited women from taking the catechism, being baptized, or studying.[12] The medieval Church castrated boys to create eunuchs for its choirs rather than use women. As late as the fifteenth century English law made it illegal for women to read the New Testament.[13]

The exclusion of women reflected, of course, the patriarchal social structure of the whole society. Religiously it had roots even in the early asceticism and ancient myths of women's impurity. Clement wrote: "Above all, it seems right that we turn away from the sight of women." He believed it was shameful for women to contemplate their own nature.[14] This shamefulness lay, of course, in women's unruly sexuality, a tradition that began in the Old Testament. It suppressed the powerful pagan heroines, and the convention of Roman law that men, as the seducers of women, were responsible for sexual crimes.[15] Beginning with Genesis, most crimes were blamed on women. Female sexuality was an irresistible force, never constructive, the source of tremendous human evil and suffering. (The good women in the Bible are always chaste.*) Eve, Delilah, Bathsheba, Salome, Lilith, Naamah: their dangerousness was heightened because they could not act as independent aggressors, but exerted their will through manipulation of men.[16] The power of these women is mythically expressed as the power of emasculation.

Christian hostility to sex expresses a fear that sex is weakening for men. (The Victorians attributed this weakening directly to the loss of semen.) Christianity extended this fear of women's sexual drives to her whole being. "Do you not know," wrote Tertullian, "that each one of

---

* Judith is one of several exceptions in the Old Testament; there are none in the New Testament.

you is an Eve? The sentence of God on this sex of yours lives in this age, the guilt must of necessity live too. You are the devil's gateway; you are the unsealer of the forbidden tree; you are the first deserter of the divine law; you are she who persuaded him whom the devil was not valiant enough to attack. You destroyed so easily God's image, man. On account of your desert, that is, death, even the Son of God had to die." Tertullian would have liked women to wear perpetual mourning.[17]

Such ideology was a weapon of war. Its purpose was to suppress women's resistance and discontent by instilling in them an immobilizing guilt and self-hatred, and by justifying men's enjoyment of their privileges. The fact that a positive counterimage of woman, Mary, was created by the Christians does not weaken the negative tradition. The coexistence of opposites is commonplace in ideologies about women. The only effective counterimage would have been a realistic woman, with both strengths and weaknesses, virtues and faults, someone both sexual and good. There is no woman like this in the Bible, though there are many such men. In describing the ideal woman, Mary, the Gospels made her physiologically impossible: what is good about Mary is that she is a virgin mother. Since no other woman can be a virgin mother, she represents an attack on, a criticism of woman's very nature.

The sex hatred of Christianity was identical with its woman hatred.[18] The unity of these two ideologies created a very powerful weapon indeed, and the widespread and deep guilt nourished by them is still a living problem. In terms of the whole Christian and patriarchal system, however, this ideological complex presented a contradiction. The condemnation of women was so total, and it offered them so little promise of redemption, that it ran the risk of driving women out of the Church altogether. The resolution is central to the birth-control question: redemption through motherhood. Completing the identifying of women and sex, Augustine made procreation the only justification for women's existence, just as it alone justified sexual intercourse for men.[19] Aquinas, who found it puzzling that women had been created at all, also found their value in procreation alone.[20] Thus the connection between sex hatred and woman hatred led to a lasting Christian emphasis on motherhood as woman's destiny. The worship of Mary strengthened this emphasis; Mary was not an antidote to, but a part of, Christian misogyny.

In many different cultures ideologies about motherhood are central to the justification of patriarchy. Taken most literally, the enforcement of chastity upon mothers is a mechanism to ensure that property remains within the paternal family. Ideologies of motherhood in fact defend fatherhood. But the property-regulation aspects of the motherhood ideology are only one of its functions; it also provides a justification for the entire sexual division of labor and thus for the whole male-supremacist system. In order to examine these functions we must define the concept of an "ideology" of motherhood.

Motherhood has three components—a biological one, describing pregnancy, childbirth, and suckling; a social one, describing child-raising; and an ideological one. The first two have been associated, often merged, in most societies. No doubt because of their original biological closeness to infants, women as a sex became socially and legally required to assume the ultimate responsibility for child-raising. Male supremacy gradually transformed that responsibility into the basis for a systematic division of labor that assigned to women the least prestigious work, most of it without any biological reason to be women's work (such as cooking, housework, service work, and so forth). Male-supremacist culture further institutionalized women's mothering through an ideology which branded the separation of childbearing from child-raising as immoral (or, more recently, psychologically harmful). The ideology made the biological processes of motherhood symbolic, so that lactation, for example, came to stand for a cultural and intellectual suckling of men as well as children. Women were the universal nourishers, givers of milk, love, and the rules of the society to a new generation. The socially defined requirements of femininity came to include the motherly characteristics—softness, self-effacement, passivity, sensitivity, and so forth—and to preclude the fatherly ones—power, assertiveness, freedom, activity, and so forth. Because these images were internalized by women (necessarily, for their own protection), they provided a disguise for the fact that the sexual division of labor is not a different-but-equal arrangement but rank discrimination. That is, the ideology implies that men cannot do child-raising, that women must mother in order to realize themselves, and that the qualities of this feminine motherliness are the essential qualities of all women, defining their possibilities and limits in social, economic, and political spheres.

This ideology was helpful in enforcing upon women a societal need for large families and a moral prohibition on birth control. Although individual women did use birth control despite this powerful prohibition, there was never an organized challenge to the ideology of motherhood until industrialization created a new economic system that did not require a high birth rate.

Several factors have made a lower birth rate economically advantageous in the more developed parts of the world in the last five centuries. They include improved diet and sanitation and thus a decline in the death rate, particularly the infant-mortality rate. Even before medical progress, however, mainly a nineteenth- and twentieth-century phenomenon, social changes made smaller families more desirable. A money economy, high costs of living for city dwellers, and the decreasing relative economic contribution that children could make reversed the traditional family economy and made children cost more than they could contribute. Some social groups were affected by these changes before others, perhaps the earliest being professionals who had to live on salaries (in contrast to those who lived on the land, which could absorb children's labor power) and to cope with the high cost of education if their children were to inherit their status.[21] Gradually urbanization produced a decline in the birth rate among all classes.

Nevertheless, the small-family standard did not immediately destroy the prohibition on birth control. This is because sexual repression and specifically the ideology of motherhood and the sexual suppression of women, though originally produced perhaps by the necessity for a high birth rate, had gained other important social functions. Like many forms of repression they were overdetermined—that is, they had several social functions each of which alone might be enough to support them. Their gradual weakening was in turn caused not only by the decline of the high-birth-rate necessity but also by other social changes that altered the nature of sexual control.

Changes in ideology about sex and womanhood proceeded gradually and at an uneven pace in different geographical areas and economic circumstances; in the Christian world capitalist development produced three stages in this ideology before the birth-control movement itself began. The first was in the Renaissance, among the newly monied aristocracy and bourgeoisie. The second, far more widespread and influential, was the cultural part of a class struggle against the aristocracy led by the commercial capitalist class throughout the sixteenth and seventeenth centuries; its attitudes about sex and women were expressed most clearly in the ideology of Protestantism, especially the most anti-Catholic sects such as Calvinist, Puritan, and Quaker. The third was a predominantly secular ideology, associated with the bourgeois class in its political ascendancy, beginning in the late eighteenth century but taking the name it is best known by from Queen Victoria. Though we can offer only the sketchiest characterizations of these three stages, characterizations which will inevitably filter out much of the complexity of the process of change, it is important to identify them. In understanding the birth-control movement we must understand the *particular* stage of sexual repressiveness that it struggled against—Victorian prudery, marked both by its uniqueness and by its heritage from earlier forms of sexual repression.

The commercial expansion of the Renaissance and the development of a money economy in the cities of Italy produced an individualist culture which could not accommodate the medieval Catholic world view of static social and economic relations. Striving to achieve ever higher status, men of wealth turned to pagan culture for a more individualist and hedonist evaluation of learning and pleasure. As the historian of the Renaissance Alfred von Martin wrote, "In times which were breaking away from the concept of the community, . . . love itself was bound to become an 'autonomous,' 'liberal art,' a law unto itself and its own fulfilment. . . ." [22] In the pursuit of love as pleasure the beauty of women became more important; indeed beauty was acclaimed as righteous in contrast to its identification with the devil in medieval ideology.[23] Such new cultural values supported the development of a new kind of prostitute—courtesans of wealth, status, sophistication, and often education. Increased social mobility made sexual consumption function as a status symbol more than had been the case in medieval Europe. As capitalist princes and soldiers saw effort and skill leading them to power, so they measured sexual "success" in terms of effort and skill. It is in Renaissance literature that a "quantitative" attitude toward sexuality first appears, measuring both masculine and feminine potency by how long, how many times, and with how many different partners. The value of wives, in status and in labor power, was not, however, significantly changed by the commercial capitalism of the Renaissance. Thus even among the newly wealthy the power relations within the family were not visibly altered.[24]

Greater public approval of birth control during the Renaissance was produced not by a smaller family ideal but by a higher valuation of extramarital sex. For this very reason the impact of the Renaissance in changing sexual values was probably confined to men of wealth and power. But since that group produced a significant literature about its new values, there is some evidence already (and undoubtedly much more to be found) about birth-control use. Pierre de Brantôme (1540–1614), a French courtier, chronicler, and abbé, in describing the sexual promiscuity of court life, wrote: "There are some who have no desire to receive the seed, like the noble lady who said to her lover, 'Do what you will, and give me delight, but on your life have a care to let no drop reach me.' Then the other must watch out for the right moment." [25] What is new in such expressions is not technique—withdrawal is as old as sexual intercourse itself, no doubt—but the proudly hedonistic attitude behind it. There were also new technological developments, however, as the rediscovery of pagan medical technology brought Arab and Persian contraceptive recipes to the attention of the educated.

During the Renaissance the men of new wealth—the bourgeoisie —tried to assimilate and even directly emulate the style of the aristocracy in the consumption of luxury goods and sexual pleasure. But as capitalists consolidated their economic dominance, most of them ceased imitating the nobility in favor of establishing new social standards more useful to their economic and political enterprises. These new social standards flowed from the need to develop and reinforce an individual character structure compatible with the new patterns of work and achievement possible under capitalism. Success in business came from willingness to take risks and to accept relative deprivation in the present in return for the hopes of long-range profits.

The work of capitalist commerce and industry required discipline, the ability to resist temptations for immediate gratification, a mentality that valued saving and reinvestment, and competitiveness. Bourgeois culture honored the personalities that exemplified these so-called virtues.

These changes were far more profound than those of the Renaissance, for they were produced by an economic revolution that affected nearly the whole Western world and were carried within a mass ideological revolution—the Reformation. Through it new sexual values reached even the artisans and peasants not yet directly influenced by the capitalist mode of production. New Protestant religions supported the new values even among those who did not desert the Catholic Church, by breaking up the hegemony of certain Catholic traditions uncomfortable for capitalism, such as the ban on usury, the hierarchical integration of the Church with the aristocracy, and the monastic ideal. By abolishing confession and making the individual directly responsible to God, Protestantism helped create a new human character structure in which morality and sin were internalized values, enforced by the individual upon himself, a character structure capable of self-denial without external compulsion.

This self-denying character structure was necessitated by the nature of the early development of capitalism. Originating in commerce, the accumulation of surplus sufficient for profitable reinvestment in capital-intensive projects (requiring, for example, the purchase of ships, raw materials, slaves, and free-labor power) demanded milking every possible cent of profit out of sales and denying consumptive expenditure. Such self-denying behavior soon became the norm of conduct for the early capitalists, who dressed plainly, lived modestly, and identified their hatred of ostentatious expenditure with their hatred of the old ruling class, the aristocracy. This new kind of self-denial, religiously best expressed in Calvinism, had nothing otherworldly about it. The doctrine of the "elect" suggested that the righteous might win their reward on this earth, in the form of material success. The postponement of gratification was aimed not at guaranteeing a better lot in the next world but at the promise of even greater rewards in this world.[26]

Among the gratifications that required postponement in capitalist culture, sex was one of the foremost; and for this reason the capitalist-Protestant cultural revolution of the seventeenth century produced a reorientation in attitudes toward birth control. Sexuality was threatening to the capitalist character structure. The spokesmen for this cultural revolution thought sex represented a spending of energy, potentially to the point of exhaustion, which at best withdrew from the store of energy needed for constant alertness to business opportunity; more perniciously it represented, they felt, a mood of playfulness inimical to the vigilant, individualistic, and competitive attitude required by capitalist commerce and industry. But far from endorsing celibacy as the ideal and marriage as the compromise—as the Catholic ascetic tradition had done—early capitalist sexual morality idealized marriage and the family as the very model of righteousness. The common use of the word "Puritanism" to connote prudery is incorrect. The Puritans were rather frank and accepting of sex in its place; its place, however, was strictly limited to marriage; and when sexual activity threatened to disrupt stable families, it was suppressed. Luther regarded bachelorhood as unnatural; not only marriage but sexual satisfaction was a positive good. Woman's calling was to become a wife, and thereby to bear children and satisfy man's sexual desire.[27]

If the confinement of sexuality within the family was more stringent during these early stages of capitalism, it was because the family was economically and socially more important than ever. As long as private property has existed, sex and reproduction have been controlled so as to regularize inheritance procedures. But in agricultural society, the family was less isolated from the larger community than it became under conditions of commerce and industry. For some time, historians accepted the generalization that in preindustrial Europe and America, the extended family was the dominant form—that is, that married children continued to live in the homes of one of their parental families, thus bringing children, grandchildren, cousins, aunts, and uncles under one roof. More recent empirical studies suggest that the nuclear family—only mother, father, and children under one roof—dominated even in many peasant communities. To measure family closeness only in terms of who lives under one roof is misleading; relationships of visiting, borrowing, sharing work, and giving emotional and financial support did not depend on living in one house. What changed most in family structure under the impact of capitalism was its relationship to the larger community. The increased division of labor within the whole society isolated families from one another and isolated individuals within families. Among members of the capitalist class and those below it trying to join it, competition undermined the capacity for deep loyalties to individuals outside the immediate family. The family was no longer merely the unit of earning a living, but also became, for the upwardly mobile, a means of accumulation of a surplus taken from other families. Family life became simultaneously the source of socialization into competitive habits and an escape from the exhaustion and unfriendliness of a competitive society.

This interpretation of the meaning of Puritan sexual regulation is supported by Puritan attitudes toward birth control, which were more relaxed than those of the Catholic tradition. Whereas Luther held to an absolute opposition to birth control,[28] Calvin placed less emphasis on the childbearing duty of women than Luther had and taught that procreation was not the primary purpose of marriage.[29] The later Protestant tradition did not include the constant attacks on these "unnatural practices" found in the Catholic Church. The reasons for the lack of vigilance against birth control are double: first, this was the period in which some communities of people developed, for the first time, an economic interest in smaller families; and second, the potential of birth control to promote sexual license was checked by more rigid enforcement of sexual chastity itself.

The process of industrialization that began in the eighteenth century set in motion several other social changes that ultimately weakened the Puritan family and sexual norm. Their immediate effect, however, was not to loosen the bonds on women and on human sexual expression but to secularize them and to apply them much more tightly to women than to men. The new cultural form of sexual repression is often called Victorian prudery, and it was the form of sexual repression that the birth-control campaigners had to contend with.

The emergence of Victorian prudery seems to be correlated with the end of the era of primitive accumulation and the beginning of industrial capitalism. Under industrial conditions, the leading capitalists no longer had to scrimp and save in order to produce a surplus for reinvestment. Indeed, the life style of the powerful bourgeoisie of the late-eighteenth and nineteenth centuries was no longer severe and modest, but often luxurious and conspicuously consuming. At the same time industrial capitalists faced a new problem, that of acquiring and holding a wage-labor force, for their enormous new wealth depended on the expansion of production. The demands for sacrifice of health, leisure, and above all autonomy made of early industrial workers were so great that traditional external forms of compulsion were inadequate to the task. Severe economic sanctions—even the imminent threat of starvation—were not always enough to bring artisans and peasants into what they saw as wage slavery, stripping them of their skills and self-direction. Convincing them to sell their labor power, to surrender control over it, required a major alteration of character structure. Nor were the new values appropriate to wage labor imposed simply by capitalists and absorbed by workers: often working-class people themselves, grasping the inevitable defeat of precapitalist modes of production, developed their own versions of internalized work discipline, using them to advance class solidarity and resistance to the speedup of the rate of exploitation.[30] Thus Victorian prudery had a complexity that represented its complex social function: a norm set by the bourgeoisie for itself, a discipline imposed on the labor force, and the working class's own adaptation to new conditions of production.

Yet to stop here would be an oversimplification. As prudery was a product of the class struggle, so it was also produced by the struggle between the sexes. Industrial production had begun profound changes in family structure. In agricultural and even commercial capitalist society, family enterprise had remained the unit of the entire economy. Whole families worked together under the authority of the husband/father; children, apprentices, servants, and wife were all assistants, differing in skill, experience, and authority, but all focusing their attention on the same problems. The economic unity of the family under its head represented to preindustrial people the natural microcosm of the political and economic organization of the whole society. Women were seen as inferior to men but not utterly different from them and not functioning in a different sphere.

As industrial production drew men out of their homes to social-ized workplaces, the economic basis of family unity began to dissolve. In most working-class families, husbands and wives were separated for the greater part of their lives, so their attention was focused on rather different problems and they developed different skills and found different comrades. When women worked in factories, their jobs were almost always sexually segregated. All adult workers became individ-ual employees, each with her or his separate wages. Wives became functionally independent of their husbands while remaining finan-cially dependent. Furthermore, as industry began to produce outside the home what women had once manufactured for themselves, women's work at home became increasingly degraded to mere clean-ing, repairing, consuming, and child-raising functions.[31]

Precisely because male authority was being weakened, the stabil-ity of the traditional family required the imposition of a repressive ideology. For women as for workers, internalized discipline was needed to supplement economic necessity. Victorian prudery was closely connected to the doctrine of a separate sphere of concerns for women. This notion that women were profoundly different from men—an idea newly emphasized after the late eighteenth century— was simultaneously a description of a new reality: a male-imposed doctrine to keep women from escaping from their homes and a women's adaptation to their new situation.

Because the rationale for Victorian prudery was the great dif-ference between the sexes, its essential definition was the double standard. Seen as a system, Victorian sexual norms did not impose self-denial and chastity on all, but exclusively on women. Meanwhile men created the greatest prostitution industry in history. It is true, of course, that Victorian moralists continued some of the Puritan hostil-ity to play, to spontaneous, unpredictable indulgence in pleasureful activity. Work had to be the first, and often the only, activity of most days; sex was reserved for bedtime, the hours of fatigue. Unlike their Puritan forebears, Victorian moralists argued that sex should be indulged in only for purposes of procreation. In response, men of all classes often patronized brothels rather than seek love with their wives. Sexual matters were slandered as dirty, immoral, and undignified and virtually removed from respectable discussion.

The very essence of Victorian respectability was hypocrisy. This hypocrisy accurately reflected the social function of prudery: an attempt to create in both working-class people and women of all classes a repression convenient for the new capitalist ruling class. (This attempt was complex as it required granting to working-class men some of the privileges of bourgeois men and to upper-class women some of the privileges of their husbands and fathers.) As it affected birth control, prudery was an obstacle partly because it defined any discussion of sexual matters as obscene. But as a system of sexual politics, prudery sought to hamper women's efforts to transcend their home-and-marriage prisons by keeping the burdens of motherhood upon them.

Thus Victorian prudery produced not only a prohibition on sexual discussion but also a cult of "motherhood." This romanticization of motherhood, like prudery itself, had many contributing factors. Partly it was a response of men and women alike to the decreasing permanence of families. New relations of production weakened ties between family members and undermined fathers' authority by making individuals economically independent. Simultaneously relationships outside the family for wage laborers and other big-city dwellers became less permanent and reliable, unlike the community patterns of mutual dependency that had prevailed in precapitalist society. All relationships, familial and otherwise, were increasingly composed of dependencies that were primarily psychological rather than material.* Furthermore, improved transportation and economic incentives to geographical mobility undermined close relationships with neighbors.

All these changes spelled greater freedom for individuals, especially those who had previously been subordinated to a master, such as children, unmarried women, apprentices. But these changes also carried the potential for loneliness and disorientation among individuals, and a resultant instability for the society as a whole which was quite alarming to many nineteenth-century working people, especially those who had recently migrated from nonindustrial areas.

* None of this should be taken to imply that family and community interdependencies vanished quickly or entirely. Many industrial workers to the present day continue to use patterns of sharing and mutual support which may be said to have originated in preindustrial communities but are now used in a fully proletarian manner to adapt to industrial conditions. My argument is only that a tendency toward increased individual independence was noticed and remarked upon by many people in the nineteenth century.

The disintegration of the economic basis of family life in no way ended its necessity as a social institution. On the one hand, the family remained, at least throughout the nineteenth and first half of the twentieth centuries, the primary means of the socialization of children into adults with personalities appropriate to the demands of industrial capitalism. Authoritarianism and willingness to accept external controls over basic life processes such as work, learning, and sex were among the lessons children learned in their families, and restriction of sexual activity to marriage was an important means of enforcement of these controls. On the other hand, the family was called upon to absorb the heavy strains that the economy placed upon individuals. The traditional sexual division of labor within the family meant that women had to carry the bulk of this new psychological burden.

Both these familial functions contributed to an intensification of the cult of motherhood, that is, the extension of motherliness to the very definition of femininity. In one function, maternal virtues justified and idealized the restriction of sex within marriage. In another function, the maternal tenderings of wives were now expected to extend beyond their children to their husbands, to turn their homes into soothing, comforting, challengeless escapes* for men returning from exhausting workdays of cut-throat competition and constant vigilance to buy cheap and sell dear, or of grinding physical labor and rigid external control. For both classes women provided compensatory services. For the upper class, women operated in addition to servants; wives' services were thus subtle, often symbolic, their subservience strengthening their husbands' class consciousness. Among the working class the subservience of wives dulled class consciousness and offered a false consciousness of superiority for their men.

In justifying this further specialization of the sexes in the division of labor, nineteenth-century ideologists offered the view that the two sexes were not only different in all things but nearly opposite. It became unfashionable among the educated to say outright that women were inferior. (By contrast a forthright male-supremacist line had dominated most discussions of the sexes, both religious and secular, before the nineteenth century.) Victorian ideology about

---

* By contrast with the typical workplace-home of the seventeenth century, crowded, hectic, and noisy.

women included the pretense that the spheres of men and women were separate but equal. This belief, in turn, was part of a larger ideological system in which women, although considered inferior in intellectual, artistic, and physical potential, were told that they were morally superior and that their greater holiness came from their innate capacity for motherliness. Such a division of qualities was convenient for a ruling class that got its profits and achievements by means of which even its own religion disapproved. Only the female half of the population was really expected to act on Christian morality. The theory that women's moral influence would temper the savagery of capitalist competition was used by the whole bourgeois class to assuage its guilt and soothe its tensions.

Motherhood was no longer an intrafamily ideology; it now had important ideological functions for the whole society. Whatever its origins, it was not specific to the upper classes but served the working class in a number of ways: It justified and explained as inexorable a break in solidarity between the sexes in that class, a break that workers were powerless to resist, since they lacked ways to arrange for child care and housework other than through the exploitation of women. It also provided real, not illusory, privileges for working-class men which many of them enthusiastically enjoyed. Finally, it offered working-class women a sense of dignity which their forcible removal from access to productive labor had stolen.

The theory of the oppositeness of the sexes was particularly marked in matters of sex. Sex drive became exclusively a part of the masculine sphere of things, and some theories even denied that sex drives existed in women. Female chastity was no longer merely a man's right but now also a woman's destiny, as a naturally asexual being; men were asked merely to moderate the extremes of their powerful sexual urge. Although purity was raised to first place among women's desired virtues, a significant number of working-class women were sacrificed in a different way to the maintenance of male supremacy and the sexual character structure that industrial capitalism created. Prostitutes were available to men of all classes, providing a sop to working-class men similar in function to wives themselves.

The motherhood ideology also defined the extent that sexuality was allowable for women: the only justifiable purpose of sexual intercourse for "respectable" women was reproduction.* The choice for women became motherhood or prostitution, as the sexual standards became so rigid that all sexual activity outside of motherhood became identified with (and often in fact led to) prostitution. Supporting this view was the new theory that women had no sex drive (in contrast to the male view of women that had dominated for most of human history—that women had powerful lusts, and in equal contrast to the Puritan view which considered it an obligation of comparable difficulty for both sexes to control their sexual urges). This myth was accommodated to the cult of motherhood through emphasis on the virtue of purity for mothers, and literally identified with motherhood through the idea that the female analog to the male sex drive was the maternal instinct. The chastity and passionlessness of women was expected to prevail within marriage just as outside it. The desire for maternity was presumably the only selfish reason that women submitted, literally, to sexual intercourse; beyond the immediate desire for children their motivation should be to please their husbands.

In the nineteenth century this strange sexual morality was being defined not only by the clergy and the political philosophers, as in previous centuries, but also by the medical profession, a new and powerful source of control over women's lives. Many doctors wrote manuals of sexual conduct aimed at women. These doctors were far from unanimous in their views on female sexuality, and some argued merely for moderation of sexual appetites and practices. Even their moderation, however, served a repressive function: writing prescriptive manuals, attempting to establish moral norms for sexual behavior in as well as outside of marriage, most of the moderates as well as the extremists emphasized the debilitating effects of sexual indulgence, defined normal sexual intercourse as that leading most directly to male orgasm, and opposed contraception.†

---

* "Respectable" had originally meant not working with one's hands, which required, among other things, being able to keep servants. Thus originally working-class people were not "respectable" by definition, in the European usage of the term. In the United States, and in Europe in the nineteenth century, there emerged a new concept of respectability which included those of the working class who had adopted the social and moral standards of the bourgeoisie, such as refraining from drunkenness and requiring female virginity until marriage.
† For a discussion of the medical prescriptive manuals, see Chapter 8.

A more complex matter is the degree of success of the ideologues in making their proposed norms work in practice. After years of assuming that the ministers' and doctors' prescriptions were women's reality, a few historians have lately looked for and found evidence that women's minds and bodies were not mere clay in the hands of their moral censors but remained resistant to this indoctrination. Middle- and upper-middle-class women, the main audience for the prudish sex manuals, in small samples of letters, diaries, and at least one survey by a feminist gynecologist, said that they often enjoyed sex and experienced orgasm.[32] Furthermore, the mask of prudery stimulated hypocrisy, and many men and women behaved and felt differently in private than in public, no doubt. Still, we know from our own experiences how helpless people can be, even in their own minds, against the norms of beauty, love, and propriety. The euphemistic avoidance of direct discussion of sexual matters made sex appear a dirty fact of life, unavoidable but unpleasant, like excretion. The moral guides urged excluding sex from consciousness as well as from behavior. Women were told that their purity of mind and body would determine not only their fate in the hereafter but also their marriageability on earth. Prudery was not merely an ideological system, for the sanctions on women who deviated were material and, often, permanent, such as spinsterhood, desertion, economic ruin, disease, and death. Physical though its basis may be, the sexual drive is susceptible to great variation and control from psychological pressures; and the anxieties attached to sex may well have produced many women who did not experience sexual drive, at least not in a form recognizable to them. Thus, however many individuals were able to resist it, Victorian sexual ideology produced, among the middle classes at least, many other women hostile to and fearful of sex.

The repression of female sexuality may have been accomplished through physical as well as psychological changes. Women learned to hate their own bodies. Many women never undressed, even when alone, and bathed under their shifts. When they submitted sexually to their husbands, they remained clothed; for many women sexual intercourse was reduced to such a quick act of penetration that they never had the time to become aroused. People never exposed to sexual stimulation may indeed have had truncated, undeveloped sexual drives. Ill health also contributed to lessening sexual energy. Lack of exercise and confinement indoors made women even of the privileged classes physically weak; terrible working and living conditions made working-class women unhealthy in other, more serious, ways. Among fashionable women, heavy corseting may have caused serious and permanent internal damage. The approach to pregnancy ("confinement" it was called and confinement it was, for a pregnant woman was considered indecent in "respectable" circles and was expected not to appear in public) prohibited exercise and weakened muscles, thus making pregnancy and parturition possibly more painful than earlier in history, and canceling out improvements gained through better sanitation and health care. Nothing can be more effective than the fear of painful and dangerous pregnancies and childbirths in depressing sexual interest.

Beyond these obstacles to sexual development, Victorian constraints on women created particular practical problems for birth control. The most effective traditional forms of birth control under women's control required handling one's genitals. The task of inserting a vaginal pessary may have been beyond the emotional capabilities of many nineteenth-century women. Prudery also interfered with the communication of traditional birth-control remedies from one generation to the next. And even the limited ingenuity and basic common sense required for developing home-remedy birth-control techniques may have been blocked by deep psychological fears of thinking about sexual matters.

The factors making birth control immoral were intensifying for the first three quarters of the nineteenth century. Although the rights of women were in many respects greater by the nineteenth century than they had been before in the Western world, the prohibition on birth control and on any open discussion of sexual matters had never been more severe. In 1873 in the United States, birth control was legally prohibited for the first time by the "Comstock law," which forbade the sending of obscene matter through the U.S. mail. Religious and political leaders denounced sexual immorality increasingly after mid-century. The greater sexual repression was primarily a response to growing rebellion against the Victorian sexual system. That rebellion, as we shall see, was closely connected to the feminist movement that arose in the 1840s—and the two rebellions had common causes. The two rebellions were related as the two forms of repression—the repression of sex and the subjugation of women—were related.

None of this repression would have been necessary if birth-control technology had been unknown. There is a prevalent myth, in our technological society, that birth-control technology came to us with modern medicine. This is far from the truth, as modern medicine did almost nothing, until the last twenty years, to improve on birth-control devices that were literally more than a millennium old. It is important to look at this heritage of traditional birth control if we are to understand the birth-control movement, for that movement took its strength from women's understanding of the suppression of actual possibilities.

2
The Folklore of Birth Control

BIRTH CONTROL was not invented by scientists or doctors, it was invented by women. It is a part of the folklore and folk culture of nearly all societies. Even though women rarely had had any socially accepted rights to decide by themselves when to bear children and when not to, birth control was usually a respectable alternative that could be employed in circumstances set by the husband or the community elders. Birth control was also practiced illegally, its technology passed on by an underground of midwives and wisewomen.

There was an extensive folklore of birth control in most societies, developed by women and handed down from generation to generation. Some of these traditions have remained so unchanged that, for example, vaginal sponges used several thousand years before Christ were still being prescribed in birth-control clinics in 1930. The fact that skills at preventing conception were so advanced, so long ago, tells us something about how much people wanted control over reproduction. New inventions, after all, do not fall from the sky. They are developed by practice—through trial and error—in response to people's needs.

These needs varied throughout history. Overpopulation on a world scale is, if it exists, a recent phenomenon. But overpopulation on a transient and small scale has often existed in many societies. Current population-control theory sometimes obscures the fact that overpopulation is related to people's level of production as well as to their level of consumption. Thus even very thinly populated regions may be overpopulated if consumption needs outstrip production. In societies where the entire economy is close to subsistence, where a week of bad weather could cause famine, what is an appropriate population one year can become a dangerous crowd the next. The same variation can occur within an individual clan or family: a child welcomed even at conception can become a resented burden by the time of its birth. "Excess" children may represent more than an inconvenience or a misfortune to their families or societies: they may, if the situation is severe enough, represent a direct threat to the survival of their parents or clanspeople. "Control" of these excess births then becomes a question of self-defense for the society.

The question of self-defense has additional, particular application to the situation of mothers or potential mothers. Until recently childbirth was a dangerous event. Furthermore, it is usually women who raise children at the expense of their own biological and psychological strength, who sacrifice for their children and suffer the emotional anguish of knowing that their children are, or might be, hungry. Of course women's feelings toward children also vary culturally as well as individually. Societal as well as familial patterns often endow mothers with greater power and prestige than childless women, and most women receive pleasure and rewards from childbearing and childraising. But these attitudes also differ greatly among individual women and among different cultures, and there is no inherent contradiction between love of children and desire for reproductive control and limitation.

There is substantial evidence that birth control has always been a "women's liberation" issue. The fact that most attempts at reproductive control were invented and practiced by women in itself suggests women's particular concern with this problem. A cataloguing of the extent, variety, and ingenuity of these practices is eloquent testimonial to the intensity of women's concern. Another relevant piece of evidence is that birth control is more widely practiced in societies where women have more power over reproduction.[1]

Because of the different interest of men and women in the practice of birth control, differences in birth-control techniques have social significance. Some techniques are more amenable than others to being used independently and even secretly by women; some give full control to men; others are more likely to be used cooperatively. Thus it is important to be specific when considering birth control. For example, a list of the types of birth control might look like this: infanticide; abortion; sterilizing surgery; withdrawal by the male (*coitus interruptus*); melting suppositories designed to form an impenetrable coating over the cervix; diaphragms, caps, or other devices which are inserted into the vagina over the cervix and withdrawn after intercourse; intrauterine devices; internal medicines—potions or pills; douching and other forms of action after intercourse designed to kill or drive out the sperm; condoms; and varieties of the rhythm methods, based on calculating the woman's fertile period and abstaining from intercourse during it.* All these techniques were practiced in the ancient world and in modern preindustrial societies. Indeed, until the modern hormone-suppressing pill there were no essentially new birth-control devices, only improvements of the old. (The historical trend, on the contrary, has been toward the elimination of certain methods as they have come to seem to us dangerous or in violation of our moral sensibilities.)

The basic principles of birth control—contraception and abortion—are simple. People have been designing homemade contraceptive formulas and performing homemade abortions for years, and many of them produced significant results. These techniques cannot compete with the pill or with today's legal abortions for effectiveness and safety, but when they were developed they were extraordinary

---

* In addition to these deliberate birth-control methods, all societies have social regulations which affect the birth rate. Late marriages, of course, produce a lower birth rate because there are more years between generations. Prestigious groups that require celibacy—such as monastics—are common in many societies. Preindustrial societies frequently have taboos on sexual intercourse for long periods after childbirth and sometimes even during lactation. There is no proof, however, that such customs are intended to have a population-control function; and indeed they are usually described as having other purposes by the people who practice them. For the sake of clarity, therefore, we have omitted them from consideration in this survey, and we are considering only methods with a more conscious birth-control purpose.

achievements. On a societal level, even a small percentage of effectiveness makes a great impact on the birth rate. Today women want to have 100 per cent certainty that their pregnancies will be voluntary, a reasonable and practicable desire. But the development of that desire was itself produced by its historic possibility. Lacking that kind of effective contraception, women in preindustrial societies did not form such high expectations.

For our purposes, however, birth-control attempts in preindustrial societies are important whether or not they worked at all. They are evidence not only of the desire to control reproduction but also of the conviction that it is proper to do so and the confidence that it could be done. Today we need to combine the sophistication of modern chemistry and medicine with the attitude of these women and men of long ago, who believed that birth control was their responsibility and took the responsibility for experimenting and judging what was best for themselves.

What we know today of the traditional use of these techniques represents only a fraction of what once existed. We have only sparse observations. Much of our information about modern preindustrial societies comes from foreign travelers, merchants, even colonizers—invaders of other cultures who are hardly sensitive to their social organization, let alone the private culture of women. Trained anthropologists produce more reliable information, but they too are often handicapped by their cultural insensitivity and, when male, by their sex. Some of our information comes from the written records of ancient societies; but these records, too, were often based on the impressions of historians whose limitations were not dissimilar from those of modern anthropologists. This chapter can only offer a sampling of inadequate information—a double handicap. But it is a highly selected, careful sampling that we offer, chosen to a specific end—to demystify the technology of birth control.

Magic

In the ancient and modern preindustrial worlds, magic was an important part of the technology of birth control. There were sacrifices to gods, incantations, potions and philters, dances and pantomimes. Some modern Western scientists have dismissed these methods, since most of them, apparently, do not work. But many "scientific" methods of birth control do not always work. Furthermore, there may be psychogenic causes for infertility—that is, mental states may cause physiological changes that prevent conception. It is possible that magical birth control did work when its user believed in it.

It is altogether incorrect to oppose magic to science. Magical rituals themselves arose out of impulses to explain and control the environment; magic and science had the same roots and may even have once been identical. Superstitions are often good examples of "scientific" or rational magic. Perhaps the first attempts to prevent conception were inspired by observing the circumstances that had actually pertained during an act of intercourse that proved sterile and then trying to reproduce those circumstances. Whatever the efficacy, the attempt is rational. Furthermore, superstitions like this are much easier formed than broken. They quickly gain the honored place of tradition whether they work or not. Consider the situation of a woman whose menstrual period is late. Wishing not to have a child she might try some magical recipe for causing abortion. If, a week later, her menstrual period comes, she might recognize the possibility of mere coincidence, that her good fortune had nothing to do with the potion she drank; but if she found herself in the same predicament another time, it would be *rational*, not merely superstitious, for her to take the potion again—just in case.

Another kind of magic is based on symbolism. In many primitive cultures human needs and patterns are projected onto other creatures and objects. Eastern European peasants, for example, turn the wheel of the grain mill backward four times at midnight; this being a reverse process, it is supposed to prevent conception. A Serbian woman closes the door with the legs of a newly born infant; she is thus closing the house, and herself, to further conception.[2] Both ancient Roman women and modern German peasant women believed that tea made from the seeds of fruitless willow trees would make them sterile.[3] Knots, a widespread symbol of sterility, are often tied in order to prevent conception.[4]

A cluster of magical beliefs found all over Europe centers around the use of the fingers, possibly as phallic symbols. A fourteenth-century writer, Frater Rudolphus, told women to sit or lie on as many fingers as they wished to have years without children. Modern Serbian peasant women would place as many fingers in a child's first bath as they wished free years. In another variant, a bride was supposed to sit on the desired number of fingers while riding in her wedding coach. Among Bosnians, a woman was supposed to slide the desired number of fingers into her girdle as she mounted a horse—and if she slid both hands inside the girdle she would be sterile forever! A more grotesque variant had it that the woman desiring sterility should carry the finger of a premature child.[5]

Another form of magical contraception was, simply, asking the gods, usually called prayer. If one believes in the existence and power of any gods, clearly this too is a rational way to try to prevent conception. And yet, ironically, this, which is still widely practiced in the "civilized" world, is probably the least "scientific" of all methods, because it is passive and powerless, instead of active and power-seeking. The magical methods that are based on trying to find out what makes conception or birth happen and then stopping it, even if they are mistaken, are far more scientific.

To the extent that magic systematically breaks away from the passivity of the human role in most religions it can be seen as humanistic and scientific, at least within its historical context. Medicine is an outgrowth of magic both logically and historically. The first doctors were magician priests, the "medicine men" or "witch doctors." In peasant societies women usually dominated the medical profession; they were the midwives and the practitioners of herbal medicine for the last thousand to fifteen hundred years of Western history. Under the influence of the Christian churches in medieval and early modern Europe, their magic fell into disrepute among the ruling classes (though not among the masses of poor people); they were called witches, were accused of having acquired their powers from the devil, rather than from their own brain power, and were hanged and burnt by the thousands.

There were many reasons for this persecution. Witches threatened the stability of the society partly because they did not conform to their assigned roles as women, and partly because their practice represented a resurfacing of the paganism below the Christian veneer. The content of their witchcraft was also threatening to the churches. As the dogma of Christianity was then conceived, medicine itself was inimical to orthodoxy, and the witches were practicing medicine. They prescribed potions and incantations and performed massages and douches for all kinds of ailments and conditions. They gave abortions and made women temporarily sterile. They generally violated the passive spirit—the acceptance of God's will—that the shepherd churches wished to encourage in their sheep.

There is a widespread misconception that witches and other folk healers used magical remedies out of their inability to diagnose or cure. Anthropologists contributed a related misunderstanding, that many "primitive" cultures used superstitious forms of birth control because they did not understand the process of conception. On the contrary, magical remedies were often prescribed and used together with physiologically effective ones, both in "primitive" and in "high" cultures. The ancient Greek physician Aëtios prescribed well-constructed pessaries to be used along with wearing as an amulet the tooth of a child.[6] Papuan women who wear a rope around their waists in order not to conceive also wash their vaginas carefully after intercourse.[7] (One might call that hedging one's bets.) Belief in imitative, or symbolic, magic by no means implies ignorance of material forces, any more than religion implies ignorance of the laws of physics.

Infanticide

In preindustrial societies the most universal solution to periodic overpopulation or overburdened mothers was infanticide, the killing of newborn babies. The anthropologist Ralph Linton argued that infanticide met the needs of primitive groups more efficiently than contraception would have.[8] Contraception, at the level of technology available to preindustrial society, results in hit-or-miss population limitation. Infanticide provided not only precise population control, but also control of the sex ratio, which was important economically because of sexual division of labor.

The measure becomes even more rational when viewed from a woman's perspective. The burdens of motherhood, particularly when unsupported by other help, and the deprivations of poverty could set up a brutal choice: my life or the child's. Though it had the disadvantage of requiring completion of a full-term pregnancy, infanticide was less risky and painful than abortion in societies without advanced medical techniques.

Many societies practiced infanticide in order to maintain their mobility, rather than because of a desire to check population. In nomadic societies the problem of transporting small children is great and could potentially slow down the group to a costly and even dangerous extent. Some Australian tribes killed every child born before its elder sibling could walk.[9] Among the highly mobile Cheyenne and other North American Plains Indians, children were spaced to prevent their interference with travel.[10]

In many sedentary societies, infanticide was practiced to cope with specific economic problems. Among the Pima of Arizona, a child born after the death of its father was killed so that the widowed mother would not be burdened with an extra child just when she had to support her family alone. Other groups customarily killed babies when their mothers died, or when they were illegitimate, deformed, or sickly.[11]

Where infanticide was legal, men almost always governed its application. To give women the right to decide the fate of babies would have meant that men would give up a key part of their patriarchal power. Even such a distinctly nonfeminist anthropologist as Sumner is quite clear about that: "The women would not be allowed by the men to shirk motherhood if the group needed warriors, or if the men wanted daughters to sell as wives, so that the egoistic motives of mothers never could alone suffice to make folkways. It would need to be in accord with the interest of the group or the interest of the men." [12]

There are a few examples of women deciding whether or not to keep a baby for their own reasons, and it is hard to evaluate, with our limited information, whether their freedom of choice was real. Early German law prescribed that the mother was entitled to decide whether to keep her baby.[13] (These German tribes were matrilineal.)

Polynesian and Australasian mothers told anthropologists and missionaries that they sometimes killed their babies in order not to have to suckle them, as they wanted to preserve the beauty of their breasts. Others said that since a husband was not supposed to have intercourse with his wife while she was nursing, he would often seek out other women during that time, and mothers would kill their babies in order to hold the attentions of their men.[14] These are women's choices, but hardly choices coming from positions of power.

Indeed, infanticide was frequently practiced as a direct expression of male supremacy. There is scarcely any society, in any historical period, where male babies have not been welcomed more than female. It is merely an extension of the opinion which made female children valueless, despised, and even burdensome that high percentages of them were systematically killed. Regular female infanticide was practiced in places as far apart as Tahiti, Formosa, India, and North Africa.[15] But it would be wrong to conclude that these societies were necessarily more male supremacist than others where girl children were preserved. The economic structure and division of labor in a society may make women's services needed without altering their subordinate status.

Despite what churchmen and moral philosophers have argued, from an anthropological point of view infanticide was not murder. In societies both primitive and highly civilized, infanticide has been legal and respectable, fully distinguished in law and in custom from criminal homicide, even from justifiable homicide. For the same reasons that the Catholics advance against abortion—that a fetus is as much a living being as an infant—one might argue that a newborn baby is no more a living being than a fetus. Certainly societies that have permitted infanticide have not defined infants as human. An English doctor, about fifty years ago, expressed this opinion of the practice:

> In comparison with other cases of murder, a minimum of harm is done by it. . . . The victim's mind is not sufficiently developed to enable it to suffer from the contemplation of approaching suffering or death. It is incapable of feeling fear or terror. Nor is its consciousness sufficiently developed to enable it to suffer pain in appreciable degree. Its loss leaves no gap in any family circle, deprives no children of their breadwinner or their mother, no human being of a

friend, helper, or companion. The crime diffuses no sense of insecurity.[16]

If infanticide is not suitable in most of today's societies, it is because we have found better methods of birth control, not because we are morally superior.

It needs emphasizing that it was not just the "primitives" whose moral codes permitted occasional infanticide. Approval and condemnation of the action are found in both preliterate and highly advanced societies. Aristotle and Plato recommended it for eugenic reasons.[17] The Romans legislated against infanticide, perhaps because as a general policy, in conformity with their imperialist policies, they sought to expand their population, whereas the Greeks preferred to curb or stabilize theirs.[18] Nevertheless, infanticide persisted throughout the Roman period as a widespread and rarely prosecuted crime. Tacitus, the Roman historian, found it odd and foolish that the Jews did not practice infanticide.[19]

For the Christians the emphasis on the eternal life of the soul in heaven or hell changed the issue greatly. It became not just a matter of human life, but of the potential damnation of an immortal soul if it passed out of the body before baptism. It followed from this that killing a newborn child was a worse sin than killing a baptized adult.[20] But even Christianity for a long time was unable to secure full conformity to its commandments in this area, and throughout the Middle Ages, in Christian Europe, infanticide by exposure was not unusual.[21]

Abortion

Abortion is just a step away from infanticide. Its appeals are strong: it liberates a woman not only from child-raising, but also from months of uncomfortable, tiring, and sometimes painful pregnancy, and from the pain and danger of childbirth. One of the arguments that antiabortionists have used to justify the prohibition on abortion and to frighten women is that abortion violates some age-old and God-given "natural law." One look at history dissolves that illusion. Almost all preindustrial societies accepted abortion, the fetus being considered a part of the mother as the fruit is a part of the tree till it ripens and falls down.[22] Over the centuries there developed a varied technology of abortion methods—magical and mechanical, external and internal. When abortions became illegal, these techniques merely went underground.

There is a striking continuity between abortion techniques used in ancient societies and those used in today's "home-remedy" * abortions. Especially among middle- and upper-class people, the availability of physicians who will perform abortions for profit—legally or illegally—obscures the persistence of home-remedy abortions. These methods are particularly prevalent among poor women: in communities deprived of access to professional medical care, the dependence on folk medicine continues.

One standard method of inducing abortion, ancient and modern, is the potion, or abortifacient. Recipes for such potions have a high proportion of magical elements and, therefore, are the least successful method of abortion. In modern usages only 7 per cent to 14 per cent of reportedly successful abortions result from internal medicine. (Most doctors, in fact, believe that folk recipes for abortifacients are almost never effective and attribute the reported successes to the coincidence of women having miscarriages from other causes.)[23] With few exceptions these recipes are part of a folk culture of herbal medicine that has been handed down among women for thousands of years. In old German folk medicine marjoram, thyme, parsley, brake, and lavender were recommended, to be taken in tea form. German, Tartar, and French women traditionally used the root of the worm fern in the same way; this plant was so well known as an abortifacient that it was prescribed by a Greek physician in the time of Nero and was called, in French, "prostitute root." [24] Other ancient recipes included a paste of mashed ants, foam from camels' mouths, tail hairs of the blacktail deer dissolved in bear fat.[25] Women in certain Hungarian districts have been said to drink gunpowder dissolved in vinegar, believing that "as it drives out a bullet from a gun, so will it drive out the foetus from the womb." [26] A modern study reported women drinking turpentine, castor oil, tansy tea, quinine, water in which a rusty nail has been

---

* I use the phrase "home-remedy" here to include self-induced abortions and those performed by friends, relatives, and community abortionists or midwives who are not doctors of medicine.

soaked,[27] horseradish, ginger, bluing, epsom salts, ammonia, mustard, gin with iron filings, rosemary, lavender, opium.[28]

The basic principle of the workings of these various brews is that to the degree they are effective at all they are indirectly effective. None of them specifically attacks the fetus. Rather they so irritate or poison the body or the digestive system that they cause rejection of the fetus as a side effect. Primitive medicine had observed and understood this phenomenon. In Fiji, an anthropologist observed, ". . . the wise women appear to know that drugs which irritate the bowel have an indirect effect upon the pelvic viscera." [29] It was not for lack of understanding, but for lack of other alternatives, that women resorted to these dangerous expedients.

Perhaps equally dangerous, but doubtless more effective, were abortions performed by inserting some instrument into the uterus. These operations were done frequently, and with great success, in preindustrial societies. For example, this instruction from the Persian physician Abu Bekr Muhammed ibn Zakariya Al-Razi in the tenth century:

> If these methods [contraceptives he has prescribed] do not succeed . . . there is no help for it but that she insert into her womb a probe or a stick cut into the shape of a probe, especially good being the root of the mallow. One end of the probe should be made fast to the thigh with a thread that it may go in no further. Leave it there . . . until the menses do appear and the woman is cleansed.[30]

Or a technique observed in Greenland:

> Certain Eskimo tribes use a thinly carved rib of walrus which is sharpened as a knife on one end, while the opposite end is made dull and rounded. The sharp end is covered with a rolled cover made of walrus skin, which is opened on both ends, and the length of which corresponds to the cutting part of the piece of bone. A long thread made of the sinews of reindeer is fastened to the upper as well as lower end of the cover. When this probe is being placed in the vagina, the sharp part is covered with the leather covering. After it has been inserted far enough, the thread fastened on the lower end of the covering is gently tugged. The sharp end thus being bared, a half turn is given the probe together with a thrust upwards and inwards, which punctures the uterus.* Before with-

---

* Like many other male anthropologists, no doubt, this one did not understand women's anatomy and, therefore, the technique of abortion. Clearly the intention was not to puncture but to enter the uterus through the cervix.

drawing the instrument, the upper thread of the covering is pulled
in order to cover the sharp end, thus preventing further injury to
the genital organs.[31]

In modern times this operation is done with knitting needles, crochet
hooks, nail files, nutcrackers, knives, hatpins, umbrella ribs, and pieces
of wire; or with a catheter (a rubber tube) if more "professional"
equipment is available. The physiological event, the irritation of the
uterus causing it to reject embryo and placenta, can also be created by
the injection of a chemical into the uterus, such as potassium soap.
Ancient prescriptions of this type called for the use of tar, cinnamon
on a tampon of linen, even pepper.[32]

Many societies practiced destroying the fetus by external means,
instructing women to engage in severe exercise: lifting heavy objects,
climbing trees, taking hot baths, jumping from high places, shaking.[33]
As late as the twentieth century Jewish women of the Lower East Side
of New York City attempted to abort themselves by sitting over a pot
of steam, or preferably hot stewed onions—a technique identical with
one prescribed in an eighth-century Sanskrit source.[34] Some ancient
techniques are significantly more dangerous. We have reports of
abortions performed by pouring hot water or hot ashes on the belly of
the pregnant woman, having her bitten by large ants, grasping the
uterus through the abdominal wall and twisting it until the fetus is
detached.[35]

> [In Torres Straits] In some cases the abdomen is beaten with big
> stones. In others the woman is placed with her back against a tree.
> Two men take a long pole, one at either end, and press with it
> against the abdomen until they crush the foetus—frequently to kill
> the woman as well. Other mechanical means are also used. . . . If a
> woman wishes to induce an abortion she ties a vine round her body,
> or a rope made of cocoanut fiber; or she climbs a cocoanut palm
> and bumps her stomach against the trunk in ascending and de-
> scending; or when she goes to her gardens she will fill a basket full
> of yams, lie on her back and put the heavy basket on her abdomen,
> or strikes it with something heavy and hard.[36]

Or this case of a Pima Indian girl who had become pregnant by a
white man:

As the gestation advanced to near the end, she was observed to have a rope hanging from the roof, upon which she pulled herself up and then dropped down. On one occasion she was seen to run wildly against the door and strike it with her abdomen. Finally a live child was born, but it died the same night.[37]

Despite the great pain involved, most women underwent abortion voluntarily. Many of these abortions were self-inflicted. The majority, perhaps, were done with the aid of an experienced helper, usually an older woman. This was the case in both primitive and advanced societies, and it is a pattern that continues today. In most cases, the helper was and is a specialist, a professional. Sometimes the women were exclusively or mainly abortionists, as in ancient Rome, where they were called *sagae* (which is, probably, the root word for the French *sage-femme*, or midwife). In the harem of the sultan of Turkey there was an official abortionist, called "the bloody midwife," who was one of the sultan's own wives. Like today's professionals, these midwives often tried to monopolize their knowledge and keep it from others. Frequently, too, the helpers were not just abortionists but general doctors for women—gynecologists. There were also cases, in primitive societies, where abortionists and doctors were men. This was less common in advanced societies, where professional male physicians, such as Hippocrates or the many great Arab physicians, condemned the practice of abortion. As a result women turned back to other women for help.[38]

What we know of the frequency of abortion in ancient societies further underscores how important they must have been to women. In the Human Relations Area Files, a major compilation of anthropological data, 125 out of 200 tribal studies reported evidence of abortion. Considering how many cases there must be in which anthropologists didn't ask, or couldn't find out, about abortion, that is an extremely high percentage. A study of the Alor people, in the East Indies, reported 10.5 per cent of 121 pregnancies were aborted; a study of a South African tribe showed that 18 per cent of women admitted abortions.[39] Women have traditionally accepted the pain and danger of abortion as matter-of-factly as they accepted the pain and danger of childbirth at other times, with the assumption that both were necessary for their own and their communities' health and welfare.

Contraception

Birth control before conception, if it can be done, is almost always less painful, physically and psychologically, than birth control after conception. It can be difficult, however. In the first place, contraception requires at least a rudimentary understanding of the process of conception. In the second place, it usually requires some forethought on the part of at least one person; and frequently an antagonistic male can actually prevent a woman from employing contraception. In the third place, the development of techniques that work requires a scientific trial-and-error process of study which is difficult under the conditions of privacy and/or superstition that frequently surround sexual intercourse. All these things considered, the contraceptive knowledge that was accumulated in the ancient world is impressive.

Some of that technology was lost to the Christian West—or at least to most of the people of the West—during the long period of church suppression of birth control. The better methods, those requiring more preparation, were probably the first to disappear. But the suppression was never complete. When the first birth-control clinics opened in Europe and America in the early twentieth century, the records showed that the majority of women coming to the clinics for the first time had used contraception previously.[40]

Potions, or medicinal brews, are a form of folk contraception that has changed very little over the ages. Despite almost universal failure to prevent conception through administering internal medicine, the same recipes used in primitive societies and in medieval Europe are used by unsuspecting women today. Because they were so close to magic, potions were often concocted of symbolically sterile ingredients, as teas made from fruitless plants.[41] Most of them are herbal teas or other vegetable concoctions and are usually harmless, unlike many common abortifacient potions that can be deadly. But there is a good deal of confusion in the tradition between contraceptive and abortion-causing processes. Some of the herbs commonly used in supposedly contraceptive potions—marjoram, thyme, lavender, juniper, angelica, all-heal, basil, hops, saffron, savory, celandine—may in fact be mild emmenagogues, stimulating the onset of menstruation, and thus appearing to cause abortion. Thus the following description of the properties of basil from a seventeenth-century English herbal: "To conclude. It expelleth both birth and afterbirth; and as it helps the deficiency of Venus in one kind, so it spoils all her actions in another. I dare write no more of it." [42]

The single most common contraceptive method in all history, and in all the world, is *coitus interruptus*, or male withdrawal—and unlike potions, effective. Here the male withdraws his penis just before his ejaculation so that his semen is deposited outside the vagina. Withdrawal was traditionally used in Africa, in Australasia, throughout Islamic society, and in Europe. Judaism and Roman Catholicism both condemned the practice, but in medieval Europe its practice was common enough to be frequently attacked in the canonical writings as a "vice against nature," one of the several species of lust.

Another related form of contraception is *coitus obstructus*, recommended in several ancient Sanskrit texts: "If one, at the time of sexual enjoyment, presses firmly with the finger on the fore part of the testicle, turns his mind to other things, and holds his breath while doing so . . ." [43] If the pressure of the finger is steady enough to block the urethra, the semen is forced into the bladder and passes out with the urine. In modern times one couple reported using this method successfully for thirteen years.[44] Still another method, *coitus reservatus*, in which the male entirely avoids ejaculation, has been used by Hindus, and reappeared as an ideal among some American utopian socialists in the nineteenth century.

These practices are, however, dependent on the will and skill of the male. They do not provide women with reproductive control. Except in cases where the entire society has urgent need of over-all population limitation, the desire for limiting conception has been strongest among women, and the best folk contraceptives were developed by women for their own use. Of these perhaps the most basic have been forms of physical action designed to expel semen from the body after intercourse, or to prevent it from reaching the uterus. In many societies it was believed that passivity during intercourse would make a woman less likely to conceive. Although there seems to be no physiological accuracy in this, its converse—that for intercourse to be fruitful the woman must be active—reveals an understandable association between passion and fertility. By the Middle Ages Christian influence had succeeded in reversing this folk belief: too much passion ought to be avoided, for it would make intercourse sterile. In many societies women engaged in violent movements immediately after intercourse in the attempt to get the semen out of the vagina. Sneezing was recommended by the physicians of ancient Greece and, as late as 1868, in an anonymous English birth-control pamphlet. It is not a particularly effective technique, and the more canny ancient doctors advised combining it with immediate douching.

Douching, which might have been an effective practice, was not very widespread. This is doubly unfortunate since many spermicidal substances were known, but were used in less effective ways. As we noted before, the Greek physician Aëtios knew the spermicidal properties of vinegar, but instead of recommending it to women as a douche, he suggested applying it to the penis. In the nineteenth century attempts to kill sperm by bathing the penis in some spermicidal lotion were common, judging by the recipes for such lotions in home-reference books. For example:

> Take bichloride of mercury, 25 parts; milk of almonds, 400 parts; alcohol, 100 parts; rose-water, 1000 parts. Immerse the glands in a little of the mixture, as before, and be particular to open the orifice of the urethra so as to admit the contact of the fluid. This may be used as often as convenient, until the orifice of the urethra feels tender on voiding the urine. Infallible, if used in proper time.[45]

Douching, if done correctly, would have been less painful. Ordinary water is spermicidal if used in large enough quantities to virtually flood the vagina. Citrus fruit juices, even greatly diluted, can immobilize sperm immediately, and women in tropical countries often employed lemon juice in combinations. Nineteenth-century U.S. recipes in women's books show that douching was known here too.[46]

The most effective contraceptive technique used in the ancient world was the pessary, especially when a spermicidal substance was employed. A pessary is a vaginal suppository that will kill spermatozoa and/or block their path through the cervix. Numerous ancient recipes for pessaries have been recently discovered, tested, and found effective. For example, one of the oldest of the extant Egyptian papyri, the Petrie Papyrus of 1850 B.C., is a medical instruction manual that includes gynecological information. It contains three prescriptions for vaginal pessaries. One calls for a base of crocodile dung; another, a mixture of honey and natron (natural sodium carbonate); the third, a kind of gum. Although none of the substances is strongly spermicidal, all are of a consistency that, at body temperature, would form an impenetrable covering over the cervix. (The use of dung in pessaries, incidentally, was widespread: it appears in Indian, African, and Islamic sources, though it does not seem to have passed into Western contraceptive lore. It is partly magical, since the animal chosen as a source was frequently one important in local magic or religion, as the crocodile in Egypt.) Islamic medical writings gave thirteen different prescriptions for pessaries. Both Islamic and Sanskrit sources suggested rock salt, a good spermicide. An Indian work of the first century B.C. suggested rock salt dipped in oil, which is even better, since the oil would retard the motility of sperm and clog the cervix. The use of oil inside the vagina is one of the most continuous patterns in folk contraception. Aristotle suggested either oil of cedar or olive oil. Women of the Midwest of the United States in this century have used lard. Marie Stopes, birth-control champion of the early twentieth century, reported in 1931 that of two thousand cases in which she had prescribed the use of oil and nothing else she had had a zero rate of pregnancy.[47]

The Greek gynecologist Soranus recognized that intravaginal applications were by far the most effective contraceptive techniques. He suggested thirty to forty different combinations of substances for manufacturing pessaries, most of which would have been significantly effective if used correctly. But he never happened upon any highly spermicidal agents, although there were several in earlier recipes. The Ebers Papyrus of 1550 B.C. prescribes a tampon made of lint and saturated with a mixture of honey and tips of acacia. The acacia shrub contains gum arabic, which is the substance used to produce lactic acid, the spermicidal agent in most modern contraceptive jellies and creams. An anthropologist in Sumatra was given a traditional contraceptive suppository which turned out to contain tannic acid, a spermicide even more effective than lactic acid.

Another form of pessary was a solid object used to occlude the cervix. This type of contraceptive was also widespread in preindustrial societies, particularly in Africa, where women used plugs of chopped grass or cloth. On Easter Island women used algae or seaweed. Balls of bamboo tissue paper were used by Japanese prostitutes, wool by Islamic and Greek women, linen rags by Slovak women. Geography ruled, and women used what they could get. The most effective natural cervical cap—the sponge—was first used by a people who lived by the sea, the ancient Jews. The sponge was the most effective contraceptive in use until the development of the rubber diaphragm. If properly used it will not only block the cervix, but will also absorb semen and can be saturated with a spermicidal fluid. Sponges were suggested by birth control clinics as late as 1930. In a study done in New York at that time, Marie Kopp found that women using sponges even without medical advice had a 50 per cent success rate.[48]

Among the most fascinating traditional forms of intravaginal contraceptives were internal condoms. These were found being used in the early twentieth century by women of the Djuka tribes of (Dutch) Guiana. The women inserted into their vaginas okralike seed pods about five inches long from which one end was cut off.

The ordinary condom, used by the male, was not historically a contraceptive. The incentive for its development was the desire for protection against venereal disease. Many tropical peoples used coverings for the penis for a variety of purposes—sometimes for protection against tropical disease or insect bites, and sometimes as marks of rank, as amulets, or merely as decoration. Such a sheath was first publicized as a specifically anti-venereal disease precaution by the Italian anatomist Fallopius (discoverer of the "Fallopian tubes"), an early authority on syphilis. In a book of 1564 he suggested a linen cloth made to fit the penis. By the eighteenth century the device had been transformed into something made of animal membrane, thus waterproof and effective as a contraceptive. By this time sheaths for the penis were widespread, were often given to men by prostitutes, and had acquired a wealth of charming nicknames and euphemisms: the English riding coat, assurance caps, the French letter, bladder policies, instruments of safety, condoms, condums, cundums, and, of course, prophylactics. Through the mid-nineteenth century books of home remedies gave instructions for making condoms, as for example:

> Take the caecum of the sheep; soak it first in water, turn it on both
> sides, then repeat the operation in a weak ley of soda, which must

be changed every four or five hours, for five or six successive times; then remove the mucous membrane with the nail; sulphur, wash in clean water, and then in soap and water; rinse, inflate and dry. Next cut it to the required length, and attach a piece of ribbon to the open end. Used to prevent infection or pregnancy. The different qualities consist in extra pains being taken in the above process, and in polishing, scenting, &c.[49]

Occasionally primitive peoples tried to practice some form of "rhythm method." To do so successfully would have required either an exact knowledge of the physiology of contraception or a sophisticated observation of a large number of cases—neither of which was likely. (A precise identification of the fertile period of the human female was not made until 1924.) Thus, for example, East African Nandi women avoided intercourse for a few days after menstruation. Soranus, too, thought the time just before and just after menstruation was the most fertile. A somewhat more effective practice was prolonging the suckling of infants, used by Eskimo, American Indian, ancient Egyptian, and modern European women with contraceptive intent.

Midwives in Java perform external manipulations that cause the uterus to tip, or become retroflexed, thus preventing conception. This procedure is usually done after either abortion or childbirth. An anthropologist visiting in 1897 found 50 per cent of the women with retroflexed uteruses, but the midwives told him that they could restore the uterus to its normal position by massage whenever a woman wanted a child.

The most ambitious forms of contraception practiced in the preindustrial world were surgical sterilizations. Some groups of Australians perform two kinds of surgery on women which make them less likely to conceive and/or bear children successfully. In one the vagina is cut open down toward the anus, making the vaginal opening wider. In another, performed on girls aged ten to twelve, the cervix is cut and forced to heal in an open position.[50] Ancient Egyptians did ovariotomies (removal of the ovaries) and Australians of the Parapitshuri Sea islands perform this operation on girls chosen to be collective prostitutes for the men of the tribe. An operation of less clear intent is subincision, also practiced by Australians. The urethra is surgically opened at the base of the penis so that both urine and semen emerge at a point just on top of the testicles. Subincision does not prevent conception, and there is no clear evidence that it is performed with any population-control intent; but it does make conception less likely with each act of intercourse and therefore could lower the birth rate, all other things remaining equal.

As we have seen, a wide array of birth-control techniques was used in preindustrial societies. It is a simple fact, but it must be emphasized if we are to understand the birth-control movement. The burden of involuntary childbearing was not the result of lack of technology but of the suppression of technology. This means that childbearing cannot be considered the cause, or at least not the simple, exclusive cause, of women's subject status. The ability to transcend the biological was present in the earliest known human societies. The imprisonment of women within their biological functions is a social, historical phenomenon to which we now turn.

3

The Criminals

THE widespread popular knowledge of birth-control technique, combined with the inherently private nature of sexual intercourse, made birth control difficult to suppress. Long before the emergence of an organized, explicit social movement for birth control, individual women, groups of women friends, and couples defied the birth-control prohibition. The prohibition never did what it was intended to do. Rather it forced women underground in their search for reproductive control. It transformed traditional behavior into criminal behavior and thereby attached to birth control some of the characteristics of all criminal activity: it raised the cost and lowered the quality of birth-control practice. Before we can appreciate the significance of the birth-control movement we must take a look at the experience of ordinary women forced to become criminals as they practiced birth control.

Without attempting to measure the amount of birth control available, the number of women who used it, or which kinds of women used which kinds of birth control, the most specific *quantitative* statement that can be made is that birth control was widespread. This is a *qualitative* study—concerned with the kinds of birth control alternatives that were available in this country and how one got access to them. It is a more subjective than objective understanding we pursue here, and thus it is important, first, to understand what it was like for individual women during the period of prohibition.

Fertility

The American fertility rate has been declining since 1800. In the midst of a period of concern about overpopulation, it is worth dwelling on that fact. Here is a recent estimate of total fertility rates for white women in the United States:

1800	7.04	1880	4.24
1810	6.92	1890	3.87
1820	6.73	1900	3.56
1830	6.55	1910	3.42
1840	6.14	1920	3.17
1850	5.42	1930	2.45
1860	5.21	1940	2.10
1870	4.55	1950	3.00
		1960	3.52[1]

The incomplete data that are available about black Americans, both slave and free women, indicate that their fertility declined at a slightly sharper rate, beginning somewhat later, probably about 1880.[2] Whereas America in the eighteenth century had one of the highest birth rates in the world and was legendary in Europe for its fertility, by the end of the nineteenth century only France had a lower birth rate than the United States.[3]

Another way to see these figures is in terms of family size. In the late eighteenth century families usually had eight children.[4] By 1900 the average family had three. Of course this does not mean that the sizes of actual, functioning families fell that far. The infant mortality and general mortality rates were high enough that despite an average of eight live births per married woman, the average household size in 1790 was 5.7 persons, or less than twice the size of average households in 1950, when it was 3.4.[5]

Yet in a study of birth control, it is the larger change, the change in raw fertility rates, that concerns us. It would be even better if we could obtain figures on the pregnancy rate, for that would give us a better estimate of actual birth-control use, as well as help us to distinguish preventive birth control from deliberate abortion and infanticide. Just as the infant mortality rate was high, so was the rate of miscarriage in the last century, and many women had to endure several unsuccessful pregnancies.

From 1800 to 1960, then, the average number of births per woman in this country fell from 7.04 to 3.52. In evaluating this change it is also important to realize that throughout this period the vast majority of women married. The percentage of women marrying seems to be increasing, with the highest proportion—95.2 per cent—counted in 1965, in the generation of women born between 1921 and 1930.[6] But even at the period of the highest numbers of permanent spinsters, 1865–1875, still 90.4 per cent of all women married, and the figure has never dropped below that.[7] Thus celibacy cannot be a reason for the sharp fertility drop.

Birth control* was responsible. The rumors about its use even in colonial days are plentiful. Abigail Adams wrote that she had deliberately spaced her children two years apart. This birth interval was also typical among the Puritans of Plymouth Colony.[8] There is nothing conclusive about the interval itself, since lactation seems to make conception slightly less likely, and breast-feeding was the norm. But women believed in the sterilizing effect of suckling and may have prolonged it for that reason.

Abortion and Infanticide

Systematic study of women's diaries of the eighteenth and nineteenth centuries may reveal more evidence of birth-control practices. The evidence of abortion and infanticide is easier to get, because those practices were criminal and often prosecuted when discovered. This

---

* It bears repeating that birth control, in this book, means any kind of action taken to prevent having children, including not only abortion and infanticide but also periodic or even sustained sexual abstinence if it is done with that intent. Contraception, by contrast, will be used to refer to specific devices or chemicals or medicines used to prevent conception.

evidence still misses a great deal, since most abortions undoubtedly occurred safely and without detection. Still, the criminal evidence offers a reasonably representative suggestion of the motives and circumstances under which women used these destructive kinds of birth control.

The stigma on illegitimacy frequently drove unmarried women to commit infanticide. Julia Spruill, writing on women in the Southern colonies, found three cases of infanticide reported in the *Maryland Gazette* on one day in 1761. In two of the three cases the mother was identified and arrested, in a third the child's body remained unidentified. It was, of course, difficult to prove whether a child had been murdered or stillborn, and the legislation dealing with this problem—such as making it a crime to conceal a child's death—suggests that the problem was large. Women convicted were usually hanged.[9]

That women consistently took such risks suggests how great must have been their desperation. Unlike abortion, infanticide was primarily a crime of very poor women, whose poverty was most always a source of that desperation. The transcript of a Boston infanticide trial of 1806, published because of public interest in the racial issues involved, tells a poignant story. Elizabeth Valpy, alone in Boston, got a job as a maid for a Dr. Jarvis and became pregnant by a black indentured servant, William Hardy, of the same household. Discovering her pregnancy, she asked the doctor for medicines for abortion, but they did not work. So the doctor turned her out of the house. She demanded that Hardy provide for her and her child-to-be. He rented lodgings for her with Mrs. Bridget Daley, in a "low" neighborhood in South Boston, where she gave birth to a girl, completely white. The child was found drowned twenty-three days later. Valpy claimed that Hardy had killed it, after taking it from her saying he would take it to a wet nurse so she could go out to work. A jury acquitted him for lack of evidence, and there was not enough evidence to bring charges against her either, though she was widely suspected.[10]

It provokes anxiety to read this story and not know the "truth" about who was the murderer. But historically this is not what matters; what matters is to understand the two persons' situation. Neither Valpy nor Hardy could simultaneously raise a child and earn a living alone, nor could they marry, owing to both their poverty and color difference. The trial was particularly brutal for the woman: witness after witness was brought in to defend Hardy by establishing Valpy's loose character and moral viciousness. Although the equal rights of the black man Hardy were rhetorically asserted over and over, Valpy was damned as a "foul, degraded harlot" for having slept with a black man.

Infanticide was still a regular occurrence in urban American society in the mid-nineteenth century.[11] Thomas Low Nichols, writing in the 1860s, speculated that the huge amounts of laudanum being sold were used not just to quiet crying children but also to kill infants painlessly.[12] Fifteen-year-old Mary Turtlot, for instance, working as a domestic for a well-to-do farm family in Warren County, New York, became pregnant by the son; her pregnancy discovered, she was discharged. The son gave her the address of a New York City abortionist, which he got from a cousin living in the city. Arriving there penniless, she persuaded the doctor to take her in as a domestic in return for his medical help; she remained in the doctor's house until arrested after the police found a seven-day-old child dead in the house.[13] Poor women like this, trapped by a double standard about sexual sin, became murderers.

Abortion was much more common than infanticide, however. This excerpt from a letter by an unmarried woman schoolteacher in South Hadley, Massachusetts, in 1859, to her parents in Derry, New Hampshire, suggests an acceptance of abortion as a common event: "Alphens' wife has been up here with her mother all summer. Poor Alphens he has got so poor that he cant keep house so he sent his wife to live on his father all winter—her poor health was caused by getting rid of a child as I suppose Alphens didnt feel able to maintain another one you must not say anything as I have only guessed it she was very large when she came here and in a short time she shrank to her normal size." [14] Elisa Adams, the author of this letter, was a rural, upper-middle-class, respectable young woman with strong family and community ties, not a poor, lonely immigrant girl in a big city, as was Elizabeth Valpy. If Elisa Adams knew that women, married women, had abortions, one might suspect that the phenomenon was somewhat widespread. In 1871 Dr. Martin Luther Holbrook wrote that American women were "addicted" to the wicked practice, and that it was especially widespread in New England,[15] where the decline in the birth rate among Yankees was most pronounced. One antiabortion propagandist, in a style clearly intended to repel and frighten, wrote: "Nowadays, if a baby accidentally finds a lodgement in the uterus, it may perchance have a knitting-needle stuck in its eyes before it has any." [16] In 1871 *The New York Times* called abortion "The Evil of the Age." [17]

Part of the reason for the matter-of-factness of Elisa Adams's letter was that most abortions were safe and successful. This is one of the most important lessons both of anthropological studies and of recent studies of the contemporary illegal abortion industry. There is probably more misunderstanding about abortion safety today than earlier in history, because the campaign for legalized abortion has naturally tended to exaggerate the mortality rate from illegal abortion. In fact, illegal abortions in this country have an impressive safety record. The Kinsey investigators, for example, reported themselves impressed with the safety and skill of the abortionists they surveyed. Today more women die in childbirth than from abortions.[18] That was undoubtedly true in mid-nineteenth century America also.

This does not mean that abortions were pleasant. They were usually quite painful, and they were sources of anxiety because they were gotten in sin, and, often, isolation. The physical risk was heightened by the illegality, just as it is today. Women facing childbirth also feared death, but the fear of dying alone, humiliated, unacknowledged in an abortion was a terrible ordeal. But if the risks were great, they were also calculated risks. Women knew them and still chose abortions in massive numbers. We must keep in mind that many nineteenth-century women and almost all women before that did not believe that abortion was a sin. Before the nineteenth century there were no laws against abortion done in the first few months of pregnancy. Until then the Protestant churches had gone along with the Catholic tradition that before "quickening"—the moment at which the fetus was believed to gain life—abortion was permissible.* The reversal of this

* Quickening is not the same thing as viability, and most estimates of the time of quickening put it far earlier than the point when life outside the womb was possible. In accordance with general male-supremacist attitudes, the time of quickening was usually set earlier for males than for females, thus in theory giving an advantage to the male population: Aristotle computed it at about forty days after conception for the male, ninety days for the female; Hippocrates put the

tradition and the antiabortion legislation of the mid-nineteenth century did not immediately alter the customary belief that an early abortion was a woman's right.

In the 1870s, when a campaign of antiabortion propaganda had stimulated investigation, *The New York Times* estimated that there were two hundred full-time abortionists in New York City, not including doctors who sometimes did abortions.[20] It may be that tens of thousands of abortions were done in New York City alone in the 1870s, one judge estimating one hundred thousand a year in the 1890s.[21] In 1881 the Michigan Board of Health estimated one hundred thousand abortions a year in the United States, with six thousand deaths, or a 6 per cent mortality rate.[22] In the 1890s doctors were estimating two million abortions a year.[23] In 1921, when statistics on these matters were more reliable, a Stanford University study estimated that one out of every 1.7 to 2.3 pregnancies ended in abortion of which at least 50 per cent were criminal.[24] As better and better statistics have been collected, they tend to suggest that earlier estimates of abortion frequency were far too low, and that the death rate estimate of 6 per cent was far too high.

These two errors—underestimating abortions, overestimating deaths—are connected, since most illegal abortions were discovered only if they ended in disaster: if the aborted woman either died or became very ill. The mortality among women from abortions was high, even if small relative to the number of abortions. The most dangerous abortions were usually not the mechanical ones—those done with knitting needles as rudimentary catheters, or by scraping the uterus—but the chemical ones, for internal medicines can cause abortion only as a consequence of general harsh treatment of the body. Yet the advertisements for abortifacients were plentiful. Newspapers printed many ads like these: "Portuguese Female Pills, not to be used during pregnancy for they will cause miscarriage." [25] As the denomination "French" almost always indicated some contraceptive device (a "French letter," as mentioned before, was a condom), so "Portuguese"

<hr>

figures at thirty and forty-two days respectively; the later Roman view was forty and eighty days. How the pregnant woman was to know the sex of her fetus is, however, not explained. The Catholic Church, in accordance with its concerns, identified quickening with the acquisition of a soul, and most Protestant groups had gone along with that definition. Thus abortion before quickening was not only not a crime, but not even a sin.[19]

always referred to an abortifacient. Another standard euphemism for abortion was "relief" or "removing obstacles." "A Great and Sure Remedy for Married Ladies—The Portuguese Female Pills always give immediate relief. . . . Price $5 . . ."[26] Many such ads were actually offering emmenagogues, medicines to stimulate menstruation when it was late or irregular. Thus they were often called "Female Regulators" and advertised without mentioning even the euphemisms for abortion.[27] In the 1830s one abortionist, known as Madame Restell, built herself fame and fortune through a veritable abortatorium in a Fifth Avenue brownstone. As she bragged, no doubt with at least some exaggeration, in her own advertisement, "Madame Restell, as is well known, was for thirty years Female Physician in the two principal female hospitals in Europe—those of Vienna and Paris—where, favored by her great experience and opportunities, she attained that celebrity in those great discoveries in medical science so specially adapted to the female frame. . . ."[28]

Abortions through internal medicine were not attempted only by professionals. Folk remedies for unwanted pregnancies were common. Even men knew them, or how to get them. Stories of men dosing their pregnant girl friends with abortifacients come from all periods of American history. In Maryland in 1652, Susanna Warren, a single woman made pregnant by "prominent citizen" Captain Mitchell, said that he prepared for her a " 'potion of Phisick,' put it in an egg, and forced her to take it. . . ." It didn't work and she brought charges against him![29] Slaves practiced abortion commonly. An antebellum doctor wrote that it was four times as frequent among blacks as among whites, and that "all country practitioners are aware of the frequent complaints of planters from this subject."[30] Though the doctor may have been underestimating the prevalence of abortion among whites, it seems at least possible that the rather exceptionally unpleasant conditions of child-raising for slave women might have made them reluctant to bear children.*

Abortions, then as now, were most common among the married and seemed frequent in all classes.[31] In 1862, when the wife of

* Indeed, if the doctor's figures are true, one would be practically forced to entertain the possibility that abortion among slaves was not only a tool of self-preservation, but also a form of resistance.

Confederate General William Dorsey Pender wrote him that unfortunately she was pregnant, he wrote her pious phrases about "God's will" but also sent her pills which his camp surgeon had thought might "relieve" her.[32]

One of the best ways to get a clear picture of a nineteenth-century abortion is to examine a particular case rather fully. The transcript of the trial of Dr. William Graves of Lowell, Massachusetts, in 1837, for the murder of Mary Anne Wilson of Greenfield, New Hampshire, offers us such a view.[33]

> *Testimony of Dr. James S. Burt:* Sometime in May latter part, 1837, I was in Greenfield and was called to see Mrs. Wilson. She said she was in a family way and wished to get relieved of her burden. I told her I had rather not give medicine for that purpose, that it would injure health or life. She said she had sent to Lowell for medicine and got a box of pills for that purpose. . . . she brought forward the box—I examined it—there were about two or three dozen common sized pills—she said it had been full. I told her she was injuring her health by doing so, and she had better not take any more of them—I also advised her to see the young man who had done it, tell him her situation and he would do the thing that was right. She said she had, but he seemed to be bashful or ugly and wouldn't do anything. I asked her how long she had been in this situation and she said about 4 months. . . . she said then she would go to Lowell, for she was informed there was a physician there who would perform this operation with safety. I asked her how she came by her news or information and she said she heard it from good authority and that it could be performed without danger and that in 4 or 5 days, she could go about her daily employ. I then told her this is a folly—it will endanger your life, your health at any rate, and I advise you not to go—it may be done, but not without danger. I then said death is your portion if you do go, in my opinion, and you had better not go. . . .

> *Testimony of Elizabeth Bean:* I am a sister of Mary Anne Wilson . . . I opened her trunk when it came back from Lowell—in it was a little slip of paper on which was written "Dr. Graves, Hurd street, No. 7." (The witness produces the paper.) It was folded together and fastened with a needle. . . .
>
> She had been married and was a widow. She had been a widow 4 years next January. . . . Mrs Wallace her daughter and son lived in the house with my sister. In her own family lived Mr

Isaac Pollard and one child of her own, 3 years old last June. . . . It was understood in the family that Mrs Wilson was courted by Mr Pollard . . . for 2 years. . . .

Testimony of N. H. G. Welton [stage-driver]: I left a lady at Dr Graves's last summer. . . . I left her just at twilight. I rang the bell for Dr Graves; he was not in; but just that moment he came up, and I said Dr, here is a lady to see you. . . . I heard the Dr say as I left them, "well, well, walk in and I will see."

Testimony of Lucinda Sanborn: I have lived at Dr Graves's for nearly 1½ years, and my business is to take charge of the house and doing the whole of the work. . . . The Monday before her death in the evening she was not so well, and Monday night she became very sick, and the abortion took place. She had severe pain in her back and bowels. . . . The abortion took place while she was in bed; we took her off, laid her onto another bed and removed the sheet. . . . We raked open the ashes in the fireplace and put the contents of the sheet into it and covered them up. . . . There was something that looked like a child which we found on the sheet. The after birth was with it. This was never removed from the fireplace; it was rather chilly, and I built up a small fire afterwards.

Testimony of Dr. Hanover Dickey, Jr.: I lived at Dr Graves's from June 17 to August 19, and boarded in the family. . . . I have previously studied with Dr Graves. . . . I chose to go into that room from curiosity . . . I went in and found the . . . lady there on the bed. . . . She said she thought herself 3 months or more advanced in pregnancy. . . . She said she did not know but she should have been freed the night before from her embarrassment. I don't know as she used the word embarrassment, but something referring to her pregnancy. . . . I saw her again Saturday, August 19 forenoon . . . —her hair was not adjusted—everything betokened suffering—her general appearance, dress and countenance—great suffering—mental and bodily. She made two statements to me—one was that she tho't she would die—the other was that she tho't her difficulties would subside, that she should be well and be able to go home in a few days. . . .

Mary Anne Wilson died on August 24, after three weeks alone in Dr. Graves's house, without communication from her parents, sisters, child, or lover. At her death, Graves hired some Lowell men to bring her in her coffin to Greenfield and turn her over to Pollard. He told her family that she had died in Boston of a "cholera morbus." But when her relatives initiated investigation, having found Graves's address—in Pollard's writing—in her trunk, Pollard disappeared.

Think of Mary Anne Wilson: widowed four years, supporting herself and child with millinery, "courted" by a boarder for two years but unable or unwilling to get his support for a child. Hardly a promiscuous woman, she paid very heavily for her "sin." Graves was convicted. It seemed he did a lot of business with people who lived "on the Appleton Corporation"—the Lowell mills. We do not know his sentence.

Although the notion of quickening was still popularly accepted during the first half of the nineteenth century, many states had already made abortion at any stage of fetal development a crime. This legislation was a severe blow to women, since abortions were usually performed in the early stages of pregnancy anyway. Indeed, next to the long tradition that abortion was a crime only after quickening, these laws appear as a repeal of a time-honored *right* of women.*

But despite the new laws, criminal abortionists were not only operating publicly, they were being acquitted by juries.[35] An antiabortion doctor complained in the 1860s: "In consequence of this professional and most criminal apathy, public sentiment has become more and more blunted, until it is now given as a reason [of nonprosecution] by the public prosecuting officers that a jury could not be found in Boston to convict of this crime, even in the most flagrant and indisputable cases of maternal death." [36] In 1903 another doctor wrote that abortionists were everywhere "sheltered by the sympathy of the community." [37]

Increasing concern over the abortion "evil" beginning in midcentury led even *The New York Times* to consider this previously unmentionable problem now fit to print. It embarked on a series of investigative reports that reveal something of the workings of the abortion industry. The professional abortionists who advertised in the papers were often medical imposters—that is, they lacked medical

---

* The first legislation banning abortion altogether did not originate in Catholic canon law, as is widely believed, but in the secular law of England in 1803. The Catholic Church only legislated similarly in 1869, and in the United States most states had outlawed all abortions during the Civil War period.[34]

degrees. On the other hand, diploma mills had been developed which sold fake degrees. Frequently the abortionists used many aliases, sometimes to avoid old prosecutions, sometimes to operate several establishments simultaneously under different names. Sometimes a woman would be named in the advertisement and might work with a male doctor, as women seeking help would be more likely to approach another woman. These two ads ran simultaneously in the *New York Herald*: "Madame Grindle, Female Physician, guaranteeing relief to all female complaints . . ." and "Ladies' Physician—Dr. H. D. Grindle, professor of midwifery . . . guarantees certain relief to ladies in trouble, with or without medicine; sure relief to the most anxious patient at one interview; elegant rooms for ladies requiring nursing. . . ." [38]

The Grindles, who catered to an upper-class clientele, asked $300 for an abortion.[39] But abortion transcended class distinctions. The abortion industry was highly stratified, and standards of cost and treatment varied enormously. Some advertisements offered medicines for five dollars. A Dr. Kemp, of Twenty-third St. at Seventh Avenue, just around the corner from the Grindles, charged ten dollars and promised to return half if the abortion wasn't successful; and indeed he did return five dollars to one patient, twenty-year-old Anna Livingston.[40] Some physicians kept an expensive office for rich ladies and a cheaper one for poor women. Much of the resentment against Madame Restell had a class basis. Once she was almost imprisoned, but "her lawyer stayed proceedings by a bill of exceptions, and now she rides over one of her judges, tosses up her beautiful head, and says in effect, 'behold the triumph of virtue!' Instead of a linsey woolsey petticoat . . . she is gloriously attired in rich silks and laces, towers above her sex in a splendid carriage, snaps her fingers at the law and all its pains and penalties, and cries out for more victims and more gold. . . ." [41]

Not all abortionists were disreputable. Dr. Graves, of the 1837 Lowell trial, had the best credentials available at that time. A Dr. Cutter, tried for abortion in Newark in the 1870s, was "one of the best known of the younger physicians in the State." [42] Nearly every physician writing or speaking on the topic would admit to being frequently asked for abortions. Clearly not all refused—at least not all the time;

even those who normally refused were undoubtedly sometimes prevailed upon by old patients and friends.

Such was the demand that not even occasional convictions suppressed abortionists' practices. Consider the case of Dr. Henry G. McGonegal. In 1888 he allegedly aborted Annie Goodwin, a young working woman living with her married sister on 126th Street in New York City. When she began to "see" a rich young man, Augustus Harrison, her sister kicked her out, and she went to live with another working girl, Sadie Traphagan. Later that year Annie moved to the boarding house of a Mrs. Collins on 127th Street, but was thrown out of there when discovered to be pregnant. She went to stay with a Mrs. Shaw, washerwoman, of 105th Street, and died there a few days later; her burial permit had been produced by Dr. McGonegal. Witnesses were able to place her in his office. An autopsy proved an abortion and McGonegal was convicted.[43] In that chronology lies the outlines of the fate of many young working women.

Four years later McGonegal, then seventy years old and free on appeal bail, was arrested again, and this time in association with quite a different social class. In this second trial he was alleged to have had the aid of Dr. Marian A. Dale, a graduate of the New York Women's Medical College, forty-four years old, who boarded with McGonegal and shared his practice. Together they had called on Mrs. Louisa Webb, the daughter of an old and respected family of Ravenswood, Long Island, mother of one and temporarily staying with her parents. Shortly after their visit she gave birth to a stillborn child and became very ill; a doctor called in by her wealthy parents was able to save her life. They pressed charges against McGonegal and Dale and also against her husband, Frank Webb, as accomplice. Frank Webb was of a lower social class than his wife, and worked as a Pinkerton at Homestead.[44]

When the medical establishment undertook a campaign against abortion in the second half of the nineteenth century, its stridence served as a further indication of the prevalence and tenacity of illegal abortions. The medical campaign was a response to several different factors: an increasingly prudish public moralism; higher health standards which made abortion-caused deaths less acceptable; and a desire to consolidate the official medical profession through attacks on unlicensed, quack and dissident physicians who were usually those more sympathetic to abortion. The medical doctors' offensive against abortion included both propaganda and lobbying for more rigorous prosecution of illegal abortionists. In 1857 the American Medical Association initiated a formal investigation of the frequency of abortion. Seven years later the American Medical Association offered a prize for the best popular antiabortion tract. Medical attacks on abortion grew in number and in the intensity of their moral condemnation until by the 1870s both professional and popular journals were virtually saturated with the issue. Physicians particularly bemoaned the widespread lay acceptance of abortion before quickening; in order to break that sympathy, they adopted a vocabulary that described abortion in terms designed to shock and repel.[45] As late as 1901 a doctor consistently referred to abortion as "antenatal infanticide." [46]

Physicians commonly attempted to frighten women away from abortion by emphasizing its dangers. Their common assertion that there was *no* safe abortion may have betrayed ignorance, but more likely it was exaggeration justified by what they believed was a higher moral purpose.[47] Yet occasionally even antiabortion doctors allowed the truth to slip out, revealing despite themselves why their campaign remained ineffective. "It is such a simple and comparatively safe matter for a skillful and aseptic operator to interrupt an undesirable pregnancy at an early date . . . ," wrote Dr. A. L. Benedict of Buffalo, an opponent of abortion, "that the natural temptation is to comply with the request.[48]

Contraception

Even today, under conditions of greater safety, abortions can be frightening, painful, and emotionally disturbing; they were more distasteful in the nineteenth century. Nevertheless, for most of history abortion had been a *primary* form of birth control. The fact that abortion was becoming for some, a last resort, a fallback when contraception failed, was a mark of the revival of contraceptive use in the nineteenth century. Here the author of an antiabortion tract gives us a fictional composite case study of a young couple's path to the abortionist:

So the young people are married. . . . they have freely given their friends to understand that it will not be convenient, for the present at least, for them to be troubled with children. They do not yet think it would be quite right to interfere with Nature when she has begun to create a human life, but they are prepared to prevent her from beginning the work. . . . They feel free to arrange for using all their time, vitality, and means in other ways; perhaps they plan a two or three years' course of travel and study in Europe, including a course of lectures and study for the wife. . . . By and by the wife is irregular. . . . What can it mean? It certainly cannot mean conception, for they have taken the strictest precautions!

They now consult—not a physician; it isn't worth while to do that—but some young married pair of their acquaintance who have had more experience than they. . . . [They] learn some points which delicacy and shame had before kept back, and they finally decide to take the next step, and try if a jolting ride or a hot bath will not correct the difficulty. Nothing further than this has been suggested to them, and they still assure themselves that it is not a case of pregnancy.

But after a week or two more they are persuaded to try some "correcting pills" or other infamous nostrum which our leading dailies freely advertise under one or another thin disguise. . . . besides, the medicine was not bought, it was a gift from the box of the more experienced friend. . . .[49]

Dr. Pomeroy's attitudes were representative of the larger part of the medical and moral establishment. He equated contraception with all unconventional women's activities. He was critical of the wife's taking a course of lectures and associated the young couple's desire for stimulating activity with frivolity; he could not accept the idea of a couple's wishing to postpone having children. He also pointed out some truths: that the couple in question was likely to be well-to-do (as opposed to the single pregnant woman who was more likely to be poor). And he saw that in the actual experience of a pregnant woman abortion was often a follow-up to unsuccessful contraception.

We have mentioned before the propagandistic use of confounding abortion with contraception. In women's experience the continuity between the two techniques of birth control was real. The present view of abortion as being more sinful than contraception developed only in the last fifty years, when contraception was rapidly becoming legal and respectable. Earlier the tendency for all birth-control methods to carry a similar moral weight—in relation to sharper present-day distinctions—was strengthened by the vagueness of the ways in which people learned the methods. One might persuade one's doctor to provide some instruction, but it would even then likely be given with embarrassment, be full of euphemism and ellipsis, making misunderstanding very likely; the doctor, especially if male, was not likely to be expert himself in the actual employment of contraceptives. There were a very few books and leaflets with explicit instructions, but it was more likely that, if one were lucky enough to find any printed matter at all, it would also be vague and euphemistic. The most frequent source of birth-control information, as Pomeroy described, was friends.

Nevertheless, contraceptive practice, like abortion, increased steadily throughout the nineteenth century.[50] Contemporary writers consistently attributed the falling birth rate to birth control.[51] When birth-control clinics first opened in the United States and Europe in the 1920s and 1930s, they collected statistics on birth-control practices used before medical advice. The findings completely substantiate the theory of widespread birth-control use. In a study done in a Newark, New Jersey, clinic in 1933, 91.5 per cent of patients had used birth control prior to the clinic visit.[52] A New York City study of 1934 showed 93.3 per cent using birth control, not counting abstinence.[53]

In all the clinic studies, *coitus interruptus*, or male withdrawal, was found to be the most common pre-medical-consultation form of birth control.[54] Doctors' remonstrations against withdrawal supply further evidence of its practice. The doctors' appeals naturally had to be to the men, and consistent with their antiabortion rhetoric, they argued that it was dangerous. The usual threat was that withdrawal caused nervousness and, ultimately, impotence.[55] One doctor even wrote that withdrawal would cause hardening of the uterus in women.[56]

Several sex reformers, both free lovers and others, advocated sexual intercourse with the male avoiding climax altogether.[57] The influence of these iconoclasts is hard to evaluate. Although they wrote many books and pamphlets which were published in large editions, nevertheless their proposals demanded a suppression of gratification by the male that would not seem destined for great popularity. Yet some people practiced it, and quite successfully. One woman from Maryland wrote about the effect on her husband of "Karezza," a system of avoiding climax described by nineteenth-century feminist doctor Alice Stockham in her book of the same name.

> For two years we had no children purposely because we were both nervous wrecks from over work . . . all this was the result of a copy of Mrs. Stockham's "Karezza" falling into our hands before marriage. People of intellect, will and conscience—despise waste of any kind—to waste the most vital power in the universe—(and concentration of vital fluid means untold force) seems most criminal to me. . . . My husband arises at 5 a.m., works till 7 p.m., does the work of any five men I could name, and is as fresh at night as when he starts out in the morning. . . .[58]

This is just one letter, but thousands of copies of Stockham's book, and equal numbers of many others, were distributed. Certainly many people must have attempted to practice this system.

The rhythm method was also widely discussed in the nineteenth century by doctors and sex moralists. Rhythm had the advantage over withdrawal that almost all found it acceptable. One must assume that it was widely attempted, but whether to consider it an actual birth-control method is problematic, since most persons were ignorant of the female fertility cycle. Observing the other mammals, they believed that human ovulation occurred either during menstruation or just before it.[59] This calendar coincided with the conventional taboo on intercourse during menstruation, but it did little to prevent conception.

The condom was second in popularity to male withdrawal, according to studies done in the 1920s and 1930s. Typically from 25 per cent to 50 per cent of the patients interviewed had used condoms. But these figures are misleadingly high, for condoms were often used sporadically, or alternatively with other birth-control methods.[60] Furthermore, unlike other contraceptives, these figures cannot support conclusions about the nineteenth century because condoms were introduced to the public in large part by World War I soldiers. Increased public consciousness about possible spread of venereal disease from soldiers' and sailors' contacts broke through official prudery to force government action. By 1919 the Army alone was spending one million dollars a year against venereal disease through sex education and prophylactics. Even fundamentalist Secretary of the Navy Josephus

Daniels was forced, after initial opposition, to authorize passing out condoms to sailors.[61] A total of 4,791,172 men served in the U.S. armed forces in this war. This could only mean the introduction of condoms into public use on a mass scale. Strengthening that conclusion, comments from women interviewed in some small oral-history projects among working-class Massachusetts and Rhode Island women suggest that many of them first learned about birth control from their husbands who had been in the service.[62] In the late nineteenth century the development of vulcanized rubber had made the manufacture of condoms easier and cheaper. Then after the First World War, latex made condoms thinner and cheaper yet, and their sales increased enormously.[63]

In the nineteenth century the douche was certainly more widely used than condoms; at least one doctor stated categorically that it was the most widely used method.[64] Although advertising contraceptives was difficult because of censorship, douching equipment had the advantage of having multiple uses, many of them medically respectable. Used for enemas and for routine internal cleansing—both procedures having become medically fashionable in the nineteenth century —syringes could be advertised openly. And they were, constantly. Particularly in magazines of the popular health movement, but also in women's magazines, general magazines, and newspapers, syringe advertisements were standard, many of them with pictures of the instrument. In some ads there was absolutely no hint of a birth-control or even a sexual use.[65] In other places advertisements were more frank:

The Fountain Syringe

The most philosophic [*sic*] of all instruments of the kind ever devised. The cheapest, most effect [*sic*] and most durable in the market. The *sina qua non* [*sic*] to hygienic practice. A thousand times more effect than pills or powders, and without the slightest danger to any person under any circumstances. . . .[66]

And in the period before the Comstock law the advertisements even waxed poetic. In the 1840s the famed Madame Restell advertised her proprietary douche preparation thus:

Important to married females—Madame Restell's Preventive Powders. These valuable powders have been universally adopted in

Europe, but France in particular, for upwards of thirty years, as well as by thousands in this country as being the only mild, safe and efficacious remedy for married ladies whose health forbids a too rapid increase of family. . . .

Her acquaintance with the physiology and anatomy of the female frame enabled her—by tracing the decline and ill health of married females scarce in the meridian of life, and the consequent rapid and often apparently inexplicable causes which consign many a fond mother to a premature grave, to their true source—to arrive at a knowledge of the primary cause of female indisposition—especially of married females—which in 1808 led to the discovery of her celebrated Preventive Powders. Their adoption has been the means of preserving not only the health but even the life of many an affectionate wife and fond mother.

Is it not wise and virtuous to prevent evils to which we are subject by simple and healthy means within our control? Every dispassionate, virtuous and enlightened mind will unhesitatingly answer in the affirmative. This is all that Madame Restell recommends, or ever recommended. Price five dollars a package, accompanied with full and particular directions.[67]

D. M. Bennett, a freethinker himself persecuted under the censorship laws, wrote in 1878, "There is probably not a druggist in the United States who has not sold female syringes." [68]

If there was any doubt about the fundamental purpose of the syringes, the censors dispelled it. Many advertisers and vendors of syringes were prosecuted for obscenity, since the Comstock law of 1873 had expressly defined all contraceptive devices as obscene. Comstock's concern with the problem was sufficient for him to employ his entrapment methods to secure the culprits: he would write under a false name asking for a syringe, and then arrest whoever sent it. Thus, for example, on May 9, 1878, Dr. Sara Chase was arrested and held for $1500 bail at the Tombs for having sold two female syringes. The charge against her included the remark that "by the syringes which she recommends and sells, she places it in the power of wives to prevent conception." [69] One of the three prosecutions of free-love anarchist Ezra Heywood, the most important propagandist of planned conception of the 1870s, was for his advertisement of a syringe. Heywood used his trials as a platform from which to argue, from his singularly feminist point of view, the right of women to reproductive self-determination; and the syringe became the virtual symbol of that right. The advertisement in his journal had been singularly forthright to begin with: "Comstock Syringe* for Preventing Conception, sent prepaid on receipt of price, $10." [71] He later wrote: "The advertisement of the 'Comstock Syringe' . . . had one sole, exclusive purpose, viz.: the proclamation of an opinion, the assertion of Woman's Natural Right to ownership of and control over her own body-self—a right inseparable from Women's intelligent existence; a right unquestionable, precious, inalienable, real—beyond words to express. . . ." [72]

Heywood's rhetoric was atypical. The advertisements for syringes were everywhere, but only the radicals attacked the taboos openly. Frequently the euphemisms veiled simple dishonesty. Dr. Edward Baxter advertised a preparation of zinc he had invented as a remedy for leucorrhoea† and "other female weaknesses," inserting the caution that "special care should be taken not to use the remedy after certain exposure has taken place, as its use would almost certainly prevent conception." [73] Others, like Dr. Frederick Hollick, attacked most douches as ineffective and potentially injurious to the vagina—unless the physician was consulted personally! The right substance had been discovered, Hollick explained, "and it is both scarce and difficult to obtain, so that it is not likely to come into general use. . . . Those who really *need* information as to the means of *Preventing Conception* may address Dr. Hollick, Box # . . ." [74]

These dishonesties express the fear of censorship and the doctors' desire for business; they are also related to class differentials in birth-control use. *Middletown*, for example, showed that whereas birth-control use was universal among the "business class" of Muncie, Indiana, less than half the working-class people used birth control, and of those less than 60 per cent used "scientific" methods.[75] Even taking into account differing attitudes between classes, part of the

---

* Noting the irony that the syringe was called Comstock, Heywood wrote: "To name a really good thing 'Comstock' has a sly, sinister, wily look, indicating vicious purpose; in deference to its N.Y. venders, who gave it that name, the Publishers of *The Word* inserted an advertisement . . . which will hereafter appear as 'The Vaginal Syringe'; for its intelligent humane and worthy mission should no longer be libelled by forced association with the pious scamp who thinks Congress gives him legal right of way to and control over every American Woman's Womb." [70]

† Leucorrhoea was the term commonly used by nineteenth-century doctors to refer to vaginal discharges of any kind.

cause of the differential must lie with the physicians. Well-to-do, "respectable" women could get their doctors, with whom they spent more time and had closer relations, to advise them on preventing conception; even when poor women did see doctors, which was rarely, the doctors they saw were much less likely to comply with such requests unless they specialized in birth control. This has been true for the whole history of the medical profession on the question of abortion: women with money were able to secure legal or safe illegal abortions. The situation was no different with contraception.

The class differential in birth-control use is more visible with intravaginal contraceptive methods, for these are likely to make women feel they need to rely on physicians. It bears emphasis that this is largely a matter of perception. Women in precapitalist societies had little difficulty in inventing for themselves various forms of pessaries, suppositories, spermicidal jellies, and so forth. Many women had lost much of that ability and self-confidence by the early nineteenth century.

What intravaginal contraceptives were people using? This is very difficult to know, limited as we are by the current small collections of evidence. The euphemisms of the advertisements are also an obstacle. Many drug stores advertised "French Remedies and Goods." [76] A genuine parody of contraception, from the New York Medical Journal of 1867, leaves no doubt that many doctors were prescribing and even inserting such devices:

> A RAID ON THE UTERUS—A distinguished surgeon in New York City, twenty-five years ago, said, when Dupuytren's operation for relaxation of the *sphincter ani* was in vogue, every young man who came from Paris found every other individual's anus too large, and proceeded to pucker it up. . . . It seems to me that just such a raid is being made upon the uterus at this time. . . . Had Dame Nature foreseen this, she would have made it iron-clad. . . . The *Transactions* of the National Medical Association for 1864 has figured one hundred and twenty-three different kinds of pessaries, embracing every variety, from a simple plug to a patent threshing machine, which can only be worn with the largest hoops. . . . Pessaries, I suppose, are sometimes useful, but there are more than there is any necessity for. I do think that this filling the vagina with such traps, making a Chinese toy-shop of it, is outrageous. [77]

The pessaries* often had as their medical justification the correction of cervical and uterine irregularities. But if there was any doubt that they were used as birth-control devices, their advertisements in lay journals should dispel it.[78] In England, where no Comstock law branded such medical devices obscene, they were advertised frankly, particularly the "soluble pessary," really a suppository. For example:

The Family Limit.
SOLUBLE PESSARY

> This check is one of the cleanest, safest, and most convenient methods extant. It requires no preparation before, or trouble afterwards. It entirely obviates the inconvenience entailed by the use of the enema. Post free, 1/6 per doz. Preventive sheaths 2/- per doz. post free.[79]

Recipes for homemade suppositories circulated commonly throughout the nineteenth and earlier twentieth century. A formula from a young woman's papers around 1920 hardly differed from an early nineteenth-century one:[80] Acid citric—6 grains; Acid boracic—1 dram; Cocoa butter—90 grains. Such formulas were often made up by druggists upon the request of customers. Women had rather high success rates with suppositories, according to surveys taken among women coming to birth-control clinics in the early twentieth century; one study showed a success rate of 54.4 per cent, approximately the same as that with the condom, and topped only by the 71.9 per cent success rate of pessaries.[81]

Sponges might have been the most effective of all, but, oddly, the clinic surveys showed them the least frequently used.[82] The reason for this is unclear, since, as one doctor commented in 1898, "The little sponge in a silk net with string attached is a familiar sight in drug stores." [83] Others argued that sponges decreased female sexual pleasure,[84] one doctor writing that the "ejaculation and contact of the sperm with the uterine neck, constitutes for the woman the crisis of the genital function, by appeasing the venereal orgasm and calming the voluptuous emotions . . ." and that perhaps the semen itself has special properties needed by the womb.[85]

Although many doctors ceaselessly attacked contraception, oth-

---

* At this time the word "pessary" was used vaguely and could refer to any intravaginal device.

ers, equally respectable, sometimes made slips that revealed their cynicism about the ideals of purity they preached. One amusing case was exposed by the freethinker D. M. Bennett, retaliating for his prosecution under the Comstock law. Bennett found an advertisement for vaseline with a statement by Dr. Henry A. Du Bois including the following: "Physicians are frequently applied [to] to produce abortion. . . . In some cases of this kind prevention is better than cure, and I am inclined to think, from some experiments, that *vaseline, charged with four or five grains of salicyclic acid,* will destroy spermatozoa, without injury to the uterus or vagina." Vaseline was manufactured by the Samuel Colgate Company, and Samuel Colgate was head of the New York Society for the Suppression of Vice, one of the main backers of Comstock's crusade. The ad even had the Colgate Company as its return address.[86]

No doubt there were many such inconsistencies. Social and economic radicals drew the conclusion, even in the 1870s, that there was a class bias in the availability of contraception. "The 'regular' * aristocratic physicians," Bennett charged, "may prevent conceptions, produce abortions, or do anything else they choose, and your agent will not disturb them. I have never heard of Comstock bringing a charge against a regular physician or a regular druggist. Druggists may import and sell contraband French goods with perfect impunity. . . . He [Comstock] is not anxious to attack the fraternity of druggists; they are too strong and could raise too much money to successfully oppose him." [87] This was the local, empirical version of a class analysis of contraception. Others made a more far-reaching, systemic charge: the ruling class needed bodies for its industry and its wars. "That is why laws have been passed making it a penitentiary offense to inform a woman how she can avoid having undesired children. The remedy is too obvious for it to be permitted by the rich, whose fortunes depend on the fecundity of the poor," wrote Jonathan Mayo Crane, an anarchist.[88]

There was indeed a class bias in the use of birth control, and as

---

* "Regular" physicians were those with degrees from established medical schools, as opposed to members of traditional or sectarian schools of healing. Bennett, himself an irregular druggist, used this term in a derogatory sense, as he believed that the main distinction of the "regulars" was their arrogance and desire to drive others out of the profession. See Chapter 8.

we shall see later birth control became, like all custom and technology, transformed by class struggle. But Crane's interpretation was too simple. The evidence does not suggest that in the nineteenth century birth control in its inclusive sense was more widely practiced by the rich. It suggests rather that the rich had access to more effective contraceptives, sponges, pessaries, suppositories, and douches, whereas poor women were forced to rely on abortion as a primary form of birth control. Many other cultural variables undoubtedly affected the distribution of contraceptive use: religion, ethnic group, community networks, availability of sympathetic doctors and/or druggists, and so forth. But these differences were marginal. Like the general differential in medical care, the differences were not so great as they are today, because the best available methods were not so good as they are today. In many areas of medicine the "regular" doctors of the nineteenth century were offering remedies inferior to those of traditional folk healers, and the birth-control views of the "regulars" were particularly backward. A requirement for effective birth control, familiarity with one's reproductive organs, may have presented more problems for upper-class women, because of prudery, than for working-class and other poor women.

Class differences in the nineteenth century were important in birth control, but they should not blind us to the basic similarity in women's experiences. Although infanticide was confined to the very poor, the number of infanticides was tiny compared with the prevalence of other birth-control methods. The desire for and the problems in securing abortion and contraception made up a shared female experience. Abortion technique was apparently not much safer among upper-class doctors than among working-class midwives. The most commonly used contraceptives—douches, withdrawal—were accessible to women of every class. And what evidence there is of the subjective experience of women in their birth-control attempts also suggests that the desire for spaced motherhood and smaller families existed in every class, and that the desire was so passionate that women would take severe risks to win a little space and control in their lives. The individual theory and practice of birth control stems from a biological female condition that is more basic even than class.

But when a birth-control *movement* began, that biological unity among women was left far behind. From the first attempts at arguing for the legalization of birth control, the birth-controllers sought reasons and justifications that expressed particular economic, social, ethnic, and even geographical identities as well as concern with the female sex. This difference between the orientation of an individual impulse and a social movement exists with every social issue. This is not only because all individuals are different and must seek their commonness from within many individualities when they choose to work together, but also because social issues are not seen in the same contexts by different persons. Birth control, a simple act of biological self-control for an individual, becomes involved with innumerable overlapping social factors when considered on a mass level. Factors such as ideal family size, wealth, cultural conditioning, religion, marital relations, child-raising arrangements, work necessities, physical space, geographical and climatic conditions mean that different social groups have different attitudes. Sharp and, for most, painful economic changes, increasing interpersonal harshness, new opportunities for women, the replacement of religion by technology—all these and many more things affected people's responses to the birth-control issue. Often, the birth-control campaigners thought they were conducting a universal movement, designed to benefit all women, but they were not, for other social factors overwhelmed women's personal desire for fewer conceptions and made them hostile to birth control. Often, too, the campaigners thought they were conducting a single-issue movement when in reality they were not, for their proposals carried implications for many other things. Perhaps every reform ultimately implies an entire political program. Certainly birth control had implications for sexual relations, for the family as an institution, for the status of women, and for the populations of continents which could not be disguised.

4

Prudent Sex
Neo-Malthusianism and Perfectionism

EVEN AS women were risking their lives and their reputations to control their childbearing, small groups of radicals, not at all widely known, were publicly challenging the prohibition on birth control. In the United States the first challenges came from socialists, today identified as "utopian socialists," ever since the Marxists applied that term to them as a criticism of their lack of strategic thought about how to transform the whole society. At the time, in the 1840s, 1850s, and 1860s, they were often called "perfectionists," because of their determination to create "perfection" here on earth. Several perfectionist groups established rural communes where they practiced reproductive control. Although they attracted very few members, their influence was greater than their size, especially on the women's rights advocates who several decades later began to agitate on the question of reproductive control.

The U.S. perfectionist socialists, oddly enough, got their birth-control ideas primarily from British Malthusians and Neo-Malthusians, neither of which group was at all perfectionist. The Malthusian tradition was by contrast markedly pessimistic and skeptical about any except minimal reforms. Despite the geographical and emotional distance of British Malthusianism from American radicals, it is important that we pause to examine its contributions to our own birth-control movement.

Malthusianism

In Britain in the nineteenth century, population growth and the possibility of its control became for the first time a public controversy. The development of a secular, capitalist "science" of economics helped remove population from the area of ineluctable natural events to an area that seemed open to human manipulation. Industrialism created a contradiction between Protestant-bourgeois attitudes of sexual prudery and fears of overpopulation. On the one hand, the bourgeoisie, dominated increasingly by industrialists, was threatened by unrest among the urban and especially the rural poor, whose economic position had been worsened by industrialization.[1] On the other hand, the bourgeoisie had created over a three-century period a culture that severely repressed sexual activity in order to inculcate discipline and self-repression into its work force. Bourgeois culture by the late eighteenth century was especially hostile to women's autonomy, and imposed limitations on women partly through an ideology that made motherhood dominant among women's roles and linked it inseparably to sex. Birth control would have destroyed that linkage, and secular and religious authorities condemned it absolutely. Thus the goals of population control and sexual control were somewhat at odds.

If the bourgeoisie was divided on the question of reproductive control because of its sexual attitudes, it was also divided in attitudes toward over-all social control. Capitalist political theory had a "radical" and a Liberal version by the late eighteenth century. "Radical" meant a democratic and somewhat more egalitarian version of Liberalism; above all, the radical streams of political thought were optimistic, asserting the possibility of the perfection of society. The Liberal tradition, by contrast, was more pessimistic. By the early nineteenth century Liberals had absorbed much of the cynicism of the Hobbesian conservatives, a cynicism appropriate to them now that they represented a dominant class. Liberals speculated that inequality and widespread poverty were inevitable and necessary to the maintenance of a high culture. Their laissez-faire economics was often but a rewording of natural-law arguments against tampering with the ordained order.

This political division was almost immediately carried into the population issue. The response to Malthus was divided doubly, between radical and Liberal attitudes toward social control, and between concern for sexual control and concern for population control. These differences made the Malthusian controversy complex. A tendency among historians to oversimplify that controversy has lumped together all Malthus's supporters in one group and all his opponents in another. In reality, a complex set of responses made Malthusianism a tradition open to many different interpretations.

Malthus's ideas on population were part of his general work as a political economist of the developing industrial-capitalist system, which he defended primarily against its mercantilist opponents. Malthus was a Liberal, and the economic forms he defended, such as the transformation of virtually all the nation's men into wage laborers, were attacked more from the Right than from the Left. Malthus appears in history as doing battle chiefly with the radicals in large part because his work on population has continued controversial. Yet in the first edition of Malthus's *Essay*, then a mere pamphlet, it is clear that the population issue was but one among many points on which Malthus disagreed with Godwin and other advocates of revolutionary utopianism.

In all his views, even as they changed, Malthus identified himself with the capitalist class and identified its welfare with the welfare of his nation. He wrote that it was impossible "to remove the want of the lower classes of society . . . the pressure of distress on this part of a community is an evil so deeply seated, that no human ingenuity can reach it." [2] An opponent of the existing British Poor Laws,* he wrote in the second edition in 1803:

A man who is born into the world already possessed, if he cannot get subsistence from his parents on whom he has a just demand, and

---

* Legislation providing for state support of the needy.

if the society do not want his labor, has no claim of *right* to the smallest of good, and, in fact, has no business to be where he is. At nature's mighty feast there is no vacant cover for him. She tells him to be gone, and will quickly execute her own orders, if he do not work upon the compassion of some of her guests. If these guests get up and make room for him, other intruders immediately appear demanding the same favor. . . .[3]

In his attacks on any hint of the traditional right of subsistence in the Poor Laws, Malthus was helping the British bourgeoisie to destroy local traditions of welfare and community responsibility, and thereby to create a working class defenseless against incorporation into industry. His work was ultimately influential in securing the passage of the Poor Law of 1834, a measure reflecting the interests of the industrial capitalists almost exclusively: it abolished "outdoor relief," forcing the poor to enter workhouses or, as their only alternative, to take low-paying factory jobs.[4] The Law of 1834 has been called Malthusian, and certainly Malthus supplied the original (and tenacious) theory that welfare provisions themselves contribute to overpopulation by encouraging reproduction among the poor,[5] a false attack still hurled at welfare legislation today.

The most important contribution of Malthusian population theory to that body of political thought lay in its assumptions, not in its calculations or policy recommendations. His formula that population increases geometrically and subsistence arithmetically does not stand up.[6] His prediction that deliberate birth limitation could not work was already being proven false in France, where birth rates had been falling for many decades.[7] Much more long-lasting as a theory, however, was the idea that overpopulation itself is the major cause of poverty. Indeed, this idea is the kernel of Malthusianism. It made "natural" disasters such as war and famine take on social meaning— they were population regulators whether so intended or not. In the particular historical period in which Malthus offered his interpretation of population and poverty, the theory justified employers' interests in offering the lowest possible wages. Indeed, the theory presented the capitalist system of forcing laborers into jobs at subsistence wages as somehow inevitable, as being determined by natural laws such as those that governed reproduction. Malthusian population theory tended to draw attention away from the organization of labor and the distribution of resources. Periodic overpopulation was presented as universal; Malthus did not notice, or did not care to mention, that the rich did not suffer from overpopulation and famine.

By denying a class analysis of poverty, Malthusian theory denied the validity of class antagonism as a strategy for change. Demands made by the poor of the rich were illegitimate; only through self-help and sexual restraint could the poor help themselves. Malthus saw this sexual restraint as doubly valuable: not only would it reduce population but it would also stimulate industriousness. (Malthus operated on the basis of a crude theory of sublimation, an assumption that the frustration of the sex urge would induce men to put more energy into their work.) Yet at the same time Malthus was suspicious of sexual restraint, as of all forms of birth control, not merely out of religious scruples but because of his primary concern for the class interests of industrialists: "Prudential habits with regard to marriage, carried to a considerable extent among the labouring class of a country mainly dependent upon manufactures and commerce, might injure it." [8] As Marx pointed out, Malthus in fact understood overpopulation as a product of the economic system, of the "Trinity of capitalistic production: over-production, over-population, over-consumption," but would not admit it.[9] Instead Malthus, while denying a class analysis to those who might use it against the system, put forward the perspective of the industrial capitalist class as if it were universal truth.

Two assumptions, then, are central to Malthusianism: that overpopulation causes poverty and that individual failings in the form of lack of restraint cause overpopulation. These two assumptions are equally central to Neo-Malthusianism and reveal the historical connection that gives the two "isms" the same name. In birth-control history Malthusianism and Neo-Malthusianism were in opposition. Malthus was opposed to contraception, which he considered a vice. "Neo-Malthusianism," to the contrary, was a name applied to early advocates of contraception. But both shared the view that overpopulation caused poverty, and it was on that premise that the Neo-Malthusians concluded that population control could prevent poverty. Both also shared the recommendation of self-help, as opposed to class struggle, as a remedy for poverty.

Neo-Malthusianism

Neo-Malthusianism in its origins was the radical version of Malthusian population theory. Based on optimistic premises, the Neo-Malthusians believed not only that population could be controlled but that its control could provide a key to the creation of a perfect society. It is sometimes said that they turned Malthus on his head. But they only reversed his religious opposition to contraception; they did not reverse his basic assumptions about the driving forces in the world, as Marx was later to do to Hegel.

Nevertheless, the Neo-Malthusians had important differences with Liberals. Primarily they accepted contraception. Anticlericalism, antimysticism and even anti-Christianity made the radicals more prepared to challenge both the conservative interpretation that Providence determined family size and the Liberal one that only restraint could do it. Also associated with radicalism was a positive, even adulatory, attitude toward science and technology which inclined them favorably toward contraceptive technology. Perhaps most important was the radicals' greater acceptance of the scientific attitude that nature could be controlled and manipulated by human effort; surely it was this urge that led the Neo-Malthusians, when they encountered some traditional contraceptive formulas, to recommend them enthusiastically to the poor as a cure for their poverty.

Neo-Malthusianism itself had two distinct stages. The first, which I shall call radical Neo-Malthusianism, was a small propaganda campaign undertaken sporadically between 1820 and 1850 by men active in other radical causes as well, such as trade unionism and workers' education. The second, by far the better known Neo-Malthusianism, flourished particularly after the 1870s and, in Britain, established a tradition that continued uninterrupted into modern population-control movements. The earlier form of Neo-Malthusianism affected American birth-control thought, while the latter form had far less influence in the United States. (Malthusian economics, of course, has been tremendously influential in the United States, but it did not arrive through the mediation of British Neo-Malthusianism.) For that reason we must examine the early, radical Neo-Malthusian ideas closely, whereas the late-nineteenth-century version is beyond our scope.[10]

The most distinct difference between the radical Neo-Malthusians and the Liberal Malthusians was the former's rejection of sexual prudery.[11] They were willing to accept not only the implications of conception-free intercourse, but also those of publication and public discussion of contraceptive methods, matters considered offensive to taste as well as to morals by most Liberals. Radicals also differed from Malthusians in their concern to defend civil liberties.

Although their libertarian views were important, radical Neo-Malthusianism was essentially a campaign to promote contraception in the hope that smaller families might ameliorate poverty. It began as a particular interpretation of Malthusian theory and later became the dominant interpretation. As it developed, its differences from Malthus's original meaning increased. When Neo-Malthusians began radical agitation in the 1820s and 1830s, they did not challenge the framework of capitalist economics and class relations. They were responding to a period of strong working-class resistance to the oppressive conditions of industrialization in Britain. The massacre of demonstrators at Peterloo in 1819 was a signpost of that unrest. In the 1820s and 1830s, Britain experienced the first attempts at mass unionization. The development of the Grand National Consolidated Trades Union —an attempt at a national industrial workers' organization—brought militant syndicalist ideas and threats of general strike to the public. Whereas some advocated increased repression as a means of preventing social upheaval, others, equally worried, searched for peaceful solutions. Neo-Malthusianism appealed to the latter.

Francis Place was the leading Neo-Malthusian of the 1820s. An artisan tailor, he had amassed enough funds to retire in 1816 at the age of forty-five and continue full-time his work in radical electoral politics. His political work was derivative of an older tradition of artisanal, individualist reformism, oriented to self-help. He was distant from and even hostile to the industrial working class, and had never even visited the industrial north of England. He did not take into account massive unemployment and was skeptical of the existence of undeserved poverty. He wanted to instruct workers "in the great truth, that it is themselves, and themselves only, who have the means to better their own condition, to increase their own respectability." [12] The content of his radicalism was political democracy for men within electoral representative institutions; in his economic thought he did not deviate from classical capitalist theory; his social thought was directed to helping the poor without fundamental redistribution of wealth. Thus it was natural that he focused his efforts for many years on providing education for the working class. The goal of public education was to make the workers better workers and to afford a tiny proportion of them the opportunity—through excelling in their work as defined by the employing class—to leave their class and reach a higher social status. Place worked for the repeal of the Combination Laws, which had banned unions, because he thought the Laws stirred up class conflict: "They made them hate their employers. . . . And they made them hate those of their own class who refused to join them. . . ." Place was opposed to labor unions, and hoped to suppress class-consciousness among the workers.[13]

In 1823 Place wrote and published four anonymous handbills urging contraception as a means of self-help for the working class.[14] In them he recommended the use of a sponge, attached to a thread, inserted in the vagina before intercourse.

> With mankind and healthy married people, sexual intercourse is as unavoidable, as it is wholesome and virtuous. But it is by no means desirable, it is indeed, a continued torture, that a married woman should be incessantly breeding or bringing forth children, often unhealthy, and born with a certainty of death in infancy and nothing but the patients [sic] of pain: as often born where there are not the means of wholesome support: and, what is still worse, where the mother is of a delicate frame, and never can produce healthy children, conception is to her nothing but torture.[15]

Even in these short leaflets, Place made clear the Malthusian basis of his economic theory, in the form of the classic wages-fund theory. "It is a great truth, often told and never denied, that when there are too many working people in any trade or manufacture, they are worse paid than they ought to be paid, and are compelled to work more hours than they ought to work. . . ."[16]

It is not our purpose here to evaluate Place's economics on its own merit, but merely to point out its social implications. For example, in his handbills Place also implied that large families were the cause of child labor, and that small families could end it. His argument was that the working class is the cause of much of its own misery and is responsible for helping itself. Self-help is the common theme in all Place's political work. Its importance lies not in its content, but in what it denies—that the capitalist class is responsible for working-class misery and that instead of "helping itself" the working class might do better to attack its exploiters.

Place's handbills won him a few enthusiastic followers, but never a general popularity. The response of most class-conscious, working-class radicals to Place's propaganda was, on the other hand, negative. Anti-Malthusianism was already established in working-class thought by the 1820s.[17] *The Black Dwarf*, a working-class newspaper especially popular among miners, attacked Place's proposals. An editorial in 1823 argued that the population of drones, who ate without working, ought to be checked, rather than cut back the number of working bees to leave more honey for the drones.[18] Early Chartists considered Place's campaign as reactionary, not differing politically from Malthusianism. The *Trades Newspaper and Mechanics Weekly Journal*, which Place had helped establish, denounced his theories as not in the best interests of the working people and not touching their real grievances.[19] Ordinary prudery was also influential in the working-class press. Place and his supporters were charged with stimulating prostitution, destroying the chastity of women, and licensing unnatural acts.

The overall significance of Place's reforms for the working class is complex. The working-class opposition to Neo-Malthusianism should not blind us to the importance of contraception for every individual, but especially for women. The early-nineteenth-century workers' publications and organizations in Britain were dominated by men. The single women, whose chastity they feared for, and the married women, who bore the children, were not asked for their opinions. Place himself was more concerned with the problems of working-class women. Furthermore, he never claimed that population control was a panacea. Later Neo-Malthusians began to claim increasingly grandiose benefits from population reduction, which culminated in mid-twentieth-century advocacy of population control as a cure for poverty and underdevelopment, but Place by contrast continued to devote his energies to a wide range of reforms in what he saw as the interest of the urban poor.

Nevertheless, Place offered contraception encapsulated in an ideology that promoted acceptance of the capitalist mode of production and distribution. He urged workers to better themselves individually by having smaller families but did not challenge a system of production that would inevitably re-create inequality no matter how small the workers' families were. Indeed, even as an individual remedy Place's recommendation was flawed, for no single small family could benefit from higher wages, even on Place's wages-fund theory, unless all or many workers similarly limited their families. Contraception was first urged upon the working class as part of a theory that denied the concept of exploitation. It is no wonder that many industrial workers rejected this inherent blame-the-victim logic.

Unable to compete with the campaign for the suffrage-reform bill of 1832 and the Chartist movement, contraception propaganda claimed the attention of radicals only sporadically in the first half of the nineteenth century. And the evidence of birth rates suggests that the impact of the publication of contraceptive information was small. Only the revival of Neo-Malthusianism in the 1870s correlated with a marked birth-rate decline, and that among the professional and business classes.[20] It is not clear that the Neo-Malthusians' political decision to aim their propaganda at the working class was ever successful. Rather, their major contribution seems to have been the creation of a new general mood in which, after much controversy and some legal struggle, contraception again became a fit topic for public discussion. Despite its intentions, British Neo-Malthusianism was ultimately most effective as a sexual-reform movement, a challenge to Victorian standards of propriety.

Perfectionism

The same could be said of American Neo-Malthusianism—that it was most influential as a challenge to the Victorian sexual system. In its development, however, American Neo-Malthusianism followed a different trajectory. Spread largely through the influence of Robert Owen, it was adopted by utopian socialists like Robert Dale Owen and Frances Wright, and religious utopians like John Humphrey

Noyes. These socialists tried to put contraception into practice within alternative socialist communities. They saw a far more revolutionary potential in contraception than the British Neo-Malthusians had perceived, and communicated this new interpretation of contraception to others.

In abbreviated form, the intellectual flow of Malthusian ideas to the United States might look like this: Malthus to radical democratic Neo-Malthusianism; through Owen to U.S. utopian socialists; through the cluster of reformers and radicals in the United States in the 1840s to the feminist movement. But though the communication of ideas is important, the acceptance of ideas depends on the social circumstances and needs of the people.

In the 1820s the United States was less industrialized than Britain and American reformers less concerned with the problems of a large working class and of agricultural impoverishment. The continuing small-farm basis of American society drew many reformers into an attempt to reject industrialism, by either struggling to retain a society based on independent farm and artisanal families as economic units, or by searching for transfamily units of collective life. From the 1820s to the Civil War, American radicals explored a variety of reform programs related to one another in their hostility to industrial capitalism; religious revivals, vegetarianism and other health cults, and utopian socialism were prominent among them. Reformers in all three types of movements recommended certain types of reproductive control. Although their first birth-control ideas were close to early British Neo-Malthusian thinking, the optimistic mode of radical thought in the United States transformed them deeply. American ideologies about reproductive control ended up rejecting the pessimistic and conservative outlook of their Malthusian origins.

Robert Owen, socialist industrialist of New Lanark, may have been a supporter of Place's neo-Malthusian ideas; his son, Robert Dale Owen, moved to the United States and became a major advocate of contraception through his New York paper, *The Free Enquirer*.[21] Dale Owen's co-editor, Frances Wright, also supported those ideas in her utopian colony, Nashoba; a feminist, Wright's ideas influenced the women's rights movement.[22] Owen's tracts, produced just a few years after Place's work, had already begun a major transformation of the

Neo-Malthusian idea. Owen, a socialist, argued for reproductive control on the grounds of women's right to self-determination. He attacked the fear that contraception would stimulate license as an example of the sexual double standard. He also attacked celibacy, sexual repression, and sexual ignorance. Owen insisted that the fundamental economic problem was not overpopulation but maldistribution of wealth and oppression of the poor. Population excess was relative, not just to the means of subsistence but also to the system of control over the means of subsistence. Population-control measures would alleviate certain local pockets of poverty temporarily, but poverty would always reproduce itself under capitalism.[23] Thus Owen's anti-capitalism and feminism placed Neo-Malthusian ideas in a different context. There was far less of helping others in his ideas and far more of a revolutionary view of society. Later reformers who incorporated contraceptive ideas in their theory and practice moved still further in this direction.

Religious groups shared this impulse. In its original sense, "perfectionism" referred to the belief of a group of upstate New York and western New England Christian revivalists in the 1830s that human beings could, through conversion, become perfect while still on earth. The leading exponent of religious perfectionism was John Humphrey Noyes, who founded a utopian colony at Oneida, New York, in the 1840s. For him and his followers, retiring to a new community allowed the rejection of worldliness and the creation of a perfect society. His purpose in forming a separate, deliberate socialist community was identical with that of many secular utopian communitarians. His perfectionism was a religious version of revolutionary utopianism, as exemplified by anarchists such as William Godwin and his followers in the United States.

In America, all radicalism was imbued with perfectionism in the early nineteenth century. The perfectionist tendency rejected the skepticism of the old world, a skepticism engendered by the solidity of class distinctions, the seeming eternalness of human sufferings, and the "lessons" of industrialization—that economic progress had to be bought with the misery of the many. In the United States many factors were different: the availability of land, the sense of starting with an open if not empty slate, the absence of an aristocracy and the promise of great social mobility combined to produce a more optimistic view of the potential of human society. Utopianism seemed practicable.

Perfectionism also produced a tendency to view individual reforms as carrying the potential for total cure of social ills. The skepticism of the old-world tradition carried with it a view of social ills as insolubly complex, whereas new-world optimism tended toward oversimplification. Characteristic of all the reformers of the early nineteenth century was the belief that a single level of change might bring the utopia into being. As Sylvester Graham recommended whole-grain and fruit diet, as Mary Gove Nichols recommended therapeutic baths, as Noyes recommended a new religion—each as a panacea—so some thought that reproductive control could solve all the problems of humanity. There was something about the hope for perfection on earth that made it difficult for reformers to encompass many variables in their analyses of problems, to contemplate the complex clusters of factors that in fact produce social change.

Two aspects of the perfectionist application of reproductive-control schemes are worth discussing here, as both created traditions of thought that continued into the twentieth century. One was the notion to use contraceptive technique to effect qualitative as well as quantitative control over human reproduction—a system later called eugenics. A second was the notion that sexual liberation could be brought about by conception-free intercourse and the technique of avoiding conception itself, and that this liberation would create perfectly contented individuals and, through them, a perfectly tuned society. Both theories involved a rejection of mechanical or chemical contraception in favor of changes in the nature of sexual intercourse itself and therefore involved whole theories of sexuality and human relations. For this reason, they were of importance for future feminist birth-control thought.

Both eugenic and sexual aspects of the perfectionist approach to reproductive control are well exemplified in the communitarian writings and practice of John Humphrey Noyes, first at Putney, Vermont, and from the late 1840s at the Oneida Community. Let us first consider perfectionist sexual ideology as preached by Noyes and others, and then return to perfectionist eugenics. Noyes imposed on his followers a sexual system that he called male continence. Under this regimen, men refrained from ejaculation. (It was a rejection of *coitus interruptus* as well as of propagative intercourse; intercourse including ejaculation was permitted only when it had been decided in advance that conception was desirable.) Male continence allowed a system of multiple sexual partners, and Noyes prohibited monogamous marriage entirely. More than a system of preventing conception, male continence was a higher form of sex, and sex was considered the highest expression of love. Expanding and deepening human sexual experience was part of perfection here on earth, Noyes insisted, just as he argued that sexual intercourse went on in heaven too.[24]

Although male continence rejected traditional male preferences in intercourse, it was neither antisexual nor antimale. It did not involve any form of physical frustration. By learning to constrict the seminal ducts—a task considered by Noyesians to be easy once learned—the male could experience orgasm without ejaculation.[25] Nor did male continence abolish male supremacy and heterosexuality as the norm of sexual expression. In Noyes's community, sexual relations could be had between any individual man and woman. But he did not tolerate homosexual relations or group sex, and men always did the asking. Furthermore, in his exaltations of the benefits of suppressing orgasm it was only male pleasure that was considered.

What was it, then, that made male continence an allegedly superior form of sexual intercourse? The answer lay in a theory of human energy frequently called animal magnetism by its nineteenth-century believers; at other times they used electrical metaphors, or hydraulic ones. The operative assumption was that the body's energy was of finite quantity and, normally, in a closed circuit; the loss of semen was weakening to the system and was not a loss readily recouped. The loss of semen caused by regular intercourse produced many afflictions, ranging from nervous anxiety to general lassitude to specific ailments. On the other hand, intercourse without the loss of semen was highly beneficial. It produced an interchange of magnetic, or electric, influences between a man and a woman which was the physiological correlate of love and which contributed good health and energy to both persons. One variation of magnetic sexual theory, "sedular absorption," had it that the reabsorption of semen into the male's system added to a man's mental, physical, and sexual strength. Even those who did not posit any particular salubrious effect from seminal fluid itself argued that the control acquired and exercised in refraining from ejaculation strengthened character and raised up the sexual experience until it gained the spiritual level of art or religious communion.[26]

Magnetation theorists saw themselves as "transcending" the "propagative plane" and reaching to more intense sexual experience. "Physical propagation is but the vestibule of sex use. . . ." [27] They were in some ways sexual connoisseurs, but in an antihedonist, radical mode. Sexual stimulation in itself they saw as wholesome. Indeed, magnetation theorists made an important contribution to ultimate popular rejection of Victorian prudery through their distinction between "amative" and "propagative" aspects of sexual intercourse—acclaiming the former and charging that the latter was often misused. Their distinction often rested on distinguishing between amative and propagative physical organs, thus distinguishing sexual feeling from propagative desire. They recognized women's sexual drive as separate from the maternal drive. Furthermore, their insistence on the healthfulness of sexual stimulation applied to both sexes, and the control they required of men helped to challenge the double standard. Avoiding ejaculation meant that men were able to continue intercourse for longer periods of time. Male-continence advocates harped on this as a feature of their system which brought special delight to women, and their publications were regularly full of glowing testimonials from women about how much they liked the system. For example:

> Since my husband became acquainted with this new theory he has endeared himself to me a hundredfold; and although our so-called "honeymoon" was passed five years ago, it was no more real and far less lasting than the ecstatic, the unspeakable happiness which is now continually mine. My prosaic and sometimes indifferent husband has changed by a heavenly magic into an ardent and entrancing lover, for whose coming I watch with all the tender raptures of a schoolgirl. His very step sends a thrill through me, for I know that my beloved will clasp me in his arms and cover me with kisses. . . .[28]

But the elements of the male-continence analysis that reflected concern with women's situations were limited. The clitoris was not identified as the female "amative" organ, but rather the vagina. In describing the process of the interchange of energies, they thought only of the friction of intercourse and did not normally consider other variations of sexual stimulation as capable of producing the desired effect. Magnetation theorists continued, as did Noyes, within a male-centered definition of "the sexual act." Indeed, their use of that phrase, still common today, expressed their confidence that there was but one normal sexual form, heterosexual intercourse. The sexual system created by these perfectionists was no threat to the male power to define sexuality. Nevertheless, in its system-building quality it was inseparable from the utopian urge to leave the existing society behind and start anew.

Male continence shared with many other reform causes of the nineteenth century the tendency to present itself as a panacea. That tendency was greatly strengthened by its association with various theories and schemes of eugenics, forms of human engineering expected to lead to perfection. Perfectionist eugenic ideas were expounded by all the American birth-control advocates, including the most rationalist of them. Robert Dale Owen wrote:

> I may seem an enthusiast—but so let me seem then—when I express my conviction, that there is no greater physical disparity between the dullest, shaggiest race of dwarf draught horses, and the fiery-spirited and silken-haired Arabian, than between man degenerate as he is, and man perfected as he might be; and though mental cultivation in this counts for much, yet organic melioration is an influential—an *indispensable*—accessory.[29]

Owen, Charles Knowlton and others emphasized the prevention of hereditary diseases through the use of birth control.[30] With these goals perfectionist utopians created a eugenic experiment—that is, to try not only to prevent bad hereditary traits but to breed deliberately for positive traits. Such a scheme had occurred to many—as exemplified in Henry Ward Beecher's comment that the surest way for a man to improve himself would be to choose his own grandparents. But other scruples against birth control prevented all but those who took sexually radical positions from attempting to put such thoughts into practice.

The sexual ideology of the Oneida Community made such an experiment possible.[31] Although Oneida gained a contemporary reputation for promiscuity, in fact sexual relations were tightly controlled. Rules governed everything: the couples that might form, the places they could go, their allotted time together, for example. Permanent couples were not permitted, and multiple sexual partners encouraged, though women at least in principle had their right to refuse guaranteed. All the members of the community were said to be married to each other collectively—Noyes called it "complex marriage"—and indeed they were all socially and economically committed to one another. Organized social pressure disciplined men who had not mastered the technique of continence, and few unwanted children were born. The desired children were produced with the intervention of Noyes and a committee who examined applicants for parenthood and assigned them to mates who would produce desirable children.

Through his eugenic system, "stirpiculture," * Noyes planned not only to expand but to improve the quality of the Oneida Community through breeding over better perfectionists. Nothing could have been a better expression of the perfectionist impulse than the notion of applying human intelligence to breeding a better race. Unlike later eugenists, the Oneidans had no dogmatic theory of genetics and paid as much attention to upbringing as to breeding. Their communist alternative to the nuclear family extended to child-raising as well as sexual relations, and they raised the "stirps" communally, their private hours with their mothers rigorously restricted. They sought to create human beings perfect spiritually, religiously, and emotionally.

There is a great distance between these schemes and British Neo-Malthusianism. The antiscientific, utopian, and even mystical attitudes of the American perfectionists seem remote from Malthus and Place. The American radicals by and large opposed contraception whereas their British counterparts accepted it. The Americans had an anti-industrial and antitechnological bias that made them suspicious of contraception; the Americans also, in their unorthodox way, were generally more moralistic and antihedonist in their sexual attitudes.

---

* The breeding of humans.

Furthermore the large land area and later industrialization in the United States meant that overpopulation did not seem a threat. The American descendants of British Neo-Malthusianism did not adhere to Malthusian economics or its contraceptive recommendations. What the Americans shared with the Neo-Malthusians was an enthusiasm for reproductive control as a means of creating larger social change. Planned parenthood for the perfectionists was a path to a new order, an instrumental and utilitarian tool, only secondarily a matter of increasing individual freedom. (Indeed, some collectivist utopians considered themselves opposed to individualism and had no commitment to expanding individual rights.) In this they were part of the population-control tradition.

The modification that American perfectionists created in Neo-Malthusian ideology made them marginally more favorable to women's rights, however. The optimism and utopianism of the American reform community nourished the feminist aspirations of many female reformers while it developed their organizational skills. When organized feminism began in the United States, it was not simply a reaction to the discrimination against women in, for example, the abolitionist movement, but was also a logical development of the idea that these women had absorbed from their male reform mentors that a perfect society could be created. If this was the general climate that produced a feminist orientation, the specific ideology that stimulated feminism was the exploration of sex radicalism by American perfectionists.

In the conditions of early-Victorian America, any rebellion against sexual prudery had to contain a recognition of female sexuality. The essence of prudery was not a blanket sexual repression, but a sexual distortion based on deepening the male-female distinction to an extent that sexualized the entire universe. Contemporary critics of prudery knew that the distortion they hated had created oversexualization more than undersexualization. We will see in the next chapter how they constructed their arguments, but it is important to observe now their conclusion: that the suppression of women was a necessary basis of the whole Victorian sexual system. In demanding the end of censorship on sexual discussion, the legalization of divorce, the abolition of prostitution, and the spiritualization of sexual relationships, the sex radicals believed that these objectives could not be achieved with women in bondage.

The perfectionist birth controllers, almost all men, were sometimes frightened by the logical trajectories of their own ideas. They were worried by the accusation that birth control would destroy female chastity and took care to answer such objections at length. (They were unconcerned at the possible loss of male chastity, by contrast.) Noyes took care to institutionalize his sexual experiments at Oneida (and previously at Putney, Vermont) within rigidly male-supremacist lines. Frances Wright became a spokeswoman for Owen's birth-control views, but her own unconventional sexual behavior left her defenseless against vicious, misogynistic attacks and ultimately destroyed her effectiveness as an advocate. Yet Robert Dale Owen seems to have realized that the direction of his sexual thought was inherently appealing to women. In 1830, shortly after having published his *Moral Physiology*, he noticed a high proportion of favorable responses from women. He wrote that he had always expected that women would appreciate his views more than men, "inasmuch as their minds are less contaminated and their moral feelings stronger." Owen went on to say that he could hardly urge women to endanger themselves by making their birth-control views public, that women could not easily oppose any dominant prejudice until they had political equality. Nevertheless, he added, "I know that we men are always more inclined to push ourselves forward and monopolize whatever we can; but it is not always those that are the most forward, who best deserve the situations they assume. There are many things which women could teach us better than men, if they would but overcome their diffidence, and turn their minds to it." [32]

Owen's request was answered. The feminist movement of the 1840s stimulated the discussion of sexual issues among women, and women began to express their views on birth control with a remarkable lack of diffidence considering the heavy condemnation they received. From the beginnings of feminist groups, women talked among themselves about their unhappiness with the entire sexual system. By the 1870s they had gained sufficient clarity about their critique of the system, and sufficient confidence in their movement, to raise publicly a birth-control demand, which they called voluntary motherhood. As we turn to examine it now we will see how deeply it was influenced by perfectionism.

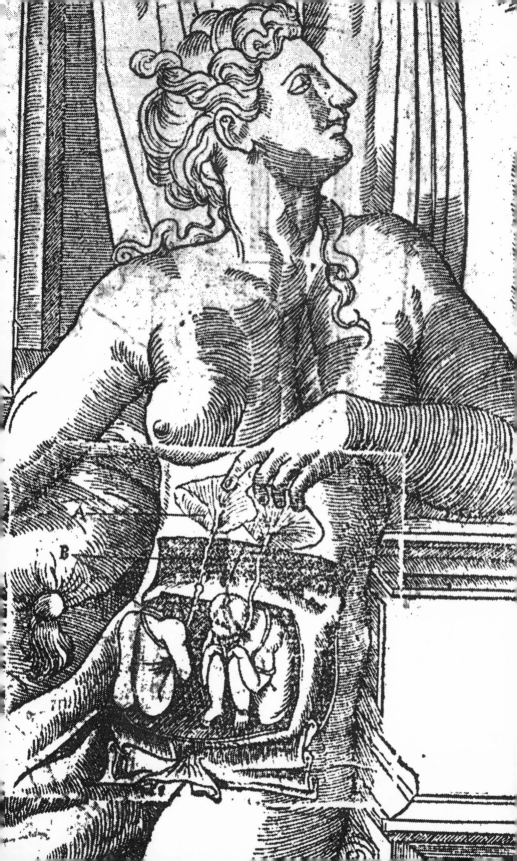

Part II

Toward Women's Power

5
Voluntary Motherhood
The Beginnings of the Birth-Control Movement

By THE 1870s the feminist movement in the United States was divided into many different organizations and loose reform tendencies. Yet among these groups there was a remarkably coherent ideology on major questions—marriage and divorce, suffrage, employment opportunity, for example—and on no question so much as on that of birth control. The standard name applied to the demand for birth control was "voluntary motherhood"—incorporating a political statement about the nature of *involuntary* motherhood and child-rearing in women's lives and a solution to the problems they presented.

The feminists who advocated voluntary motherhood were of three general types: suffragists (divided between two national organizations and many local groups), moral reformers (in causes such as temperance, social purity, church auxiliaries, and women's professional and service organizations), and members of small free-love groups. The political distance between some of these feminists was great—as between the socially conservative churchwomen and the usually atheistic and anarchistic free lovers, for example. Thus their relative unity as

feminists and voluntary-motherhood advocates seems the more remarkable.

Free-love groups in the 1870s were the closest successors to the
perfectionist reform groups of the first half of the century. The
free-love movement was always closely related to free thought, or
agnosticism, and was characterized by a passionate resentment of the
Christian established churches, especially in their power to influence
law and create restrictive social and cultural norms. They called
themselves free lovers as a means of describing their opposition to legal
and clerical marriage which, they believed, stifled love. Free-love
groups were always small and sectarian and were usually male-domi-
nated, despite their ideological feminism. They never coalesced into a
large or national organization, but represented the dying remnants of
a preindustrial period of utopian reform. Their very self-definition
built around their iconoclasm and isolation from the masses, the free
lovers could offer intellectual leadership in formulating the shocking
arguments that birth control in the nineteenth century required.[1]

The suffragists and moral reformers, on the other hand, concerned to win mass support, became increasingly committed to social
respectability; as a result they did not generally advance far beyond
prevalent standards of propriety in discussing sexual matters publicly.
Indeed, as the century progressed the social gap between these people
and the free lovers grew, for the second and third generations of
suffragists had become increasingly respectable (whereas in the 1860s
and 1870s the great feminist theoreticians, such as Elizabeth Cady
Stanton, had been intellectually closer to the free lovers, and at least
one of these early giants, Victoria Woodhull, was for several years a
member of both the suffragist and the free-love camp). But even the
quest for respectability did not stifle these feminists completely, and
many of them said in private writings—in letters and diaries—what
they were unwilling to utter in public.

The similarities between free lovers and suffragists on the question of voluntary motherhood should be understood then not as
minimizing the political distance between them, but as showing how
their analyses of the social meaning of reproduction for women were
converging. The sources of that convergence, the common ground of
their feminism, were their similar experiences in the changing condi-

tions of nineteenth-century America. Most were educated Yankees of professional, farm, or commercial families, responding to severe threats to the stability, if not dominance, of their class position. Both groups were disturbed by the consequences of rapid industrialization —the emergence of great capitalists and a clearly defined financial oligarchy, the increased immigration that provided cheap labor and further threatened the dignity and economic security of the Yankees. Above all they feared and resented the loss of their independence and would have undone the wage-labor system entirely had they been able. Free lovers and suffragists, as feminists, welcomed the decline in patriarchal power within families that followed upon industrialization, but they worried, too, about the possible disintegration of the family and the loosening of sexual morality. They saw reproduction in the context of these larger social changes and in the context of a movement for women's emancipation; and they saw that movement as an answer to some of these large social problems. They hoped that giving political power to women would help to reinforce the family, to make the government more just and the economy less monopolistic. In all these wishes there was something traditional as well as something progressive. Their voluntary-motherhood ideas reflected this duality.

Since we bring to our concept of birth control a twentieth-century understanding of it, it is important to stress the fact that neither free lovers nor suffragists approved of contraceptive devices. Ezra Heywood, patriarch and martyr, thought "artificial" methods "unnatural, injurious, or offensive." [2] Tennessee Claflin, feminist, spiritualist, and the sister of Victoria Woodhull, wrote that the "washes, teas, tonics and various sorts of appliances known to the initiated" were a "standing reproach upon, and a permanent indictment against, American women. . . . No woman should ever hold sexual relations with any man from the possible consequences of which she might desire to escape." [3] *Woodhull and Claflin's Weekly* editorialized: "The means they [women] resort to for . . . prevention is sufficient to disgust every natural man. . . ." [4]

On a rhetorical level the main objection to contraception was that it was unnatural, and the arguments reflected a romantic yearning for the "natural," rather pastorally conceived, that was typical of many nineteenth-century reform movements. More basic, however, in the women's arguments against contraception was an underlying fear of the promiscuity that it could permit. And that fear was associated less with any woman's fear for her own virtue than with her fear of other women—"fallen women"—who might undermine her husband's fidelity.

To our twentieth-century sensibility it would seem that a principle of voluntary motherhood that rejects contraception is a principle so theoretical as to be of little real impact. What gave it substance was that it was accompanied by another, potentially explosive, conceptual change: the reacceptance of female sexuality. Both free lovers and suffragists, interestingly, staked their claims here on the traditional grounds of the natural. Free lovers argued, for example, that celibacy was unnatural and dangerous—for men and women alike. "Pen cannot record, nor lips express, the enervating, debauching effect of celibate life upon young men and women. . . ." [5] Asserting the existence, legitimacy, and worthiness of female sexual drive was one of the free lovers' most important contributions to sexual reform; it was a logical correlate of their argument from the "natural" and appeal for the integration of body and soul.

Women's rights advocates, too, began, timidly, to argue the existence of female sexuality. Isabella Beecher Hooker wrote to her daughter: "Multitudes of women in all the ages who have scarce known what sexual desire is—being wholly absorbed in the passion of maternity—have sacrificed themselves to the beloved husbands as unto God—and yet these men, full of their human passion and defending it as righteous & God-sent lose all confidence in womanhood when a woman here and there betrays her similar nature & gives herself soul & body to the man she adores." [6] Alice Stockham, a spiritualist and feminist physician, lauded sexual desire in men and women as "the prophecy of attainment." She urged that couples avoid reaching sexual "satiety" with each other in order to keep their sexual desire constantly alive, for she considered desire pleasant and healthful.[7] Elizabeth Cady Stanton, commenting in her diary in 1883 on the Whitman poem "There is a Woman Waiting for Me," wrote, " . . he speaks as if the female must be forced to the creative act, apparently ignorant of the fact that a healthy woman has as much passion as a man, that she needs nothing stronger than the law of attraction to draw her to the male." [8] Still, she loved Whitman, and largely because of that openness about sex that made him the free lovers' favorite poet.

According to the system of ideas then dominant, women, lacking sexual drives, submitted to sexual intercourse in order to please their husbands and to conceive children. There was a nervousness about this view, however, expressed in the ambivalence of asserting both that women naturally lacked sexual drive and that they must be protected from exposure to sexuality lest they "fall" and become depraved, lustful monsters. This ambivalance perhaps came from a subconscious lack of certainty about the reality of the sexless woman, which was a construct laid only thinly on top of an earlier conception of woman as highly sexed, even insatiably so, that prevailed until the late eighteenth century. Victorian ambivalence on this question is nowhere more tellingly revealed than in the writings of physicians, who viewed woman's sexual organs as the source of her being, physical and psychological, and blamed most mental derangements on disorders of the genitals.[9] Indeed, they saw it as part of the nature of things, as Rousseau had written, that men were male only part of the time, but women were female always.[10] In a system that limited women's opportunities to make other contributions to culture, it was inevitable that women should be more strongly identified with sex than were men. Indeed, females were frequently called "the sex" in the nineteenth century.

The concept of the maternal instinct helped to make Victorian sexual attitudes more consistent. In many nineteenth-century writings we find the idea that the maternal instinct was the female analog to the male sex instinct; as if the two instincts were seated in analogous parts of the brain, or soul. Thus to suggest, as these feminists did, that women might have the capacity for being sexual subjects rather than mere objects, feeling impulses of their own, automatically tended to weaken the theory of the maternal instinct. In the fearful imagination of the self-appointed protectors of the family and of womanly innocence, the possibility that women might desire sexual contact not for the sake of pregnancy—that they might even desire it at a time when they positively did not want pregnancy—was a wedge in the door to denying that women had any special maternal instinct at all.

Most of the feminists did not want to open that door either. Indeed, it was common for nineteenth-century women's rights advocates to use the presumed special motherly nature and sexual purity of women as an argument for increasing their freedom and status. It is no wonder that many of them chose to speak their subversive speculations about the sexual nature of women privately, or at least softly. Even among the more outspoken free lovers, there was a certain amount of hedging. Lois Waisbrooker and Dora Forster, writing for a free-love journal in the 1890s, argued that although men and women both had an "amative" instinct, it was much stronger in men, and women— only women—also had a reproductive, or "generative," instinct. "I suppose it must be universally conceded that men make the better lovers," Forster wrote. She thought that it might be possible that "the jealousy and tyranny of men have operated to suppress amativeness in women, by constantly sweeping strongly sexual women from the paths of life into infamy and sterility and death," but thought also that the suppression, if it existed, had been permanently inculcated into woman's character.[11]

Modern birth-control ideas rest on a full acceptance, at least quantitatively, of female sexuality. Modern birth control is designed to permit sexual intercourse as often as desired without the risk of pregnancy. Despite the protestations of sex counselors that there are no norms for how often people should engage in intercourse, the popular view always has such norms. Most people in the mid-twentieth century think that "normal" couples indulge several times a week. Given this concept of sexual rhythms, and the accompanying concept of the purpose of birth control, the free lovers' rejection of artificial contraception and "unnatural" sex seems to eliminate the possibility of birth control at all. Nineteenth-century sexual reformers, however, had different sexual norms. They did not seek to make an infinite number of sterile sexual encounters possible. They wanted to make it possible for women to avoid pregnancy if they badly needed to do so for physical or psychological reasons, but they did not believe that it was essential for women to be able to indulge in sexual intercourse under those circumstances.

In short, for birth control they recommended periodic or permanent abstinence, and the tradition of "magnetation" theories of sex among the perfectionists made this seem a reasonable, moderate procedure. The proponents of voluntary motherhood had in mind two distinct contexts for abstinence. One was the mutual decision of a couple; the other was the unilateral decision of a woman. Let us consider them one at a time.

In the context of the nineteenth century's patriarchal society, the "mutual decision of a couple" often meant the will of the male. Thus abstinence chosen by a couple normally meant that the husband accepted self-imposed celibacy, either continuous or through a form of rhythm method. Some medical observers had correctly plotted the woman's fertility cycle, but the majority of physicians, accepting a logic of analogy from lower mammals rather than direct observation of humans, had got it quite wrong. (It was not until the 1920s that the ovulation cycle was correctly plotted, and the 1930s before it was generally understood among American doctors.) Ezra Heywood, for example, recommended avoiding intercourse from six to eight days before menstruation until ten to twelve days after it.[12] Careful use of the calendar could also provide control over the sex of a child, Heywood believed: conception in the first half of the menstrual cycle would produce girls, in the second half, boys.[13] These misconceptions functioned, conveniently, to make arguable Heywood's and others' ideas that celibacy and contraceptive devices were *both* dangerous.

Some voluntary-motherhood advocates explored another form of abstinence—male continence, or avoidance of ejaculation. Ezra Heywood, for example, endorsed the Oneida system, but was repelled by Noyes's authoritarian leadership and his ban on monogamous relationships.[14] Dr. Alice Stockham developed a more woman-centered approach to male continence, "Karezza," in which it was necessary for the woman as well as the man to avoid climax.[15]

Concern with sexual self-control was characteristic of the free lovers' point of view. It came to them mainly from the thought of the utopian communitarians of the early nineteenth century, but it was most fully developed theoretically by Ezra Heywood. Beginning with the assumption that people's "natural" instincts, left untrammeled, would automatically create a harmonic, peaceful, ecological society— an optimism certainly deriving directly from liberal philosophical faith in the innate goodness of man—Heywood applied it to sexuality, arguing that the natural sexual instinct was innately moderated and self-regulating. Heywood denied the social necessity of sublimation. On one level, Heywood's theory may seem inadequate as a psychology, since it cannot explain phenomena such as repression and the fact that adults have greater self-control than children. As a social critique, however, it has explanatory power. It argues that the society and its attendant repressions have distorted the animal's natural self-regulating mechanism and have thereby created excessive and obsessive sexual drives. It offers a social explanation for these phenomena usually described in psychological terms and holds out the hope that they can be changed.

Essentially the same as Wilhelm Reich's theory of "sex-economy," the Heywood theory of self-regulation went beyond Reich's in providing a weapon against one of the ideological defenses of male supremacy. Self-regulation as a goal was directed against the prevalent attitude that male lust was an uncontrollable urge, an attitude that functioned as a justification for rape specifically and for male sexual irresponsibility generally. We have to get away from the tradition of "man's necessities and woman's obedience to them," Stockham wrote.[16] The idea that men's desires are irrepressible is merely the other face of the idea that women's desires are nonexistent. Together the two created a circle that enclosed woman, making it her exclusive responsibility to say No, and making pregnancy her God-given burden if she didn't, while denying her both artificial contraception and the personal and social strength to rebel against male sexual demands.

Heywood developed his theory of natural sexual self-regulation in answer to the common anti-free-love argument that the removal of social regulation of sexuality would lead to unhealthy promiscuity: ". . . in the distorted popular view, Free Love tends to unrestrained licentiousness, to open the flood gates of passion and remove all barriers in its desolating course; but it means just the opposite; it means the *utilization of animalism,* and the triumph of Reason, Knowledge, and Continence." [17] He applied the theory of self-regulation to the problem of birth control only as an afterthought, perhaps when women's concerns with that problem reached him. Ideally, he believed, the amount of sexual intercourse that men and women desired would be exactly commensurate with the number of children that were wanted. Since sexual repression had had the boomerang effect of intensifying human sexual drives far beyond "natural" levels, effecting birth control now would require the development of the inner self-control to contain and repress sexual urges. But he expected that in time sexual moderation would come naturally.

Heywood's analysis, published in the mid-1870s, was concerned primarily with excessive sex drives in men. Charlotte Perkins Gilman, one of the leading theoreticians of the suffrage movement, reinterpreted that analysis two decades later to emphasize its effects on women. The economic dependence of woman on man, in Gilman's analysis, made her sexual attractiveness necessary not only for winning a mate, but as a means of getting a livelihood too. This is the case with no other animal. In the human female it had produced "excessive modification to sex," emphasizing weak qualities characterized by humans as "feminine." She made an analogy to the milk cow, bred to produce far more milk than she would need for her calves. But Gilman agreed entirely with Heywood about the effects of exaggerated sex distinction on the male, producing excessive sex energy and its excessive indulgence to an extent debilitating to the whole species. Like Heywood she believed that the path of progressive social evolution ran toward monogamy and toward reducing the promiscuous sex instinct.[18]

A second context for abstinence was the right of the wife unilaterally to refuse her husband. This idea is at the heart of voluntary motherhood. It was a key substantive demand in the mid-nineteenth century when both law and practice made sexual submission to her husband a woman's duty.[19] A woman's right to refuse is clearly the fundamental condition of birth control—and of her independence and personal integrity.

In their crusade for this right of refusal the voices of free lovers and suffragists were in unison. Ezra Heywood demanded "Woman's

Natural Right to ownership and control over her own body-self—a right inseparable from Woman's intelligent existence. . . ." [20] Paulina Wright Davis, at the National Woman Suffrage Association in 1871, attacked the law "which makes obligatory the rendering of marital rights and compulsory maternity." When, as a result of her statement, she was accused of being a free lover, she accepted the description.[21] Isabella Beecher Hooker wrote her daughter in 1869 advising her to avoid pregnancy until "you are prepared in body and soul to receive and cherish the little one. . . ." [22] Elizabeth Cady Stanton had characteristically used the same concept as Heywood's, that of woman owning her own body. Once asked by a magazine what she meant by it, she replied: ". . . womanhood is the primal fact, wifehood and motherhood its incidents. . . . must the heyday of her existence be wholly devoted to the one animal function of bearing children? Shall there be no limit to this but woman's capacity to endure the fearful strain on her life?" [23]

The insistence on women's right to refuse often took the form of attacks on men for their lusts and their violence in attempting to satisfy them. In their complaints against the unequal marriage laws, chief or at least loudest among them was the charge that they legalized rape.[24] Victoria Woodhull raged, "I will tell the world, so long as I have a tongue and the strength to move it, of all the infernal misery hidden behind this horrible thing called marriage, though the Young Men's Christian Association sentence me to prison a year for every word. I have seen horrors beside which stone walls and iron bars are heaven. . . ." [25] Angela Heywood attacked men incessantly and bitterly; she was somewhat ill-tempered, though not necessarily inaccurate. "Man so lost to himself and woman as to invoke legal *violence in these sacred nearings, should have solemn meeting with, and look serious at his own penis until he is able to be lord and master of it, rather than it should longer rule, lord and master, of him and of the victims he deflowers.*" [26] Suffragists spoke more delicately, but not less bitterly. Feminists organized social-purity groups and campaigns, their attacks on prostitution based on a larger critique of the double standard, to which their proposed remedy was that men conform to the standards required of women.[27]

A variant of this concern was a campaign against "sexual abuses," which in Victorian euphemistic language could mean deviant sexual practices or simply excessive sexual demands, but not necessarily violence or prostitution. The free lovers in particular turned to this cause because it gave them an opportunity to attack marriage. The "sexual abuses" question was one of the most frequent subjects of correspondence in free-love periodicals. For example, a letter from Mrs. Theresa Hughes of Pittsburgh:

> . . . a girl of sixteen, full of life and health when she became a wife. . . . She was a slave in every sense of the word, mentally and sexually, never was she free from his brutal outrages, morning, noon and night, up almost to the very hour her baby was born, and before she was again strong enough to move about. . . . Often did her experience last an hour or two, and one night she will never forget, the outrage lasted exactly four hours.[28]

Or from Lucinda Chandler, well-known moral reformer:

> This useless sense gratification has demoralized generation after generation, till monstrosities of disorder are common. Moral education, and healthful training will be requisite for some generations, even after we have equitable economics, and free access to Nature's gifts. The young man of whom I knew who threatened his bride of a week with a sharp knife in his hand, to compel her to perform the office of "sucker," would no doubt have had the same disposition though no soul on the planet had a want unsatisfied or lacked a natural right.[29]

From an anonymous woman in Los Angeles:

> I am nearly wrecked and ruined by . . . nightly intercourse, which is often repeated in the morning. This and nothing else was the cause of my miscarriage . . . he went to work like a man a-mowing, and instead of a pleasure as it might have been, it was most intense torture. . . .[30]

Clearly there was a level of hostility toward sex here. The observation that many feminists hated sex has been made by several historians,[31] who have usually failed to perceive that their hostility and fear of it came from the fact that they were women, not that they were feminists. Women in the nineteenth century were urged to repress their own sexual feelings, to view sex as a reproductive and wifely duty. But they also resented what they had experienced, which was not an abstraction, but a particular, historical kind of sexual encounter: intercourse dominated by and defined by the male in conformity with his desires and in disregard of what might bring pleasure to a woman.

Furthermore, sexual intercourse brought physical danger. Pregnancy, childbirth, and abortions were risky and painful experiences in the nineteenth century; venereal diseases were frequently communicated to women by their husbands. Elmina Slenker, a free lover and novelist, wrote, "I'm getting a host of stories (truths) about women so starved sexually as to use their dogs for relief, and finally I have come to the belief that a CLEAN dog is better than a drinking, tobacco-smelling, venereally diseased man!" [32]

Sex-hating women were not simply misinformed, or priggish, or neurotic. They were often responding rationally to their material reality. Denied even the knowledge of sexual possibilities other than those dictated by the rhythms of male orgasm, they had only two choices: passive and usually pleasureless submission, with high risk of undesirable consequences, or rebellious refusal. In that context abstinence to ensure voluntary motherhood was a most significant feminist demand. There was a medical superstition that women could not conceive unless they felt sexually aroused; it is understandable that Dr. Alice Stockham, for example, proposed deliberate sexual coldness as a form of birth control. [33]

What is remarkable is that some women recognized that it was not sex, but only their husbands' style of making love, that repelled them. One of the women who complained about her treatment went on to say: "I am undeveloped sexually, never having desires in that direction; still, with a husband who had any love or kind feelings for me and one less selfish it *might* have been different, but he cared nothing for the torture to *me* as long as *he* was gratified. [34]

Elmina Slenker herself, the toughest and most crusty of all these "sex-haters," dared to explore and take seriously her own longings, thereby revealing herself to be a sex-lover in disguise. As the editor of the *Water-Cure Journal*, and a regular contributor to *Free Love Journal*, she expounded the theory called Dianaism, or Non-procreative Love, sometimes called Diana-love and Alpha-abstinence. [35] It meant free sexual contact of all sorts except intercourse.

> We want the sexes to love more than they do; we want them to love openly, frankly, earnestly; to enjoy the caress, the embrace, the

glance, the voice, the presence & the very step of the beloved. We oppose no form or act of love between any man & woman. Fill the world as full of genuine sex love as you can . . . but forbear to rush in where generations yet unborn may suffer for your unthinking, uncaring, unheeding actions.[36]

Comparing this to the more usual physical means of avoiding conception, *coitus interruptus* and male continence, reveals how radical it was. In modern history general public awareness of the possibilities of nongenital sex and of forms of genital sex beyond standard "missionary position" intercourse has been a recent, post-Freudian, even post-Masters and Johnson phenomenon. The definition of sex in terms of heterosexual intercourse has been one of the oldest and most universal cultural norms. Slenker's alienation from existing sexual possibilities led her to explore alternatives with a bravery and a freedom from religious and psychological taboos extraordinary for a nineteenth-century Quaker reformer.

In the nineteenth century neither free lovers nor suffragists ever relinquished their hostility to contraception. Free speech, however, was always an overriding concern,* and for that reason Ezra Heywood agreed to publish some advertisements for a vaginal syringe, an instrument the use of which for contraception he personally deplored, or so he continued to assure his readers.[37] Those advertisements led to Heywood's prosecution for obscenity, and Heywood defended himself with his characteristic flair by making his position more radical than ever before. Contraception was moral, he argued, when it was used by women as the only means of defending their rights, including the right to voluntary motherhood. Although "artificial means of preventing conception are not generally patronized by Free Lovers," he wrote, reserving for his own followers the highest moral ground, still he recognized that not all women were lucky enough to have free lovers for their sex partners.[38]

Since Comstockism makes male will, passion and power absolute to *impose* conception, I stand with women to resent it. The man who would legislate to choke a woman's vagina with semen, who would

---

* Radicals were usually united in their opposition to Comstock's censorship. The National Liberal League, for example, formed in 1876 to promote secularism, mounted a petition campaign for repeal of the Comstock law and collected over fifty thousand signatures.

> force a woman to retain his seed, bear children when her own
> reason and conscience oppose it, would waylay her, seize her by the
> throat and rape her person.[39]

Angela Heywood, Ezra's wife, enthusiastically pushed this political
line.

> Is it "proper," "polite," for men, real *he* men, to go to Washington
> to say, by penal law, fines and imprisonment, whether woman may
> continue her natural right to wash, rinse, or wipe out her own
> vaginal body opening—as well as legislate when she may blow her
> nose, dry her eyes, or nurse her babe. . . . Whatever she may have
> been pleased to receive, from man's own, is his gift and her
> property. Women do not like rape, and have a right to resist its
> results.[40]

Her outspokenness, vulgarity in the ears of most of her contemporaries, came from a substantive, not merely a stylistic, sexual radicalism. Not even the heavy taboos and revulsion against abortion stopped
her: "To cut a child up in woman, procure abortion, is a most fearful,
tragic deed; but *even that* does not call for man's arbitrary jurisdiction
over woman's womb." [41]

It is unclear whether Heywood, in this passage, was actually
arguing for legalized abortion; if she was, she was alone among all
nineteenth-century sexual reformers in saying it. Other feminists and
free lovers condemned abortion and argued that the necessity of
stopping its widespread practice was a key reason for instituting
voluntary motherhood by other means. The difference on the abortion
question between sexual radicals and sexual conservatives was in their
analysis of its causes and remedies. While AMA doctors and preachers
were sermonizing on the sinfulness of women who had abortions,[42] the
radicals pronounced abortion itself as undeserved punishment, and
women who had them as helpless victims. Woodhull and Claflin wrote
about Madame Restell's notorious abortion "factory" in New York
City without moralism, arguing that only voluntary conception would
put it out of business.[43] Elizabeth Cady Stanton also sympathized with
women who had abortions, and used the abortion problem as an
example of women victimized by laws made without their consent.[44]

Despite stylistic differences, which came from differences in goals, nineteenth-century American free-love and women's rights advocates shared the same basic attitudes toward birth control: they opposed contraception and abortion but endorsed voluntary motherhood achieved through periodic abstinence; they believed that women should always have the right to decide when to bear a child; they believed that women and men both had natural sex drives and that it was not wrong to indulge those drives without the intention of conceiving children. The two groups also shared the same appraisal of the social and political significance of birth control. Most of them were favorably inclined toward Neo-Malthusian reasoning (at least until the 1890s, when the prevailing concern shifted to the problem of underpopulation rather than overpopulation).[45] They were also interested in controlling conception for eugenic purposes. They were hostile to the hypocrisy of the sexual double standard and, beyond that, shared a general sense that men had become oversexed and that sex had been transformed into something disagreeably violent.

But above all, their commitment to voluntary motherhood expressed their larger commitment to women's rights. Elizabeth Cady Stanton thought voluntary motherhood so central that on her lecture tours in 1871 she held separate afternoon meetings for *women only* (a completely unfamiliar practice at the time) and talked about "the gospel of fewer children & a healthy, happy maternity." [46] "What radical thoughts I then and there put into their heads & as they feel untrammelled, these thoughts are permanently lodged there! That is all I ask." [47] Only Heywood had gone so far as to defend a particular contraceptive device—the syringe. But the principle of women's right to choose was accepted in the most conservative parts of the women's rights movement. At the First Congress of the Association for the Advancement of Women in 1873 a whole session was devoted to the theme "Enlightened Motherhood," which had voluntary motherhood as part of its meaning.[48]

The general conviction of the whole feminist community that women had a right to choose when to be pregnant was so strong by the end of the nineteenth century that it seems odd that they were unable to overcome their scruples against artificial contraception. The basis for this reluctance lies in their awareness that a consequence of effective contraception would be the separation of sexuality from reproduction. A state of things that permitted sexual intercourse to take place normally, even frequently, without the risk of pregnancy, inevitably seemed to nineteenth-century middle-class women to be an attack on the family. In the mid-Victorian sexual system, men normally conducted their sexual philandering with prostitutes; accordingly prostitution, far from being a threat to the family system, was a part of it and an important support of it. This was the common view of the time, paralleled by the belief that prostitutes knew of effective birth-control techniques. This seemed only fitting, for contraception in the 1870s was associated with sexual immorality. It did not seem, even to the most sexually liberal, that contraception could be legitimized to any extent, even for the purposes of family planning for married couples, without licensing extramarital sex. The fact that contraception was not morally acceptable to respectable women was, from a woman's point of view, a guarantee that such women would not be a threat to her own marriage.

The fact that sexual intercourse often leads to conception was also a guarantee that men would marry in the first place. In the nineteenth century women needed marriage far more than men. Lacking economic independence, women needed husbands to support them, or at least to free them from a usually more humiliating economic dependence on fathers. Especially in the cities, where women were often isolated from communities, deprived of the economic and psychological support of networks of relatives, friends, and neighbors, the prospect of dissolving the cement of nuclear families was frightening. In many cases children, and the prospect of children, provided that cement. Man's responsibilities for children were an important pressure for marital stability. Women, especially middle-class women, were also dependent on their children to provide them with meaningful work. The belief that motherhood was a woman's fulfillment had a material basis: parenthood was often the only creative and challenging activity in a woman's life, a key part of her self-esteem.

Legal, efficient birth control would have increased men's freedom to indulge in extramarital sex without greatly increasing women's freedom to do so. The pressures enforcing chastity and marital fidelity on middle-class women were not only fear of illegitimate conception but a powerful combination of economic, social, and psychological factors, including economic dependence, fear of rejection by husband and social-support networks, internalized taboos, and, hardly the least important, a socially conditioned lack of interest in sex that may have approached functional frigidity. The double standard of the Victorian sexual and family system, which had made men's sexual freedom irresponsible and oppressive to women, left most feminists convinced that increasing, rather than releasing, the taboos against extramarital sex was in their interest, and they threw their support behind social-purity campaigns.

In short, we must forget the twentieth-century association of birth control with a trend toward sexual freedom. The voluntary-motherhood propaganda of the 1870s was associated with a push toward a more restrictive, or at least a more rigidly enforced, sexual morality. Achieving voluntary motherhood by a method that would have encouraged sexual license was absolutely contrary to the felt interests of the very group that formed the main social basis for the cause—middle-class women. Separating these women from the early-twentieth-century feminists, with their interest in sexual freedom, were nearly four decades of significant social and economic changes and a general weakening of the ideology of the Lady. The ideal of the free lovers—responsible, open sexual encounters between equal partners—was impossible in the 1870s because men and women were not equal. A man was a man whether faithful to his wife or not. But women's sexual activities divided them into two categories—wife or prostitute. These categories were not mere ideas but were enforced in reality by severe social and economic sanctions. The fact that so many, indeed most, free lovers in practice led faithful, monogamous, legally married lives is not insignificant in this regard. It suggests that they instinctively understood that free love was an ideal not to be realized in that time.

As voluntary motherhood was an ideology intended to encourage sexual purity, so it was also a pro-motherhood ideology. Far from debunking motherhood, the voluntary-motherhood advocates consistently continued the traditional Victorian mystification and sentimentalization of the mother. It is true that at the end of the nineteenth century an increasing number of feminists and elite women—that is, still a relatively small group—were choosing not to marry or become mothers. That was primarily because of their increasing interest in professional work, and the difficulty of doing such work as a wife and mother, given the normal uncooperativeness of husbands and the lack of social provisions for child care. Voluntary-motherhood advocates shared the general belief that mothers of young children ought not to work outside their homes but should make mothering their full-time occupation. Suffragists argued both to make professions open to women and to ennoble the task of mothering; they argued for increased rights and opportunities for women *because* they were mothers.

The free lovers were equally pro-motherhood; they only wanted to separate motherhood from legal marriage.[49] They devised pro-motherhood arguments to bolster their case against marriage. Mismated couples, held together by marriage laws, made bad parents and produced inferior offspring, free lovers said.[50] In 1870 *Woodhull and Claflin's Weekly* editorialized, "Our marital system is the greatest obstacle to the regeneration of the race." [51]

This concern with eugenics was characteristic of nearly all feminists of the late nineteenth century. At the time eugenics was mainly seen as an implication of evolutionary theory, which was picked up by many social reformers to buttress their arguments that improvement of the human condition was possible. Eugenics had not yet become a movement in itself. Feminists used eugenic arguments as if they instinctively felt that arguments based solely on women's rights had not enough power to conquer conservative and religious scruples about reproduction. So they combined eugenics and feminism to produce evocative, romantic visions of perfect motherhood. "Where boundless love prevails, . . ." *Woodhull and Claflin's Weekly* wrote, "the mother who produces an inferior child will be dishonored and unhappy . . . and she who produces superior children will feel proportionately pleased. When woman attains this position, she will consider superior offspring a necessity and be apt to procreate only with superior men." [52] Free lovers and suffragists alike used the cult of motherhood to argue for making it voluntary. Involuntary motherhood, wrote Harriet Stanton Blatch, daughter of Cady Stanton and a prominent suffragist, is a prostitution of the maternal instinct.[53] Free-lover Rachel Campbell cried out that motherhood was being "ground to dust under the misrule of masculine ignorance and superstition." [54]

Not only was motherhood considered an exalted, sacred profession, and a profession exclusively woman's responsibility, but for a woman to avoid it was to choose a distinctly less noble path. In arguing for the enlargement of woman's sphere, feminists envisaged combining motherhood with other activities but never rejected motherhood. Victoria Woodhull and Tennessee Claflin wrote:

> Tis true that the special and distinctive feature of woman is that of bearing children, and that upon the exercise of her function in this regard the perpetuity of race depends. It is also true that those who pass through life failing in this special feature of their mission cannot be said to have lived to the best purposes of woman's life. But while maternity should always be considered the most holy of all the functions woman is capable of, it should not be lost sight of in devotion to this, that there are as various spheres of usefulness outside of this for woman as there are for man outside of the marriage relation.[55]

Birth control was not intended to open the possibility of childlessness but merely to give women leverage to win more recognition and dignity. Dora Forster, a free lover, saw in the fears of underpopulation a weapon of blackmail for women:

> I hope the scarcity of children will go on until maternity is honored at least as much as the trials and hardships of soldiers campaigning in wartime. It will then be worth while to supply the nation with a sufficiency of children . . . every civilized nation, having lost the power to enslave woman as mother, will be compelled to recognize her voluntary exercise of that function as by far the most important service of any class of citizens.[56]

"Oh, women of the world, arise in your strength and demand that all which stands in the path of true motherhood shall be removed from your path," wrote Lois Waisbrooker, a feminist novelist and moral reformer.[57] Helen Gardener based a plea for women's education entirely on the argument that society needed educated mothers to produce able sons (not children, *sons*).

> Harvard and Yale, not to mention Columbia, may continue to put a protective tariff on the brains of young men: but so long as they must get those brains from the proscribed sex, just so long will male brains remain an "infant industry" and continue to need this protection. Stupid mothers never did and stupid mothers never will furnish this world with brilliant sons.[58]

Clinging to the cult of motherhood was part of a larger conservatism shared by free lovers and suffragists: acceptance of traditional sex roles. Even the free lovers rejected only one factor—legal marriage—of the many that defined woman's place in the family. They did not challenge conventional conceptions of woman's passivity and limited sphere of concern.[59] In their struggles for equality the women's rights advocates never suggested that men should share responsibility for child-raising, housekeeping, nursing, or cooking. When Victoria Woodhull in the 1870s and Charlotte Perkins Gilman in the 1900s suggested socialized child care, they assumed that only women would do the work.[60] Most feminists wanted economic independence for women, but most, too, were reluctant to recommend achieving this by turning women loose and helpless into the economic world to compete with men.[61] This preference was conditioned by an attitude hostile to the egoistic spirit of capitalism; but since the attitude was not transformed into a political position, it often appeared in the guise of expressing women's failings rather than the system's faults. Failing to distinguish, or even to indicate awareness of a possible distinction, between women's learned passivity and their equally learned distaste for competition and open aggression, these feminists also followed the standard Victorian rationalization of sex roles, the idea that women were morally superior. Thus the timidity and self-effacement that were the marks of women's powerlessness were made into innate virtues. Angela Heywood, for example, praised women's greater ability for self-control, and, in an attribution no doubt intended to jar and titillate the reader, branded men inferior on account of their lack of sexual temperance. Men's refusal to accept women as human beings she identified, similarly, as a mark of men's incapacity: ". . . man has not yet achieved himself to realize and meet a PERSON in woman. . . ."[62] In idealistic, abstract terms, no doubt such male behavior is an incapacity. In the historical context it was an expression of false consciousness on Heywood's part because she omitted to mention the power and privilege to exploit women that the supposed "incapacity" gave men.

This omission reveals a false consciousness characteristic of the cult of motherhood: a consciousness that ignored or denied the privileges men received from women's exclusive responsibility for parenthood. For the "motherhood" of the feminists' writings was not merely the biological process of gestation and birth, but a whole package of social, economic, and cultural functions. Although many of the nineteenth-century feminists had done substantial analysis of the historical and anthropological origins of woman's social role, they nevertheless agreed with the biological-determinist point of view that woman's parental capacities had become implanted at the level of instinct, the famous "maternal instinct." That concept rested on the assumption that the qualities that parenthood requires—capacities for tenderness, self-control and patience, tolerance for tedium and detail, emotional supportiveness, dependability and warmth—were not only instinctive but sex-linked. The concept of the maternal instinct thus also involved a definition of the normal instinctual structure of the male that excluded these capacities, or included them only to an inferior degree; it also carried the implication that women who did not exercise these capacities, presumably through motherhood, remained unfulfilled, untrue to their destinies.

Belief in the maternal instinct reinforced the belief in the necessary spiritual connection for women between sex and reproduction and limited the development of birth-control ideas. But the limits were set by the entire social context of women's lives, not by the intellectual timidity of their ideas. For women's "control over their own bodies" to lead to a rejection of motherhood as the *primary* vocation and measure of social worth required the existence of alternative vocations and sources of worthiness. The women's rights advocates of the 1870s and 1880s were fighting for those other opportunities, but a significant change had come only to a few privileged women, and most women faced essentially the same options that existed fifty years earlier. Thus voluntary motherhood in this period remained almost exclusively a tool for women to strengthen their positions within conventional marriages and families, not to reject them.

6
Social Purity and Eugenics

THE SOCIAL-PURITY movement intended to abolish prostitution and other sexual philandering. That the movement also contributed to the acceptance of birth control in this country may, therefore, seem odd. Social purity really meant sexual purity,* and that meant confining sex within marriage and moderating its indulgence even there. Contraception, by removing the "risk" of illegitimate pregnancies and even of venereal disease from nonmarital affairs, undermined some of the props of that sexual morality. Social-purity advocates were unequivocally opposed to contraception. But so too, as we have seen, were most sex radicals—free lovers, utopians, and feminists.

Because few in the nineteenth century advocated or even accepted the separation of sexuality from reproduction, there was a remarkable unity between sex radicals and sex conservatives on the issue of birth control. Indeed, the attempt to use categories such as "radical" and "conservative" in regard to sexual issues becomes questionable on close examination. Just as many interpreters of the

* "Social" was the standard euphemism for sexual. For example, Elizabeth Cady Stanton said that she was addressing the "social question" when she spoke on prostitution or sexual abuses.

sexual attitudes of the nineteenth-century feminists focused on their "prudery," applying twentieth-century attitudes to it and missing its political content, so the sexual attitudes of the social-purity advocates have been shallowly interpreted.

The birth-control ideas of social-purity advocates were remarkably feminist. Social purity was a direct continuation of one line in voluntary-motherhood thought: the use of eugenic arguments to support the necessity for women's control over their reproductive capacities. The eugenic propaganda used by the social-purity movement is an important and neglected part of American intellectual history, inasmuch as two decades later eugenics became one of the most influential fads in American culture, both academic and popular. Social-purity advocates began the attempt to use eugenic logic to increase women's power and dignity; yet ultimately eugenic thought did more harm than good to feminism and voluntary motherhood.

Social Purity

Social purity had intellectual roots in early temperance and moral reform, in abolitionism, in left-wing Protestantism, and in utopian radicalism. Like many of these earlier nineteenth-century causes, social purity had a double-edged political blade: it was liberal in its commitment to legal equality for all persons and to a single standard of morality, but conservative in its desire to enforce traditional, rural, Yankee, Calvinistic moral values on the whole society. Energized by the women entering organized reform activity and threatened by the specter of "regulated" prostitution, the movement first formed in opposition to legalization of prostitution. That danger having been averted, in the 1880s social-purity reformers began to campaign for lowering the age of consent, prosecuting customers of prostitutes as well as the prostitutes themselves, reforming prostitutes, providing police matrons and sexually segregated prisons, stopping abortion, censoring pornography, and spreading social-purity education.[1]

This list of issues suggests that the attraction of the social-purity cause for women was not peripheral but fundamental. The closer we look, the harder it is to distinguish social-purity groups from feminist ones. Feminists from very disparate groups were advocates of most major social-purity issues—women committed to such varied causes as suffrage, free love, and temperance, for example.[2]

What they most obviously had in common was a current of fear and hostility toward sexuality. Their frequent attacks on "lust" and "sexual excess" have made them appear as sex-haters to many twentieth-century readers, including historians. Here is Clara Cleghorne Hoffman of the National Women's Christian Temperance Union (NWCTU) addressing the International Council of Women in 1888:

> In thousands of homes everything seems to be perfectly pure, perfectly moral . . . and yet . . . hundreds go forth from these homes to swell the ranks of recognized prostitution, while thousands more go forth into the ranks of legalized prostitution under the perfectly respectable mantle of marriage. The fires of passion and lust lurk in these homes like the covered fires of Lucknow, only needing the occasion, only needing the temptation, to burst forth into flame, carrying death and destruction to every pure, and true and lovely attribute of heart and soul.[3]

One historian has defined that view as "pansexual," observing that sexual drives seemed to them omnipresent and ever present and that social progress depended upon sublimating these drives.[4] That interpretation leaves many feminist/social-purity ideas unexplained, however, because it incorrectly assumes a Freudian view of sexuality. Social-purity advocates did believe that sexual drives could interfere with work discipline and could subvert the necessary societal commitment to hard work, competition, and social status earned by worldly success. But that belief, which dates back at least to early Puritanism, is not the same as a pansexual, Freudian theory which postulates that the sex drive is identical with the "life force," that it is the *only* creative drive of human beings. This distinction is important because without it the singular contribution of feminism to social-purity thought is lost. Feminists believed that men had developed excessive sexual drives which contributed to the subjection of women and hence limited the development of the whole civilization. From this they drew the inference that excessive sex drive had to be *eliminated*, not merely checked or sublimated, in order to create a pure and sexually equal society. Nor did this goal seem to them unrealistic. Social purity grew from a "new abolitionism" directed against prostitution to a totalistic reform movement intent upon transforming the consciousness, changing the basic "needs," to use a twentieth-century term, of society. Social-purity advocates considered that transformation possible precisely because they believed that the current set of "human needs" was itself a social product, not a biological instinct.

If there is such a thing as "natural" human sexual behavior we do not and cannot know what it is; sexual behavior is always culturally regulated. For women, normal sex in the nineteenth century meant either marriage or prostitution. In both institutions sex meant a form of intercourse dictated primarily by male desires and by the myth that women had no legitimate sexual needs; in both it carried the risks of venereal disease, unwanted conception, dangerous and painful parturition or abortion. Throughout every reform movement that touched on the "social" question, including the free-love movement, feminist influence tended to coincide with an attack on "excessiveness" in sex. But this did not mean that the authors of these attacks hated sex absolutely. Rather they were concerned to make women's risks calculated, to create some limitations on men's unilateral right to define every sexual encounter.

This feminist orientation was not the only one within social purity. It was a complex movement, really a coalition. Differences were sharp on some issues, such as censorship. Toward the common end of abolishing sexual sin, some social-purity reformers were convinced of the necessity of freeing society from pornography, others of the importance of encouraging sex education and candid speaking. Another important issue of division within social purity was the proper place of women. Despite the general commitment to a single standard, there were many who opposed woman suffrage, equal employment opportunities, and higher education for women. On the other hand, there was a distinctly feminist strain within social purity, mostly women,* whose writings and speeches were as militant as anything the suffrage movement produced. Voluntary motherhood itself was not a controversial issue, and almost all the social-purity advocates endorsed

* Unlike the free-love movement, where many of the most militant feminists were male.

it in principle. But the feminists within the movement were more passionate in their demands for voluntary motherhood, gave it higher priority, and, most importantly, were more inclined to support deviations from the standard act of sexual intercourse.

When social-purity reformers endorsed voluntary motherhood, they often altered the customary feminist rhetoric slightly. Free-love and women's rights advocates tended to argue mainly that voluntary motherhood was a woman's right. Social-purity advocates often spoke more religiously. Sin, wrote Lady Henry Somerset in 1895, begins with the unwelcome child.[5] Belle Mix, in an official pamphlet of the National Purity Association, began by quoting Saint Paul and went on to say "Enslaved motherhood is the curse of civilization. . . ."[6] Whereas the antisexual attitudes of the Christian founders had been directed mainly against women, the social-purity imprecations were turned against men. Elizabeth Lisle Saxon, vice-president of the National Woman Suffrage Association for Tennessee, speaking on social purity in 1888, said, "For two thousand years we have preached Christ and practiced Moses, in all our dealings with woman—stoning her to death and letting the man go free."[7] Mix went on, in her pamphlet, to praise the "rebellion of woman against the lustful domination of man. . . ."[8]

Hereditarian Thought

Nearly everyone who supported voluntary motherhood was concerned with the welfare of children, and nearly all thought that unwanted or unwisely spaced children might suffer. In the 1890s these concerns were often expressed in the language and logic of eugenics. Birth-control advocates had used eugenic arguments since early in the century to argue the advantages of reproductive control.[9] As a form of simple hereditarian thought eugenics is as old as humanity. The resemblance of children to their parents has, in every culture, produced a folklore of heredity, from "Tuesday's child is full of grace," to astrology, to taboos against incest. Hereditarian thought in the nineteenth century was still largely folkloric in that it had not yet distinguished accurately between hereditary and nonhereditary characteristics. It was employed primarily in an optimistic, perfectionist vein, to demonstrate the possibilities of improvement of the human condition; environmental and reproductive control were not distinct. The looseness and flexibility of this pre-Mendelian hereditarian thought continued throughout the nineteenth century, permitting eugenics to be used to fit the biases of any of its users—that is, the threat of bad heredity could be used to enforce any moral code. But in another respect hereditarian thought changed drastically after the 1870s, becoming associated with a social and political pessimism used to justify the miseries and inequalities of the status quo. While still lacking a sound genetic base, eugenic thought emphasized the primary importance of heredity in opposition to environmentalist schools of thought. In medicine, law, sociology, criminology, psychology—in nearly every social science—hereditarian arguments were used to explain social problems by individual failings and to doubt the efficacy of social reforms to solve those problems. At the very end of the century an upsurge in nativism produced a self-conscious eugenics movement dedicated to maintaining the supremacy of the Yankees.

It is important to bear in mind this overall trajectory of hereditarian thought in order to place the social-purity advocates. Using hereditarian arguments, they were still in the perfectionist vein of American reformism. Eugenics helped them integrate their grievances into a unified program for reform; if vice was itself hereditary, once abolished it would be gone forever. Thus, for example, Benjamin Flower wrote that bad heredity created lust which created prostitution; if prostitutes could be prevented from bearing children their ranks would not be replenished.[10]

Beyond suggesting birth control as a means of abolishing existing vice, the same people also suggested that involuntary motherhood produced vice. It would be hard to find a single piece of writing on voluntary motherhood between 1890 and 1910 that did not assert that unwanted children were likely to be morally and/or physically defective. Frequently, the eugenic argument for voluntary motherhood was expressed through assuming rhetorically the point of view of the child (a device similar to the "rights-of-the-fetus" propaganda of the 1970s abortion opponents). Moses Harman, a free lover, wrote *The Right to*

Be Born Well,[11] and Margaret Deland, a popular writer, wrote of "the right of children *not* to be born." [12]

Free-love advocates—that is, opponents of marriage—used eugenic arguments to defend their more daring sexual proposals. Lillian Harman, for example, justified divorce with eugenic logic: ". . . [the] state has barred the way of evolution, has rendered natural selection of the best human characteristics impossible, by holding together the mismated. . . ." [13] Tennessee Claflin and Victoria Woodhull had argued in 1870 that the entire marital system was an "obstacle to the regeneration of the race." [14] Many sex radicals thought that illegitimate children were usually superior as they were the children of love.[15] But even conservative social-purity advocates consistently argued that love between parents made children superior and that the offspring of unloving couples were likely to be defective.[16]

These judgments were based on a misconception that permeated all eugenic thinking from 1890 until at least 1910—the belief in the inheritability of acquired characteristics.[17] On this basis, for example, Dr. George Napheys, an early voluntary-motherhood advocate, argued in 1869 that the mood of the woman at the time of intercourse "has much power in the formation of the foetus, both in modifying its physical constitution and in determining the character and temperament of its mind." Able to speak about sexual matters with impunity in the years before the federal antiobscenity statute, Napheys quoted Shakespeare that a "dull, stale, tired bed," would create a "tribe of fops," and Montaigne to the effect that prolonged continence before conception would create especially gifted children.[18] Many writers, both lay and medical, endorsed the notion that the circumstances and mood of the intercourse itself could affect the child's character.[19] Nearly all the books of guidance for pregnant women taught that "mental impressions" received by the pregnant mother would be transmitted to the fetus and argued that pregnant women should be protected from all disturbances.[20]

Several specific applications of this genetic theory served to reinforce particular causes of the social-purity advocates. One was discussion of the hereditary damage caused by drinking. There was perhaps no social question on which there was such unanimity among reformers—feminists of all kinds, social-purity advocates both feminist and antifeminist, free lovers, and conservative Christian moralists—as the question of alcohol. All agreed that parental drinking, both during or after conception, could cause severe genetic damage to the child, and that intemperance was itself hereditary.[21] * The argument that alcohol was a "race poison" was standard in both temperance and prohibition movements.[23]

It is possible to identify several common bases for the opposition to alcohol, each of which bears on the voluntary-motherhood question as well. Reformers reviled drunkenness as a state in which humanity was "lowered" beneath any possibility of spiritual aspirations or attainments. Voluntary motherhood through continence represented precisely a spiritual ideal, a victory of self-control. Alcohol not only lessened self-control, it stimulated lust. Social-purity advocates preferred that sexual feelings be an expression of the "highest" spiritual love. Their antialcohol tirades expressed a longing for "purity," an ideal that contained both sexual and also cultural meanings, and that was essentially pastoral, related to a preurban, preindustrial way of life. The traditionalist strain in antialcohol sentiment should not be overstated or used to suggest that temperance was simply an anti-working-class campaign. There was another strain in temperance that was widespread among the working class itself—woman's resentment of the saloon both as a symbol and weapon of male supremacy. In the nineteenth century working-class men drank in saloons, not at home; the saloon was an exclusively male preserve.[24] Men's long absences from their homes were directly oppressive to the women who were confined there, and threatening to the family, which was for so many women the only supportive environment. The husband's drunken presence at home was, however, equally oppressive. It led to physical and psychological mistreatment of women and children, caused financial irresponsibility, and deprived women of needed companionship. Drunkenness certainly made husbands less sensitive to the need for family limitation and to wives' personal happiness.

These attitudes were joined in another cause in which eugenic arguments loomed large: the attacks on "sexual abuse." One of the

* The moderation of Dr. Benjamin Grant Jefferis, who wrote in 1894 that although habitual drunkenness would produce defective children, "a single glass of wine or brandy on the wedding night can have no possible effect on the sperms already formed," [22] was exceptional.

key motifs of social purity in the 1890s was that sexual immorality was just as bad—nay, worse—inside marriage as outside it. The criticism by free lovers and feminists that marriage was used to license rape was taken up even by the most conservative social-purity advocates. They charged that husbands' excessive sexual demands on their wives were a serious social problem,[25] and criticized the brutality of husbands insistent on "vindicating" their "manhood" on their wedding night.[26]

Sex radicals differed from respectable social-purity advocates in their language and frankness, not in their message. "I know of one case where a man when his wife was so near her confinement that he did not care to enforce his claim in the natural way, forced her to relieve him by making a 'sucker' of her and she would vomit with the disgust and nausea thus caused," wrote Lois Waisbrooker, a freethinker and free-love novelist, in 1890.[27] Behind this story lay the assumption, also universal among social-purity advocates, that sexual intercourse during pregnancy was immoral and would produce terrible consequences for the child. A woman during gestation should be "set apart to holy and sacred uses," wrote Hoffman of the NWCTU.[28] The result of the indignity that Waisbrooker reported above, following eugenic logic, was that "the child was a poor sickly thing that seemed so disgusted with food that they could hardly get enough down to keep it alive." [29]

What social-purity advocates defined as a sexual abuse or excess was in part determined by prudish sexual standards, and in part by their discomfort with the separation of reproduction and sexuality. But their definition of both abuse and excess also included any situation in which the woman was unwilling—a view uniquely feminist and crucial to voluntary motherhood. Antifeminist as some of the social-purity advocates may have been in their condemnation of woman's higher education or employment outside the home, they could not countenance the doctrine that a woman owed sexual obedience to her husband. In this respect, their desire to check male lust imbued the entire social-purity movement with some important feminist convictions.

The addition of hereditarian thought to this set of attitudes could be used to make them even more feminist. For example, Dr. Joseph

Greer, writing in 1902, reprinted a letter allegedly sent to him by a patient:

> I was married when only sixteen. . . . He was twenty-two;
> strong, healthy, and with large sexual demands. . . . I thought him
> exacting and selfish, and he thought me unaccommodating and
> capricious. . . . If I refused, his great, strong fingers would sink into
> my flesh and force would compel submission. . . . He meant to be a
> good husband and thought he was. He gave me "a good home,"
> and I did not have to work, and all he asked was what marriage is
> supposed to secure to every husband. He did not intend to be
> unreasonable and thought and said, "The sooner you do as I say the
> sooner we will have peace." I thought so too, and tried hard to be
> an obedient wife. I would resolve not to resist again, but the Scotch
> blood was strong; there was too much freedom in my nature, and
> before I knew it I was fighting away "tooth and nail." As a result I
> would be bruised and beaten, and perhaps made sick and have a
> doctor before I got over it. Two little babies were literally killed
> before they were born, and the one that did live I have seen often in
> convulsions from "sexual vice," either a transmitted tendency or a
> birthmark due to the infernal nastiness I was forced to witness
> during pregnancy. When at last I watched his little life go out, I
> knew that he was spared a life of imbecility or idiocy, and I could
> not mourn. . . .[30]

Greer's letter illustrates an important point about the propaganda against sexual excess: the men guilty of it were not considered monstrous, but normal. Eliza Bisbee Duffey, who insinuated feminist ideas into her dozens of marriage and household-guidance books for women, wrote that forty-nine out of fifty men had sexually abused their wives.[31] Many of these social-purity advocates offered a *social* analysis of men's lustfulness as something *learned.* Furthermore, the attack on men's lust in the name of social purity often included an assertion of women's suppressed sexual instinct. Dr. Elizabeth Blackwell wrote of the "radical physiological error" that "men are much more powerfully swayed by this instinct of sex, than are women.[32]

In the 1870s free lovers had developed the hypothesis that the excessive sexual drive of the human male was the dialectical result of the repression and attempted rejection of sexuality in Christian society.[33] In the 1890s social-purity advocates, though hostile to free love, were repeating similar views. The excessively sexual male might be normal as an individual in relation to his society, but the whole human species was aberrant: "The Satyr (male or female) who cannot see one of the opposite sex without the production of physical excitement, is not strong, but irritable; the nature is diseased." [34] Every woman's struggle for the right to refuse her own husband came to be seen as part of an evolutionary process, a process in this case conceived as restoring a previous "natural man." Bad hereditary consequences provided social-purity advocates reasons for checking male sexual selfishness more persuasive than the mere principle of women's integrity.

What is more, the problem—the oversexing of the male—was blamed on societal male supremacy. Some of the social-purity advocates explained the sexual "diseasedness" of the society in terms of the subjection of women. The gynaecentric theories of Charlotte Perkins Gilman and Lester Frank Ward were the culmination of this line of thought.[35] Gilman believed that the passing of the power to choose a mate from the woman to the man was a major cause of the hereditary decline in the human race—a theory that was shared by many other social-purity advocates.[36] And, of course, the social-purity campaigners charged that the double standard functioned in a dangerously dysgenic manner.[37] Ward even repeated the hypothesis of some feminists that the subjection of women to the excessive sexual demands of men had produced monthly menstruation as an evolutionary mutation, undesirable in his view, away from the more infrequent rhythm common among lower mammals.[38]

A Feminist Eugenics?

Eugenic thinking thus provided empirical arguments for previously abstract contentions that the status of women was an indicator of civilization. The polemical function of eugenic arguments for feminists was often to give teeth to their moralism, to provide a punishment with which to threaten those who would ignore or despise women's demands for equality and a single standard of morality. "Maternity is an awful power, and . . . it strikes back at the race, with a blind, fierce, far-reaching force, in revenge for its subject status." [39] Here

Helen Gardener was apparently referring to genetic deterioration; elsewhere her threat could equally have been carried out through children's simple imitativeness: the "pretended subservience but resentful acquiescence of wives helps to account for the mendacity of their offspring." [40] Speakers at the National Purity Congress in 1894 declared prostitution to be a simple consequence of the double standard, and the double standard as the chief obstacle to race progress. The physical and spiritual uncleanness of fathers made their offspring inferior.[41] "Race progress," to those fledgling eugenists, was another name for the "civilization" concept they had argued before; race was not understood as a specifically biological term. Suffragist Harriot Stanton Blatch argued in 1891 that the three primary conditions for "race progress" were voluntary maternity, including financial independence for women, broader education for women, and assurance of women's sole authority over their children.[42]

When that line of thought was followed to its limit, eugenic logic could prove that women's subjection was the specific cause of all the social suffering in the world.

> . . . towards her own emancipation from all slaveries, economic dependence on man included . . . in order that she may worthily fulfill her function of motherhood; in order that she shall no longer be compelled to become the unwilling creator and builder of mental and moral dwarfs and imbeciles—in order that she may no longer be compelled to help supply the gallows, the prison, the poorhouse, the house of ill-fame, with birth-predestined victims." [43]

Moses Harman, who was a leading early eugenist as well as a free lover, blamed the development of American imperialism partly on women's subordination. In an article of 1908 in his _American Journal of Eugenics_, combining populist and feminist arguments in a manner characteristic of these Midwestern social-purity advocates, he listed the four major causes of imperialism as (1) concentration of the ownership of land, (2) an undemocratic monetary system, (3) the subjection of women and the consequent development of a slave-owning mentality in man, and (4) denial of women's control over reproduction and the consequent increase in the number of degenerate offspring.[44] In his point number three, Harman connected the individual male consciousness in a male-supremacist system with the larger consciousness that underlay and justified the imperialist policies of male-supremacist governments and economic systems. In this feminist-eugenic logic women's subjection had corrupted men, and they in turn had passed on that corruption, physical and mental, to successive generations.

We are now in a position to understand one of the important peculiarities of the thought of these early eugenists. They believed that the independence of women would *automatically* produce a eugenic effect. Some thought education might be needed first: "If a girl were brought up with any rational knowledge of herself and of the pains and perils as well as the pleasures of maternity, the dangers of indiscriminate procreation in her case would be reduced to a minimum." [45] But others, such as Harriot Stanton Blatch, thought women were natural eugenists: "In contrast to this, the man's commercial view of race production, stands the women's intuition backed by reason: She asks, first, will the child be welcome? second, what will be its inheritance of physical, mental, and moral character? third, can the child be provided for in life?" When the first and second questions are answered in the affirmative, the third problem would take care of itself.[46] Such confidence in the automatic and immediate benefits of women's emancipation reflected a dominant nineteenth-century view that in the competitive world created by capitalism, women had somehow remained unsullied by individualism. Women represented pure, selfless good, as opposed to the egocentrism developed as a survival instinct by men. Essentially the view of the sentimental "cult of true womanhood," it was used by feminists to argue that women should have the opportunity to make public contributions through the exercise of virtues they had developed as their survival instincts—tenderness, self-effacement, the expression of emotion.[47] The qualities of virtuous womanhood were almost fully contained in the concept of motherhood. The nineteenth-century view did not distinguish between biological and social motherhood because it considered the social (and cultural and economic) work of motherhood dictated by biological instinct.[48]

The maternal instinct and its realization, motherhood, thus reflected a whole female politics. The lack of distinction, even in the "expert" genetics of that day, between hereditary and learned charac-

teristics, left these feminist eugenists free to develop an all-encompassing view of women's contribution to humanity. They used eugenic
ideas to place *both* hereditary and environmental concerns in opposition to an earlier view of reproduction which attached little prestige or
skill to childbearing or child-raising.[49] They were trying to make
motherhood a profession—Charlotte Perkins Gilman called it "child-
culture." [50] It was a "profession" that combined genetics and child
psychology. In her Presidential Address to the National Council of
Women in 1891, Frances Willard spoke of "scientific motherhood,"
referring to heredity, prenatal and postnatal psychology and health.[51]

   In this new rhetoric the reformers were, of course, changing and
in some sense undermining their own argument that women were
"natural" eugenists. Gilman argued for "unnatural motherhood,"
charging that what women had done naturally for so many centuries
was insufficient.[52] Feminists used the new-found importance of child-
raising to win gains for women. ". . . so long as the laws of heredity
last no man can give free brains to his children if their mother is the
victim of superstition and priestcraft," wrote the freethinker Helen
Gardener in a plea for women's education.[53]

   Stepping even further away from the earlier nineteenth-century
view of the moral superiority of the woman/mother, feminist eugenists
attacked the selflessness and emotional generosity hitherto the very
essence of the sentimental ideal of womanhood. The submissiveness of
women, in social as well as sexual matters, was itself dysgenic, they
charged. Self-sacrifice in women is a violation of duty to unborn
children, said a National Purity Association pamphlet.[54] In one of her
widely read books of short stories, published in 1890, Gardener wrote:
". . . so long as motherhood is serfhood, just so long will this world be
populated with a race easy to subjugate, weak to resist oppression,
criminal in its instincts of cruelty toward those in its power and
humble and subservient towards authority and domination." [55] Sexual
surrender to one's husband is identified with political surrender to
tyranny; voluntary motherhood was the correlate of political independence. Self-denial and surrender to one's husband's selfishness,
Eliza Duffey wrote, is the worst thing to do for one's unborn child.[56]
Women's self-abnegation fosters selfishness in others. "Unreasonable
and unreasoning patience is a sin." [57]

There were practical purposes in these arguments. Feminist eugenists used the importance of a skilled motherhood to argue for women's education.[58] Along with most social-purity advocates they demanded sex education.[59] They argued against the diluted education that was conventionally supposed to prepare women for motherhood, saying that it left them with no wisdom to pass on to their children.[60] And of course they insisted that a wise and eugenic motherhood had to be voluntary.

As a general motif, then, we can see that in the eugenic arguments for birth control of the 1890s, as in the first public voluntary-motherhood statements of the 1870s, the orientation of birth control was pro-motherhood. The goal was to make motherhood better, not to challenge its place as the number-one career of women. In the development of this argument, as we have seen, the feminists changed slightly the concept of motherhood, emphasizing its social and cultural, and de-emphasizing its biological, aspects. They hoped that in so doing they might win popular acceptance of the voluntary-motherhood principle *within* the conventional view of women's place as primarily in the home.

In that attempt they failed. Every eugenic argument was in the long run more effective in the hands of antifeminists than of feminists. Motherhood was "proved" to be weakened, rather than improved, by higher education for women; those who argued that work outside the home devitalized motherhood had the best of the debate against those who supported job opportunities for women. By the turn of the century, widespread familiarity with certain rather superficial but provocative statistics—that educated, upper-class women were having fewer children than uneducated, poor women—had turned the voluntary-motherhood argument on its head and produced the "race-suicide" argument, to the effect that voluntary motherhood was *lowering* the quality of the nation's population.

So powerful seemed these "proofs" that many erstwhile feminists followed their own eugenic arguments to extremely antifeminist conclusions. Many feminist social-purity advocates, for example, endorsed the race-suicide fear of the first decade of the twentieth century, criticizing women for not having enough children, arguing that higher education and professional employment for privileged women were enticing the most able women away from motherhood.[61] The old arguments got turned around. Anna Garlin Spencer, attacking sexual vice, cited as one of its destructive consequences the "lamentable" fall in the birth rate.[62] Elizabeth Blackwell condemned the English divorce law for its double standard in these terms: "The very grave National danger of teaching men to repudiate fatherhood, and accustoming women to despise motherhood and shrink from the trouble involved . . ."[63] Even free lovers used the argument from motherhood in antifeminist ways. Moses Harman, a much-jailed free lover, wrote that this generation of women were not yet worthy of freedom; they should learn "honorable maternity" first.[64] And he endorsed Theodore Roosevelt's attack on women's "selfishness" in preferring small families.[65] The maternal instinct had become a means for manipulating women.

Was it that eugenic ideas had a logic of their own, leading inexorably in an antifeminist direction? One might argue this by pointing to the discrediting of Lamarckian in favor of Mendelian genetics. The effect of this change was to transform eugenics into a strictly hereditarian social theory in which environmental changes such as female education, respect for women, and sexual independence of wives were not significant. But eugenics was never, despite its pretensions, a strict translation of genetic theory into social theory. Indeed, no such strict translations are possible. Eugenists could have responded to Mendelian genetics by going entirely in the other direction, toward child psychology and public health. Eugenic ideas were always the tools of politics, and political needs defined these ideas.

Eugenics became predominantly antifeminist and anti-birth-control because antifeminists seized control of and redefined some of the basic eugenic concepts. It is not as if the antifeminist side won the debate about women's employment and education because of the superiority of their arguments. They won because of the greater effectiveness of their organization and propaganda and the greater sympathy of the articulate public with their point of view. In using eugenic arguments, feminists had tried to win more political and social power for women with the support of many male-dominated institutions and professions—churches, schools, doctors, for example. To do this they had to seek change while appearing to accept their traditional social roles as mothers and housewives, using the argument developed in the first half of the century that reforms such as voluntary motherhood would enhance their effectiveness in these traditional roles. The same thing is true of social-purity ideas. Although an important part of the antisexual bias in social purity came from women resenting their sexual subjection to men, social-purity advocates always insisted on restricting sexuality within the conventional nuclear family, which was already proving so restrictive to women. The social-purity view had always tended to raise up motherhood into a cult; eugenics merely gave a scientific basis to it. Ultimately women's chafing in their roles as housewives and mothers forced them to give up both eugenic and social-purity arguments. Within the old social structure they could go so far and no further, and by the end of the nineteenth century, at least in the area of control over their own reproduction, they had reached a limit. Their propaganda for fewer children, children only when wanted, the right to refuse or even to redefine sexual intercourse, steadily intensifying since the 1870s, had created a backlash.[66]

This backlash would not be particularly interesting or relevant to our argument if it occurred only among men. But it also occurred among women, for whom it was a genuinely conservative response to the threatening implications of change. It was this response that led so many feminists into the antifeminist traps of eugenics. Objective social conditions made many women uncomfortable with a rejection of the cult of motherhood or the full separation of sexuality from reproduction. Let us try, very briefly, to review these conditions.

With birth control, as with many other kinds of power that women might have had, the persistence of traditional roles often precluded them not only from winning the right to it but even from wanting it. A central fact in the lives of most women until at least World War II was that seeking a "life" outside the home, whether in employment or volunteer labor, presented them with a painful choice: either doing a double job—paid laborer by day, unpaid laborer by night—or suffering from criticism and self-hatred as an "unnatural" woman who avoided motherhood or even marriage. Most women found either alternative unbearable and continued laboring alone in their homes. The importance of this female dilemma to birth control has been proven by recent demographic analysis: among all the variables that create differentials in the birth rate at a given historical moment, the employment of married women outside the home has been the most significant. Of course, outside activities for married women are correlated with other factors, primarily class; but with all other variables controlled, employment was the most likely to reduce a woman's fertility.[67] For working-class and most middle-class women, motherhood was in fact as well as in ideology the most important and enjoyable part of their lives and work. (The married women who did move outside their homes and motherhood to more public tasks did so only because they could hire other women to do their housework and take care of their children. Thus the minority of women who were able to manage both marriage and a "career" did so by exploiting an equal number of women as maids.) The assumption of many contemporary feminists, looking back at the past, that women were anxious for work outside their homes but prevented from getting it by their husbands' opposition and the scarcity of jobs, is not borne out by the facts. Working-class women often preferred their unpaid housework to the dreadful jobs that were available to them and to the "second shift" that awaited them at home after their jobs. Only higher education and professional work brought women enthusiastically out of their homes, and the proportion of women with those options was tiny.

If a lack of attractive alternatives was an obstacle to a widespread challenge to the cult of motherhood, a further one was created by women's experience of sex itself. For many women belief in the glory of motherhood and the nobility of the maternal instinct were necessary to make continued submission to their husband's sexual demands compatible with the new dignity they sought. Indeed, if one compares the connotations of the words "motherhood" and "womanhood" in nineteenth-century middle-class usage, one of the chief differences is that the former had more dignity. True womanhood connoted frail virtue, needing protection; true motherhood was strong, enduring, independent. That dignity was based on a real power, as dignity usually is: mothers had some power over the lives of their children. No wonder so many women were so self-sacrificing in their maternal roles; they were gaining something very significant. When maternity was

not an expected consequence of and justification for sex, many feminists, as we have seen, expressed a fervent wrath against male sexual
demands. If many women were ambivalent about separating sexuality
from reproduction, about surrendering their specialness as mothers,
these attitudes were not signs of intellectual confusion, but a rational
response to their objective situation.

By the early twentieth century, however, some feminist reformers
were increasingly impressed by the negative aspects of the motherhood
cult. The "new feminists" were separated from social-purity advocates
by the divorce issue among others. The latter offered up hysterical and
romanticized defenses of the family in opposition to divorce; the
feminists turned toward a view of the family less as supportive for
woman than as strengthening her chains. Increased public acceptance
of hereditarian ideas brought into high relief the inconsistencies of
earlier attempts to build a case for the advancement of women on
assumptions of women's innate differences from men. The pretense
that those differences made the sexes different-but-equal was wearing
thin. As long as one group has all the political power, theories of
innate differences always function most effectively as arguments for
the status quo.

Eugenic thought had always contained the assumption that reproduction was not just a function but the purpose, in some teleologi-
cal sense, of women's life. Furthermore, as eugenics moved toward
greater emphasis on heredity as opposed to environment, it moved
away from an emphasis on woman's labor and skill as a mother, and
back toward a view of her as a breeder, of her motherly function as
part of nature. It was not just that the cult of motherhood was itself
limiting, but also that feminist attempts to make it more prestigious
and to qualify it as skilled labor failed; as an ideology motherhood was
becoming more animal-like and less human. Reproduction was raised
from a biological precondition of human striving and achievement to
the goal of human life itself. This is evident in the eugenic rhetoric of
"improving the race." The idea that the human "race" was in genetic
decline reversed a humanist tradition that had measured human
achievement in terms of learned culture. That was the tradition that
had given birth to feminism, and feminism could not survive without
it. The only hope for women as for any subject group was to progress

beyond their parents or ancestors. The notion that lay behind race suicide—that the value of a child must be determined by the social status of its parents—condemned the working class, native and foreign, and all women to the status quo of subjection.

7

Race Suicide

IN MARCH 1905 the President of the United States attacked birth control. Theodore Roosevelt condemned the tendency toward smaller families as decadent, a sign of moral disease. Like others who worried about race suicide, he specifically attacked women, branding those who avoided having children as "criminal against the race . . . the object of contemptuous abhorrence by healthy people." [1]

Although Roosevelt did not invent the term "race suicide," it quickly became the popular label for his ideas. Indeed the weight and publicity naturally given to the views of the President, and a President so newsworthy, made birth control a public national controversy, and Roosevelt became one of the chief spokesmen for the race-suicide theory. The sharpened and broadened attack on birth control produced stronger defenses of it than ever before. Placed on the defensive, feminists and voluntary-motherhood advocates revealed their motivations and ideology more openly than they had before. Roosevelt's bombast led many hitherto cautious suffragists to speak out publicly for birth control for the first time. At the same time the race-suicide theorists expressed more clearly what was threatening to them in birth control.

The race-suicide episode, a controversy that lasted from about 1905 to 1910 at its height, was not only illuminating but influential on the future of birth control. While it forced conservative feminists to incorporate the demand for birth control into their programs, it simultaneously narrowed the appeal of birth control to educated and prosperous women. The outspoken feminist defense of birth control and the narrow class terms in which it was put were connected and mutually reinforcing. To show this connection we must consider both the arguments for birth control and the evidence about its use. The race-suicide alarm did not emerge out of the imagination of Roosevelt or any other social conservative, but was a backlash, a response to actual changes in the birth rate, family structure, and sexual practice. Contemporary perceptions of these changes were not always accurate. But both sides of the dispute recognized that fundamental changes were, by the early twentieth century, affecting a significant minority of the U.S. population, and that small families and birth-control use were not a temporary aberration but a secular trend, and possibly even a new norm.

The Threat to the Race

By the early twentieth century several different reactions to demographic changes and birth-control use had been subsumed under the slogan "race suicide." One was an objection to the practice of birth control because it was sinful. Another was an objection to family limitation on the grounds that the nation needed a steadily growing population and large, stable families. A third was the fear that the Yankee "stock," which displayed the lowest birth rates, would be overwhelmed, numerically and hence politically, by immigrants, non-whites, and the poor. Fourth, there was the view that birth control represented a rebellion of women against their primary social duty— motherhood. These four strands were never entirely distinct and tended to reinforce one another. Sin and small families weakened social cohesiveness and moral fiber, which encouraged and enabled women to stray from their proper sphere—home and children. Women's wanderings weakened the family, which in turn led women to stray further, in a vicious cycle of social degeneration. The Yankee upper classes, who believed themselves destined for political and economic leadership, saw this degeneration as weakening their position vis-à-vis those who continued to reproduce in larger numbers. The situation was culturally and morally fatal because, proportionately, the most valuable sectors of the citizenry were shrinking and the least valuable expanding.

The fear of race suicide was at least four decades old by the time of Roosevelt's imprecations. Fears about immigrants and the poor reproducing faster than the Yankee elite had been current since before the Civil War.[2] Physicians in particular noticed demographic patterns. Nathan Allen, a New England doctor, reported that in 1860 the foreign-born population of Massachusetts produced more children than the Yankees and that in 1877 a full 77 per cent of the births in all New England were Catholic.[3] Another physician wrote that the birth rate was declining in "our most intelligent communities."[4] Medical journals carried many similar articles of warning.[5]

In 1891 Francis Amasa Walker, a noted academic economist, made the first comprehensive statistical case against race suicide.[6] As superintendent of the 1870 and 1880 censuses, Walker had observed a declining birth rate among white native-born Americans and a steadily high birth rate among the foreign-born. He concluded that there was a direct relationship between immigration and the falling birth rate among the native-born: observing the poverty and wretchedness of the immigrants, and the necessity of competition with these unkempt newcomers for employment, the native-born shrank from bringing children into the world to experience those unpleasantnesses. In his book *Poverty* a decade later, Robert Hunter drew the logical, if extreme, conclusion from Walker's figures that continued immigration, combined with a continuation of the current trend in the native-born birth rate, would result in the complete substitution of one kind of people for another throughout the United States. Hunter also pushed his analysis of census figures in another direction by showing the class differential in the birth rate among native-born Americans. The poor, he feared, would crowd out the rich.[7]

As the United States entered into overseas expansion, the differential birth rate took on international implications. Demographer-sociologist Edward A. Ross saw parallels between U.S. problems and those of other imperial powers. "In South Africa," he wrote, "the whites stand aghast at the rabbit-like increase of the blacks." He feared that our "more fecund rivals" would outstrip us in "colonizing the waste places" and that our prosperity would likely be "darkened by the pressing-in of hunger-bitten hordes." [8]

Simultaneously, other social critics emphasized the more domestic aspects of the race-suicide problem—women's avoidance of their proper role. But the criticism of women, unlike nativist and racist fears, was primarily directed at relatively privileged women. For example, higher education for women was a favorite target. It had been attacked by antifeminists since its inception, on the grounds that it unfitted women for motherhood. Demographic statistics added to these charges the weight of quantification. College-educated women married less often, married later, and had fewer children than their less privileged sisters.[9] By 1917 only half of all the graduates of women's colleges in the United States were married.[10]

There is some evidence that the more intellectual the schooling, the lower the birth rate: in 1909 only 16.5 per cent of the Radcliffe class of 1900 were married.[11] The birth rate went down for married college graduates too, showing that birth control was at least part of the cause. One writer calculated in 1904 that the average number of children of married alumnae was 1.8.[12] Of course the birth rate for male college graduates was low too: in 1902 the president of Harvard had done his part to raise the anxiety level about race suicide with his pronouncement that Harvard graduates were not even replenishing their own numbers, with only 75 per cent marrying, 25 per cent of those childless, and an average of only two children for the rest. But the corresponding female birth rates were even lower.[13]

Race suicide was similarly used to condemn work outside the home for women.[14] Antifeminists frequently argued that college education and employment reduced women's health and therefore their biological fertility.[15] Though the heavy labor that many working-class women did might have produced this effect, the professional work and educational experience of the prosperous women whose birth rates were decreasing certainly did not. Others, recognizing the likelihood that the birth-rate reductions had voluntary causes, attacked the practice of birth control. They accused women of selfishness and self-indulgence in avoiding their "duty," thus revealing their own recognition that childbearing and child-raising were arduous, thankless tasks. The implications of these charges were that women unilaterally were avoiding conception, presumably by using birth-control devices without the complicity of their husbands, or by refusing themselves sexually to their husbands, or by bamboozling their husbands into accepting their "selfishness." A doctor defined the problem as woman's "social ambition" for a "false social position" and "attainment of luxury." [16] In any of those cases, the source was the same: the newfangled independence of women. Roosevelt wrote: ". . . a desire to be 'independent'—that is, to live one's life purely according to one's own desires . . . in no sense substitutes for the fundamental virtues, for the practice of the strong, racial qualities without which there can be no strong races." [17] Clearly the definition of "strong racial qualities" reflected the social and political values of the definer. A physician active in the attack on birth control lamented that the two groups of women who did not breed were those with the best minds—intellectuals—and those with the best bodies—prostitutes.[18]

These views reflected a double standard. The very attitudes that were attacked in women—social ambition, desire for wealth—were applauded in men. Individualist, self-aggrandizing, and materialist values were the norm in the world of men—in politics and economics. In the world of women they were unnatural and sinful. In order to preserve the "race" nature had ordained not only a division of labor but an ultimate division of values as well, that required of women absolute selflessness. The antiindividualism of the attack on women is noticeable in the strange absence of "right to life" arguments about unborn children, despite the common device of linking and even confusing contraception with abortion.[19]

A variant of the objection to women leaving their sphere was a fear for the subversion of the home and family. Roosevelt spoke of this passionately. "The whole fabric of society rests upon the home. . . ." [20] He associated the ideal home with a large family. Six children were the minimum number for people of "normal stock";

those of better stock should have more.[21] William S. Rossiter, chief clerk of the Census, thought that the large family had been one of the key sources of the "finer elements of American character." [22]

Many strands of race-suicide thought—belief in large families, women's domesticity, nativism and racism, Yankee chauvinism both domestic and international—were unified in the minds of the believers. They were parts of an organic world view, made aggressive because it was on the defensive. Both the defensiveness of the viewpoint and the convergence of different attitudes within it are particularly clear in Roosevelt's own thought. Roosevelt is doubly important here—as a representative of race-suicide thought and as a powerful influence on it. His intellectual development is a microcosm of the tendency of Wasp chauvinism and male chauvinism to reinforce each other against threats.

The young Roosevelt had been in favor of women's emancipation. His senior essay at Harvard in 1880 was called "The Practicability of Equalizing Men and Women Before the Law"; his biographer Pringle quotes some extraordinary passages from it.

> . . . even as the world now is, it is not only feasible but advisable to make women equal to men before the law. . . . A son should have no more right to any inheritance than a daughter. . . . Especially as regards the laws relating to marriage, there should be the most absolute equality preserved between the two sexes. I do not think the woman should assume the man's name. The man should have no more right over the person or property of his wife than she has over the person or property of her husband. . . . I would have the word "obey" used not more by the wife than the husband.[23]

These views were quite advanced for the day. It is possible that they represented the temporary influence of his fiancée at the time, Alice Lee; shortly afterward, as a New York State Assemblyman, he was not an active partisan of woman suffrage.[24] Still, the first instances in which he expressed fears for the birth rate were during his campaign to justify the United States' seizure of the Philippines.[25] He wrote then to Henry Cabot Lodge: "Did I write you of my delight at meeting one Hiram Tower, his wife and his seventeen children?" [26] For Roosevelt virile men, womanly women, and large families were necessary conditions for the world supremacy of the Yankees.

When, as President, Roosevelt began his series of direct attacks on birth control, he fell naturally into the then-fashionable eugenic rhetoric about the importance of building the "race." * In January 1905 he attacked both the low birth rate and the increased divorce rate as leading to race suicide.[27] In March 1905, addressing the National Congress of Mothers, he repeatedly condemned the selfishness, self-indulgence, and "viciousness, coldness, shallow-heartedness" of a woman who would seek to avoid "her duty." Roosevelt compared woman's reproductive obligation to a soldier's duty.[28] If she did not do it, "no material prosperity, no business growth" could save the race.[29] In his authoritarian image of society it was clear where women belonged, and heightened militarism and imperialist passion required tightening their bonds.

Feminist Self-Defense

The race-suicide attacks led feminists to reject the cult of motherhood, which they had previously shared with more conventional women. By focusing not simply on the principle of voluntary versus involuntary childbearing—a principle abstract enough to be meaningless—but on small versus large families, race-suicide theorists forced feminists to address the more basic issue of whether women ought to devote themselves exclusively to child-raising. Prior to the race-suicide controversy, that issue had been avoided because voluntary-motherhood advocates had argued for birth control on the grounds that it would produce a better motherhood and a purer race. Suffragists had emphasized the nobility of motherhood as a symbol for a female selflessness with which they argued the political expediency of women's rights.[30] The desire for respectability which made them avoid the birth-control issue led them to lean on the "Motherhood" refrain, for they perceived that motherhood was the only permissible social role in which all women could command respect. There was no form of special pleading that American feminists found so hard to reject as

* Eugenic rhetoric of this period and Roosevelt's personal rhetoric were often ambiguous in their use of the word "race"—it could mean the human race, or the white race; the emotional significance of this usage lay in the fact that it connoted both meanings simultaneously, encouraging a tendency to identify the human race with the white race.

that of motherhood—that is, female parenthood mystified and spiritualized, defined as the ineluctable destiny and fulfillment of woman-
kind.

Roosevelt's public attacks made the continued use of this line of
argument uncomfortable for a newer generation of feminists. Race-
suicide ideas included even the most conservative goals of feminism—
such as suffrage—in a generalized condemnation of women leaving
their domestic sphere. Many women felt themselves personally attacked as well, in an era when a large proportion of middle-class
women were seeking careers and remaining single. Roosevelt's attacks
reverberated in widespread popular recognition of new values and
practices and stimulated a wave of criticism against feminists, spinsters, childless women, and even mothers of small families. The
hysteria lasted many years. For example, when feminist Catherine
Waugh McCulloch made a speech denouncing the race-suicide scare
in 1911, she received obscene and threatening postcards.[31] The birth
rate had been falling steadily for many decades, birth-control devices
and abortions were widely, if disguisedly, advertised, and smaller
families were visible in most middle-class neighborhoods.[32] Roosevelt
did not invent the race-suicide hysteria. But as President he was able
to put it into the forefront of public concern.

Even such a broad attack did not produce a unified response. The
motherhood mystique was familiar, and most feminists clung to it. A
few took the side of the race-suicide alarmists and remonstrated with
other women to do their duty. Julia Ward Howe was representative of
that view. She offered, in defense of her sex, the observation that lack
of money and the growing expenses of child-raising were partly
responsible; but she believed that this in turn was because people were
selfish, cared too much for personal and not enough for civic success.
Sacrifice was necessary. "It is the sense of this duty which gives
especial dignity to parentage." [33] Motherhood guarantees to a woman,
she wrote, an

> unlimited part in the future of her race. . . . She has learned the
> sweetness of self-sacrifice. . . . Now let us for a moment contrast this
> picture with that of a woman who is never weaned from the intense
> personality of her start in life. . . . She may win personal distinction
> and high fame. She may surely deserve them, but she will be in

danger of following the false way which begins and ends in self. If the fates deny her marriage, or leave it bare of offspring, let her win to arms some motherless child. . . . I would not exaggerate even so great a blessing as that of maternity. . . . Many women in our days have a gift and callings which detain them far from the pains and pleasures of the nursery. . . . I should be the last to undervalue their labor and their reward. But to young mothers not yet weaned from the vanity of girlhood I would say: "If this great blessing of maternity shall visit you . . . do not whine at its fatigues and troubles. . . ." [34]

Howe and others like her accepted the double standard: they did not challenge the selfishness of men who avoided children.

Other feminists, probably the majority, accepted race-suicide assumptions but reinterpreted the evidence so as to shift the blame. Thus Ida Husted Harper, a leading suffragist, responded to these fears by charging that men, not women, were responsible for smaller families.[35] Elsie Clews Parsons, a feminist anthropologist, blamed the problem on legal and social policies that forced women to choose between motherhood and other interesting, useful work; she was angered specifically by a ruling of the New York State Board of Education against married women teachers.[36] Parsons and many others agreed that small families were a misfortune.[37]

Some feminists accepted the eugenic logic of race-suicide theory but argued for different correctives. The quality of offspring and the racial health of the nation remained their primary concerns. But they asserted, for example, that the most careful studies showed that educated women were healthier, not weaker.[38] They raised traditional eugenic bogies: that unwanted children would be likely to be inferior and/or neglected; that children also had a right not to be born if they would be weak or deprived or defective; that only a voluntary and intelligent motherhood in a marriage of equals was capable of producing good citizens.[39] Martha Bensley, later to become active in a national birth-control organization, argued in 1905 that perhaps it was just as well that the very best and the very worst human specimens did not reproduce, pointing out that children did not necessarily inherit the pre-eminence of extraordinary parents.[40] An article of 1904 signed by "An Alumna" ventured the suggestion that the low mar-

riage rate among university alumnae might be eliminating the potentially unhappy marriages![41]

Putting the eugenic arguments to their own uses, other feminists
argued that smaller families were healthier. The phrase "fewer but
better" became common.[42] Ida Husted Harper attacked large families,
charging prolific parents with weakening the race, by producing
deprived children, sending them to work instead of school, and
eventually filling the poorhouses. As to the command "Multiply and
replenish the earth," we have only men's word for it, she wrote,
handed down to us by the "masculine hierarchy" of the churches.[43]
Other feminists criticized the hypocrisy of the race-suicide moralists
who ignored the poverty and sufferings of children already born. The
Reverend Anna Howard Shaw, suffragist leader, pointed to the *true*
race suicide caused by disease, food adulteration, impure water, filthy
cities, poor schools, child labor, and drunkenness.[44] Socialists and
anarchists also took this line of reasoning and in addition charged that
the call for large families was conditioned by the capitalists' desire to
fill their factories and armies.* [45] Susan B. Anthony went so far as to
introduce the threat of overcrowding, an unfamiliar idea in an era
when birth-rate decline was the general fear.[46]

Other feminists rejected the entire eugenic framework and argued instead on the basis of women's right to self-determination. But
their line of argument remained abstract; they did not discuss small
families or childlessness. "All this talk, for and against and about
babies, is by men. One would think the men bore the babies, nursed
the babies, reared the babies. . . . The women bear and rear the
children. The men kill them. Then they say: 'We are running short of
children—make some more. . . .' " Thus stormed Charlotte Perkins
Gilman, the major feminist theoretician and writer of the turn of the
century.[47] Catherine McCulloch thought that it was "unbecoming for
men to talk about this subject and make demands upon women. . . .
The question of having children should rest entirely with women."[48]
Ellen Key, a much published and very influential European voice in

---

* If this failed to take into account that the race-suicide theory concerned a declining birth rate
among the upper classes specifically, they can hardly be blamed, since the phrase "race suicide"
was used in the popular media in many different ways, often as a slander on any form of birth
limitation.

this country, also argued that the declining birth rate was a consequence of the devaluation of mothering. The challenge and rewards of motherhood, she said, had not grown commensurately with women's expectations.[49] Even before Roosevelt's fulminations, Moses Harman had written that the birth-rate decline represented a strike by women: "If they cannot get employment as mothers on their own terms, if they cannot have children without putting their necks under the yoke of marital bondage, they will not have children at all."[50] Harman's interpretation of "marital bondage" came from his conviction that all state regulation of private relationships was wrong. But with a broader interpretation, marital bondage—including the material conditions that limited women and especially mothers—was acknowledged throughout the feminist community. Elsie Parsons attacked the system that forced women to choose between motherhood and other work—a system enforced by law, custom, and lack of opportunity. Refusing motherhood was indeed a strike against those conditions.

The concept of a birth strike was widely known. Educated women had Lysistrata as a model, of course, and indeed Charlotte Perkins Gilman's anger at raising children to feed men's armies was a common theme, particularly provoked by Roosevelt's imperialist policies. A modern version of *Lysistrata*, *The Strike of a Sex*, by George Noyes Miller, an English Neo-Malthusian, was circulating in the United States in the 1890s.[51] In Miller's fantasy the women of an entire community leave their husbands until the men adopt "Zugassent's Discovery" or "Karezza"—avoidance of orgasm, or male continence. However militant the birth-strike discussion, it still used refusal of motherhood as a lever to gain something else, a lever that could be relinquished when the end was won. In birth-strike logic, birth control was a temporary expedient, not a permanent change in the female condition.

The most radical response to the race-suicide attack was one that reinterpreted woman's role and "duty" in the society. Offered tentatively, in language far less militant than Gilman's, the defense of small families and childlessness was far more radical because it was a direct challenge to motherhood. Ida Husted Harper wrote in 1901 that motherhood represented a huge sacrifice of other kinds of talents and might not be the right choice for every woman. Some marriages *ought*

to remain childless, she wrote.[52] In 1905 another woman, who signed herself "A Childless Wife," wrote that she believed herself more useful to society childless than as a mother because she made a social contribution through her profession.[53]

Though the challenge to motherhood was the minority position among feminists, it was influential and frightening because it implied profound changes in social values. To the extent that it was a challenge to motherhood but not to marriage, it tended to separate sexuality from reproduction and implicitly to license more sexual activity. It chipped away at the ideology of differences between the sexes, differences often comforting both to men and women. When Roosevelt called childless women "selfish," he was calling up a powerful bogey; this was an ultimate kind of selfishness because it involved in the contemporary understanding a betrayal of the entire human race for the sake of self. Feminists who refused to accede to this condemnation were implicitly condemning all those women who had accepted maternal selflessness as their source of self-esteem. And indeed some such women sensed this condemnation and resented it, feeling that their labors as full-time mothers were being discounted.[54]

This reaction was especially generated by the fact that the issue was becoming increasingly a question of motherhood versus career. Feminists responding to race suicide attacks focused increasingly on the question of professions for women. The "Childless Wife," as we have seen, justified her childlessness by her profession. Ida Husted Harper wrote that women *ought* to work.[55]

The jobs that these spokeswomen had in mind, professional jobs, were available only to educated upper- and middle-class women. Because they were taking a utilitarian line—that childbearing might not be the best way for women to serve society—they had to focus on jobs that commanded respect. Their arguments lacked persuasiveness with working-class women. By and large the jobs that were available to working-class women were not preferable to full-time mothering and housewifery, and married working-class women usually took jobs out of necessity. This does not, of course, imply that working-class women had no interest in winning acceptance for birth control and smaller families. From what we know of the prevalence of abortion among working-class married women, their concern was great and their willingness to take risks to have fewer children equally great. Even without outside employment as a desirable alternative, the labor of mothering could be made far less oppressive with fewer and more widely spaced children.

But the race-suicide controversy occurred primarily on terms set by middle-class feminists defending their interest in activity outside their homes. As a result, the controversy had the effect, at least temporarily, of moving birth-control propaganda still further away from working-class communities than it had been several decades earlier. Women dedicated to improving the lot of the working class, especially those in the Socialist party, were silent during this controversy. *The Socialist Woman* and *The Progressive Woman*, Socialist party women's journals published monthly from 1907, said nothing at all about birth control during this controversy despite their strong calls for women's rights on issues such as equal work and equal wages. In her 1912 book *The Sorrows of Cupid*, which covered many other problems of sex and marital relations, Kate Richards O'Hare, a leader of the Socialist party women's movement, ignored the birth-control question. She accepted the Rooseveltian premise that the shrinking family was a misfortune and blamed it on working-class poverty, ignoring the fact that the lowest birth rates were among the wealthy. Instead, she defended working-class women against charges that they had lost the maternal instinct.[56] None of the women active in the socialist movement in this period, though many of them were very feminist, believed that birth control was an urgent concern for working-class women.[57]

The Root of the Problem

What caused so-called race suicide? Effective remedies to social problems must address themselves to root causes, and the race-suicide theorists naturally argued their proposals in those terms. Two causal theories prevailed at the time, and still prevail. One was the view that feminism was the culprit; the second was an economic explanation.

Those who attacked the "independence" and "selfishness" of women saw such attributes as the individual reflection of a vicious doctrine that violated nature. In refusal of motherhood it seemed personal and ideological feminism were joined: women's unnatural and false yearnings were threatening the entire race. Something about the feminist movement had communicated that particular threat to its enemies from its very inception. In 1867 an anti-Reconstruction writer saw it as a regional phenomenon because feminism at that time was largely confined to the Northeastern United States:

> The anti-offspring practice has been carried in New England and wherever New England ideas prevail. It is the esoteric, the interior doctrine of the woman's rights movement. These female reformers see that if they are to act the part of men in the world, they must not be burdened with the care of young children. So they have resolved to marry, but to limit, in certain ways well understood in France,* the number of their offspring. . . . in proportion as women's rights ideas prevail, are parents becoming ashamed of large families. It is not that the New England women are unable to bear as many children as formerly, but that they will not.[58]

This view reveals one kind of effect the women's rights movement was having, but it is not necessarily an accurate description of the movement. Opponents of a movement commonly exaggerate the movement's influence. Catherine Beecher had written in 1871:

> This woman movement is one which is uniting . . . all the antagonisms that are warring on the family state.† Spiritualism, free love, free divorce, the vicious indulgences consequent on regulated civilization, the worldliness which tempts men and women to avoid large families, often by sinful methods, thus making the ignorant masses the chief supply of the future ruling majorities.[59]

Here was the entire race-suicide nightmare, foreseen thirty years before Roosevelt discovered it, and the blame laid squarely upon the women's rights movement. Though the women's rights movement in the early twentieth century did not in fact advocate birth control or rejection of the family, its opponents perceived its influence in the reproductive behavior of even nonfeminist women. The small-family

* France had had a falling birth rate longer than any other Western country, and that fact was well publicized in the United States, with the result that popular writers often tended to assume that all knowledge of contraceptive techniques originated in France.
† This phrase, "the family state," is perhaps significant in view of the later analysis by professional sociologists, a constant refrain in Roosevelt's speeches, that the family is in fact a microcosm of the state and its logical and necessary training ground.

norm was a concession, they believed, to a rebellion of women. Recently, one historian has used the phrase "domestic feminism" to refer to an alteration in the balance of power within the family in favor of women, and attributed the birth-rate decline to it.[60]

An alternative explanation for the race-suicide phenomenon was an economic one, and it was the prevalent theory among contemporaries. Writers noticed that children had been an asset in agricultural societies, whereas industrialization and urbanization made large families no longer economically advantageous.[61] Journalist Lydia Kingsmill Commander interviewed thirty-eight physicians practising in the New York City area about "the causes of the prevalence and popularity of the small family" and found uniformly economic explanations. Here are some of their observations:

> Children are an expensive luxury. They cost a lot to raise; they are late in getting to work, because of the long training they must have; and few parents get anything back from them. . . . What I mean is that nowadays raising children is all outlay, financially speaking. . . .
>
> . . . the secret of success in the new world is education and years of training. The fittest to survive in our civilization are the trained and educated. Brain rules, not brawn. This is the American idea, and it involves small families, for so much cannot be given to a large number.

And the reverse:

> The large families of the Italians are easily understood when we realize that almost nothing is spent raising the children, and they begin to work almost as soon as they can walk. You will find that newsboys and bootblacks always come from large families. . . . The Italians are just like animals. They produce as freely and naturally and they expect their children to look out for themselves almost as early as animals do.
>
> These people [German, Irish and English poor on the East Side] look upon their children as a sort of insurance. The man has just a certain number of years to work. Then rheumatism, consumption, an accident or some such trouble attacks him, and he cannot work full time. . . . By this time his children are getting old enough to "earn a couple of cents," and the family pulls through. A large family is an advantage to people of that type.[62]

There are no independent women avoiding maternal responsibilities in these vignettes. Indeed, in several of the articles we meet women who wanted more children but felt that their husbands could not afford them.[63] Recently historians Joseph and Olive Banks have offered a similar economic explanation of the birth-rate decline in England. The Banks's study found that married women's fertility was associated with the class position of their husbands, not with feminist ideas.[64]

Which theory was right? What did cause race suicide? The second question is made more difficult by the asking of the first. By seeking an either/or explanation, choosing between feminism or new economic needs among urban people, observers have overlooked the connections between the two phenomena. Just as city dwellers, particularly educated professionals, had new values and a life style more favorable to women's equality than peasants,[65] so feminism both in principle and in practice had an economic basis. To put it another way: to answer the question "what caused the decline of fertility" by saying "women," or "feminism," merely raises other questions: What caused feminism? What changed the women?

Feminism itself grew from the upward mobility that made smaller families more economical. A closer look at the birth rates of women college graduates shows this. First, the female college students in these early years of women's higher education (roughly, the last quarter of the nineteenth century) were themselves upwardly mobile socially. Education represented for them a challenge; they went to college carrying the burden of proof of their abilities, often over the objections of those who felt their education would be wasted; frequently the students were feminists themselves. For these women, to ask whether the cause of their low marriage and birth rate was feminism or class mobility would be to introduce a false distinction. Second, among the female college students—even among students from the same college—birth rates varied according to class in the same way that they did in the whole society. And third, a high proportion of females in college themselves came from small families and had already been influenced by attitudes favorable to small families.[66]

Smaller families were both cause and effect of feminism. Women's desire for more leisure to use in the areas now open to them (charity work, organization work, jobs) made fewer children preferable. And their husbands' economic calculations produced the same view of desirable family size. These "new-middle-class" husbands, satisfied with smaller families, were also less concerned with other ostentatious displays of wealth. More and more they identified professional and educational attainment as signs of status.[67] This made them ask different things of their wives as well as their children. The phenomenon of educated and ambitious women remaining unmarried, characteristic of the late nineteenth century, began to change quickly in the twentieth century. Women who were educated, experienced, even mentally energetic were increasingly acceptable as wives to educated men.[68]

An expression of the juxtaposition of feminist and economic sentiment for smaller families can be found in an article of 1903 signed "Paterfamilias." Insisting that his *main* reason for opposition to Roosevelt's large-family sentimentality was his recollection of the oppression large families meant for women in earlier America, he spoke frankly of his personal economic calculations.

> I have four children. . . . It happens that we are able to care for four, not quite in the style in which two could have been maintained, but to all intents and purposes quite well enough for them, and sufficiently well for us to maintain our social position, which is very dear to us, though to some such a statement may seem folly. If a time should come when we had to give up our present style of living (which, practically, means our friends, since in that event we would not and could not continue present relations with them), I would consider it, perhaps, the most serious day of my life. So far as can be judged at present, the only thing that might threaten such an event would be the appearance say of a couple of more children. I presume there are those who will think that this is an ignoble statement; but it is not only true, but it is true of about every family of which I have any personal acquaintance, except in those rather numerous instances where there are no children at all. . . .

About his ambitions for his children, Paterfamilias was equally blunt: If a young man "is to be anything more than a hewer of wood and a drawer of water, it must needs be that he become fitted for the race in the best manner possible. Perhaps his best chance will be with the great corporations where only experts are wanted in the paying positions. . . ." [69]

Paterfamilias was not alone. Many important establishment spokesmen supported the small-family trend and were not alarmed by race suicide. *World's Work*, an early twentieth-century business journal, editorialized that the birth-rate decline might be a good thing, implying more appreciation of the individual child.[70] (This psychology—appreciation of the individual child—is the correlate of the economics Paterfamilias outlined, of increasing expenditure on each individual child.) *Harper's Weekly* editorialized in 1903 against race suicide when Harvard president Eliot reported his fears of Harvard's inability to replenish itself from among its peers,[71] but four months later shifted to support the idea of having only the children that one could afford to raise well.[72]

The economic and the feminist explanations for the decline of the birth rate are inextricably connected. The economic reorganization that made smaller families more economical also made upper- and middle-class women eager for broader horizons, which in turn made them desire smaller families. The changes were in fact gradual, the product of the entire course of American economic development. The race-suicide alarm was a response to the transformation of an entire society, and the alarm tells us as much about the old values as about the new. It was a conservative response, as hostile to the new, professional values of Paterfamilias as to feminism. These conservatives were genuinely threatened by actual social changes and simultaneously overreacting to their own fears, imagining a challenge to white male hegemony far greater than actually posed by changes in birth rates. It will be easier to distinguish between what was really happening and what the race-suicide theorists thought was happening if we review, briefly, the actual demographic and family changes. The development of demography and the passage of time has given us today a longer view of those events.

The most fundamental perception of the race-suicide theorists still stands as correct: women in the nineteenth century bore progressively fewer children. The fertility rate for white* women fell from

* We do not have a comparable statistic for all women, but see following footnote on the black birth rate.

7.04 in 1800 to 4.24 in 1880 and 3.56 in 1900. At the beginning of the twentieth century only France, notorious home of contraception and other vices, had a lower fertility rate than America.[73]

A second perception was equally valid: that the decline in fertility was deliberate. Nearly all the people involved in the race-suicide controversy, on all sides, asserted or assumed that birth-control practices were widespread.[74] Physicians, who were probably in the best position to judge in the era before sex-behavior surveys, reported the same.[75] The demographers agreed.[76]

A third belief of race-suicide theorists is more controversial today: that the fertility rate was much lower among "respectable," Wasp people than among blacks, immigrants, working-class, and below-working-class people. This judgment is controversial because it depends on how one defines the categories of the population. For example, although the immigrant birth rate remained relatively high in relation to the Wasp native-born rate, a little noticed fact is that blacks had the greatest birth-rate decline of all.* Though new immigrants had, on the whole, higher birth rates than old Americans, the birth rate of all immigrants fell in relation to their length of residence in the country. Furthermore, the urban and rural birth rates declined in approximately equal ratios.[78] Whereas effective contraceptive practices were common in the middle and upper classes, abortion was common in all classes—with a high maternal mortality rate, to be sure, but effective in lowering the birth rate nonetheless.[79] By stressing or suppressing the birth-rate statistics of certain social groups over others, one could arrive at a picture of the race-suicide "problem" that would prove any of a number of theories of its causes—economic, ethnic, feminist, or religious, among others.

It is true that the birth rate fell first among educated, professional people. Where the women of that class had lower birth rates than the men, it was of course because they were less likely to marry; but it is

---

* Although the danger of a huge black population increase was frequently raised by Southerners (and repeated by Northerners, as by Ross, in relation to South Africa), the facts are that the black population of the South was increasing much more slowly than the white. In 1870 there were 5 million blacks in the South, and in 1910 8.7 million, whereas there were 8.6 million whites in 1870 and 20.5 million in 1910. Even Dr. Billings, Director of the Census Bureau's Division of Vital Statistics and publicizer of race-suicide dangers, pointed out this decrease in black birth rate, although he then attempted to account for it by inaccuracy in census statistics, an inaccuracy which presumably he did not think affected the white statistics.[77]

not obvious that the reasons for remaining unmarried were exactly identical with the reasons for having fewer children. The assumption of contemporaries that the phenomena of spinsterhood and small families had identical causes reflects their own bias about the proper role of women and the identity of marriage and reproduction.

A fourth belief shared by most race-suicide theorists—that there had been a sharp decline in birth rates in the *late* nineteenth century— was wrong. On the one hand, birth rates had been declining steadily and gradually since 1810, the differential between classes and ethnic groups remaining reasonably constant. On the other hand, from as early as 1905 the gap in birth rates between classes and ethnic groups began closing: college graduates' birth rates actually rose and other birth rates fell steadily until at least 1965.[80]

Re-evaluating these race-suicide tenets demonstrates several things. Although changes of the greatest magnitude were taking place, they had been occurring for so long that it would be hard to attribute them to the influence of an organized feminist movement. The birth-rate differential was in fact only a lag. The suddenness of the race-suicide alarm was due partly to the impact of immigration—the sudden and massive introduction of people from rural and preindustrial situations; just as in the twentieth century migration of blacks from the South to North produced similar alarms about the birth rate. The societal changes that make large families no longer advantageous— the high cost of education, food, and rent and the end of productive child labor—take time, often a whole generation, before the new values they produce are internalized. Parents' willingness to accept small families requires their understanding that children will not provide them security in their old age, either because they will be unwilling to do so or, more rarely, because their security will come from other sources.[81] Furthermore, new industrial workers tried to utilize preindustrial family patterns to meet new economic needs, patterns such as extended families and the contribution of grown working children to the parental income. In most new economic situations, people try at first to use their old values and social patterns in new ways and only surrender them after long resistance. The notion that children represented wealth and security was a particularly tenacious conviction. Naturally those who had most to gain from giving up the large-family life style—such as the upwardly mobile and professional—made that change first.

There is another reason that these changes appeared to contemporaries to be more sudden than they were. Gradual and incremental social change does take qualitative leaps when previously exceptional patterns become new norms. The illusion of suddenness led some to search for sharp causes; the birth-rate differential led some to anticipate a continuing divergence between different social groups in population patterns. Race-suicide theorists believed the small-family trend would produce social disaster if it was not stopped. But even at the time a few social critics found perspectives from which to appreciate both the long-term origins of the changes and their inevitability, and even equated them with progress.

Some argued, in short, that there was no race suicide. Socialist eugenist Scott Nearing wrote that the "race murderers" were really race saviors, since birth control was establishing a new equilibrium between birth rates and declining death rates.[82] A "brilliant and thoughtful Hebrew lawyer of Boston," probably Louis Brandeis, writing under a pseudonym, argued that although the birth rate was inevitably falling as a result of "the advance of civilization," the fact that children lived longer and that social childhood was extended more than compensated.[83] Another writer thought it odd that the "suicide" of the rich was feared when the far greater problem was continued high mortality among children of the poor.[84]

These dissident voices agreed that important demographic changes were taking place but perceived that "race suicide" was a misnomer, deflecting attention from the true social significance of the changes. Indeed, "race suicide" was worse than a misnomer—it was a red herring. It was a way of refusing to accept the implications of democracy without clearly rejecting democracy. It provided a focus for distress among Yankee business and professional classes about the growth of working-class and non-Yankee groups and about shifts in family and sex-role patterns (that is, the increase in married women wage-earners) produced by industrialization and the feminist movement. Since traditional religious and moral scruples and belief in the system's economic need for population growth would not yet allow seeking remedy by urging birth control upon the poor, it was necessary to turn in the other direction and ask of prosperous women that they restore upper-class families to a competitive size. Women became the scapegoats.[85]

Blaming prosperous women for the declining birth rate was the reverse side of blaming immigrant groups for keeping theirs up. The race-suicide theorists saw the overall changes in their society as a whole. A physician writing about inadequate reproduction among women of the "better class," put many things together:

> The family idea is, indeed, drifting into individualism. . . . Now [woman] has weaned herself from the hearthstone, and her chief end is self. Pray! What has brought about these changes? By the invention of the sewing-machine, by the introduction of ready-made clothing, and by that damnable sin—the avoidance of off-spring, our women are no longer compelled to stay at home—the home-tether is broken. . . . [The sin of avoiding offspring] comes from fashion, from cowardice, from indolent wealth and shiftless poverty.[86]

Poor women *and* rich women were to blame, in the view of race-suicide theorists. Hostile to the social disruptions of industrial society but lacking a class analysis of capitalism, race-suicide theorists often turned from blaming the industrial working class to blaming *all* women for the social evils of the whole economic system.

The race-suicide propagandists had no success. Few women responded to Roosevelt's castigations by giving up their birth-control devices. On the contrary, the lasting result of the race-suicide controversy was that many feminists and professional women previously silent on the subject now committed themselves publicly and lastingly to birth control. Furthermore, the birth-control arguments they put forward were more woman-centered than any since the first timid voluntary-motherhood assertions of the 1870s. They wanted women to have options other than full-time motherhood—at least those women who could afford it.

The qualification is as important as the basic demand, however. Although the race-suicide controversy released a strong feminist endorsement of birth control, it also brought to the forefront those issues that most separated feminists from the working class and poor. This

happened in two ways. First, the feminists were increasingly emphasizing birth control as a route to careers and higher education—goals out
of reach of the poor with or without birth control. In the context of the
whole feminist movement, the race-suicide episode was an additional
factor identifying feminism almost exclusively with the aspirations of
the more privileged women of the society. Second, the pro-birth-control feminists began to popularize the idea that poor people had a
moral obligation to restrict the size of their families, because large
families created a drain on the taxes and charity expenditures of the
wealthy and because poor children were less likely to be "superior."
Though the idea that birth control was an attack on the working class
and the immigrants was not new, this episode supplied more solid
evidence for it than ever before, and popularized the fear. Consider
this letter to the editor of a pro-birth-control journal in 1907:

> Dear Doctor . . . I want to say that I am surprised to here a Man of
> your supposed intelligence to ask in sincerity if it would not be
> better to criminally limit the off spring of the Poor, what would you
> gain by adding crime to poverty? it has never been held a crime
> (even in N.Y.) to bee Poor. . . . Human life is more than money, is
> a man justified in killing his own children be cause his business
> failes? then the history of our country and the history of the Human
> race would read verry diferent if we was to exclude from its pages
> all the workes of our grate men who was born in obscure poverty we
> would cut out the workes of the immortal Lincolen.[87]

Such defensiveness and suspicion toward birth control is still common,
and one of its historical sources is here in the race-suicide controversy.

8

Continence or Indulgence
The Doctors and the "Sexual Revolution"

Eₐᵣₗy IN THE twentieth century, simultaneously with the race-suicide controversy but less public, another dispute about the implications of birth control raged. Confined primarily to the pages of medical journals, it concerned the moral and physical healthfulness of continence. In more contemporary language, was doing without sex harmful?

The question had arisen because of increased acceptance of the principle of voluntary motherhood. But at the turn of the century the major respectable form of birth control was sexual abstinence. This could mean, and many physicians and moralists explicitly prescribed, abstinence from one conception until the next time that another conception was desirable and possible. It could alternatively mean abstinence during the periods when a woman was likely to be fertile—the "rhythm method." But the exact female ovulation cycle had not yet been successfully calculated, and medical opinion was mounting, no doubt based on women's sad experiences, that the rhythm method did not work.[1] "Continence" came to refer specifically to abstinence for the purpose of birth control.

Whether continence was "harmful" depended, of course, on one's view of the nature of the sex drive. The two extreme opinions were that sex was an absolute physiological necessity, like food, or that it was a dispensable item, like liquor. Another dimension of disagreement was whether the sex drive was the same in both sexes or entirely different in men and women. In short, the arguments about birth control in this period led to basic social and moral questions about sexuality.

Many of the participants in these discussions were doctors. Looking backward, this perhaps seems natural, as birth control today seems so much a medical issue. If one were to have looked forward into the future from the year 1870, however, voluntary motherhood did not particularly seem a medical issue. Furthermore, most doctors in the nineteenth century had been opposed to birth control of any sort. Thus before focusing on the "continence-versus-indulgence" debate of 1910 and thereafter, we will have to trace the role of medicine in the spread of birth control.

In the nineteenth century the leaders of the American medical profession had been reluctant, to say the least, to accept birth control. Instead, they frequently identified promotion of contraception with quackery and immorality. As Norman Himes, historian of birth-control technology, remarked, "One way to gain a reputation for supermorality . . . was to condemn birth control in portentous tones with much moral exhortation to purity, and in violent language." [2] The sexual conservatism of the doctors was in part merely representative of their social class. It also had special origins: in establishing themselves as professionals with a cooptive authority to admit or exclude others, doctors made particular use of their power over women. Physicians not only obtained a monopoly on the treatment of upper- and middle-class women's diseases and pregnancies, forcing out midwives and popular healers, who had been the social repository of birth-control knowledge; they also invented syndromes of diseases which explained away their patients' depressions and resentments and helped make physical fragility, weakness, sickliness, and consequent hypochondria part of the convention of bourgeois femininity.[3] Birth control, part of the growing self-assertion of women generally, particularly annoyed doctors. Women were taking back control of an aspect of their bodily functioning into their own hands.

Indeed, much of the medical establishment responded hysterically to voluntary motherhood. Doctors used their social status as experts to denounce birth control. In the face of easily available evidence to the contrary, some asserted to the public, and presumably to their patients, that there was no method of contraception that worked. H. S. Pomeroy, writing in 1888, was typical:

> It is surprising to what an extent the laity believe that medical science knows how to control the birth-rate. Just here let me say that I know of but one prescription which is both safe and sure— namely, *that the sexes shall remain apart.* So thoroughly do I believe this to be a secret which Nature has kept to herself, that I should be inclined to question the ability or the honesty of any one professing to understand it so as to be able safely and surely to regulate the matter of reproduction. . . .[4]

In this very book Pomeroy reveals his awareness of the widespread use of "prevention" throughout the population; clearly his moralism had overwhelmed his scientific curiosity.

Doctors also commonly asserted that contraception was physically harmful, and the harm was often described as a mortal threat. Edward J. Ill [*sic*] wrote in the *American Journal of Obstetrics and Diseases of Women and Children* in 1899 that contraceptive practices led to permanent sterility.[5] A Michigan doctor, Eliza Barton Lyman, wrote in 1880 that contraception led to hardening of the uterus.[6] Nor were these warnings confined to the medical press. Since the 1860s doctors had been writing popular books and articles attacking birth control.[7]

One rhetorical device employed by these physicians was to confuse birth control with abortion.[8] At other times they called birth control "onanism" (since it was fruitless intercourse, "wasting seed"), thus associating its condemnation with the Bible. Women who used birth control were brutally maligned: "Legitimate prostitutes," Dr. Ill called them; "the depth of moral degeneracy in such cases can only be imagined."[9] Dr. McArdle in 1888 branded sexual intercourse with the use of contraceptives "marital masturbation."[10] Abbot Kinney, in a popular antiabortion tract of 1893, wrote: "Sexual intercourse, unhallowed by the creation of the child, is lust . . . wife without

children is a mere sewer to pass off the unfruitful and degraded
passions and lust of one man." [11]

Such misogyny was usually accompanied by a defense of the
double standard. Kinney, transforming common moralistic views into
physiological language, wrote that nature had created the hymen as a
sign of woman's purity, because purity was so much more important
for women than for men.[12] But so extreme was the physicians' fear of
voluntary motherhood that many condemned even sexual abstinence
for women.[13] Abbot Kinney was among several who charged that not
having children was in itself unhealthy: a woman still childless at
twenty-five would have a "continuous tendency to degeneracy and
atrophy of the reproductive organs." [14]

Not all doctors shared these repressive attitudes. Medicine was far
from homogeneous during the nineteenth century. Indeed, the creation of uniform standards and education for doctors was the focus of a
significant upheaval among doctors, for healing had traditionally been
a craft, a skilled labor, performed with as much personal variation and
latitude as other artisanal crafts. Furthermore, the craft of healing had
once, centuries before, been dominated by women. The nineteenth
century saw the establishment of male hegemony in medicine, and
simultaneously of medicine as a prestigious profession. Doctors attempted to establish their profession, like a church, differentiating a
group of "regular" doctors from "irregulars," standardizing education
in European techniques, including "heroic" medicine—bleeding, surgery, powerful emetics; eventually they won establishment through a
state-licensing system. In the course of this campaign the regulars
attempted to discredit the older, folk tradition of healing by identifying it with quackery, implying that it was not only universally
ineffectual but universally dishonest as well.[15]

Victory did not come quickly or easily to the new professionals,
however. They were faced with the stubborn attachment of traditionally minded people to the older healing practices; and in the eighteenth century this came to include the ideological conviction that
especially in gynecological and obstetrical matters, women ought not
to be attended by men. Then in the 1830s the young medical profession met direct rebellion. A popular health movement began at that

time in the United States, a movement at once a reassertion of older traditions and an expression of a new class hostility to the emergence of powerful professional elites. Describing that peculiar combination of rebellion and traditionalism in the movement, the medical historian Joseph Kett wrote that popular health campaigners "saw their movement as wresting medicine from the doctors and completing the great revolution which, beginning with the Reformation, freed government from the lawyers and despots and religion from the priests." [16] Ehrenreich and English, feminist historians, have described it as "the medical front of a general social upheaval." [17] Begun by a few charismatic individual reformers, such as Sylvester Graham and Samuel Thomson, the movement quickly spun off many local groups, either followers of one or another of these medical prophets or originators of their own medical systems for health and happiness. Many of these groups were women's groups—"Ladies' Physiological Reform Societies." [18] The popular-health movement emphasized preventive hygiene, having good reason to distrust the uncertain cures of that period. Many "natural" cures became associated with the movement —water cures, homeopathy, animal magnetism, physical culture, and herbal medicines, for example. By mid-century many irregulars were creating their own sectarian medical schools and awarding their own degrees; and as the century went on the medical sects became increasingly dogmatic and narrow. The word "irregular" was used to describe everyone from herbalists to osteopaths, from partisans of popular-health principles to shysters.

The regulars eventually established the hegemony of their medical approach. Their success was not always the public's gain. Ignorant of germ theory and with only rudimentary understandings of physiology, the regular physicians of that period often relied upon harsh drugs, bleedings, and surgery for cures that were frequently dangerous and/or ineffective. The herbal medicines that the regulars condemned as fraudulent often contained substances now recognized as genuinely valuable. The hygienic recommendations of the sectarians—for example, frequent bathing; whole-grain cereals; more vegetable and less animal foods; loose, warm clothing; fresh air and exercise; avoidance of tobacco and alcohol—were often more sound than the book-learned methods of the regulars.

Two important aspects of this popular-health movement are at the center of our concern. One is that it produced some of the first frank medical tracts about birth control in the United States. The second, closely connected to the first, is that the movement was often feminist: in the preponderance of women in the movement, in its challenging of the conventional medical version of a restrictive definition of women's place, and in its asserting of the right of women to become doctors and the propriety of their doing so. In 1847 the *Boston Medical Surgical Journal* thought that ninety-nine out of a hundred patients of the "quacks" were women.[19] Many groups in the popular-health movement specifically directed their appeals to women, considering them the primary victims of the violent methods of the regulars. It was sectarians who pioneered a new approach to pregnancy, attacking the tradition that required confinement inside a house, proscribed any physical exercise, and insisted on protection from the slightest psychological stimulation. Ironically, although some irregulars fought prudery in encouraging education about sex, pregnancy, and childbirth, they often asserted that it was improper for men to be gynecologists or obstetricians. In part that view disguised their real purpose—asserting women's right to work in medicine. "We cannot deny that women possess superior capacities for the science of medicine . . . ," one medical reformer wrote.[20] But we have learned from our discussion of the voluntary-motherhood movement how misleading such a one-dimensional analysis would be. Prudishness was not a disguise for feminism; it was an integral part of feminist thought until at least the 1890s. Furthermore, the prudish antagonism toward male doctors had a basis in women's desire to protect themselves from humiliation. In the late twentieth century the women's liberation movement has begun to bring to light the fact that women have often been humiliated in medical examinations by men—at worst by sexual molestation and more commonly by arrogance and disregard of women's own feelings and physiological self-understanding. There is every reason to suspect that in the nineteenth century women's powerlessness in such situations would have been even greater.

The issue of birth control cannot be separated from the question of power. For its opponents, particularly its male opponents, birth control was a symbol and a basis for female power. It was also a symbol of the power of irregulars. The two fears reinforced each other. Preventive hygiene programs combined with birth control and abortion formulas and female midwifery in threatening to restore women to their traditional roles as healers. As Kett puts it, the irregulars "replaced the infirmary with the family." [21] One way they did this was through writing medical manuals aimed at the public, particularly wives and mothers, offering them help and confidence to do their own diagnoses and treatment.

It would not be correct, however, simply to reverse the establishment view and make the irregulars into progressive reformers. They had among them many dishonest, avaricious, and ignoble men, as the regulars did. Especially in the field of birth control many were quacks, selling pills, douche powders, and other nostrums* which they must have known were ineffective. When their abortion patients sickened or died, regular and sectarian doctors alike frequently tried to conceal their role, even if it meant leaving the woman helpless. Greater closeness to a community may have made the lay healers more sensitive to social needs, whereas greater concern with prestige may have made the regulars more cautious. The irregular healers were objectively part of a different, more democratic, medical tradition, but they were not always subjectively committed to those principles. Few of them were conscious that their medical views and practices might be considered to have political implications. Nevertheless, their different situations—needing larger practices, since they could not charge as much as the regulars, being accustomed to seeing themselves as less prestigious, and being closer to communities of poor people— may have made the irregulars do more for the birth-control cause than the regulars. Certainly the irregulars were more active as publicists of birth control. The popular-health movement had stimulated the publication of books of health and hygiene for the public, many including birth-control information. Both honest sectarians and unscrupulous quacks published such books in mid-century.

An example of the latter was A. M. Mauriceau, a charlatan who described himself as a "professor of Diseases of Women" with offices at 129 Liberty Street, New York City. He published *The Married Woman's*

---

* A nostrum is a prepared remedy or tonic the composition of which is secret.

Private Medical Companion in 1847. Its preface used the rhetoric of the popular-health movement: ". . . to extend to every female, whether wife, mother or daughter, such information as will best qualify her to judge of her own maladies, and, having ascertained their existence, apply the proper remedies." [22] In 1871 Mauriceau and his wife were practicing abortionists. A *New York Times* reporter who had investigated them and had been explicitly promised a sure, safe abortion, wrote that the Mauriceaus spent sixty thousand dollars a year on advertising their business.[23] *The Married Woman's Private Medical Companion* sold well and may have been as big a financial success as the abortion business. Its contraceptive information is vague ("The principle . . . is to neutralize the fecundating properties in semen . . . ," probably referring to a douche or suppository),[24] making it necessary for a patient to see the doctor in order to get more explicit directions.

In the same time period, on the other hand, irregulars published similar health manuals full of sound and useful advice, both general and contraceptive. In the 1850s books such as *The People's Lighthouse of Medicine* and J. Soule's *Science of Reproduction and Reproductive Control* recommended condoms, douche powders, withdrawal, the rhythm method, and vaginal sponges.[25] One of the more influential of these early works was Frederick Hollick's *The Marriage Guide*, published in 1860. Hollick regularly lectured on "physiological science" to women's groups. It was probably this activity, as much as the content of his book, that led some who he branded "Medical *Old Fogies*" to attempt, unsuccessfully, to suppress the book.[26] Hollick was by no means open-minded about contraception. He condemned withdrawal as physiologically harmful; considered douching ineffective unless done with spermicides, in which case it could injure the vagina; objected to condoms for their desensitizing effect on the male. The process of elimination suggests that he gave out some kind of pessary or suppository.[27] His philosophical defense of birth control was strong:

> It may appear to some persons . . . that there is danger in making such facts as these known, because, they say, young persons knowing that there are times when they can indulge with safety [he has just discussed the female fertility cycle] will be led to do so . . . It seems to me also that it is forming a very low and degrading opinion of young persons, especially of females, to suppose that they are only.

kept from indulgence by fear of the consequences. If their virtue is solely dependent upon this, it is scarcely deserving of the name. . . ." [28]

This supportive and respectful attitude toward women pervades Hollick's work and that of many irregulars in these publications. They often rejected the double standard and many of them harped on the importance of sexual pleasure for women. Their greater liberalism on sexual issues did not necessarily indicate any greater integrity or politicization than that of the regulars. The sexual ideology of both groups was formed by professional interests and business pressures. The irregulars were primarily doctors to women, especially women of poor and modest income and class. The health and hygiene books were intended specifically for female buyers, both because they dealt with female medical problems and because mothers continued to be the primary source of medical care for their families. The success of these manuals, with their birth-control formulas and their relatively enlightened views of sexuality, suggests above all the existence of a demand by women for such information for such a perspective.

In the second half of the nineteenth century the popular-health movement diminished in size and popularity. Medical sectarianism and hygienic and medical fads lost their political content. The irregulars no longer organized popular-health groups; they no longer spoke politically against the monopolization of medicine by a self-regulating profession; and they lost their association with women's rights. Quackery continued, however, as a business. The manufacture and sale of patent medicines, home health manuals, health spas, and various health gadgets (electrical belts, special baths, posture supports, and so forth) flourished. In 1873 the Comstock law prohibited the interstate mailing of obscene material, and it specifically defined birth control as obscene. Selling contraceptives became dangerous just as the movement of irregulars lost its motivation for taking risks. These factors created a major setback in the spread of contraceptive information.

Still there were some exceptional doctors who resisted the commercialization of irregular medicine and were willing to challenge the censorship laws. Most important of this group in the late nineteenth century were the three doctors Foote, father Edward Bliss, son Edward Bond, and daughter-in-law Mary Bond Foote. The Footes differed from other pro-birth-control doctors in that they were conscious, articulate social reformers. Because their contribution was so great and their reforming style so typical of late nineteenth century medical reformers, it seems important to describe their work.

Born into a poor family in 1829, Edward Bliss Foote worked as a printer's devil and then a journalist before attending medical school in Philadelphia. In 1858, two years after his graduation, he published a popular medical guide. In it he was still very much a follower of traditional medicine, prescribing herbal potions, electricity cures, inhalations and baths.[29] His early sympathies with spiritualism and phrenology gave way later in his life to liberal Unitarianism and evolutionism. Always a civil libertarian, he spent many years fighting the Comstock law. Comstock meant for Foote not only obscurantism but also direct personal oppression, since Foote had built his career as a writer and reformer in part on public advocacy of prevention of conception and free speech about sexual matters. Having been able to express himself relatively freely for at least fifteen years before the Comstock law, he found its passage a maddening obstacle to his work.

Foote was an ardent feminist—in the tradition of the popular-health movement. His writings on birth control and sex emphasized women's rights. "It is my conscientious conviction that every married woman should have it within her power to decide for herself just when and just how often she will receive the germ of a new offspring," he wrote after his arrest.[30] Quoting from *Revolution*, newspaper of Susan B. Anthony and Elizabeth Cady Stanton, he gave a description of female infanticide in China as a lesson in the consequences of prohibiting birth control.[31]

In Foote's time, medicine was an open and competitive field, and Foote ran his medical office like a high-profit factory. Thus he advertised constantly: for example, "Dr. E. B. Foote and His Assistants May be Consulted daily from 9 a.m. to 6 p.m. (excepting Sundays), in the English or German Languages. . . ."[32] He established his own publishing company to put out his books. His establishment, at 120 Lexington Avenue (at Twenty-eighth Street) in New York City contained a small phamaceutical factory where thousands of dollars' worth of medicinal roots and plants were processed into patent medicines. "The floor below the laboratory," wrote the *New*

York Independent, "is occupied by the stenographers . . . who are employed in attending, under the direct dictation of the Doctor, to the immense correspondence, which often exceeds one hundred letters per day. . . . The Doctor has originated and perfected a series of questions relating to the physical conditions of invalids. These questions are so thorough and complete that when they are answered by patients at a distance, the Doctor is able to make a complete diagnosis and prescribe for his patients with about the same facility that he could do were they present." [33]

Apparently one kind of advice Foote sent out to these correspondence cases was contraceptive information.* In 1876 he was arrested for having sent such a letter in response to a decoy inquiry sent by one of Comstock's agents. (Entrapment was a standard and frequent Comstock technique.) The pamphlet he sent "was set up in pearl type, so as to make it only thirty-two pages of about the size of a letter envelope, in which it was invariably sent *sealed, under letter postage*. . . . The pamphlet took strong grounds against producing miscarriage or abortion. . . . Shortly after the Congressional law . . . a similar one was passed in our own State (New York), forbidding the devising or supplying of any means whatever for the prevention of conception. The doctor was assured by his legal adviser that this clause would never be enforced against physicians. . . ." But Foote was convicted and fined three thousand dollars.[34] Foote's prosecution had, and was intended to have, a chilling effect upon other pro-birth-control doctors. Although actual dissemination and use of contraception probably did not fall off, birth-control education did.

Foote occupied a unique position: an irregular who in his later life won the respect of the established profession. His son, Edward

---

* Foote may actually have contributed to the development of contraceptive technology. He wrote: "The first reliable means for the use of the wife was an invention of my office, having been imperfectly suggested by an associate physician and developed by myself some 15 years ago. Application was made at that time for a patent (!), which was refused on the ground that it was a question in the mind of the Commissioner whether the invention was not one which might be employed for immoral purposes. Without the protection of a patent it was, as might have been expected, extensively counterfeited. . . ." [35] His son later wrote that "the best mechanical means yet devised, though commonly described as a 'French' article, was really invented and elaborated in the office of . . . Dr. E. B. Foote, Sr." [36] Since it is unlikely that Foote, Jr., would be so naïve as to claim that his father had invented the "French letter," or condom, he was probably referring to a pessary of some sort. The medical historian of contraception, Norman Himes, thought it was a rubber cervical cap.[37]

Bond Foote, became a respected, if liberal, regular doctor, also active as a civil libertarian (particularly in the field of sexual matters—he was founder of the Free Speech League and a campaigner for the repeal of the Comstock law). He, too, argued for birth control as a woman's right to "control of her person." [38] Dr. Mary Bond Foote, his wife, was a lecturer and crusader for birth control, women's equality, and welfare legislation.[39] By the early twentieth century the two younger doctors Foote seemed unusual because traditions of the popular-health movement had been forgotten. Feminists in the medical profession were oddities then.

The uniqueness of the Footes in the nineteenth century points to the rule: the regular doctors did very little to advance the birth-control cause. First, they did not advance contraceptive technology. (See Chapter 1.) Second, the regular doctors did little to educate women about their sexual and reproductive systems, but, on the contrary, contributed to developing and maintaining fears and mystification. Third, and equally important, while many doctors did give birth-control help and even abortions to individual patients, they publicly attacked birth control. There was no necessary contradiction between doing this and "helping" individual patients who found themselves in difficult situations—precisely *because* most of the doctors concerned were humanitarian and principled. They disapproved of birth control on high principles of morality and health; but they could understand that in exceptional cases the principles might need to be flexible. Indeed, part of the doctors' anti-birth-control propaganda was a response to their awareness of increased birth-control use. At another level, the attack came from a new perception of their own place as doctors in the society, a sense of responsibility and privilege as the guardians of sexual morality and as the arbiters of situations in which exceptions might need to be made.

Perhaps the best analogy for this new self-image of a profession is to say that the doctors were the new ecclesiastics. Especially in the increased concern of the entire medical profession for the diseases of women, many believed to be genital in origin, the line between physiology and morality became fuzzy. In 1908 Robert Latou Dickinson, later to become president of the American Gynecological Society, wrote in an article called "Marital Maladjustment: The Business of Preventive Gynecology": "Our high function as confessors and advisers of the saintly half of the race, and the imperative need, at times, of one step within the Holy of Holies, is impossible without intimate speech, gentle, reverent, direct." [40] Religion was an "unrecognized branch of higher physiology," wrote another doctor of the same era.[41] Throughout the whole society in the nineteenth century, an overwhelming concern with sex, specifically with the difficult but urgent necessity of checking the anarchic sex drive, was reflected in the narrowing of previously general moral terms—such as virtue, propriety, decency, modesty, delicacy, purity—to exclusively sexual meanings.[42] Given the increase of physiological knowledge, it was only appropriate that the medical establishment should replace the church as the authority on sex. That authority simultaneously aided the new medical establishment in distinguishing itself from the irregulars of the popular-healing tradition.

For many doctors, playing churchmen merely required translation of ecclesiastical into medical language. What had been sin became physically injurious. In an earlier chapter we commented on the concept of vice as including sin but also carrying the connotation of destructiveness. We can now see that concept as a transitional one, between a purely metaphysical morality and a purely "empirical" commitment to science. Thus in the late nineteenth and early twentieth century physicians began to write and speak about "hygiene," by which they meant sexual morality. Schools gave classes in hygiene. "Social hygiene" meant the control of venereal disease. And somewhat later, "feminine hygiene" became a euphemism for contraceptive douches. (Today with mass acceptance of contraception, "feminine hygiene" has reverted to a strictly cleaning or purifying meaning.) Injuries supposedly caused by contraception, such as venereal disease, were just punishments for sin. Augustus Kinsley Gardner, Boston gynecologist and moralist, wrote, in a single sentence, that condoms degraded love and produced lesions.[43] The lesions or other physical debilitations were "God's little allies" in promoting chastity.[44] It was almost as if doctors felt a subconscious satisfaction, a justification, when their patients developed infections.

The victory of the medical regulars in establishing full control over the medical practice in the United States naturally supported this high sense of moral leadership. In the first two decades of the twentieth century, aided by the influence of German medical science, money from the Carnegie Corporation, a system of accreditation of medical schools, and the wide powers granted to the American Medical Association, the regulars drove midwives and lay healers out of business. Reforms spurred by the AMA improved the standard of health care available to some—prosperous—Americans. Medical re-examination of birth control was a concomitant of these reforms. This re-examination took place among doctors who had already widely internalized a sense of their own responsibility as guardians of sexual morality. Their debates about the healthfulness or harmfulness of sexual continence were translations of deep moral concern, and their words betrayed their sense of self-importance. As is the case with most ideologists, their self-evaluation was exaggerated. The major breakthroughs in public acceptance of birth control were caused by social changes—the continued underground spread of birth-control knowledge and the campaign against venereal disease during World War I—not by intellectual debates. Still, those debates shed light on social changes. The doctors' search for a convincing moral affirmation of plentiful sexual intercourse was like a flag marking still invisible subterranean upheavals.

Just as medicine in America was generally influenced by German science—which reached this country largely through American medical students studying in Germany—so the spread of contraceptive information in Europe was influential here. The first birth-control clinic had been established in 1882 in Holland. In France a Neo-Malthusian conference was held in 1900. In Germany, too, contraception was widely practiced, and it was a common observation that a veritable birth strike was taking place, so rapidly had smaller families become the norm. The birth-control struggle was no smoother in Europe than in America over the long run, for in the second decade of the twentieth century repressive legislation was passed in reaction, in both Holland and France.[45] But in 1900 the United States seemed backward in this field, and some physicians were stimulated to try to catch up.

In 1912 Abraham Jacobi, known to many as the father of

pediatrics, was elected president of the AMA. One of the country's most distinguished physicians and medical reformers, in his presidential address he spoke against war, for a campaign for industrial health, and for required venereal-disease tests before marriage. He specifically endorsed birth control, calling particular attention to the injustice of its prohibition while the well-to-do already had access to contraception.[46]

Jacobi's address had an impact. Yet it was more a product than a cause, a culmination not a beginning, of the revival of medical birth-control activism. Jacobi was influenced by his revolutionary background as a youth in the German revolution of 1848, and by his feminist wife, Dr. Mary Putnam Jacobi. Yet Jacobi was "organized" into his support for birth control, as were many others, by the remarkable William Josephus Robinson, who had been editing two pro-birth-control journals since 1903—the *Medico-Pharmaceutical Critic and Guide* and the *American Journal of Urology*. Starting with his first pamphlet in 1904, he wrote at least two dozen books on sex and birth control before his death in 1936. Probably no doctor in America has been so influential as a publicist in winning support for birth control and in defining its future development—toward contraception.

Like Foote before him, Robinson was able to combine something of the tradition of the popular health movement with the most advanced scientific medicine, especially from Germany. Robinson served as president of the Berlin Anglo-American Society and was a member of the Internationale Gesellschaft für Sexualforschung (International Association for Sex Research). A civil libertarian, remarkably free of anxiety about his own respectability, Robinson was never a free lover, though he published free-love writings and, more importantly, respected their thought. He took over some of the ideas of the irregular doctors: thus, for example, he recommended going naked inside one's own house for health reasons, believing that the skin needs light.[47] Yet he frequently attacked quacks and midwives.[48] His style was restrained, lacking the moral righteousness of the sex radicals (and political radicals). Yet he constantly attacked the conservatives of the medical profession for their hypocrisy on sexual questions.[49]

Like so many doctors before and after him, Robinson received many requests for contraceptive information. In his journal he announced that he would send such information to other doctors only.[50] But since he much later, in a privately printed and circulated memoir, admitted to having done abortions ("cleaned out uteruses"!),[51] it seems safe to assume that he also gave birth-control information to private patients. Certainly he knew that many other doctors did so. In his writings he tirelessly argued the case for birth control. He considered it, he wrote, "the most important problem affecting the welfare of humanity." [52] He often gave his reasons in lists, as did so many of the nonideological birth-control supporters. That is, he claimed every conceivable benefit from birth control: women's health, children's health, reduction of abortion, happy marriages, improving the over-all human stock, reducing sexual "neurasthenia" caused by *coitus interruptus* and worry, population control, family planning. Later Robinson became one of those single-minded devotees of the cause who sometimes presented birth control as a panacea. The tendency to see it that way was characteristic of those who came to it without another overriding ideology, such as feminism or Malthusianism.

In most of the earlier history of American birth-control agitation, the advocates had approached birth control with a larger radical social ideology. The voluntary-motherhood proponents were feminists, envisioning a new order of sexual power relations, the free lovers were anarchists, the utopians were religious socialists. At the other extreme were the Malthusians, their equally ideological stance disguised because they supported the maintenance of prevailing power relations. Robinson stood between these extremes because for him sex reform was the overriding concern, the key in itself to a better society; and birth control was the key to sexual liberation. Unlike his predecessors but like many of his successors in the birth-control movement, Robinson was a single-issue reformer. Robinson fought for birth control under different guises, flexibly redesigning his arguments to fit current social trends and crises. During the Theodore Roosevelt administration, he wrote and published on the race-suicide question. In the 1920s he turned to eugenics. In between he responded to the question of continence when others raised it.

Until the 1880s sexual reformers almost unanimously condemned contraception and supported continence. Then in 1881 Edward Bliss Foote reopened the issue, pointing out the inefficiency of continence as a means of ensuring voluntary parenthood. He argued, first, that only the "most intelligent and conscientious" would be able to maintain continence, and thus the paupers and criminals would continue producing unwanted children; second, that continence could be physiologically damaging, since the sexual organs lost their power through inaction; and third, that sexual intercourse was in itself good and healthful and did not need reproduction to justify it. The dominant feminist reformers attacked him sharply. He kept their respect by his open-mindedness in printing their attacks in his magazine, the *Health Monthly*. Foote was not so far distant from their point of view anyway, for his defense of sex was couched in spiritualist terms. Every individual had an animal magnetism, and each person's was different; the exchange of these magnetic forces through social contact was invigorating, physically and mentally, and that exchange was at its most perfect in the act of sexual intercourse.[53] For him as for the feminists, sex had to be justified by some higher purpose.

In the last decades of the nineteenth century a few more doctors repeated that continence was not the best solution, and even injurious. In the first decade of the twentieth century that opinion was aggressively asserted. The doctors' debate on the subject was nowhere better capsulized than in Robinson's *Medico-Pharmaceutical Critic and Guide*. This magazine, more in the tradition of the popular-health journals than in the mode of contemporary professional journals, published many letters and articles from subscribers, and many lay persons were among its readers. Robinson, consciously or unconsciously, worked out many of his ideas through this discourse with others before presenting them in his books.

The development of the continence debate is revealing. In 1904 and 1905, public birth-control discussions were almost all couched in terms of the problem "small or large families," prompted by the race-suicide controversy. In January 1906 Robinson asserted that safe "contracepts" existed and their use was justifiable.[54] In the next months many responses and amplifications from other doctors focused on spelling out the medical indications* for contraception. In 1907

---

* "Indications" is the term for the medical appropriateness of a given prescription. In the birth-control discussions, it is but another example of the use of medical terms to correspond directly to concepts expressed earlier in moral terms. For an "indication" usually means a

Robinson editorialized that prevention of conception was humanity's most important problem.[55] In 1911 he began reporting his findings that whereas periodic continence seemed to produce no ill effects, prolonged abstinence had a tendency to cause relative impotence and premature ejaculation,[56] thus opening up a discussion of continence as a form of birth control.

The responses that Robinson's editorials provoked made the *Critic and Guide* a compendium of the main sexual attitudes in the liberal parts of the medical profession. In addition to various evaluations of the strength of the sexual drive, there emerged a sharp disagreement on the double standard, for in his attack on continence Robinson had spoken of its dangers for the male but not the female. He thought the difficulties of continence were mainly felt by men and defended this potential deviation from the single standard by asserting that he wished to eschew moralism and to be practical.[57] Another doctor reiterated the belief that continence was particularly hard on men and pointed out that in any case women suffered no physiological loss of potency from continence.[58] Some argued for it physiologically, like Dr. Warbasse, who pointed out that it all depended on what was meant by continence. True continence would have to mean, he wrote, not just abstention from coitus but also from all stimuli "which result in libidinous turgescence of the organs of copulation"; if this were done there should be no special difficulties for men.[59] There were feminist responses too, as in one letter complaining that "Women with imperative sexual desires are classed as Nymphomaniacs. Should not men with imperative sexual desires be classed as Satyromaniacs?"[60]

The question of the double standard inevitably led to a related question, that of sexual monogamy itself. This was another issue that always underlay that of birth control: sex without fear of conception could take an important risk out of promiscuity. Almost all the sexual-reform movements of the nineteenth century, especially those with a feminist orientation, had been unanimous in their commitment to the principles of monogamy and marital fidelity, and this commitment was one reason they preferred abstinence to contraception as a

---

specific symptom; a "contraindication," a physiological fact that might make the drug dangerous or ineffective. In birth control the "indications" include such things as poverty and overwork of the mother—factors that a doctor was no better equipped to judge than anyone else.

form of birth control. Now, in the early twentieth century, many social and political radicals were reconsidering the monogamy principle. Beginning in the 1890s, some of the remaining free-love journals began exploring "varietism" in love.[61] These latter-day free lovers contributed frequently to Robinson's journal. Edwin C. Walker wrote that "the proponents of the single standard have been handicapped from the beginning of the race by the needless burden they took upon themselves. They essayed the impossible task of bringing all men into and holding them in the narrow groove of monogamy."[62] Dr. James F. Morton, a free-love physician, also objected to Robinson's acceptance of a double standard but added that the "recognition of equality between the sexes is no guarantee that new fetters are to be put on the male, when the more natural sequence would seem to be the removal of the shackles with which the female has so long been bound."[63]

Endorsement of "varietism" at this time was limited to those who considered themselves sex radicals. But as related to the birth-control issue their position differed only in degree from that favoring "indulgence." With one partner or several, the sacrifice of the principle of continence would force birth-control advocates to look to contraception.

So serious was the threat that a veritable lobby for continence was organized to combat the weakening moral standards. A rash of sex-education books for young men, with venereal disease as a primary concern, appeared in the years 1890–1920, the vast majority of them preaching continence.[64] Under the aegis of the YMCA, Dr. M. J. Exner got 358 of America's "leading medical authorities and foremost physicians" to sign the following declaration:

> In view of the individual and social dangers which spring from the widespread belief that continence may be detrimental to health, and of the fact that municipal toleration of prostitution is sometimes defended on the ground that sexual indulgence is necessary, we, the undersigned, members of the medical profession, testify to our belief that continence has not been shown to be detrimental to health or vitality; that there is no evidence of its being inconsistent with the highest physical, mental and moral efficiency; and that it offers the only sure reliance for sexual health outside of marriage.[65]

This declaration is significant in many respects. First, its interpretation of continence contrasts sharply with the use of the term just a few decades previously: now confining intercourse within marriage was enough to satisfy the requirements of continence! Second, the defensiveness of the declaration contrasts similarly with the statements of doctors of the late nineteenth century. In the late nineteenth century most doctors were warning that frequent intercourse, in or out of marriage, was debilitating; here Exner and his allies were trying to reassure their readers that continence was not debilitating. The doctors were no longer merely attacking sexual indulgence. They were attacking the ideology of indulgence as a superior form of morality. The continence lobby was behaving like the partisans of a lost cause.

Among doctors, then, early-twentieth-century controversies focused on three issues—continence versus indulgence, monogamy versus variety, and the problem of venereal disease—all central to the future development of birth control. The medical participants in these discussions shared one important assumption—indeed, the assumption that made their discussions possible: the need for a moral position on these questions. William J. Robinson's tentative request that moralism be avoided was dismissed out of hand by the great majority of doctors, who did not believe that they should abdicate their responsibility for moral leadership in sexual matters.[66] No one doubted that there should be a general moral policy on contraception and that doctors should decide it. The pro-birth-control doctors were operating out of the same professional self-image as the medical opponents of contraception. Thus, despite the reluctance of many of its members, the medical profession became the first established moral authority in the United States to endorse the separation of sex from reproduction through contraception. Because of the birth-control question, doctors played a significant role in the changed sexual attitudes and practices that have been called a "sexual revolution." Though it was the birth-control issue that projected physicians into the sexual controversies of the first decades of the twentieth century, their receptivity to new sexual standards was a function of their class position.

From the vantage point of physicians the old sexual standards included, as we have seen, a double standard of accepted sexual behavior for men and women, but also an ideal of continence for both. Continence meant entire abstinence from sex outside of marriage and limited indulgence within marriage. Continence was an ideal at the very core of the whole sexual morality, for it represented not only a form of birth control but a virtue in itself. Continence was a form of self-control, and self-control to the Victorian bourgeoisie represented one of the highest human ideals. This was a strenuous self-control, perhaps more accurately described as self-repression. (The dominance of this model of virtue can be seen in its acceptance even by the archenemies of the Victorian morality, the free lovers. In questioning the right of external authority to regulate individual behavior, they preferred to see morality enforced by the individual upon himself, by the "superego"; they were thus in the very vanguard of the self-control ideology.) Doctors contributed their own expertise to the general sentiment for self-control in criticisms of masturbation, abortion, and sexual excess in marriage. Repression of one's bodily urges led, like other forms of self-control, to spiritual awakening and strength of character. There was something beneficial not only in avoiding the bad effects of vice, but in the process of self-denial itself.

When the birth-control issue was reopened in the early twentieth century, a major reorientation was evident among physicians: even those opposed to contraception rejected self-control as an ideal. This rejection underlay not only new sexual practices, but also a new image of the ideal human character. Good "character" was no longer judged by the ability to postpone gratification. The ability to enjoy sensuous things was tolerated, encouraged, even romanticized. Contraception provided a material basis for this, making one form of self-denial dysfunctional. But contraception did not cause the change; indeed, there were no significant technological improvements of importance in this period. A few American doctors, like Foote, privately developed improved pessaries, suppositories, and douche preparations, but the basic technology had been unchanged for decades in Europe, affected only by the development of vulcanized rubber in the mid-nineteenth century. The Mensinga pessary (vaginal diaphragm), important because it could be inserted by a woman alone, was not commonly prescribed by U.S. doctors before Margaret Sanger introduced it into her clinic.[67] The sources of the more widespread acceptance of contraception and sexual pleasure must be sought outside of technological change.

Several historians have compared the nineteenth-century ideology of self-control with the saving of semen and the saving and reinvestment of money.[68] Without arguing that each nineteenth-century male regarded his penis as a bank, we can be sure that businessmen saw a connection between habits of personal self-control and those of economic industriousness; and that men of the middle and upper classes felt that sexual self-repression built character strength, which was then usable in other trying situations. These classes believed that sexual self-denial was a virtual requirement for womanly respectability, although, as we have seen, the forms of that self-denial were not always the same. The capitalist class established cultural standards, communicated through schooling, religion, entertainment, and many other channels, which offered these standards to people of the working class as well, in variant forms suitable for men and women. That standards of repression were apparently somewhat less adopted by the poor and by wage laborers in general reminds us of an important fact about these and all cultural standards: they are adopted not merely as pretty or appealing ideas but only when actual experience confirms their usefulness. The ideology of self-control remained so long as it was a useful guide to economic success or at least survival in capitalist society.

The transformation of capitalism from within had created, by the early twentieth century, a new set of economic experiences which rendered less useful a repressive view of sexuality and other personal indulgences. These new experiences affected not so much adults, whose behavioral and moral codes had been deeply inculcated for years, but youth, and therefore took the form of a generational rebellion when actual sexual behavior began changing in a noticeable way. Many factors combined to produce these new economic experiences: monopolies effectively destroyed the possibilities of success through new business enterprise; the decline of business opportunities for those with great ambition and initiative was matched by the rise of professional and managerial opportunities for educated, cautious men willing to accept prestige and wealth without great power or independence; a series of worsening business crises due to overproduction forced efforts to expand consumption; the combination of immigration, the ruin of farming, and the squeeze on small businessmen produced an ample industrial labor force that, having lost any other alternatives, no longer needed to be forced into wage labor. These and other forces created problems no longer soluble by the internalization of industrious and penurious habits. Indeed, there were problems now better solved through consumption and indulgence in immediate gratification. The new society needed citizens who spent rather than saved, in the phallic as well as the commercial sense.

Physicians were well suited to play a leading role in rejecting the self-control values for a fuller acceptance of frequent sexual indulgence. As doctors, they were more aware than most people of the prevalence of sexual indulgence in Victorian society, beneath the hypocritical obeisance to chastity. As men, they experienced the pleasures of that indulgence without the direct physical risks and burdens that women carried as a consequence. But above all their professional status and life style made the more relaxed sexual standards seem to them appropriate. The establishment and licensing of their own particular profession had produced a coherent regular medical establishment. European training was common among prestigious U.S. physicians, and the general revival of interest in European medicine produced a cosmopolitan influence throughout the profession. Undergraduate education also contributed a broadening influence and brought to young doctors-in-training understanding and sympathy for other areas of liberal-arts thought. More important, it brought them to identify with other liberal professions. Medicine was seen less as a craft and more as a high form of learning, service, and even leadership. The increasing status and wealth of physicians raised their self-esteem and introduced a sense of superiority not only to the working class but to the business classes as well, while strengthening their felt commonalty with other professionals. Like lawyers and professors, twentieth-century physicians felt increasingly released from the competitive, materialistic standards of success that had dominated the late-nineteenth-century prosperous classes. The professionals' status came from their education and was accompanied by an ideology of helping and leading others; they had no need for an ideology or a character structure emphasizing saving, investment, or striking hard bargains. A moral system of repressing gratification or enjoyment was unnecessary to their own motivation for work and achievement, and they were prepared to explore more tolerant and permissive moral standards. Of course there was no simple correlation between joining the medical profession and accepting a "sexual revolution," and myriad individual variables explained the positions of individual doctors. The process of questioning, then rejecting, the strictures of the system of self-control was an intense and often painful process, which only a minority experienced. But the influence of this minority, its professional status and outlook, is unmistakable in its arguments and through them, as we shall see later, on the whole birth-control movement.

Far from rebelling against moralism or authority, the pro-birth-control physicians tended to replace one moral system with another, equally prescriptive. Influenced by European sex theorists, they argued for birth control by arguing against continence, and acclaimed free sexual "expression" as leading to liberation. They echoed in their statements an assumption that sexual restraint, as all repression, was damaging to the total human psyche. As self-control once led to salvation, now it led to damnation—ill-health, neurasthenia, debilitation (the same evils once attributed to masturbation and sexual excess). This change was a shift in emphasis, not a reversal. The majority of physicians, from the most conservative to the most radical in sexual matters, retained a preference for moderation. The content of moderation, however, shifted radically. In the mid-nineteenth century there were doctors who thought that for sexual intercourse to take place only when conception was desired was a reasonable rhythm; by the early twentieth century there were doctors who found twice a week a reasonable rhythm. The major change in this measurement of moderation resulted from a whole new view of good character, one that no longer viewed the libido as antagonistic to the needs of civilization and social discipline.

The doctors' conception of this newly acceptable libido was entirely male. As we have seen, their acceptance of greater sexual permissiveness seemed to lead to a backing down from commitment to the single standard. The repressions of the nineteenth century had been primarily directed against male philandering; for women, moral, religious, and medical imprecations against "indulgence" were almost unnecessary, so serious were the social, biological, economic and psychological risks, not to mention the frequent lack of pleasure in sex, that kept women from yielding to temptation or from experiencing temptation in the first place. Not only was the impulse that needed rescuing from repression primarily a male one, but the repression itself had been supported by many women's interest groups. It was partly empirical observation that led some of the anticontinence spokesmen to pronounce the single standard "impractical."

Thus the sexual-reform views of twentieth-century doctors expressed an important historical shift in the views of moral leaders. In the nineteenth century progressive sexual thought—advocacy of sex education, healthy diet, exercise, an open and nonprudish attitude toward reproductive functions, for example—had been associated with feminism. The few female doctors were always in the forefront of these campaigns; and the more numerous male doctors involved were always favorable to feminist causes. In the early twentieth century those attacking the ideal of continence were frequently hostile to feminism, sometimes pillorying feminists as sexually frustrated women who got that way by denying their true destinies.

This change was significant. The twentieth-century understanding of Victorian prudery often associates it with ladylikeness, indeed with a female style imposed upon male society. It is more correct to understand prudery as a historical moment in a struggle between women's attempts to defend their interest in familial fidelity and men's attempts to preserve their traditional sexual privileges. The latter won, and the resulting unstable compromise rested on an essential hypocrisy in men's behavior. Understanding this clearly, feminists and pro-feminists led the attack on prudery, analyzing it not as a female system but as a part of women's oppression. By the early twentieth century the partial victories of this attack on prudery had forced a reorientation. Having succeeded in demolishing many sexual taboos, the feminists did not succeed in imposing a sexual single standard. Rather they saw public acceptance of male sexual indulgence, without a reorientation of the social order sufficient to give women equivalent freedom, independence, and power.

It is for this reason that many of the leading feminists were hostile to sexual permissiveness in the pre–World War I period. Charlotte Perkins Gilman, the most important theoretician of the feminist movement at this time, clung to the belief that the oversexing of men was the creation of male supremacy and that women's interests lay in the restoration of a society of chastity with much less energy and emphasis placed on sex.[69] This was her position even about monogamous sexual relations. "Varietism" she would have considered abhorrent, for monogamy seemed to her the only organization of sexuality worthy of being called human.

Gilman's antagonism to sexual "indulgence" was simultaneously a traditionalist, prudish fear of change and a forthright defense of women's interests. As the "sexual revolution" affected the actual sexual behavior of millions of Americans between 1910 and 1930, both aspects of this feminist response were overwhelmed; and the defeat of this anti-sexual-revolution orientation, as part of the decline of the whole feminist movement, was the inevitable death of a world view, which had become outmoded by social changes, as well as a setback for women. As we will see later, many of Gilman's fears about the antiwoman aspects of the New Morality were confirmed. And even in these early years before massive social changes were evident, women close enough to the disputes to be aware of these permissive ideas often feared and criticized them.

Even within the free-love movement there emerged a women's opposition to the advocacy of "indulgence" and "varietism." A woman from Brooklyn wrote in a free-love journal in 1897 that "sexual freedom, in the present stage of its development, means greater slavery for the average woman who embraces it. So long has she been the tool and slave of man, sexually, that she needs protection from herself. . . ."[70] In many such letters women argued that they could not become sexually free and equal to men merely by a change in law or mores. They saw "sexual freedom" not as liberating or progressive at all but as *reactionary*, a returning to the double standard and license of the eighteenth century. A decade later, when these issues reached out beyond the small free-love circles into conventional communities, a woman from Missouri wrote this to Dr. Robinson's journal:

> I see that some of you doctors say, that the sexual instinct in man is imperative and should be gratified. Others say it is a natural function and that a moderate indulgence is beneficial, while too

much is harmful. Still others argue that perfect continence is the right thing, tho nearly all will admit that it is almost an impossibility for most men to live that way. . . .

You doctors understand these things from a man's point of view, because you know the passions you have to overcome yourselves, and you understand it scientifically, but do you think you understand the woman's feelings and the place which these qualities in man force her to occupy? Do you realize that the spirit of possession and jealousy she has, must have been handed down to her thruout countless ages perhaps? And isn't the training of the ordinary so called respectable girl of this country such that she grows up believing that she must keep herself clean and chaste sexually; that somewhere in the world there is a man who will one day claim her for his wife from among all the other women of the world: that he will expect and demand that she has been continent in sexual affairs. . . . Is it any wonder then that when she grows older and wiser as to the true state of the husband's feelings in these matters, that she feels deceived . . . if he is honest enough with her to admit after several years of married life that she does not thoroly gratify him sexually, and that his nature demands and cries out for this relation with other females, what is the wife to do? . . .

There is one thing that I cannot understand any more than some of the others. Why has man himself in the ages preceding this allowed the social conditions we now have to gradually grow up? Why has not some custom been maintained whereby he could have had this gratification in a lawful and legal way? Why have men themselves made bigamy a crime, and punish those who commit adultery?

If the women had been raised by polygamous parents, had the men always been allowed to have had many wives, or kept mistresses openly and publicly, there is no doubt but what women could now have looked on these things much more liberally than they do. . . .[71]

This woman was probably not a feminist. She was humble before the doctors, pleading that she was too weak, too unprepared, to deal with marital infidelity. Her expressions of respect for doctors had no sarcasm. Nevertheless, she rejected a logic that blamed women themselves for their inability to welcome sexual "freedom." She thought that, somehow, men were to blame.

9
Birth Control and Social Revolution

A Sexual Revolution?

After about 1910 a radical shift in sexual attitudes occurred among leading intellectuals and reformers, who were greatly influenced by European sexual theorists. Although there were American traditions of sex radicalism, they were rather unsystematic. Most were sectarian proposals for sexual reform, few of them encompassing entire social analyses. The Europeans, by contrast, offered more empirical, "scientific" investigations of sexual behavior through psychology and anthropology. Or, like Edward Carpenter and Ellen Key, they continued in the old, utopian style but had powerful social movements behind them (such as Fabian socialism and feminism), unlike the tiny sectarian groups of the American sex reformers.

The greatest "scientific" influence for sexual-liberation thought in the United States was that of Freud, though it was an influence based on quite erroneous interpretations of his work. The complexity, the pessimism, and the full radicalism of Freud's work never penetrated the United States at all, and even in Europe much shallower interpretations of Freud soon began to dominate. Although Freudian psychology was in its essence the unraveling of the effects of repression, Freud was inclined to view repression as the inevitable cost of human progress, or at least as part of a total system that could be altered only by changing its fundamental structures of power. Indeed this pessimistic view was close to the attitude toward sexual repression characteristic of the nineteenth-century Victorian moralists and physicians.[1] But American sex radicals transformed Freud's ideas into support for a campaign against sexual repression. They argued that Freud's psychological studies showed the inevitable "return" of repressed sexual drives in destructive forms, thus mobilizing Freud's authority against continence as a practical route to voluntary parenthood. Still uneasy with a straightforward hedonist position toward sex, that is, that pleasure was a good in itself, American reformers preferred the notion of sex as an irresistible drive, dangerous to interfere with.[2]

The reformers' critique of sexual repression was part of a growing attack on hierarchy, authoritarianism, and all forms of social repression. Feminism, the critique of male tyranny, was thus a kindred social ideology, and the European sex theorists were usually pro-feminist. Havelock Ellis, Edward Carpenter, and Ellen Key, three major spokespeople for the "New Morality," all considered sexual liberation to be primarily dependent on women's sexual liberation, which in turn required women's independence and opportunity to seek full, creative lives. Carpenter, like the free lovers before him, perceived male supremacy behind much of the brutality of civilization—

> men so fatuous that it actually does not hurt them to see the streets crammed with prostitutes by night, or the parks by day with the semi-lifeless bodies of tramps; men, to whom it seems quite natural that our marriage and social institutions should lumber along over the bodies of women, as our commercial institutions grind over the bodies of the poor and our "imperial" enterprise over the bodies of barbarian races . . .[3]

—and thought only sexual equality could correct these grotesque injustices. Like many of the sex radicals of his era, Carpenter was anticapitalist. He was convinced that women could not win equality under the "commercial system," "with its barter and sale of human labor and human love for gain." It seemed to him, furthermore, that the women's cause was the cause of all the oppressed, that freedom for women required communism.[4] Ellis and Key also believed in women's right to economic independence. But none of them thought total equality likely or desirable. All believed that women's biologically specialized function—childbearing—was their destiny as well. Arguing that pregnancy and nursing would inevitably prevent women from ever achieving intellectual and economic equality with men, Ellis and Key also insisted that avoidance of the maternal function was unhealthy and abnormal, itself a form of repression. Key believed it was the obligation of every woman to have three or four children and to devote ten years of her life to child-raising exclusively.[5]

This limited feminism reflected the limitations of this body of sexual theory. Hostile to all repression, or so they thought, these sex radicals imagined a "natural" human existence in which there was no necessity for repression at all.

> The poet sang of "Nature red in tooth and claw." But we realize today that—if we are to adopt the conventional distinction—it is . . . Nature rather than Man that comes before us as the exalting and civilizing element in the world's life. Men—the men we thought the most civilized in the world—are to-day over a great part of the earth rending each other hideously by means of the most terrible weapons that intelligence can devise. . . .[6]

A program calling for return to the natural is no program at all, but a fantasy. A program for sexual liberation and women's liberation requires an analysis of the social regulation of sex and sex roles, to identify what the vested interests in the repressive arrangements are and how they could be changed. The analysis of Ellis and Key, by contrast, suggested that repression was just a bad habit, not a function of exploitation. Inimical equally to class struggle and sex struggle, they were anticapitalist and anti-male-supremacist but counted on a cooperative socialism to which people of all classes and both sexes would be persuaded.

Ellis, Key, and Carpenter came from pre-Marxist romantic socialist and feminist movements. Their ideas reached the United States first through intellectuals with similar backgrounds, but many of the latter were being transformed by an entirely different kind of socialist movement dominant here—a mass movement with a working-class base. In the years before the First World War, almost all intellectuals seeking radical social change were drawn into some kind of relationship to that movement, and this meant that sex-reform ideas would be tested against the needs of many working-class men and women. European sex radicalism entered the American birth-control movement through this filter and was changed in the process from a utopian, abstract libertarianism to a program offering immediate material aid to working-class women and raising a set of demands against the state.

The enthusiasm of the birth controllers in this period came from their conviction that birth control was an idea whose "time had come." They observed and sensed social changes that led to mass acceptance of contraception and demands for reproductive self-determination. The most immediate of these changes were the shrinking birth rate, smaller families, increased use of contraception, and increased public admission of the use of birth control. An example of the many signs that birth control was "here to stay" was the publicity given to two court cases in which women accused of theft were released by sympathetic judges in 1916. One in New York City and one in Cleveland, both defendants argued that they had stolen to feed their children; the first was given a suspended sentence and the second acquitted; both judges argued in their opinions, delivered from the bench, for spreading birth-control information among the poor.[7]

Behind this attitude was an acceptance, even among birth-control opponents, of the fact that the practice was unstoppable. Public opinion spiraled: the more evidence of birth-control use became public, the more birth control became acceptable. A second factor, evident in the judges' opinions, was what we might call a neo-race-suicide view: the prosperous would use birth control anyway, so keeping it from the poor was socially destructive. A third and probably most important factor was a generally more positive attitude toward sex itself.

Some historians have argued that there was a "sexual revolution" in the early twentieth century. Whether these changes in sexual behavior and attitudes constituted a revolution or not, they created a new concept of birth control. Birth control now meant reproductive self-determination along with unlimited sexual indulgence. This new definition—quite different from that of voluntary motherhood—understood sexual activity and reproduction as two separately justified human activities. Either might be considered immoral under certain circumstances, but they did not need to be connected. The eventual mass acceptance of this new morality required the conviction not only that sexual indulgence without the risk of pregnancy was a good thing, but also that fear of illegitimacy was not necessary to maintain an acceptable public morality. This new morality could challenge the weight of tradition, law, and Christianity because it conformed to the needs or strong wishes of many people, and because social changes had made the traditional morality uncomfortable. The sex philosophers like Havelock Ellis were influential only with people already uncomfortable with Victorian restrictiveness; the physicians who challenged the health of continence were reflecting rather than creating social changes. Free love was no longer a utopian ideal as it had been in the nineteenth century. It was being practiced among intellectuals, radicals, bohemians, professionals, and even office workers in big cities. Unmarried people spent nights together, even lived together; unmarried women took lovers whom they were not even engaged to, often many consecutively, sometimes more than one at a time; a few experimented with drugs such as peyote, and many women drank and smoked with men; sex was discussed in mixed groups; and all these things were done without disguise, even with bravado.

Historians for a long time associated this "sexual revolution" with the flappers, jazz, and speakeasies of the 1920s, and only more recently discovered that sexual changes began in earnest before World War I.[8] The reason for the original chronological mistake was that greater sexual latitude became a mass phenomenon in the 1920s, and new forms of sexual behavior were both "sold" through the mass media as fashionable and used to sell other products through modern advertising.

Before the war the nature of the sexual revolution was very different. It was not only not commercialized, but anticommercial. Confined to small groups of urban sophisticates, it was a process of experimentation that was self-conscious and ideological. One of its most important locales was Greenwich Village. Once an immigrant neighborhood, the Village became a center of bohemianism with the decision to move the Liberal Club there in 1913. The move was a self-conscious attempt to create a community for radical intellectuals.

> . . . artists and writers had always lived here—but in tiny groups and cliques, mutually indifferent, or secretly suspicious of each other. . . . how would the new invaders . . . university people, students and professors, the social workers, the newspaper men and women . . . ever get acquainted with those shy and timid aborigines, the artist folk? . . . "Why . . . shouldn't intelligent people to-day have the same chance to know each other that the church and the tavern gave their grandparents?" [9]

Perhaps the intellectuals and professionals took on the artists' traditionally erratic personal relationships, whereas artists adopted philosophic justifications for their preferences.

They were unified by the fact that their work and career goals made the nineteenth-century family norm constricting. Josephine Herbst wrote: "If a fine martial spirit existed between the sexes, it was a tonic and a splendor after so much sticky intermingling and backboneless worship of the family and domesticated bliss." [10] For some the discomfort in the old forms had created conscious ethical rejection of the traditional values; others perceived themselves as simply "enjoying life" a little before "settling down." Some, especially women, would have preferred traditional marriage but could not find it; others thought they preferred it but could not tolerate it once they tried. There were many differences, but all were breaking out of the constrictions of a bourgeois norm that dictated monogamous and permanent marriage, with the man the sole wage-earner, and the woman a full-time, housebound wife and mother. The rejection of traditional families also deprived people of important sources of security, however, and community-building endeavors were a natural response— both formal ones like that in Greenwich Village and the informal bondings and groups that emerged among bohemians in many big cities.

Though men and women both were in rebellion against the family, the rebellions of the two sexes took different forms. Men were often rejecting economic responsibilities and business careers for the chance to be footloose and pursue less lucrative but more meaningful vocations as artists, intellectuals, reformers, or even revolutionaries. Their sexual rebellion was less intense, for the double standard had already permitted a certain amount of philandering without overly harsh consequences. In the area of sexual activity, women's rebellion was much sharper, for the traditional norms had given them no sexual latitude whatever. Even pro-feminist Victorian standards had prescribed that a woman could have sexual relations with only one man in her lifetime, and if she wanted to limit her pregnancies, with him only occasionally. A culture that was re-evaluating sex as a positive human experience made such limitations intolerable.

Changes in women's sexual behavior constituted the very essence of the sexual revolution. That fact has been obscured by the tendency of most historians to place men at the center of all large changes, and more specifically by the Kinsey and other reports on sexual behavior which drew attention to changes among both sexes. But in the first three decades of this century *the* significant change was that women were claiming some small part of the sexual freedom man had long had. Contemporary observers were clear about that fact. V. F. Calverton associated the New Morality with the "New Woman." [11] Schmalhausen spoke of the "strange sexual awakening of woman." [12] Attacks on illicit sexuality were especially concerned with adolescent females.[13] The basis for the weakening of prostitution between 1910 and 1920 was not the conversion of men to purity; it was the conversion of women to "indulgence." Sex studies done in the 1920s showed a tendency toward "convergence" between male and female rates of nonmarital sexual intercourse. Though men and women were both becoming more likely to have nonmarital sex, the change for women was proportionately greater. Most significant, men were more likely to sleep with the women they would later marry, thus making virginity a less universal requirement for a marriage partner, while the men's rate of intercourse with people other than future spouses remained almost stationary.[14]

It has proven difficult to determine the actual quantity of increased sexual activity in this period. But a few sex and demographic studies have given us some useful clues and bits of relevant data. For example, the premarital pregnancy rate probably fell significantly between 1800 and 1880 and then picked up again.[15] A sex study done in 1925 found that of middle-class married New York City women, thirty out of fifty of those born after 1890 had had nonmarital sex, whereas only seventeen out of fifty born before 1890 had.[16] Another study done in the 1930s asked 777 college-educated women about premarital sexual intercourse. It found that women born between 1890 and 1899 (women, therefore, coming to sexual maturity between 1910 and 1920) had twice as high a percentage of premarital intercourse as those born before 1890:[17]

Birth date	Per cent of premarital coitus
pre–1890	13.5
1890–1899	26
1900–1909	48.8
1910–on	68.3

A Kinsey study found the same doubling percentage for women born after 1900:[18]

Birth date	Per cent of premarital coitus
pre–1900	26.6
1900–1909	51.3
1910–1919	56.1
1920–1929	51.2

One of the few early twentieth-century sex studies to collect data on homosexuality suggests that the sexual revolution was exclusively heterosexual: lesbian activity did not seem to increase for women born after 1890.[19] This finding is based on a very small sample—2200 college-educated women—but it is supported by rapidly accumulating evidence of the prevalence of intense emotional relationships between women in the nineteenth century. Probably because they did not define physical expressions of affection between women as sexual, nineteenth-century women felt free to hug and kiss and sleep in beds together; they wrote and spoke to each other in words of passionate endearment.[20] We do not and probably will never know how many women actually had genital sexual contact with one another, but it is certain that many women had opportunities to slide gradually into love-making situations. General and imprecise as this observation may be, it is extremely significant, since we are focusing here primarily on changes in women's sexual behavior. Culturally we are describing not just changes in the frequency or situation of sexual intercourse but a transformation of the ideology and emotional experience of love and sex as well, so that we must focus not just on intercourse but on whole relationships. We must notice that the sexual revolution was not a general loosening of sexual taboos but only of those on nonmarital heterosexual activity. Indeed, so specifically heterosexual was this change that it tended to intensify taboos on homosexual activity and did much to break patterns of emotional dependence and intensity among women. Greater freedom of emotional and sexual expression with men made women view their time spent with women friends as somehow childish in comparison, or at least less sophisticated and less adventurous. In other words, the sexual revolution produced a social as well as sexual emphasis on heterosexuality.

Women's gains from these changes were by no means clear and unequivocal. Their new sexual license exempted them from some of the immediate penalties of sexual surrender to men. It did not make them men's equals, sexually or in any other way, and it did not give them the power to evaluate clearly what they really wanted for themselves sexually. Economically, socially, and politically, sexually "free" women were as powerless as conventional women (with the exception of those who built careers for themselves). As with all women, their survival and success largely depended on pleasing men; those in bohemian communities merely had to meet new male demands. Bohemian men used philosophic principles of sexual liberation to coerce women. Floyd Dell wrote:

> . . . girls wanted to be married, not only for conventional reasons, but also because sexual relations outside marriage aroused in them feelings of guilt which made them miserable. . . . The . . . spiritual hocus-pocus which sufficed instead of a wedding-ring to give a girl a good conscience, seemed to consist in quotations and arguments from Edward Carpenter, Havelock Ellis, and other modern prophets, arguments designed to show that love without marriage was infinitely superior to the other kind, and that its immediate indulgence brought the world, night by night, a little nearer to freedom and Utopia. . . .[21]

Over and over in memoirs as well as in contemporary comments from these prewar bohemian days, we hear the lament of women who felt used and ultimately weakened by the new sexual freedom. Historian Caroline Ware analyzed it thus: Men could "fit the facts of freedom and experimentation . . . into the tradition of the double standard . . . which remained an essential part of their attitude. . . . The very girls whom men persuaded to sleep with them by a learned discourse later became objects of their contempt, and their conversation when no women were present would have done credit to any similar bourgeois group." [22] Meridel LeSueur, who came to the Village in 1916 at age sixteen, recalled that "free sex nearly ruined men." She was like many young immigrants there, vulnerable because of her desperate desire to be a writer. Theodore Dreiser chased her at a party, and when she steadfastly refused him sexually, he told her that she would never be a writer unless she got rid of her prudery.[23] A chief spokesman for the sexual revolution, Samuel Schmalhausen, saw these problems: "His [man's] most crafty technique for the diminution of her personality is the quasi-comradely exploitation of her sexuality— which he can now rationalize as a simple behavior of perfect equals." [24]

One cannot, after all, separate sexual behavior from people's experience of love. Even the men—at least the "highbrow" ones—usually associated their affairs with love. They fell in love over and over; or alternatively they were endlessly unsure of their capacity to love. The ideology and practice of love was changing along with that of sex. In the late eighteenth and early nineteenth centuries, another "sexual revolution"—the birth of prudery—had also carried with it a transformation of love. Love became pre-eminently a spiritual union, as free of lust as it was possible to make it. Ironically it was the nineteenth-century sex radicals, free lovers and spiritualists, who carried that desexualized definition of love to its extreme. They wanted even to desexualize sex, arguing through analogies to magnetism and electricity that the most important purpose of sexual union was the exchange of spiritual energies. Dialectically, this had enabled them to put sex back into an honorable place within love. Now twentieth-century sex radicals were making sex the very center of love. As love became more sexualized, its imagery divorced from the ideal of purity, it also became more transient—or, more accurately, its transience became acceptable. The bohemians were fascinated with the disappearance and the fragility of love, with its rarity. They were quick to see everyday human relationships as imperfect.

> All the women I have been close to . . . have been in a way cripples, of broken beauty. With them I have often felt a profound sympathy and a nearness, because they were cripples like me. I could not, however, really love them, for it seems to me that complete beauty only can be completely loved.[25]

Expressions like this, by novelist and Village-dweller Hutchins Hapgood, were common in this period. In effect, they defined love out of the existence of most people for most of their lives. Love came to describe a moment's emotion. John Reed's telegram of rejection of Mabel Dodge from Paris read, *"J'aime X.L. Pardonnez-moi et sois [sic] heureuse"* ("I love X.L. Forgive me and be happy.")[26]

For women, it had been precisely the function of the family to protect them against the transience of love. Only men could afford that kind of transience. For women, economic and social discrimination and responsibility for children meant that desertion by men left them extremely vulnerable. Sexual freedom made birth control important for women; the possible impermanence of love made birth control an absolute necessity. It was not a solution to the problem of sexual inequality, but it was a small help.

In all this rapid change, women's frequent unhappiness and men's frequent opportunism were perhaps inevitable. The sexual revolution, like real revolutions, brought violence and suffering, which must accompany the destruction of any traditional social institutions. And like many rebels, the bohemians were excessive. Their sexual behavior was often promiscuous. Max Eastman called this period the adolescence of the twentieth century.[27] Like adolescents, the bohemians were fickle and extremist; they overstated their rejection of their parents' values. Many of them drew back after a few years of experimentation, sometimes to more moderate positions and sometimes all the way to traditionalism. Some of this drawing back was part of the process of change, a naturally uneven process at best. A larger part of it was the product of a general rightward turn in the society in the 1920s. The traditionalism that recurred then, however, was not a full return to nineteenth-century norms. On the contrary, the sexual freedoms claimed by bohemians in the prewar period began, in the 1920s, to be extended to masses of urban and even small-town Americans. The difference was that the bohemians had been rebels and the children of the flapper era were conformists.

To understand this difference we must notice the political and social context of bohemianism. The new bohemians were often newcomers to the big cities, but few were from poor European or American working-class backgrounds—Emma Goldman and Margaret Sanger stood out as exceptions. Most were from prosperous, native-born professional or business families. Floyd Dell remarked that they were usually the children of important men in their home towns, often college-educated; often too they were in flight from marriages and careers laid out for them by their successful parents.[28] But despite the rather upper-class base of bohemianism, it was given political shape and significance primarily by the rapid rise of working-class militancy in the prewar period. The Villagers were especially influenced by the revolutionary union, the Industrial Workers of the World (IWW); and by mass industrial strikes. In a period of rapidly escalating class struggle the bohemians' own struggles against cultural repression and bourgeois values seemed to them a part of the working class's fight against capitalism. Their exploration of sexual freedom, odd forms of dressing, and even peyote seemed to them a part of a process of reaching toward a nonauthoritarian, democratic society. Many Villagers left off their individual rebellions to do support work for the Women's Trade Union League. Working-class revolutionary leaders like Bill Haywood and Emma Goldman were the featured guests at parties. Even wealthy Mabel Dodge, in her always white, beautifully draped gowns worked to organize a mass rally for the Paterson strikers in Madison Square Garden. And these were not seen as humanitarian actions. Rather a sense of unity with a sharp class struggle, a struggle in which the working class was destined to be victorious, gave the bohemians the optimism and sense of purpose they needed to create a cohesive community.

Another major factor in the political content of this pre–World War I radicalism, among the working class and intellectuals, was that women played a key role—for the first time in American history—in these movements. Not only was women's rebellion the essence of the sexual revolution but of the entire new bohemianism as well. Hutchins Hapgood wrote, "When the world began to change, the restlessness of women was the main cause of the development called Greenwich Village, which existed not only in New York but all over the country." [29] This should not be construed to suggest that bohemianism was dominated by women or feminist views; on the contrary men often used women's rebellion for their own purposes. But it was the motion among women, the risks they took themselves, that placed them in vulnerable positions. The rejection of marriage, of the traditional family, of propriety in dress and behavior—the whole gamut of rejections that marked the bohemians' radicalism—began because women offered themselves to men and to a larger social and political community without the usual protections of these institutions. Understood even less by most historians has been the dependence of the great strikes of the prewar period on women. Although the IWW in the West had been primarily a male, even a masculinist, movement, it made its impact in the East through its willingness to support massive workers' uprisings in female-dominated industries. In the Paterson, New Jersey, silk-mill strike of 1913, the New York shirtwaist strike of 1909, and the Lawrence textile mill strike of 1912, women constituted from nearly half to the overwhelming majority of workers; and in incident after incident women proved themselves the more militant and persevering of strikers. Political leadership remained almost exclusively in the hands of men (to the disadvantage of the working class as a whole, one might add). But again it was women's action in stepping, sometimes forcibly, out of traditional restrictions, that made possible the class unity that gave the strikes such great strength.

The significance of this movement toward unity of men and women, working class and intellectuals, is that it created a potential for a simultaneous attack on capitalism from many fronts. Certainly intellectuals never had the power to change the society or to create a viable alternative to capitalism. But the reorientation of the intelligentsia to look toward working-class militancy and leadership was an important step in the U.S. socialist movement. And the destruction of that unity was a serious setback. The separation of middle-class intellectuals from workers was perhaps inevitable and less serious; the decline of women's militancy within both classes was more damaging, for it made possible the ultimate severing of the sexual revolution from any over-all social radicalism and the containment of sexual change within the capitalist system. It is difficult to evaluate this containment precisely because it has been so complete; sexual license today seems not only a part of, but even to strengthen, capitalist exploitation and alienation. To view this containment in the correct historical perspective, we must recall the whole context of the period from 1910–1920, the sense of being in a prerevolutionary situation that many felt. For them sexual rebellion was inseparable from social rebellion; in the French Revolution, the European revolutions of 1848, the Paris Commune, and, they were soon to see, the Russian Revolution—in every revolutionary situation—feminism and sex-liberation theory had arisen within the class struggle. This is because in revolutionary situations all power relations, including those between the sexes and between young and old, are opened to examination. (The fact that victorious revolutionary movements have also produced a Puritanism, in the true historical sense of emphasizing hard work and self-sacrifice, as Hobsbawm and others have pointed out, does not contradict this.)[30] The struggle involved in bohemian sexual rebellion was not simply that of individual adolescents against Victorian parents. They were attacking a family system that was a material prop of capitalism, the locus of the reproduction of much, perhaps most, of exploitable labor power—which is, after all, the only commodity absolutely necessary to the system.

It was not obvious then that the sexual revolution could be separated from social rebellion. The success of the surgery was partly fortuitous: beginning with World War I, political events helped right-wing forces divide and weaken the Left. War-induced patriotism combined with the Russian Revolution to allow identification of socialism with un-Americanism. Wartime politics permitted the imposition of severe legal repression and the creation of hysterical "public opinion" against the Left. Some members of the bohemian community were persecuted directly, like Emma Goldman and the birth controllers themselves, as we shall see. But the primary source of the decline of the radical bohemians was the crushing of the working-class Left, which had given them their vigor and coherence. It was relatively easy to demoralize the bohemians anyway, for, as Floyd Dell put it, many of them were only "slumming" from their real lives as gentlemen and scholars.[31] Most of them did not have a material need to transform the society—merely a preference, which they could live without.

In the long run the key factor in separating the sexual revolution from the Left, however, was the spread of the sexual revolution on a new basis to the American working class. This process was not the result of a plan by conservatives, but an organic development of the capitalist economy. Regular business crises throughout the nineteenth century had at first reflected the chaotic financial system of the country while industry provided steady growth—profits for the capitalists and rising wages for the working class; depression did not signify deep or lasting unemployment. But after about 1907 the economy entered a period that might be described as semistagnation, in which industrial production could not continue steadily because of the failure of markets to expand equally. Wages were not keeping up with the cost of living, unemployment reached high levels (12 per cent frequently), and production sank in relation to capacity. World War I marked the beginning of a steady industrial expansion based on the production of war materials and, afterward, durable consumer goods, sold through the rapid expansion of advertising. This was a prosperity dependent on continued artificial expansion of the market—that is, finding consumers for new products—and on installment buying. What the advertisers were selling was not just specific products, but a whole consumptionist attitude among the American working and middle classes. There was also a political aspect to this endeavor, for businessmen and their ideologists of the 1920s looked to mass consumption to refute the socialist critique of capitalism.[32]

Advertisers, of course, used the promise of sexual allure and success to encourage the buying of specific products. More important, as sexual freedom reached the working-class majority, it itself became a commodity. Young people indulged in dating, necking, nonmarital sexual intercourse not as a rebellion but as a predigested new social fashion. They did it because "everyone else" was doing it. They sensed the inadequacy and irrelevance of their parents' moral standards, but they did not participate in developing new standards. As a result the sexual exploits of youth in the 1920s had an unhappy air about them. Hutchins Hapgood summed up the difference as he felt it: Before

World War I "there was still healthy vigor and moral idealism underlying the effort. So that the total result was a working out of the situation into a more conscious companionship, greater self-knowledge, and a broader understanding of the relations between the sexes. . . ." He branded the 1920s mood, by contrast, as "sexual demoralization." [33] This demoralization was deepened by the war, fed not only by death and suffering but by a sense of their purposelessness.

> The War was another Black Death that came upon the world. . . .
> And it brought with it not the Dance of Death but the Dance of
> Priapus. . . . The western world is made with this dance. . . .
> Every year, every month, the dance takes new forms, assumes new
> disguises. Each form is more futile than the other. Each change is
> more sexual. . . . *Cynicism has become the new faith.* . . . "A World
> War lies between us and our fathers. . . ." This World War, then,
> shot into shreds the old ideals, the old morals, the old customs.[34]

The war appeared as a turning point though it was not the ultimate cause.[35]

When freer sexual standards reached Muncie, Indiana, in the mid-1920s, as described in the Lynds' study, *Middletown*, they produced all the confusion and disorientation of the original sexual revolution but none of the political content or sense of discovery. Middletown residents perceived these sexual changes as something that happened to them, not something they pioneered. The sexual revolution was brought to Middletown by mass culture. Roughly thirty-five hundred to four thousand copies per month of sex-adventure magazines came into Middletown, a town of thirty-five thousand. In them Middletowners read stories and articles such as "The Primitive Lover" ("She wanted a caveman husband"), "Can a Wife Win with the Other Woman's Weapons?" and "Indolent Kisses." Motion pictures were probably an even greater influence. The automobile weakened one of the greatest barriers to premarital sexual adventure —lack of privacy. Of thirty girls charged with sex crimes in 1924, nineteen had committed their alleged offense in an automobile.[36] As early as 1913 social-purity writers had noticed the institutionalized basis of loose behavior—billiard halls, ice-cream parlors, popular songs, amusement parks, "schools of sexual immorality, with clever and persistent teachers." [37] The prewar bohemians had invented their own immorality, consciously attacking a restrictive culture they hated. The 1920s American masses were being fed a predigested new culture, more homogenized and capitalized than ever before.

Original or not, these new values made contraception more acceptable. Increased openness of speech about sexual matters made it easier to ask for contraceptives. The fact that women less often expected to be protected or to exclude themselves from exposure to sexual topics made it easier for them to learn about contraception and to accept the validity of sexual experience without reproductive consequences. Even if women did not honestly desire sex for themselves, or did not think they should, they were frequently told that they should use their sex appeal to win other objectives. This new sense of *using* sex was a mere twist away from the nineteenth-century view that women ought to *submit* to please their husbands and keep them from prostitutes. In both cases sex was an instrumentality to another end, not an end in itself or a part of a whole relationship. The mass culture of the 1920s told women to learn to grip and manipulate their husband's interest through their attractiveness. In Middletown people went to films and read articles with titles like "Married Flirt," and "How to Keep the Thrill in Marriage." [38]

The emphasis on sex did not, however, challenge the idea of woman's place being in the home. Advertisers appealed to the frustration and tedium of housewifery, offering beauty products and "labor-saving" devices, but never with the orientation of escaping from housewifery altogether or spreading the housework among more family members. The changed technology was meanwhile making full-time housework a steadily more alienated, proletarianized job: the manufacturing and creative aspects of housework, women's individual control over their work and ability to use skills (such as fine baking, cooking, sewing, and nursing) were eroded and replaced by industrialized, prepackaged products and services ranging from canned foods to a variety of cleaning aids to ever-changing ready-to-wear fashions and cosmetics. New modes of production were historically making housework ever more tedious, in the guise of making it easier, shorter, and more alluring. But meanwhile no way out of full-time housework was offered or even acknowledged for married women, and their over-all frustration deepened. Freedom of sexual expression was allowed only if it did not challenge the essential family structure; premarital sex and adultery were tolerated because they offered no challenge and even, temporarily, shored up the rotting timbers of housewifery. The sexual revolution certainly offered no liberation to working-class and middle-class housewives.

A more serious challenge to the family was produced by another aspect of the industrial economy—the need to increase productivity without increasing labor costs. This had its impact primarily on unmarried women, who were drawn in rapidly increasing numbers into the wage-labor force. In 1870 1,900,000 women were employed; in 1890 4,000,000. By 1910 the number had doubled.[39] Over the long run probably no single factor did more to change the sexual behavior of unmarried women than their entrance into the labor market, especially if it meant living away from home. Protecting the morals of unmarried working girls in the big cities became a major worry for social workers, reformers, and moralists; they built boarding houses and YWCAs and attempted to lure the young women into supervised living. But the greatest charm of the big cities for young women was privacy, and the YWCAs reported over and over that women preferred private apartments if they could get them.[40]

An open neighborhood in this as in other ways, Greenwich Village attracted many such young workers. Landlords there allowed groups of women to share small apartments. The old Village bohemians even complained about the influx of "green" working women.[41] Once in the big cities, young women often outnumbered single men. They most frequently worked in sexually segregated occupations, where they did not quickly find husbands. Furthermore, the persistent conviction that a man should marry only when he could support his wife often led to lengthy postponement of marriage. In this period employed women were still overwhelmingly single: only about 5 per cent of wives worked for money outside their homes.

Within the wage-labor force, clerical work expanded more rapidly than any other kind of employment for women after 1880. In 1880 women numbered only 4 per cent of clerical workers; in 1890 they were 21 per cent; by 1920 they were 50 per cent.[42] The working conditions of offices differed greatly from those in factories. Typists and secretaries often had close contact with men. Their subculture emphasized dressing well, and although they were poorly paid they earned more than almost all factory workers. Many young secretaries spent so much of their salaries on clothes that they literally had to skip eating for periods of time; urban employed women also frequently spent a high portion of their earnings for the luxury of an apartment and the relative privacy it afforded. Even without overspending, many independent women workers had to count on being taken out to dinner several nights a week in order to make ends meet.[43] The other side of these new circumstances was the disappearance of many traditional restraints. Not only were parents absent, but close, prying neighbors had also gone. Church and school influences were distant. Even older brothers and sisters, who had once helped sanction traditional moral values, could no longer. Big cities generally provided physical and social privacy in ways that small towns never had, for the married or unmarried. At the same time the old-fashioned view of independent working women as not quite respectable hung on and combined with the male double standard to make them fair game.

Inextricably related to the increased privacy for sexual activity among unmarried women was the decline of prostitution. During and after World War I a nationwide campaign by reformers for the suppression of red-light districts—that is, tolerated prostitution—was nearly universally successful. The success was both a consequence of these sexual changes and also a contributory cause of them. It also contributed to the pressure for birth control. For men, the unacceptableness of hiring prostitutes, and the acceptableness of love-making with unmarried women for free, grew together and reinforced each other. Prostitutes had access to birth-control information and devices through their own underground; for the new sexual system to work, other women needed access to the same information. Campaigners against prostitution counseled early marriage. But to make early marriage an economic possibility, in an era when husbands were still expected to support their wives, contraception was as necessary as it was to illicit affairs.

Another important factor in the increased acceptability of contraception was the scourge of venereal disease and the campaign against it. V.D. had, of course, been a serious problem in the United States throughout the nineteenth century. Widespread prostitution meant that many innocent women were infected by their husbands, and for feminists and voluntary-motherhood advocates this injustice loomed large in their attack on the double standard. Medical discoveries of the consequences of syphilis and gonorrhea showed that they were even worse than had been previously understood,[44] and in the early twentieth century some physicians began educational campaigns for their prevention. Soldiers had always spread V.D., even in peacetime. World War I worsened the problem considerably. Between September 1917 and February 1919 there were over 280,000 cases of V.D. reported in the U.S. Army and Navy.[45] In 1914 one expert estimated that over half the male population of the country had had gonorrhea.[46] The main reason for the spread of V.D. among the armed forces was, of course, increased recourse to prostitutes.

Thus before the World War the anti-V.D. campaign was tied to antiprostitution work, indeed to the social purity movement; the key recommendations were abolition of prostitution (or, occasionally, the licensing and inspection of prostitutes)* and continence propaganda.[48] So serious was the problem that one well-known social-purity writer urged soldiers to masturbate if they could not manage continence! [49] Then in 1909 the compound 606, or Salvarsan, was demonstrated to be effective in destroying syphilis spirochetes. As early as 1912 a War Department general order required that soldiers take prophylactic treatment for suspected V.D.[50] Condoms—far more effective than chemical treatment—had been available for centuries, rubber condoms since the mid-nineteenth century. What made condoms more objectionable was that they had to be given out before the fact to be useful, possibly encouraging intercourse, and that they had a clear contraceptive capability. But the pressure to employ such effective devices was irresistible. The Navy had been distributing condoms before shore leaves since early in the century. Josephus Daniels, of fundamentalist persuasion, attacked the practice and vowed to discontinue it when he became Secretary of the Navy, but he too was forced to reinstitute it.[51]

---

* In the nineteenth century, when licensed and regulated prostitution was being tried in Europe, American feminists and social-purity advocates had mounted an effective campaign against the system. They prevented its establishment here except in one case: St. Louis established an inspection and licensing system in 1870. But in 1874 the social-purity forces succeeded in repealing it.[47]

The impact of World War I and the circulation of condoms represents a microcosm of the spiraling relationship of contraception to the whole sexual revolution. The availability of contraceptives licensed sexual activity and the new acceptability of sexual activity licensed contraception. Katherine Bement Davis's monumental sex study published in 1929 established a correlation (though based on a small sample) between knowledge of contraception and premarital sex.[52] We have already mentioned the importance of military service in World War I as a source of contraceptive information. Demobilization greatly increased the civilian market for condoms. V. F. Calverton did a private study of condom distribution in Baltimore and found that two to three million a year were sold before the war and approximately 6,250,000 in the mid-1920s. Furthermore, he believed that 50 per cent of those buying contraceptives in Baltimore were unmarried.[53] Thus did the U.S. government promote "sexual revolution."

But in doing so it was only accelerating long-term tendencies. As is often the case in looking back, we can get a sense of the social change by noticing what its opponents thought. Traditional social-purity advocates had been growing steadily more defensive since 1910. Even their gratification at the victory over prostitution was ruined by their sense of an impending corruption that would be even worse. They described the decline of sexual morality in the vocabulary of crisis and revolution. They had a sense of emergency, of values crumbling so rapidly that they must be shored up quickly or be lost forever.[54]

A Mass Movement

The movement that first coalesced around the slogan "birth control," a phrase invented by Margaret Sanger in 1915, was a force of people fighting for their own immediate needs, and because of this it had an intensely personal dimension for its participants. The fact that the birth controllers often stood to gain immediately in their personal lives from legalization of birth control did not narrow their vision but strengthened their commitment. They united their personal experience and emotional understanding with political thought and action. They created a politics based on women's shared experience which had the potential to unite masses of women. At the same time the birth controllers transcended women's immediate needs. They were not seeking incremental improvements in their sex lives or medical care; they did not view birth control as primarily a sexual or medical reform at all, but as a social issue with broad implications. They wanted to transform the nature of women's rights—indeed, of human rights—to include free sexual expression and reproductive self-determination.

In challenging the traditional limits of people's control over their own lives, they used birth control to make a revolutionary demand, not a reform proposal. They did not want just to limit their pregnancies; they wanted to change the world. They believed that birth control could alleviate much human misery and fundamentally alter social and political power relations, thereby creating greater sexual and class equality. In this they shared the voluntary-motherhood analysis—that involuntary motherhood was a major prop of women's subjection—and added a radical version of a Neo-Malthusian analysis—that overlarge families weakened the working class in its just struggle with the capitalist class. They also demanded sexual freedom.

The birth controllers were putting forward these demands at a time when American radicalism was at one of its peaks of strength and breadth. Indeed, the birth-control movement that began in 1914 was a part of a general explosion of resistance to economic and social exploitation. Joining that resistance, birth controllers appealed for support to the powerless, particularly to women and to working-class and poor people in general, because they believed that lack of control over reproduction helped perpetuate an undemocratic distribution of power.

Strategically their analysis tried to draw together the women's movement and the working-class movement. The leading birth controllers between 1914 and 1920 were both feminists and socialists and wanted to unite their respective goals and constituencies. Many of them came to the birth-control cause from multi-issue reform or revolutionary movements, ranging from the suffrage organizations to the IWW. Few were themselves working class, although some important leaders—Margaret Sanger is only one—had working-class origins. Their experience of the common oppression of women in sexual and reproductive matters convinced them that they could transcend their class differences and create a movement that would fight for the interests of the least privileged women.

They failed in this grand intention, but that does not mean that their analysis and strategy were completely wrong or that their experiences are useless to us today. Their belief that birth control could create a new freedom and dignity for women and a new right for all people was not wrong just because it was incompletely realized.

By 1914 the radical movement in the United States was unified to a large extent in a single Socialist party. From 10,000 members in 1901 it grew to include 118,000 in 1912. Its voting strength was many times greater—almost 6 per cent of the total in 1912—and by 1912 it had elected twelve hundred public officials and regularly published over three hundred periodicals.[55] No other political party in American history has ever fought as consistently for women's rights (such as woman suffrage, employment opportunities, equal legal rights).[56] Especially after 1910 many feminists entered the Party and began agitating for more active political work by and for women. Women's committees were organized in many locals, socialist woman-suffrage societies were created, and a few women were elected to the National Executive Committee.[57]

The Socialist party's conception of what women's rights were, however, agreed in all respects with those advocated by liberal feminists. Like suffragists, most socialists accepted the conventional definition of woman's proper sphere and activities—home, motherhood, housework, and husband care. There was no general support in the Socialist party for birth control or for any reforms that threatened to alter or even to question traditional sexual roles and division of labor. In clinging to their traditional views of the family, socialists often cited as their authority the early Marxist view that drawing women out of their homes was one of the evils of capitalism that socialism would put right. The revolutionaries in the Socialist party, more inclined to reject the conventions, were concerned even more exclusively than the rest of the Party with class struggle in the workplace, and consequently had little interest in questions of domestic relations. The Party's women's journal, *Socialist Woman*, published in Girard, Kansas, did not have a single article that discussed the principle of voluntary motherhood before 1914. (Indeed, even when the journal got a letter asking them to take up the question, the editors declined to publish it.)[58] Socialist women concerned with sexual issues, even regular contributors to Party periodicals, published their writings on birth control elsewhere.[59]

Despite its great influence in the birth-control movement, the Socialist party never formally endorsed birth control. Indeed, before 1912 the issue was never the subject of major debate within the Party, so great was the disapproval of creating internal divisions. The rejection of anything but the most limited feminist goals by the Socialist-party majority reflected a larger split in the whole U.S. radical and reform community between socialism and the women's movement. That split deepened in the early twentieth century. Previously, almost all supporters of birth control had been socialists of a sort. Voluntary-motherhood advocates of the 1870s had been critical of capitalist values and social organization, as had utopian communitarians who practiced birth control; many American feminists by the end of the nineteenth century had concluded that women's emancipation would require a higher level of economic justice than capitalism could provide; most European sex radicals were socialists. But as Marxian scientific socialism began to dominate, and the organized socialist movement gained a working-class constituency, emphasis on class differences and class struggle tended to diminish the importance of sex equality as a program. Many feminists, although thoroughly anticapitalist, refused to follow socialist theory into a denial of their own experience of sex oppression.

This ideological split occurred under conditions of industrialization which deepened class differences among women as among men. A feminist analysis that in the 1870s seemed broad enough to include all women, by the early twentieth century could appeal only to upper-class women. By 1910 working-class women were more distant from the suffrage organizations in their point of view as well as in their actual political loyalties than they had been in the 1870s. On the other hand, the Marxian socialist movement in America had rejected many of the feminist and sex-radical traditions of utopian and other romantic socialisms. Furthermore, within the Marxist organizations, the tendency to emphasize unions and organizing at the workplace left men without pressing reasons to appeal to women, most of whom remained outside the labor force. The complaints of even the most antifeminist of socialist women leave no doubt that arrogance and disrespectful attitudes toward women were widespread among socialist men. Thus anyone trying to formulate a socialist *and* feminist theory about the importance of birth control faced serious difficulties: a conservative and elite woman-suffrage movement and a rather blindly antifeminist Socialist party.

Despite its limitations, however, the existence of the Socialist party was one of the most important, probably necessary, conditions for the emergence of the radical birth-control movement in the second decade of the century, in that it brought together almost all radicals and reformers in touch with the working class or concerned with working-class power. Without this opportunity to reach and to learn from working-class women, the sex radicals would have continued to pursue sterile, theoretical formulations, contributing at most to a bohemian life style among urban intellectuals. On the other hand, the sexual conservatism of the Party's male leadership could not contain the growing restlessness produced among women by their changed circumstances.

Some Midwestern socialists still cherished some of the feminist traditions of pre-Marxian socialism, for instance, Virginia Butterfield. Her book, *Parental Rights and Economic Wrongs*, published in Chicago in 1906, argued that birth control was a form of self-defense against capitalism. In agricultural society children were a form of wealth, and therefore birth control was economically unnecessary, she argued; under conditions of industrialism birth control became necessary because capitalism's system of unjust distribution made people poor. Ideally, socialism would again make birth control unnecessary! She believed that socialism would also restore the "natural equilibrium of the sexes" by allowing men to earn enough so that all women could stay at home, and that this restoration of a natural condition would end marital unhappiness and the necessity for divorce.[60] Until then, however, women's refusal to bear children under conditions of oppression was a form of rebellion. Indeed, since procreation was one of the highest forms of human labor, birth control became, for Butterfield, a form of workers' control! * Many socialists turned their attention to the prohibition on birth control and asked: Whom does it serve? Many concluded that the ruling class kept birth control from the working class in the interest of continued exploitation. One reason was war—a large population of underlings was needed for cannon fodder.[62] Another was that a reserve army of labor was used to keep wages down.[63] To the charge that birth control might weaken the working class by decreasing its size, they pointed to historical events in which the unemployed and poor—a lumpen proletariat—had played an antirevolutionary role.[64]

The limitations of these analyses reflected the general limitations of socialist theory regarding women. The debate about whether the working class would benefit from increasing or shrinking its size implicitly left most women beyond consideration, since they were outside the wage-labor force or the armed forces.

A few U.S. radicals, Margaret Sanger and Emma Goldman among them, were able to advance beyond this partly because they were influenced by several European developments. In Protestant countries with mass working-class socialist parties, there were many birth-control clinics. In Holland a trade-union-sponsored birth-control clinic had operated since 1882. In Germany birth control had been an important issue in the Social Democratic party since early in the century, and the demands of Party rank-and-file women had forced the Party leadership to give up its opposition to endorsing birth control.[65] Even in Catholic France, socialist Paul Robin had organized a clandestine international Neo-Malthusian† conference in 1900. Both Goldman and Sanger, attracted more by anarchism than by the Social Democratic parties, were at first less impressed by the clinics than by the theories of sexual freedom. They transformed these ideas into an action program, a program of sex education.

---

* Although Butterfield's identification of reproduction with production is unique, several socialist women of this period were concerned with the social importance of other aspects of women's unpaid labor in the home. Party journals sometimes discussed the economic value of housework under capitalism, suggesting that it represented perhaps the most extreme form of exploitation.[61]
† Until several decades into the twentieth century Europeans continued to use "Neo-Malthusianism" as the generic name for birth control whether or not they accepted the social and political perspective of the Neo-Malthusian organizations and tradition.

In this period sex education was not merely action but militant action because it involved breaking the law. The Comstock law still barred "obscene" materials from the mails, and most noneuphemistic sex discussion—such as naming the human genitalia—was considered obscene. Defying such laws was a form of what the IWW called direct action, people acting directly against state and capitalist power, not petitioning or negotiating but taking what they needed. Women needed sex education. Feminists and sexual-freedom advocates agreed that women's ignorance of their bodies was debilitating and that deference to conventions about what was good for "ladies" to know deepened their passivity and political fearfulness.

In the United States a campaign of sex education formed a bridge between pro-birth-control ideas and an organized movement for birth control. Sex manuals had been plentiful since the mid-nineteenth century, but their style had begun to change in the 1900s. Even the conservative writers, while remaining moralistic, introduced detailed physiological descriptions and sometimes drawings of reproductive anatomy.[66] Midwestern socialists and feminists of Virginia Butterfield's tradition had been the first to appreciate the importance of sex education and had written dozens of books in the first decades of the twentieth century.[67] Somewhat later, demands for sex education appeared within the Socialist party itself. One particularly effective spokeswoman and practitioner of sex and birth-control education was Antoinette Konikow, a Russian immigrant physician. She had been one of the founding members of the Socialist party and later one of the five members of its Women's Commission. She practiced medicine in Boston after her graduation from Tufts Medical School in 1902; and although Boston was then as now an overwhelmingly Catholic city, with little support even within its radical community for sexual unconventionality, she was outspoken for birth control and probably did abortions.[68] Konikow wrote for the *New York Call*, a daily socialist newspaper, arguing that sex education was an important task for socialists.[69] Dr. William J. Robinson also wrote for the *Call* on sex hygiene; he and Konikow were the first to focus their sex-education articles on birth control.[70]

The most notorious for her outspokenness on sexual questions was Emma Goldman. Goldman, more than any other person, fused into a single ideology the many currents that mingled in American sex radicalism. She had connections with European anarchism, syndicalism, and socialism; she knew and was influenced by American utopian anarchists and free lovers such as Moses Harman; she was also familiar with American feminism and with dissident doctors such as Robinson.[71] In 1900 she had attended the secret conference of Neo-Malthusians in Paris and had even smuggled some contraceptive devices into the United States.[72] In New York Goldman was tremendously influential on other women radicals, as a role model and a practitioner of the new morality. One woman strongly influenced by Goldman was Margaret Sanger. Sanger later tried to hide that influence. Always needing recognition and fearing rivals for power and importance, Sanger underestimated Goldman's contribution to birth control in her later writings. Sanger met Goldman when Goldman was a magnetic and dominating figure nationally and Sanger an insecure young woman lacking a cause and a political identity. Sanger still clung to more conservative sexual ideas, and Goldman must have been shocking to her, at the least.[73]

Moving to New York City in 1911 and searching for something to do, Sanger's background as a nurse made it natural for her to take an interest in sex education. She began writing articles for the *New York Call*. At about the same time she was hired as an organizer for the Women's Commission of the Socialist party (with a small salary) and elected secretary of the Harlem Socialist Suffrage Society. In both capacities she began making speeches and was so enthusiastically received when she spoke on health and sex topics that she began to specialize in these areas. Questions and responses at the meetings and letters to the *Call* gave Sanger reinforcement and a sense of appreciation.

On the other hand, Sanger was disappointed in her more "orthodox" socialist organizing, working with striking laundry workers and trying to garner support for a legislative campaign for a wages-and-hours bill. She resigned as an organizer in January 1912.[74] But her dissatisfaction with her Socialist-party work did not at first push her more deeply into sex-education activities; rather she was drawn, as were so many radical intellectuals at the time, toward the greater militancy of the IWW, with its direct-action tactics. When the strike of

Lawrence, Massachusetts, textile workers, supported by the IWW, broke out in January 1912, Sanger became involved in support work for the strikers, which she continued until June 1912.[75]

Sanger resumed her articles in the *Call* in November 1912 with a series, "What Every Girl Should Know." It was more daring than the first series, which had been called "What Every Mother Should Know" and had been designed to help mothers tell their children about sex and reproduction, largely through analogy to flowers and animals.[76] The second series spoke more fully of human physiology, especially the female sexual and reproductive apparatus, and argued that the "procreative act" was something natural, clean, and healthful.[77] But when Sanger turned to the problem of venereal disease, which had for decades been discussed in public only with euphemisms such as the "social problem" and "congenital taint," the Post Office could take no more. They declared the article unmailable under the Comstock law. The *Call* responded by printing the headline of the column—"What Every Girl Should Know"—and in a big, blank box underneath it, the words, "NOTHING, by order of the Post-Office Department." [78] (The Post Office ban was lifted two weeks later on orders from Washington and the article actually appeared in the *Call* on March 2. In one of the finer ironies produced by the rapid changes in attitudes of those years, this very article was reprinted—without credit to the author—by the U.S. government and distributed among troops during World War I.)[79]

Up until this time, however, Sanger had not discussed birth control in writing. Her sex-education work was again interrupted by a more urgent demand for her services—the Paterson silk-workers' strike that began in February 1913. The workers asked the IWW for help, and Big Bill Haywood sent Sanger and Jessie Ashley (a socialist, feminist lawyer later to be active in birth control) to Paterson to organize picket lines.[80] Sanger worked there until the strike's failure in the summer. She did not write anything further on sexual hygiene that year, and in October sailed for Europe with her husband and children. In Paris she began the first stage of her "research" into birth control—the sociological phase. Not yet interested in libraries and sexual theory, she spoke with her neighbors, with the French syndicalists that Bill Haywood (also then in Paris) introduced her to, with druggists, midwives, and doctors. She collected contraceptive formulas. She discovered that birth control was respectable, widely practiced, and almost traditional in France. Women told her that they had learned about contraception from their mothers.[81] In fact, birth-control advocates in the United States such as William J. Robinson had been publishing articles about the low birth rate and widespread contraceptive use in France for years.[82] Emma Goldman knew these facts about France. All this, however, was new to Sanger in 1913. For the rest of her life, birth control was to be her single, exclusive passion.

What were the sources of this decision, or conversion, of Sanger's? Years later she herself portrayed it as a rather sudden conversion and attributed it to an incident that had happened a year earlier in her work as a visiting nurse: an encounter with a poor Jewish family in which a beloved wife died from one pregnancy too many.[83] She also wrote that before going to Paris she had already spent a year in New York libraries and the Library of Congress futilely searching for contraceptive information.[84] Apparently, Bill Haywood himself urged her to go to France to learn.[85] There can be no doubt that she was hearing about birth control frequently and that it had the basic approval of people she respected. Even in the Paterson strike it was in the air. Elizabeth Gurley Flynn recalled a meeting for women strikers at which Carlo Tresca, an IWW organizer, "made some remarks about shorter hours, people being less tired, more time to spend together and jokingly he said: 'More babies.' The women did not look amused. When Haywood interrupted and said: 'No, Carlo, we believe in birth control—a few babies, well cared for!' they burst into laughter and applause." [86]

One key difference between Sanger and her radical friends who saw the importance of birth control was that she was dissatisfied with her role as a rank-and-file socialist organizer and was searching for something more like a career. Many biographers have commented on Sanger's drive for recognition. Among men in most situations that kind of drive would have seemed so commonplace that it would have gone unmentioned. Sanger instinctively understood that the recognition she needed required a special cause, a specialization. As a nurse, she felt comfortable building on expertise and experience she already had.

But the reason she chose contraception rather than venereal disease or sex education was her recognition of the potential historical and political meaning of birth control. Most American socialists at this time, primarily oriented to class relations, saw birth control in Neo-Malthusian terms, that is, in terms of economics. They were concerned to help raise the standard of living of workers and thus increase their freedom to take political control over their own lives. Measured against this goal, birth control was at most an ameliorative reform. Seen in terms of sexual politics, however, birth control was revolutionary because it could free women entirely from the major burden that differentiated them from men, and made them dependent on men. Sanger did not originally have this perspective. Although female and concerned about women's rights, her political education had been a male-defined one. She gained this perspective in Europe from the sexual-liberation theorists like Havelock Ellis. Ellis literally tutored Sanger. His idealism about the potential beauty and expressiveness of human sexuality and his rage at the damage caused by sexual repression fired Sanger with a sense of the overwhelming importance, urgency, and profundity of the issue of birth control, a sense lacking in most other American radicals.

The entire future course of birth control in the United States was influenced by Sanger's European "education" on birth control. And yet the conviction, curiosity, and drive that led her to her research in Europe would almost certainly have led someone else there if Margaret Sanger had been diverted. Sanger's European trips took place in the midst of a flurry of activity for sexual change in the United States which began before Sanger's influence was great and which would inevitably have led to a birth-control campaign before long. Sanger was stimulated by it and returned to shape it, but in all respects she was a part of a movement, not its inventor.[87]

In 1937, when the first general history of contraception was published, Benjamin Reitman, once Emma Goldman's comrade and lover, wrote a letter of protest to its author, charging that the book had suppressed the radical origins of the birth-control movement. It was a passionate and an amusing letter, and largely correct.

My Dear Himes.

You made me weep.
Because your article
On the history
    Of Birth Control
was inaccurate
    Superficial
    "Highschoolish"
And you gave no evidence
Of attempting
To learn the facts.

You delved into history.
    But failed to get data from the living.
    Moses Harmon*
Was the true father of American Birth Control
His grand Children are living
And have lots of splendid material. . . .

You "muffed" all the fine material
In the early Socialist, Anarchist & I.W.W. literature.
The tremendous amount of Free Love literature
Passed you by.
There are several hundred pamphlets
On B.C. that you evidently know nothing about.
The technique of B.C. propaganda
In America is a Mystery to you. . . .

I mean your prejudice against the RADICALS
Is so great that you COULD not give them credit.
    Emma Goldman
More than any one person in America
Popularized B.C.
She was Margaret Sanger's INSPIRATION
No that ain't the word.
Margaret imitated her and denied her.
Emma was the first person in America
To lecture on Birth Control
in one hundred Cities. . . .

The physicians, Social Scientists, Clergy & etc.
Became interested in B.C.
Only after the Radicals had "broken" the ground.
And gone to jail.

* Moses Harman, free lover and anarchist from Kansas, arrested and imprisoned for birth-control advocacy. See Chapter 6.

The inclosed pamphlet
Was distributed by the millions.
Free.
　In hundreds of Cities in America
It went through many many editions
Was copied and recopied. . . .
The decline in the Birth Rate
Was influenced by this pamphlet
More than any other one piece of literature.
　Including Margaret's "Family Limitation" . . .

　B.L.R.*
Was arrested
　For distributing the pamphlet
In New York City (60 days)
Rochester, N.Y. (freed)
Cleveland, Ohio (six months)
He was picked up by the police in many cities
But was let go.

Big Bill Shatoff
　Who was an I.W.W. Organizer
Translated the pamphlet
Into Jewish and most all
　Of the Radical Jews had copies.
In the early days of the Communists' activity
In Russia this pamphlet
Had a tremendous circulation in Russia . . .

GET THIS INTO YOUR HEAD.
This was all done as part of the radical propaganda.
ANTI WAR
ANTI MARRIAGE
　ANTI CHILDREN BY ACCIDENT . . .

I see no hope for your Medical Scientific group to make any real
Contribution to history or ****

Enough for today
Ben L. Reitman[88]

Allowing for exaggeration due to nostalgia, loyalty to Goldman,
and the pique of a radical who saw "his" movement taken over by
conservatives, the essence of Reitman's claims is nevertheless correct.
The author—Norman Himes—defended himself by pointing out that

* The author, Dr. Benjamin L. Reitman.

he had written a *medical* history of contraception and was primarily concerned with those who made medical and technological contributions. Nevertheless, it is true that historians and biographers have overlooked or underestimated the radical roots of the American birth-control movement. Sanger herself contributed to that distortion. She was ignorant, in the early years of her career, of the free-love and feminist roots of birth-control propaganda, and later she sought to diminish the socialist participation in the movement when she wrote and spoke about it.[89]

After about 1910 Goldman regularly included a birth-control speech on her tour offerings. In it she placed birth control in the context of women's rights and opposition to conventional legal marriage. Like all radicals of her era, she used eugenic arguments: "Woman no longer wants to be a party to the production of a race of sickly, feeble, decrepit, wretched human beings. Instead she desires fewer and better children. . . ." On the other hand, she also spoke about homosexuality, criticizing social ostracism of the "inverts," as homosexuals were commonly called at that time. Her sexual and feminist theories were not only far more radical than those of the birth controllers who followed her, but also far more systematic, integrated into her whole politics. "To me anarchism was not a mere theory for a distant future; it was a living influence to free us from inhibitions . . . and from the destructive barriers that separate man from man." [90] Reitman was himself a birth-control campaigner, not a mere companion to Goldman, and he did indeed, as he claimed, serve sixty days shoveling coal on Blackwell's Island and six months in an Ohio workhouse for distributing birth-control leaflets.[91]

Goldman and Reitman distributed a small, four-page pamphlet called *Why and How the Poor Should Not Have Many Children*. It may have been written by Goldman or Reitman, or possibly by William J. Robinson. It described condoms, instructing the user to check them for leaks by blowing them up with air; recommended rubber cervical caps, diaphragms (also called pessaries or womb veils; in the early twentieth century there was no standard nomenclature for these various devices), which could be bought in drugstores, but urged fitting by a physician for reliability. It suggested three contraceptive methods that could be homemade: suppositories, douches, a cotton ball dipped in borated vaseline. (It advised against relying on the rhythm method but unfortunately still defined the safe period as the two weeks between menstrual periods.) The political argument of the pamphlet was brief: although normal people love and want children, society today is a "wretched place" for poor children, who are not only a burden to their mothers and families, but also "glut the labor market, tend to lower wages, and are a menace to the welfare of the working class. . . . If you think that the teaching of the prevention of conception will help working men and women, spread the glad tidings." * American sex radicals, despite their militant rhetoric, had not so far defied law and convention by publishing such explicit contraceptive advice. Goldman and Reitman's ideas about birth control were not new. Their sense of the political importance of taking risks to spread it was, however.

Though Goldman and her associates were the first radicals since the free lovers to act in defiance of the law, they were not able to make birth control a mass cause. Goldman's connections made her seem the right person for that task. But Goldman was also an extremist, and as a result she was often isolated. Partly because she took outrageous positions and partly because she was personally egocentric, Goldman left most of her admirers behind. If they were feminists, they were often from the educated classes, individualist by habit and ultimately more deeply committed to professional and artistic careers than to full-time revolutionary organizing. If they were revolutionaries, they were often men, skeptical about the importance of sexual and women's rights issues.

Though she began later, Margaret Sanger was much more effective as an *organizer* for birth control. Lacking Goldman's intellectual daring and originality, she drew supporters to her, at first, through assuming a role in which she was more convincing than Goldman: that of victim. In the first years of her career, people frequently commented on Sanger's apparent fragility and vulnerability; only as they came to know her did her stamina, tenacity, and personal power impress them. Intellectuals repelled by the abrasive style of Goldman and her comrades could adore Margaret Sanger. Max Eastman, for

* Note that this pamphlet was written before the term "birth control," coined by Sanger, was in use.

example, hailed Sanger as a hero in *The Masses* but refused to speak at a Carnegie Hall meeting to welcome Goldman out of jail after she had served sixty days for distributing birth-control pamphlets, because, he said, he would not appear with Ben Reitman. "Reitman was a white-fleshed, waxy-looking doctor, who thought it was radical to shock people with crude allusions to their sexual physiology." [92] Nevertheless, Sanger's debut as a birth-control activist was tactically and substantively right within the pattern plotted out by Goldman and the IWW. Sanger began with provocative, illegal action, and, once arrested, organized support for her defense.

The key difference between Sanger's and Goldman's strategies in 1914 was that Sanger chose to act independently of any leftist organization—indeed, independently of even any close collaborators. The path that led the Sanger-inspired birth-control movement away from the Left thus began with Sanger's first actions, though they may not have been consciously intended in that direction. When Sanger's divergence from the organized Left led to total separation, it was as much because the Left had rejected birth control as because Sanger and her followers had rejected the Left. Nevertheless, the roots of the split can be found at the beginnings of the birth-control movement itself.

Sanger returned from Paris to New York in December 1913, deeply influenced by her discovery that birth control was widely accepted in Europe and by support for birth control among some French syndicalists. She did not return to Socialist-party work but decided instead to publish an independent, feminist paper. *The Woman Rebel*, which appeared seven times in 1914 until it was suppressed by the Post Office, emphasized birth control but was not a single-issue journal. It raised other problems of women's sexual liberation: "The marriage bed is the most degenerating influence of the social order, as to life, in all of its forms—biological, psychological, sociological—for man, woman and child." [93] Although concerned with the whole gamut of injustices that the capitalist system created, *The Woman Rebel* focused mainly on its effects on women. But it also sharply attacked the nonsocialist suffrage movement and various "bourgeois feminists." For example, of Katherine Bement Davis, then New York City Commissioner of Corrections (and later, ironically, a sociologist of sexual behavior who worked with Sanger on several sex-education projects), *The Woman Rebel* wrote: "We have no respect for the type of so-called 'modern' and 'advanced' woman who becomes a willing and efficient slave of the present system, the woman who curries favors of capitalists and politicians in order to gain power and the cheap and fulsome praise of cheaper and more fulsome newspapers." [94] Also characteristic of the journal was a supermilitancy, surpassing even the IWW in its rhetorical support of violence. An editorial asked women to send rifles instead of messages of solidarity to striking miners in Colorado.[95] An article in the July issue was the last straw that led the Post Office to declare the journal unmailable, although when Sanger was indicted, two counts of obscenity were also brought against her.[96]

The Woman Rebel did not represent a tendency in American feminism or socialism at this time. It was rather a singular, unrepeated attempt by Sanger to combine her IWW-influenced commitment to direct action with her deepened feminism and sense of the radical potential of birth control. At any rate, it did not last long—and its sudden demise may well have been in part Sanger's intention. She claimed that she wanted to be arrested in order to force a legal definition of what was "obscene." [97] In fact, she may have recognized the journal's lack of political viability.

But *The Woman Rebel* had given Sanger space and stimulus for further political exploration. She was able to correspond with leading European and American feminists in the name of a publication; rejected by many of them, she discovered the pro-birth-control tradition among many quasi-religious groups such as spiritualists and theosophists. She coined the phrase "birth control." When prevented from mailing the journal, Sanger drafted a detailed birth-control pamphlet, *Family Limitation*, and got IWW member Bill Shatoff to print one hundred thousand copies. She got a few hundred dollars to pay for it from a free-speech lawyer who administered a fund left by Edward Bond Foote (Sanger called him "A certain Dr. Foote," again illustrating her ignorance of the American birth-control tradition).[98] Sanger arranged that the *Family Limitation* pamphlets would be sent out by IWW comrades on receipt of a prearranged signal from her. She thought thereby to release the provocative information they contained after she was already in jail.[99] This would make an effective climax to her work, for *The Woman Rebel* was never able to print actual contraceptive information. The pamphlet not only recommended and explained a variety of contraceptive methods—douches, condoms, pessaries, sponges and vaginal suppositories—but even gave a suggestion for an abortifacient. While promising that birth control would make abortion unnecessary, she nevertheless defended women's rights to abortion, something she was never to do at any later time. In this period her attitude toward sexual issues was consistent with her general militance. Still using IWW anarcho-syndicalist rhetoric, she wrote in the pamphlet, "The working class can use direct action by refusing to supply the market with children to be exploited, by refusing to populate the earth with slaves." [100]

But when her case came to trial, Sanger changed her strategy. Fearing that she would lose publicity because of the dominance of war news, and perhaps also that juries would be unsympathetic at this time, she decided to flee and went via Canada to London under an assumed name.[101] In the United States the illegal pamphlets were mailed out as she had planned. With them went a letter asking that the pamphlets be passed on to "poor working men and women who are overburdened with large families. . . . Thousands of women in the cotton states bearing twelve to sixteen children request me to send them this pamphlet. Thousands of women facing the tortures of abortion . . . Three hundred thousand mothers who lose their babies every year from poverty and neglect . . . Are the cries of these women to be stifled? Are the old archaic laws to be respected above motherhood, womanhood! The mothers of America answer no. The women of America answer no!" [102]

Sanger remained in Europe from October 1914 to October 1915. She spent that time researching the history, philosophy, technology, and practice of birth control, working in archives and libraries and visiting clinics and doctors in Holland, France, and England. Havelock Ellis directed and encouraged her work in a relationship made only more intense and nourishing to her because it was a love affair.[103] Ellis had sympathy for neither revolution nor the working class. His influence in diminishing Sanger's attraction to the revolutionary Left was communicated to her not only through his political views, but also through the life style and charm of the British Neo-Malthusians she met through him.[104] (In Britain the sex radicals did not have connections with a revolutionary, class-conscious Left.) After she returned she herself never resumed the consistently revolutionary posture she had held until 1914. In this second trip to Europe, the basic outlines of Sanger's entire future work took shape. She became committed unwaveringly to birth control as a single issue. She would offer feminist or pro-working-class arguments for birth control when they were helpful, along with many other arguments, but she never again saw her identity as mainly within a socialist, or even a generally radical, movement. For all its rhetoric, *The Woman Rebel* had already been a step away from the radical community.

Her reputed radicalism hereafter became more specifically the sex radicalism she learned from Ellis and his circle. But this radicalism was not the hedonistic sex-for-enjoyment ideology of the mid-twentieth century. Sanger's sexual views always remained within the romantic school of thought that had reached her from the European sex radicals and American free lovers. Her orientation was always to treat sexual activity as a form of communication, expressing love through extrasensory impulses. In their desire to rescue sexuality from its degraded reputation under the reign of prudery, Sanger and the sex radicals, better called sex romantics, virtually reversed the Victorian view of sexuality: from an animal passion it became a spiritual one, at least potentially. There were degrees of the development of one's sexual nature which presumably were determined by more than technical expertise. The stages of development represented depth of communication and emotional intensity which in turn reflected men's consideration of women. (This consideration was necessary because Sanger did not argue for women's equal assertiveness in sexual encounters.) In Sanger's own sex manual, published in 1926, she entitled intercourse "sex communion," the use of a religious term revealing her tendency to spiritualize the sexual act. "At the flight, body, mind and soul are brought together into the closest unity. 'No more are they twain, but one flesh,' in the words of the Bible."

> . . . sex-communion should be considered as a true union of souls, not merely a physical function for the momentary relief of the sexual organs. Unless the psychic and spiritual desires are fulfilled, the relationship has been woefully deficient and the participants

degraded and dissatisfied. . . . the sexual embrace not only satisfies but elevates both participants. The physical demands are harnessed for the expression of love.[105]

Sanger's work in sex education helped to alleviate the guilt of married couples and to give women an ideology with which to encourage—but hardly to demand—that men be considerate and proceed more slowly. But this sex education could hardly be considered radical in that it did nothing to challenge the conventional Victorian structure of sex relations, which were confined to the nuclear family and rested on male assertiveness and female passivity.

Furthermore Sanger's politics did not tend toward a socialist, and certainly not toward a Marxist, feminism but rather toward a mystique about womanliness, the successor to nineteenth-century feminist notions of the moral superiority of women (a precursor of what is known as "radical feminism" in the 1970s). Sanger believed in the "feminine spirit," the motive power of woman's nature. It was this spirit, coming from within, rather than social relations that drove women to revolt.[106] She often thought of women as fundamentally different from men. She wanted to help poor women but had no particular commitment to the working class as a class, not even to its female half, let alone its male; she simply did not see class relations, the relations of production, as fundamental to women's problems.

If any leader could have drawn Socialist party and feminist support together behind birth control, Sanger was not the one. Of course, Sanger's relative social and sexual conservatism greatly contributed to the acceptance of birth control as a specific reform. Similarly, her narrow focus and single-mindedness contributed to its legalization. But in 1914 neither the ultimate dominance of this conservative, single-issue approach nor the central role of Sanger was yet evident.

Before Sanger returned to the country, a spontaneous and decentralized movement of birth-control agitation and organization appeared in the Eastern, Midwestern and Western United States. It was stimulated by the news of Sanger's indictment, which was carried in newspapers through the country, in such distant places as Pittsfield, Massachusetts, and Reno, Nevada. Some newspapers described Sanger as an IWW editor. Local socialist groups were distributing Sanger's and other birth-control leaflets.[107] Local birth-control organizations were established in several places in 1915 long before Sanger's return to the United States and her first speaking tour.[108]

Two kinds of political groups were primarily responsible for the birth-control agitation in 1915: women's Socialist-party groups and IWW locals. In many places people had been introduced by Emma Goldman to Sanger's pamphlet, Sanger's name, and sometimes *The Woman Rebel*, just as later Goldman was to raise money for Sanger's defense on her speaking tours.[109] Elizabeth Gurley Flynn spoke about birth control in the Northwest and pledged local IWW and other anarchist support if Sanger would go on a speaking tour there.[110] Socialists saw Sanger, or adopted her, as one of their own and flooded her with letters of support and, inevitably, advice. Eugene Debs was one of the first to write and promised her the support of a "pretty good-sized bunch of revolutionists." [111] Goldman, in her motherly way, wanted to take Sanger under her wing, not only recommending a tactical plan for Sanger's trial but suggesting, "Hold out until I come back the 23rd of this month. Then go away with me for 2 weeks to Lakewood or some place . . . we'd both gain much and I would help you find yourself. . . ." [112] Others like Kate Richards O'Hare, Rose Pastor Stokes, Georgia Kotsch, Caroline Nelson, Rockwell Kent, Alexander Berkman, William J. Robinson, Jessie Ashley, and many lesser-known socialist organizers sent her messages of support and spoke on her behalf.[113] Liberals supported her too: for example, *The New Republic* published several editorials in her favor after March 1915.[114] In May 1915 birth-control supporters held a large meeting at the New York Academy of Medicine, urging public birth-control clinics. Many liberals spoke there.[115] But in March 1915, when a primarily liberal group organized the National Birth Control League (despite its name, the NBCL was never more than a New York City group), they would not support Sanger or any law-defying tactics. (They also excluded Goldman and other radicals.)[116] To the end of 1915 at least, those who supported Sanger and did local birth-control organizing everywhere except New York City were socialists.

In September 1915 William Sanger, Margaret's estranged husband, was tried for distributing her *Family Limitation* pamphlet. (He had been entrapped by a Post Office agent who requested a pamphlet.)[117] Sanger was convicted in a dramatic trial in which he defended himself. The trial was dominated by radicals, who shouted at the judge until he ordered the police to clear the courtroom. Messages of support came from various parts of the country. From Portland, Oregon, a strong IWW city that was a veritable hotbed of birth-control fervor, came a handwritten petition:

> 1. A woman has the right to control her own body even to the extent of deciding when she will become a mother.
> 2. Unwelcome or unfit children ought not to be born into the world.
> 3. Motherhood is dignified and noble only when it is desired and a joy. . . .
> 4. Scientific knowledge of sex-physiology can never be classified as impure or obscene. Those who do so classify it, proclaim only the impurity of their own minds.

The first signer added after his name: "The industrial system which needs children as food for powder or factories may desire unlimited propagation, but the masses who suffer in poverty have no right to add sufferers to the already too many competing for bread." [118] In these phrases were summarized fifty years of different birth-control arguments as they had reached the grass roots in the United States: women's rights, hereditarian social thought, social purity transformed by a faith in science and human dignity, and Neo-Malthusianism. It was such letters that made William Sanger believe his trial a great success, making "birth control a household word [sic]." [119] The responses that flowed in to the Sangers showed that the concept of birth control, if not the term, was already widely known and supported. It was as if people had been waiting for leadership to ask them for help.

Margaret Sanger came home from London soon after her husband's trial. Seeking support for the trial she faced, she found that her husband's confrontational conduct at his trial had aroused many strong opinions as to how she should conduct her trial. The flurry of letters offering to tell her how to run the trial emerged from gallant but male-chauvinist assumptions that she was in need of help. Most of her friends urged her not to follow her husband's example (pleading not guilty and acting as his own lawyer) but to plead guilty and use a lawyer.[120] Goldman, on the other hand, begged her to resist those counsels, branding that line of defense cowardly.[121] One of her medical "supporters" preached to her about her duty to her children.[122] Sanger stood firm in her plan to plead not guilty.

The differences among birth-control supporters over what Sanger's trial tactics should be repeated differences that had become evident within the organization of the NBCL. In that original split it seemed that Sanger herself belonged to the ultra-left faction identified with the IWW. But Sanger's own public-relations activities in the fall of 1915 were not ultra-left at all. She had a "distinguished-guests-only" dinner at the Brevoort Hotel and in her speech gave an apologia for her militant tactics, explaining that her methods had been unorthodox merely in order to secure publicity.[123] Instead of devoting time to preparing her defense, she worked on publicity; and the steady growth of public support for her led to the government's dismissing the charges against her on February 18, 1916.[124] On April 1 Sanger left for a three-and-a-half-month speaking tour across the country. By its conclusion she was nationally famous. Newspaper coverage of her speeches was copious and often enthusiastic. Her occasional misadventures were usually transformed into successes: refused halls in Akron and Chicago, arrested and jailed in Portland, Oregon, and locked out of her hall in St. Louis by Catholic Church pressure, she responded like a seasoned political campaigner, turning always from the defense to the offense. She turned birth control into a free-speech as well as a sexual-liberation issue and won support from important liberal civil libertarians.[125] She sought to establish effective coalitions of liberal and radical groups for birth control.

Still, the grass-roots work in organizing for birth control was being done by radicals. In Cleveland (the first major city to organize a birth-control group, and a place where the birth-control campaign was later to be especially successful),[126] workers' groups sponsored Sanger's tremendously successful speeches and led the birth-control movement. In St. Paul the Women's Socialist Club led the birth-control movement,[127] and in Ann Arbor, Agnes Inglis, a socialist activist, organized a group.[128] Even the relatively staid Massachusetts Birth Control League was led by socialists.[129] In small towns as well as big cities socialists were organizing for birth control.[130] And although Sanger varied her appeals to particular audiences, she made several sharp attacks on the conservatism of privileged groups. When the snobbish Chicago Women's Club cancelled her speaking engagement, she attacked it, saying she did not care to speak to a "sophisticated" audience anyway. "I want to talk to the women of the stock yards, the women of the factories—they are the victims of a system or lack of system that cries out for corrections. I am interested in birth control among working women chiefly." [131]

In 1916 birth control in the United States was a radical movement and a large movement. Birth control as a political demand had demonstrated an ability to involve not only educated but also working-class women in a participatory social movement. Elizabeth Gurley Flynn wrote to Sanger that she found everywhere in the country the "greatest possible interest" in birth control. ". . . one girl told me the women in the stockyards District [Chicago] kissed her hands when she distributed [Sanger's birth-control pamphlet]." [132] In 1913 in Tampa, Florida, Flynn had visited a cigar factory with Spanish-speaking workers where the reader* was reading aloud a pamphlet on birth control.[133] Letters from women all over the country came pouring in not only to Sanger but also to others who were identified in newspapers as birth-control activists, letters asking for contraceptive information and thanking them for the fight they were making. Often they were fearful: "I nearly had nervous prostration after I had mailed you my letter asking for that 'information' . . ." [134] Or: "Please send me one of your Papers on birth control, I have had seven children and cannot afford any more. Please don't give my name to the Papers." [135] Usually they poured out the difficulties of their lives, with their most intimate sexual problems and most externally caused economic problems intermingled—as they indeed always are in real life.

> I was married at the age of eighteen. Now I am married for seven years and I have four children. . . . I am a little over twenty-four and already skinny, yellow and so funny looking and I want to hold my husband's love. . . . He tried to help me but somehow I got caught anyway and a baby came. We didn't have any money to get rid of it and now when I look on her little innocent, red face I am glad I didn't kill it. . . . When you was in Chicago I wanted to go to see you but I had no nice clothes and I knew I would make you feel ashamed if I went dressed shabbily. . . .

* Cigar makers traditionally pooled their money to employ readers to entertain them as they worked.

> I have six children, am forty-one years old . . . have reason to
> believe my husband has a venereal disease. . . . To all of my
> pleadings my husband turns a deaf ear. He beats me, curses me and
> deserts us for weeks at a time when I refuse intercourse. . . . The
> place we call home is only a hovel. . . . I must live with him to get
> his support until my youngest children are older (youngest is
> eighteen months . . .) but to live with him I must indulge him
> sexually and whatever protection I get I must provide myself.[136]

Many of the letters expressed exasperation at the class injustice behind
the fact that they were deprived of birth control information. "Tell me
how it is the wealthier class of people can get information like that and
those that really need it, can't?" [137] And many others plunged immediately into political action, like Mrs. Lulu MacClure Clarke of St.
Louis, who wrote to Sanger:

> I have been through suffrage wrangles all my adult life, in back-
> woods communities and [among] the vicious of a city and I know
> how very chivalrous indeed men can be when any new freedom is
> asked for by women, and this is harder for them to swallow. . . . I
> cannot help financially, altho I would like to. We are just working
> people, but I am writing to various friends about it and tonight I
> mailed a letter to the Post-Dispatch of my city. . . . But even if
> women cant help much, don't know how to speak in public or write
> for the press, etc., yet they are awakening up all over the nation and
> waiting for someone to lead the way. I think—in fact, I know—
> there is a well-spring of gratitude to you—that they think you are
> fighting for them and they wait hoping and praying. . . . I am glad
> you have a husband who is a help and not a hindrance. Tell him I
> send him my heartiest goodwill and best wishes. If there is anything
> that you think I could do, please let me know. And oh, Please dont
> give up or get discouraged. . . .[138]

Direct Action

Not only was there a potentially large movement here, but its
people were ready for action. What they wanted personally, the
minimum demand, was to be given information in defiance of the law.
Beyond that, women in many places quickly moved to a strategy that
logically followed—opening illegal birth-control clinics to give that
illegal information to others. There was a practical reason for this: the

best contraceptive—a vaginal diaphragm—required a private fitting. Sanger was already convinced of the efficacy of "direct action." She gained support for this plan by what she learned on her national tour.[139] In many ways that tour was as much a learning experience for Sanger as a teaching one. In Ann Arbor, Michigan, socialist Agnes Inglis had a de facto clinic functioning before Sanger returned to New York.[140] In St. Paul socialist women announced plans for a clinic in June.[141] Sanger herself dreamed of a "glorious 'chain' of clinics" throughout the country.[142]

Returning to New York City in July 1916, Sanger organized a clinic of her own in the Brownsville section of Brooklyn. Brownsville was then a Jewish and Italian immigrant neighborhood, an extremely poor slum. Sanger worked with her sister Ethel Byrne, also a nurse, and Fania Mindell, whom Sanger had recruited in Chicago. The three women rented an apartment and gave out to every family in the district a handbill printed in English, Yiddish, and Italian. They were not prepared to fit women with contraceptives, but only to "give the principles of contraception, show a cervical pessary to the women, explain that if they had had two children they should have one size and if more a larger one." [143] Women were lined up outside when the clinic opened on October 16. As many Catholics came as Jews. Sanger asked one Catholic woman what she would say to the priest at confession. "It's none of his business," she answered. "My husband has a weak heart and works only four days a week. He gets twelve dollars, and we can barely live on it now. We have enough children." [144] Most of the neighbors were friendly and supportive. The baker gave them free doughnuts and the landlady brought them tea. By the end of nine days, the clinic had 464 case histories of women on file.[145]

Then, inevitably, one of the patients turned out to be a police-woman. She seemed prosperous; Fania Mindell suspected her but did not turn her away. The next day she returned as Officer Margaret Whitehurst, arrested the three women, and confiscated all the equipment and case histories. Tried separately, Ethel Byrne was sentenced to thirty days on Blackwell's Island. Byrne immediately announced her intention to go on a hunger strike. (The hunger strikes of British suffragists were at this time an international symbol of feminist resistance.) Like the British suffragists, she was force-fed by tubes through the nose; the combination of her starvation and the brutality of the force-feeding left her so weakened she required a year to recuperate.[146] At Sanger's trial women who had visited the clinic testified. Although legally they supported the prosecution, giving evidence that they had indeed received contraceptive advice without medical indication, politically they helped the birth-control cause by their clear testimonials to the misery of involuntary pregnancy.[147] Sanger also was sentenced to thirty days but conducted herself cooperatively. When she was released on March 6 her friends met her singing "The Marseillaise." [148]

Many activists were arrested and jailed for their birth-control activities—at least twenty besides Sanger on federal charges alone. Carlo Tresca, an Italian-American anarchist, was sentenced to a year and a day for advertising a book called L'Arte di non fare i figli ("The Art of Not Making Children") in his radical labor paper, Il Martello. (American Civil Liberties Union intervention got his sentence commuted after he served four months.)[149] Emma Goldman was also jailed for giving out contraceptive information. There was, of course, class injustice in arrest, convictions, and sentences. Jessie Ashley, Ida Rauh Eastman, Bolton Hall, and Rose Pastor Stokes gave out birth-control pamphlets publicly at mass meetings at Carnegie Hall; although Ashley, Eastman and Hall were arrested, Stokes—a millionaire's wife—was not.* [150] Carl Rave, an IWW longshoreman, was jailed in San Mateo, California, for three months for selling Sanger's Family Limitation. He complained that Professor Holmes of the University of California (probably a eugenist) proclaimed the need for compulsory birth control on the front page of the papers with impunity.[152] Others took risks as abortionists, though none was prosecuted on such charges. In addition to Dr. Konikow in Boston these included Dr. Marie Equi in Portland, Oregon, a lesbian who later served ten months in San Quentin for making an anticonscription speech during World War I.

---

* Stokes was upset about this discrimination in her favor. Ashley wrote, reassuring her: ". . . they think you *want* to be arrested and they are loath to increase the notoriety of the b.c. propaganda. They think your trial would be as widely advertised as Margaret Sanger's or Emma Goldman's. In any case it seems to me to the advantage of all of us to keep you out of jail. While you are free you can go about doing your work, and yours is now more effective than Ida Rauh's or mine. After all, everyone knows there *is* injustice and we don't have to demonstrate that, *that* is not what we are trying to accomplish. . . ." [151]

Police and prison guards were often hostile and violent to the birth-control prisoners, especially the women, for their advocacy of birth control seemed to violate every male fantasy about what women should be like. The detective arresting Agnes Smedley in 1918 told her that "he wished he had me in the south; that there 'I would be strung up to the first lamp post'; I would be lynched. I tried to tell him that he was on the wrong side of the trenches . . . ," Smedley recalled, but he only threatened her again.[153]

Legal persecution always promoted publicity but sometimes also produced concrete victories. Birth-control prisoners often propagandized their sister prisoners. Agnes Smedley wrote from the Tombs, "Kitty, Mollie Steiner, and I have wonderful meetings when we can dodge in some corner or hall. Kitty is turning the place into a birth-control branch. And she has held a meeting. And her friends are writing out demanding that their parents and friends vote Socialism!"[154]

Commitment to action was strong among these birth controllers. As socialists, most of them believed that working-class strength was the key to political progress, and thus they wanted above all to reach working-class people with their message and service. As feminists, they wanted to improve the position of women. They believed that the subjugation of women supported capitalism directly by creating profit, and indirectly by weakening the socialist movement: depriving it of half its potential constituency and allowing socialist men to cling to privileges that corrupted. All of them, even the non-Marxists, shared an interest in improving the lives of poor people in the present and did not try to fob them off with promises of postrevolutionary paradise. Their work in trying to reach working-class women was made more difficult by their own class origins. Most of the leadership of this movement was from professional, even capitalist, backgrounds. Their superior confidence and articulateness often made them better talkers than listeners. But their humanitarianism, their desire to eliminate material misery, was not a symptom of elitism. Indeed it was shared by those among them of "lower" origins—like Stokes, Goldman, Equi, and Sanger. It was also a conscious tactical choice, a rejection of the myth that greater misery makes workers more revolutionary.

Similarly, the plan to agitate among working-class people, particularly women, on an issue so private and so removed from production was a conscious tactical choice, one based on political experience. Sanger had been struck by the strongly positive reaction among socialist constituencies to her writing and speaking on sexual hygiene. Flynn and Bloor had worked with women, sometimes women who were not wage workers themselves but workers' wives, in many strike situations and had perceived the deep connections between family support and workers' militancy. Robinson had been receiving for over a decade the kind of personal letters that began flooding in to Sanger and the birth-control organizations after 1915—letters attesting to the mutually reinforcing nature of sexual, economic, and political helplessness. A systematic evaluation of five thousand such letters sent to Margaret Sanger after the publication of her *Woman and the New Race* in 1920 showed that they were overwhelmingly from working-class and poor women. The most common occupation given for husbands was "laborer," the most common salary fifteen dollars per week. One-third of the women were themselves wage-earners, as compared to the over-all national average of 23 per cent in 1920. Eighty per cent of the writers had married before the age of twenty, and averaged five children.[155] These organizers thought birth control could improve the economic situations and family stability of the poor and give women in particular more free choice and greater alternatives. Focusing on the connection between the sexual and economic oppression of working-class women was a strategy for organizing. Its goal was to create a significant women's force within a socialist movement.

Socialist feminist birth controllers in the prewar years developed educational propaganda that used birth control as a political issue. For example, Rose Pastor Stokes wrote a didactic script, "Shall the Parents [*sic*] Decide?" which tried to capture the revolutionary impact that birth control could have. In it a factory owner, who has already attacked birth control for its threat to deprive him of cheap labor, fires his worker, Mrs. Jones, for coming late. Mrs. Jones is burdened with many children to take care of and was late because of her grief over the death of one of her children! Helen, another worker in the plant, is incensed at the firing and organizes a wildcat strike to demand Jones's job back. The owner orders his friend the police chief to have Helen arrested, but Helen sneaks out her back door, with the help of her mother, because she is scheduled to speak at a birth control rally. Accidentally meeting the owner's mistress, Helen gives her emotional support when she is rejected and offers a political analysis of her unhappy position. When the factory owner tries to buy off his mistress with money, she gives it to Helen for her bail.[156] The themes of women's solidarity and women's sexual exploitation were both important in the writings of many of these early birth controllers. Sanger had written a short story in 1912, before her conversion to birth control, about a young nurse whose first employer tries to rape her. It concluded with a plea for working girls to stick together and defend one another.[157]

From their earliest efforts, however, these organizers learned that this task would not be easy. As early as June 1915 Caroline Nelson spelled out in a letter to Sanger the difficulties she had already encountered:

> It seems strange, but it is almost impossible to interest the workers in this. . . . So that our League here consists mostly of professional people. . . . I myself think that if the Leagues are ever to amount to anything, they must send trained nurses into the workers' districts, who speak the language of the district, whatever that may be. . . . I still hold that it would be beneficial to change the name. You know the workers are so afraid of being suspected of immorality, and they love the word—Moral—with an affection worthy of something better than it stands for today. That is why I cling to the name of—New Moral. After all, what we must do is to catch the worker's wife and daughter. . . . Dilettante Birth Control Leagues may help as the workers take their morals from the upper class, but they will not go far, they will not reach down to the bottom. . . . Yes, dear Margaret, this is the mere beginning of working women to do our work. The working men have gone around in a vicious circle, until today they are engaged in the very lawful occupation of killing each other, and where they are not killing each other they are running around begging for a job to feed their starved families. All this, after seventy-five years of revolutionary propaganda and scientific economy and academic discussion that the working woman had [no] interest in, chiefly because they were not practical, and did not touch her life, and the radical woman is chiefly an echo of the radical man, even in the sex question. . . .[158]

But Nelson's frank appraisal of the difficulties did not diminish her commitment. Indeed, her analysis led to the conclusion that there was no choice but to continue to fight for birth control, for she seemed convinced that unless women of the working class could be aroused to assuming some political leadership the entire cause of socialism would be doomed. Though not a feminist, Nelson had developed in her thinking from two years previously when she still saw birth control primarily in socialist Neo-Malthusian terms: the rich have birth control but try to keep it from the working class.[159] By 1915 she saw birth control not merely as an economic device but as fundamental to women's liberation. Thus like many other birth-control activists, though members of the Socialist party, she also looked to the woman-suffrage movement for approval and support of her work. Though they were successful to an extent—the first to be interested in birth control did indeed recruit from within the ranks of the Party and even of NAWSA—they also met with disapproval and even opposition from both sources.

Opposition and Setbacks

Conservative feminists and antifeminist socialists often disapproved of birth control, usually for very different reasons, occasionally for similar ones. Their common reasons probably expressed the deepest-rooted social fears regarding the implications of birth control.

Many conservative feminists were simply timid. In 1915 Sanger and Elsie Clews Parsons tried and failed to get fifty well-known women to state publicly that they believed in birth control and practiced it. "I was told to wait," Sanger said, "until we got the vote, I was told to wait until I became better known. . . ."[160] Frequently conservative feminists accepted race-suicide fears and worried about the dysgenic effects of birth control. Often they clung to the view that motherhood was a woman's vital source of dignity in a world that all too often denied it to her. In 1917 Anna May Wood, president of the D.C. Federation of Women's Clubs, said she opposed birth control because "Motherhood glorifies Womanhood and . . . any teaching that would tend to take from each woman the desire for motherhood is not ennobling the race."[161] Others thought contraception would

destroy the family. "Men no longer feel the 'urge' to marriage," wrote
Dr. Eliza Mosher, editor of the *Medical Woman's Journal*, in 1925.
"They can get on without wife and home and children, with much less
expense and with all sexual gratifications desired without untoward
consequences, and this largely through birth control education. . . .
contraceptives are carried about, even by some high school boys and
girls, just as they carry 'hip flasks.' . . ." [162] Conservative feminists,
especially older ones, feared sexual promiscuity. They feared it often
for women's sake, not on abstract moral grounds, believing that
marriage and monogamy were a woman's hard-won protection
against the merciless selfishness of men. They were in favor of the
voluntary-motherhood principle, of course, but suspicious of contraception. They clung to notions that the human race had become
oversexed, that sexual intercourse ought to be for reproduction, and
that too much sexual activity was physically and spiritually weakening. The characteristic nineteenth-century suspicion of sexual pleasure
itself shone through sometimes, as in this letter from California
feminist Alice Park. She had just finished reading a liberal sex book
recommended by Mary Ware Dennett of the Voluntary Parenthood
League (which succeeded the NBCL), and was furious:

> . . . of all the androcentric—inherited bias and self-opinionated
> pronouncements—this is the very top notch. Sex books are most of
> them in this class. But they do tend to move along from the dark
> ages to a degree. . . . I am always expecting a good one to be born.
> Intercourse every night and morning and sometimes noon—with
> satisfaction to both parties—PRAISED. Handling the clitoris—ad-
> vised. Intercourse to advanced years—hoped for—benefits recited.
> Intercourse in pregnancy—frequent—etc. Really I can't remember
> in Forel or any other author—even the much quoted Martin
> Luther—anything approaching this . . . it will certainly be liked
> by those whose wish is father to the thought of more and more
> intercourse until life would consist of nothing else.[163]

No doubt many older feminists shared these attitudes. But for
many their larger commitment to women's rights made them reluctant to reject the birth-control movement entirely. Park continued to
argue for inserting into some VPL literature that "intercourse may be
wisely and healthily limited." [164] Carrie Chapman Catt declined to

give her name as a sponsor to the American Birth Control League (Sanger's organization founded in 1921), but wanted to be sure that Sanger understood the ambivalence of her position:

> . . . please be assured that I am no opponent even though I do not stand by your side . . . in my judgement you claim too much as the result of one thing. Most reformers do that. Your reform is too narrow to appeal to me and too sordid. When the advocacy of contraception is combined with as strong a propaganda for continence (not to prevent conception but in the interest of common decency), it will find me a more willing sponsor. That is, a million years of male control over the sustenance of women has made them sex slaves, which has produced two results: an oversexualizing of women and an oversexualizing of men. . . . There will come some gains even from the program you advocate—and some increase in immorality through safety. The gains will slightly overtop the losses however, so I am no enemy of you and yours. . . .[165]

While Catt was repeating what Charlotte Perkins Gilman had written twenty years previously, Gilman herself was defending her views against new kinds of attacks—from the New Morality spokespeople. It is not "Puritanism," she wrote, to say that gluttony is unhealthy, in sex as in other indulgences. And she too was suspicious of contraception. "While men talk of sex, they mean only intercourse; for a woman it means the whole process of reproduction, love and mating." [166] Gilman continued to view the ideology of sexual freedom as merely a reorientation within the structures of male supremacy. What she had witnessed of the sexual revolution in practice, of the apparent insignificance of women's voting to change their over-all position, bore out her fears. She was not arguing that sexual "liberation" was an exploitive male conspiracy, but only that social power was indivisible, and unless it was shared among women and men in all areas, men would simply weave individual reforms into the fabric of sexism. Freud was popular, she charged, because he justified and legitimized man's "misuse of the female. . . . It was natural enough that the mind of man should evolve a philosophy of sex calculated to meet his desires. . . ." [167] Despite these fears Gilman could not, any more than Catt, reject the birth-control demand. For Gilman it was always the highest priority to increase the area of women's choice. As an old woman, in 1932, she testified before U.S. Congress hearings for

legalized birth control, and consistently spoke and wrote for legalization.[168] Her persistent fears of sexual permissiveness were founded not
on timidity but on an insightful assessment of the continuing general
suppression of women. What had changed in the society that made
these attitudes now seem a cranky, old-fashioned prudery?

The fact is that very little had changed. More women were in the
work force, receiving independent pay envelopes, but they were still
underpaid and forced into the worst jobs. They had won the vote, in
the middle of the birth-control agitation, just as many socialist-feminist women had concluded that it would give them little real power
anyway. What seems odd, in fact, is that so many feminists of
sexual-liberation persuasion had somehow imagined that the assertion
of female sexuality could erase deeply rooted male supremacy in the
culture and in the economy. Did they imagine that power relations
ceased to exist in beds, that men shed their culturally determined
attitudes and expectations at the bedroom door? Even the most
socialist of these birth controllers, those who well understood that
women's powerlessness was the product of a total economic and social
discrimination, failed to recognize the infiltration of sexism into sex
itself. They thought of the "risks" of sexual intercourse in terms of its
consequences: involuntary pregnancy, venereal disease, the physical
and economic dependency of pregnant women. They forgot the
"risks" of sexual intercourse itself. A classic argument of the nineteenth-century feminists had been that in marriage women sold themselves, as sexual as well as house servants, in return for security; and
that consequently the withholding of sexual favors was one of the few
powers that women had, a form of strike. The logic of sexual "liberation" made such withholding reprehensible, even selfish. The provision of good contraception often in fact made the situation even more
difficult for women, depriving them of an excuse for saying no. There
was nothing inherent in sexual "freedom" that challenged the double
standard, and in fact the double standard was easily adapted to allow
the manipulation of women in new ways.

The creation of sexual equality in heterosexual intercourse itself
will require literally generations of sex equality in practice and
education. Women's sexual objectification of themselves will not be
eradicated easily under the best of circumstances. The socialist-femin-

ist birth controllers of the second decade of this century would have readily admitted that they had barely scratched the surface toward uprooting male supremacy. The most likely explanation for this enormous inconsistency on the part of the birth controllers is that, like many vulgar Marxists before and after, they believed that involuntary pregnancy and sexual repression were not symptoms but causes of women's subjection. They did not understand that women's resistance as well as men's pressure had created the sexual and family system now being transformed, and that many women as well as men had cause to fear and regret that transformation. Carrie Chapman Catt was right—they claimed too much as the result of one thing. It is not necessary to accept Gilman's view that humanity had become over-sexed in order to question whether sexual reform alone could fundamentally change women's status.

Within the socialist movement, objections to birth control came from a different source. Many socialists found any concentration on women's problems dangerous because it deflected attention from the main issue of the class struggle: wage slavery. Although claiming that capitalism was the cause of the "sex problem"—by which they meant both sexual inequality and sexual immorality—many socialists nevertheless did not think that political agitation around sexual issues could effectively attack capitalism. After the revolution socialism would take care of these problems. Sanger complained that socialists were forever telling her to wait, just as the feminists had. " 'Wait until women have more education. Wait until we secure equal distribution of wealth.' Wait for this and wait for that. Wait! Wait! Wait!" [169] Antoinette Konikow challenged this attitude too: "Socialists cannot persist in sitting on the fence wisely and monotonously repeating: 'Socialism will change that.' They must go ahead and begin to shift things, ready for the change, or someone else will take their place in the onward movement of the world as far as the sex question is concerned." [170] But even Rose Pastor Stokes, who became a communist in the 1920s as Sanger became an increasingly conservative reformer, adopted the wait-until-the-revolution view after World War I. She wrote to Sanger in 1925:

> At this time, when the greatest of all wars is preparing, when the contending capitalist groups will need cannon-fodder as never

before in their destructive history, it is to my mind certain that no amount of agitation and earnest effort will force the desired [birth-control] legislation upon the capitalist governments.

It is my conviction that by working for the abolition of capitalism, for the establishment of Soviet Governments we bring nearer the triumph of the [birth-control] cause. . . . Those Soviet Governments would themselves hasten to pass B.C. legislation (as Russia is doing today) in the interests of the race and the mothers of the race.[171]

It was not merely that socialists did not care about women's liberation. Many socialists—leaders and rank and file—opposed the principles and goals of birth control. Although most supported the principle of voluntary motherhood, many believed that under socialism prosperity would make women willing to have as many children as came naturally. At the same time they supported the division of labor that made women solely responsible for child-raising and men solely responsible for production. In these views they were at one with the conservative feminists, who wanted to retain the "sacredness" of motherhood and who believed that industrialism was destroying it. The socialist version of this longing for an imaginary preindustrial family paradise was based on the Marxian tenet that capitalism and the bourgeoisie had destroyed the family. These socialists disavowed projects for communal living and other family alterations that would have freed women to leave their homes. As Victor Berger summarized this viewpoint, under socialism "women will not only be restored to the home, but enabled to *form* a home." [172]

Sanger complained about such views after a difficult confrontation with some Fresno socialist men: ". . . the fact that women shall not desire to be breeders under a Socialist Republic no more than she wants to be today is difficult for them to see. There is harder work to do among the 'dyed in the wool' radical than with the average person. He has Marxian blinders on his eyes and will not see." [173]

Some socialists also shared restrictive sexual attitudes with conservative feminists. The following extract from a letter to Rose Pastor Stokes in 1916, when she was a birth-control activist, from New York Party comrades is typical of that view:

. . . We have full confidence in your sincerity and devotion to the cause of freedom, but, Dear Comrade, we consider it a waste of time and energy on such a tomfullary as the B.C.L. venture. . . . We believe in one standard of morality, but, we are not willing to bring down the females to that low standard that men set, but we do want to help pull the men to the women's standard, but, again the B.C.L. propaganda can not and will not do. You know or you ought to know that, the generative organs as well as any other organ of the human body has its own particular function to perform, and that of the generative organ in particular is for perpetuation, and nothing else. . . . We hold . . . that the desire of sexual interrelation is the unconscious desire for "parenthood and perpetuation," and rather than destroy the fruit of that unconscious desire, it would be more expedient to deny one self that very desire.[174]

When Sanger published her sexual-hygiene articles in the *New York Call*, many readers protested. "I for one condemn the idea where a mother should show through the columns of a newspaper her nakedness to her children," Mrs. L.B. of Greenpoint, Brooklyn, wrote.[175] Caroline Nelson had met these attitudes since 1915:

. . . while they want to get the information in secret, they cannot discuss it in public without giggling and blushing and this holds good to our very learned radical men, or at least some of them. . . . I must say with great shame to our labor editors that the capitalist editors in many instances have been much more liberal and sensible on this question than they have, which shows that our class is not yet out of the woods of gullibility with its sewage minds, and sewage minds are not clear instruments of thinking.[176]

These antisexual attitudes were hard to separate from outright male chauvinism. Most socialists were not prepared to acknowledge the existence of male supremacy within the working class. They often disguised their defense of male privilege with criticisms of population control as a capitalist plot. One typical letter argued:

Will you kindly question yourself and see that it is better to relieve the poor than to bring more destruction. Naturally we all-appreciate the fact that we would be free from having children, but it only brings a more adulterious generation and gives married women a freedom to wander more into the sin of the world.[177]

Some socialist leaders opposed birth-control propaganda because they hoped that eschewing sexual radicalism would make their economic radicalism more palatable. That is, socialist economics combined with defense of family, home, and motherhood would presumably make a wider appeal to the American public. Here again, socialist tactical thinking was not so different from that of the suffragists, who also wished to avoid association with antifamily doctrines. Both socialism and suffragism had been charged with advocating free love in the late nineteenth and early twentieth centuries; both socialism and suffragism had defended themselves by condemning free love.[178]

The free-love charge was a constant thorn to the birth controllers. Margaret Sanger was frequently accused of free loveism, and always denied it.[179] The origins of birth control as a women's movement *were* in free love. Some socialists not only recognized this but thought it best to accept that legacy, trying perhaps to redefine it. Those who took this view were inclined to the perception that youth involved in sexual rebellion might be an important socialist constituency.[180] Others believed that refusing to face the necessity for fundamental change in family and sexual norms would ultimately betray the interests of women. Josephine Conger-Kaneko of the Socialist party argued that women and the whole Party had to give up "bourgeois respectability" in order to make a thoroughgoing women's rights struggle.[181]

But most Socialist-party people feared being forced back into isolation by attacks from the Right branding them as immoral. They felt this danger because changes in sexual behavior had made free love a real threat. Because the sexual revolution meant increased sexual activity among women, many men stood to lose from it. It threatened to rob them not only of the pleasures of exclusive privilege, but of the security of women's dependency on marriage.

Birth control was an easy focus for all this fear of sexual change. The attack was strong enough to prevent birth control from becoming an official program of either the Socialist party or any national women's rights organization.

At the same time other factors caused a rapid diminution of the power of socialist and women's rights movements. This political shift affected the future course of birth control greatly. The decline of women's rights movement was probably hastened by its one victory— the woman suffrage amendment to the Constitution. The National American Woman Suffrage Association had mobilized a powerful lobby, its work orchestrated by an excellent politician, Carrie Chapman Catt, and focused on the single issue, suffrage. But the narrowing focus of women's rights had weakened the movement. Large social changes created a distinctly antifeminist mood among the American middle classes in the 1920s. The sexual revolution itself was partly responsible in that the increased sexual orientation of women made political activity seem even more unacceptable than usual to many of them. Greatly expanded commodity production and advertising industries appealed to women as consumers in two roles primarily—housewives and beauty objects—thus contributing to make other activities seem uncomfortable to women. The false ideology of prosperity added to the unfashionableness of appearing discontented. Within the remnant women's organizations, the controversy over an equal-rights amendment to the Constitution (first introduced in Congress in 1923) ended by pushing feminism even further into a minority corner, as the majority of socially concerned women opposed the equal-rights amendment for fear of jeopardizing protective labor legislation for women. A false dichotomy was set up which opposed feminism to progressive labor reform.

Organized feminism was also weakened by repression of socialism which began with the First World War. So virulent was the patriotic hysteria that any views critical of American society appeared disloyal; in this regard feminists were only slightly better than socialists. Many feminists and some socialists supported the war, but this did not help the reputation of their causes, especially since some feminists and socialists were outspoken critics of the war. The patriotism led to jingoism, not only against Germans but to some extent against all non-Wasp immigrants. Many radicals, including Goldman, were deported. Dr. Robinson, a pacifist, was ostracized in his profession. Dr. Equi was jailed. There were also many local persecutions and even lynchings of antiwar radicals. Calculating men of power, long anxious for a tool to check the increasing strength of their class enemies, stimulated and guided antiradical hysteria to a systematic and effective attack on socialist leaders and organizations.

Under attack the socialist movement could not respond effectively because it was split between pro-war and antiwar politics. After November 1917 another division—regarding attitudes toward the Russian Revolution—rapidly led to a final split. Furthermore, the

Russian Revolution and Civil War helped antisocialists brand socialist ideas as alien and violent.

Thus two separate factors pushed the birth-control movement away from the organized Left—the attacks on birth control by socialists and feminists and the independent decline of socialism and feminism.* These two factors together forced the birth-control movement to assume the form of independent organizations, local and national. That independence meant that even though large numbers of socialists and feminists were committed to birth control, they were unable to bring with them into the movement the benefits of the large world view and broad constituency of their movements of origin. Organizational connections with such groups as the Socialist party, the IWW, NAWSA, the Women's Party, the socialist suffrage leagues, and the WTUL could have brought political experience and discipline into the birth-control movement. Organizational estrangement from such groups and their constituencies made the task of creating a socialist-feminist politics in the birth-control movement extremely difficult. Birth control as an issue presented problems new to socialist and feminist organizers. It required efforts to change the law, efforts to seek favorable court rulings, tactics of breaking the law, and above all the means to provide services—birth-control information and devices. Outside of utopian communities and ill-fated workers' cooperatives, the American Left had had little experience with the provision of services through counterinstitutions like birth-control clinics. Fundamentally, birth-control advocates were confused and ambivalent about whether they felt that the practice of birth control or the illegal agitation for birth control was the factor that would do most to change the society; they therefore had difficulty setting their own priorities for political action.

* Perhaps that decline was not so independent; perhaps had the socialist and feminist organizations taken more supportive positions toward birth control, they would have been rewarded with the increased allegiance of neglected but large constituencies, particularly women and young people. But these are mere speculations.

Part III

From Women's Rights to Family Planning

10
The Professionalization of Birth Control

THE SOCIALISTS and sex radicals who began the birth-control movement before the First World War were amateurs. With few exceptions, mostly men, they had no professional or socially recognized expertise in sexology, public health, demography, or any related fields. (If they were professionals at anything, it was radical agitation!) They fought for birth control because it was self-evidently in their own interest as women. The intellectual work that had influenced them most in their birth-control views was philosophy, radical ethics sometimes grounded in political appraisals of social problems. Birth control was, for them, pre-eminently a political and moral issue.

But after the war, the birth-control movement changed. The local birth-control leagues with radical and socialist leadership lost their momentum. Birth control became an increasingly centralized cause, dominated from New York City by Sanger's American Birth Control League and Dennett's Voluntary Parenthood League. The strategies that dominated—opening clinics and lobbying for legislation—required large sums of money, and the power of the wealthy in the organizations increased accordingly. People accustomed to working in respectable, even elegant, charity organizations joined the movement. Birth-control leagues began to sponsor balls and expensive white-tie dinners. Simultaneously the weakening of the organized Left deprived the birth-control movement of leadership that might have created alternative tactics and strategies. Respectable legal tactics produced different results from militant law-defying ones. The latter attracted radicals and angry, poor people; the former attracted more prosperous people, those eager for reform but not desperately in need of fundamental social change. It was not always possible for more conservative reformers to forgive birth control's early associations with bohemianism, radicalism, and illegality. In efforts to break those associations, birth-control organizers in the 1920s often condemned and publicly disassociated themselves from radicals.

The main factor behind this new conservatism of the birth-control movement was the entrance of professionals into the cause on a large scale. Professionalization was not the only important development in the birth-control cause in the 1920s, but it was the single most influential one. The professionals took over birth-control groups less often by driving out the radicals (though this did happen in a few places), than by joining a cause that radicals had deserted. For most socialists, the war itself, then the Russian Revolution and the defense of the American Left against repression seemed more pressing issues from 1918 on.

The reason the radicals thought it politically correct to change their causes so quickly was that most of them had seen birth control as a reform issue rather than a revolutionary demand, something requiring less than fundamental change in the society. The tendency to distinguish between fundamental and superficial change, between revolution and reform, was characteristic of those influenced by a Marxist analysis of society. These Marxists argued that certain aspects of social reality determined others, and the prevalent Marxist interpretation had placed matters of sexual and reproductive relations in the "superstructure," among other cultural phenomena determined ultimately by the "base" (economic relations). In the postwar development of Marxism, rejection of the absolute distinction between "base" and "superstructure" has been an important theme. Contemporary Marxist feminism is reviving that critique of "vulgar," simplistic

Marxism. In the World War I reform era it was already clear to many feminists that changes in sexual and reproduction patterns would produce far-reaching changes in daily life, class consciousness, and even class composition that could not be dismissed as "superstructure" and therefore not primary or urgent. But they could not, in that historical era, integrate this into a Marxism that then saw the world exclusively through the eyes of men.

Thus it was partly due to the flatness of the existing Marxism that many feminists were attracted to liberal reformers, who perceived birth control as fundamental. Doctors saw it as a health measure, and naturally doctors viewed human health as a fundamental, not a superficial, condition of social progress. Eugenists' hereditarian views led them to consider reproduction the fundamental condition of social progress. Therefore, members of both groups, once converted to the birth-control cause, devoted themselves to it with passion and perseverance.

Professionals entering the birth-control movement brought with them a unique self-image and consciousness that made their reform work an integral part of their careers. They believed, by and large, that they worked not only to earn a living but simultaneously to help humanity and improve society. Since they saw the content of their work as important, and were not merely concerned with earning wages, they viewed their paid work and their volunteer activities as a unified whole. Clearly, such a view is made possible by the opportunity professionals have to do creative, self-directed work. There is no mystery about the relative absence of this consciousness among working-class people or businessmen. The professional attitude toward work is largely dependent on not being paid by the hour and, for higher professionals, the opportunity to determine their own work schedules. Furthermore, many of the professionals active in birth control—particularly doctors—were not wage workers at all, but self-employed. For both kinds of professionals—employed and self-employed—participation in reform activities, if respectable enough, could add to their prestige.

The desire to make a contribution to civilization led many professionals to go beyond their places of employment to seek wider social influence. For many professionals, seeking political influence seemed a contribution, not an indulgence, because they believed society needed them. Especially in the early twentieth century many professionals believed that their superior intelligence and education entitled them to a larger share of political leadership than their numbers in the population would automatically create in a democracy. Their ideal society was meritocratic. Edward L. Thorndike, a eugenist-educator, wrote in 1920, "The argument for democracy is not that it gives power to men without distinction, but that it gives greater freedom for ability and character to attain power." [1] Henry Goddard, who introduced the intelligence test to the United States, thought that democracy was "a method for arriving at a truly benevolent aristocracy." [2]

Behind this politics was, first of all, the assumption that superior intelligence and education were coincident with superior political virtue. Professional psychologists in the 1920s were engaged in developing intelligence tests, and the bias of these tests was consistently hereditarian and meritocratic: they measured ability to solve the kinds of problems urban professionals met with the kinds of solutions urban professionals would approve. Indeed, the Stanford-Binet test, for years the standard, classified intelligence in terms of what was "required" for five occupational groupings, the professions considered the highest. (The others were semiprofessional work, skilled labor, semiskilled labor, and unskilled labor, in descending order.) [3]

Professionals did not assume that intellectual superiority came entirely from innate ability. On the contrary, they perceived that rigorous training in intellectual discipline, general knowledge, and tested methodologies had given them skills unavailable to the masses. They did not see their monopolization of this expertise and knowledge as special privilege because they were committed to equal opportunity. They did not usually perceive the effective social and economic barriers that kept most people from these opportunities. But they never doubted that their expertise and knowledge were useful guides for social policy. They did not hesitate to build professional organizations, institutions, and programs of self-licensing which excluded others from their privilege and influence, because they had confidence in the universality, objectivity, and social value of the expertise they possessed.

The original social basis for the professionals' confidence in their objective dedication to rationality and expertise had been their economic independence. Most professions had traditionally been independent, selling services, not hourly labor. By the twentieth century the professionals' sense of themselves as independent and therefore loyal only to self-defined standards of truth was a mystique held over from a previous era and was no longer supported by reality. The professionals of the 1920s were literally a different class from the professionals of a century before. Not only was a decreasing proportion of them self-employed (by 1940 only 16 per cent),[4] but all of them were increasingly dependent on funds, research direction, and political priorities set by the capitalist class through its corporate foundations and its influence on government. Their antibusiness values sometimes made professionals identify with the highest, and despise the lowest, strata of capitalists. Through the progressive movement, in fact, professionals, often provided the agency and the justification for the transfer of political power from local small capitalists to professional representatives of national capitalists. In the 1920s they helped transform the birth-control movement in the same way, from a popular radical cause to a reform that operated to stabilize, rationalize, and centralize corporate social planning.

In the birth-control movement professionals sought to solve by objective study what had previously been ethical and political questions. In order to lend their support or even their names to a cause, they needed to be satisfied that it was honest, its strategies careful, and its tactics appropriate to their dignity. They distrusted leaders who did not share their own values, skills, and social status. Their influence transformed birth-control leagues from participatory, membership associations into staff organizations.

Had the professionals merely changed the structure and methods of the birth-control movement, their influence could not have worked. Structure and methods in social movements cannot be separated from goals. Despite their posture as reformers who sought changes for the benefit of the whole society, or for the less fortunate in it, in fact professional men brought to the birth-control movement their own political beliefs and social needs. Molded by different training and practice but also by class origin and individual experiences, these beliefs were by no means identical among professionals, even within one profession. But leading professionals shared a common set of values, with meritocracy at its root. The professionals of the 1920s believed that some individuals were more valuable to the society than others. Whether environmentalists or hereditarians or both, they doubted that superior individuals were equally distributed within all classes and ethnic groups and believed that scientific study could determine where talent was most likely to occur. Birth control appealed to them as a means of lowering birth rates *selectively* among those groups less likely to produce babies of great merit.

Professionals also saw themselves as social benefactors, eager not just to legalize birth control for themselves and their wives, but also to install it as social policy. Their commitment to individual liberty was tempered by their recognition that some people were wiser than others, that good social policy would not necessarily result from allowing each individual to make private decisions about such matters as birth control. Furthermore, many professionals (doctors, social workers, clergymen, educators, and psychologists, for example) were placed by their jobs in positions where they could influence others. Accepting meritocratic political views, they naturally taught them to others.

Many saw some of their clients as part of the problem. Such a view strongly influenced the relationship of many doctors to women patients, of social workers to clients, of ministers to their congregation. Eugenists particularly, with their analysis of social problems as hereditary, tended to see people as the problem. Their view was sharply distinguished from a more democratic view that saw people as *having* problems many of which were caused by social inequality; professionals often preferred to solve problems by checking the autonomy of individuals in the interest of what they saw as wise social policy. Thus for example many doctors were willing to prescribe contraceptives for individual women whom they judged to be justified in limiting conceptions, while opposing the general legalization of birth control. The professional's tendency was to trust his own judgment, even about others' lives. They not only disapproved of but feared a democracy that meant that all individuals, despite their educational or intellectual qualifications, would have equal power in the society; they genuinely feared the unfortunate political decisions that might result. Goddard wrote in 1920: "The disturbing fear is that the masses—the seventy or even eighty-six million—will take matters into their own hands." Rather they should be directed by the four million of superior intelligence.[5] This self-conscious elitism reflected not only fear but also an effort to reassure themselves of their differences from the "masses." Indeed, professional reformers usually yearned for more influence and bemoaned the fact that they were not listened to. Their sense of the necessity of their controlling the policies of a movement such as birth control came both from their sense of superior worth and their suspicion that they were ignored.

These values were not usually duplicated among the wives of professionals. Although they shared the class prestige and status of their husbands, they did not generally see themselves as contributing expertise to the birth-control or any other social movement. They were essentially amateurs. The college education that most of them received did not automatically lead to a career but gave them skills and self-confidence which they applied to running local and national birth-control organizations. The minority of women who were practicing professionals shared, of course, many of the attitudes of their male peers—sometimes more strongly because their sense of personal uniqueness and therefore merit was greater, sometimes more tentatively because of their identification with other women and their inferior status in their professions. But on the whole the professionalization of the birth-control movement produced a division of labor along sexual as well as class lines. The "amateurs," almost all women, became the staff and organizers of the birth-control groups; the professionals, almost all men, functioned as directors and consultants, influencing policy without sharing in the actual organizational work.

Other professionals also joined and influenced the birth-control campaign. Two other important groups were clergymen and social workers. Among Protestants and Jews a growing revisionism—anti-Fundamentalist or Reform in orientation—allowed many religious leaders to accept reform solutions to social problems and to view moral decisions as individual matters. Churches with prosperous congregations most frequently endorsed birth control,[6] because of both the more professional orientation of their ministers and the attitudes of their members. Perhaps the most common theme among pro-birth-control religious leaders was concern for the health of the family. In their role as counselors, ministers, and rabbis they were aware of growing family instability. In clerical acceptance of freer sexuality and contraception, a key factor was the theory that sexual repression was a cause of that instability. Without challenging conventional sex roles, churchmen began to emphasize, even romanticize the importance of good sexual relations within marriage.[7] They altered the nineteenth-century religious antisexual view by, as historian David Kennedy put it, "understanding . . . sex as an instrumentality for the preservation of marriage." But these pro-birth-control ecclesiastics were a minority, though prestigious. The winning-over of organized religion was not fully accomplished for several decades.[8] The Catholic Church meanwhile remained firm in its opposition to contraception.[9] Direct exposure to the acute problems of poor women also drew social workers to birth control, as, for example, Alice Hamilton, who "discovered" it while working at Hull House (a settlement house established by Jane Addams in Chicago).[10] But as a group social workers were converted to birth control only slowly in the 1920s. In general after about 1910 social workers were distancing themselves from overt political involvement. On Sanger's national tour in 1916, the Hull House staff told her they were "not interested." (She in turn denounced "charitable institutions" for using "well-intentioned palliatives," like quack doctors "treating a cancer by burning off the top" while disease spreads underneath.)[11] When the Women's Trade Union League brought other reformers into support of women's strikes, social workers remained aloof. In order to win the prestige that had been denied them because of their traditional amateur status and domination by the female sex, social workers in the 1920s were seeking professional organization and respectability.[12] Sanger and the ABCL actively sought social workers' support, and did win some influential supporters and semisupporters, such as Julia Lathrop, president of the National Conference of Social Work.[13] But in large part it was to require the drastic problems of the Depression to win over the profession as a whole.

Two groups of professionals had a particularly great influence on the 1920s birth-control movement: doctors and eugenists. The latter group did not make up, of course, a professional occupation in itself, although private foundations began in the 1920s to make it possible for an increasing number of scholars to work full time on eugenic research. The eugenists were largely university academics in various fields—genetics, demography, economics, psychology, and sociology in particular. Scholarly eugenic organizations, however, brought them together and gave them a collective consciousness as strong as that among doctors.

The leadership of Margaret Sanger was an important factor in facilitating, even encouraging, the professionalization of the birth-control movement. Despite a tactical radicalism, which she learned from and shared with other socialists, Sanger's approach to birth control was distinguished by her willingness to make it her full-time, single cause. From her return from Europe to face trial for _The Woman Rebel_ in 1915, until her trial for the illegal Brownsville clinic in 1917, an ambivalent political posture helped her to retain the support of many disparate political groups. She simultaneously pursued direct action and defiance of the law and, with a "low profile" on her radical ideas, organized financial and public-relations support from conservative and wealthy reformers. At the same time Sanger was preparing an organizational structure to give her ongoing power.

In the fall of 1916—even while she had been working on the Brownsville clinic—she founded the _Birth Control Review_. She recruited Frederick Blossom, a professional charity fund-raiser from Cleveland, to come to New York as its paid editor and manager.[14] In December she founded the New York Birth Control League (NYBCL) as an alternative to the National Birth Control League (NBCL), organized by Mary Ware Dennett, and Blossom also worked for Sanger's organization. An ugly disagreement and then split between Sanger and Blossom exploded in 1917. Whoever was in the right—and it seems likely both of them acted badly—the quarrel demonstrated Sanger's rigid need for personal control and separated her still further from the radical movement. Blossom quit when he could not have his way and took the records and small bank account of the _Review_. Sanger brought formal charges against him. Blossom had been a member of the Socialist party, and other socialists in the NYBCL were infuriated at Sanger's turning to the capitalist state to solve her quarrel; they formed an investigation committee which condemned Sanger and exonerated Blossom. Ironically, Blossom's subsequent behavior led the IWW to conduct another investigation in 1922 which condemned him for the break with Sanger.[15]

Whatever the actual issues involved, Sanger did not quail before the disapproval of her former socialist comrades. Ironically, some of them had defended Sanger's need for personal control on the grounds that she was trying to create a movement with radical politics. Dennett's NBCL had always excluded people identified with the far Left and avoided radical tactics like civil disobedience, and Sanger's radical reputation had arisen partly in being distinguished from Dennett. But even before the break with Blossom and his socialist supporters, Sanger had begun to move in another equally conservative direction, though it was not widely perceived as such at the time.

From the beginning of planning for her Brownsville clinic she had sought a doctor to prescribe and fit contraceptives. New York state law at the time would have permitted her to legalize the clinic by putting it under a physician's supervision, and this was an important part of her motivation. Section 1142 of the New York State Penal Code made it a misdemeanor to give out any contraceptive information, but section 1145 allowed lawfully practicing physicians to prescribe devices for the cure and prevention of disease. Sanger believed that this provision intended to allow only the prescription of prophylactic measures against venereal disease, and wanted to challenge and broaden its interpretation. But Sanger's conviction that contraception required the attendance of a physician was based on a belief deeper than mere legal tactics. Since she was a nurse herself, it seems odd that she should have doubted that a nurse could fit a diaphragm as well as a doctor. Her earliest medical tutor, Dr. Johannes Rutgers of Holland, had taught her to fit a diaphragm; she herself fitted some of his patients while in The Hague. While she was there, Rutgers was training midwives in contraceptive technique so that they could start birth-control clinics elsewhere.[16] Nevertheless, Sanger argued to the end of her career—even after laws no longer stood in her way—that every applicant for birth control should see a doctor. After the forcible closure of the clinic, Sanger quickly returned to the search for medical support for her work. As early as January 11, 1917, a year before

Sanger was brought to trial for the Brownsville Clinic, her New York Birth Control League was urging modification of the laws to permit physicians only to give out birth-control information.[17] Dennett's NBCL, with its more respectable image, was nevertheless fighting for a more thoroughgoing legislative reform—a bill simply removing birth control from any definition of obscenity.

Margaret Sanger's leadership was particularly responsible for making birth control a medical issue in the United States. In the 1920s she also courted recognition and support from another group of professionals—the demographers, geneticists, and other academics who led the eugenics movement. But in promoting professionals to increasing importance in the birth-control movement, Sanger just helped along a trend that would have happened without her. She was not responsible for the decline of the feminist movement, although her individualist and dominating style of working did not help to build solidarity with surviving feminist groups. She was not responsible for the repression, division, and shrinking of the socialist movement; her opportunist alliances with antisocialists and conservatives for the cause of birth control were partly necessitated by the refusal of male-domi-nated socialism to incorporate birth-control and women's liberation issues into their programs. All these factors plus the economic weaken-ing of the working class created a political power vacuum where the socialists had been. Sanger did not wish to give up her birth-control campaign, nor could she fill that vacuum by herself; she had to find support. Sanger has often been criticized for her urge to dominate and her liking for power, weaknesses she clearly had. But not even she had the personal influence to substitute for a movement, or to articulate the needs of masses of American women when the masses were silent and depoliticized.

Doctors

Despite the efforts made by pro-birth-control doctors in attacking sexual continence, most physicians remained opposed to contraception in the early 1920s. The predominant position among prestigious doctors was not merely disapproval but revulsion so hysterical that it prevented them from accepting facts. As late as 1925 Morris Fishbein, editor of the *Journal of the American Medical Association*, asserted that there were no safe and effective birth-control methods.[18] In 1926 Frederick McCann wrote that birth control had an insidious influence on the female, causing many ailments; and that although "biology teaches" that the primary purpose of the sexual act is to reproduce, the seminal fluid also has a necessary and healthful effect on the female.[19] Many doctors believed that they had a social and moral responsibility to fight the social degeneration that birth control represented. The social values underlying their opposition were often extremely conservative. ". . . fear of conception has been an important factor in the virtue of many unmarried girls, and . . . many boys are likewise kept straight by this means. . . . the freedom with which this matter is now discussed . . . must have an unfortunate effect on the morals of our young people. It is particularly important . . . to keep such knowledge from our girls and boys, whose minds and bodies are not in a receptive frame for such information." [20] George Kosmak, a prominent gynecologist, attacked the birth controllers for their affiliations with anarchism and quackery. Although he acknowledged that physicians should have the right to prescribe contraception in those extraordinary cases in which it was necessary to save life, he reasserted that sexual abstinence ought to be the means of avoiding not only unwanted children but also deleterious sexual excess.

Running throughout Kosmak's attack was an expression of strong elitism. Sharing eugenic assumptions about innate inequalities in the population, he did not, however, buy the race-suicide argument that overbreeding among the "inferior" was a danger.

> . . . those classes of our social system who are placed in a certain position by wealth or mental attainments, require for their upkeep and regeneration the influx of individuals from the strata which are ordinarily regarded as of a lower plane. . . . it is necessary for the general welfare and the maintenance of an economic balance that we have a class of the population that shall be characterized by "quantity" rather than by "quality." In other words, we need the "hewers of wood and the drawers of water," and I can only repeat the question that I have already proposed to our good friends who believe in small families, that if the "quantity" factor in our population were diminished as the result of their efforts, would they

be willing to perform certain laborious tasks themselves which they now relegate to their supposed inferiors. Might I ask whether the estimable lady who considered it an honor to be arrested as a martyr to the principles advocated by Mrs. Sanger, would be willing to dispose of her own garbage at the river front rather than have one of the "quantity" delegated to this task for her?

Kosmak's concern to guard accustomed privilege also applied to the particular prerogatives of his profession and reflected the professional ideology that expertise should decide social values.

> . . . the pamphlets which have received the stamp of authority by this self-constituted band of reformers . . . are not scientific and in most instances have been compiled by non-scientific persons. . . . Efforts to impress the public with their scientific character need hardly be dignified by further professional comment, and yet they are a source of such potential danger that as physicians we must lend our assistance in doing away with what is essentially indecent and obscene. . . . Shall we permit the prescribing of contraceptive measures and drugs, many of which are potentially dangerous, by non-medical persons, when we have so jealously guarded our legal rights as physicians against Christian Scientists, osteopaths, chiropractors, naturopaths and others who have attempted to invade the field of medical practice by a short cut without sufficient preliminary training such as is considered essential for the equipment of every medical man? Will we not by mere acquiescence favor the establishment of another school of practice, the "contraceptionists," . . . if as physicians we do not raise our voices against the propaganda which is spreading like a slimy monster into our homes, our firesides, and among our young people?

In protecting his profession Kosmak was very like a craft unionist; in his sense of responsibility for morality, his point of view was uniquely professional. The sexual values that the anti-birth-control doctors cherished were not so different from nineteenth-century conservative values: that the major function of women and sexual intercourse both was reproduction of the species; that the male sex drive is naturally greater than the female, an imbalance unfortunately but probably inevitably absorbed by prostitution; that female chastity is necessary to protect the family and its descent; that female chastity must be enforced with severe social and legal sanctions, among which fear of pregnancy functioned effectively and naturally.

Physicians arguing for a higher valuation of human sexuality as an activity in itself had gained support by 1920, not only among radicals. A leading spokesman for this point of view among prestigious physicians was gynecologist Robert Latou Dickinson. He had used his medical expertise to comment on social problems for several decades previously. In 1902 he had written on masturbation, urging a less hysterical view of its dangers;[21] in 1895 he had defended women's bicycling against those who argued that it might foster the masturbation habit.[22] He believed that mutual sexual satisfaction was essential to happy marriage. As early as 1908 he was giving instruction in contraception as premarital advice to his private patients.[23]

Dickinson encouraged his Ob/Gyn colleagues to take greater initiatives as marriage and sex counselors. In his 1920 address as president of the American Gynecological Society he recommended that the group take an interest in sociological problems. He too disliked the radical and unscientific associations of the birth-control movement. But unlike Kosmak he preferred to respond not by ignoring the movement but by taking it over, and he urged his colleagues to that strategy as early as 1916.[24]

Sensitive to the difficulties of pulling his recalcitrant colleagues into a more liberal view of contraception, Dickinson began his campaign with a typical professional gambit. In 1923 he organized a medical group to *study* contraception, with the aim of producing the first scientific and objective evaluation of its effectiveness and safety. He consciously used antiradicalism to win support for the plan. "May I ask you . . . whether you will lend a hand toward removing the Birth Control Clinic from the propaganda influence of the American Birth Control League . . . ," he wrote to a potential supporter in 1925.[25] So firm was Dickinson's insistence that the group would merely study, without preformed opinion, that he was able to get Kosmak himself to serve on the committee. He got financial support from Gertrude Minturn Pinchot, who had been the first president of the NBCL until she was alienated by the movement's radicalism, and a qualified endorsement from the New York Obstetrical Society.

Dickinson did not merely *use* antiradicalism; it was in part his genuine purpose. His Committee on Maternal Health, as his "study" project was called, was a reaction to Margaret Sanger's continuing efforts to open and maintain a birth-control clinic. Continuing her search for medical authority, when she planned a second clinic beginning in 1921 she projected it primarily as a center for the medical study of contraception; the women who would receive contraception would be its research subjects! Called the Clinical Research Bureau, it opened in January 1923. It had a physician as its supervisor, but she was a woman, not a gynecologist but formerly employed by the state of Georgia as a public-health officer—in other words, she did not have professionally impressive credentials. Furthermore, Sanger had insisted on considering social and economic problems as sufficient indications for prescribing contraception. Thus, because of Sanger's alternative, many doctors, while remaining suspicious of birth control, supported Dickinson's endeavor as a lesser evil.

At first Dickinson's group was hostile to the Sanger clinic. They tried to get Sanger and Dr. Dorothy Bocker, head of the Clinical Research Bureau, to accept the supervision of a panel of medical men, but failed. In 1925 Dickinson wrote a report scathingly critical of the value of Bocker's scientific work.[26] But several factors intervened to lessen this hostility and even bridge the gap between Sanger and the Committee on Maternal Health. One was the fact that the CMH clinic found it difficult to get enough patients with medical indications for contraception. The CMH insistence on avoiding publicity and open endorsement of birth control made women reluctant to try the clinic, anticipating rejection and/or moralistic condemnation of their desire for birth control. Furthermore, it was still extremely difficult to obtain diaphragms, which had to be smuggled into the country. By 1926 three years of work had produced only 124 incomplete case histories. Meanwhile Sanger's clinic saw 1655 patients in 1925 alone, with an average of three visits each.[27]

Another factor leading toward unity between the two clinics was Sanger's conciliatory, even humble, attitude toward Dickinson and other influential doctors. Her organization, the American Birth Control League, had been courting medical endorsement since its establishment in 1921. The League accumulated massive medical mailing lists, for example, and sent out reprints of pro-birth-control articles from medical journals.[28] Sanger's wealthy second husband paid a $10,000 yearly salary to a doctor, James F. Cooper, to tour the country speaking to medical groups for the ABCL.[29] Although even he was not immune from attacks as a quack,[30] he commanded the attention of male physicians as no woman agitator could ever have done. And Cooper's prestige was enhanced by his sharing the speakers' platform with prestigious European physicians at the International Birth Control Conference held in New York in 1925 under ABCL auspices. Indeed, the prestige of the Europeans—whose medical establishment was far more enlightened on the birth-control question than the American—was sufficient to entice the president of the AMA, William A. Pusey, to offer a lukewarm endorsement of birth control at that conference.[31] The ABCL kept exhaustive files, not only of letters but also from their clipping service, on every physician who appeared even mildly favorable to birth control. By 1927 they had 5484 names.[32] These were collected from the thousands all over the country who wrote asking the ABCL for help. The writers were asked for the names of doctors near them; the ABCL then wrote the doctors asking whether "it is your custom to give contraceptive advice in your regular course of practice, to those patients who in your judgment need it." The names of those who responded positively were then sent to applicants from their vicinity.[33]

In response to criticism of her clinic from the Dickinson group in 1925, Sanger, avoiding any defensive reaction, asked the Committee on Maternal Health to take over and run the clinic, hoping in return to be able to get licensing from the State Board of Charities. Dickinson demanded in return the removal of all propagandistic literature and posters, to which Sanger agreed. The scheme failed anyway, because Sanger's radical reputation and opposition from the Catholic Church led the State Board to refuse a license.[34] Dickinson, on the other hand, made his professional influence clear and useful to Sanger by procuring for her a $10,000 grant from the Rockefeller-backed Bureau of Social Hygiene.

Undoubtedly the largest single factor drawing doctors into the birth-control movement, however, was Sanger's support for a "doctors-only" type of birth-control legislation. Sanger had apparently been strongly influenced by Judge Crane's 1918 decision in her trial for the Brownsville clinic. In it he had upheld her conviction under the New York State law on obscenity but suggested the possibility of a broad interpretation of section 1145 of the act which made an exception for physicians prescribing contraception for the cure or prevention of disease, by defining disease broadly, as any pathological bodily change. Since then Sanger and her ABCL had worked, both on a state and a federal level, for legislation that would simply strike out all restrictions on doctors' rights to prescribe contraception, giving them unlimited discretion. The ABCL also proposed an amendment to section 211 of the U.S. Penal Code exemption from Post Office restriction on all medical and scientific journals, all items prescribed by physicians, and all items imported by manufacturers, wholesalers, or retail druggists doing business with licensed physicians.[35]

Mary Ware Dennett and her colleagues in the Voluntary Parenthood League, meanwhile, continued to campaign for an open bill, exempting discussion of contraception from all restrictions for anyone. VPL arguments against the doctors-only bill were substantial. "Yes, of course we believe in medical advice for the individual, but again how about the large mass of women who cannot reach even a clinic? . . . Mrs. Sanger's own pamphlet on methods finds its way through the American mails . . . and *it is not a physician's compilation.* . . . Mrs. Sanger herself testified 'that the Clinicial Research Department of the American Birth Control League teaches methods so simple that once learned, any mother who is intelligent enough to keep a nursing bottle clean, can use them.' " [36] Furthermore, Dennett argued, the doctors-only bill left "the whole subject . . . still in the category of crime and indecency." [37] Not only did it accept the definition of sexuality without reproduction as obscene, but it also removed the technique of birth control from a woman's own control. If women could not have direct access to birth-control information, they would have to get their information from doctors along with censorship at worst and moral guidance at best. Tactically, the doctors' bill also had serious repercussions. As Antoinette Konikow wrote, the very advantage that its supporters liked—that it would make birth control seem safely controlled—was its worst feature "because it emasculates enthusiasm. To the uninformed the exemption seems hardly worth fighting for. . . ." [38] The very substance of the politics doctors brought to the birth-control movement tended to squash lay participation in the movement.

Many doctors, of course, believed that they had an ethical duty to oppose an "open bill." Sharing the views expressed by Kosmak in 1917, their sense of professional responsibility and importance led them to anticipate all sorts of moral and physiological disasters should contraceptive information and devices be generally available. Strategically, Dickinson feared that an open bill would increase religious opposition to birth-control legalization.[39] Sanger's opposition to Dennett's bill combined condescension, conservatism, and compromising practicality. "I have come to realize," she wrote to Dennett supporter James Field in 1923, "that the more ignorant classes, with whom we are chiefly concerned, are so liable to misunderstand any written instruction that the Cause of Birth Control would be harmed rather than helped, by spreading abroad unauthoritative literature." To Dennett Sanger wrote that "clean repeal" was impossible because it would have to mean removing abortion from the obscenity category as well, something which Sanger knew could never win and which she probably did not personally accept. "You," she wrote to Dennett, ". . . are interested in an abstract idea . . . I am interested in women, in their lives. . . ."[40]

The effect of concentration on a doctors-only bill can be seen by examining the work of a local birth-control league. Although there were of course many differences in the histories of the local leagues, we are emphasizing here certain developments that were common to most of them while illustrating them with specifics from the Massachusetts case. A birth-control group had emerged in Boston in 1916 with the arrest of a young male agitator, a Fabian socialist, for giving a police agent a pamphlet, *Why and How the Poor Should Not Have Many Children.* Supporters of the accused, Van Kleeck Allison, organized a defense committee which later became the Birth Control League of Massachusetts (BCLM). The League members were from the beginning a coalition of radicals (Allison's fellow Fabians and members of local Socialist-party groups) and liberals (social workers and eugenic reformers in particular). As elsewhere, no doctors—with the exception of the revolutionary socialist Dr. Antoinette Konikow—were conspicuous in the movement in its first years.[41] Some were attracted to the cause by civil-libertarian principles, as the Reverend Paul Blanshard; he took the ground that the right to speak out on birth control should be defended even by those who opposed birth control itself.[42] More commonly, League members argued the socialist Neo-Malthusianism prevalent among Socialist-party birth controllers. Ella Westcott, a settlement-house worker, argued from her observation of the poor struggling with overlarge families and resorting to dangerous abortion attempts, since they were denied access to safe and effective contraception. Simultaneously, some of the upper-class reformers talked of using birth control to restrict reproduction among the "unfit." [43]

Despite the variety of people in the BCLM, they agreed in 1916 and 1917 on tactics designed to make birth control a public issue and a popular cause. They tried and often succeeded in getting publicity in the popular press, they held mass meetings and public debates, and they contacted nine hundred women's clubs around the state in efforts to recruit supporters. They accepted support from all quarters and featured speakers as far left as Frederick Blossom, of Sanger's *Birth Control Review*, and Theodore Schroeder, of the Free Speech League of America, a group organized by radicals and associated with Emma Goldman.[44] From the beginning, however, some of the socialists in the BCLM encountered a tension between offering a genuinely radical social alternative and using the support of conservative but powerful people to win immediate gains. Influential eugenists, mostly Harvard professors, were quickly attracted to the cause. One of them, Charles Birtwell, proposed in 1917 to replace the League with a eugenic organization that would be "so big and supported by so many people of influence that the authorities would never think of attacking us. . . ." [45] Cerise Carman Jack, a Harvard faculty wife of radical leanings, expressed her conflicts about the tension between her radical ideas and her desire to win. "It is the same old and fundamental question," she wrote Birtwell, "that everyone who has any independence of mind encounters as soon as he tries to support a really radical movement by the contributions of the conservative. . . . The Settlements have . . . found it out and have become . . . crystalized around activities of a non-creative sort; the politician has found it out and is for the most part content to lose his soul in the game. . . . [But] half-baked radicals . . . [tend to] have nothing to do with any movement that savors of popularity and . . . think that all reforms must be approached by the narrow path of martyrdom." [46]

Unable to resolve that problem, many radicals throughout the country lost interest in birth control in favor of what then seemed more pressing issues—the War, the Russian Revolution, the repression against the Left. Cerise Carman Jack was typical of many women of similar views when she decided in 1918 that the most important and strategic direction for her political efforts should be defense work against political repression. Birth control could wait; it would come anyway after the revolution, would "come so spontaneously wherever the radicals get control of the government, just as the war has brought suffrage . . . now is the time to work for the fundamentals and not for reform measures." [47]

In Massachusetts, as in many places, the immediate effect of the defection of radicals and the entrance of professionals into the birth-control leagues was a period of inactivity. In 1918 birth-control supporters among high professionals were still the minority. Most doctors, lawyers, ministers, and professors found birth control too radical and improper a subject for public discussion. Besides, they feared race suicide. But throughout the 1920s quiet but steady concentration on a doctors-only bill by remaining birth-control activists transformed medical opinion. Despite Massachusetts' special problem of strong Catholic pressure against birth control, the League got twelve hundred doctors to endorse its bill. [48] The principle of doctors' rights even led the by now exclusively liberal and conservative Massachusetts Birth Control League to defend the ultraradical Dr. Antoinette Konikow. She regularly lectured on sex hygiene to women, demonstrating contraceptives as she discussed birth control; she was arrested for this on February 9, 1928. She appealed to the now defunct League and her defense in fact rehabilitated the League under its old president, Blanche Ames Ames. Konikow was a difficult test case for the League to accept: a Bolshevik and regular contributor to revolutionary socialist periodicals, she was also not at all elegant and, as we have seen, was rumored to be an abortionist. [49] Nevertheless, the principle at stake was too important for the doctors to ignore: the prosecution of any physician under the obscenity statutes would have set a dangerous precedent for all physicians. The Emergency Defense Committee formed for Konikow worked out an extremely narrow line of defense: that she was not exhibiting contraceptive devices within the meaning of the law but was using them to illustrate a scientific lecture and warn against possible injuries to health.[50] This line worked and Konikow was acquitted.

The verdict stimulated renewed birth-control activity and a new BCLM nucleus drew together with the goal of persuading doctors to support birth control and passing a doctors-only bill in Massachusetts. A new board for the BCLM was chosen, and ten out of the sixteen new members were physicians. The lobbying activities took all the League's time, and there was virtually no public visibility in this period. Konikow herself was extremely critical of this policy. She saw that commitment to it required maintaining a low profile and specifically meant giving up the project of a clinic. She argued, in fact, that opening a clinic would in the long run do more to bring the medical profession around than a long, slow legislative lobbying campaign.[51] Konikow's criticisms angered the League people. Possibly in retaliation, they refused to lend her the League mailing list of fifteen hundred names to publicize her new book, *The Physicians' Manual of Birth Control.* (She had been given not only a mailing list but also a letter of endorsement by Mary Ware Dennett from the Voluntary Parenthood League.) Konikow's angry protests described a whole new kind of organization from the original local birth-control leagues: ". . . the relations between the Executive Board and the membership are so distant that the members do not know what the official policy of the organization is. . . ."[52]

As Konikow had predicted, one of the consequences of this new kind of organization was failure. Whereas the BCLM had become narrow and elitist, the opposition from the Catholic Church was based on mass support. The BCLM had become less an organization than a professionals' lobbying group. Furthermore, no matter how decorous and conservative the League's arguments for birth control, they could not escape redbaiting and other forms of scurrilous attack. Cardinal O'Connell said that the bill was a "direct threat . . . towards increasing impurity and unchastity not only in our married life but . . . among our unmarried people. . . ." The chief of obstetrics at a Catholic hospital said that the bill was "the essence and odor that comes from that putrid and diseased river that has its headquarters in Russia." Another opponent charged that this was a campaign supported by Moscow gold.[53] A broad opposition defeated the doctors' bill. Even non-Catholic attackers recognized the radical potential of birth control, particularly the removal of one of the main sanctions for female chastity—involuntary pregnancy. Even had birth control never had its reputation "damaged" by association with socialists, anarchists, and free lovers, its content could not be disguised. This was the weak point in the conservative strategy of the BCLM, even measured as against its own goals. Birth control was subversive of conventional morality in its *substance*, and thus no form of persuasion could fool those who benefited from the conventions. The meaning of birth control could not be disguised by describing it as a medical tool.

Although the Catholic Church played a particularly large role in Massachusetts, doctors-only bills were defeated in every state in which they were proposed, even in states without large Catholic populations.[54] Indeed, the pattern of development of the BCLM was echoed in many local birth-control leagues. After the radical originators of the movements left for other causes that seemed to them more pressing (or in a few instances were pushed out by professionals and conservatives), the birth-control leagues sunk into lower levels of activity and energy. The impact of professionals—particularly doctors—on birth control as a social movement was to depress it, to take it out of the mass consciousness as a social issue, even as contraceptive information continued to be disseminated. Furthermore, the doctors did not prove successful in the 1920s in winning even the legislative and legal gains they had defined as their goals. Although some birth-control organizers, such as Jack of the BCLM, felt that they were torn between radical demands and effectiveness, in fact there is reason to question whether the surrender of radical demands produced any greater effectiveness at all.

The Massachusetts example, though typical of the national struggle for legislation legalizing birth control, was not representative in the development of birth-control clinics. By 1930 there were fifty-five clinics in twenty-three cities in twelve states.[55] In Chicago a birth-control clinic was denied a license by the City Health Commissioner, but the League secured a court order overruling him and granting a license. Judge Fisher's 1924 decision in this case marked out important legal precedents. His opinion held that the project was a clinic under the meaning of the law; that there existed contraceptive methods not injurious to health; that the actions of the Health Commissioner (who had cited biblical passages in his letter of refusal to license!) amounted to enforcing religious doctrines, an illegal use of power; that the obscenity statutes only sought to repress "promiscuous" distribution of contraceptive information; that "where reasonable minds differ courts should hesitate to condemn." [56]

As the clinic movement mushroomed around the country, however, conflict continued about how and by whom the clinics should be controlled. In New York Sanger still resisted relinquishing personal control of her clinic to the medical profession. No doubt part of her resistance came from a desire to control things herself, especially since she had lost control of the ABCL and the *Birth Control Review* by 1929.[57] But part of her resistance, too, came from disagreement with the doctors' insistence on requiring medical indications for the prescription of contraceptive devices. Her Clinical Research Bureau had consistently stretched the definition of appropriate indications; and if an appropriate medical problem that justified contraception could not be found, a patient was often referred to private doctors, for whom prescribing contraceptives would be less dangerous.[58] Sanger was willing to avoid an open challenge to the law on the question of indications, but she was not willing to allow close medical supervision to deprive physically healthy women of access to contraception. Sanger always retained a critical view of medical control. As late as 1940 she wrote to Dr. Clarence Gamble, "I am absolutely against our educational or propaganda or organizational work being in the hands of the medicos. . . . Being a medico yourself you will know exactly what I mean because you are not strictly medical." [59] Yet nationally her work had the objective impact of supporting medical control. The only birth-control help the ABCL ever offered individuals was directing them to sympathetic physicians. At ABCL-sponsored birth-control conferences nonmedical people were excluded from the sessions that discussed contraceptive technique.[60] The VPL protested against this policy; but the VPL was also excluded from these conference programs.[61] There was resistance to these policies in some local birth-control groups. Caroline Nelson, for example, the IWW birth controller of the prewar period, still active in California, complained in 1930 of nothing more nor less than an effort to get the laymen out of the field to leave it to the doctors. Now we have this Conference called by Margaret Sanger, who wants the dissemination of the information limited to doctors, which means that every doctor can demand the arrest and prosecution of every layman who hands it on. Fine! The whole proposition has been evolved outside the medical profession. They have tried with all their professional sneers to hold it back, and refused to include it in their medical curriculum. Now when they find that they can't hold it back, they want to appropriate it and police the layman.[62]

But Sanger's control over the national conferences, lobbying efforts, and publicity was complete, and the increasing medical control was not checked.

So completely was birth control identified with the medical profession that it is sometimes difficult for us today to imagine what else it could have been. A contemporary population-control expert whose international experiences gives him a perspective on the limitations of a medical approach to birth control described Sanger's impact like this:

Partly because of the medical orientation of Margaret Sanger, and primarily because of legal difficulties under which the movement in this country has labored, a very strong medical bias dominates the movement in the United States. Among other things it has meant a concern with "maximum protection" . . . the clinical system . . . examination rooms, case histories and white coats. It has also meant a highly conservative attitude toward abortion, sterilization, publicity and non-medical personnel.[63]

In addition, we must consider among the effects of medical domination the ultimate control over indications for birth control, over attitudes about motherhood, over sex education and sexual morality. Sanger resisted the doctors' supervisory powers on the question of indications, but she did not contemplate community-controlled clinics, in which the clients could determine the scope of activities and politics.

But Sanger faced a serious problem: without medical approval her clinics were illegal and vulnerable. In New York she continued to seek a license to guarantee the safety and stability of her clinic. When she withdrew the clinic from the auspices of the ABCL in 1928, Sanger once again approached Dickinson requesting that he find her a medical director whose prestige might help obtain a license. Dickinson in reply demanded that the clinic be entirely turned over to a medical authority, suggesting New York Hospital. Sanger was convinced that such an affiliation would hamstring her work and refused it. Then, in April 1929, the clinic was raided by the police. As at Brownsville thirteen years before, a plainclothes policewoman asked for and was supplied with contraceptives. She even came for her second checkup to make sure her diaphragm was fitting her well—then returned five days later with a detachment of police, arrested three nurses and two physicians, and confiscated the medical records. The last action was a mistake on the part of the police, for it united the medical profession behind Sanger and in defense of confidential medical records. Furthermore, the policewoman had been a poor choice because the clinic doctors had indeed found that she had pelvic abnormalities that provided a proper medical indication for giving her a diaphragm. The case was thrown out of court. (Some time later the policewoman returned to the clinic, off duty, to seek treatment for her pelvic disorders!)[64]

This episode produced good feelings between Sanger and the doctors who had supported her, and Dickinson followed it up with a last attempt to persuade her to give up the clinic—this time into the hands of the New York Academy of Medicine rather than a hospital. Sanger was probably closer to acceding now than she had ever been, and might have done so had it not been for countervailing pressure she was getting from another group of professionals—the eugenists. Though easily as conservative as the doctors in terms of the feminist or sexual-freedom implications of birth control, they were solidly in Sanger's camp on the issue of indications. They could not be content with a medical interpretation of contraception, that is, that its function was to prevent pathologies in mothers. The eugenists were after the kind of impact birth control might have when disseminated on a mass basis; they wanted to improve the quality of the whole population, not just protect the health of women. They also felt a certain amount of professional rivalry with the physicians. Eugenists had been among the earliest of the nonradicals to support birth control, and some of them had spoken out for it publicly even before the war. They perceived the doctors as joining the cause after it was safe, and then trying to take it over from its originators.[65] Though politically conservative, their intensity of commitment to their reform panacea—selective breeding—allowed them to accept Sanger's militant rhetoric and her willingness to challenge and stretch the law. At the same time the eugenists had a great influence not only on Sanger but on the whole birth-control movement.

Eugenists

Eugenic ideas had attracted reformers of all varieties for nearly a century. In nineteenth-century eugenics, as we have seen, there was no opposition between environmentalism and hereditarianism. These early eugenists believed that individual improvements acquired through an improved environment could be transmitted to offspring; and also that corrupt social relations would produce physically and mentally deformed individuals. The scientific discrediting of the theory of the inheritance of acquired characteristics changed the political implications of eugenics, however, and more narrow applications of it became dominant. Margaret Sanger described the development of eugenics succinctly: "Eugenics, which had started long before my time, had once been defined as including free love and prevention of conception. . . . Recently it had cropped up again in the form of selective breeding." [66] The new eugenics, "selective breeding," was elitist, intending to reproduce the entire American population in the image of those who dominated it politically and economically. The new eugenics was not a reform program but a justification for the status quo. Its essential argument—that the "unfit," the criminal, and the pauper were the products of congenital formations—suited the desire of its upper-class supporters to justify their own monopoly on power, privilege, and wealth.

New genetic theories promised reliable methods of prediction, and therefore control, of the transmittal of some identifiable physical traits, and they stimulated a great deal of scientific research into human genetics. The first eugenics organizations were research centers, such as the Eugenics Record Office and the Station for Experimental Evolution. As eugenics enthusiasts developed specific political and social proposals for action, they established organizations to spread the gospel generally and do legislative lobbying particularly. The first of these was the Eugenics Section of the American Breeders Association, set up in 1910; in 1913 human breeding became the main focus of the Association which changed its name to the American Genetic Association. Several other organizations were established in the next decade.[67]

The personnel of these organizations consisted largely of professional men, particularly university professors. Their professionalism was by no means identical to that of doctors. Whereas doctors have remained, to this day, one of the last self-employed professional groups, teachers were one of the first groups to become salaried workers. Their reduction to employees brought with it strong responses, especially among university professors who sought to preserve their prestige and status. In the 1920s professors and university administrators complained bitterly over their lack of recognition and their inability to attract recruits of the highest quality.[68] The new eugenics was attractive to university professors because of their frustration at this status loss. Eugenics provided them with an ideology that defended their superior status and sought to increase their prestige through mobilizing fear about the consequences of continued democratization. As a greater percentage of Americans sent their children to the universities, the professors had to focus more on teaching and less on the abstruse scholarship that separated them from—and, in their eyes, raised them above—the work of ordinary people. Their longing for full-time research opportunities was one reason that professors welcomed the intervention of large corporate foundations into American education.

Corporate foundations changed the content and structure of higher education in the twentieth century, and their impact gave support to the eugenics movement. The foundations, of course, were not the first channel for business influence on educational institutions. Business gifts to education grew rapidly after the Civil War, and between 1872 and 1905 business gifts were already the largest single source of income for colleges.[69] But the development of foundations magnified these contributions so much that they created a qualitative change in the degree of direct corporate influence on education. Between 1893 and 1913 education received 43 per cent of foundation gifts. Furthermore, these gifts were directed increasingly to the elite schools (between 1902 and 1934 73 per cent of the gifts went to twenty institutions). Carnegie and Rockefeller in particular were responsible for far-reaching changes not only in university curriculum but, through the reshaping of university admissions requirements, in secondary education as well.[70] Foundations helped to unify universities and business, drawing businessmen onto university boards of trustees and professors onto the boards of foundations.

In no academic field was the coalition between corporate capital and scholars developed more fully than in eugenics. In the 1920s eugenics was a required course in many American universities.[71] The widespread adoption of eugenics as a scholarly field represented the capitulation of university scholarship to a fad, allowing the eugenists' skills to become a commodity for sale to a high bidder. The backers of eugenic research and writing included the wealthiest families of the country. The Eugenics Record Office was established by Mrs. E. H. Harriman.[72] The Station for Experimental Evolution was paid for by Andrew Carnegie.[73] Henry Fairfield Osborn, a gentleman scholar and founder of the New York Museum of Natural History, was a main financial backer of the eugenics societies; in the late 1920s Frederick Osborn, nephew of Henry Fairfield, assumed leadership in the cause and financed a research program for the Eugenics Research Association.[74]

Despite the direct influence of big business on eugenics, the cause carried with it some of its historic aura of radicalism for many years, an aura which sometimes disguised its fundamentally conservative content. Eugenists did promote some genuinely progressive reforms, such as requiring syphilis tests before marriage. But the eugenists' appearance of being progressive reformers was based primarily on their use of apocalyptic warnings (for example, "race suicide," "menace to civilization") and perfectionist visions ("a world of supermen"). Many conservative and religious people objected equally to this tone, to syphilis tests, and to more coercive programs such as compulsory sterilization of criminals and the insane; and this opposition tended to rally progressives to the eugenics camp. Furthermore, in the programs and logic of many eugenists, heredity and environment continued to be imprecisely distinguished and as a result many socialists, feminists, and sex radicals continued into the 1920s in a "popular eugenics" tradition that offered proposals based on the inheritance of acquired characteristics. They endorsed programs for the prevention of birth defects; they included demands for prenatal medical care for women under the aegis of eugenics.

After the First World War, however, academic eugenists consistently avoided all except strictly hereditarian interpretations of eugenics. In clinging to their hereditarian assumptions,* they stood in opposition to the tradition of social reform in America. Eugenists justified social and economic inequalities as biological; their journals featured articles about "aristogenic" families, as if the existence of several noted gentlemen in the same family proved the superiority of their genes. Their definitions of what was socially worthy naturally used their own professional and upper-class standards of success. The professional bias can be seen particularly clearly in their emphasis on intelligence. Standard eugenic concepts of inferiority—such as "degeneracy"—consistently equated lack of intelligence with viciousness and intelligence with goodness.[75] "Among the 1000 leading American men of science," eugenist Paul Popenoe wrote, "there is not one son of a day laborer. It takes 48,000 unskilled laborers to produce one man distinguished enough to get in *Who's Who*, while the same number of Congregational ministers produces 6000 persons eminent enough to be included. . . ."[76]

Aristogenic stock was missing not only from the working class as a whole, but also from non-Yankees in particular. Here is a typical explanation of the problem from a standard eugenics textbook first published by Bobbs-Merrill in 1916:

> From the rate at which immigrants are increasing it is obvious that our very life-blood is at stake. For our own protection we must face the question of what types or races should be ruled out . . . many students of heredity feel that there is great hazard in the mongrelizing of distinctly unrelated races. . . . However, it is certain that

* I call these assumptions because nothing in the genetic theory they relied upon, even as it progressed to Mendel's mathematically sophisticated and predictive models, provided any basis for judgment about the relative impact of heredity and environment in producing characteristics such as feeble-mindedness, insanity, laziness, and other common eugenic bugaboos.

under existing social conditions in our own country only the most
worthless and vicious of the white race will tend in any considerable
numbers to mate with the negro and the result cannot but mean
deterioration on the whole for either race. . . .[77]

Consider the following—typical—passage from *Revolt Against Civilization: The Menace of the Under Man* by Lothrop Stoddard, one of the
most widely respected eugenists:

But what about the inferiors? Hitherto we have not analyzed their
attitude. We have seen that they are incapable of either creating or
furthering civilization, and are thus a negative hindrance to progress. But the inferiors are not mere negative factors in civilized life;
they are also positive—in an inverse destructive sense. The inferior
elements are, instinctively or consciously, the enemies of civilization. And they are its enemies, not by chance, but because they are
more or less uncivilizable.[78]

The eugenics movement strongly supported immigration restriction[79] and contributed to the development of racist fears and hatreds
among many Americans. In 1928 the Committee on Selective Immigration of the American Eugenics Society recommended that future
immigration should be restricted to white people.[80] The movement
also supported the enactment of antimiscegenation laws throughout
the South,[81] and Southern racists used the respectability of eugenics to
further the development of segregation.[82]

Like other social Darwinists, the eugenists were enamored of the
process of natural selection and the survival of the fittest which they
believed it produced. They tended to romanticize the "health" of
animal and premodern societies in which nothing interfered with these
processes.[83] On this point the eugenists were caught in a contradiction
however: the logic of their argument led to a laissez-faire ideology, but
the reforms they sought required intervention not only into social
policy (such as immigration restriction) but into one of the most
intimate aspects of human life—reproduction. The contradiction had
been bequeathed them, so to speak, by the immediate predecessor of
eugenics itself—the race-suicide theory. Race-suicide spokesmen had
wanted to stop dysgenic population tendencies by encouraging those
of "better stock" to refrain from using birth control and to have large
families; in the 1920s eugenists merely added to this another proposal

—to discourage reproduction among those of "inferior stock." They called this two-part program "positive" and "negative" eugenics, encouraging and discouraging reproduction in different social groups.

When they turned their attention to positive eugenics, most eugenists were antagonistic to birth control. To appreciate this conflict fully, one must remember that the eugenists were concerned not only with the inadequate reproduction of the "superior," but also with a declining birth rate in general.[84] As late as 1940 demographers worried that the net reproduction rate of the United States was below the replacement level.[85] Many eugenists clung to mercantilist notions that a healthy economy should have a steadily growing population. In the area of negative eugenics, they approved of birth limitation of course, but preferred to see it enforced more permanently—through sterilization and the prohibition of dysgenic marriages.

The feminist content of birth-control practice and propaganda was especially obnoxious to the eugenists. They endorsed the race-suicide critique of the growing "independence" of women. Eugenists were frequently involved in propaganda for the protection of the family, and in antidivorce campaigning.[86] The most common eugenic position was virulently antifeminist, viewing women primarily as breeders.[87] One typical eugenist wrote in 1917: ". . . in my view, women exist primarily for racial ends. The tendency to exempt the more refined of them from the pains and anxieties of child bearing and motherhood, although arising out of a very attractive feeling of consideration for the weaker individuals of the race, is not, admirable as it seems, in essence a moral one." [88]

Although most eugenists were opposed to birth control, some were not, and all saw that they had certain common interests with the birth controllers. Some believed that though sterilization would be necessary in extreme cases, birth control could be taught to and practiced by the masses. Especially the younger eugenists and the demographer-sociologists (demography was not at this time a distinct discipline) were convinced that the trend toward smaller families was irrevocable, and that the only way to counteract its dysgenic tendency was to make it universal. Finally, they shared with birth controllers an interest in sex education and freedom of speech on sexual issues.

If these factors contributed to close the gap between eugenists and birth controllers, the attitudes of the leading birth controllers contributed even more. Whereas eugenists by and large opposed birth control, birth controllers did not make the reverse judgment. On the contrary, many birth-control supporters agreed with eugenic goals and felt that they could gain from the popularity of eugenics.

Identification with eugenic goals was, for many birth controllers, based on familiarity with the nineteenth-century radical eugenic tradition. Most of them did not immediately apprehend the transformation of eugenics by the adoption of exclusively hereditarian assumptions. Some radicals were critical of the class basis of eugenic programs, as was socialist Henry Bergen, who wrote in 1920:

> Unfortunately eugenists are impelled by their education and their associations and by the unconscious but not less potent influences of the material and social interests of their class to look upon our present environment . . . as a constant factor, which not only cannot be changed but ought not to be changed.[89]

But most socialists accepted the fundamental eugenic belief in the importance of inherited characteristics. Thus British birth controller and socialist Eden Paul wrote in 1917 that the "socialist tendency is to overrate the importance of environment, great as this undoubtedly is. . . ." [90] And IWW birth-control organizer Caroline Nelson wrote in the *Birth Control Review*: "We no longer believe that the child comes into the world psychologically blank, but with an ancestral soul that potentially contains the strength or weakness of the past." [91]

Nelson was not denying the importance of environmental influences altogether, but clung to the older eugenic view of the confluence of environmental and hereditary factors. The problem was that in admitting any place to hereditary factors at all, radicals made it difficult to argue that the deepest existing inequalities were environmentally produced. This was particularly noticeable on issues of racial or ethnic differences, where the Left shared deep prejudices with the Right. In the same article in which Bergen identified the class function of eugenics, he endorsed the goal of using eugenic programs to improve the white race.[92] In a socialist collection of essays on birth control published in 1917 we find passages like this:

> Taking the coloured population in 1910 as ten millions; it would in 1930 be twenty millions; in 1950, forty millions; in 1970, eighty

millions; and 1990, one hundred and sixty millions. A general prohibition of white immigration would thus, within the space of about eighty years, suffice to transform the Union into a negro realm. Now although individual members of the Afro-American race have been able, when educated by whites, to attain the highest levels of European civilisation, negroes as a whole have not hitherto proved competent to maintain a lofty civilisation. The condition of affairs in the black republic of Haiti gives some justification for the fear that negro dominance would be disastrous.[93]

Like the rest of the Left, the feminist birth controllers tended to accept racist and ethnocentric attitudes. Like most middle-class reformers, the feminists also had a reservoir of anti-working-class attitudes. The American feminist movement had its own traditions of elitism, in the style of Elizabeth Cady Stanton's proposal for suffrage for the educated.[94] Many feminists had been active in the temperance movement and saw immigrants and working-class men as drunken undesirables. Anti-Catholicism in particular, stimulated by Catholic opposition to prohibition and women's rights, had been an undercurrent in the women's rights movement for decades. Southern feminists used the fear of the black vote as an argument for female suffrage, and were supported by the national woman-suffrage organizations in doing so.[95] Birth-control reformers were not attracted to eugenics *because* they were racists; rather they had interests in common with eugenists and had no strong tradition of antiracism on which to base a critique of eugenics.

Sanger, too, had always argued the "racial" values of birth control, but as time progressed she gave less attention to feminist arguments and more to eugenic ones. "More children from the fit, less from the unfit—that is the chief issue of birth control," she wrote in 1919.[96] In *Woman and the New Race*, published in 1920, she put together statistics about immigrants, their high birth rates, low literacy rates, and so forth, in a manner certain to stimulate racist fears.[97] In *The Pivot of Civilization*, published in 1922, she urged applying stockbreeding techniques to society in order to avoid giving aid to "good-for-nothings" at the expense of the "good." She warned that the masses of the illiterate and "degenerate" might well destroy "our way of life." [98] She developed favorite eugenic sub-themes as well, such as the cost to the society of supporting the "unfit" in public institutions and the waste of funds on charities that merely put Band-Aids on sores rather than cure diseases. Society is divided into three demographic groups, she argued: the wealthy, who already practiced birth control; the intelligent and responsible, who wanted birth control; and the reckless and irresponsible, including "the pauper element dependent entirely upon the normal and fit members of society." [99] She shifted her imagery about such social divisions, for later in the 1920s she cited a "Princeton University authority" who had classified the U.S. population as consisting of twenty million intellectual persons, twenty-five million mediocre, forty-five million subnormal, and fifteen million feeble-minded.[100] The racism and virulence of her eugenic rhetoric grew most extreme in the early 1930s. In 1932 she recommended the sterilization or segregation by sex of "the whole dysgenic population." [101] She complained that the government, which was so correctly concerned with the quality of immigrants, lacked concern for the quality of its native-born.[102]

Eugenics soon became a constant, even a dominant, theme at birth-control conferences. In 1921, at the organizational conference of the American Birth Control League, many eugenists spoke and charts were exhibited showing the dysgenic heritage of the infamous Jukes and Kallikak families. In 1922 Sanger went to London for the Fifth International Neo-Malthusian and Birth Control Conference as its only female honored guest. Yet not a single panel was devoted to birth control as a woman's right nor did Sanger raise this point of view. In 1925 Sanger brought the Sixth International Conference to New York under the sponsorship of the ABCL. The impact of its control was to make the emphasis more eugenic and less Neo-Malthusian, but there was no increase in concern with women's rights. Not a single session was chaired by a woman; only about one out of ten speakers was a woman. Four out of the total of eleven sessions focused specifically on eugenics, none on women's problems.[103]

Meanwhile the propaganda of the ABCL was becoming more focused on eugenics at the expense of women's rights. The introductory brochure used during the 1920s lists as point number one of "What This Organization Does to Inform the Public" the publishing and distributing of literature and the conducting of lectures "on the disgenic [sic] effect of careless breeding." The program of the ABCL included a sterilization demand and called for "racial progress." [104]

The *Birth Control Review*, the ABCL publication, reflected the influence of eugenics from its inception in 1917. Although eugenists of the older, radical tradition dominated in its first years, it also printed without editorial comment a eugenic anti-birth-control argument, virtually a race-suicide argument, in its very first volume.[105] By 1920 the *Review* openly published racist articles.[106] In 1923 the *Review* editorialized in favor of immigration restriction on a racial basis.[107] In the same year the *Review* published a study called "The Cost to the State of the Socially Unfit." [108] In 1920 Havelock Ellis reviewed Lothrop Stoddard's *The Rising Tide of Color Against White World-Supremacy*—favorably.[109] Stoddard was at this time on the Board of Directors of the American Birth Control League. So was C. C. Little, another openly racist eugenist. President of the Third Race Betterment Conference, he justified birth control as an antidote to the "melting pot," a means of preserving the purity of "Yankee stock." [110] Also closely involved with the ABCL and writing regularly for the *Review* was Guy Irving Burch, a director of the American Eugenics Society and leader in the American Coalition of Patriotic Societies. He supported birth control, he wrote, because he had long worked to "prevent the American people from being replaced by alien or Negro stock, whether it be by immigration or by overly high birth rates among others in this country." [111] A content analysis of the *Review* showed that by the late 1920s only 4.9 per cent of all its articles for a decade had had any concern with women's self-determination.[112]

There were, of course, continuing conflicts between birth controllers and eugenists. One of the most common sprang from the tendency of the former group to argue for birth control as if it were a panacea in general and a total solution to the problem of the "unfit." Edward East, for example, wrote to Sanger in 1925 objecting to her exaggeration and pointing out that "there will be many children of no value whatever to the community no matter what laws are passed and no matter what educational propaganda is put forth. . . . No matter what you say Birth Control is only a part of a eugenical program." [113] At other times Sanger's continued commitment to civil disobedience as a tactic alarmed the eugenists. As late as 1932 she happily quoted in a newsletter what some Congressman told her, off the record: "You'll never get this bill passed in Congress; get yourself arrested again, that's the only way to get the law changed." [114] But Sanger's tactical militancy was one thing; she rarely had conflicts with the eugenists about political goals. Her residual concern for women's emancipation was not radical enough to seem objectionable to them.

It is important to understand the birth controllers' conversion to eugenics and their desertion of feminism. They did not disavow their earlier feminism so much as find it less useful because of the more general change in the country's political climate. Had they had deeper feminist or antiracist convictions, they might have found eugenic ideas more uncomfortable. But feeling no discomfort, they found eugenic ideas useful. They could get from the eugenists a support that they never got from the Left. The men who dominated the socialist movement did not perceive birth control as fundamental to their own interests, and their theory categorized it as a reform peripheral to the struggle of the working class. Eugenists, on the other hand, once they caught on to the idea of urging birth control upon the poor rather than condemning it among the rich, were prepared to offer active and powerful support.

As academics and sexual theorists, eugenists were often concerned with matters of free speech and in the early years of birth control many eugenists were drawn into legal-defense work when birth controllers were prosecuted. In Massachusetts, for example, Harvard professor Edward East got involved in the defense of Van Kleeck Allison in 1916. Other academic eugenists supported overt birth-control propaganda and clinics. University of Chicago professor James Field worked with a clinic-organizing project as early as 1914. University of Michigan president C. C. Little was an early member and activist in the Detroit Birth Control League.[115]

In planning the First National Birth Control Conference for November 1921, Sanger had made an active attempt to recruit support from academics and scientists in particular. She won endorsement from economists and sociologists like Irving Fisher, Edward A. Ross, Ellsworth Huntington, Warren Thompson, F. H. Giddings, Thomas Nixon Carver, and Raymond Pearl—all eugenists.[116] At a concluding meeting at Town Hall, Lothrop Stoddard helped her take the podium in defiance of a police ban. By exposing these professors to arbitrary suppressions of free speech, she drew them into a deeper commitment to the cause, even to condoning civil disobedience. As a means of increasing her exposure in academic circles, Sanger conducted a university speaking tour in 1925, going to Yale, Bryn Mawr, Harvard, Tufts, Columbia, the University of Chicago, and elsewhere.[117]

Sanger was aided in her efforts to win over academics by the support of British Neo-Malthusians, some of great prestige, such as Harold Cox, Member of Parliament and editor of the *Edinburgh Review*. Different economic and social conditions meant that the British upper classes were concerned with overpopulation when Americans were still worried about underpopulation. Despite this difference, British Neo-Malthusians and American eugenists shared many attitudes and ideas. They represented the same classes, by and large; they were concerned not to let unbalanced population growth alter the social and political stability of their respective societies. Cox came to the United States to deliver the keynote speech at the 1921 Conference. At the Sixth International Neo-Malthusian and Birth Control Conference, held in New York in 1925, Charles Vickery, British Neo-Malthusian, delivered the presidential address; eugenists such as Edward East, Raymond Pearl, and Henry Pratt Fairchild and even firm opponents of birth control such as demographer Louis Dublin shared platforms with the Neo-Malthusians. By thus presenting at least the appearance of openness to her critics, Sanger won the respect of many academics. Two years later she organized, almost single-handledly, the First World Population Conference in Geneva. Again she brought American eugenists to confer with European Neo-Malthusians. So great was her conviction that she needed the unity of these two groups that she submitted to the humiliation of having her name removed from the conference program by its chairman, Sir Bernard Mallet (formerly Registrar-General of Great Britain and president of the Royal Statistical Society). "The names of the workers should not be included on scientific programs," Mallet said; the workers were all female and nonprofessionals. Another delegate told Sanger that Sir Bernard had been warned by Sir Eric Drummond that "these distinguished scientists would be the laughingstock of all

Europe if it were known that a woman had brought them together."
Sanger not only accepted the snub but took it upon herself to persuade
the other women to do so.[118]

Just as Sanger accepted a back seat here, ABCL women in
general lost their leadership positions to men (although women members remained in the majority). This takeover by men was an inevitable manifestation of the increasing influences of professionals.

The men, however, were not united. Although doctors and eugenists could mesh their concerns for individual and racial health in
propaganda, they did not see eye to eye on the practice of the clinics.
Particularly as regards indications, as we have seen, the doctors
wanted to preserve narrow medical justifications for prescribing contraceptives, whereas eugenists and many lay birth controllers wanted
to use contraception to ameliorate social, psychological, and economic
problems as well. Beyond this, the eugenists were eager to use birth-
control clinics to collect data on family patterns, birth-control use,
changing attitudes, sexual behavior, and genetic history. In this interest the eugenists were in the forefront of the social sciences; many were
leaders in the development of improved quantitative and statistical
techniques in the social sciences.[119] The foundations generously funded
such statistical studies.[120] Eugenists feared and opposed medical supervision of clinics because it threatened to interfere with their data
collection.[121]

Most birth-control clinics appreciated the eugenists' support for
disseminating contraceptives in the absence of pathological indications. The clinics also acceded to eugenists' research interests. Many
clinics conducted inquiries into the hereditary histories of their patients and presumably advised the women as to the desirability of
having children.[122] In 1925, responding to suggestions from her eugenist supporters, Sanger reformed her clinical records to show the
nationality, heredity, religion, occupation, and even trade-union
affiliation of patients.[123] In 1929 Harvard eugenist Edward East wrote
to Sanger, "I suppose it would be a delicate matter, but it would be a
very interesting thing, from the standpoint of science, if your clinical
records . . . show the amount of racial intermixture in the patient.
Perhaps, without embarrassing questions, it would be possible to make
a judgment as to whether the person was more or less pure black,

mulatto, quadroon, etc." Sanger agreed, anticipating no difficulties, "as already colored patients coming to our Clinic have been willing to talk." [124] (It is noteworthy that the eugenists' passion for race categorization did not prevent them from accepting most inexact measurements, such as "judgment.") A review of the work of seventy birth-control clinics in Britain and the United States, published in 1930, proudly demonstrated that they reached a disproportionately large number of working-class women, and claimed a eugenic effect from doing so.[125]

The birth controllers also influenced the eugenists, of course. Sanger described the relationship thus:

> . . . eugenics without birth control seemed to me a house built upon sands. It could not stand against the furious winds of economic pressure which had buffeted into partial or total helplessness a tremendous proportion of the human race. The eugenists wanted to shift the birth-control emphasis from less children for the poor to more children for the rich. We went back of that and sought first to stop the multiplication of the unfit.[126]

Thus in one paragraph is condensed the transformation of birth-control politics: the poor, "buffeted into partial or total helplessness" by economic pressure, are rechristened the unfit.

With such an attitude toward the poor, it is not surprising that the clinics encountered difficulties in teaching working-class women to use birth control properly. Some such women were unteachable, Sanger and several other birth control leaders agreed. They particularly had trouble with "the affectionate, unreflecting type known to housing experts, who, though living in one room with several children, will keep a St. Bernard dog." For these women, sterilization was recommended.[127] Another area in which the snobbery of the birth-control workers was manifest was in their attitude toward working-class men. They projected an image of these husbands as uncontrolled, uncontrollable, sex-hungry, violent sexual aggressors, with no regard or respect for their wives, who would never agree to contraception. Certainly the reasons such men might have for hostility to birth-control clinics were not taken seriously.[128]

But medical supervision of the clinics had created similar problems in reaching the poor with birth control, and Sanger and other clinic partisans ultimately saw more usefulness in the propaganda of eugenics than in the more reserved style of doctors. Furthermore, the eugenists could not exercise the kind of direct control over clinics that the doctors could, lacking the institutions like hospitals or medical academies, and were thus willing to share control with birth controllers like Sanger. If Sanger and her colleagues ultimately chose to work with the eugenists, it was because it seemed to them the only realistic option. They would greatly have preferred cooperative working relationships with both groups; and perhaps, had this been possible, they might have retained more direct power in their own hands by playing off the two groups of professionals against each other. As it was the ideological disagreements and, even more, the jurisdictional rivalry of the two professions prevented this.

Ultimately, the rivalry held back the clinic movement. Although contraception became widespread in the 1930s, most middle-class people continued to get their help from private doctors. Working-class people, on the other hand, often did not get it at all. This last is, of course, part of the general inadequacy and unequal distribution of medical care in the United States. Poverty usually tends to limit the use of medical facilities to the treatment of emergencies and acute or painful conditions, and minimizes access to preventive health services. Although the right to birth control is not a medical issue, the actual delivery of most contraceptives must be done in medical situations. The movement for birth-control clinics was thus in itself a break with the private capitalist medical system in the United States, and its failure was a part of a general failure of American medicine. Physicians' attitudes toward the birth-control movement—their demand for exclusive control and restrictive distribution—was a microcosm of the general attitude taken by the medical profession.

In terms of the birth-control movement specifically, the clinics did not spread widely because the people who had become the backbone of the cause did not need them. Increasingly, the clinics were operated by groups of professional and well-to-do people for the poor. They were charities, not self-help organizations. Eugenic logic had convinced many of these educated people that this particular charity was very much in their own interest; that without population limitation the poor and the unwashed could become a political threat. The members of the ABCL were not the main clients of the clinics they had sparked, but went to private doctors. The attitude of many doctors toward their private patients continued, well into the mid-twentieth century, to parallel that of many elite nineteenth-century doctors: although they opposed the "promiscuous," "indiscriminate" dissemination of contraception, they did not question their own discrimination and even thought it important that private doctors should be able to make exceptions to the policies they supported as general rules. Well-to-do women were able to secure diaphragms without medical indications from doctors who may themselves have opposed making it possible for clinics to use the same principles. The discretionary right of the individual doctor was a privilege as cherished by the profession as that of privacy—and the latter, of course, protected the former.

Although rivalry between medical and eugenic professionals held back the clinic movement, the ultimate decline of eugenics as a mass cause weakened it still further. Eugenics was the driving ideology transforming a charity into a political cause. The passion behind eugenics led even conservative people to condone law-breaking, and the content of its politics brought money into the birth-control clinics.[129] But though the decline of eugenics deprived the birth-control clinics of some of their support, the over-all success of the birth-control cause contributed to the decline of eugenics. American eugenics was also tarnished by Nazi eugenic policies, which identified eugenics in the popular view with fascist ideology and practice. Furthermore, scientific criticisms of Galtonian genetics stripped away some of the academic respectability that had clothed eugenic racism. Although some leading eugenists continued to function as a conservative sect, they lost much of their professional following in the 1930s.[130] Some eugenists tried to reinterpret their credo in "value free" ways. Some wrote about the decline in the quality of the population without using the word "eugenics." [131] In 1933 the *Journal of Heredity* produced an editorial disassociating the magazine, for the first time, from eugenics; the magazine was now prepared "to give favorable consideration to analyses that might demonstrate fundamental unsoundness in present eugenic efforts." [132] (An indirect, but nonetheless damaging, admission of their earlier bias, and of the capitulation of a whole academic discipline to political opportunism.)

Part of the reason that professionals could defect was that they had someplace else to go. Birth control had become a movement that could do much of the eugenists' work for them. Henry Pratt Fairchild, president of the American Eugenics Society, told the annual meeting of the Birth Control Federation (successor to the ABCL) in 1940: "One of the outstanding features of the present conference is the practically universal acceptance of the fact that these two great movements [eugenics and birth control] have now come to such a thorough understanding and have drawn so close together as to be almost indistinguishable." [133] In part the transfer of many eugenists into birth-control organizations was the phenomenon of unemployed specialists needing jobs and new sources of recognition. But in part, too, they were men genuinely concerned with a problem—race deterioration—looking for ways to solve it. Important changes in the birth-control organizations made the eugenists comfortable in them. From the eugenists' point of view, the essential change was the acceptance that birth control should be a question of public policy, not just private right.

Eugenics, in the long run, was a type of population-control thought, similar to Neo-Malthusianism. The former had been concerned with quantity and quality whereas the latter had restricted its focus to quantity. But both aimed to manipulate reproduction on a large scale in order to control a society's development. Neither employed women's or even individual rights; on the contrary both had been quick to argue that individuals do not have those rights if they interfere with the best interests of the whole society. The loss of a women's rights emphasis left the birth-control movement, as we have seen, without a guiding ideology, open to any justification that increased its importance beyond that of many other charities and minor ameliorative reforms.

National Organization

The influence of the professional birth controllers also transformed the nature and constituency of the birth-control organizations themselves. In the pre–World War I period, the birth-control leagues were almost all local, tied together by a loose sense of common purpose and a few traveling speakers and organizers. By the mid-1920s one organization—the American Birth Control League—could claim national scope and hegemony. The ABCL, created by Sanger and her protégé Frederick Blossom in 1921, lasted until 1938 and by 1927, at its peak, had thirty-seven thousand dues-paying members from every state.[134] Although supporting itself through a membership, in its operations the ABCL was primarily a staff organization and a centralized one. Policies and projects were decided on and executed by a paid staff and national officers; local birth-control groups were affiliates, but there was no structure for their participation in decision-making.

The national dominance of the ABCL was achieved largely through the contribution of its professional supporters. The ABCL was the center of most national lobbying and litigation; much professional research and most local clinics in the 1920s were affiliated with it in some way. Affiliated branches and projects were required to contribute to the national 50 per cent of contributions and 25 per cent of dues, in return for which the ABCL supplied birth-control literature at minimum cost, trained organizers and speakers for special campaigns, and gave technical assistance in the establishment of clinics.[135] In addition individual members of the national organization were sought. The ABCL built the respectability of birth control through national and international conferences and sustained publicity campaigns, using prestigious professionals to promote the cause.[136] Sanger continued through the 1920s to operate as an individual proselytizer for birth control, even a superstar, and by the 1930s she was estranged from and resented by many ABCL officers. But in the 1920s the ABCL was Sanger's primary organizational tool for projecting herself and her ideas.

The organizational direction of the ABCL can be appreciated more sharply by comparison with the rival national birth-control organization, the Voluntary Parenthood League. The VPL was organized primarily by Mary Ware Dennett, an ex-suffragist who had disapproved of Sanger's style and tactics since 1914. Actually, Dennett had created the first American birth-control organization, the National Birth Control League, in March 1915, while Sanger was in

Europe. Never reaching beyond New York City, the NBCL died in 1919, weakened by the war's impact in deflecting reform energies to other causes. Shortly afterward Dennett created the VPL, dedicated exclusively to lobbying for legislative reform. For a time the VPL even published a paper rivaling the ABCL's *Birth Control Review*.[137] Between 1925 and 1927 the VPL gradually collapsed. Its appeal was limited by its insistence on legislative lobbying as its exclusive program, for birth-control clinics were more visible, more confrontational, and more capable of stimulating and absorbing local reform energies.

The VPL cannot, however, be characterized as simply more conservative than the ABCL. The differences between the two groups were complex, based on personal rivalries between the leaders as often as on principle. But in this, as in many other political situations, we should not allow the existence of personal conflicts to reduce the importance of political differences. Dennett, always a liberal, had never even flirted with radicalism. Perhaps for that reason Dennett was more consistently committed to fighting for the legalization of birth control on free-speech grounds, whereas Sanger's early exposure to radical critiques of bourgeois civil-liberties theory made her prefer direct argument for the importance of birth control and practical compromises that would bring it closer. Dennett and her organizations opposed the doctors-only bills because they would leave birth control within the realm of the legally obscene and deny the general public access to contraceptive information. Indeed, Dennett fought the whole concept of legal obscenity, a challenge Sanger never made. Perhaps for this reason, too, Dennett disliked the phrase "birth control." Her slogan, "voluntary parenthood," was a rephrasing of the nineteenth-century "voluntary motherhood," emphasizing individual rights but de-emphasizing women's rights. Prosecuted for distributing her pamphlet *The Sex Side of Life* in the late 1920s, Dennett was defended by the American Civil Liberties Union and strengthened her association with civil libertarians (while Sanger drew closer to doctors and eugenists).[138]

Dennett's emphasis on free speech brought her support from liberals but left her and her followers on the fringes of the most important currents in social thought. Not that she was uninterested in the practical case for birth control; on the contrary, she shared most of

Sanger's and the ABCL's ideology. Dennett and the VPL propaganda defended sex without reproduction. Contraception was a good thing because sex itself was a good thing—if infused with love and "idealism." [139] Like Sanger, Dennett wrote on sex education.[140] It is true that Dennett wanted, slightly earlier than Sanger, to disassociate the movement from radicalism. Dennett's group included many rich, amateur reformers; but Sanger too had organized society women into a Committee of 100 to defend her in 1916. The influence of capitalists did not produce a significant difference between the Dennett and Sanger birth-control tendencies. It was Sanger's greater closeness to professionals, indeed her active courting of participation from doctors and eugenist-academics, that moved the ABCL away from civil-liberties arguments toward an integrated population program for the whole society.

In attracting professionals, the ABCL had to overcome the taint of radicalism that clung to Sanger for decades. Though it is often hard to shake such reputations, Sanger had particular difficulty doing so because her personal style was combative. And she had, after all, been arrested for deliberately defying the law, whereas Dennett's organizations had never endorsed civil disobedience. Indeed, the NBCL and VPL at first even avoided seeking court cases to set new precedents and limited themselves to advocating new legislation. Meanwhile Sanger, long after she shed her socialist and feminist ideas, refused to commit herself to staying within the law. No matter how she changed the content of her speeches, Sanger was identified by most who knew of her as a radical, at least until the end of the 1920s. Many doctors considered her untrustworthy even after she had campaigned years for a doctors-only bill.

The clinic strategy provided a continuing basis for this suspicion. The successful operation of birth-control clinics in the 1920s required at least bending the law, and the clinics' decisions about who should be given contraceptives required some dissembling in most cases. Certainly the meaning of the law was always open to interpretation, and Sanger had thought for many years to win the latitude the clinics needed through widening existing legal loopholes that gave doctors discretion in cases where pregnancy could be dangerous to a woman's health. But Sanger wanted that discretion used generously and found that doctors often preferred to employ it restrictively. Her refusal to give up tactics of civil disobedience was a major cause of her failure to get the full support of the medical profession for these clinics, although the most important problem was undoubtedly physicians' hostility to providing health care as salaried workers rather than through private practice.

Sanger's commitment to civil disobedience in defending her clinics did not, as we have seen, include any program for radical social transformation. Her use of "direct action" contains an important lesson about the distinction between militant tactics and radical goals. Although the two are often confused, they are in reality quite separate. There were many historical precedents for Sanger's combination of militancy and conservatism. In both Britain and the United States the most violent suffragists were the more conservative in their social and political goals. Earlier, the Anti-Saloon League, despite its window-smashing tactics, had not demanded social change as radical as the Women's Christian Temperance Union, whose tactics consisted mainly of education and consciousness-raising. Sanger herself often chose militance because it brought her publicity. Sexual reform by definition required shock tactics, for a part of the problem was that sexual matters were considered best not discussed at all. But adoption of law-breaking and convention-defying tactics did not necessarily indicate a thorough challenge to the sources of law and convention in the society.

Before the war militant tactics for birth control had been associated with a radical content. Influenced by IWW direct-action ideas, birth controllers believed that people could take their lives in their own hands: reject laws over which they had no control by distributing contraceptives and contraceptive information, hold mass meetings in defiance of prohibitions, court arrest and conduct political trials. The war brought a sharp break in this activity. Nationally and locally, most birth-control leagues died between 1917 and 1919 and were re-established in the 1920s. Where the same organizations did continue, they also experienced sharp changes in constituency and policy. Before the war the major activities of the local leagues were five: distribution of contraceptive information; propaganda about the virtues of birth control; mass meetings about birth control; legal defense;

the planning and operating of birth-control clinics. After the war the mass meetings and illegal distribution of contraceptive information virtually disappeared. The continued locus of direct action—clinics—were not seen by the birth controllers as civil disobedience, because an important part of the fight was their claim that the clinics were legal, under medical discretionary powers. So completely had their illegal tactics been emptied of political meaning that these questionably legal clinics could be operated with the ideology of traditional women's charity projects. With their repeated argument that contraception would check the massive illegal abortion trade, they convinced themselves that they were fighting crime, not perpetrating it.

Increasingly the ABCL organized its local affiliates through upper-class women's clubs, even high-society charity groups. In 1926 ABCL organizing in Philadelphia was focused mainly on women of the Main Line, a group of extremely wealthy suburbs.[141] In Grand Rapids, Michigan, Mrs. C. C. Edmonds, of 1414 Wealthy St., S.E., was collecting "influential people" for a local group.[142] New York meetings were held in the Bryn Mawr Club.[143] These details pile up, drawing an unmistakable picture of a rich women's organization.

The new respectability of the birth-control movement shaped the constituency of the ABCL. In 1927 questionnaires were mailed to a random fifth (7800) of ABCL members and of these 964 were completed.[144] This sample may have tended to raise the apparent class level of the members as more educated people were more likely to reply, but even allowing for some degree of distortion the results are significant. Politically the membership was slightly more Republican than the whole country, the men more inclined to be Republican than the women. (Fifty-five per cent of men were Republicans, 19 per cent Democrats; the women's figures were 46 per cent and 25 per cent.) One-third of the members were from cities of more than fifty thousand people; 43 per cent of the members were within five hundred miles of New York City, although this proportion had declined from 60 per cent in 1922, suggesting increasing penetration of the whole country with birth-control interest and knowledge. The organization seemed not to be dominated by big cities, with half the membership from population centers of less than twenty-five hundred. ABCL techniques in procuring members, however, require a reinterpretation of this phenomenon. Throughout the 1920s ABCL responses to letters of inquiry about birth control either explicitly or implicitly told writers that they could not receive information unless they joined the League. "The information that you desire can only be given to League members," said a form letter signed by Sanger.[145] Thus big-city dwellers, more likely to have access to clinics or local birth-control organizations, had less incentive to join the national organization; ABCL membership could not, therefore, be said to be representative of the over-all distribution of people interested in birth control as a cause.

The average age of the members was thirty, the mean age thirty-five—suggesting that they were mostly of childbearing age but not newly-weds; the average member had been married five years and had two children. (Compare this, for example, to the figures given in Chapter 9 for the women writing to Sanger and others asking for birth control help, who had an average of five children and of whom 80 per cent had married before the age of twenty.) Nor was there a significant proportion of immigrants, as there might have been among urban working-class people: the members were seven-eighths native-born and of those 74 per cent had native-born parents; of the foreign-born, over half were from Canada and Northern Europe. The survey director assumed, although he did not specifically ask, that the members were all white. Ninety per cent were Protestants; Jews and Catholics numbered only 5 per cent each. The low percentage of Jews, a group once disproportionately well represented in the movement, reflects the more small-town and prosperous social base of the organization.

The questionnaires also asked the members what other organizations they belonged to, and these figures too demonstrate a respectable, Wasp prosperous base. The other organization they most often belonged to was the Red Cross—one-third of the respondents checked this. Urban males tended to belong to Rotary or Kiwanis clubs; whereas 19 per cent of rural males belonged to the Anti-Saloon League. Urban women most often belonged to local women's clubs (23 per cent), and 10 per cent of them belonged to the League of Women Voters. Rural women, naturally, did not belong to many organizations at all. A much higher percentage of men were socialists than the women—7.3 per cent as compared with 3.3 per cent. Since the party affiliations were not correlated with other indices, we have no way of knowing what other characteristics might have distinguished this rather high proportion of socialists from other ABCL members. Certainly the fact that a higher proportion of men than women were socialists indicates not only the imbalance within the Party, but the male attitude toward birth control, for nonradical men on the whole still perceived this as a women's issue. Only 17 per cent of the sample was male, 83 per cent female.

Although men were not the major constituents of the ABCL, those that were tended to have a higher social status than the women. A full 49 per cent of male members were professional men; of the remaining 51 per cent, 11 per cent were in "trade," 8 per cent clerical, 10 per cent agricultural and 14 per cent industrial. (The categories chosen by the questionnaire were most un-class-conscious and tended to group people by economic sector rather than personal status.) Of course a very high percentage—86 per cent—of the women were housewives. But the husbands of female members also had a distinctly lower class status than the male members: of husbands only 19 per cent were professional, for example. Education revealed the same general high status of male ABCL members: 47 per cent were college graduates as opposed to 14 per cent of females. (The educational level of husbands was not asked for.)

Although men made up only 17 per cent of the members, they made up 25 per cent of the financial backers and a majority of the National Council. Of Council members 36 per cent were in *Who's Who*: nine clergymen, nineteen scientists, twenty physicians and twenty-one other professionals; ten women members of the Council also had husbands in *Who's Who*.

This adds up to an organization of predominantly Wasp middle-class people, a high proportion from small towns; an organization with the number of male leaders far greater, proportionately, than the male members, and with the percentage of male members who were professionals far in excess of the percentage of professionals in the country. The survey's findings were confirmed by the practice and propaganda of the ABCL, which also reflected the powerful influence of professional men in the organization. Symbolically, the ABCL even listed its National Council members by profession: scientists,* physicians, "other professionals," and "lay" members. The women on the Council, of course, were almost all in the "lay" category, where they accounted for thirty-six out of forty. On the other hand, the women did all the work, both as staff members on the national and local organizations and as volunteers. The men tended to serve as professional volunteer consultants.[146] At another time, with a thriving feminist movement, these laywomen might have formed an ideological bloc powerful enough to offer strategies and policies different from those of the two dominant professional groups, eugenists and doctors.

Professionals had the influence they did for several reasons. First, they were at their peak power thus far in U.S. history. Relative prosperity in the urban north was rapidly expanding the career opportunities for educated men; the reforms produced by the Progressive period (1901–1917) increased their political power. Second, they had created a coherent social perspective, one that crossed disciplinary lines. The coherence of their views gave them a collective influence greater than that of their individual numbers. Third, supporting this coherent social perspective and increasing power was the establishment of the separate professions as controlled, standardized, and sometimes even licensed guilds, and of the professions in general as groups with guaranteed, if varying, status. The establishment of the professions was a function of their declining independence. By the 1920s academics, social workers, scientists, and to a lesser extent doctors and lawyers were in a dependent relationship to the corporate industrial leadership of the country. Fourth, this dependence nevertheless gave professionals limited control over certain resources—foundation and government grants and contracts, and private and governmental service programs, for example—the manipulation of which in turn gave them great influence in organizations they entered.

These factors also defined the content of professionals' reform efforts. Despite their sense of themselves as seeking a good society on

* Of these scientists, almost every one was identifiable as a eugenist through his (there were no women) writings and/or organizational affiliations.

the basis of independent, objective criteria of justice, they were unable to entertain notions of social reorganization that challenged the existing class and sexual order. Although many of them wanted to use birth control to improve people's lives, most of them believed that by and large those people on the bottom would inevitably remain on the bottom. Few thought that women's social roles and functions should be fundamentally altered relative to men. They might work hard and devotedly within their professions to improve the conditions of all, but not to change the relative power of social groups.

The only check on professional influence would have been a broader-based, popular birth-control movement. No social group of equal size could contest the power of the professionals; only a much larger group could have done that, either a working-class movement or a feminist one. The former was unimaginable by 1920. Even the union movement lost ground in the 1920s; working-class movements demanding larger social change had been severely beaten in the repressive period that followed World War I. Furthermore, the men who dominated all forms of working-class organization at that time were hostile to and/or uninterested in birth control.

The source of the feminist failure in birth control is complex. In addition to many external factors, a contradiction within the feminist movement itself was sharply debilitating; that is, the vision of a new sexual order which this feminism contained was threatening to many of its advocates. We have seen how in the nineteenth century contraception—the severing of sex from reproduction and hence from family control—was not in the interest of the majority of women. In the 1920s that situation had changed. Sex outside of marriage had been incorporated into a relatively stabilized new family structure, and contraception itself was accepted by most women. But the potential volatility of a continued social movement frightened the relatively privileged women who became reformers in the 1920s. Whether themselves "career women" or, more commonly, leisured wives able to do volunteer work, they were a generation reaping the benefits of a relative social emancipation, one that applied only to their class. They could have "help" with the housework or at least with the children; they could get effective contraceptives to reduce the number of their children; they enjoyed social acceptance for their work in the public arena, including public speaking, traveling alone, supervising others. On the other hand, they had not experienced the raising of expectations which was to influence their daughters and granddaughters, expectations which made the continued inequality with men of their class frustrating and galling. Perhaps even more than their nineteenth-century suffragist predecessors, they felt enormously different from the working-class poor whom they tried to help.

The problem was that their very estrangement from the less privileged majority of women cost them their own coherence as feminists. The essence of feminism has always been a view of all women as united by certain problems and strengths, the "bonds of womanhood." [147] When class distinctions make this vision of a common womanhood impossible, they dissolve the basis for any feminist analysis or strategy. Taking advantage of their class privileges for their own personal advancement, the prosperous reformers of the 1920s lost the mass base that could have made them a powerful influence. Without a constituency demanding change, they became merely a group of individuals, whereas their male professional rivals in the birth-control organizations had the power of the capitalist class behind them. Their inability to spark a mass movement made them simultaneously unable to create even a coherent militance among a small group, for they had no larger goals that distinguished them from their male colleagues.

Furthermore, the timidity of these prosperous women reformers of the 1920s created a spiral away from working-class women: the less radical and far-reaching their demands, the less attraction they had for the poor; the fewer poor women participated in birth-control groups, the less impetus there was for a militant approach. When public opinion was studied in the 1930s, working-class women appeared quite favorable to birth control. But as we have seen in opinion polls of the 1960s and 1970s, support for women's rights as measured by attitudes on specific issues and problems is separate from identification with or desire to participate in feminist organizations. Most women thought birth control was an opportunity they would like to have available, but they perceived it as any other commodity; few saw it as part of a program of democratization of the society.

11

The Depression

THE GREAT DEPRESSION of the 1930s had a large and mixed impact on the development of birth control. Declining incomes frightened many middle- and upper-class Americans into practicing family limitation and accepting it morally and sexually. Despite economic hardships, however, the movement for birth control did not become a grass roots, popular cause, nor one that involved working-class people in significant numbers. There was desire, and pressure, for good birth control among poor and working-class women, but it was channeled into a movement run and staffed primarily by professional men, wealthy women, and middle-class reformers. In this pattern birth control was not an exception to the general history of social movements during the Depression. Even among labor, where there were mass and explosive pressures from the bottom, the movements were ultimately contained within reform ideologies and institutionalized into existing power structures. Part of the reason that the Depression's social movements did not transform the United States profoundly was the single-issue quality of each, the fact that birth control was separated from the workers' movement, for example. Leading birth controllers were mostly indifferent to the labor movement; the labor movement was suspicious of birth control as being both too radical and too conservative—radical in its sexual implications and conservative in that it used Neo-Malthusian and eugenic assumptions. This mutual suspicion existed because of the absence of a feminist spirit in either birth control or the Left generally. Where women's needs and rights were central, workers' issues and birth control were part of a common strategy; where male domination went unchallenged, they seemed in opposition.

Almost completely isolated from the Left, birth controllers in the Depression turned to the government and tried to integrate birth control into New Deal welfare programs. In this effort the birth controllers' approach to social problems underwent a gradual but important change. The economic crisis changed the dominant ideology that explained social problems such as poverty, by discrediting eugenic theories of hereditary inferiority and substituting environmentalist views. Applied to birth control, this shift implied less emphasis on reducing the population of the inferior and more emphasis on helping the underprivileged through family planning. Historically speaking, it was a shift back toward Neo-Malthusianism.

Nevertheless, rejection of hereditarian ideas did not destroy the elitism of the birth controllers. Rather they grew closer to a new, liberal view of social problems which continued to blame the victims. Specifically, many birth controllers adopted the ideas of some "social pathologists" who wrote primarily in the late 1920s and 1930s. While denying that hereditary disabilities inhered in certain classes, or that they were the major sources of social problems, this new analysis still located the source of the problems in the disabilities, albeit environmentally caused, of individuals.[1] Flowing from this analysis were recommendations for helping the poor by increasing their individual ability to compete for jobs through education, socialization to middle-class norms of propriety, and reduction of family size. The goal was to move certain individuals up in the class structure. By not acknowledging the existence of a class structure, the social planners who offered these recommendations ignored the fact that moving some individuals up would merely leave others on the bottom. They did not face the structural problem that the society always produced a bottom.

At its depths the Depression rendered this approach to poverty and other problem useless, and forced a set of massive, structural remedies. The Work Projects Administration (WPA) and the Civilian Conservation Corps (CCC), for example, did not teach people skills on the assumption that their lack of skills was the cause of their unemployment. Similarly birth controllers could not consistently argue that large families were the cause of the extensive impoverishment around them. But these massive remedies were temporary, and the predominant view among New Dealers was that the economic system was sick, not permanently disabled. Its return to "health" with World War II produced a return to individual-help solutions. What is surprising was the extent to which blaming-the-victim attitudes and analyses prevailed among birth controllers during the Depression itself. On the whole the transformation from hereditarian to environmentalist analyses of the relation between birth rates and economic status had few consequences. The "environment" was scrutinized in terms of influences on each individual, not in terms of systemic class and sex relations.

Depression Eugenics

The giving up of eugenic ideas came with difficulty, for they had served the birth controllers well. But loyalty to the old eugenic assumptions was weakened by international political developments: Nazi eugenic policies—forced sterilizations and the subsidization of large "Aryan" families—were increasingly identified with totalitarianism. Furthermore, the experience of sudden, massive unemployment and economic ruin weakened social Darwinist views of American economic justice. Even those who had accepted the veneer of prosperity in the 1920s began to doubt in the 1930s that being of "good stock" was a guarantee of success even in the long run. Those who had long been poor saw themselves joined by many others, and both groups suspected that their economic problems were not due to personal, hereditary or moral, failings, but had social causes.

Nevertheless, eugenists stubbornly continued to promote Malthusian and hereditarian explanations of the problem. Birth-rate differentials "proved" that the "excess" people were mostly among the poorest. These calculations hid assumptions that excess population caused poverty and that those in poverty somehow deserved to be there. In April 1933 a total of 4,445,338 families were collecting funds from the Federal Emergency Relief Administration (FERA), and early studies estimated that they had a birth rate 50 to 60 per cent higher on the average than those not on relief.[2] By 1935 "relief babies" had become a public scandal. Taxpayers' money was not only being used to support the poor, but to produce more of them—this was an implicit charge being made in a variety of public arenas, from *Time* to the *Birth Control Review.*[3]

The "relief babies" logic was not new. Margaret Sanger used that refrain frequently in the 1920s. Arguing that birth control would cut public costs and thus taxes, she said, "We are a nation of business men and women"; we should use good business methods and cut our overhead.[4] Nor was it new that public dependents had higher birth rates than the average.[5] But the sheer magnitude of unemployment in the 1930s gave the problem urgency it had not had before. Previously race-suicide arguments—namely, that the "best stock" would be overwhelmed by the faster breeding of the "unfit"—had threatened the future, not the present, and lacked persuasiveness with those who did not consider themselves of the best stock. During the Depression the problem of "relief babies" threatened to hit people immediately, in the pocketbook, and to hit everyone.

Birth controllers seized upon the relief crisis with gusto. "You are absolutely right that the economic situation is our greatest ally," one woman physician wrote to the president of the American Birth Control League in 1935. "The most sensitive nerve center in which to hit the public is their pocketbook. Sick poor mothers and the high mothers' death rate leave them cold." [6] Clarence C. Little, pro-birth-control eugenist and ex-president of the University of Michigan, demanded birth control as an end to the "present tendency that pays money to non-productive and idle persons." [7] Another planner proposed legal limitation of families to two children with penalties for more as a cure for unemployment.[8] Margaret Sanger plotted escalating relief expenditures on a graph in her speeches.[9] Professor James Bossard, a sociologist and social-work expert, asked rhetorically, "Do those who are aided by society owe anything to society in return?" The answer —their debt to society—was to control their fertility.[10] The ABCL unanimously adopted a resolution on the crisis at its 1935 annual meeting:

Whereas, the cost of public relief in the United States is now over 125 million dollars a month, and

Whereas, scientific research has shown that families on relief have about 50% more children than similar families not on relief, and

Whereas, these children add to the burdens both of their already over-burdened parents and of the taxpayers,

Therefore, be it resolved that the American Birth Control League unite with the American Eugenics Society in formulating and securing the adoption of the most effective plans for providing that as a matter of routine, all families on relief shall be informed where they may best obtain medical advice in a strictly legal fashion as to ᵗhe limitation of families by methods in accordance with their religious convictions.[11]

As they had done for decades, birth controllers used hereditarian arguments. To Eleanor Dwight Jones, president of the ABCL, it was obvious that the relief babies were of the "unfit," and that "social unfitness is, by and large, hereditary." [12] Despite the dimensions of the economic crisis, one birth-control leader was so blinded by personal privilege as to argue that "the man who shows no judgment about the number of children he sires is likely to be the man who loses his job in a crisis, perhaps because he lacks judgment all along the line." [13] Paul Popenoe, a pro-birth-control eugenist, tried to make his views "objective" through IQ measurements proving that welfare children and their mothers were less intelligent.[14]

The eugenists were especially enraged that the birth rates of those on relief did not decline and in some cases went up. Between 1929 and 1932 the birth rate among families whose economic status dropped from moderate to poor was higher than that of families who continued in moderate circumstances. This phenomenon, seen as an irrationality, was proof of inferiority to the measurers.[15] Not only the birth rate but also the marriage rate, which was falling among the more prosperous, sometimes rose among poor immigrants and blacks.[16]

Although birth controllers saw these problems as evidence for the importance of spreading contraception, not all drew the same conclusion. The alliance that Sanger had created with professionals was still shaky in several areas. Many found birth control too radical and objected to its capacity for licensing illicit sexuality and its interference with the divine or natural law of sex and reproduction. Under-population was still a common fear among those who gauged normal-ity by nineteenth-century trends of steady population expansion. Some physicians were anxious to preserve their exclusive control over reproductive medicine and felt threatened by the birth controllers' recommendation of contraception as a social and economic reform as well as a medical prophylactic. Above all, many eugenists continued to fear the dysgenic effect of the rapid spread of contraception among the upper classes while the poor continued to produce large families.

Indeed, the first years of the Depression not only intensified the eugenists' attack on birth control but seemed, temporarily, to weaken the relative influence of the pro-birth-control eugenists. In 1932 Henry Fairfield Osborn, a veritable dean of eugenics, delivered a major attack on birth control at the Third International Congress of Eugen-ics in New York. "BIRTH CONTROL PERIL TO RACE SAYS OSBORN," *The New York Times* headlined.[17] "The country which has birth control in its most radical form is Russia, where it is connected with a great deal of sexual promiscuity. . . . Let us therefore consider birth control as one of the more or less radical departures from fundamental principles of our present social structure, not only in the religious but the ethical and moral fields." He criticized the feminist as well as the "dysgenic" component of birth control from a social Darwinist perspective. Al-though birth controllers say their aim is to free women of suffering, they fail to realize that "women's share in the hard struggle for the existence of the race is a very essential element. . . . To relieve the animal or plant organism of its struggle-for-existence pressure is an extremely dangerous experiment, for . . . the struggle for existence is the *sine qua non* of every great human or animal quality."[18] Few eugenists condemned the birth-control movement as totally as Osborn had done, but many continued to press for "positive eugenics" pro-grams in addition: that is, they wanted to encourage more reproduc-tion among the "best stock." The eugenists considered themselves in advance of the birth controllers in projecting a whole population policy, not just a single reform.

The ABCL, through the *Birth Control Review*, responded to Osborn with fury, arguing quite correctly that although contraception could give people the means to avoid reproducing, it was necessary to look elsewhere for their motivations—to the "quality of our lives." The birth controllers challenged none of Osborn's basic assumptions, however: his eugenic categories (the "fit" and the "unfit"), his assumption that a growing population was normal, his concept of "promiscuity," his facts about the Soviet Union.[19] Indeed the ABCL began to argue that birth control was a flexible tool providing greater human choice and control over reproduction in every direction. Birth-control clinics began to offer infertility therapy to couples who wanted children but had been unable to conceive.[20] Increasingly, the clinics' propaganda was directed toward "child spacing" rather than smaller families.[21]

Meanwhile, the early 1930s produced a number of demographic studies with conclusions potentially damaging to the birth-control cause. Without challenging their assumptions, the birth controllers could not easily defeat their eugenic accusations. The development of statistical techniques in demography made possible ever finer breakdowns of census information, and foundation money paid for ambitious data-gathering projects. The questions these demographers asked of their informants, and of their data, once gathered, were motivated by their own eugenic fears, so that studies concentrated on birth-rate differentials. Furthermore, they usually left out any analysis over time, and their apprehension of historical trends was minimal. For example, surveys emphasized the differential birth rate—lower among prosperous, educated, white, native-born people—and often ignored the tendency now several decades old for the birth rates of rich and poor to converge. Thus Frank Lorimer reported in 1932 that the professional classes had a "replacement rate" of only 76 per cent whereas unskilled workers had a rate of 117 per cent.[22] In 1930 Edgar Sydenstricker and Frank Notestein published their study of differential fertility which showed an "inverse" ratio of birth rate to class status. They listed the number of children per one hundred wives [*sic*] for the following classes.[23]

Urban		*Rural*	
Professional	129	Owners	247
Business	140	Renters	275
Skilled	179	Laborers	299
Unskilled	223		

But Frank Notestein also knew, and pointed out in a private "round table" discussion on the eugenic effect of contraception, that birth rates were declining fastest among groups previously most fertile.[24] Socialist-leaning sociologist Joseph Folsom pointed out that a look at the European experience* showed a clear trend toward reducing the differential birth rate to zero.[25] But these trends were not usually integrated into the popularized versions of demographic alarms.[26]

Eugenists denied that birth control could be a solution for two reasons. The first was that the poor were morally irresponsible, possibly even vicious, and would not control their fertility. Welfare recipients were sometimes accused of having children deliberately to get the added relief payments—even as little as $1.15 a week;[27] the Metropolitan Life Insurance Company reported that relief was the *cause* of the birth-rate increase.[28] The second was that the poor could not use birth control properly; and in an era when the vaginal diaphragm was the only effective women's contraception, this hypothesis carried considerable weight. This had been Pearl's position in the 1920s,[29] and it was reiterated by many other scholars in the 1930s. Some recognized the need for development of simpler and also cheaper methods.[30] But many merely repeated eugenic formulas thoughtlessly and uncritically. A common rhetorical device was a confusion of the rather large over-all birth-rate differential between the urbanized and prosperous and the rural or newly urban poor, with the numerically much smaller problem of reproduction among those with handicaps. In their attacks the eugenists frequently described the problem as if the poor and fertile were all feeble-minded. As Dr. T. R. Robie expressed it:

> I feel that I come from a very superior community because there one has the privilege of owning a garden. But from having this garden, I know how much faster weeds can grow than roses. There has been nothing said tonight about a way to stop the undesirables from over-running us. . . . We talk about education, yet how can we educate feeble-minded mothers not to have children? We have got to look further.[31]

---

* Western European countries experienced approximately the same demographic patterns as the United States—rapid population growth in the early years of industrialization, followed by birth-rate declines—but several decades earlier.

Such views were the more ill-founded since there was not much evidence that most of the defects the eugenists feared—feeble-mindedness and insanity for example—were, in fact, hereditary; worse, many of their categories of undesirability did not describe objective congenital handicaps at all, but only characterized antisocial behavior, as in the concept of "degeneracy."

The fact that the vaginal diaphragm was the object of this skepticism is important, for the diaphragm is a "rich-folks contraceptive." It is difficult to use without privacy, running water, and full explanation and fitting, luxuries not available for many Americans. The diaphragm was the most effective available contraceptive in the 1930s and certainly ought to have been offered to every birth-control client. But some simpler female methods, such as a vaginal sponge moistened with some spermicidal substance, had significant effectiveness rates and ought to have been made available as alternatives. In Miami, Florida, maverick birth controller Dr. Lydia Allen DeVilbiss used the sponge method very successfully when combined with home instruction.[32] DeVilbiss was a racist and her conviction that black women were of lower intelligence than whites led her to construct an apartheid system of birth control: different devices prescribed for whites and blacks.[33] Such racist practices were not uncommon in birth-control clinics, as we shall see later in this chapter. But the experimentation that DeVilbiss did with easier contraception for poor people could have been pursued in a nonracist way. The ABCL rejected DeVilbiss's experiments not because of an opposition to her racism but because it did not find her work medically respectable.[34]

It is surprising, too, that birth controllers did not pay more attention to the advantages of the lowly condom—cheap, disposable, easy, quick, and pocket-sized. The condom has a lower effectiveness rate than the properly used diaphragm, but a much higher effectiveness rate than the improperly used or unused diaphragm.*

---

* It is a wry commonplace among today's birth controllers that diaphragms are not effective when left in the drawer. That is exactly the problem with the diaphragm: its use often represents an annoying interruption which people "take chances" in order to avoid. But recent calculations of the effectiveness rates of contraceptives *as actually used* (thus excluding non-use, but including improper use) show a small difference between condom and diaphragm: the former producing 14.9 unwanted pregnancies per 100 woman per year, and the latter 12.0 unwanted pregnancies.[35]

One reason for the neglect of the condom was fear of licensing sexual immorality. The condom was well suited to be, as it indeed became, the chief contraceptive for "sinners." It was easy to get and required no doctors or special instruction. Indeed it is *because* the diaphragm was a medical device, requiring fitting and instruction in a clinic, that its distribution could be controlled. Until the late 1960s most birth-control clinics would not aid unmarried women; and most women, married or not, had no access to clinics. The struggle over medical versus social and economic justifications for contraceptive prescriptions reflected not merely a fear for population size but also for the potentially immoral consequences of contraception.

That the birth control clinics aimed their appeal almost exclusively at women was a legacy, of course, of their early feminist heritage. But by the 1930s the birth controllers had virtually ceased expressing any concern with the women's rights aspects of birth control. It is all the more ironic and unfair, then, that they did not question the assumption that women should take the sole responsibility for birth control. The assumption also contributed to their failures, for they were asking women to take on this responsibility without arguing that it was specifically in their interest.

The clinics usually failed to offer women the support and counseling they needed to include a diaphragm regimen in their sex lives. For example, the more common reason given by clinic patients for their failure to continue using birth control was "problems in marital adjustment." [36] There was a significant gap between the rate of women's exposure to contraception and their successful practice of it. For example, studies of several clinics showed that a mere two years after clinic visits, only 43–45 per cent of women were still using any part of the clinical birth-control methods they had learned.[37]

But the eugenists' argument that poor and "stupid" women could not practice contraception was not supported by the evidence.[38] Although studies showed higher effectiveness rates among the rich and well educated, they also showed significant effectiveness among the poor and very poor.[39] There were many reasons for the higher contraceptive effectiveness among more prosperous women: better facilities at home; husbands desiring to limit their families; possibly less traditional moral or religious standards about sex, lessening the sense of guilt and/or shame; and especially better instruction and medical advice in the first place. Women getting birth-control devices from private doctors were likely to get more personal attention, and better educated women, whether at private doctors' offices or clinics, were more likely to articulate their questions, doubts, and misunderstandings. Sharp differences in contraceptive effectiveness rates even within groups of the same class, religion, and ethnic origin suggested the importance of the kind of instruction women received and of incalculable personal and local factors.

The eugenic conclusion that the poor were stupid and immoral provided ammunition for a renewed campaign for sterilization during the Depression. "Birth control or contraception cannot be depended upon to save us from the children of the very groups whom we are most eager to restrict," said Rabbi Sidney Goldstein at a eugenics conference in 1936.[40] The eugenics movement had introduced state laws for the compulsory sterilization of "degenerates" as part of a program that most progressives supported. By 1915 thirteen states already had compulsory sterilization laws. Birth controllers had also supported sterilization as a form of birth control for the feeble-minded and others clearly unable to use contraception.[41] By 1932 twenty-seven states had sterilization legislation. But sterilization proponents were discouraged that only 12,145 people had been sterilized under these laws.[42] With a new organization, the Human Betterment Foundation, begun in 1928, eugenists stepped up their campaign for sterilization in the 1930s. Paul Popenoe, one of the leading eugenists and sterilization advocates, estimated that ten million Americans ought to be sterilized; his estimate was based on the results of IQ testing.[43] Another theme in sterilization propaganda was the waste of taxpayers' money in providing public institutional care and other "charity" for the "socially inadequate"; some even cited the economic loss of the wages that institutionalized patients did not earn! [44] The sterilization campaign tended to identify economic dependence with hereditary feeble-mindedness or worse. In the context of an alarm about relief babies, it reinforced fears that those with high birth rates were incompetent to use birth control.

To these objections to birth control—that the poor couldn't and wouldn't use it, that the rich used it too much—the response of the birth controllers was to prove that the poor wanted birth control and could use it. Today there is little room for doubt about that proposition. One proof was in the mounting evidence that birth rates were falling fastest in those groups with remaining high birth rates, especially as a response to urbanization. Another could be seen in the public-opinion polls about ideal family size. For example, a 1939 report on birth control among professionals cited 3.2 children as the ideal, but a *Ladies' Home Journal* poll produced almost identical results with 3.3 children as the ideal.[45] Studies done in the 1950s and 1960s have shown that poor people usually have more "excess" children—in terms of their own preferences—than higher-income people.[46] There is no reason to doubt that the same held true in the 1930s.

A third kind of evidence was in the enthusiastic response of working-class people to birth-control clinics.[47] The high percentages of women who did not return for follow-up visits and did not continue to use contraception properly had many causes other than lack of desire for further control—including unpleasant experiences at the clinics, hostile social pressure from husbands, relatives, and priests, and difficulties in using contraceptives. Furthermore, a large falling off in contraceptive use after initial clinical visits was characteristic of women of all classes.[48] Social workers consistently reported both high interest in contraception among working-class women and problems in using it. "In the follow-up work of the . . . cases which I have just completed I find many patients have used the method a short time or not at all. Some became confused as to technique, others lost confidence. Often they did not return to the clinic because of lack of carfare." Women were surprised when clinical workers took an interest in them, a surprise obviously based on long experience of disinterest. "Invariably, when I put on my coat to go," wrote one birth-control caseworker, "the patients comment, 'how nice of Mrs. Sanger to send some one, I didn't know the clinic was so interested in us.' "[49] Birth-control casework—visiting women in their own homes—was extremely rare (whereas in countries where birth control has been effectively introduced to the poor, home visits have been the basis of the strategy, as in China). Clinical workers and observers understood the necessity of casework,[50] but could not get the funding for it.

Money had always represented a problem for birth-control clinics. In the first years few doctors had been willing to associate with a cause so risqué; respectability had not yet brought in funds on a scale grand enough to pay doctors the salaries they could command elsewhere. Birth-control clinics were not yet receiving large foundation grants.* Despite the influx of professionals into the movement, the actual operation of local clinics, except for a few high-powered projects in New York and Baltimore, was still primarily in the hands of amateur female reformers; their financing had not yet been professionalized. Now, just as it became most urgent to reach the poor, the Depression made raising funds more difficult, and made the poor unable to pay.

The New Deal and Birth Control

Both sides of the Depression's impact—lack of funds and eagerness to spread birth control among relief clients—contributed to a new tactic in the strategy of birth controllers: selling social workers on the importance of birth control. The increase in the number of social workers, as relief and other public-assistance programs grew, also made that group seem an even more important channel for the cause than previously. Social workers were likely converts both because of the orientation toward service that led them to their profession in the first place and because of their direct and sometimes painful exposure to family poverty in their jobs. Responding both to their own common sense and to direct requests from clients, caseworkers flooded their supervisors and the birth-control organizations with requests for birth

---

* Columbia University economist and social reformer Caroline Robinson, who studied seventy birth-control clinics in the late 1920s, criticized them for "an inferiority complex" in their fund-raising attempts. "They should publish less apologetic and more conventional booklets, decked out with all the paraphernalia of finance, audit, and a treasurer's address somewhere in Wall Street, thus affirming their right to march with all the other health charities and depending calmly on the first-class arguments they are able to muster as well as on the first-class scientific men who have within the last three or four years become eager to lend their names to the movement." [51]

control information and authorization to give it out. At social-work conventions, ABCL booths were flooded with questions—on techniques, locations of clinics, names of helpful doctors, speakers on birth control, and so forth. At the 1935 National Convention of Social Work, one-fifth of those attending registered at the booth.[52]

ABCL leaders understood the impact of the Depression and made a systematic attempt to win over social workers. Emily Vaughn wrote in the *Birth Control Review* that "a major blessing may be pulled out of a major depression": a recognition that "prevention is better than cure." [53] Both in their professional organizations and at their agencies, social workers were heavily leafletted. The ABCL organized three or four panels at most social-work conferences throughout the 1930s. In December 1935 the ABCL staged a mass meeting at Carnegie Hall to demand that relief agencies give birth-control information, with speakers including Professor Eduard Lindeman, a leader of the social-work profession.[54]

Some birth-control leaders, still eugenically oriented, criticized welfare services, charging that philanthropy without birth control was dysgenic. These charges often reflected extremely conservative social values. Speaking at an ABCL panel at a 1932 social-work conference, Frank H. Hankins, sociologist and economist, argued:

> Suppose now we take a look at the extreme environmentalist view of the causes of poverty . . . that the ills of poverty as well as . . . delinquency, crime, prostitution, venereal disease . . . are due almost entirely to the circumstances in which individuals grow up. . . . Certainly one cannot subscribe to the absurd extremes to which the environmentalist view has been pushed. . . . The restriction of the fertility of the less successful elements in modern society constitutes an important relief measure.[55]

Sometimes the birth controllers' line amounted to a direct attack on relief programs, charging that they led to the "survival and increase of the unfit. . . ." [56] Indeed, some eugenists who spoke for the birth control cause were opponents of any kind of welfare programs,[57] and some birth controllers attacked the New Deal specifically. Margaret Sanger wrote in 1935:

> As long as the procreative instinct is allowed to run reckless riot through our social structure. . . . as long as the New Deal and our

paternalistic Administration refuse to recognize this truism, grandiose schemes for security may eventually turn into subsidies for the perpetuation of the irresponsible classes of society.[58]

By and large birth controllers were favorable to the New Deal. Most were political liberals, and furthermore as professionals many benefited directly from the expansion of state-provided services. Sanger attacked the New Deal because she was so single-minded about birth control and was antagonized by the Administration's timidity and Roosevelt's personal ambivalence about birth control. The "underconsumption" theory of the cause of the Depression, which influenced Roosevelt's "brain trust," had incorporated the underpopulation theory promoted most vociferously by Louis Dublin, demographer and statistician for the Metropolitan Life Insurance Company.[59] Sanger also suspected Roosevelt of caving in to Catholic pressure against birth control.[60] But despite the existence of good reasons to criticize the New Deal, the over-all impact of the attacks coming from the birth controllers was to aid the right-wing opposition to the liberal Roosevelt administration, rather than to join with liberal or radical criticism of the inadequacy of New Deal programs. The birth controllers frequently raised their demands in terms of competing with welfare programs for funding, rather than argue for more spent on services generally.

Public-relief programs did indeed drag their feet on incorporating birth-control services. In 1934 the ABCL sent a case worker to the South in response to appeals from relief administrators, and she found them unanimously enthusiastic about birth control.[61] But they felt unable to act officially. A 1935 survey of local administrators of the Federal Emergency Relief Administration showed not one willing to admit for the record that he or she gave birth-control advice.[62] An attempt to get a birth-control clinic accepted as a WPA project failed.[63] Key officials such as Harry Hopkins, head of the FERA; Ray Lyman Wilbur, Secretary of the Interior; Katherine Lenroot, head of the Children's Bureau; and Thomas Parran, Surgeon General of the Public Health Service all refused to support birth control publicly, even in principle. Administrators of private charities shared this reluctance.

This continuing disingenuousness about birth control put individual social workers in a difficult position. They never knew when their discretionary powers might be withdrawn, or when they would be reprimanded or even punished for what their supervisors tacitly accepted.[64] As long as officials chose to hedge, to protect themselves from political attack, social workers could become the scapegoats, as one journalist pointed out:

> . . . the social worker is merely a liaison officer . . . between the ruled and the rulers. . . . In general it seems neither just, pertinent nor useful to attack social workers for their failure to come out forthrightly and officially for the expansion of contraceptive service. . . . Unofficially, social workers . . . are not merely convinced, they are acting; they are everywhere and increasingly referring relief cases to the available clinics, sometimes at the very risk of their professional careers and their jobs.[65]

Behind official recalcitrance was, in some cases, strong opposition from the Catholic Church, which made politicians with Catholic constituencies especially fearful of the issue (and these politicians included Roosevelt, of course).[66] Another source of official reluctance on birth control was the radical reputation of the cause. In 1930 and again in 1937 a public-relations consulting firm hired by the ABCL reported that birth control was being held back as a cause by Sanger's radical reputation.[67] Government officials expressed distaste for the term "birth control." Secretary of the Interior Ray Lyman Wilbur told eugenist–birth-controller Henry Pratt Fairchild that the notion of birth control was far too controversial for the government, and that another name could not disguise it as long as Margaret Sanger was associated with it.[68] A Florida physician trying to organize birth control clinics wrote to the ABCL in 1935 that the name " 'birth control' . . . is still a red rag to the masses." [69] Furthermore, the combination of eugenic and underpopulation fears among welfare bureaucrats and social workers continued to support antagonism to birth control.[70]

The defeat of official skepticism was due in part to popular pressure and in part to the realization that birth control among the prosperous classes was here to stay. Propaganda urging the "fit" to have more children had been repeated since the 1870s, and with great intensity in the first years of the twentieth century, but made no impact whatsoever. Upper-class birth rates fell steadily and reached a new low in the Depression. Furthermore, demographers and eugenists increasingly realized that repression of the organized birth-control movement would not solve the problem. Well-to-do people did not depend on birth-control clinics for their contraceptives, but on private doctors, and there was no practicable way of interfering with the work of such a well-organized profession. The clinics revealed that a high percentage of women attempted some form of birth control before seeking clinical advice; and apparently the higher the class of the clinic patients, the more often they had used birth control previously. As Dr. Regine Stix commented in 1937, "It wasn't the birth controllers who taught people to use contraception." Furthermore, she said, "The things in general use, other than those prescribed by doctors, are extremely effective. The least effective method used cut the pregnancy rate in half." [71] The Depression showed more clearly than before that the reasons for smaller families were mainly economic self-interest—a motivation difficult to challenge effectively in the American economic system.

Another factor, both consequence and cause of the "birth-control-is-here-to-stay" phenomenon, was the commercialization of contraception. By the 1930s the manufacture of contraceptives was a large industry, retailing through millions of outlets. In 1936 the fifteen chief manufacturers of condoms were producing one and a half million a day at an average price of one dollar a dozen. [72] A survey done in Florida during 1932 showed condoms being sold in 376 kinds of places other than drug stores—including gas stations, garages, restaurants, barber shops, news stands, and grocery stores. [73] One survey showed about $25,000,000 spent on condoms in 1936; [74] another showed $436,000 spent on "feminine hygiene" products (douches) in 1933, the nadir of the Depression, with advertising expenditures off over 20 per cent. [75]

The contraceptive industry of the 1930s was an extreme, if inevitable, example of commercial exploitation of popular ignorance. Although federal laws prohibited the mailing of contraceptive information, euphemisms such as "feminine hygiene" or "the intimate side of a woman's life" made possible the advertisement of products not only ineffective, but potentially dangerous. The major danger was from chemical douches which frequently created vaginal irritations. Lysol was such a product, advertising in *McCall's* in July 1933:

> The Most Frequent Eternal Triangle
> A HUSBAND   A WIFE
> and her
> FEARS
>
> Fewer marriages would flounder around in a maze of misunderstanding and unhappiness if more wives knew and practiced regular marriage hygiene. Without it, some minor physical irregularity plants in a woman's mind the fear of a major crisis. . . .[76]

There were also a variety of vaginal tablets and suppositories supposed to produce a shield across the cervix—mostly ineffective.[77] Preying particularly on people denied access to better information, firms employed door-to-door peddlers who made completely fraudulent claims, offering, for example, diaphragms without fittings or proper instruction; one firm told women that the device could be exchanged at the nearest birth-control clinic if it didn't fit. Another firm sent saleswomen to the very poor with an intrauterine device almost certain to be dangerous if inserted by oneself. Advertisements were manipulative, even brutal:

> She was a lovely creature before she married. . . . But since her marriage she seems forever worried, nervous and irritable. . . . Poor girl, she doesn't know that she's headed for the divorce court. . . . And, yet, that tragedy could be so easily avoided, *if she only knew.*[78]

One common racket was the sale of two products: the "B-X Monthly Relief Compound" was alleged to bring "soothing, satisfying Glorious Relief" with the "B-X Special Multi-Strength Treatment" recommended if the purchaser complained that the first didn't work.[79] Others told simple lies, as this ad for Hygeen vaginal tablets:

> Some time ago a group of prominent English physicians, thoroughly alarmed at the increasing variety and nature of various feminine hygiene products offered to the public—set about to determine which one was the safest and most effective. . . .
> So this group of English physicians under the auspices of the English Medical Society, had the Oxford University, Department of Anatomy and Zoology, determine under Dr. John R. Baker . . .
> THE RESULT OF THIS MOST THOROUGH INVESTIGATION REVEALED

THIS SAME HYGEEN TABLET HOLDS FIRST PLACE AMONG ALL THE
PRODUCTS INVESTIGATED.

There was no English Medical Society and the investigation was a
complete fabrication; the tablets consisted of baking soda, tartaric
acid, sand, starch, and a small amount of an organic chlorinated
product, not an effective spermicide at all.[80]

The contraceptive industry boomed during its prohibition* just as
the liquor manufacturers had during Prohibition. Manufacturers' and
retail profits were enormous in comparison to those on other pharmaceutical items. For the three leading brands of condoms in the late
1930s (Rameses, Sheiks, and Trojans), the average gross retail profit
was 72.5 per cent, wholesale 33.3 per cent, and the manufacturer's
average markup was 120 per cent. Profits were equally high on
diaphragms and spermicidal jelly products. For example:

Average Diaphragm	*Molded*	*Dipped*
Cost to manufacture	$.25	$.18
Price to wholesaler	$1.20	$.60
Price to druggist or doctor	$1.50	$.75
Price to consumer	$3.00 to	$1.50 to
	$5.00	$2.50

Average 3-oz. Tube of Vaginal Jelly	
Cost to manufacture	$.11
Price to wholesaler	$.40
Price to druggist or doctor	$.60
Price to consumer	$1.00 and up

These were not the prices of fly-by-night, small operators but of the
largest pharmaceutical houses and druggists.[81]

Despite high profits, the increasing commercial success of birth
control contributed to its ultimate legalization. The toleration of
public euphemistic advertising while noncommerical discussion of
contraception in popular journals remained illegal was a galling irony.
The birth controllers continually attacked that injustice. The fact that
the "patent medicine" contraceptives were not only ineffective, but

* Manufacture of contraceptives was not federally prohibited, only their interstate mailing, but
this weaker prohibition produced black-market conditions nonetheless.

often dangerous, deepened the unity of birth-control organizers with the medical profession.

The birth controllers' reaction against commercialization was not to combat it with demands for public sex education, but to lobby for doctors' privileges. Sanger, for example, argued not only against commercialization but against all "indiscriminate dissemination of birth control." [82] Furthermore, in the campaign against commercialization the biggest drug companies—frequently referred to by birth controllers as the "reputable" companies—tended to support restriction of sales to doctors. Their size made them reluctant to face legal difficulties, whereas smaller, transient companies sought quicker profits.* [83] The more professional orientation of the larger firms found them discriminated against in some avenues. For example, one large pharmaceutical house wanted to run an advertisement in a women's magazine urging women to consult their doctors for contraceptive advice; no magazine would take the ad, even those that ran euphemistic ads for feminine hygiene.[84] But the fact is that private doctors and scholarly medical journals were free to prescribe and discuss contraception. Although a legal basis for prosecuting doctors existed, under most state if not federal laws, no such prosecutions were attempted and most doctors felt safe to do what they believed was medically proper in their private practices.[85]

The more serious obstacles to birth control were not legal but social and economic. Despite the fact that a 1937 poll showed 79 per cent of U.S. women believed in birth control,[86] those who did not have access to private doctors regularly were effectively deprived of contraceptive information. Clinics served only a negligible fraction of the population.

The professional and upper classes, on the other hand, did get the birth-control information they needed. Had this not been the case, Sanger might have been able to mobilize a more effective lobbying campaign. Despite a brilliant organizing effort, Sanger's National Committee for Federal Legislation on Birth Control failed to push any

---

* It is important to bear in mind, however, that legalization and medical control of contraception ultimately gave the large pharmaceutical houses exclusive control over the contraceptive market, and ended all competition; prices of vaginal diaphragms, spermicide creams, and condoms remain today greatly inflated and provide enormous profit margins.

legislation through the Congress. A doctors-only bill was passed out of the Senate Judiciary Committee in 1934, but was quashed when Senator Pat McCarran, of anticommunist fame, demanded that it be held over for reconsideration to the next session. Sanger's efforts did, however, make possible victory in the courts in 1938. A test case had been designed to provide for litigation against customs officials, who had tended to enforce bans on "obscene materials" more rigidly than the Post Office. Sanger had arranged to have a package of pessaries mailed to Dr. Hannah Stone of the New York Clinical Research Bureau from Japan, and U.S. Customs seized the shipment. Holding against the government on appeal, Judge Augustus Hand used medical testimony in his opinion, arguing that in 1873 at the time of the passage of the Comstock law, information on contraception was poor, and that Congress would not have considered contraception immoral had it understood all the facts.[87]

This decision removed all federal legal bans on birth control. But it did not touch state legislation against birth control, and it did not solve the moral, social, and economic problems in providing birth control for U.S. citizens. The federal decision was based, furthermore, on narrow grounds. Sanger's work in congressional lobbying and at the Senate hearings on her bill had brought to the attention of public leaders the prestigious pro-birth-control opinion in the medical profession. This sense that birth control had been endorsed by the "experts" informed the judge's opinion. Indeed, it declared birth control not obscene *because* it was a medical tool. The opinion avoided any discussion of changing sexual morality or women's rights. The birth-control movement had won this victory by purporting to represent the medical profession. As a result, nonmedical birth-control programs gained little from the decision. The progress of projects such as birth-control education for relief recipients depended more on economic and social pressures on the New Deal administrators.

In the final analysis, however, judges, doctors, government administrators, and pharmaceutical houses entering the contraceptive business were all persuaded by an enormous change not only in public opinion but in public demand for birth control. The top-down birth-control programs of the New Deal were responses to bottom-up pressures. Just as all New Deal measures were in part a stabilization program undertaken by the governors to pacify the governed, and in part a concession to demands raised by the victims of capitalism's temporary collapse, so birth-control measures were both a stabilization program and a response to demand.

The popular demand for birth control would have been much stronger, naturally, had women been more organized during the Depression. Still, when working-class and other poor women did get together, they sometimes raised the demand for birth control spontaneously; and when birth-control clinics were made available, they responded enthusiastically.[88] Clinic workers in Bangor, Maine, reported that one woman, a mother of seven, arrived at the clinic on a bitter winter day in 1937, having walked five miles in only a thin coat. They had to warm and feed her before she could see a doctor.[89] One birth-control clinic worker in Brooklyn told about an incident when a working-class woman she was visiting, after a brief discussion about birth control, asked to be excused for a few minutes; she returned with six more women and said, "They want to know about birth control.[90] In Paterson, New Jersey, a Working Women's Council organized to establish a birth-control clinic. Mill workers were active in the initial efforts. They invited a woman from the Montclair, New Jersey, ABCL clinic to speak and she stressed the need to work quietly and avoid newspaper publicity in order not to provoke opposition. A social worker at the meeting reported that then a "poorly dressed" woman jumped up and in "scanty English she said, 'We want publicity; we expect opposition; we will fight it; we want to reach the women like myself.' " [91] Anecdotes such as these suggest that where working-class women became involved, they were not only enthusiastic but tended to a more confrontational, militant style of organizing.

Letters continued to pour in to Sanger and the ABCL asking for help. Birth control was a subject of discussion in many local papers, including the popular press. When a woman's page columnist on the Columbus, Ohio, *Citizen*, for example, published Margaret Sanger's address as a source for birth-control information, Sanger got over five hundred letters in a few days. Here are two typical excerpts:

> I have 8 children and the oldest is 14. My husband works on relief, because his job is shut down. . . . Please tell me the secret about

birth control. When you write about it, please write to me in plain words because I don't know what it means in big words.

I am a farmer's wife in the drouth area and we have not had a crop for four years. My husband worked on the WPA, but now all the farmers have been layed off, so we are very hard up. . . . It spoils married life to be worried all the time over having more babies. . . .[92]

These letters tended to support what the polls had shown since the early 1920s: that support for birth control was surprisingly high even in rural and small-town communities which seemed very conservative on other issues. The high proportion of mail from rural areas reflected in part the inaccessibility of local birth-control advice. Furthermore, the most powerful organized opposition to birth control came from the Catholic Church, relatively weak in rural areas and strongest in large working-class parishes. Catholic women consistently used birth control less and attended clinics less than Jewish or Protestant women; nevertheless many working-class Catholic women used contraceptives. A report on a New York City clinic with a predominantly poor Italian Catholic clientele showed 63.5 per cent had used birth control before coming to the clinic, as compared with approximately 90 per cent of Protestant clients in a Harlem clinic. Other studies showed comparable statistics.[93]

The interest of working-class women, even Catholics, in birth control did not represent a rebellion against a traditional family role. As letters and interviews showed, women wanted control over pregnancies to improve and make easier their traditional home work, not to escape it. The increase in birth-control use during the Depression was not caused, as it had been in past decades among professional-class women, by the search for more education and better employment. Yet the desire for birth control came overwhelmingly from women, not men, and was not quite identical with the so-called economic motives that we have discussed earlier. For working-class as opposed to more prosperous women, reducing family size and extending the gaps between children was not just a matter of the budget but also of working a little less hard and in a less alienated fashion: having more control over the conditions of housework and child care, being able to do good, skilled housework and child care. It was a motivation not entirely different from that of an artisan or skilled worker who prefers to be able to do a good job.

Some women viewed their childbearing capacity as a form of social labor. In a few cases working-class women threatened, in fact, to use birth control as a weapon. For example, in 1937 twenty Lower East Side New York City housewives picketed City Hall against procrastination in the construction of promised public housing, and announced they would have no more babies until their demands were met.[94] This threat had ancient and repeated precedents; it represented a form of resistance to having one's child-raising labor and the product—children—expropriated by men. But in the context of the sharp class struggle that prevailed in the United States in the 1930s, such "birth strike" threats took on other political potentials and were used in the struggle not against individual men but against the state.

In many ways the demand for and use of birth control among working-class women in the Depression coincided with an increase in their class consciousness. Birth-control use almost always represented, in fact, a raised self-evaluation of women's own work as child-raisers, a change that increased women's self-identification as workers, even without being wage laborers. These changes in self-image presaged the possibility of greater sexual equality within the working class. Despite the rapid commercialization of contraception and exploitation of the demand for it in the 1930s, birth-control use was nevertheless a great step toward more power for many working-class women.

Some New Dealers and social workers supported and encouraged the birth-control demands of working-class women. Social workers convinced settlement houses in New York City to provide contraceptive services.[95] In Connecticut social workers organized a mobile contraceptive clinic in a van to reach housebound women.[96] New Deal admirers of the Soviet Union sometimes urged emulation of its birth-control policies.[97] Many Left and liberal New Deal birth controllers rejected hereditarian theories of poverty and justifications for birth control.

Nevertheless, most social workers' attitudes remained condescending, since their motivation was to help others rather than themselves, and since their professional positions nurtured in them the conviction that they knew what kind of help was good for the poor.

They focused on birth control as a tool against poverty; thus there was an essentially Neo-Malthusian theory implicit in their policies. Birth control became mainly a welfare program, only secondarily a human right.

Furthermore, many social workers tended to see their clients not as *having* problems but as *being* problems. No matter how environmentalist their analysis of the problem's genesis, they still saw it as located within the individual. They believed that accumulated experiences of poverty and powerlessness damaged people, deprived them of skills, and that it was this deprivation which, by preventing them from competing equally, caused their poverty. They called such people "disadvantaged," "underprivileged." Although not their fault, it was their problem, to be corrected by changing them. By contrast one might have argued that the problem was of the rich, not the poor; that in class society some people were always "disadvantaged"; that this problem of inequality could only be solved by correcting the behavior, and the structural privileges, of the rich. The view of most birth controllers not only denied that the rich were the problem but did not even consider the possibility that the problem lay in the interrelations between rich and poor. This is because their view involved an isolation of social problems from one another, a refusal to look at the over-all structures of the society. By contrast an examination of the many interconnected and mutually reinforcing factors creating poverty would have led inevitably to an analysis of class exploitation and male supremacy as systems. Social problems would be seen as systemic, not individual at all; individuals could have been offered birth control without requiring that they blame themselves for their problems.

An example of ignoring systemic problems in New Deal–era birth-control propaganda was its virtual denial that reproduction was particularly a woman's problem. The program of the National Committee on Federal Legislation for Birth Control, for example, listed four reasons for birth control—to help family spacing, to decrease poverty, to stop illegal abortions, and to eliminate mental and physical deficiency.[98] ABCL documents similarly omitted any mention of women's rights; for example, a 1934 pamphlet listed eight necessities for family health, in this order: prevention of venereal disease; complete elimination of abortion; reduction of maternal and infant mortality; sex education; early marriage [*sic*]; prevention of conception for unhealthy, exhausted, or economically unprepared women; sterilization of the insane and feeble-minded; good marital sexual adjustment.[99] For women birth control was presented as a remedial aid in the case of abnormal personal problems: "unhealthy, exhausted or economically unprepared." The truth is, of course, that women's problems were not abnormal and personal but normal and social; that they needed birth control as a right, not a cure for a disability; that birth control was a needed defense against a male-supremacist system and economic inequality, not personal inadequacy.

Denying the existence of sexual discrimination actually made it more difficult to convince women of the importance, and potential, of birth control. The birth controllers presented contraception antihistorically, as if it had just been invented and was a means of improving society as it was now structured, ignoring birth control's capacity to affect class and sex conflicts within the society. It was as if social inferiority, now that it was no longer considered hereditary, were randomly distributed; the problems were in people themselves—their diseases and deficiencies—not in patterns of deprivation produced by the social structure. This kind of analysis, even if environmental in its assessment of the causes of deficiencies, functioned equally with eugenics to undermine collective struggles to change the over-all distribution of power.

Another impact of this "blaming-the-victim" sociology on birth control as a movement was to continue the pattern of professionalization. Viewing individuals as the problem was also a way for social workers and bureaucrats to retain control of the service programs they offered. Welfare programs placed birth control in the context of social worker–client, subject-object, relations, discouraging mass participation in the programs. Already in the 1920s the influx of professionals had moved birth control organizationally away from local leagues with amateur participation toward national staff organizations. That tendency continued in the 1930s. Margaret Sanger left the ABCL altogether and put her energies into the National Committee for Federal Legislation on Birth Control, a lobbying organization with less room for mass participation than ever before. Indeed, the NCFLBC was not even a membership organization; the extent of amateur participation possible was subscription to its newsletter. In one of her first actions with the new organization, Sanger hired a prestigious New York public-relations firm to advise her on tactics.[100] She became, with her lieutenants, an expert Washington "pol." She accumulated endorsements from organizations claiming to represent twenty million voters;[101] she attempted to attach pro-birth-control amendments as riders to relief bills (using the high birth rates of relief recipients as justification); she organized state-by-state pressure applied to any legislator that seemed even potentially winnable. Ultimately she failed, and no federal legislation for birth control was passed (although she managed to smother in committee H.R.5370 in 1935, which would have made the receipt of contraceptive information illegal). But the lobbying tactics became a permanent part of the new style of the birth controllers.[102]

This kind of work required money, and Sanger also devoted an increasing amount of effort to fund-raising among the rich. Winning over upper-class women was part of the legislative strategy, for while the labor power in the movement remained primarily women's, the influence of class status was all the more advantageous. In a 1935 magazine article, "Birth Control Goes Suave," one reporter described the new birth-control movement:

> Evidence that the cause has reached the dignity of a grown-up movement was offered at the recent banquet of the National Committee on Federal Legislation for Birth Contol in the Hotel Mayflower in Washington. Limousines drew to the door in a prosperous relay, debouching a confident and well-bred crowd. Women predominated, society-page cameras clicked. Significant was the cordiality between dinner guests and the occasional Congressman they encountered among the potted palms. . . . No one expressed anger or impatience at the snail's pace methods necessary for doing business with out government. No one was *gauche* enough to recall the naive and impolite methods once used, when birth control leaders courted arrest and forced test cases on embarrassed magistrates. . . . Margaret Sanger's movement had tacitly announced that it was ready to play ball. . . .
>
> Women of the type now appearing in the birth control movement have had social training in drawing-room diplomacy, and they carry their tact with them into legislative halls. They are deft at fund-raising—their childhood friends are the heads of corpora-

tions, the publishers of newspapers. . . . Many a man . . . will reach for his checkbook when the appeal comes from his hostess of the week before. The owner of a radio station or a magazine chain, inaccessible to most callers, listens politely to the plea of a woman who heads the membership committee of the Junior League, which his daughter would like to join.[103]

The fund-raising events were sometimes so snobbish that they even antagonized professionals. Harry Hansen, for example, *New York World-Telegram* literary editor, wrote to Sanger: "Your formal invitation to the H. G. Wells dinner [held at the Waldorf-Astoria] looks to me like one of those Big Business Rackets. Hence I withdraw my name from your so-called reception committee." [104] So involved was Sanger with this pretentious style that she did not defend herself on the reasonable grounds that she was trying to raise money, but tried to convince Hansen that he belonged on the reception committee because of his literary merit:

> You were asked to be on the Reception Committee not because I wanted $10.00 from you or wanted your financial support at all. There will be many literary people on the Reception Committee invited to the Dinner to sit at the speakers' table. There will be others—bankers and other persons who can pay and who . . . find it cheap at that. I do not know whether you attended the Tagore or Einstein dinners at which there were cover charges of $25.00 and $100.00 respectively.[105]

For Sanger this style of organizing had become more than a tactic. She believed now in using important people to apply pressure on the government, and despite her continued legislative failures did not again try to bring about mass action. She did not, for example, try to mobilize masses of women to come to Washington to testify that birth control was their right; rather she relied on the persuasive abilities of society women and male experts to convince legislators that birth control was good for what ailed the country. Perhaps, indeed, she feared the possibilities of mass action. Certainly she relied on supporters who had such fears, and Sanger herself undoubtedly feared the possibility that popular organization would challenge her personal hegemony. While traveling, she ignored local birth-control organizations that did not acknowledge her national leadership and the political line she laid down, and she excluded them from conferences. Sanger's relations with co-workers were those of master to apprentice, or employer to employee, and her apprentices and employees were frequently discontented. The files of her Clinical Research Bureau in New York City held many letters of complaint from workers, torn because they believed in the cause they were working for while they resented being treated like proletarians. Workers were poorly paid, allowed no participation in decision-making, even deprived of information that would allow them an overview of their work—turning their work, in fact, into alienated labor, or piecework. They complained of speedups, Sanger insisting that they were not working as fast as they could. Workers were fired without notice or explanation.[106]

The ABCL organizing style did not differ fundamentally from Sanger's. It too concentrated on getting endorsements from the rich and prestigious and neglected educational or organizational development of local chapters. ABCL president Eleanor Dwight Jones usually argued that reducing the population of the "unfit" was the main task of the movement.[107] The ABCL and Sanger's Clinical Research Bureau merged in 1938 into the Birth Control Federation of America, and the new organization established policies designed at "Professionalizing" its work. These new policies included the introduction of time sheets for the staff, to clock working hours and also to evaluate the time spent on particular activities, thus enabling cost-benefit analysis of the work. In efforts clearly designed to check decentralization the BCFA prohibited staff members from undertaking any work without clearing it with the national director; and even ordered elected board members not to make suggestions to local leagues without clearing them with the national director.[108]

Birth Control and Government: Race and Class Politics

The top-down organization of birth control, both in politics and procedures, was intensified by its integration into the programs of governmental social-welfare agencies. During the Depression small-scale birth-control programs developed on three governmental levels: state, and occasionally city, public-health programs; federal relief

programs; and a population-control program in a Third World colony
of the United States. Let us consider each in turn.

The first state to offer birth-control services through its public-
health program was North Carolina in 1937, and it was followed by
South Carolina, Virginia, Georgia, Mississippi, Alabama, and Florida.[109] Despite control by health officials, birth control was offered to
women for economic and social as well as medical reasons. On the
whole, contraceptive advice was offered only to indigent mothers;
others were directed to physicians.[110]

These were not the leading but by and large the most backward
states in social-service programs. Their pioneering role in government-
sponsored birth control was conditioned by the absence of large
Catholic constituencies, and stimulated by racism. A generally high
Southern birth rate was higher among blacks. Black families, both
urban and rural, were among those hardest hit by the Depression in
the South: they were the first fired, the first evicted, the first foreclosed.
Like other poor people they did not respond to economic pressure by
lowering their birth rates, so the Depression added to the racist fear of
being overpopulated by blacks. The North Carolina public-health
officer who initiated the program described his technique for convincing recalcitrant country health officers that birth-control clinics were
needed: check your vital statistics, he would suggest, confident that
they would discover a high proportion of black births and that they
would then come around.[111] In Miami, Florida, separate birth-control
clinics for whites and blacks were organized. The separate-but-equal
pretense broke down quickly when the blacks, given autonomy in
their clinic, ignored the "advice" of the white directors. Dr. DeVilbiss,
furious, took away its funding: "Our colored clinic did not turn out
the way we thought it would so it should not be mentioned this time
[on the ABCL list of affiliated clinics]. We shall likely have to
re-organize it. I wonder if southern darkies can ever be entrusted with
such a clinic. Our experience causes us to doubt their ability to work
except under white supervision." [112] State leagues affiliated with the
ABCL, later with the Planned Parenthood Federation of America,
continued segregated into the 1940s.[113] There was a history several
decades long of racist use of eugenic rhetoric and theory. In the
Southern states, eugenics had provided justifications for antimiscege-

nation laws passed in the twentieth century.[114] Echoing the conservative eugenists, Virginia officials in the mid-1920s thought birth control inimical to their maintenance of their racist society. An official of the State Board of Health wrote to the ABCL:

> I believe that Mrs. Margaret Sangster [sic] and her group have done far more to ruin the future of our country than all other methods combined, unless it be the amalgamation of the white and negro races, now rapidly in progress. The evidence which I have is that the universal adoption of the methods advocated by you has done much to increase immorality among the unmarried, who have no fear of consequences. . . . You may now be securing the adoption of such measures by the feeble-minded and lower type, but I very much doubt it. You have, however, met with overwhelming success among the higher type. . . . [This] will mean their ultimate deterioration, just as it occurred in Rome.[115]

Yet in the 1930s the same Virginia authorities promoted birth control. Methods changed, goals did not: they had become convinced that the "lower type" would accept contraception and the "higher type" would never give it up.

Although racism in the South was built on segregation, it rested on the exploitation and impoverishment of a large proportion of whites as well, and the continuing arrogance of "good" Southern families toward "white trash." The demographic characteristics of Southern blacks—high birth rates, not lowered by increasing economic pressure—described Southern poor whites as well, though to a slightly lesser degree. State programs tried to bring birth control to them also. North Carolina, for example, persuaded several large textile mills, employing mostly whites, to distribute slips in payroll envelopes telling workers that company nurses would provide contraceptive information.[116] (One might wonder at the efficacy of introducing birth-control propaganda to workers through their bosses.)

Racism and the defense of class distinctions were integrated into an over-all eugenic view of Southern population and health problems as overreproduction of the "unfit," a view which lumped together all forms of undesirable inferiorities. "In a study of 1500 women admitted to the obstetrical wards .   . 39 per cent of the whites and 70 per cent of the negroes were found to be feeble-minded or at least of a mental age of only eleven years or less," argued a Miami birth-control clinic, later supported by the City Department of Health and the Public Health Nursing Service.[117] A fund-raising letter said:

Dear Friend and Taxpayer,

You were taxed in round numbers TWO MILLION DOLLARS for the care of pauper, indigent sick and the criminal classes in Dade County for 1933. . . .
    500 indigent mothers in Dade County have been instructed in eugenic birth regulations. . . .[118]

Racism, then as now, is not a Southern problem. Indeed, the tendency to project it exclusively upon the South has been a device of Northern racism. In 1939 the Birth Control Federation of America, responding to the cooperativeness of Southern state public-health officials, designed a "Negro Project," arguing that Southern poverty was a major national problem and one which could be ameliorated through birth-rate reduction. This project was a microcosm of the elitist birth-control programs whose design eliminated the possibility of popular, grass roots involvement in birth control as a cause. "The mass of Negroes," argued the project proposal, "particularly in the South, still breed carelessly and disastrously, with the result that the increase among Negroes, even more than among whites, is from that portion of the population least intelligent and fit, and least able to rear children properly." [119] Despite the pretense of concern with the unfit *among* Negroes, this statement was immediately followed by a chart showing the over-all increase of the black as opposed to the white population. The eugenic disguise fell off to reveal overt white supremacy. "Public health statistics," the proposal went on, "merely hint at the primitive state of civilization in which most Negroes in the South live."

The project was to hire three or four "colored Ministers, preferably with social-service backgrounds, and with engaging personalities" to travel through the South and propagandize for birth control. "The most successful educational approach to the Negro is through a religious appeal." As Sanger wrote, in a private letter, "We do not want word to go out that we want to exterminate the Negro population and the minister is the man who can straighten out that idea if it ever occurs to any of their more rebellious members." [120] The ministers would enlist the aid of black physicians—who were expected to offer their services gratis—and would attempt to organize a "Negro Birth Control Committee" in each community. A general steering committee was to supervise the whole project, but the birth-control leaders had no qualms about their reluctance to surrender control even to the hand-picked local blacks. Clarence Gamble, author of the proposal and negotiator of its eventual funding by Mary Lasker, wrote in a private memo: "*Colored Steering Committee.* There is great danger that we will fail because the Negroes think it a plan for extermination. Hence lets appear to let the colored think it run it [*sic*] as we appeared to let south do the conference at Atlanta." [121]

The relationship between the projects and local doctors was equally illuminating as to the BCFA mode of operation. Since no doctors were at first to be paid, the proposal would allow them to recompense themselves at the expense of their patients: ". . . offer interested physicians a limited supply of free material which they are at liberty to charge a private patient for, but which must be given without charge to an indigent patient." Eventually Sanger and Mary Lasker revised the project to include hiring a doctor. Gamble agreed to "a subsidy to a local colored doctor to put his weight behind the new regime," [122] but preferred to spend BCFA funds on education only, through the ministers. When the project was operative Gamble clashed with South Carolina Public Health Director Seibels: Gamble did not want his funds "diluted with a lot of general health work," whereas Seibels thought the general health work was essential to the program.[123] Gamble's principle was adherence to the narrowest, single-issue orientation. Though he himself did not believe that birth control alone could solve problems of poverty and discrimination, that was the educational content of the project.

In content and organization the BCFA's "Negro Project" functioned to stabilize existing social relations. It worked through conservative community leaders such as ministers and doctors. Nor did it challenge the commercial relationship of doctors to patients by paying doctors to work with the poor. From New York the BCFA sought support for the Project by writing to everyone in the *Colored Who's Who.*[124] The birth-control propaganda in the South was removed from any politics that might have given it a socially progressive meaning: women's rights, civil rights, or any social analysis of southern poverty.

Lack of a larger analysis doomed even well-meaning birth controllers to the perpetuation of racist and elitist attitudes in all their work, not only in projects specifically aimed at blacks. An ABCL field worker wrote about the Southern women she encountered: "They are almost child-like in their faith in the clinic workers and what can be done for them." She was outraged at their poverty: "It is difficult to believe that so much poverty and misery can exist in such a playground as Miami with all its wealth and gaiety"; but she was quick to find solutions in the puny efforts being made: "However, during the Season generous donations are made for hospitalization and contraceptive work. . . . With laws no longer hindering and a method which is simple and obtainable everywhere under-privileged mothers can at last be free from over-frequent child bearing and establish for themselves and their children a decent standard of living." [125] With such an analysis a woman's failure to establish a decent standard of living was naturally to be blamed on stupidity or irresponsibility.

The sympathetic but condescending attitudes of this birth-control worker were paralleled among many caseworkers and public-health nurses in federal as well as local programs. As the Depression continued, a few federal agencies had begun surreptitiously funding birth-control work. In the late 1930s a confidential memo in Sanger's files listed two federal birth-control projects under the Farm Security Administration: one, paying public-health nurses to bring contraceptive information to poor farm women, and the other, paying them to bring such information to the California migrant labor camps.[126] In addition to these authorized programs, many caseworkers were directing clients to private clinics and doctors for contraceptive advice. Acting without explicit authorization, such caseworkers also lacked training in dealing with sexual issues. Furthermore, they were usually educated people coming into contact for the first time with the illiterate, demoralized, and resentful poor. No doubt many of the latter did not receive the social workers with welcome and trust. The social workers, on the other hand, could not always avoid a condemning attitude toward the poverty, dirt, and fatalism with which their clients often lived.[127] Even the most sympathetic workers often

responded to the extremely poor with a blinding condescension, as in
the report of this social worker on her visit to a migrant worker's
family in California:

> One of my first cases was a family reported to our agency for neglect
> of children. . . . It was a sort of improvised commune, which the
> poor and migratory had found for themselves. Here they could
> unload the dilapidated Fords and turn the children loose. The
> luxuries of the place included one water faucet, serving the colony
> of thirteen tents—apparently the only sanitary convenience.
>   I found the family I sought established in two tents, the pots
> and pans hanging in a row along a tent beam, the washing
> steaming over a stove made from an old oil can. Five scrawny
> children hung about. Two of them, I learned, were registered in
> school, but were temporarily on vacation for lack of shoes. Three
> were babies, one obviously defective. The mother was loyal to her
> brood, tired and dispirited as she was.
>   "But why do you have so many children," I asked bluntly.
>   She shrugged her shoulders.
>   "My husband not very bright, not make much money. But he
> do the best he can. . . . Too bad," [she said] apologetically, "some
> of the children not very bright too. . . ."
>   Before the winter rains descended, the mother of five was again
> big with child.[128]

Among all the myriad problems faced by this woman, the social
worker had little basis for her judgment that lack of birth control was
central. Unable to offer contraception herself, she tried and failed to
find a doctor to provide a diaphragm and fitting. She then tried to
arrange a sterilization for her client, but was disappointed again to
find that the county hospital would not do it; this inquiry apparently
took place before any discussion with the woman about what she
wanted. There is no report of offering condoms to the husband, or of
speaking to the husband at all (although the source we have is only a
fragment of a report).

Beyond the social worker's understandable helplessness to offer
concrete birth-control assistance, there is another problem in her
condescending attitude. She finds it somehow odd, or at least worth
mentioning, that the woman loves her children; indeed, she describes
their relationship in animal terms—she was "loyal to her brood." The
social worker's report that the woman said her husband was "not very

bright" seems so unlikely, both in language and attitude, that one is inclined to question whether it was an accurate report at all or a projection of the social worker's own attitudes. Admittedly a novice at her job, she was responding humanly and naturally to a circumstance that shocked her. Better education about the problems of poverty might well have improved her sensitivity to the situation, but it was not available, because the whole relief program was an emergency measure taken by a government not permanently committed to public responsibility for social welfare. Without the premise that all the ingredients of a decent standard of living, including but not limited to birth control, are a citizen's right, the administrators of relief measures were bound to see their work as charity and their clients as inferior. Some contraceptive information reached poor women through relief nursing and social work, but its extent was small—the total amount spent by the federal government directly on birth control was $11,000, according to Sanger's confidential memo—and its justification an emergency situation, designed to help individual emergency cases at the discretion of individual nurses and social workers. This was hardly a program of making birth control a right.

The Depression did, however, bring about one governmental attempt to introduce a massive birth-control program, not in the continental United States but in Puerto Rico. We cannot here discuss the administration of population control in Puerto Rico, but the political debate about its inception raised issues that soon became of importance on the mainland itself. Since the early 1920s Margaret Sanger had visited Third World countries to explain the contribution that birth control could make toward alleviating poverty. In Japan, China, Korea, Hawaii, India, and Bermuda, among other places, she stimulated national birth-control organizations. In several underdeveloped countries, liberal governments supported birth-control programs, though lack of funds usually made them minimal. Then in the 1930s a major campaign was fought for the legalization of birth control in Puerto Rico, finally won in 1937 over strong opposition from the Catholic Church. U.S. pressure was extremely important, if not defining, in this victory.* [129]

* One conclusion that seems unavoidable from this episode is that Catholic opposition—unchallenged by other religious institutions in Puerto Rico—was not insuperable when governments had other powerful motives for supporting birth control.

Whereas Catholic opposition was based on antisexual and anti-woman attitudes, Puerto Rican nationalism produced another opposition to birth control that was neither. Nationalists perceived birth control as a U.S.-manufactured ideology, a form of cultural imperialism, and above all a means of deflecting attention from the deepest problems of the island and a permanent solution to them. One of the more moderate opponents of the pro-birth-control legislation, J. Enamorado Cuesta, Secretary of the Nationalist Party, wrote as follows:

> There is no denying that overpopulation . . . is at present a problem to us. . . . it is directly at the door of American capitalism that the blame must be laid for everything that is wrong in Porto Rico today. . . . when American intervention was started, while sanitary conditions were certainly not very good, still our people owned their land, the produce they exported. . . . in thirty-four years of American intervention . . . with the cooperation of American-made native and continental legislative bodies, the people have been dispossessed of their land and brought to the condition of paupers. . . .
>
> This does not mean that I am systematically opposed to birth control. But our real problem lies in the actual control by American capital of practically all our wealth. . . . We may, and we may not, enact birth control laws (I think we would) as soon as the American flag is lowered from our public buildings.[130]

Cuesta's position was that though overpopulation may have contributed to Puerto Rico's poverty, it was not the cause; Puerto Rico's underdevelopment was caused by U.S. imperialism. Any proposed solution that did not reach to the root cause, that did less than free Puerto Rico entirely from U.S. imperialism, would be a mere palliative. He was not opposed to the palliative; he did not wish, however, to surrender his demand for the whole cure.

Cuesta's position could only be refuted by denying his analysis of the cause of Puerto Rico's problems. Other internationalist critics of birth control have sometimes confused imperialist motives in birth-control programs with the value of contraception as a technology, and have minimized the issue of birth control as an individual human right. Their confusion, however, was created by the smothering of the issue of individual rights in the arguments for the value of birth control. Although this had begun to happen in domestic eugenic arguments for birth control produced in the 1920s and 1930s, it was carried much further in the discussions of birth control as a cure for economic underdevelopment. For example, a committee of the American Child Health Association, appointed by President Hoover, reported that Puerto Rico had 174,650 "too many" children.[131] Perhaps this was merely a clumsy formulation; but the mentality that would lead a demographer to calculate the number of "extra" children is one that is not particularly concerned with individual rights and human emotions. In May 1939 a report of Roosevelt's Interdepartmental Committee on Puerto Rico labeled overpopulation the basic cause of "the Puerto Rican problem." The Committee proposed a mass campaign to reduce the birth rate at least to the level of the death rate. "All other endeavors to improve the health conditions of Puerto Rico must be organically tied to, and made contingent upon, effective birth-control work." [132] This Puerto Rican program was in many ways the embryo of today's massive U.S. population-control programs. Their common denominator is the treatment of birth control as a weapon in the arsenal of economic planners. It was almost a full reversal of the nineteenth-century conception of birth control, voluntary motherhood, in which technology followed the human and especially female desire for self-determination; now technology leads and individual will is to be made to follow by the application of powerful persuasive techniques. Birth control became a lever for the manipulation of the economy much as advertising is used to stimulate consumption.

There was also an embryonic domestic version of this new conception of birth control as an economic tool. Although the United States was not an underdeveloped country like Puerto Rico, still the severe crisis of the 1930s had given it one of the characteristics of underdevelopment—"overpopulation" in the form of massive and persistent unemployment. The Depression was not a temporary collapse but the beginning of a permanent inability of private corporations to provide full employment without government assistance. The demographers began speaking of the danger of overpopulation in the 1940s, after decades of worrying about underpopulation, and their change of mind was stimulated as much by unemployment as by birth-rate changes. Even before they were postulating general overpopulation, however, while the differential birth rate was still the problem they noticed, they began to suggest that birth control might alleviate or at least lessen the unemployment problem.

Margaret Sanger, usually in the vanguard of new birth-control arguments, asserted in a major speech in 1935 that unemployment was not a temporary but a permanent problem, which only birth control could correct. She identified the cause as technology.[133] More sophisticated economists realized that unemployment was not created by technology, but by the capitalist mode of production.

Some professionals interested in birth control realized that the Depression represented a major turning point for the economy, and anxiously leaped at the new uses of birth control that it meant. As Professor James Bossard, a sociologist, observed:

> The demand for unskilled labor has been declining . . . but it is in this group . . . that the reproductive rates are highest. . . . As the demand for unskilled, low intelligence labor decreases, corresponding readjustments must be made in the supply of this type of labor, if we are to avoid the crystallization of a large element in the population who are destined to become permanent public charges. This points again directly to birth control on a scale which we have not yet fully visioned.[134]

Like so many professional eugenists before him, Bossard slipped from concern for the unemployment of the unskilled to the hereditary assumption that the low-born were only suited to unskilled jobs. This kind of slippery assumption is what lay behind Sanger's blaming unemployment on technology: assuming that class is largely a matter of heredity, neither she nor Bossard could perceive that another form of economic organization might have made technological advance beneficial to all by providing better education for better jobs. But within the system set up by their assumptions, they had latched on to a new way to manipulate the employment market, a new variable open to social control—the supply of people itself.

This was a major factor behind birth control's ultimate achievement of respectability. The Depression—capitalism's worst crisis to date—began the transformation of birth control into an official program for economic improvement, without social unrest. The transformation of birth control over the decades is encapsulated in the title of an article by Guy Burch, leading eugenist and later population controller: "Birth Control vs. Class Suicide." [135] Four decades previously the cry had been that birth control *was* race suicide, as its practice by educated, prosperous women challenged sex roles, sexual inequality, and the family structure within their class. In the 1930s birth control became the alternative to class suicide, a means of heading off the militancy of an increasingly powerful working class. Yet in both eras the impact of birth control was double. In the 1900s race suicide represented not only a women's rebellion but also a deepening of class divisions among women. In the 1930s, birth control not only represented an effort to prevent social explosion but also, simultaneously, was an explosion of new demands and expectations from among working-class and poor women. These complexities have been part of the history of birth control since its inception, and continue today.

12
Planned Parenthood

IN 1938 rivalry in the birth-control movement was ended with the reunification of Sanger's friends and enemies in the Birth Control Federation of America. In 1942 the new organization changed its name to the Planned Parenthood Federation of America (PPFA). It was the only national birth-control organization until the abortion-reform movement that began in the late 1960s, and its new name—Planned Parenthood—defined a new concept of birth control that dominated in the United States until then.

Planned parenthood posed as apolitical, offering no over-all program for social change. But in confining itself to a single issue and in its interpretation of that issue, it functioned to preserve and strengthen the existing view of the success of U.S. capitalism in providing the potential for democracy, prosperity, and freedom for all. The central contribution of the planned-parenthood organizations to social stability was through their attempts to strengthen the family. Planned parenthood took the family, not the woman within it, as the unit for the application of reproductive control. As voluntary motherhood had envisioned the restoration of a stable preindustrial family, in a literally reactionary orientation, as birth control had considered rejecting the family, or at least revolutionizing the power relations within it between man and woman, parent and child, as part of a revolutionary orientation, now planned parenthood set about stabilizing the family in a reformist orientation. Planned parenthood implicitly denied that the family itself was a source or transmitter of injustice, ignoring sexism within it and its function in socializing children to sexist and elitist relations outside it. In the 1940s it became clear that whatever vestigial concern with over-all social injustice remained in the PPFA, its leaders were primarily concerned with social instability as a far greater evil; they were concerned to correct specific inequities, but only within the safety of continued social peace.

Reform and defense of the family were the earmark of planned parenthood, its defining difference from earlier birth-control programs. Yet planned parenthood was also part of a gradual progression away from a feminist and socialist birth-control program, a progression begun in the 1920s with the influx of professional personnel and values into the ABCL. Planned parenthood in the 1940s expressed a distinct second stage in that progression—the incorporation of reproductive control into state programs as a form of social planning. The PPFA commitment to planning must be understood in two ways: planned child spacing and family size, and governmental population planning. In the movement toward large-scale social planning of population, the 1940s was a midpoint between the seeds sown in the Depression and harvested in the 1950s and 1960s with massive federal support for population-control programs. A program that called for governmental support and policy planning could not contribute to social change that altered the fundamental power structure of the society.

The PPFA in the 1940s was not yet calling for a population-control policy, because there was not yet agreement that overpopulation was a serious problem. The demand was for planning, not specifically reduction in numbers, and it was a planning that involved qualitative as well as quantitative views of what was a desirable population. It is this qualitative set of norms that provides the unity between the large-scale population planning and the small-scale planned families that PPFA urged. Both involved the imposition of standards of excellence based on upper-middle-class income and educational levels and aspirations, and of policies directed to reforming and preserving the existing social structure.

This was not a conservative but a reform program. Like the ABCL in the Depression, the PPFA attracted the support of liberals in the government, those from capitalist and professional classes who welcomed and even fought for reforms to make the economic and social system more generous and tolerant. This was true not only of their desire to raise the standards of living of the poor through family planning, but also of their increased recognition—at least among those aware of these issues—that women might be happier with more sexual fulfillment. Part of the PPFA program of family stability was the recognition of mutual sexual enjoyment as an important cement in marriages and of women's sexual repression as a dangerous, explosive frustration. The key difference in their sexual ideology from that of their nineteenth-century predecessors was that the latter thought sexual control led to stability whereas the PPFA people thought sexual expression led to stability. Neither group endorsed a program of sexual exploration that led away from the family (although the institution of the family by the 1940s comprehended divorce and remarriage).

The reforms promoted by Planned Parenthood were desperately needed. Planned Parenthood made a valuable contribution to the independence, self-esteem, and aspirations of many women. Nevertheless, Planned Parenthood both reflected and contributed to the decline of a popular birth-control movement, which had been part of a program to change the whole society. The PPFA is hardly responsible for this failure; the ultimate cause was the general weakening of socialist and feminist struggles in the country after the First World War, and the adoption of the birth-control movement by reformers representing other class and sex interests. Under professional control, Planned Parenthood offered people birth control wrapped in a propaganda package that accepted existing power relations. It challenged neither the sexual inequities within the family, nor the sexual or class inequities of the medical system, nor the imposition of over-all cultural patterns by a dominant minority.

Dialectically, the success of Planned Parenthood in what it did do—making contraception more accessible, and thereby freeing many women from unplanned pregnancies—helped create the conditions for a revived feminist movement, which in turn produced a second feminist birth-control movement in the late 1960s. An attentive look at the themes of the 1940s will show that they are still among the defining issues of birth-control politics today.

A New Name, A Clean Image

The radical associations of the name "birth control" seemed inescapable to many in the movement in the 1920s and 1930s. Opponents still called Sanger a free lover, a revolutionary, an unwed mother. Some supporters tried to coin new names for the movement: "Children's Charter," "Better Families," "Child Spacing," "Family Planning" were a few. Many of these suggestions had a meaning similar to that which was finally victorious; they lacked only the catchy alliteration of "Planned Parenthood." All the names proposed took the focus away from women and placed it on families or children. All were designed to have as little sexual connotation as possible.

"Planned Parenthood" was a name that had been proposed from within the ABCL from at least 1938.[1] That it was not adopted until 1942 was due in part to opposition from Margaret Sanger. Within the birth-control movement the name change was supported largely by the eugenists. But the specific name was chosen by public-relations consultant D. Kenneth Rose, originally hired by Sanger. Despite her objections, the switch to "Planned Parenthood" flowed directly from Sanger's own policies.[2]

One of the arguments for the new name was that it connoted a positive program unlike the negativism implicit in "birth control." This idea that "birth control" was a negative phrase reflected mainly eugenic influence. Eugenists used a distinction between "positive" and "negative" eugenics and considered birth control a tool in the latter program; positive eugenics meant encouraging more reproduction among the "fit." In 1941 the medical director of the Birth Control Federation of America took this distinction, twisted it slightly, and applied it to birth control itself. He called for the addition of a "positive" birth-control program, the "encouragement of a sound parenthood, in all economic classes, as a major means by which this nation can be maintained strong and free." [3] His implication was that birth control in itself was unpleasantly negative and inadequate.

Beyond this there was another kind of "negativism" in the tradition of birth control, especially one lingering from the voluntary-motherhood tradition. Feminists had begun their birth-control agitation emphasizing the right of women to refuse their husbands sexually. Voluntary-motherhood advocates interpreted this refusal in a political sense, understanding women's power of negation as the necessary condition for their winning the power of assertion; and they understood the power relations within the family to be a microcosm of the power relations of the whole society. Planned-parenthood advocates, by contrast, sought to treat the family, and in particular the married couple within it, as a unit, capable of common decisions. They consciously wanted to de-emphasize the feminist connotations that still clung to birth control. Antifeminists have always seen women's complaints as negativism; indeed, the complaints of any oppressed group are often branded negativism. The term "planned parenthood" was positive in the sense of being uncomplaining, positing no aggrieved parties seeking justice.

"Planned parenthood" seemed a more positive concept than "birth control" especially to those who were general advocates of the importance of planning. Presumably "birth control" left matters such as population size and quality to the anarchism of individual, arbitrary decision. The propaganda of the birth-control organizations from the late 1930s through the late 1940s increasingly emphasized the importance of over-all social planning. A Birth Control Federation of America poster read: "MODERN LIFE IS BASED ON CONTROL AND SCIENCE. We control the speed of our automobile. We control machines. We endeavor to control disease and death. Let us control the size of our family to insure health and happiness." Sanger used the planning rhetoric too. National economic and social planning, she argued in 1935, requires "family security through family planning. . . ." [4] In a CBS radio speech in 1935 she pointed out, accurately enough, "Every good housewife accepts the idea of planning for the comfort of her household. She plans her budget. . . . She tries to plan for sickness and unemployment. . . ." [5] Thus family planning was argued for on both the grandest and the smallest of scales. Common themes were planning the use of the nation's "human resources"; the waste of overpopulation, particularly "overproduction of people" among those families that could ill afford them; and the necessity to understand the consequences of population changes for economic problems.[6] "Haphazard childbirth" wastes resources, "planned childbirth" saves resources, wrote Woodbridge Morris, Medical Director of the BCFA.[7]

Many social and economic changes had boosted the respectability of planning since the inception of the birth-control movement. The New Deal represented only a quantitative, not a qualitative, intensification of the state's intervention into people's lives. The laissez-faire, individualist image of freedom was defended only by extreme conservatives in the post–World War I period of monopoly capital. Although Nazi and Soviet state planning, including that in the area of reproduction, generated opposition in the United States, they also produced admiration; even among its enemies the Soviet Union commanded respect for its economic, and later military, achievements. The late 1930s produced a qualitative change, however, in the prestige of state planning. The response of reformers to a myriad of new issues was to demand the development of an over-all governmental policy on each. The planned-parenthood advocates, even before they adopted their new name, emphasized that contraception was a tool to achieve a goal greater than mere individual freedom.[8]

The application of planning to *birth* control helped transform it into a *population*-control movement, a transformation nearly total by the early 1960s. In the 1940s PPFA leaders still saw large-scale population concerns as secondary to those of family health, but the two were converging. "Planned Parenthood is an invitation to apply a basic social and scientific concept to the improvement of the family unit—and thereby our whole population . . . ," said a PPFA pamphlet.[9] Leading social worker Eduard Lindeman insisted as early as 1939 that population planning should "become an integral part of social and economic planning." [10] The birth-control organizations demanded a "sound national population policy," whatever that meant.[11] And indeed it was not at all clear what population planning meant, for almost all those who mentioned it were quick to denounce the "authoritarian" population planning used in Germany. They called for a "democratic population program" to "mobilize our human resources." The BCFA urged the development of a National Population Commission.[12] They were thinking in terms of demographic study and projection of long-range trends, moving toward recommendations about optimum growth rates and family sizes.

However ill-defined the nature of socially controlled reproduction, the demands for it assimilated the whole movement more closely than ever to the general economic planning of the bourgeoisie. In March 1943 a mass mailing from the PPFA to lawyers and businessmen spoke of the importance of population in planning for the postwar era. "Any sound peace plan must take into consideration population trends and natural resources, when we face such divergencies as the population of India. . . . Sound planning for business expansion on a national scale must also consider carefully not only the numerical growth of people, but their purchasing power." [13] The considerations necessary to capitalists and political leaders could never be strictly quantitative. What was overpopulation in one place might be good for business in another. The tradition of population-control thought had never defined it as a merely quantitative problem, and the dominant trends among the most recent demographers were eugenic.

Furthermore, to the extent that the government began to take official cognizance of population problems, it still did not consider birth controllers the relevant and proper experts. The best the birth controllers could do was to get pro-birth-control eugenists to represent them. Henry Pratt Fairchild had been their spokesman to the Hoover administration, and as late as 1941 when Mrs. Roosevelt held a White House meeting on population, it was Fairchild and Frederick Osborn of the American Eugenics Society who argued the case for birth control.[14] The eugenists no longer used racial or ethnic identifications but often referred to income levels. "ONE HALF OF ALL BABIES ARE BORN TO THE LOWEST INCOME FAMILIES," proclaimed a BCFA poster. It did not, incidentally, compare this number of births to the percentage of low-income people in the population; the implication was that low-income people ought to have few children. As a Planned Parenthood pamphlet put it, parents should build families "commensurate with their abilities to provide for them adequately." [15] When a prospective parent says this to herself, it is common sense; when a birth-control organization says it, with an explicit or implied "ought," it is a policy of urging different family sizes upon different classes.

World War II

The emphasis on planning had strengthened the population-control and eugenic slant of the birth-control movement. World War II further strengthened that orientation and de-emphasized contraception as a means of expanding individual and especially female rights. Civil liberties and individualism are often weakened in militarily mobilized societies. In this war domestic policies had a continuity with New Deal policies that made government planning and control easily accepted. The major PPFA pamphlet on birth control during the war declared:

PLANNING FOR VICTORY

The American people today need no further evidence on the necessity for quality in man power and materials to win the war. It sees, at last, that victory cannot be won without *planning*. . . .

Planned Parenthood, with your understanding and support can, in 1943, be made to mean that more healthy children will be born to maintain the kind of peace for which we fight.[16]

Nevertheless, despite its assimilation now two decades old to eugenics and population control, birth control still had a reputation as individualistic, selfish, and weakening to society. Birth controllers feared the impact of a "war psychology" upon their movement. They remembered the antiradicalism that had accompanied the First World War, its great cost in lives and the resultant concern for population growth; they anticipated a reassertion of the logic that in a time of national crisis childbearing was a woman's contribution. Several years before the United States entered the war, the Birth Control Federation of America began planning a propaganda offensive designed to counteract wartime anti-birth-control sentiment.

The wartime slogans of BCFA (and after 1942 Planned Parenthood) publicity centered around birth control's contribution to na-

tional strength. It tried to squelch the lingering Malthusian association of national well-being with numbers, replacing it with a
qualitative definition of strength. Sanger called for "national security
through birth control." [17] She spoke of the national weakness created
by the high birth rates among the poor, and the international insecurity created by surplus population in Germany, Italy, and Japan.[18]
After war broke out in Europe, the emphasis on national strength
divided into three themes: birth control's contribution to the economy,
to Americans' physical health, and to their mental health through the
stability of marriage and the family. All were interrelated and all
shared an emphasis on the good of the collective and a marked
de-emphasis on individual rights.

Regarding the economy, BCFA and PPFA publicity argued that
in modern war, as in industry, machines had come to be more
important than men, and that even in the infantry military strength
was often a matter of quality rather than quantity. It argued that the
expenditures on "relief babies" were even more dangerous to the
economy in wartime than before. One BCFA memo calculated costs,
anticipating a hypothetical argument that five hundred birth-control
clinics could be closed at a yearly saving of approximately $2500 each,
creating a total of $1,250,000 which could be used for war work. "The
average cost to the community of a baby born is $100. The average
clinic serves 500 women. If 60 per cent had unwanted babies, the cost
to the community would total $15,000,000 annually. To save
$1,250,000, we would saddle the United States with $15,000,000
additional expense. Rather than do this, we would redouble our
efforts. . . ." [19] Another memo proposed arguing for birth control as a
solution to the social disorders that might flow from economic disar-
ray: the curtailment of world trade due to the war could be expected
to deprive the United States of needed markets and raw materials;
these losses would in turn create unemployment and greater social
unrest, for which a decline in the birth rate would be a helpful
palliative.[20] This rather frank plea for birth control as a crutch for
weakened imperialism did not find its way into public statements of
the organizations.

Closely related to economic arguments was concern for supporting the proper morale on the home front. Here, too, birth control

could make a contribution. "A nation's strength does not depend upon armaments and man power alone; it depends also upon the contentment . . . of its people. To the extent that birth control contributes to the health and morale of our people, it makes them less receptive to subversive propaganda, more ready to defend our national system." [21] President Roosevelt had said the same thing in one of his "fireside chats": that unless the social reforms of the New Deal were preserved, the people's morale would be weakened and they would be less resistant to foreign propaganda. The BCFA staff by this time saw themselves as an unofficial part of the reforms of the 1930s, and when appealing to the Democratic majority they often identified themselves with the New Deal. They were still worried about their radical image, however, especially in relation to wartime xenophobia. By May 1941 a BCFA field-work director wrote to a national staff member, "Can you think of a way to identify B.C. with 'Being an American?' . . . Out of New York 'Being an American' is what folks are boasting about." [22]

World War II nationalism, however, had a more liberal political content than the nationalism of the Theodore Roosevelt administration or of the First World War, two periods that had set back the birth-control movement substantially. The view that the Second World War was a struggle of democracy against totalitarianism was especially appealing to the liberals and reformers of the birth-control movement. One BCFA staff member wrote that birth control was a part of the fight for personal liberty against authoritarian governments. She said that in preparing for defense we should not sacrifice one of the rights we were defending.[23] The pronatalist, "positive eugenics" policies of the German and Italian governments seemed the very essence of fascism to the birth controllers. "The Stork Is the Bird of War," headlined an article of 1938 attacking the rewards given to prolific mothers in Germany and Italy.[24] This went beyond the argument that overpopulation caused belligerence; it was based on a distinction between authoritarian and democratic methods of population control. That birth control was an integral part of our democratic and free way of life became a basic theme in early wartime publications.[25] Margaret Sanger spoke out against the Soviet Union for its reintroduction of controls on birth control and abortion; using the sharpest criticism in her vocabulary, she compared Mussolini, Hitler, and Stalin to the Catholic Church.[26] But, interestingly enough, the birth controllers did not find it necessary to denounce fascist "negative eugenics" policies—forced sterilization of Jews, for example—though this may have been because such programs were less well publicized in the United States or because they had no supporters here.

Ironically, criticism of fascist and even communist population and family policies, and their suppression of women's rights, may have made it easier for the PPFA to ignore the problems of women in the "democracies." When, for example, the birth-control organizations discussed women workers, their numbers expanded by war production, their concern was extremely narrow and often slanted toward serving the employers. In a 1944 PPFA pamphlet plant managers were asked to consider the "industrial loss incurred through the lessened efficiency of married women deprived of a normal sex life through fear of conception." Personnel managers were urged to put Kotex- and Tampax-dispensing machines in the bathrooms and warned that women often used menstruation as an excuse for not working.[27] Elsewhere women workers were described as expensive investments to be protected through proper care including birth control.[28] Describing the general situation of birth control in wartime, Henry Pratt Fairchild's only comment about women workers was: "It needs no special argument to demonstrate the dangers of interruption and restriction of production if women are unable to exercise rational control over reproduction. It has been found in a few plants surveyed that absenteeism due to pregnancy or induced abortion is creating a problem which may increase as more women move into war industry." [29] Nowhere in BCFA or PPFA material was there a suggestion that women were discriminated against, at the job or at home. If women were singled out in the propaganda, it was to suggest that birth control was a woman's duty, not her right.

The contribution of birth control to health became another important argument in the general theme of building national strength. Health replaced "good stock" as the measure of the quality of our population. From 1940 on, BCFA and PPFA spokespeople declared health the major immediate objective of birth-control work.[30] The unfitness of many conscripted men brought the backwardness of

U.S. public-health standards to public attention, and the birth controllers argued that planned children would be healthier. The "waste of human resources" theme was applied to the 40 per cent rejected by the armed forces. One PPFA leaflet calculated a total human waste of 37 per cent, including 9 per cent who died unnecessarily, 3 per cent crippled, 1 per cent with TB, 15 per cent retarded, 8 per cent "maladjusted," and 1.4 per cent delinquent.[31] This dysgenic problem was attributed to "lack of control of the size of family in relation to health and income." [32] Clearly birth control did contribute to health. The PPFA's emphasis, however, was not on individual welfare but on individuals as items in social planning—"human resource management." During World War II many social scientists contributed analyses of the over-all weaknesses and strengths of the human resources of the United States and its enemies—for example, national-character studies—as well as analyses of the labor force and workers' attitudes used for industrial psychology. Considering human beings as "resources," they viewed people as instrumentalities toward ends defined by rulers, and the PPFA health emphasis shared that orientation.

Furthermore, in its new emphasis on health, Planned Parenthood continued its eugenic traditions. Class, or income level, now replaced "stock" as the determining criterion, but many planned-parenthood arguments rested on the assumption that the children of the poor would be less healthy than the children of the rich; and since they did not suggest that better nutrition or medical care could change these health destinies, their arguments continued to reinforce hereditarian views. At least one PPFA staff member was perturbed enough about this content in birth-control propaganda that she complained to the national director. She acknowledged that the propaganda was less elitist than it had once been, but she still thought that the tendency of the PPFA to make a family's economic status a "paramount criterion regarding desirability of reproduction" was a continuing problem. "We know too little about heredity," she wrote in 1943, "and certainly by implying that people without wealth have no right to have children, we are open to criticism. . . . True, we appeal to some people by expressing such views, but we can appeal to them on other, sounder grounds." [33]

Although the hereditarian assumptions of PPFA propaganda in the 1940s were expressed mainly in class terms, racial differentials in the birth rate were by no means ignored. World War II accelerated the migration of blacks to Northern industrial cities. The incorporation of blacks, mainly men, into industry and then the Army created the conditions for a renewed civil-rights struggle which drew the attention of white reformers. At the same time New Deal programs brought to the attention of white liberals and radicals the disproportionate poverty of blacks. For example, 1940 studies estimated that half the black population of the United States was undernourished; that blacks had an infant-mortality rate 60 per cent higher than whites; that tuberculosis and syphilis were five to six times more prevalent among blacks. Black mothers had twice the white rate of mortality in childbirth.[34]

For both eugenic and social-welfare motives, birth controllers tried to increase the availability of contraception in black communities. Birth-control clinics included in public-health programs in Southern states had reached proportionally fewer blacks than whites, despite their intentions. In the North the clinics and organizations were primarily in white communities. In response, the ABCL had begun in the 1930s a campaign specifically directed toward blacks. True to its over-all orientation, the ABCL first courted the support of black professionals. Special "Negro Issues" of the *Birth Control Review* began to appear after June 1932, publishing testimony by black men of note (rarely women) supporting birth control. A Negro Advisory Council and a national Negro Sponsoring Committee were established; in 1944 PPFA hired a full-time "Negro Consultant."

A PPFA policy adopted in 1947 instituted a kind of Affirmative Action program for the organization, insisting that, beyond hiring staff and choosing board members on the basis of ability alone, there should be "qualified representation . . . for any racial group which is consistently represented in its geographic area" or "which constitutes a considerable clientele." Furthermore they were to exclude racists: "No staff member should be employed who does not possess the emotional acceptance and intellectual understanding of the problems represented in the minority groups of the Community."[35] The deeper aspects of the race problem, however, were not those of overt discrimination, severe as that might have been, but the structural aspects of racism and their impact on the significance of birth control. Throughout the 1930s and 1940s the resistance of many blacks to birth control was reflected in the arguments of both black and white birth-control spokesmen. They were continually countering charges that birth control was a policy designed to reduce the size of the black population, thus weakening it politically.[36] That charge—in its extreme form a charge of genocide—must be taken seriously. It has been repeated up to the present time by many who suspect both the intentions and the objective consequences of birth-control programs, and it is hardly odd that representatives of an extremely poor and exploited group might find some security in numbers. The opposing, pro-birth-control view argued in response that a richer, healthier black population would be collectively as well as individually stronger, that numerical size is not the main source of political clout. This disagreement was based on the confusion—indeed the virtual identification—of birth control with eugenics. Continually de-emphasizing birth control as an individual right, birth controllers themselves had made their program safe only for the privileged of the society who did not fear eugenic views, because their own class set the standards.

Despite their fears, black women have usually responded enthusiastically to contraception when clinics were available to them.[37] Their health, like that of most of the poor, was indeed worse, and in general they welcomed increased control over reproduction. But the reasons for their poorer health were primarily environmental, not hereditary, and birth control could provide only a small improvement. A few birth-control advocates, such as sociologist Joseph Folsom, argued for better over-all health services to complement birth control. Some Planned Parenthood workers recommended that PPFA call for better housing and expanded health programs.[38] PPFA statements did not adopt this line but sometimes pointed out, on the contrary, that birth control could make up for the inevitable curtailment of health and welfare programs due to war expenditures.[39] In an even more blunt acceptance of wartime cutbacks, one BCFA memo warned that the poor would need birth control in order to survive, since New Deal relief funds were likely to be cut.[40]

In failing to show the complexity of the relation between family size, health, and class, Planned Parenthood was responsible for some misleading propaganda. A common example was the presentation of statistics on family size and/or child spacing and infant mortality. A large BCFA poster, "PROPER CHILD SPACING PREVENTS INFANT DEATHS," compared death rates for babies one year apart (146.7 per 1000 live births) to those spaced two, three, and four years apart (rates 98.6 per 1000, 86.5 per 1000, and 84.9 per 1000, respectively). Such statistics imply that close births *cause* infant mortality, whereas the truth is that closely spaced births are common among people with generally poor health care, nutrition, and housing, and it is these latter factors which more likely cause higher mortality rates. This confusion of symptom with cause, and the removal of birth control from the general health context, has been the tendency of the modern birth-control movement. It disguises the fact that good birth control usually goes along with a generally higher standard of living which in turn produces good health, educational achievement, and a second generation with a high standard of living.

Although they did not wish to dilute their arguments for birth control by campaigning for improved general health care, Planned Parenthood workers knew they would gain through inclusion of birth-control services in existing general health programs. A particular wartime problem that offered them an opportunity for this was venereal disease. Precedents for the distribution of condoms having already been established in the First World War, the armed forces quickly added V.D. prevention programs to their scope of work. But V.D. was also spreading within the United States, and it provided a wedge for increased governmental participation in birth-control problems. A Navy captain appointed by the White House to serve as liaison with Planned Parenthood representatives forwarded recommendations that birth-control work be done by the Public Health Service, the Children's Bureau through its maternal- and child-health programs, the Works Projects Administration through its V.D. prevention program, the Defense Health and Welfare Service of the Federal Security Agency, and the Food and Drug Administration (testing contraceptives). Captain Stephenson also recommended federal financing of a long-term research program and of a test case against the Comstock law to be brought to the Supreme Court.[41] Little of this was initiated except direct anti-V.D. work, but the campaign for it won many supporters within the government, helped counteract fears of Catholic opposition, and brought closer the time when birth control was to become eligible for federal support.

In general the emphasis on health was part of a BCFA and PPFA campaign to convince professionals in the health field that birth control should be part of the services they offered, whether in governmental public-health-service programs, private clinics, or individual practices. A second and more controversial aspect of that campaign argued that birth control was an important ingredient in mental-health programs. This argument, too, was strengthened by war experiences, especially family instability. Social workers and sociologists were warning of the war-associated causes of the destabilization of family life: fatherless children, employed mothers, geographical mobility, "marry-and-run" weddings.[42] Their fears were borne out. Marriages, births, and divorces increased sharply. The marriage rate had gone up 5.7 per cent by 1940, and another 20 per cent by 1941; in the month after Pearl Harbor the rate went up 50 per cent. The birth rate went up steadily for the years 1940 to 1943 (17.9, 18.9, 20.5, and 22 per cent).[43] Unwanted conceptions probably grew even more than the birth rate, since the number of illegal abortions was believed to have increased, especially in the large cities.[44] Premarital relations between the sexes changed rapidly during the war. "Dating" became the norm and a part of the double standard in its practice was modified— women began sharing expenses and taking the initiative in proposing activities. Taboos against sex in dating relationships were eroded.[45] The armed forces had given up preaching continence, and even those who advocated social purity in World War I now recognized the inevitability of soldiers' sexual indulgence.[46]

These changes in attitude and behavior punctured the ideal of an untroubled, abiding family life. The ideal had never existed in reality, but it was nonetheless powerful as an image, and the fear of social instability was intensified by anxieties caused by the recent depression and present world war. If good morale on the home front was important to the war effort, it seemed that family stability should provide that morale. Birth controllers argued that unwanted conceptions and "excess children" threatened family stability.[47] They talked of "reinforcing family values." [48] Birth control would produce "wholesome family life." [49] The journal of the National Conference on Family Relations, an organization whose leaders often also worked in the BCFA and PPFA, called family life a national problem of the greatest urgency, central to the national defense. Particularly concerned with cynical army morality, they called for inculcation of members of our armed forces with attitudes compatible with healthy family life.[50]

This emphasis on the family was new to birth control. Yet it was the logical culmination of changes in the social concept of birth control over the past two decades as a reform that would stabilize, rather than destabilize, society. The feminist orientation toward birth control had expected, even welcomed, a certain measure of destabilization, particularly of the family, as essential to women's liberation. The birth controllers' World War II propaganda contained nothing critical of women's role in the family, nor any suggestion of expanding women's opportunities through controlling pregnancies. The over-all goals of Planned Parenthood, developed during the war, did not mention women's rights. Indeed, PPFA mass leaflets described women's appropriate family role in conventional, sexist terms. A cartoon pamphlet, "The Soldier Takes a Wife," claiming to deromanticize marriage, urged "companionship" through these descriptions of what to look for in a wife: "She may be good at jive but a 'Sad Sack' at the skillet. She may be a dud at the piano but an ace with the needle. She may look like an angel at midnight but how about when she wakes up without her make-up?" [51]

The family stability they sought locked women into their traditional spheres. It is striking, but logical, that this image of the family persisted during a period when widespread employment of women and absence of men jolted many into creating new living situations outside conventional nuclear families. Women showed remarkable ingenuity in finding alternative sources of stability—with roommates, collective living and eating situations, extended families, and the like. They also struggled for day care and equal treatment on the job, causes that PPFA did not enter. The official PPFA attitude toward women war workers was at best opportunist and at worst hostile: the birth controllers predicted that married women doing paid work would need birth control more than ever, and that thereby the birth-control organizations might even benefit from the war.[52] But nothing in their propaganda suggested that these work opportunities were desirable (though this was the view that predominated among the workers).[53]

Margaret Sanger, retired in Tucson, Arizona, and playing a diminishing role in Planned Parenthood affairs, was by this time almost an old-fashioned feminist by comparison to the rest of the organization. In 1942, for example, she protested a regulation of the Women's Army Corps against WACs having babies, there being no such regulation applied to Army men.[54] The unfortunate WACs were in a double bind, for Army men were issued contraceptives and the WACs were not. Sanger issued a statement attacking this discrimination as well, although PPFA Public Relations Director Scull tried to prevent her from doing so and criticized her for not specifying each time that only married WACs should receive contraceptives (a requirement certainly not made of men).[55] Sanger's speeches of the late 1930s and 1940s retained some of the feminist rhetoric of the past, calling for "rebellion" and "struggle." Sanger held on to her grudges, too. Shown a proposal in 1940 for a National Marriage and Family Institute which was to include Dr. Kosmak as a charter member, she scribbled angrily in the margin, "Oh my god Why always honor the reactionary and keep him afloat. My interest would stop right at sight of his name." *[56] By contrast, the orientation of the birth-control organizations by this time was to make alliances and to seek support from all influential, respectable people, no matter what their historical role or their over-all politics, and required only the lowest common denominator of agreement.

Sanger's differences with the organizations boiled down to an instinctive militance she could not shed. Birth control's success had only confirmed her conviction that gains were won and public opinion changed through confrontation and open conflict. This militancy and outspokenness did not define major political disagreements with the organizations that now harvested what she had cultivated. Sanger's concern for women's problems had never appeared to her in any way

---

* Kosmak was a notorious antifeminist and diehard opponent of birth control during the second and third decades of the century. See Chapter 10.

antagonistic to her growing commitment to eugenics and the social planning of population. If she was opportunistic, she never violated her own principles. She was eclectic, but consistent. As late as 1939 she repeated what she had first said in 1919: that birth control could solve the key social problems through eugenic regulation, if only

> statisticians and population experts as well as members of the medical profession had courage enough to attack the basic problem at the roots: That is not asking or suggesting a cradle competition between the intelligent and the ignorant, but a drastic curtailment of the birth rate at the source of the unfit, the diseased and the incompetent. . . . The birth control clinics all over the country are doing their utmost to reach the lower strata of our population, but as we must depend upon people coming to the Clinics, we must realize that there are hundreds of thousands of women who never leave their own vicinity . . . but the way to approach these people is through the social workers, visiting nurses and midwives. . . .[57]

Sex and the Feminine Mystique

In one area Planned Parenthood continued a woman-centered orientation, and that was in matters of sex. In the past birth-control organizations and agitators had argued for the acceptance of women's sexuality. After World War II the Planned Parenthood Federation incorporated the goal of female sexual fulfillment into its program. Planned Parenthood led the way in bringing the medical, social-work, and mental-health establishments to support the sexual rights of women, and thereby changing "public opinion."

We must measure this contribution historically, however, and in its over-all social context. PPFA sex counseling and sex education was developed during the late 1940s and 1950s, a period of political reaction and great economic expansion. Wartime production finally brought the United States out of the Depression. At home the postwar era was prosperous if measured by the gross national product, disposable personal income, and purchases of consumer durables. A high rate of inflation and of increase in productivity meant, however, that the working class paid for the prosperity, gaining very little in real wages and losing on issues of working conditions; despite some large strikes, many of them successful, the working class and its allies were weakened in this period and made vulnerable to a sharp political attack on radicals and the labor movement. First communists were driven out of the unions, then the power of the unions themselves was restricted by federal legislation, and the red scare then extended to non-working-class liberals and leftists through the McCarthy investigations. The importance of all this to birth control was similar to that of political events in the post–World War I period: it created a political and cultural situation potentially hostile to the radical overtones of birth control.

One aspect of the post–World War II culture that particularly affected Planned Parenthood was a new image of femininity called by Betty Friedan the "feminine mystique." Communicated through the mass media, the schools, the psychiatric and medical establishments, indeed through all the channels that create norms of sex roles, the mystique resurrected Victorian images of femininity. The physical differences between the sexes were presented in a kind of biological determinism as determining a whole set of exaggerated sex roles, the defiance of which could only lead to unhappiness, neurosis, failure, even sickness. Women's biological capacity for motherhood made it improper for them to attempt any other career. On the other hand, a true woman, according to the mystique, would be able to make an important and fulfilling contribution to civilization through her "homemaking" and her edifying influence on her children and husband. The transformation of housework into routine, alienated janitorial services was attributed to women's own failings rather than to the process of industrialization; indeed the manufacturers and advertisers of industrially manufactured goods argued to the housewife that their products could help her restore creativity to her housework, although it was the mass manufacture of those commodities which had stripped the creativity from housework in the first place. The source of the power of the feminine mystique was partly in the economic need of the manufacturing sector to raise consumption rates in order to prevent an economic downturn after the end of war production. Simultaneously, demobilization presented serious unemployment potential unless women could be forced out of the industrial jobs they had been able to get during conscription, and the "women-belong-in-the-home" line helped justify the process of depriving women workers of their senior-ity rights and laying them off. Thus the feminine mystique was not merely a typical postwar retrenchment response, but also an economic tool.[58]

The actual impact of the feminine mystique is difficult to evalu-ate, although this is the crucial question. Certainly women of all classes continued to function as profitable consumers for the manufac-turers who needed their services in this respect. On the other hand, women were not so easily driven out of the labor market, because other economic forces drew them in, and the proportion of women working for wages continued to rise in the late 1940s and 1950s. (Women driven out of better-paying industrial jobs by demobilized men simply went back into the poor-paid, nonunionized jobs, particu-larly in the service sector, that they had held before the war.) But most of these working-class women, like men, took jobs out of economic necessity, not because of the influence of this or that ideology of woman's place. Educated women, on the other hand, may indeed have been dissuaded from seeking the professional employment they were trained for by a sense of duty to family and self. For all women, however, it seems certain that one effect of the feminine mystique was a deepening sense of inadequacy and frustration as the promise of fulfillment failed to materialize.

One aspect of that frustration was sexual. The feminine mystique implicitly offered women ecstatic love as the reward for the surrender of their larger ambitions, and few husbands could meet the high standards of the fantasies engendered by the mystique. Furthermore, the functions of men dictated by the sexual division of labor in the society rendered them often incapable of loving or sexual generosity. Meanwhile the commercial culture surrounded women with images of free, enchanting sexuality just around the corner. For the middle-class housewife, with household aids, servants, and/or babysitters freeing her time somewhat, resentment of sexual deprivation was practically an inev-itable response. Some sought sex outside their marriages, with a result-ing high rate of adultery and divorce. Others sought psychiatric help. As Betty Friedan wrote, "Sex is the only frontier open to women who have always lived within the confines of the feminine mystique." [59]

Many of these women were clients at Planned Parenthood clinics, and some brought their sexual frustrations to the attention of clinic staff. Reluctantly at first, but later with eagerness, the birth-control clinics began to offer counseling. They did this with an implicit sexual program analogous to the over-all politics of Planned Parenthood: a tendency to isolate the problem—whether it was unwanted pregnancies or lack of orgasm—from larger social structures, thus accepting the surrounding social circumstances as given. In comparison to alternative analyses of sexual problems that were available previously, the Planned Parenthood version of sexual liberation for women avoided the issues of women's rights and male supremacy. This avoidance, however, made solutions impossible, for women's sexual problems were caused by a complex network of sexist patterns of behavior that pervaded marriages and even "affairs." In their attempts to treat sex as an isolated problem, the birth-control counselors offered, despite their intentions, a therapy that perpetuated the feminine mystique. Let us take a closer look at the ideology Planned Parenthood projected, in words and in practice, on sex and the family.

In 1947 the PPFA produced an official statement on its Marriage Education and Counseling Program.[60] It read in part:

> Any descriptive account of the current marriage and family scene, if it is honest, will reflect the same insecurities and uncertainties that are part of the social and economic readjustment in postwar America. One would like to think of the family as a retreat from the chaos of day-to-day conflict and strain . . . but the family is not a thing apart. . . . The juvenile delinquency figures and the resurgence of "gangs" in our big cities are part of it; so also is the increase in venereal disease among civilian groups—disproportionately high for adolescents. Unmistakably part of it are the current divorce statistics . . . one out of three marriages. . . .
>
> Further, the challenge is a double one, for the forces of reaction are at work. Our concern is not just for the family; it is for a democratic family! Newspaper headlines to the effect that we must legislate divorce out of existence and keep women so busy having children that they won't have time to get into trouble, are not uncommon today.
>
> A more thoughtful approach rejects the current hysteria . . . deplores the authoritarian approach . . . recognizes that one can't enforce happy marriages by laws, by strangling personality development . . . that indiscriminate fecundity is itself a fascist notion.

This statement of the problem, of the need for a counseling program, reflected the influence of the war—in stimulating fear both of family instability and of authoritarian solutions. In defining the nature of the counseling PPFA would offer, the statement reflected, too, the increased complexity of birth-control thought after several decades of organization. Denying that contraception was a panacea, the statement attacked the "assumption that given a good contraceptive most marital difficulties would be solved." On the contrary, "sometimes the use, even the very decision to use a contraceptive, unwisely arrived at, introduces conflicts and anxieties." The statement placed sex at the center of many human problems. PPFA counseling would not be focused exclusively on sex, the statement said, but would not deny the basic importance of good sexual relationships and would accept sexual maladjustment as the point of departure for counseling.

From the beginning, then, PPFA counseling advocates were responding to two different problems: over-all social instability, and individual sexual problems among women attending birth-control clinics. Their identification with the still somewhat controversial psychiatric appraisal of sex as central to human relationships provided them with a connection between these social and individual problems. An emphasis on individual adjustment as the key to stability pervaded the Planned Parenthood approach to both social and individual problems. While rejecting "authoritarianism," PPFA publications and counselors did not encourage women to risk instability or "maladjustment" in order to develop. Identification with a women's liberation movement might have suggested that instability and maladjustment, in some degree, are the inevitable costs of social change. But there was no feminist movement to offer that analysis. Both socially and individually, these birth controllers sought to solve problems and ameliorate suffering without rocking the larger societal boat.

Planned Parenthood approached these tasks in two ways: through propaganda and through counseling. Although similar assumptions underlay both approaches, the counseling tended to focus on sexual problems whereas the publications discussed family, economic, and social values more explicitly. Let us look first at some PPFA propaganda of the 1940s. A renewed effort to win support from Protestant and Jewish clergymen centered around the preparation of a pamphlet designed for them to use in premarital interviews, *The Clergyman Talks with the Bride and Groom about Family Planning*.[61] The pamphlet had long verbatim excerpts from Hannah and Abraham Stone's forthright sex manual, and had been offered for criticism and final editing to prominent churchmen in order to win clerical endorsements. The PPFA staff accepted, for example, one minister's suggestion to omit the word "sensuality." They adopted another proposal to soften the Stones's assertion that a good sex relation is "essential" to a happy marriage, making it only "most desirable." In this as in most PPFA publications the policy was not to give actual birth-control information but to argue the moral and social benefits of birth control and to refer those wanting it to clinics and doctors.

The main point of the pamphlet was that birth control and good mutual sexual adjustment were central to a happy marriage. The authors of the pamphlet did not share the feminists' assertions of the nineteenth century that women should control sexual activity, a view primarily designed to allow women to check what they considered to be excessive male lust. In the 1940s male lust was not seen as excessive or oppressive to women in any respect; women were expected, on the contrary, to reach and express parallel levels of desire themselves. On the other hand, the mutuality recommended in marriage did not extend beyond the sex act itself. The pamphlet offered no reason to challenge tradition in matters of economics, housework, child-raising, or other aspects of marriage traditionally nonmutual.

Most Planned Parenthood publications assumed that all sex, and therefore all birth control, belonged inside marriage; and that equality in sex could be achieved without a fundamental alteration of marriage itself. These were in themselves not only sexually conservative but antifeminist assumptions. They implicitly opposed acceptance of the "sexual revolution" of the post–World War I era, and they explained away the depressions and hostility of frustrated housewives as products of sexual maladjustment and refusal to accept the female role. They were in no way antagonistic to the feminine mystique.

This area of PPFA ideology was publicized largely through the psychiatric profession. Beginning in the early 1940s a number of psychiatrists were recruited to speak out for birth control as conducive to mental health. Their arguments were rendered decidedly antifeminist by the assumption that marriage must be primary and central in women's lives. Dr. Marynia Farnham, a zealously antifeminist psychiatrist and public spokeswoman, on occasion, for PPFA, specifically attacked spinsters. In her *Modern Woman: The Lost Sex*, published in 1947, she demanded that single women should be barred by law from teaching since a "great many children have unquestionably been damaged psychologically by the spinster teacher, who cannot be an adequate model of a complete woman. . . ." [62] In a speech for Planned Parenthood in 1943 she attacked the single women who play men's roles.[63] Behind these condemnations lay the assumption that celibacy was damaging; and behind that the assumption that single women had to be, or ought to be, celibate.[64] Planned Parenthood's policy of not serving unmarried women was carried at this time to the impractical extreme of refusing to send out the pamphlet *The Doctor Talks with the Bride*, designed for premarital sex education, to unmarried women.[65]

When most psychiatrists discussed the value of birth control within marriage, they did not mention the value of freeing women for activities outside their homes which might promote women's personal development. Rather they emphasized the chilling effect of fear of unwanted pregnancy on the sex act itself.[66] Psychiatrists sometimes insisted on women's right to sexual fulfillment; but they did not seem to acknowledge rights to other areas of fulfillment, or to recognize that women's frustrations in other areas might be expressed in sexual coldness toward the husbands and family situations that restricted them. Marynia Farnham argued, like a nineteenth-century feminist, that the problem of reproductive control lay at the root of woman's position; but in her development of that theme she was more reminiscent of an early twentieth-century race-suicide alarmist: Since reproduction is woman's "primary function," it should not be outside her control: ". . . one of the most morbid aspects of the so-called 'modern' woman's development . . . [is the] steadily increasing tendency on the part of intelligent and well-trained, as well as intellectually alert, women to assert their independence at the cost of abandoning the function for which they are inherently responsible and biologically fitted. This exhibits itself in a variety of forms . . . [including the spectacle of married women who want the] emotional and social prestige of marriage . . . [but are] unwilling to tolerate all the burdens of a woman's life and elect either to bear no children or at most one or two." [67] Such views differed from the race-suicide hysteria in the observations offered by Farnham and other psychiatrists that women who wished to avoid motherhood would probably make poor mothers anyway. Such an analysis might seem sensible enough were it not for the vicious condemnation of these women: ". . . the woman who cannot find satisfaction in adult relations in life, who is incapable of succeeding in living a woman's role, who is constantly in revolt against her submission and who is unable to achieve sexual gratification with her husband cannot possibly be a satisfactory parent. . . . She will only find it necessary to obtain gratification through an excessive attachment to her children, particularly her sons." [68]

These psychiatrists thought the value of birth control was to promote good sex, not to offer women options other than full-time motherhood. Indeed they perceived good sex as inseparably connected to women's acceptance of their "true" roles. At a time when the ideology that woman's place was in the home was reclaiming dominance, Dr. Farnham postured as an iconoclast in arguing to remove the stigmata from women who worked as full-time homemakers and child-rearers.[69]

Furthermore, viewing sexual adjustment in isolation from women's general problems, as these psychiatrists did, led to blaming women, especially aberrant or rebellious women, for their own unhappiness and for family instability. This was evident, for example, in the birth controllers' opportunistic use of the widespread concern over juvenile delinquency in the 1940s. A *Look* magazine article of 1947 quoted PPFA leaders that their four main enemies were death and disease, divorce, juvenile delinquency, and sterility.[70] Birth controllers argued that unwanted children were more likely to be delinquent. But they did not connect unwanted children with other socially determining factors like poverty, bad schools, and adult crime; rather they emphasized the mother's psychology and mother-child relationships. The PPFA *Outline for a Course in Planned Parenthood* argued that "the mother's lack of affection or compensatory over-solicitude is said by psychiatrists to establish tendencies to destructive attitudes." [71] The PPFA Twenty-sixth Annual Meeting had Rhoda J. Milliken, director of the Women's Bureau of the Washington, D.C., Police Department, arguing that unwanted children tended toward criminality.[72] David Loth, PPFA public-information chief, argued that "excess" children tended to become delinquent, and produced marital conflict, sibling jealousy, and family instability.[73] These themes were part of, and contributed to, the attack on working mothers as productive of delinquency, an aspect of the feminine mystique that peaked in the 1950s. The attacks were marked by a singular superficiality in analyzing the problem. Removing from the spotlight the contribution of men, poverty, unemployment, and urban rot to delinquency, these critics blamed women exclusively. The assumptions that there was such a thing as excess children and that unplanned children were "unwanted" were not supported by actual inquiry into the feelings of the parents or children involved. These assumptions further removed birth control from the area of individual rights and strengthened its association with policies imposed by social planners.

The educational work of Planned Parenthood not only ignored the women's frustrations that had been the original source of the birth-control movement, but even deepened them by contributing to the view that individual women were to blame for their own unhappiness. In its clinical programs, however, PPFA offered not only contraception, but also counseling, both important tools with which women could change their situations. It is worth examining the latter and attempting to evaluate its social impact.

Experiences in providing contraception drew doctors and nurses into sex counseling. Social prudery seemed only to make women more anxious to spill out their sexual miseries once they were in a safe and sympathetic situation.[74] Routine questions at clinic intake procedures often revealed deep wells of pain and astonishing sexual ignorance, even among mothers of many children. Indeed, in their sex counseling there was little distinction between therapy and education. (In the 1970s the therapy done in clinics such as Masters and Johnson's, and the educational publications of the women's liberation movement, such as *Our Bodies Ourselves*, owe much to the experience and experiments of birth-control work.)

Women whose names became publicized as birth-control advocates began receiving appeals for help by mail from the beginning of the movement, asking not only for contraceptives but also for sexual advice. Many were appeals for abortions, such as this letter of June 1916 to Rose Pastor Stokes:

> Dear Benefactress—Would you be pleased to include our little family. . . . I am an elevator runner, in the Hotel Savoy, and am salaried at $25 monthly. . . . We are threatened with a possible newcomer to our fold—my wife is two months and no show. . . . if you could only benefit us with your kind advice. . . . —Helen and John Sweeney.[75]

Others had nothing to do with birth control. Here one of Sanger's assistants summarizes a particularly thorny problem:

> I am afraid to tackle this one without some advice. The girl is 20 years old, had had a terrible home life, so she says. . . . She finally met a man who as she says, ruined her. She became pregnant and was aborted. She now says that she is engaged to marry a man who has studied medicine two years. She is afraid he will know she has had another adventure and wants to know whether he can tell or not. She says she has told him there is nothing in her past etc. and wants to know whether she should marry him or give him up.[76]

With a good deal of assistance, Sanger attempted to answer these appeals. In the 1920s she wrote in her own name but by the 1930s she had developed the Margaret Sanger Motherhood Advice Bureau and used form letters to speed the work—refusing to offer abortion help, for example, or referring the writers to birth-control clinics or doctors. In 1931 she described the Bureau as a direct extension of birth-control clinic work. She called it "a unique undertaking—the first of its kind in this country." [77] Of course it was not that, for advice bureaus of this type were older, and they in turn merely succeeded neighborhood "wise-women," who had once served this purpose. Sanger's boasts were indicative of a new desire to professionalize this counseling service, yet without surrendering it to psychiatric control. For her, the professionalization of this "advice bureau" was a form of democratization, making a service available on a mass scale, quite different from the inclination of the psychiatric establishment. (And indeed the provision of counseling services through birth-control clinics, opposed at first by the psychiatric establishment, eventually helped force an expansion of the limits of what was professionally reputable therapy.)

Sanger's responses to the written appeals for help offer a faithful microcosm of her overall sexual views and a useful basis of comparison with later Planned Parenthood views. Sanger's approach remained that of nineteenth-century free-love ideology which asserted the spiritual, honorable qualities of sex and the simultaneous dangers of its degradation into something low. To the woman who worried about her past affair and abortion, Sanger replied:

> You must not think of yourself or your relations with Tom, whom you have loved, in the wrong light. If you loved him and he loved you, any relations between you were just as holy and as pure in the sight of God as if a marriage certificate had been given you. . . . It is love between two people that sanctifies marriage. There are many marriages today that are not so sanctified. . . .[78]

Yet she was no exponent of unmarried love, arguing generally that "sex belongs to love and love belongs to marriage."[79] And she tried to dissuade a woman from bearing a child alone. "I can understand how a very honest, straightforward, independent woman must despise the necessity for deceit, but isn't that just giving vent to our own inward satisfaction. . . . My own suggestion would be if it were possible, to go away to England or some place, the last three or four months and have her baby, or . . . to say she is married. . . ."[80] She consistently opposed masturbation and insisted that will power could get rid of the habit. "If you are sincere in your statement that you wish to overcome the habit of masturbation which you acquired during childhood, . . . try to interest yourself in some social, athletic or other group . . . and as you develop such interests . . . your impulses and thoughts will center less upon your own body and gradually they will be diverted to more important matters."[81]

Heavy as Sanger's barrage of written appeals was, it was small compared to the expressions of sexual discontent encountered at the birth-control clinics. Clinicians seeking to provide effective contraception would have been hard put to refuse at least to discuss problems so closely related to birth control. Dr. Hannah Stone, medical director of Sanger's New York City clinic, the Clinical Research Bureau (CRB), had kept careful data on "adjustment to marriage" which had begun to reveal the dimensions of the problem: only 60 per cent of her patients had a "normal" attitude toward intercourse; 19 per cent were indifferent and 20 per cent hostile to intercourse; only 42 per cent said they usually had an orgasm, and indeed the doctors frequently had to explain the meaning of that word.[82] In 1931 she and her husband, Dr. Abraham Stone, opened a Marriage Consultation Center under the auspices of the New York City Labor Temple, and women from the birth-control clinic were referred there. The large numbers of women needing help, however, led Stone and her co-workers to try incorporating counseling into the clinic's services. From 1932 on the Clinical Research Bureau was providing consultations on marriage problems.[83] The service was free if the woman was a birth-control client at the clinic; otherwise the average fee was five dollars. Women with marital problems were often advised to come in for additional consultations with their husbands.

An equally important part of the program was premarital consultations, a form of individualized sex education. The discussion of sexual topics with unmarried women was still a controversial matter, even in the medical profession, in the 1930s. The "premaritals" had been accepted in part because of the support of eugenists, who viewed them as a necessary means for investigating possible hereditary taints which should halt the marriage or at least parenthood. Thus Dr. Robert Latou Dickinson, an important advocate of premarital consultations, adopted the eugenists' view that they should take place before the announcement of engagement and definitely before a wedding date had been set. But Dickinson himself realized that the demand for premarital interviews was mainly a demand for contraceptive information among engaged couples,[84] and the Clinical Research Bureau got hundreds of requests for such consultations. The Bureau developed a standard format of examination and consultation. Although they offered surgical dilation or rupture of the hymen if desired, they usually directed the woman to come back three to four weeks after her marriage to be fitted with a diaphragm.[85]

Counseling services were also being offered by many birth-control clinics elsewhere in the country,[86] but with little publicity. Toward the end of the 1930s the recognition of the need for counseling became so great that it stimulated a public program, but creating this required, for the PPFA leadership, years of careful negotiations with and reassurance of both psychiatric and social-work professional organizations. Both professions were anxious to preserve their control over the content as well as the personnel of counseling. PPFA medical director C. C. Pierce was forced to defy the demand of a psychiatrist called in for consultation that any applicant for counseling had to have a preliminary interview with a psychiatrist.[87] It was 1947 before the PPFA was able to produce a public statement on its marriage-counseling program.[88]

Although the program was called "marriage counseling" and was intended to relate planned-parenthood services to over-all family life through homemaking and health services, sex education, mental hygiene, and child welfare,* in fact the service offered was primarily sex counseling. This restriction was perhaps unavoidable, were the small, private clinics to be able to help any one person sufficiently to have any impact. Most of the other kinds of services mentioned, such as homemaking or child welfare, required resources far beyond the capability of the shoe-string clinics. Had the clinic workers been deeply committed to these causes, the most they could have done would have been to help organize and focus pressure on other institutions, particularly the government, to provide better services. To offer sex education on a public scale (as opposed to its integration into individual and small-group counseling) would have required political struggles against censorious authorities such as school boards, churches, and the police. The basis of the restriction of the program was that the clinics no longer wanted to be involved in any adversary relations to state or private institutions. Indeed, the majority of the clinics had not wanted to dilute their impact with any issues other than contraception at all; their introduction of counseling was a capitulation to overwhelming pressure from their clients and those in direct contact with the clients.

Sex-centered marriage counseling, then, was offered at many clinics, nationwide, by the early 1940s. The style and content of the counseling sessions varied, but certain generalizations hold. The counseling was short term, ranging from single consultations, to occasional or regular sessions for a relatively brief time, to "classes" with a

---

* A proposal by one PPFA staff member to call for "child care" as a necessity for family health, included in an earlier draft of the counseling-program description, was modified in the final version to "child welfare."

specified number of meetings. The national PPFA tried to enforce high standards for the counselors, including a graduate degree and job experience, in a concession to the opposition from psychiatrists and social workers, although physicians without counseling experience were often employed. Without trying to deny the great variation that must have existed among clinics, I want to focus here on the experience of counseling at the Clinical Research Bureau in New York City, later called the Margaret Sanger Research Bureau.

For doctors Lena Levine and Abraham Stone, who directed them, these counseling services did not long remain a minor addition to birth-control work. Stone envisioned the clinics as expanding their definition so greatly that birth control would be just one of several functions. Levine argued that most people, not just the exceptional, might need counseling.[89] Levine and Stone were both convinced that for most couples being told to "do what comes naturally" would not produce mutual satisfaction.

> It is generally taken for granted, for instance, that men and women know instinctively how to perform the sex act, yet this is often not the case. Among primates, the act of coitus is not an instinctive behavior pattern but a technique acquired through association, imitation, experimentation, and learning.[90]

The problem was that modern culture had set up numerous social obstacles, in the form of censorship and guilt, to effective sexual learning. Thus their view of therapy was particularly close to education, seeking to remedy the ignorance-creating aspects of society. Indeed, *most* sexual failure, Levine and Stone believed, was due to ignorance.[91]

The importance of the basic education offered in these counseling sessions can hardly be overestimated. Levine and Stone used sculptured models of the genital and reproductive systems. They found frequent examples of debilitating ignorance. Few clients knew exactly what or where the clitoris was. A man married many years, unable to effect complete penetration, confessed that he was not entirely sure where the vagina was.[92] The two doctors' comfortableness with discussions of sexual physiology and technique was contagious, and both female and male clients heard themselves, often with some surprise, speaking about their own experiences in the same direct, specific manner.

To aid this educational work these and other birth-control doctors wrote a number of manuals on marriage and sexual technique. Perhaps the most important was *A Marriage Manual* by doctors Hannah and Abraham Stone,* first published in 1935. Nothing could better illustrate how much the approach to sexuality of the birth controllers had changed than comparing the Stones' work to Sanger's own *Happiness in Marriage*, published in 1926. Sanger wrote nothing at all on the technique of physical love but confined herself to romantic philosophy about courtship, honeymoon, and the marriage relation itself. Women should maintain a playful elusiveness during courtship, not surrendering to a young man's more insistent sexual urges. Although youth's reaction against prudishness is good, there are severe dangers in too much intimacy, emotional as well as sexual, during engagement.[93] The responsibility for a proper marital adjustment is primarily the woman's: "She must dominate the relation. . . . she must create the happiness of their life together. The future depends on the woman's attitude toward sex." [94] Looking at this from the vantage point of the Stones' work, less than ten years later, Sanger seems again deep in the nineteenth-century tradition. She consistently emphasizes self-control, the need to spiritualize sexual relations; she is uncomfortable with physiological discussion. At the same time her view of marital relations reflects the view of the "sex radicals" of 1910–1920, that male lust is healthy, women's inhibitions neurotic. She kept the romanticism but lost the hostility to a male-defined sexual rhythm characteristic of the nineteenth-century feminists.[95]

The Stones were doing something completely different. Not that theirs was an amoral, strictly technical manual; nor that they would have disagreed with Sanger. But sex, for them, was not something that needed to be spiritualized. And their view of the nonsexual aspects of a good marriage emphasized different features from Sanger's: "I quite agree with you that sex alone does not make a marriage . . . there must of course be present mutual love and affection, a community of ideas, of interests, of tastes, of standards, an adequate economic

* Hannah Stone was always the more deeply involved in birth-control work, since her joining the CRB in the 1920s; but she died in 1941.

arrangement and a satisfactory adjustment in many personal, family and social relationships." [96] The approach of the Stones and Dr. Levine in their writings and counseling was down-to-earth, family-centered, emphasizing moral responsibility and stability, and reassuring. (*A Marriage Manual* carried a message to lovers similar to that Dr. Spock carried to mothers: whatever you're inclined to is probably all right.) Their message was that sexual happiness lay within every individual's reach; although objectively battling the effects of a repressive culture, they did not protest or criticize or attribute blame for this repression, nor did they encourage even the most unhappy to vent anger. Theirs was not the sex manual of a sex-radical movement or a feminist movement; it was the sex manual of a planned-parenthood movement. Even in the midst of a great depression it assumed the possibility of a secure, stable, and if not prosperous, then at least hopeful, family life. Their happy, confident outlook made the Stones and Levine remarkably successful as counselors, one suspects. Certainly clients were enthusiastic about their sessions, and many reported improvements in their sex lives.

One of the most influential aspects of their counseling work, and the aspect about which we have today the greatest documentation, was group marriage counseling. This was an experiment which Abraham Stone and Levine approached with some caution, aware, as they put it, that "marriage counseling has always been considered to require strict individualization. . . . In reviewing our histories, however, we were increasingly impressed with the fact that the problems presented by couples coming for marriage counseling fell into several specific categories. . . ." [97] They were recognizing, essentially, that these sex problems were not personal but social. They compiled a list of the common complaints of women coming to the clinic:[98]

Lack of sex desire.
Difficulty in becoming aroused.
Arousal only after much precoital play.
Lack of any sensation in coitus.
Orgasm only from external play, but not from coitus.
Fear of intercourse.
Fear of pregnancy.
Infrequency of sex relations.
Painful intercourse.

Orgasm achieved only in certain positions.
Husband's anxiety over wife's lack of response.
Husband's objection to wife's need of precoital play.
Husband's loss of sexual interest because of wife's frigidity or
slowness of response.

Stone's and Levine's primary motivation in trying group therapy
was to save time and be able to help more people. In groups of six to
eight, the women met three times at one-week intervals, then once six
months later; their husbands met once, and once again six months
later. Dr. Levine, an experienced psychiatrist, was concerned from the
outset with the interaction that would take place among the clients.
To avoid "possible conflicting attitudes," they tried to choose couples
of similar age, class, and cultural backgrounds. But neither doctor
intended to create a general discussion or encounter group. The
doctors led each session strongly. At the first a fifteen-minute physiology lecture began the two-hour session; at the second, the doctor
reviewed, then called for progress reports; at the third, the doctor
lectured on the effects of early-childhood socialization into sexual
inhibitions.[99]

It is clear from the transcripts of these sessions, however, that the
group discussions developed an intensity, energy, and openness far
beyond what the doctors had anticipated. Indeed, Stone and Levine
were rather surprised at their own success without precisely understanding it. The power of the groups lay in the fact that the doctors
were not only contributing their significant knowledge and experience
in a frank manner, but also creating situations in which women and,
to a lesser extent, men could learn from one another. Evidence of that
mutual learning can be found in nearly every transcript. The most
basic form of it was the abatement of a sense of inadequacy as woman
after woman, man after man, expressed the same fears and failures.
The men consistently revealed embarrassment that they could not
maintain erections long enough, and a pathetic relief when the doctors
assured them that the average duration of an erection was two
minutes.[100] Among the women the relief assuaged more generalized,
even total, anxieties, for the women blamed themselves for their own
lack of satisfaction. On the average, two-thirds never had orgasms;*

* These groups were formed of those with sexual problems, expressed during interviews at

others felt that they were failures, even perverts, because they could not have "vaginal" orgasms or orgasms during intercourse; almost all felt inadequate because they were sexually disinterested much of the time, or too tired to respond at the end of an evening. In these discussions the comfort they got was not mainly from the doctors, who frequently labeled these symptoms as neurotic, but from one another. Often the mutual support helped women transform their own self-hatred back to its origin, resentment of their husbands for their insensitivity and sexual selfishness. The men occasionally expressed fear of this transformation (though on the whole their gratitude for the sexual honesty encouraged by the sessions dominated). One man remarked of his wife, "She came here and listening to other women and came to the conclusion she had no problem." [101]

The rapport and openness among the women developed in only three meetings was remarkable. In their first meetings women frequently plunged immediately into frank and painful complaints. "I have been married fifteen months, and have not gotten any satisfaction yet. I am aroused when my husband plays with me, but as soon as he enters I lose all feeling. I lose it and I don't get it back again, and I get disgusted. Often I start crying." [102] At the third session, women sometimes expressed a desire for the groups to continue. "It's not fair, giving us just a taste." [103] Although there is no evidence that women continued to meet without the doctors, they did in many ways take small measures of control over the group themselves. One group criticized the CRB for not providing contraception for unmarried women.[104] Some clients assumed a counseling role toward others, sometimes taking positions sexually more radical than those of the doctors, as when one woman said to another, who had been valiantly trying to achieve a vaginal orgasm, that maybe she should not care about it, perhaps not every woman needed to have a vaginal orgasm.[105] Often the women sought to employ the doctors for their ends, asking them to give particular messages to the husbands, in their separate meetings. Sometimes the women clients said they themselves felt too timid to carry the information; more frequently they wanted the weight of the doctors' status to make a dent they themselves could not create.[106]

---

birth-control clinics. There should be no inference here that these groups are necessarily representative of the general female population.

The women's eagerness to communicate with their husbands was due to the importance of what Stone and Levine were teaching them. The key messages were primarily technical: that it was normal for women to require long periods of "foreplay" to reach arousal; that the vagina was normally quite insensitive in young women (we will discuss the doctors' explanation for this below); that stimulation of the clitoris was extremely important in achieving arousal and orgasm; that men and women should not be expected to sense what was sexually pleasing to the other, but should be told; that honesty in describing responses was the only route to a mutually pleasing sexual relationship; that a wide variety of sexual activities could be normal and pleasing. Some of these ideas were not new to the urban, predominantly Jewish couples who attended the sessions, though their repetition by a doctor was a source of great reassurance. Some of the ideas, for some people, were totally new, particularly the sexual importance of the clitoris; and for many that message—that a woman's clitoris was her most sensitive sexual organ—gave them the courage to try making love in a new way, with remarkable results. "My wife and I have felt like newlyweds," said one man who had just learned what and where the clitoris was.[107]

The transcripts show that instruction about the clitoris was the most important message taught in these sessions, because it was a license for women to heed their own feelings; it was the message that led most consistently to actual change. We should not oversimplify this, for clitoral sexuality had complex ramifications, many of them disturbing to women. Experiencing orgasm for the first time, many women felt badly that their orgasms were separated from their husbands' and took place outside of intercourse; many also recognized that expectations for simultaneous, vaginal orgasms were false and noticed how they had been created. Clitoral stimulation at least temporarily relieved women of the fear of conception and undoubtedly led to relaxation; on the other hand, women were uneasy with the feeling that their bodily rhythms should determine the dynamic of the love-making and felt unable to make the men "wait." The clitoris was not a magic button that miraculously created a new sexual experience. But the discovery of that one small organ, its capacity for feeling so long feared and suppressed, was the main theme of these sessions.

The enthusiasm of both participants and leaders of these sessions leaves no doubt about their success, although we should not exaggerate their novelty. Where women are not artificially separated by housing and work patterns, they have often formed informal, supportive discussion groups. In the 1870s Elizabeth Cady Stanton and other voluntary-motherhood advocates organized women-only discussion groups, and the degree of frankness in them seems to have been as great, relative to current social definitions of propriety, as that in the consciousness-raising groups a century later. But Stanton's groups had a women's movement and a burgeoning feminist consciousness bringing them together. The Stone-Levine groups were brought together not as participants of a movement but as *clients* of experts. It is a tribute to the importance and achievements of the planned-parenthood clinics that they brought sexual conflicts and frustrations into the open. But at the same time the fact that the counseling groups grew out of clinics, themselves part of a national program, set some limits on the discussion that might not have been present otherwise. This judgment must be carefully measured, since many of the limits were imposed by the experience and acculturation of the participants themselves. Still, in many areas the session leaders authoritatively defended sexual conventions today widely considered disproven or at least biased. The leaders maintained a narrow focus, preventing exploration of the interconnectedness of sex and the rest of life, and preventing locating the source of sexual problems in alterable social conditions. Many male-supremacist assumptions went unchallenged.

Despite their emphasis on the importance of clitoral excitement, Stone and Levine taught the superiority of the so-called vaginal orgasm. Their psychoanalytic interpretation of this issue represented an attempt to combine what they had observed and heard in years of practice with the categories of female psychosexual development laid down by Freud and, by the 1940s, dominating the U.S. psychiatric establishment. There were two kinds of orgasms, clitoral and vaginal; the former was immature, the latter difficult to achieve partly because girls did not normally masturbate in the vagina—vaginal sensitivity had to be developed. Clitoral orgasms were better than none, to be sure, but both Stone and Levine urged a continual striving for vaginal orgasm achieved during intercourse. The technique they suggested to accomplish this "transference of sensitivity to the vagina" was intercourse in positions that allowed simultaneous clitoral stimulation.[108]

It was several decades later, of course, that the Masters and Johnson studies showed that there was only one kind of orgasm, brought on by stimulation of the clitoris. For decades previously doctors had observed and written that the clitoris was the seat of all observable female sexual stimulation.[109] In the face of that knowledge, continued belief in the vaginal orgasm had an ideological basis: the desire to maintain heterosexual intercourse, nearly certain to provide orgasm for the male, as the norm, indeed the very definition, of the "sex act." Thus for Stone and Levine, the emphasis on the achievement of vaginal orgasm had as a corollary that certain sexual practices were perversions. It is true that they had narrowed the area of perversity greatly, admitting as normal a frequency and breadth of sexual activity that would have been unacceptable to most nineteenth-century sexual reformers. In their efforts to encourage naturalness and self-expression, the Stones had come up with a definition of perversion based on intention: perversity was the absence of attempt at "normal" heterosexual relations. Thus clitoral stimulation was acceptable if it was preliminary to intercourse, and even clitoral orgasms if they were a stage in a woman's progress toward vaginal orgasms; if the clitoral orgasm was accepted as a sufficient form of sexual satisfaction, it was perverse. In the abbreviated style used by the secretary who transcribed the sessions, Stone was quoted as follows: "If want to take in mouth and kiss and it is preliminary diversion, not perversion. If always becomes end in itself would be beyond normalcy." [110] This view further implied a rejection of all homosexual activity, and a condemnation—if kindly and understanding—of masturbation as well. (Kinsey later criticized Stone for his inaccurate and conservative views on masturbation and the clitoral orgasm.) [111]

In supporting relatively conventional ideas of perversion and continuing to use the vaginal orgasm as the definition of female sexual maturity, the doctors maintained a male definition of sexuality itself. Indeed, throughout the counseling sessions the doctors worked to suppress or deflect challenges to male-defined sex which their own therapy had stimulated. When women ventured to express resentment at having to fit their husbands' rhythms, Dr. Levine advised accepting a man's failings, counseled against nagging or trying to change him. The Stones and Levine tended to offer psychological rather than physiological analyses of maladjustments. "In most instances . . . the failure to reach an orgasm is psychological in origin," the Stones concluded in 1940. "For one reason or another, the woman sets up a barrier against complete surrender and abandon during the sexual act." [112] When a woman complained about losing excitement when her husband stopped touching her clitoris, Levine retorted, "You lost it because you thought it would be gone." [113] "Do you feel a complete woman?" she asked another unhappy client. Or, "Maybe if you were more of a woman . . ." to another.[114] For those already capable of clitoral orgasms, she advised suppressing the orgasm: since the average woman only achieves one orgasm during a single encounter it is important to stop the "foreplay" prior to a clitoral orgasm in an effort to make possible a vaginal orgasm.[115]

On the other hand, in the sessions with the men, the doctors did little to check their tendency to blame their wives for the problem— even though it was usually the women's lack of satisfaction that *was* the problem. "She is always tired." Or, worse, "She's trying to be normal." [116] The helpful specific advice offered to the men—to extend the time of foreplay, try clitoral stimulation during intercourse, and so forth—did not alter the fundamental assumptions that intercourse was the core of the sex act and that women's inability to reach orgasm during intercourse was a maladjustment.

Inconsistently, the doctors clung to this view while also believing that male and female sexuality were essentially different. They emphasized the slowness of women's normal sexual-arousal period; the periodicity of women's sexual desire (as opposed to the putative constancy of men's); the complex psychosexual development of women which required them, as children, to transfer libidinous impulses from mother to father; and the necessity to develop sexual sensitivity in a naturally insensitive organ, the vagina. It was as if nature had set up every possible obstacle to mutual heterosexual satisfaction. A reasonable conclusion from these assumptions might have been that homosexual activity was more likely to prove satisfying to women, or that lack of female satisfaction was a normal condition. That the Stones and Levine clung to an ideal of "adjustment" that required overcoming such major obstacles must be attributed to their inability to discard conventional categories despite the lack of evidence for them. (The work of Kinsey, Masters, Johnson, and other recent sex researchers has since disproven many of the categories. Men and women alike have hormonal and libidinous cycles; the vagina never becomes sexually highly sensitive; it is normal for women not to reach orgasm during intercourse. All human orgasms are remarkably similar: the two analogous organs, clitoris and penis, respond to rhythmic stimulation.)

Perhaps their strong identification with the birth-control cause made it more difficult for them to look at women's sexual experiences openly. Since modern contraception was designed to make unlimited intercourse possible, it was not unnatural that they focused on intercourse itself as the center of sexual normality. The development of mechanical contraception had made the twentieth-century birth controllers less aware than the nineteenth-century voluntary-motherhood advocates of the importance of other forms of sexual expression, both genital and nongenital. Stone and Levine noticed that it was necessary to distinguish between women's desire for "lovemaking" and for intercourse.[117] But they interpreted the former as an incomplete, immature impulse. The Stones accepted the categorization suggested by Albert Moll and Havelock Ellis twenty years before of the contrectation or tumescence impulse, the desire to touch and caress, and the detumescence impulse, the desire for orgasm.[118] These categories were based on inadequate understanding of the female orgasm and the assumption that, like the male, it led to immediate detumescence, a sense of completion. Thus the doctors labeled women as sexually immature for not sharing a peculiar male impulse; on the other hand, when women did actively seek orgasm, in the manner successful for the great majority of women, the doctors condemned that too, albeit gently, as not fully womanly.

As Stone and Levine focused on psychological, rather than physiological, explanations for women's sexual disinterest or frustration, so they also tended to discard environmental explanations. The most common of these among women was tiredness. Levine rightly understood that tiredness was a psychological as well as a physical problem; that men were less "tired" when it came to sex because they more regularly got pleasure out of it. The women clients usually instinctively understood the truth of this. As one woman put it, "I get tired when I even think of it." [119] Yet Levine's approach to this problem mixed a certain amount of blame with her advice as to how to achieve orgasm. Tiredness was an alibi, she said.[120] Yet there were so many "alibis": lack of privacy from in-laws and children, money worries, feelings of being unloved and unappreciated, lack of child care, for example. The exclusive focus on sexuality was useful and may well have been the most productive choice given the limits of what the doctors, the clinic, or the whole birth control movement could offer; nevertheless, it contained a certain unreality in terms of the lives of the particular women. The sexual problems could not be separated from other problems.

The narrow approach to sexual problems of the clinical counseling led, inevitably, to elitism, for women whose economic and social lives were relatively privileged were those most likely to be helped by focused sex counseling. A subjective snobbery was also evident in the case reports of many counselors. A typical entry from the Clinical Research Bureau records: "Consultation with Miss Lichtenstein and fiancé—to be married on Saturday—rather poor type—poorly educated—not very intelligent." [121] There seems some evidence of a double standard in responding to the numerous appeals for abortions that came to the clinic. Abortions were, of course, illegal and extremely dangerous for the clinic; therapeutic abortions were sometimes arranged, but most applicants were rejected absolutely. The clinic workers would, however, sometimes go out of their way to arrange "therapeutic" abortions, even for nonmedical problems, if the candidate impressed them. For example:

> Miss Eide is a Norwegian, without relatives, who is unmarried, and is five weeks pregnant. Expected to be married in March, but when her fiancé discovered her condition he deserted her. She is a woman of education, came here wanting termination. . . . Then arranged with Dr. Appel for a D & C. Patient is out of work and has only $100 in the bank. . . . We explained to her the confidential nature of our assistance and she promised not to violate our confidence. Was not charged for conference. . . .[122]

Furthermore, the sexual problems were entwined in power struggles between husbands and wives, even in the best of marriages. Women's resentment of their husbands for imposing male sexual expectations and rhythms reflected many other resentments: their inability to get out of the house, the burden of housework and child care, their lack of interesting work, their husbands' lack of sensitivity and emotional generosity. Stone and Levine saw no place for a feminist analysis of marital maladjustments, despite the fact that both doctors, in their writing and therapy about sex, paid more attention to women's own experiences than most others doing marriage counseling. Levine was particularly quick to brand women's resentments and rebellions as signs of a desire to dominate. For example:

> Mrs. S: I try to be analytical about it. Had orgasm once and tried to think what was different. Allowed myself to kiss and be kissed without restraint. Not able to repeat it even though tried. I don't know why. I don't like his breath or his mouth open and prefer it closed. Always seem to find some petty reason. Always feel he gets ahead of me and I resent it and if he would let me get ahead of him even in kissing. It leads to inner resentments.
>
> Dr. Levine: Would you like to run the marriage?

In this case, Mrs. S. tried to defend herself:

> There's always a slight competition between two people. He's quite outgoing person. Accomplishes a great deal. . . . I have to keep going to meet his standards. Subtly makes me feel badly if I don't keep up. . . . If I don't look at it too carefully, we really get on very well together. Sometimes find as a woman a lot is asked of me. Have to do everything to make a perfect wife and he, in turn, has to be a perfect husband. (Referring to husband's standards.) [123]

Mrs. S. was walking a delicate line: relaxed and relatively open in the discussion, she was probing to understand the source of her sexual problem, yet also reassuring herself of her marriage, keeping a lid on her resentment. Levine supported her in the suppression, not at all in the expression, of anger.

Under the circumstances, Levine's desire not to open these marriages up to thorough examination was probably considerate. The problem was not with the doctors, but with the limitations of clinic-referred, very short-term therapy (and possibly of all psychotherapy).

Many of these women had total marital problems, and many of those were created by their over-all social circumstances as working-class and middle-class women. Their opportunities limited by sex discrimination even in prosperous times, the Depression had intensified the pressure on them. Postwar prosperity had not produced substantial benefits for these women, most of them unemployed. Many of the husbands had served in the war, and the wives had lived through wartime loneliness and hardship, expecting and hoping for a better life after the men's return. But the reunification of their families had not taken away their restlessness and disappointment in their lives.

Despite the warm and helping intentions of doctors Levine and Stone, and no doubt of hundreds of other birth-control marriage counselors, the objective limitations of what they could offer created a blaming-the-victim effect. Other leaders of the counseling movement within Planned Parenthood were even less sympathetic to women's sexual problems. An example is in the approach of Emily Mudd, one of the national leaders of the marriage-counseling profession. The women attending birth-control clinics, she wrote, fell into three groups: those who use contraception successfully and easily, those who are failures as contraceptors, and those who try but return with dissatisfactions and complaints.

> The majority of those who register dissatisfaction . . . are drawn from that group of women who, largely because of their childhood influences and training, are unable to relate themselves freely to the sexual aspect of life. For want of a better term we might call them "the complainers." Their inability to accept sex . . . or, in more technical terms, their "frigidity" varies . . . (1) the self-centered, narcissistic type of woman; (2) the passive, accepting type; and (3) the woman who is resentful but desirous of change.

Only type three could likely be helped by counseling, Mudd thought.[124] Perhaps these categories were useful to clinic workers in helping to provide an initial approach to women with problems. Beyond a bare beginning, however, they could only have been barriers to understanding, for they merely condemn while obscuring the possible sources of resentment and unhappiness. Like Stone and Levine, Mudd was of the Freudian school and emphasized the importance of early-childhood experiences. This may well have been a correct analysis of the root of a problem, but in situations providing short-term therapy it could not offer much help, and tended to exclude even the consideration of present environmental factors contributing to women's feelings of resentment and trapped-ness.

For women to assert as equals their needs in the bedroom required a sense of equality that had to pervade the kitchen, nursery, and study as well; only over-all equality in status, wealth, and power could produce equal self-confidence in sex. Furthermore, for women to assert their sexual needs was not merely to reach for equality but to summon the strength to throw off the heavy burden of centuries of male-supremacist sexual-behavior patterns, a weight that had been at its greatest a mere century previously. The universality of male-supremacist culture meant that even the most egalitarian-minded women and men reproduced inequalities in their sexual encounters. The women felt guilty about making the men wait; the men felt inadequate for not being able to keep their erections longer; both resented each other for being made to feel inadequate; both resented themselves for not living up to the ecstatic expectations they had formed of orgasm.

The sex therapists of the 1940s could not carry out a sexual revolution because a sexual revolution could only be accomplished by a successful feminist revolt. The birth controllers had involved themselves in a contradictory task: to encourage women's sexual liberation while not encouraging their efforts to liberate themselves from societal inequality. The more timid sex reformers of the pre–World War I era had more impact. Although seldom discussing sexual anatomy or technique, they had supported women in more daring sexual assertions because they were simultaneously challenging a whole series of conventions of femininity and propriety. (And studies show, in fact, that sexual behavior changed much more in the second and third decades of the century than at any time since.[125]) The birth controllers of the 1940s no longer wanted to challenge many conventions. Indeed, the main thrust of their campaign was toward family stability. In sexual relations stability usually meant the status quo. Radical changes in sexual relations, like most other radical changes, did not come easily, but produced painful, wrenching jolts, broken marriages, and loneliness; radical sexual change was not conducive to stable, planned families.

In its inability to support larger change in the relations between the sexes, the birth-control movement had become self-limiting. If sexual liberation was always dependent on women's general liberation, birth-control usage was too. The evidence was not so clear on this question in the 1940s as it is in the 1970s, but the essential factors in the situation were the same. The accessibility of birth-control information did not seem to affect family size as greatly as many other factors, such as economic status and women's work. People motivated, because of the structure of their lives, to limit their childbearing would seek out birth control, and to them Planned Parenthood was valuable; people lacking that motivation would not use birth control despite its availability. Unmarried women, despite strong motivation to avoid pregnancies, would often not use birth control even when it was available because of the guilt they felt about their sexual activity.

The help in achieving sexual satisfaction that the birth controllers were offering in the 1940s was useful to some women, but it ironically also produced frustration. The attention it focused on the possibilities of sexual pleasure was a luxury of relatively privileged people, with leisure and privacy. Sexual ecstasy seemed realistic to those relatively free of more pressing problems, such as ill-health and poverty (and even the clinic clients, as we have seen, could not maintain that clear focus on sex because of such other distractions). At the same time the sexual focus reflected, and encouraged, a general focus of women on their home life. Planned Parenthood urged sexual fulfillment while it also urged mothers to stay at home, there to be responsible for better but smaller families. Sexual fulfillment became an increasing national concern simultaneously with the feminine mystique. Psychologists, the advertising industry, the schools, all the opinion-forming artillery of the nation sought to influence married women, especially mothers, who pursued employment or activity outside their homes. Such women and their husbands were threatened with juvenile delinquency and maladjustment, divorce, and social ostracism. At the same time single women were denied appealing models of unmarried life. That the feminine-mystique propaganda campaign eventually failed was due to economic pressures more powerful than the backlash against woman's power—that is, the increasing need for low-wage labor and the over-all continued decline in men's real wages, which made the two-income family increasingly a necessity. The campaign succeeded, however, in making many working-class and middle-class women feel conflicted and guilty.

The sexual-liberation emphasis was by no means inevitably hostile to the feminine mystique, but was often part of it. Planned Parenthood sex counselors took care that their sex-education program could not stimulate "promiscuity." The birth-control clinic clients were required to be married, as marital monogamy was the explicit norm for men and women, and premarital chastity for women the preferred standard. The assumption of the therapists was that single women should have no sex life. Furthermore, the counseling offered through the birth-control clinics retained medical direction; all the women involved had previously been examined for gynecological problems as well as given diaphragms. Physiological education and sex counseling were seen as natural extensions of medical services into the field of mental health; both physical and psychological problems could hinder good sexual adjustment in marriage. Offering this kind of service outside a general social-welfare program and without a larger political education about women's problems had an impact that supported the feminine mystique. It suggested that the frustrations women felt need not poison their sexual relations; it suggested that poverty and overwork need not damage the sex lives of the working class; it suggested that sexism was not incompatible with sexual ecstasy.

From a longer historical view this Planned Parenthood sex counseling was in some respects within a long tradition of feminist-led sexual reform and in other respects outside the tradition. The 1940s sex counseling was feminist in that it continued the century-old struggle against Victorian prudery. From the voluntary-motherhood advocates of the 1870s to the birth controllers of the second decade of the twentieth century to the Planned Parenthood workers of the 1940s, there is clearly a progression toward more frankness about the physiological aspects of sex and more acceptance of women's sex drives. Yet politically the earlier sex reformers were far more radical in the breadth of their interpretation of their own work. The voluntary-motherhood advocates were challenging male tyranny over all sexual and family life. The birth controllers were questioning marriage; they criticized the family itself as an institution that replicated and reproduced the existing authoritarian class and sex relations of the society. Planned Parenthood's sex counseling was influenced by continued scientific collection of information on sexual behavior that showed that the marital and sexual norms so deplored by the earlier sex radicals were indeed disintegrating, or rapidly changing, as evidenced by escalating divorce and adultery rates. The 1940s sex counselors could only oppose these trends blindly, unable to perceive in the pain and loneliness of disintegrating relationships the signs of the inadequacy of the old models of marriage. Though they lacked a strategy to shore up permanent, monogamous male-dominated marriage, they continued moralistically to reaffirm its value in the face of incontrovertible evidence of its weakening.

Planned Parenthood's defense of traditional marriage was an understandable response to a general nervousness about social instability that had been heightened by the war. Sex and marriage counselors could see that the reaction against prudery, while necessary and, in their view, "healthy," had been a strongly individualist reaction, leading toward atomization and social disintegration. What they did not see so clearly was that there had previously been a countervailing force to this disintegrative tendency: the several waves of feminism which offered movement toward an alternative along with attacks on the old sexual and marital system. The feminism of the 1870s had sought to remake marriage in the image of its traditional claims: permanent and monogamous, with dignity and power for women within it, retaining the separate functions of the sexes, and instituting a single standard. In one sense the voluntary-motherhood advocates were reactionary because they associated the empowerment of women with the restoration of a preindustrial, family-centered society. But at the same time they were driving wedges into the old patriarchal unity of the couple. Descrying rape within marriage, insisting on women's right to refuse, often recommending separate beds and even bedrooms, they were not sentimentalizing marital togetherness or the couple as an inseparable unit. Furthermore they were actively building women's organizations and a women's community and sisterhood that provided sources of support alternative to those of marriage. The feminist birth controllers of the second decade, by contrast, actually looked forward to a weakening of the traditional family through the increasing socialization of work outside the home. They too insisted upon a single standard, but they sought it in the removal of repression, not in its equal distribution. They welcomed industrial society, with its class, generational, and sex conflicts. They experimented with alternatives to marriage and the family, seeing in those experiments part of a search for new power relations in the society. They tried to create space for satisfying sexual and social lives for single people and to create women's and workers' organizational forms that could supply some of the support that families had always given. Theirs was a revolutionary strategy, however, and they spurned halfway measures. Failing to create a revolution, they also failed to create organizational forms that could assume defensive postures, could dig in for a lasting struggle for birth control and women's rights. They left the birth-control issue to the professional social planners.

These professionals, who directed Planned Parenthood, were faced with a difficult situation. We have seen how the Victorian restrictive and hypocritical sexual and marriage system began, in the 1920s, to unravel fast. A challenge originally fueled by women's unrest was channeled through commercialization and corporate-controlled mass media into a nonexperimental, consumptionist set of sexual standards, as conformist as the old. By the late 1940s these new standards had been incorporated into a virtually unchanged marriage system, which merely included as normal the possibility of divorce and remarriage. Adultery and illegitimacy continued in secret. The normal role of women in these sequential families remained the same— full-time housewife and mother (although the actual content and conditions of women's labor in the family changed greatly.) The feminine mystique idealized love and marital intimacy and spurned forms of collective support—particularly among women—outside the family and heterosexual relationships. Sisterly love was projected as an outdated, infantile sentimentality, and even as unnatural. Lacking fundamental changes in sexual power relations, women remained vulnerable to a new set of male sexual demands.

Because they were not feminists, even the best of the Planned

Parenthood workers inevitably oversimplified the sexual and reproductive problems they encountered. As a consequence they tended to isolate sexual and reproductive problems from women's over-all position. Furthermore they offered no alternatives to the current marital norm or even suggestions for modifying it. As individuals they cannot be blamed that no feminist movement remained to give a context to their work. Organizationally, Planned Parenthood helped to integrate birth-control ideas into mainstream social planning and thereby further separated birth control from any remaining feminist orientation. Yet, ironically, in the long run Planned Parenthood also contributed to the eventual rebirth of a feminist movement by making birth control widely acceptable.

13

A Note on Population Control

AFTER 1950 a new perspective came to dominate the birth-control organizations, that of population control. Descended from Malthusianism, population control, as we have seen, had distinctly separate roots from the birth-control movement. Yet Planned Parenthood provided a bridge between the two both organizationally and ideologically. Its emphasis on family size as a factor contributing to family stability and prosperity foreshadowed today's revived Neo-Malthusian emphasis on population size as contributing to societal stability and prosperity. Planned Parenthood in fact represented the suppression of birth control as a bottom-up social movement, replacing it with a project of health, economic, and social planning by experts. Thus Planned Parenthood made the population-control campaign possible, having created its organizational and financial base.

But just as the planned-parenthood emphasis arose in response to specific contemporary social problems—World War I, the repression of working-class and feminist radicalism after the war, the Depression—so too population control arose as a result of specific historical changes. When I speak of population control here, I am referring to the programs and policies advanced primarily by the United States, sometimes through international organizations such as the United Nations, in the last few decades. These programs urge birth-rate reductions upon underdeveloped countries as a tool in economic development and upon poor people within the developed capitalist countries as a weapon against poverty. Before the 1950s the generic population-control idea had gone through several stages. Common in classless hunting-and-gathering societies, population control was then a collective survival strategy. At the end of the eighteenth century Malthus provided a population-control ideology for the ruling class. In the 1950s, for the first time, population control became an important part of the foreign policy of the world's greatest superpower.

These modern programs are still basically Malthusian. They rest on the conviction that population growth may wipe out not only agricultural growth but all economic development. Beyond this the population-control programs rest on particular sets of priorities about the needs of the poor. With birth-rate reduction as the highest priority, the policies assume that the prevailing class structure should not be altered (although it may be stabilized through allowing some mobility for individuals to rise out of their class); that only gradual, nonrevolutionary political change is to be encouraged; that relations between the sexes should be allowed to shift only gradually and within the existing class structure. Thus population control becomes not only a force *for* economic development, but *against* revolutionary change.

Like the original Malthusianism, modern population control arose as a program of defense of the ruling class. In late eighteenth-century Britain, peasant and working-class discontent was rocking the established government. Poverty was increasing owing to capitalist industrialization, the destruction of the peasants' livelihood, and the creation of an economically helpless working class; Malthus provided both a rationalization for and an attempted solution to the social stress by blaming the problem on overpopulation. After World War II the U.S. government, as leader of the capitalist world, was threatened by international discontent as formerly colonial peoples demanded independence and sought economic development through nationalist and often socialist economic reorganization, which would have limited or even ended the continued economic exploitation of Third World peoples by Western capitalists. Population control again provided both a rationalization for the failure of capitalism to provide economic growth for the Third World masses and a proposed solution to the social stress. Born of the Cold War, the population controllers considered stopping communism not only the highest priority but also, it seemed from their propaganda, the main reason that economic progress in the Third World was desirable. For example, *The Population Bomb*, a pamphlet of the Hugh Moore fund, first published in 1954 [1] and reprinted frequently until the mid-1960s, featured such arguments as this: "There will be 300 million more mouths to feed in the world four years from now—most of them hungry. Hunger brings turmoil—and turmoil, as we have learned, creates the atmosphere in which the communists seek to conquer the earth." [2] Thus the "altruism" of U.S. population-control programs was not very convincing in the Third World.

Population control reached Third World countries and peoples as a program of U.S. foreign policy and therefore, in the experience of many Asians and Latin Americans in particular, as an aspect of imperialism. Population control was, in the 1960s, absolutely first priority within U.S. nonmilitary foreign aid; indeed, receiving any foreign aid usually obligated receiving nations to undertake population-control programs in accordance with U.S. State Department specifications.

Understanding that population control has been abused in the service of imperialism does not erase real problems of overpopulation. Overpopulation *is* a problem in some parts of the world. The important point, however, is that overpopulation is not the only or even the main cause of poverty. In some of the poorest areas of the world population is very sparse; in others it is dense. Even countries opposed to the ideology of population control, such as China, have adopted policies to counter pronatalist pressures and to encourage small families.

Overpopulation, far from causing poverty, is more frequently a result of poverty. Addeke Boerma, former director-general of the United Nations' Food and Agriculture Organization, once argued that the best means to reduce birth rates would be through effective public-health programs that could ensure the survival of first-born babies.[3] Historically birth-rate decline has by and large been a consequence, not a cause, of economic development. In every industrialization, birth rates fell after changes in the mode of production lowered infant mortality, made children less valuable and more expensive economically, and increased demands and opportunities for women's employment outside their homes. On the other hand, even in socialist countries, the continuation of peasant agricultural production and social organization perpetuates the incentive for large families.[4]

There is, of course, no hidden hand that guarantees that population size will be appropriately regulated by individual desires alone. Density of population in relation to land and to productive capacity is not the only, or at this time the most important, measure of overpopulation. Ecologically, overpopulation is more importantly a question of the consumption of energy and other resources. By this measure the U.S. population is much more destructive to the world's resources than many poorer nations with higher birth rates and higher population densities, and internationally the few rich often drain more of the earth's capacity than the many poor. If everyone in the world used as much energy, for example, as the U.S. average, the resulting production of energy would be seven times what it is now and would produce enormous and unforeseeable pollution.[5] Just as population questions cannot be separated from the whole natural system of which human beings are a part, so ecological questions cannot be separated from social organization.

Population control alone cannot solve the problems created by an economic system that continually reproduces and deepens poverty and inequality. Nor could population control and ecological reforms together solve the problems created by an economic system that crazily expands the production of wasteful commodities and coerces people, through their alienation from their own labor, into ever greater dependence on such commodities. Societies and governments can regulate birth rates and resource consumption. But there is no evidence that such regulation in isolation from radical social reorganization would create significant improvements for the world's masses or long-term resolution of dangerous threats to the ecology.

The use of population control as part of an imperialist foreign policy is outside the scope of this book. But although contemporary population control is not a part of the birth-control movement, it is a part of its opposition. Population-control ideology has invaded the popular consciousness about reproductive control in the United States to such an extent that it has clouded the vision of an independent struggle for reproductive freedom. The identification of population control with birth control is not a result of the obtuseness of the public but of the actual convergence of the two causes, primarily the surrender of feminist orientation by birth-control leaders and the substitution of elitist—in both sex and class terms—values. Let us look briefly at that convergence.

As the birth controllers grew ever closer to the eugenists in the 1920s and 1930s, they also grew close to population control in the 1940s and 1950s. Indeed, viewed from the perspective of professional demographers and birth-control reformers, population control was the successor to eugenics in every respect—ideologically, organizationally, and in personnel. Eugenists were almost always supporters of imperialism, in Britain in the late nineteenth century and in the United States in the early twentieth century. Indeed, eugenists developed a uniquely hereditarian justification for imperialism, arguing that it allowed a healthy competition among the races which established the superiority of the more civilized.* The eugenists, however, were stuck with a contradiction, for although they believed imperialism itself to be healthy, they considered wars dysgenic, since they killed off the "best" young men. Population control helped resolve this contradiction by offering a nonmilitary tool for controlling colonies. Eugenics and imperialism were also connected through an evolving racism, directed especially against whatever group was the most truculent subject of, and hence threat to, white world supremacy. In the course of the twentieth century the dominant form of U.S. racism was directed first at immigrants, later at blacks, and more recently at

---

* Eugenists have always had an ambivalent attitude toward social Darwinism. Their ideology was a rejection of *laissez faire* in favor of intervention to improve on natural selection, but they justified this intervention on the grounds that the process of natural selection had already been derailed by civilization. Their value system, however, was identical with that of the social Darwinists—equating "fitness" with success; the eugenists were only less sure that untrammeled competition would always produce the success of the fittest.

Third World peoples even while they remained in their own lands. Population-control propaganda in the last two decades mixed concern for the poverty of these Third World peoples with fear of the power of their "teeming" numbers.

Both organizationally and individually, eugenists became population controllers between 1930 and 1950. In the late 1940s the Milbank Memorial Fund, one of the main backers of eugenic and birth-control research, began to support research and writing about overpopulation in underdeveloped countries.[6] In 1952 Frederick Osborn, a leading eugenist, organized the Population Council.[7] Osborn later set up the Population Association of America, and his cousin Fairfield Osborn later became a leader of Planned Parenthood–World Population. The Rockefeller Foundation, key funder of eugenic work, joined Milbank in 1936 in giving Princeton (Henry Fairfield Osborn's and John D. Rockefeller III's alma mater) an Office of Population Research. In the 1940s the OPR became a kind of sanctuary for eugenist demographers. Kingsley Davis, Clyde Kiser, Frank Notestein, Dudley Kirk, and Frank Lorimer all worked there. When Rockefeller financed the Population Council, these five men moved to it immediately. (Rockefeller had also sent a man, Charles-Edward Amory Winslow, into the Planned Parenthood Federation at its inception.) Out of the ten men on the Population Council's demographic and medical advisory boards, six had been associated with eugenics.[8] In 1955, attempting to shore up the declining popularity of eugenics, the Population Council undertook to support the *Eugenics Quarterly* for the next three years if matching grants could be found. The Population Reference Bureau, which had functioned since 1929 as a eugenics organization, was made over into the population-control model.* [9] Soon afterward it received grants from Rockefeller, followed by grants from many other great foundations—Ford, Mellon, du Pont, Sloan, Standard Oil, and Shell among others. Similar monies came into other organizations now devoted to population control—the International Planned Parenthood Federation, Planned Parenthood–

---

* Its organizer, Guy Burch, had been active in the campaign for immigration restriction; one of the most persevering and fervent in his views, in 1939 he was campaigning against the admittance of "non-Aryan" children, Jewish orphans who were Nazi refugees, into the United States.[10]

World Population, the Population Crisis Committee, and the Committee to Check the Population Explosion.[11]

In the transition from eugenics to population control, the separation between birth-control and population-control organizations was lost. Indeed, all the major population-control organizations of the 1970s were born from the Planned Parenthood Federation. In 1948 Sanger got the Brush Foundation (with its head, Dorothy Brush, previously a funder of eugenic work) to finance, along with the Osborns, the International Planned Parenthood Federation. Its headquarters, in London, were provided free of charge by the English Eugenics Society.[12] IPPF work was focused on international population control. In 1961 the U.S. PPFA launched a new division called Planned Parenthood–World Population which dominated PPFA's whole orientation for the next decade. Until the women's liberation movement, feminist birth-control propaganda and services were practically nonexistent in the United States.

On the other hand, population-control propaganda, regarding both domestic and international birth rates, became widespread in the 1950s and 1960s. Two major factors underlay the selling of population control in the United States. One was the decision, around 1960, of leading population-control exponents and backers, such as John D. Rockefeller III, to make the U.S. government support population-control services, thus shifting the cost to the taxpayers. In order to accomplish this they naturally had to convince at least vocal parts of the public that population control was in their interest. The second factor behind the campaign to build overpopulation fears in the country was the desire to cut the birth rates of the poor, particularly nonwhites, in the United States. Stemming from the same hereditarian and blaming-the-victim assumptions as eugenic programs always had, population-control propaganda carried sometimes overt, sometimes covert, racist and elitist messages. A particularly bad, but by no means atypical, example was the 1969 mass-advertising campaign of the Committee to Check the Population Explosion:

> How many people do you want in your country? Already the cities are packed with youngsters. Thousands of idle victims of discontent and drug addiction. You go out after dark at your peril. . . . Birth

control is the answer. . . . The evermounting tidal wave of humanity challenges us to control it, or be submerged along with all of our
civilized values.* [13]

These ads called their program birth control, not population control.
The suggestion that urban crime is related to overcrowding is not
unreasonable as a partial explanation, but the proposal to solve the
problem through population control is worse than impractical. In the
context it is an implicit denial of the possibility of attacking the poverty and injustice that lie behind these problems. It is blaming the
victim again: the problem is not the crime but the criminals; let us
have fewer of the kind of people who become criminals. In the rhetoric
of this ad it is clear, if unspoken, who are the people that need birth
control: the urban poor, particularly blacks and other nonwhites.

If the victims of our class society have seen in birth control a plot
to exterminate them, there is a great deal of evidence, contemporary
and historical, to support their analysis. It is not an irrational fear,
especially as the use of coercion increases in population-control programs. Today, population controllers discuss ever more frequently the
possibility that effective population control can never happen voluntarily. Reviewing a decade of well-funded "family planning" programs in Latin America, one of their chief architects writes that there
is no evidence of birth-rate reduction on that continent. The women
who attend the family-planning clinics there are primarily those who
used contraception even without the clinics and who furthermore have
already had an average of five pregnancies.[15]

As a result of this kind of evidence, population controllers increasingly advocate various kinds of coercion in their programs.[16] They
have discussed a range of sanctions including forced sterilization after
a given number of children. The more common use of material
incentives is merely another form of coercion, especially when the
rewards are accompanied by incomplete explanations, and especially

* Although the more academic Population Council and the Population Reference Bureau did
not formally endorse these ads, many of their leaders did. Eugene Black, on the board of Planned
Parenthood and once vice-president of Chase Manhattan and head of the World Bank, signed
the ads, as did Frank Abrams, former chairman of Standard Oil of New Jersey (owned by
Rockefeller) and a director of the Population Reference Bureau. Of fifty-eight regular signers of
the ads, thirty-six were previously part of the population-control establishment, fourteen others
were closely associated with Planned Parenthood, and four of the remaining eight were close
associates of the Rockefellers.[14]

given the diffidence that uneducated peasants often feel before outsiders of authority—doctors, for example. When people living on a subsistence economy, with the threat of starvation never far and a constantly high incidence of malnutrition and painful disease, are offered things of great value in return for their signature or verbal agreement, they cannot be said to have made a free choice.

Such coercive methods are already common. In India men are bribed with cash, transistor radios, and other commodities to accept vasectomies. "The cash reward proved to be a major attraction for the poor of Kerala, whose monthly earning is less than a third of the reward," reported *The New York Times*.[17] India, Korea, Pakistan, Taiwan, Ceylon, Egypt, and Turkey developed programs offering incentive payments for accepting vasectomies or IUD's.[18] Payments were made not only to the patients but also to doctors and other family-planning workers. By paying the latter a piece rate, as it were, they were encouraged to serve as many patients in a day as possible and to persuade reluctant ones to accept more permanent forms of birth control; the resulting potential degradation in the quality of medical care offered was considered a problem of lower priority.* Beyond this, individuals not employed by the clinics were offered "finder's fees," veritable bounties for bringing in patients willing to be sterilized or fitted with an IUD. The population-control organizations themselves have reported widespread corruption, failure to inform patients of side effects, bribery, and so forth. Women were known to have IUDs inserted and remove them themselves (a painful and risky procedure) in order to have another inserted to get another payment. But it is irrational to criticize the abuses in such a system when the system itself is structurally coercive.

Coercion, though less open and widespread, is increasingly used in the United States. Just as Third World countries were required to operate population-control programs if they wished to keep receiving U.S. foreign aid, so poor women in the United States are often pressured to accept sterilization in order to keep getting welfare payments. In the United States today nonwhite welfare recipients

---

* That paying doctors a piece rate did not seem immoral and liable to subvert medical standards is because it is only an extension of the whole capitalist organization of medicine, in which doctors are entrepreneurs whose earnings escalate if they spend less time with each patient.

have had approximately one-third more sterilizations than the total of non-welfare-receiving women.[19] Federally-sponsored birth-control programs use heavy pressure on poor and nonwhite women both in the continental United States and in Puerto Rico: for example, visiting women still in maternity wards after childbirth to get their agreement to sterilizations. (The law requires a lapse of only seventy-two hours between birth and sterilization agreement.) Women suffering primarily from inadequate housing, inadequate nutrition, and inadequate medical care, from poverty in short, are told that reducing their family size and/or unwanted pregnancies will better their lives.[20] Presumably, their profligacy in producing children is the cause of their poverty.

Coercive population control is stimulated and then made acceptable by racism. Racist fears of black power have been easily symbolized by black population increases. Nonsensical ideas such as the "cheapness" of life among Asians and highly documented analyses of the "different" structure of the black family such as the matriarchy theory have served to justify the use of coercion to reduce the nonwhite birth rate. These myths are accepted because they provide some sort of explanation for some of the actual social problems in the United States. Unemployment, crowded and ill-kept cities, inadequate recreational space, for example, are in part due to relative overpopulation, relative that is to the supply of jobs, housing, and beaches that the present political economy provides. The increasing numbers of blacks, Puerto Ricans, and other Spanish-speaking people in cities, combined with their militant civil-rights struggles, appeared to correspond with the relative impoverishment and degradation of many whites. More, the job and housing markets and school systems of cities are thoroughly and often deliberately segregated, producing real cleavage and suspicion among racial and ethnic groups. The problems are real; proposing population control as their solution can only exacerbate racism. Indeed, proposing population control as a solution to problems caused by racism—such as crime and poverty—is, objectively, a contribution to that racism, whatever the intentions of the proposers.

It would be a mistake to conclude from this that whites are not also the targets of population-control programs. Throughout the United States, in white as well as black communities, family-planning clinics have been introduced as services to the poor, who could benefit much more from all-around health clinics. Women may be able to get treatment for problems directly related to the reproductive system such as vaginal infections, but they cannot get pediatric care, general internal medicine, or even emergency care from the family-planning clinics. In this country as in the Third World population-control programs have had the effect, whatever the intentions of their supporters, of emphasizing small families disproportionally to their actual contribution to people's well-being.

Universally population-control programs have been antifeminist. Population controllers often claim to support female emancipation but only on terms that they would define for women. For example, in Puerto Rico, model for the population controllers, where 35 per cent of women have been sterilized, abortion remains illegal, for abortion becomes too often a tool in women's own command. In the United States, for example, privileged white women often have difficulty finding doctors to sterilize them whereas working-class and especially nonwhite women are often sterilized against their will. The population controllers have not campaigned against illegitimacy legislation or for public day care or any other programs that would increase women's power to have real reproductive choice. Throughout the world, population-control programs decreasingly use diaphragms and even pills and favor IUDs and operations which are not in women's control. The population-control view of women's "emancipation" is the imposition of norms of U.S. bourgeois behavior onto women. The feminist view, by contrast, imagines women's emancipation as a process designed and created by women themselves.

No matter what kinds of coercive pressures are used to induce the acceptance of population control, it is going to be resisted. At the World Population Conference of August 1974, planned by U.S. population controllers, an on-the-spot alliance of Third World representatives and individual critics of Neo-Malthusianism not only resisted the plans of the conference organizers but forced the rewriting from the floor of the assembly of the "World Plan of Action," to de-emphasize population control and reject international norms of family size.[21] Population control is resisted equally effectively by illiterate peasants who not only resent the imposition of alien norms but more important calculate that smaller families are not in their interest in situations where children are valuable contributors to a family's meager security.[22] But if the level of coercion is high enough, as in the sterilization programs of Puerto Rico, this combined political and personal resistance may still be defeated. Both in the United States and world wide there is evidence that women are being sterilized without their consent or with consent extracted under conditions of stress, misconceptions, and/or inadequate information.[23]

Despite such direct attacks on women's rights, population control has nevertheless been blamed on feminism at times. This is another destructive aspect of population control, and a most painful irony for feminists. As those on the receiving end of population control grow more resistant, some of their anger has been deflected from its true target, imperialism, to a potential ally, feminism. In this way the ideological system created by population control has divided its opponents. Although feminists have not usually supported coercive population control, they have not fought hard enough against it or dissociated themselves clearly enough from it. Anti-imperialist organizations have sometimes accepted the identity of birth control and population control, blithely denying the existence, even in potential, of population problems and implicitly denying the importance of women's rights to control their own bodies. The fusing of the concepts of birth control and population control in mass propaganda functions to smother the movement for reproductive freedom. Beyond this, in the over-all struggle for freedom from domination, feminism and anti-imperialism have an objective basis for unity, in an opposition to all forms of domination. Population control has helped to mask it.

14

Sexuality, Feminism, and Birth Control Today

THE STRUGGLE for reproductive self-determination is one of the oldest projects of humanity, one of our earliest collective attempts to alter the biological limits of our existence. Women died in this struggle, and still do, though their deaths today are due more to prohibitions and illegalization than to necessary risks in birth control. (The mortality rate from illegal abortion, for example, is much higher than that from legal abortion, and the mortality rate in childbirth itself is higher than both.) But most pregnancies in the world are still unplanned, and perhaps unintended, though not necessarily unwanted. Indeed, the equation of desire with planning, the assumption that unplanned means unwanted, is part of a false view of self-determination. Self-determination does not mean exercising intellectual mastery at all times over bodily, earthly processes, though the capacity for that mastery expands our human possibilities. Self-determination—liberation, that is—is an historical concept itself. What people want for themselves and what they find oppressive and will resist have changed over the centuries. Industrial forms of production have indicated a potential for an easier and more creative human existence that leads people today to fight against the drudgery and suffering that has been the human experience for all of history. Even people in unindustrialized areas sense the possibilities that surplus and control over natural obstacles could give them.

It is in terms of the historical possibilities and needs of today that the failure to realize human reproductive self-control is frustrating. Many of the necessary tools already exist, and others could be developed quickly given the right priorities. Lack of contraception is now part of underdevelopment. But even in a country where contraception is widely used such as the United States, reproductive self-determination is far from realized. I have argued that this is because reproductive freedom cannot be isolated from other human freedoms. Reproductive patterns everywhere are determined by sexual morality, by the over-all status of women, by class formations, and by the nature of the struggles for social change.

It was in defense of class and sex privileges that birth control was originally prohibited. The accumulation of private property, first in the form of land, created the first prehistorical social force for increasing family size; through their sons fathers became patriarchs and could accumulate wealth indefinitely. "Right to life" theories have never represented the interests of the young. Today the powers and privileges that can be passed on to succeeding generations through the family are more varied: property, education, confidence, social and political connections. But the essential nature of class divisions is unchanged and depends on the generational passing down of status. Thus in class society children are never individuals and cannot escape the expectations, high or low, attached to their fathers' position.

The interference of class society with reproductive freedom affects not only propertied fathers anxious to perpetuate their power. Poor people frequently assuage their own frustrations by seeking vicarious satisfaction through their children. Women of all classes, denied creative work, achievement, or recognition for themselves, live through their children. Childlessness spells for many people not only loneliness but the threat of economic insecurity in old age; whereas the hope, often subconscious, for immortality through the family reflects not only the desire to pass on property or prestige, but often an emotional need to make a mark as a human being, to feel one's life as significant and lasting. Child-raising seems, deceptively, to offer an area of control, an area in which adults have power to create human value according to their own, not their employers', direction. These factors make children potentially the victims of adults' unsatisfactory lives. These pressures systematically push reproduction decisions beyond the reach of technological solutions. Only the liberation of children from the burdens of being useful to adults can make child-bearing a free choice, emanating from the desire to perpetuate human life, not oneself.

Beyond these pressures which all adults feel, childbearing is particularly problematic for women. Children are delightful and burdensome. Weighing the delights against the burdens is a process that women could accomplish without great stress were it not for enormous external pressures toward motherhood. Most people, men and women, feel some desire for children and the gratification of producing them and watching their growth. Children are beautiful, far more beautiful than most adults, especially in industrial capitalist society, where adults are changed by tedious work and insecurity into repressed, cautious, fearful animals. Children bring pleasure and some temporary relief from isolation. For women the attraction is heightened by the opportunity to produce a child in their own bodies, an exhilarating experience.

Against these factors are the difficulties of child-raising, especially for poor women and employed women in a society that offers little public support for children. But the consideration of these drawbacks is hampered by a mythology of motherhood, a series of pronatalist cultural pressures. Childless women often feel like failures, whereas childless men are not as likely to. Girls are socialized from their own infancies to anticipate motherhood. Women learn to like themselves in mothering roles, which allow them experiences of love and power not easily found in other situations. These maternal attitudes do not emanate merely from learned ideas and ideologies, but from a fundamental female character structure formed through earliest experiences and reinforced in daily life throughout youth and adulthood. Few women escape it entirely; few women can reject or change all of it once they reach adolescence.

The motherhood mystique, as opposed to the genuine pleasures of motherhood, contributes to the maintenance of a sexual division of labor that requires women to do confining, unpaid domestic work. At the same time the mystique is used by women in their own interests— that is, it is a rational ideology for women's survival and for maximizing the creative and enjoyable aspects of their lives. Full-time motherhood, when it is possible, is for most women preferable to the other job alternatives they have. In wage labor women have been relegated to the most menial, boring, and low-paying work—assembly line, typing, selling, housework, serving. Systematic discrimination in access to education, the content of education, and avocational activities such as art, politics, and sports, usually prevents women from even aspiring to more engaging, creative social or private activity. Child care, for all its difficulty, is inherently less alienated and more creative than most alternatives; it offers the mother at least a semblance of control over her working conditions and goals. Of course much of the skill and creativity of parenthood has been eroded just as most other work in this society has been degraded. Control over child care has been alienated from parents both through socialized institutions such as schools and through commoditization—children's "needs" mass-produced and sold back to parents in the form of toys, ever higher standards of cleanliness, prescriptive theories of child psychology—virtually forced on women through high-pressure advertising. Despite this degradation of the work of motherhood, women have not fled from it in disgust but have entered the wage labor force only out of necessity, because they need the money. Doing wage labor for most women means working two shifts, spending evenings and weekends doing housework; and part-time jobs are hard to get. If full-time unpaid motherhood is financially possible, even temporarily, it is no wonder that so many women choose it, or more accurately, fall into it.

"Falling into motherhood" is the more accurate description on several levels. The unpredictable nature of conception makes pregnancies difficult to schedule exactly. More important, the lack of firm choice reflects the lack of decent alternatives. When all the options are rather bad, intense preferences are not formed, and it becomes a natural response to avoid a decision altogether, leaving events to chance, to nature, to God. It is no wonder therefore that "excess fertility"—births in excess of what the parents themselves say they wanted—is higher among working-class, poor, and nonwhite women, for they have the fewest desirable alternatives. Inferior medical and birth-control services worsen their predicament; but many women do not use birth control even though it is available, they know about it, and they have no binding religious or moral hostility to it.

A particularly prevalent example of the tendency to respond to a no-win situation by avoiding the semblance of decisions is among young unmarried women. They are not only buffeted by contradictory pressures about motherhood and its alternatives, but placed in a double bind by the sexual aspects of a continuing double standard. Guilt feelings about sex lead many young women, not only Catholics, to the nondoctrinal, emotional view that contraception is a sin. The secular version of this dogma is that it is wrong to have intercourse without "taking your chances." Pregnancy is a risk that must be taken, a punishment that it is dishonorable to avoid. The pill has diminished this view somewhat, since it can be taken routinely every morning, separated from sexual activity entirely. The diaphragm is too difficult for many young women. To carry it with one, to have to admit to a man that one has a contraceptive device, is to take a responsibility for one's sexual behavior that many young women are not prepared for. It is easier and more "normal" for men to be lustful and assertive, for women merely to surrender, to be carried away by a greater force. To acquire and use a diaphragm means that a woman must accept herself as a sexual, heterosexual being, to admit that she plans to continue sexual activity indefinitely. It is easier to deal with guilt about sex by viewing one's adventures as one-time-only slips, promptly repented—over and over.

This is just one side of a double bind. The other side is that women resist the exploitive aspects of the sexual double standard. Women's guilt feelings are not mere relics of a dead morality: they are withdrawals from danger. One's reputation is somewhat safer now in the United States than a generation ago, but men still brag about their conquests. Being single is frightening to women, whereas men fear its opposite—being trapped. Women's fear of singleness is also not a vestige or a superstition. Single women are discriminated against and disadvantaged, in comparison to both married women and single men, socially and economically as well as by vulnerability to direct physical danger. The emotional ravages of these inequities are reflected in the terror of being a spinster that nearly every woman feels. Being without a man is threatening to a woman's very identity, to her self-esteem, because singleness objectively weakens her position. For women, therefore, heterosexual relations are always intense, frightening, high-risk situations which ought, if a woman has any sense of self-preservation, to be carefully calculated. These calculations call for weapons of resistance, which may include sexual denial. One effect of easily accessible contraception is to deprive women of that weapon. Another weapon is pregnancy itself, for the social ethic that requires marrying and supporting a woman who is pregnant is somewhat stronger, though not thoroughly reliable, than the ethic of loyalty to women as sexual partners. Women get pregnant "accidentally on purpose" as a way of punishing themselves. But they are also protecting themselves and sometimes punishing men. In reproduction men share the costs of male supremacy and women's resistance to it. Nothing more than reproduction illustrates that unless women can be free, men will never be. Pregnancy is woman's burden and her revenge.

In these double-bind situations, sexual and economic, "decisions" about childbearing take place with varying levels of ambivalence. Most "unplanned" pregnancies are partly wanted and partly unwanted. A frequent solution to ambivalance is passivity—not using contraception, or using it haphazardly. This is a rational response when no alternative is desirable. Those family planners who speak of irrationality, of women not understanding their own interests, do not themselves understand the problem. Self-determination cannot exist if none of the options is attractive. Reproductive options cannot be separated from economic, vocational, and social choices.

Although all the factors of women's lives affect reproductive decisions, sexual norms play an especially important role. Birth control separates reproduction from sexuality. For this separation to be desirable, both sexes must be able to enjoy sexual activity for its own sake. Though the capacity for sexual pleasure is simple and universal among humans, its realization has been elusive for most women. Understandably, the birth-control movement was always connected to a more disguised campaign for female sexual liberation. The modern women's liberation movement re-emphasizes, openly, women's sexual self-discovery. Even though the technology of birth control in itself contributes to women's sexual independence, it also deprives women of some important weapons, as we have just seen. If women's gains in sexual freedom outweigh the losses over the last century, it is not because of technological advance but because of the feminist movement.

There is a fundamental unity among the contributions of several waves of feminism to women's sexual liberation. A struggle for sex education since the mid-nineteenth century laid the basis for the de-repression of female sexuality. Cultural values and even physiological knowledge changed radically from the manuals of the popular-health movement of the 1840s to the social-purity writers of the 1890s to *Our Bodies Ourselves* of 1973, but all sought to throw off the blanket of suppression and lies about women's psychological and physiological sexuality. Furthermore, the end of all these efforts was the restoration of the legitimacy of female sexual pleasure, though the definition of its proper form changed historically. Since at least the 1870s feminist groups used forms of "consciousness-raising," that is, discussions among women which revealed the interface between "personal" and "political" problems, sexual problems always looming large among them. Feminist groups have continually attacked, for example, conventional fashions in dress, apprehending that the transformation of women into decorations helped to lower their self-esteem and, ironically, stunt their sexual development, keeping them eternally objects and never subjects. Feminists in all periods have emphasized the strength and flexibility of women's bodies as against their beauty, attempting to break the exclusive association of the female body with sexuality; simultaneously, feminists tried to reintegrate sexuality into full human relationships and fought the commoditization of sex which required the sacrifice of women as prostitutes to men's distorted sexuality.

The feminists' political approach to sexual and to personal problems produced an alternative to blaming-the-victim analyses of the "woman problem." Freeing women's minds to some extent from faulting themselves for their dependence, prudery, or loneliness, it enabled women to look more aggressively for alternatives to constricting conventions. In every historical period one effect of feminism has been to raise the status and the latitude of socially permissible activity for single women. Feminism's influence also helped married women to change the power relations within their marriages (and they found the strength to challenge their husbands' privileges and the conventions partly because feminists had shown them the possibility of a life outside marriage). The modern women's liberation movement has reaffirmed both celibacy and multiple sexual partners for women. The modern movement has also given birth to a lesbian-liberation movement, possibly the most important contribution to a future sexual liberation. It is not that feminism has produced more lesbians. There have always been many lesbians, despite high levels of repression; and most lesbians experience their sexual preference as innate, nonvoluntary. What the women's liberation movement has created is a gay-liberation movement that politically challenges male supremacy in one of its most deeply institutionalized aspects—the tyranny of heterosexuality. The political power of lesbianism is a power that can be shared by all women who choose to recognize and use it: the power of an alternative, a possibility that makes male sexual tyranny escapable and rejectable.

These sexual changes brought about by feminism were based on changing economic relations. Industrialization, the weakening of the family and patriarchal power within it, the rise of a small-family norm, and the increase in women's employment—all these and many related changes were the sources of both feminism and greater sexual freedom and equality. The impact of these changes is complex and it is only on average that it shows a gain for women, for there have been setbacks. Furthermore, the tendency toward sexual freedom and equality is constantly being threatened with deflection, even reversal.

The relative weakness of this liberating and equalizing tendency is partly due to the mistakes of the feminist movement itself. For example, since the early twentieth century feminists often isolated their own particular needs from those of all women. They wandered into utopian experiments, trying to create living sexual situations of total equality and freedom by relying on individual wealth or status, or even by sheer will power, falling back into cynicism when these visions proved failures. Lesbian and straight feminists imagined they could create relationships entirely free of sex roles, just as free lovers believed women could cast off all their marks of subordination at once. The focus on sex is understandable because sex seems one of the few areas of human experience still in our own control in an era of totalitarian control over so much else, and because sex is one of the few sources of intense, natural pleasure remaining in an all-commoditized world. But the isolation of sexual-liberation struggles, though understandable, weakens these very struggles in the long run. Not only does it hold back the development of understanding of the social and economic influences on sexuality, but it fails to challenge the two largest forces that corrupt human sexual potential—class exploitation and male supremacy.

The isolated focus on sexual liberation has been seized and manipulated by capitalists in their ever-extending search for profits. In the twentieth century capitalism has transformed our whole society into a universal market. Little remains that is not bought and sold, and sexual pleasure itself, both that produced by individual human beauty and that from caresses, has become commoditized. Even those who would prefer to give and take freely have been affected by a consciousness of sexual exchange value. Furthermore the market produces its own, distorted, sexual needs through an advertising system that can virtually coerce large segments of targeted groups to buy, and then to need, new products and services. Part of this expansion of the market has been the manipulation of fears of sexual inadequacy and desire for sexual ecstasy—always made more powerful by the scarcity of other satisfactions—to sell products unrelated to sex, such as automobiles, kitchen appliances, prepared foods.

Thus the story of the breaking away from Victorian sexual repression over the last century has a double aspect: one of liberation and another of the reimposition of new forms of social control over the human capacity for free and inventive sexual expression. Those two aspects correspond, on the one hand, to the collective and individual rebellions of people, primarily women, against their masters, rebellions represented nowhere more forcefully than in the birth-control movement, and, on the other hand, to the economic and political needs of the capitalist system. That the former aspect may yet prove victorious is due in part to the fact that the capitalist economy has developed weakening contradictions within itself. The expansion of commoditization has brought many more women into the wage-labor force through the expansion of consumer-goods production and of clerical and service work, labor sectors filled primarily by women workers. The increase in women's employment has been quantitatively so great that it has produced a qualitative change: being permanent members of the labor force is now the norm for women. This change appears irreversible. It is not a response to a short-term labor-supply problem, as in wartime, but a result of two long-term economic tendencies: one, that workers are getting a smaller proportion of the value they produce than they did fifty years ago, so that it now requires two wages to maintain an average working-class family (or, to put it another way, the victories of the working class in winning a shorter working day are now being wiped out as the number of hours of labor *per family* is going up); two, the degradation of the quality of labor, so that the only expanding sectors of the labor force are those jobs with the lowest levels of skill, pay, and working conditions—jobs often earmarked for women.

We are just beginning to perceive the dimensions of the sexual changes produced by this basic restructuring of the labor force. As the norm that men alone support their families is altered, men will lose much of their social power in the family. Increased women's employment means that adult couples, though not necessarily parent-child ties, are losing their economic necessity and women are becoming more reluctant to accommodate themselves to male privileges. Women's growing consciousness of themselves as workers will strengthen their sense of equality with men of their own class and stimulate resistance to their continued sexual exploitation by men. As we saw before, no other variable seems to provide such a direct incentive to birth-control use, in all classes and ethnic groups, as women's employment. Birth-control use is more a measure of women's increased self-esteem and sense of opportunity than a cause of it.

The suffering in the process of this transformation has already been and will continue to be great. Liberating only in potential, the dissolving of family ties produces loneliness and despair, which in turn render people more susceptible to manipulation and self-destructive behavior. Sexual health, measured either physically or psychologically, is in some respects deteriorating, as evidenced in spreading venereal disease, rape, and sexual encounters stripped of obligations between people as subjects. In other areas the balance between helpful practicality about sex and its dehumanization is a delicate one. Frank discussion of sexual technique is vital, a needed extension of sex education, a continuation of the best traditions of feminism and sex radicalism. Yet the marketing of sex cookbooks for the "connoisseur" is moving, as commoditization always does, in an antihuman direction, that is, it is carving up the human experience so that sex becomes severed from economic, social, political, and emotional life. Prostitution is reaching out from its hard core to the provision of more ambiguous sexual services for cash, as in massage parlors and "modeling," or even not for cash but for forms of barter as in swinging and "personal" advertisements for companionship.

The problem with the commercialization of sexual pleasure is not merely that it fosters fragmented sexual experience. These new permissive standards and practices remain fundamentally deformed by male-supremacist practices and attitudes and a heightened instrumentalism, people using one another as mere tools for personal satisfaction. It could hardly have been otherwise with a commercially produced sexual "revolution." The rapid shifts in women's economic roles produced by capitalism did not immediately reduce the over-all male chauvinism in the society, but rather thrust women ill-prepared into a male world of work and play. Women's problems in the sexual encounters of the 1970s are not so different from those we described in the sexual revolution of the second decade of the century. Without equality women run great risks in "casual" affairs because of their economic needs for marriage and their equally sharp emotional needs for affirmation; nor do women usually get sexual satisfaction in forms of intercourse based only on the physiology and rhythm of the male orgasm. The pretense of equality in the face of basic inequality merely contributes to the inequality.

Male supremacy is now under attack, its traditional supports being eroded by capitalism itself, but its beneficiaries are defending it by modifying it to suit new economic conditions. As men once took advantage of the sexual double standard and the enforced chastity of their wives, now they often take advantage of the mythical single standard to belittle and pressure women who resist their sexual preferences. Thus the area of sexual relationships remains now, as it was in the nineteenth century, a major battlefield for feminists.

In this context birth-control struggles are but small skirmishes. Nevertheless if we insist that birth control does not mean population control or birth-rate reduction or planned families but reproductive freedom, then the issue looms larger. As it is but a piece of a larger social change, it can never be realized until that larger program is a reality. Every one of the conditions that would make reproductive freedom possible—the elimination of hereditary class and privilege, sexual equality, and sexual liberation—is a radical program in itself. From this it follows that reproductive freedom is most likely to be achieved as a rider, so to speak, on the coattails of broad social movements.

Ironic though it may appear, it would have been better for the cause had birth control never formed a separate movement. Its separation as an issue from the over-all problems of women and of the poor—worse, its separation from the victims of those problems—led to an increasingly narrow definition of its goals, settling eventually for technological reform within the status quo rather than freedom. The majority of those who lack reproductive freedom experience the problem as part of a system of social and economic problems, in which, most often, lack of birth control is not the major one. Thus the chances of winning long-term broad popular support for a single-issue birth-control campaign are not good and never were.

The high points of the birth-control struggle in the past came with its maximum integration into larger political movements—the exploding "woman movement" in the mid-nineteenth century and the Socialist party in the second decade of the twentieth. In the 1970s birth control emerged strong again as a leading demand of the women's liberation movement. Women's liberationists sought birth control that was usable by women for themselves because it went along with the rediscovery of women's humanity in the struggle for total equality. This revolt has been rather successful in its long-run strategic goal—encouraging women to resist their problems collectively and politically—but less successful in the short-term task of winning reforms. Very little has been gained in the field of birth control. No new male contraceptives have yet been developed; women have been encouraged to rely primarily on hormonal pills and intra-uterine devices, both dangerous. The main achievement has been the legalization of abortion, and this represents a significant victory. It has lowered the price of abortions sharply and made abortions available in the public clinics and hospitals that poor people must use. But it is a shaky victory and the backlash against abortion is growing. Worse, legal abortions are being forced on poor women, especially nonwhite women. Even the most libertarian reforms, such as legalized abortion, are but tools. Women can use them to build better lives, but those with power can also pick them up and attack women with them. This whole book has been, in a sense, a documented plea for the importance of a total program of female liberation, for a never-ending vigilance to view birth control and sexual activity in the context of the over-all power relations of the society, especially sex and class relations.

In the United States in the 1970s two alternative views of reproductive control have emerged to challenge the liberating emphasis of birth control. One is the opposition to abortion, the "right to life" movement. The attribution of human rights to the fetus is not a new idea but repeats nineteenth-century anti-birth-control views which, revealingly, fused abortion with contraception. Perhaps sperm and ova have rights too. This is not to deny the existence of real moral issues about life or to deny the reasonableness of a position that fetuses ought not to be destroyed. But right-to-life advocates do not usually fight for "life" in any systematic way. As a social force the movement represents not Catholics in general but the threatened Church hierarchy and its right-wing supporters. Right-to-life forces have generally opposed the kinds of social programs that would make abortion less frequent: child care, sex education, contraception, and so forth. Right-to-lifers are not usually pacifists, though pacifism is the only over-all philosophy that could make their position on abortion honorable and consistent. They oppose the specific forms of "killing" that amount to women's self-defense. They are reacting not merely to a "loosening of morals" but to the whole feminist struggle of the last century; they are fighting for male supremacy. Often they support it because it is the only system they know which can provide family and social stability, and many right-to-life supporters do not fully understand the implications of their views. Yet many do understand, too, and even among Catholics many women have rejected the right-to-life position. Opponents of abortion have been repeatedly defeated at the polls—in fact they have won no elections as of this writing. Catholic women preponderately support legalized abortion—that is, they support women's right to choose for themselves. The right-to-life movement is not a mass movement and it cannot mobilize women in large numbers, particularly not working-class women who need and practice abortion in higher proportion than other women. Although the antiabortion movement often appears strong in working-class neighborhoods, its leadership is always part of the top-down leadership structure administered through the Church and the political-party machines. Furthermore, right-to-life groups nearly always line up behind other right-wing causes: support for the Vietnam war, for racist anti-school busing protests, for example. The right to life is not the issue of abortion; the issue is women's rights.

A second form of opposition to reproductive self-determination is population control. The damage it has inflicted on the birth-control cause has been the greater because it has been confused with birth control, and because that confusion was based on some shared interests—better contraception, legalized contraception, and sterilization. But even these specific interests diverge as soon as one digs at all below the surface. Population controllers have encouraged the evaluation of contraceptives simply on the basis of their effectiveness in preventing conception, time after time winking at their health hazards. Thus, for example, the notorious testing of contraceptive pills with very high hormonal levels on Puerto Rican and other Third World women. A feminist birth-control approach must make the whole woman the subject of the reforms at all times: an effective contraceptive that is dangerous is of no use at all. Population controllers support the legalization of contraception and sterilization, but not necessarily of abortion or any forms of birth control that let women make their own choices exclusively. Population controllers have not fought for funds for sex education or general women's health programs. Birth-rate reduction always came first. The coincidence or antagonism of this goal to women's overall freedom was incidental, to be made use of or ignored as the case might be.

Historically all reproductive-control movements were responses to social unrest, challenging class inequality and sex inequality. But some in the movements sought to justify these inequalities, whereas others sought to end them. This is the fundamental difference, the difference obscured by the confusion between population control and birth control. It is not the population question itself that divides the two fundamentally opposed movements, and those committed to egalitarian solutions would do well to remain open-minded on the issue of population growth. Among those who have supported birth control in the struggle for equality there is an essential unity of interests between those who have fought primarily for women and those who have fought primarily for the working class. (And as we have seen there were some who fought for both.) Involuntary childbearing has burdened all women, but it has burdened poor women most, and the sexual inequality that resulted has helped perpetuate all other forms of inequality and weakened struggles against them. Reproductive self-determination is a basic condition for sexual equality and for women to assume full membership in all other human groups. Historically both feminist and working-class supporters of birth control have differed, too, from population controllers in seeing their struggle as two-sided. Tending to blame the victim, population controllers fused the object of their humanitarianism with the enemy. Birth controllers fought against a ruling class which, they understood, had imposed upon women a subordination to reproductive functions that was neither natural nor eternal.

Despite the apparent dominance of population-control–eugenics advocates for much of the last century, in fact that group has accomplished very little. The legalization of contraception and abortion in the United States was primarily the result of the feminist movement and has benefited all women greatly. Population control has achieved little on a global scale; although its coercive application has done violence to many thousands of women, the resistance to it has been victorious in most places. We must not make the mistake of assuming that all women who accept population control's proffered contraception, even sterilization, are its victims. To resist population control does not necessarily mean being forced into producing many children; a more practical form of resistance may occur when women use contraceptive knowledge to help make their own decisions about childbearing.

In all social movements every gain by the exploited has been manipulated, "coopted" by the rulers. Women fought for sexual freedom only to find themselves imprisoned in new forms of sexual exploitation; women fought for jobs only to find themselves exploited more intensely; women fought for education only to find it used to keep them in their subordinate places.

But these manipulations are not part of an unending chain. Their limits are set by the strength and intelligence of the political opposition to them. Indeed, the twists and turns of the rulers of women, attempting to adapt their supremacy to new situations, help to educate their subjects. The lesson to be learned is that reproductive freedom cannot be separated from the totality of women's freedom.

Reference Notes

Chapter 1. The Prohibition on Birth Control

1. Genesis, 38:7-10.
2. Norman Himes, *Medical History of Contraception* ([1936] New York: Gamut Press, 1963), pp. 71–73; David M. Feldman, *Birth Control in Jewish Law* (New York: New York University Press, 1968), Chapter 8.
3. Feldman, *Birth Control*, pp. 169–70. Recipe and indications for the Cup of Roots are given in the *Babylonian Talmud, Tractate Shabbath*, trans. I. Epstein (London: Soncino Press, 1938), 109b–111a, II, pp. 532–39.
4. Feldman, *Birth Control*, Chapter 3 passim, p. 53 particularly. This is discussed in the *Babylonian Talmud, Seder Nashim, Tractate Yebamoth*, trans. Israel W. Slotki (London: Soncino Press, 1936), 65b–66a, I, pp. 436–40.
5. Feldman, *Birth Control*, pp. 297–98 and passim.
6. Mary Daly, *The Church and the Second Sex* ([1968] New York: Harper Torchbooks, 1975), pp. 79–82.
7. Quoted in John J. Noonan, Jr., *Contraception: A History of Its Treatment by Catholic Theologians and Canonists* (Cambridge: Harvard University Press, 1965), p. 42.
8. Quoted in Demosthenes Savramis, *The Satanizing of Woman*, trans. Martin Ebon (Garden City, New York: Doubleday, 1974), p. 51.
9. Ibid., Chapter 7; Glanville Williams, *The Sanctity of Life and the Criminal Law* (New York: Knopf, 1957), pp. 51–57.
10. Savramis, *Satanizing of Woman*, Chapter 7; Williams, *Sanctity of Life*, p. 55; Noonan, *Contraception*, pp. 240 ff.

11. Noonan, *Contraception*, p. 426.

12. Chapman Cohen, *Woman and Christianity, the Subjection and Exploitation of a Sex* (London: Pioneer Press, 1919), p. 47.

13. Ibid., p. 47.

14. Ibid., p. 44; Daly, *Church and the Second Sex*, pp. 87–88.

15. Cohen, *Woman and Christianity*, p. 38.

16. See Eva Figes, *Patriarchal Attitudes* (New York: Fawcett, 1970), especially p. 42.

17. Quoted in Cohen, *Woman and Christianity*, p. 44.

18. For corroboration of this view, see Savramis, *Satanizing of Woman*, and Daly, *Church and the Second Sex*.

19. Daly, *Church and the Second Sex*, p. 85.

20. Ibid., p. 91.

21. Joseph Ambrose Banks, *Prosperity and Parenthood: A Study of Family Planning among the Victorian Middle Classes* (London: Routledge & Kegan Paul, 1954).

22. Alfred von Martin, *Sociology of the Renaissance*, trans. W. L. Luetkens ([London, 1944] New York: Harper Torchbooks, 1963), p. 73.

23. Pietro Bembo, paraphrased by Emily James Putnam, *The Lady* ([New York, 1910] Chicago: University of Chicago Press, 1969), p. 200.

24. Von Martin, *Sociology of Renaissance*, p. 72; Reimut Reiche, *Sexuality and Class Struggle* (New York: Praeger, 1971), pp. 40–41n.

25. Quoted in Himes, *Medical History of Contraception*, p. 190.

26. See R. H. Tawney, *Religion and the Rise of Capitalism* (New York: Harcourt, Brace & World, 1926); Christopher Hill, "Protestantism and the Rise of Capitalism," in F. J. Fisher, ed., *Essays in the Economic and Social History of Tudor and Stuart England in Honour of R. H. Tawney* (Cambridge: Cambridge University Press, 1961); Hill, *Society and Puritanism in Pre-Revolutionary England* (New York: Schocken, 1964), for examples of this interpretation.

27. Savramis, *Satanizing of Woman*, pp. 78–79.

28. Noonan, *Contraception*, p. 353.

29. Vern Bullough, *The Subordinate Sex* (Urbana: University of Illinois Press, 1973), p. 199.

30. For examples, see E. P. Thompson, *The Making of the English Working Class* (London: Victor Gollancz, 1965); Paul Faler, "Cultural Aspects of the Industrial Revolution: Lynn, Massachusetts, Shoemakers and Industrial Morality, 1826–1860," *Labor History* 15, no. 3 (Summer 1974), 367–94.

31. There have been no over-all studies of the rise of industrial capitalism from the perspective of women, but my interpretation has been influenced by Alice Clark, *The Working Life of Women in the 17th Century* (London: Routledge, 1919).

32. For the findings of the survey and on the medical opposition to Victorian prudish extremism, see Carl N. Degler, "What Ought to Be and What Was: Women's Sexuality in the Nineteenth Century," *American Historical Review*, Winter 1974, pp. 1467–90. For other evidence of women's resistance to prudery, see Chapter 5.

Chapter 2. The Folklore of Birth Control

---

1. This greater power was often found in matrilineal societies—where descent is figured through the mother—and in matrilocal societies—where a married couple goes to live in the wife's native place. Both matrilineality and matrilocality tend to divide the loyalties, obligations, and power of men between their family of marriage and their family of birth, divisions that frequently result in men's periodic absences and greater autonomy for the women. It is not that patrilineal and patrilocal societies do not practice birth control—they

do. But men's concern is more often with over-all population problems, whereas women tend also to worry about their own need for more space between births.

2. Norman E. Himes, *Medical History of Contraception* ([1936] New York: Gamut Press, 1963), pp. 175, 177.

3. Herbert Aptekar, *Anjea: Infanticide, Abortion, and Contraception in Savage Society* (New York: William Godwin, 1931), p. 119.

4. Himes, *Medical History of Contraception*, pp. 6, 9, 20, 174.

5. Ibid., p. 175.

6. Quoted in ibid., p. 95.

7. Ibid., p. 20.

8. Private letter to Himes, quoted in ibid., p. 52.

9. Aptekar, *Anjea*, pp. 159–60.

10. William Graham Sumner, *Folkways* ([1906] New York: New American Library, 1940), p. 271.

11. Edward Westermarck, *The Origin and Development of the Moral Ideas* (London: Macmillan and Co., 1906), 2:401; Raymond Firth, *We, the Tikopia: A Sociological Study of Kinship in Primitive Polynesia* (London: Allen & Unwin, 1936), pp. 527–30, Chapter 12; Burton Benedict, "Population Regulation in Primitive Societies," in *Population Control*, ed. Anthony Allison (London: Penguin, 1970), pp. 173–75.

12. Sumner, *Folkways*, p. 269.

13. Ibid., p. 272.

14. Westermarck, *Moral Ideas*, 1:399.

15. Sumner, *Folkways*, pp. 273–74.

16. Quoted in Glanville Williams, *The Sanctity of Life and the Criminal Law* (New York: Knopf, 1957), p. 18.

17. Thomas R. Malthus, *An Essay on Population* (London: J. M. Dent, 1960–61), 1:141–42; Sumner, *Folkways*, p. 272; Himes, *Medical History of Contraception*, p. 79.

18. W. E. H. Lecky, *A History of European Morals from Augustus to Charlemagne* ([London, 1869] New York: Appleton, 1877), 2:27.

19. Malthus, *Essay on Population*, 1, Chapters 13 and 14; John J. Noonan, Jr., *Contraception: A History of Its Treatment by Catholic Theologians and Canonists* (Cambridge: Harvard University Press, 1965), pp. 85–86.

20. Lecky, *European Morals*, 2:23; Williams, *Sanctity of Life*, p. 16.

21. David Bakan, *The Slaughter of the Innocents* (Boston: Beacon, 1972), pp. 35–36; Westermarck, *Moral Ideas*, 1:411–13.

22. Westermarck, *Moral Ideas*, 1:415.

23. Paul H. Gebhard, Wardell B. Pomeroy, Clyde E. Martin, and Cornelia V. Christenson, *Pregnancy, Birth and Abortion* (New York: Harper Brothers, 1958), pp. 193–96.

24. Himes, *Medical History of Contraception*, pp. 170–71.

25. George Devereux, "A Typological Study of Abortion in 350 Primitive, Ancient, and Pre-Industrial Societies," in Harold Rosen, ed., *Abortion in America* (Boston: Beacon, 1967), p. 129.

26. Aptekar, *Anjea*, p. 140.

27. This particular recipe has one of the oldest histories of any piece of birth-control lore. In the second century A.D. the Greek gynecologist Soranus prescribed drinking the water from the fire bucket of the smith after every menstrual period to cause sterility. In medieval Europe the prescription appeared in the writings of Arnold of Villanova in the late thirteenth century. The active ingredient of such a solution would presumably be iron sulphate; there is no reason to believe that it would have either contraceptive, sterilizing, or abortifacient effect. It is, however, an emmenagogue—a substance tending to stimulate the onset of menstruation. It should be obvious why this faculty might make women attribute abortifa-

cient qualities to it. See Himes, *Medical History of Contraception*, pp. 92, 162; and Aptekar, *Anjea*, p. 120.

28. Gebhard et al., *Pregnancy, Birth and Abortion*, p. 195.
29. Aptekar, *Anjea*, p. 145.
30. Himes, *Medical History of Contraception*, p. 138.
31. Aptekar, *Anjea*, pp. 142–43; also described by Devereux, "Typological Study of Abortion," p. 128.
32. Himes, *Medical History of Contraception*, p. 179; George Devereux, *A Study of Abortion in Primitive Societies* (New York: Julian Press, 1955), p. 129.
33. Devereux, *Study of Abortion*, pp. 123–24.
34. Himes, *Medical History of Contraception*, p. 138.
35. Devereux, *Study of Abortion*, pp. 123–33.
36. Aptekar, *Anjea*, p. 141.
37. Alex Hrdlicka, *Physiological and Medical Observations* (Washington, D.C.: Bureau of American Ethnology, Bulletin No. 34), p. 166.
38. Devereux, *Study of Abortion*, pp. 136–37.
39. Harry L. Shapiro, "An Anthropologist's View," in *Abortion in a Changing World*, ed. Robert E. Hall (New York: Columbia University Press, 1970), 1:183; Benedict, "Population Regulation," pp. 173, 184.
40. Marie E. Kopp, *Birth Control in Practice: Analysis of Ten Thousand Case Histories of the Birth Control Clinical Research Bureau* (New York: McBride, 1934), p. 133; Lella Secor Florence, *Birth Control on Trial* (London: Allen & Unwin, 1930), p. 91; Raymond Pearl, "Contraception and Fertility in 4945 Married Women: A Second Report on a Study in Family Limitation," *Human Biology* 6 (1934): 355–401, for examples.
41. Nicholas Culpeper, *Complete Herbal* (London, n.d., reprinted London: W. Foulsham, n.d.), pp. 39–41.
42. Himes, *Medical History of Contraception*, pp. 109–10, 116–17, 151. All the information on contraception that follows, unless otherwise indicated, is taken from Himes. His excellent index should help interested readers read more about any of the details mentioned here.
43. Quoted by Himes, *Medical History of Contraception*, p. 118.
44. *International Journal of Sexology* 6, no. 3, 187–88.
45. *The United States Practical Receipt Book: or, Complete Book of Reference* (Philadelphia: Lindsay & Blakiston, 1844), p. 29.
46. Ibid.
47. Marie C. Stopes, "Positive and Negative Control of Conception in Its Various Technical Aspects," *Journal of State Medicine* (London) 39 (1931): 354–60.
48. Kopp, *Birth Control in Practice*, p. 133.
49. *United States Practical Receipt Book*, p. 87.
50. Aptekar, *Anjea*, pp. 122–26.

Chapter 3. The Criminals

1. Ansley J. Coale and Melvin Zelnik, *New Estimates of Fertility and Population in the U.S.* (Princeton: Princeton University Press, 1963), Table 2, p. 36, quoted in Daniel Scott Smith, "Family Limitation, Sexual Control and Domestic Feminism in Victorian America," *Feminist Studies* 1, no. 3–4 (Winter–Spring 1973), 44.
2. Wilson H. Grabill, Clyde V. Kiser, and Pascal K. Whelpton, "Demographic Trends: Marriage, Birth and Death," in Michael Gordon, ed., *The American Family in Social-Historical Perspective* (New York: St. Martin's Press, 1973), pp. 390–91.

3. Smith, "Family Limitation," pp. 5–6; Smith, "The Demographic History of Colonial New England," in Gordon, *American Family*.

4. Grabill et al., "Demographic Trends," p. 375.

5. Ibid., p. 379.

6. Smith, "Family Limitation," p. 2.

7. Wilson H. Grabill, Clyde V. Kiser, and Pascal K. Whelpton, *The Fertility of American Women* (New York: John Wiley, 1958), p. 46.

8. John Demos, *A Little Commonwealth: Family Life in Plymouth Colony* (New York: Oxford University Press, 1970), p. 68.

9. Julia Spruill, *Women's Life and Work in the Southern Colonies* (Chapel Hill: University of North Carolina Press, 1938), pp. 323–25.

10. *A Sketch of the Proceedings and Trial of William Hardy, on an Indictment for the Murder of an Infant, November 27, 1806, Mass. Supreme Judicial Court* (Boston: Oliver and Munroe, 1807). I am indebted to Nancy Cott for calling this transcript to my attention.

11. Horatio Robinson Storer, *Why Not? A Book for Every Woman* (Boston: Lee and Shepard, 1868), pp. 16, 34–35. Also see, for example, *The Police Gazette*, May 28, 1892, for a story typical of its sensationalist reporting: Mary Wertheimer is indicted, along with her two boyfriends, for the death of her three-month-old baby.

12. Thomas Low Nichols, *Human Physiology: The Basis of Sanitary and Social Science* (London: Trübner, 1872), pp. 21–27.

13. *New York Times*, September 4, 1871, p. 8.

14. I am indebted to Joanne Preston for showing me this letter from her family collection.

15. Martin Luther Holbrook, *Parturition Without Pain: A Code of Directions for Escaping from the Primal Curse* (New York: Wood and Holbrook, 1871), p. 16.

16. Quoted in Horatio Robinson Storer, *Criminal Abortion: Its Nature, Its Evidence and Its Law* (Boston: Little, Brown, 1868), pp. 57–58.

17. *New York Times*, August 23, 1871, p. 6.

18. Edwin M. Schur, *Crimes Without Victims; Deviant Behavior and Public Policy: Abortion, Homosexuality, Drug Addiction* (Englewood Cliffs, New Jersey: Prentice-Hall, 1965), pp. 28–29.

19. Glanville Williams, *The Sanctity of Life and the Criminal Law* (New York: Knopf, 1957), pp. 148–52.

20. *New York Times*, August 23, 1871, p. 6.

21. Benjamin Grant Jefferis and J. L. Nichols, *Light on Dark Corners: A Complete Sexual and Science Guide to Purity* (New York, 1894, reprinted 1919 as *Search Lights on Health*), p. 138.

22. Quoted in V. F. Calverton, *The Bankruptcy of Marriage* (New York: Macauley, 1928), p. 187.

23. Jefferis and Nichols, *Light on Dark Corners*, p. 138; A. Lapthorn Smith, "Higher Education of Women and Race Suicide," *Popular Science Monthly*, March 1905, p. 470.

24. Arthur William Meyers, "The Frequency and Cause of Abortion," *American Journal of Obstetrics and Gynecology* 2, no. 2 (August 1921).

25. Quoted in Meade Minnigerode, *The Fabulous Forties* (New York: Putnam, 1924), pp. 101–102.

26. *New York Times*, August 23, 1871, p. 6.

27. For example in Adelaide Hechtlinger, *The Great Patent Medicine Era* (New York: Grosset & Dunlap, 1970), pp. 76 and 188.

28. Quoted in Minnigerode, *Fabulous Forties*, pp. 103–104.

29. Quoted by Spruill, *Women's Life and Work*, pp. 325–26.

30. Dr. E. N. Pendleton, "On the Susceptibility of the Caucasian and African Races to the Different Classes of Disease," in *Southern Medical Reports* 1 (1849): 338.

31. Storer, *Why Not?*, pp. 67–68; Storer, *Criminal Abortion*, p. 58; H. S. Pomeroy, *The Ethics of Marriage* (New York: Funk & Wagnalls, 1888), p. 57.

32. Quoted in Ann Scott, *The Southern Lady: From Pedestal to Politics, 1830–1930* (Chicago: University of Chicago Press, 1970), p. 38.

33. *Examination of Dr. William Graves before the Lowell Police Court from September 25 to September 29, 1837, for the Murder of Mary Anne Wilson* . . . , n.d., n.p.

34. Williams, *Sanctity of Life*, pp. 148–52.

35. Storer, *Criminal Abortion*, pp. 54–55. See also remarks of N.Y. District Attorney at trial of Dr. Michael A. Wolff, January 25–27, 1871, in *New York Times,* January 26, 1871, p. 3.

36. Quoted in M. S. Iseman, *Race Suicide* (New York: Cosmopolitan Press, 1912), p. 137.

37. George J. Engelmann, "Education Not the Cause of Race Decline," *Popular Science Monthly* 63, no. 2 (June 1903).

38. Augustus St. Clair, "The Evil of the Age," *New York Times*, August 23, 1871, p. 6.

39. Ibid.

40. Ibid., February 27, 1872, p. 6.

41. Orson Squire Fowler, *Love and Parentage* . . . (New York: Fowler and Wells, 1844), p. 69.

42. *New York Times*, May 6, 1871, p. 8.

43. Ibid., November 30, 1892, p. 10.

44. Ibid., July 28, 1892, p. 2.

45. Pomeroy, *Ethics of Marriage*, pp. 84–85.

46. Emma Frances Angell Drake, *What a Young Wife Ought to Know* (Philadelphia: Vir Publishing Co., 1901), p. 130.

47. For example, Mrs. R. B. Gleason, *Talks to My Patients* (New York: Wood and Holbrook, 1870).

48. *Medico-Pharmaceutical Critic and Guide* 9, no. 2 (June 1907): 59–63.

49. Pomeroy, *Ethics of Marriage*, pp. 62–65.

50. William Alcott, *The Physiology of Marriage* (Boston, 1856), p. 180; Arthur W. Calhoun, *A Social History of the American Family from Colonial Times to the Present* (Cleveland: Arthur H. Clark, 1917–19), 2:157–59, 209–10 and 3:34–35, 238–45; Joseph J. Spengler, "Notes on Abortion, Birth Control, and Medical and Sociological Interpretations of the Decline of the Birth Rate in Nineteenth Century America," *Marriage Hygiene* (Bombay, India), November 1935, pp. 159–60; Richard Shryock, *Medicine in America, Historical Essays* (Baltimore: Johns Hopkins Press, 1966), p. 117n.

51. For example: H. B. McKelveen, "The Depopulation of Civilized Nations," American Medical Association, 46th Annual Meeting, May 7–10, 1895; Richard Shryock, "Sylvester Graham and the Popular Health Movement," in *Mississippi Valley Historical Review* 18, no. 2 (September 1931): 176n; George J. Engelmann, "The Increasing Sterility of American Women," *Journal of the AMA* 37 (1901): 890, 1532; for more references see Spengler, "Notes on Abortion," p. 166n.

52. Himes, *Medical History of Contraception*, pp. 336–37.

53. Marie E. Kopp, *Birth Control in Practice: Analysis of Ten Thousand Case Histories of the Birth Control Clinical Research Bureau* (New York: McBride, 1934), p. 133.

54. Himes, *Medical History of Contraception*, pp. 335 ff.; Kopp, *Birth Control in Practice*, p. 134.

55. Abbot Kinney, *The Conquest of Death* (New York, 1893), p. 99; Frederick Hollick, *The Marriage Guide, or Natural History of Generation: A Private Instructor for Married Persons and Those About to Marry Both Male and Female* (New York: C. W. Strong, 1860), p. 336; Augustus Gardner, in *The Knickerbocker* 55 (1860): 49; George H. Napheys, *The Physical Life of Woman: Advice to the Maiden, Wife and Mother*, 5th ed. (Philadelphia: George Maclean, 1870), pp. 97–98; Eliza Barton Lyman, *The Coming Woman: or, The Royal Road to Physical Perfection* (Lansing, Michigan: W. S. George, 1880), pp. 242–46.

56. Lyman, *The Coming Woman*, pp. 242–46.

57. For example: Alice Stockham, *Karezza: Ethics of Marriage* (Chicago: Stockham, 1898); John Humphrey Noyes, *Male Continence*, 2d ed. (Oneida, N.Y.: Office of the *American Socialist*, 1877), pamphlet.

58. Letter from Mrs. A. B. Saulsbury, Ridgely, Md., May 1917, to Margaret Sanger, in Sanger Papers, Library of Congress.

59. Napheys, *Physical Life of Woman*, pp. 96–97, for example, put ovulation just before menstruation; Mrs. P. B. Saur, *Maternity: A Book for Every Wife and Mother* (Chicago: L. P. Miller, 1891), p. 151, put it during menstruation.

60. Himes, *Medical History of Contraception*, pp. 335 ff.

61. Edith Houghton Hooker, "The Case Against Prophylaxis," *Journal of Social Hygiene* 5, no. 2 (April 1919): 178; John McPartland, *Sex in Our Changing World* (Garden City, N.Y.: Blue Ribbon Books, 1947), p. 108.

62. Oral histories done by Priscilla Long and Linda Gordon with older women of the Boston and Providence areas, at Schlesinger Library, Harvard University.

63. Himes, *Medical History of Contraception*, pp. 200–201.

64. David E. Matteson, in *Medical and Surgical Reporter* (Philadelphia) 59 (December 15, 1888): 759.

65. For example, advertisement from *How to Live and Breathe*, ed. Moses Brown, Boston, January 1860.

66. Advertisement from *The Laws of Health*, Wernersville, Pa., May 1878.

67. Quoted in Minnigerode, *Fabulous Forties*, pp. 103–104.

68. D. M. Bennett, *Anthony Comstock: His Career of Cruelty and Crime* (New York: author, 1878), p. 1080.

69. Ibid., pp. 1073–75.

70. Ezra Heywood, *Free Speech: Report of Ezra H. Heywood's Defense before the United States Court, in Boston, April 10, 11 and 12, 1883* (Princeton, Mass.: Co-operative Publishing Co., 1883), p. 17.

71. Ibid., pp. 3–6.

72. Ibid., p. 16.

73. Bennett, *Comstock*, p. 1067.

74. Hollick, *Marriage Guide*, pp. 337–39.

75. Helen and Robert Lynd, *Middletown* (New York: Harcourt, Brace, 1929), pp. 123–25.

76. Bennett, *Comstock*, p. 1032.

77. Extract from the address of Dr. W. D. Buck, Prest. [*sic*] of the New Hampshire State Medical Society for 1866, in "Varia" in *New York Medical Journal* 5 (1867): 464–65.

78. For example, *Omega*, August 1899.

79. Advertisement in Marie C. Fisher, *Ought Women to Be Punished for Having Too Many Children?* 2d ed. (London: R. Forder, 1890).

80. Notebooks of Josephine Herbst, Beinecke Library, Yale University. I am indebted to Elinor Langer for this reference.

81. Kopp, *Birth Control in Practice*, p. 133.

82. Ibid., p. 134, for example.

83. *Sexual Hygiene* (Chicago: Clinic Publications, 1902), pp. 186–90, quoted in James Reed, "Robert L. Dickinson and the Committee on Maternal Health," unpublished paper, Chapter 2, p. 43.

84. John Cowan, *The Science of a New Life* (New York: Cowan, 1874), Chapter 3.

85. Augustus Kinsley Gardner, *The Conjugal Relationships as Regards Personal Health and Hereditary Well-being, Practically Treated*, 9th ed. (London, 1923), pp. 100–101.

86. Quoted in D. M. Bennett, *An Open Letter to Samuel Colgate Touching the Conduct of Anthony Comstock and the New York Society for Suppression of Vice* (New York: D. M. Bennett, 1879), p. 9.

87. Ibid., p. 11.

88. Jonathan Mayo Crane, in *Lucifer*, no. 1088 (March 28, 1907).

Chapter 4. Prudent Sex: Neo-Malthusianism and Perfectionism

---

1. Eric Hobsbawm and George Rude, *Captain Swing* (New York: Pantheon, 1968), pp. 42–43.
2. Thomas Malthus, *An Essay on Population*, 1st ed. ([1798] London: Macmillan, 1926), p. 95.
3. Ibid., 2d ed. (1803), pp. 531–32.
4. Maurice Dobb, *Studies in the Development of Capitalism* (London: George Routledge & Sons, 1946), pp. 274–75; Kenneth Smith, *The Malthusian Controversy* (London: Routledge & Kegan Paul, 1951), p. 297. These comments should not be construed to mean that Malthus supported only "official" bourgeois economics. He also, for example, defended the unproductive consumption of the aristocracy.
5. J. R. Poynter, *Society and Pauperism* (London: Routledge & Kegan Paul, 1969), pp. 225–27, 324.
6. Ronald L. Meek, Foreword to *Marx and Engels on Malthus* (London: Lawrence & Wishart, 1953), passim.
7. Indeed, in a later edition of his *Essay*, Malthus was forced to acknowledge that deliberate reproductive restraint might be workable. See Gertrude Himmelfarb, "The Specter of Malthus," *Victorian Minds* (New York: Knopf, 1968), pp. 102–105.
8. Malthus, *Principles of Political Economy* (London, 1836), p. 254.
9. Karl Marx, *Capital* (New York: Modern Library, n.d.), 1:696*n*.
10. An intelligent popular summary of later British Neo-Malthusianism can be found in Peter Fryer, *The Birth Controllers* (London: Secker & Warburg, 1965).
11. Throughout this section my interpretation of Place and the radical Neo-Malthusians is primarily indebted to E. P. Thompson, *The Making of the English Working Class* (London: Victor Gollancz, 1965), esp. Chapter 16. See also Norman Himes, "Jeremy Bentham and the Genesis of English Neo-Malthusianism," *Economic Journal, Historical Supplement*, January 1936; Himes, "The Place of John Stuart Mill and Robert Owen in the History of English Neo-Malthusianism," *Quarterly Journal of Economics*, August 1928; Himes, Introduction to Francis Place, *Illustrations and Proofs of the Principle of Population* ([1822] London: Allen & Unwin, 1930). In considering why the Neo-Malthusian radicals rejected the prevalent sexual standards, we find a combination of two historical influences. John Stuart Mill, himself a second-generation radical and supporter of contraception, was critical of Victorian prudery from a principled and philosophical vantage point; a feminist, he understood the connections between sexual repression and the subordination of women. Francis Place, by contrast, a self-educated former artisan, had probably never been influenced as deeply by prudish sexual standards. Prudery was a bourgeois invention of the late eighteenth century and did not automatically, immediately, or universally convince the lower classes. European workers and peasants had strong autonomous cultural traditions that made them resistant to Victorian sexual ideology. Furthermore, prudery did not serve their needs so fully as those of the bourgeoisie. Men of the peasant and working classes did not face a rebellion among their women, for their women did not have the leisure, education, and resultant raised expectations that created frustration among bourgeois women; male peasants and workers did not have to use sexual ideology to control women who were already trapped by the material conditions of their lives. This is not to suggest that Francis Place, for example, was an advocate or practitioner of a hedonistic life. Sexual freedom was not his concern, and he believed in the importance of general sobriety. But he was no prude; he could easily call a thing, even a sexual thing, by its right name, and he did not share in the sensibility growing among the bourgeoisie at that time that sexual things were shameful. Thus when Neo-Malthusian theory came to his attention, Place wrote a leaflet with plain instructions for inserting a vaginal sponge. Jeremy Bentham, on the other hand, also suggesting a contraceptive sponge, disguised his recommendation so that only the already initiated could have guessed his meaning.
12. From Place mss., British Museum, quoted in W. E. S. Thomas, "Francis Place and Working Class History," *Historical Journal* 5, no. 1 (1962): 62.

13. Ibid., p. 65.

14. For evidence regarding Place's authorship, see Norman Himes, "The Birth Control Hand-bills of 1823," *Lancet*, August 6, 1927, pp. 313–23.

15. Ibid., p. 317.

16. Ibid., p. 316.

17. John Peel, "Birth Control and the British Working-Class Movement," *Bulletin*, Society for the Study of Labor History, no. 7 (1963), p. 16; Thompson, *English Working Class*, pp. 620–21, on Cobbett.

18. Quoted in Fryer, *Birth Controllers*, p. 79.

19. Norman Himes, "McCulloch's Relation to the Neo-Malthusian Propaganda of His Time: An Episode in the History of English Neo-Malthusianism," *Journal of Political Economy*, February 1929, pp. 77 and 75; see also Fryer, *Birth Controllers*, p. 82.

20. J. A. Banks, *Prosperity and Parenthood* (London: Routledge & Kegan Paul, 1954).

21. *The Free Enquirer*, October 16, 1830, and October 23, 1830, for example.

22. Ibid., July 22, 1829, and March 5, 1831; and William Randall Waterman, *Frances Wright*, Columbia University Studies in History, Economics and Public Law 115, no. 1 (1924): 158–59.

23. Robert Dale Owen, *Moral Physiology: or, A Brief and Plain Treatise on the Population Question* (New York: Wright & Owen, 1831); Charles Knowlton, *Fruits of Philosophy: or the Private Companion of Young Married People* (Boston: A. Kneeland, 1833); see also Richard William Leopold, *Robert Dale Owen: A Biography* (Cambridge: Harvard University Press, 1940).

24. John Humphrey Noyes, *Male Continence* (Oneida, New York: Office of the *American Socialist*, 1872); Raymond Muncy, *Sex and Marriage in Utopian Communities* (Bloomington: Indiana University Press, 1973), p. 168.

25. The physiological possibility of that practice has, incidentally, been confirmed by Kinsey in 1949. See Alfred C. Kinsey, Wardell Pomeroy, and Clyde Martin, *Sexual Behavior in the Human Male* (Philadelphia: W. B. Saunders, 1949), pp. 158–69.

26. For example, Alice Stockham, *Karezza: Ethics of Marriage* (Chicago: Stockham, 1898); R. D. Chapman, *Freelove a Law of Nature* (New York: author, 1881); Octavius Brooks Frothingham, *Elective Affinity* (New York: D. G. Francis, 1870). Most of this material is in ephemeral literature.

27. Lois Waisbrooker, *From Generation to Regeneration: or, The Plain Guide to Naturalism* (Los Angeles, 1879).

28. Quoted in Margaret Sanger, "Magnetation Method of Birth Control," unpublished paper in Sanger Papers, Library of Congress.

29. Owen, *Moral Physiology*, pp. 21–22.

30. Norman Himes, "Eugenic Thought in the American Birth Control Movement 100 Years Ago," *Eugenics* 2, no. 5 (May 1929): 3–8.

31. Henry J. Seymour, *The Oneida Community, A Dialogue* (Oneida, n.d.), pamphlet.

32. *The Free Enquirer*, December 18, 1830, p. 61.

Chapter 5. Voluntary Motherhood: The Beginnings of the Birth-Control Movement

---

1. The interested reader may refer to the following major works of the free-love cause: R. D. Chapman, *Freelove a Law of Nature* (New York: author, 1881); Tennessee Claflin, *The Ethics of Sexual Equality* (New York: Woodhull & Claflin, 1873), pamphlet; Claflin, *Virtue, What It Is and What It Isn't; Seduction, What It Is and What It Is Not* (New York: Woodhull & Claflin, 1872); Ezra Heywood, *Cupid's Yokes: or, The Binding Forces of Conjugal Life* (Princeton,

Mass.: Co-operative Publishing Co., 1876); Heywood, *Uncivil Liberty: An Essay to Show the Injustice and Impolicy of Ruling Woman Without Her Consent* (Princeton, Mass.: Co-operative Publishing Co., 1872); C. L. James, *The Future Relation of the Sexes* (St. Louis: author, 1872); Juliet Severance, *Marriage* (Chicago: M. Harman, 1901); Victoria Claflin Woodhull, *The Scare-Crows of Sexual Slavery* (New York: Woodhull & Claflin, 1874); Woodhull, *A Speech on the Principles of Social Freedom* (New York: Woodhull & Claflin, 1872); Woodhull, *Tried as by Fire: or, The True and the False Socially: An Oration* (New York: Woodhull & Claflin, 1874), pamphlet.

2. Heywood, *Cupid's Yokes*, p. 20.

3. Claflin, *Ethics of Sexual Equality*, pp. 9–10.

4. *Woodhull & Claflin's Weekly* 1, no. 6 (1870): 5.

5. Heywood, *Cupid's Yokes*, pp. 17–18.

6. Letter to her daughter Alice, 1874, in the Isabella Beecher Hooker Collection, Beecher Stowe mss. This reference was brought to my attention by Ellen Dubois of SUNY-Buffalo.

7. Alice Stockham, *Karezza: Ethics of Marriage* (Chicago: Stockham, 1898), pp. 84, 91–92.

8. Theodore Stanton and Harriot Stanton Blatch, eds., *Elizabeth Cady Stanton as Revealed in Her Letters, Diary and Reminiscences* (New York: Harper & Brothers, 1922), 2:210 (Diary, September 6, 1883).

9. For a good summary of the medical literature, see Carroll Smith-Rosenberg and Charles Rosenberg, "The Female Animal: Medical and Biological Views of Woman and Her Role in Nineteenth-Century America," *Journal of American History* 60, no. 2 (September 1973): 332–56.

10. J. J. Rousseau, *Emile* (New York: Columbia University Teachers College, 1967), p. 132. Rousseau was, after all, a chief author of the Victorian revision of the image of woman.

11. Dora Forster, *Sex Radicalism as Seen by an Emancipated Woman of the New Time* (Chicago: M. Harman, 1905), p. 40.

12. Heywood, *Cupid's Yokes*, pp. 19–20, 16.

13. Ibid., pp. 19–20; *Woodhull & Claflin's Weekly* 1, no. 18 (September 10, 1870): 5.

14. Heywood, *Cupid's Yokes*, pp. 14–15.

15. Stockham, *Karezza*, pp. 82–83, 53.

16. Ibid., p. 86.

17. Heywood, *Cupid's Yokes*, p. 19.

18. Charlotte Perkins Gilman, *Women and Economics* (New York: Harper Torchbooks, 1966), pp. 38–39, 42, 43–44, 47–48, 209.

19. In England, for example, it was not until 1891 that the courts first held against a man who forcibly kidnapped and imprisoned his wife when she left him.

20. Ezra Heywood, *Free Speech: Report of Ezra H. Heywood's Defense before the United States Court, in Boston, April 10, 11, and 12, 1883* (Princeton, Mass.: Co-operative Publishing Co., 1883), p. 16.

21. Quoted in Nelson Manfred Blake, *The Road to Reno: A History of Divorce in the United States* (New York: Macmillan, 1962), p. 108, from the *New York Tribune*, May 12, 1871 and July 20, 1871.

22. Letter of August 29, 1869, in Hooker Collection, Beecher-Stowe mss. This reference was brought to my attention by Ellen Dubois.

23. Elizabeth Cady Stanton mss. no. 11, Library of Congress, undated. This reference was brought to my attention by Ellen Dubois.

24. See for example, *Lucifer, The Light-Bearer*, ed. Moses Harman (Valley Falls, Kansas: 1894–1907) 18, no. 6 (October 1889): 3.

25. Victoria Woodhull, *The Scare-Crows*, p. 21. Her mention of the YMCA is a reference to the fact that Anthony Comstock, author and chief enforcer for the U.S. Post Office of the antiobscenity laws, had begun his career in the YMCA.

26. *The Word* (Princeton, Mass.) 20, no. 9 (March 1893): 2–3. Emphasis in original.

27. See for example, the National Purity Congress of 1895, sponsored by the American Purity Alliance.

28. *Lucifer*, April 26, 1890, pp. 1–2.

29. *The Next Revolution: or, Woman's Emancipation from Sex Slavery* (Valley Falls, Kansas: Lucifer Publishing Co., [1890]), p. 49, pamphlet, unsigned but probably by Moses Harman.

30. Ibid., pp. 8–9.

31. Linda Gordon et al., "Sexism in American Historical Writing," *Women's Studies* 1, no. 1 (Fall 1972).

32. *Lucifer* 15, no. 2 (September 1886): 3.

33. Alice Stockham, *Tokology: A Book for Every Woman* ([1883] New York: R. F. Fenno, 1911), pp. 152–53.

34. *The Word* 20 (1892–93), passim, for example.

35. For example, *Lucifer* 18, no. 8 (December 1889): 3; 18, no. 6 (October 1889): 3.

36. Ibid. 18, no. 8 (December 1889): 3.

37. Heywood, *Free Speech*, p. 17.

38. Ibid., p. 16.

39. Ibid., pp. 3–6. "Comstockism" is again a reference to Anthony Comstock. Noting the irony that the syringe was called by Comstock's name, Heywood wrote: "To name a really good thing 'Comstock' has a sly, sinister, wily look, indicating vicious purpose; in deference to its N.Y. venders, who gave it that name, the Publishers of *The Word* inserted an advertisement . . . which will hereafter appear as 'The Vaginal Syringe'; for its intelligent, humane and worthy mission should no longer be libelled by forced association with the pious scamp who thinks Congress gives him legal right of way to and control over every American Woman's Womb." At this trial, Heywood's second, he was acquitted. At his first trial, in 1877, he had been convicted, sentenced to two years, and served six months; at his third, in 1890, he was sentenced to and served two years at hard labor, an ordeal that probably caused his death a year later.

40. *The Word* 22, no. 9 (March 1893): 2–3.

41. Ibid.

42. For example, Horatio Robinson Storer, M.D., *Why Not? A Book for Every Woman* (Boston: Lee and Shepard, 1868). Note that this was the prize essay in a contest run by the AMA in 1865 for the best antiabortion tract.

43. Claflin, *Ethics of Sexual Equality*; Emanie Sachs, *The Terrible Siren, Victoria Woodhull, 1838–1927* (New York: Harper & Brothers, 1928), p. 139.

44. Elizabeth Cady Stanton, Susan Anthony, Matilda Gage, eds., *History of Woman Suffrage*, 1:597–98.

45. Heywood, *Cupid's Yokes*, p. 20; see also *American Journal of Eugenics*, ed. M. Harman, 1, no. 2 (September 1907); *Lucifer*, February 15, 1906; June 7, 1906; March 28, 1907; and May 11, 1905.

46. Elizabeth Cady Stanton to Martha Wright, June 19, 1871, Stanton mss. This reference was brought to my attention by Ellen Dubois of SUNY-Buffalo; see also Stanton, *Eight Years After, Reminiscences 1815–1897* (New York: Schocken, 1971), pp. 262, 297.

47. Stanton and Blatch, *Stanton as Revealed in Her Letters*, pp. 132–33.

48. *Papers and Letters*, Association for the Advancement of Women, 1873. The AAW was a conservative group formed in opposition to the Stanton-Anthony tendency. Nevertheless Chandler, a frequent contributor to free-love journals, spoke here against undesired maternity and the identification of woman with her maternal function.

49. *Woodhull & Claflin's Weekly* 1, no. 20 (October 1, 1870): 10.

50. Woodhull, *Tried as by Fire*, p. 37; Lillian Harman, *The Regeneration of Society*. Speech before Manhattan Liberal Club, March 31, 1898 (Chicago: Light Bearer Library, 1900).

51. *Woodhull & Claflin's Weekly* 1, no. 20 (October 1, 1870): 10.

52. Ibid.

53. Harriot Stanton Blatch, "Voluntary Motherhood," *Transactions*, National Council of Women of 1891, ed. Rachel Foster Avery (Philadelphia: J. B. Lippincott, 1891), p. 280.

54. Rachel Campbell, *The Prodigal Daughter, or, the Price of Virtue* (Grass Valley, California, 1885), p. 3. An essay read to the New England Free Love League, 1881.

55. *Woodhull & Claflin's Weekly* 1, no. 14 (August 13, 1870): 4.

56. Dora Forster, *Sex Radicalism*, pp. 39–40.

57. From an advertisement for her novel, *Perfect Motherhood: or, Mabel Raymond's Resolve* (New York: Murray Hill, 1890), in *The Next Revolution.*

58. Helen Hamilton Gardener, *Pulpit, Pew and Cradle* (New York: Truth Seeker Library, 1891), p. 22.

59. Even the most outspoken of the free lovers had conventional, role-differentiated images of sexual relations. Here is Angela Heywood, for example: "Men must not emasculate themselves for the sake of 'virtue,' they must, they will, recognize manliness and the life element of manliness as the fountain source of good manners. Women and girls demand strong, well-bred generative, vitalizing sex ability. Potency, virility, is the grand basic principle of man, and it holds him clean, sweet and elegant, to the delicacy of his counterpart." From *The Word* 14, no. 2 (June 1885): 3.

60. Woodhull, *The Scare-Crows*; Charlotte Perkins Gilman, *Concerning Children* (Boston: Small, Maynard, 1900).

61. See for example Blatch, "Voluntary Motherhood," pp. 283–84.

62. *The Word* 20, no. 8 (February 1893): 3.

Chapter 6. Social Purity and Eugenics

1. The only general work on social purity is David Pivar's *Purity Crusade* (Westport, Conn.: Greenwood, 1973). I owe some of these general views to his work, but my over-all interpretation is based on a widespread reading of many books, articles, and ephemeral literature, the most important of which are in the footnotes that follow. For the earlier roots of women's social-purity organization, see Carroll Smith-Rosenberg, "Beauty, the Beast and the Militant Woman: A Case Study in Sex Roles and Social Stress in Jacksonian America," *American Quarterly* 23 (October 1971).

2. The three groups were, of course, not all equally influential. The NWCTU was enormous, perhaps the largest women's organization in U.S. history. Free lovers, on the other hand, were a few tiny groups.

3. Clara Cleghorne Hoffman, speech in *Report*, International Council of Women, assembled by the National Woman Suffrage Association (Washington, D.C.: NWSA, 1888), pp. 283–84.

4. Pivar, *Purity Crusade*, p. 173; and in Pivar's dissertation, "The New Abolitionism: The Quest for Social Purity," University of Pennsylvania, 1965, pp. 127–45.

5. Lady Henry Somerset, "The Unwelcome Child," in *Arena* 12, no. 1 (March 1895): 42–49.

6. Belle Mix, *Marital Purity*, pamphlet no. 2 of the National Purity Association, n.d., p. 3.

7. Elizabeth L. Saxon, in *Report*, International Council of Women, pp. 249–50.

8. Mix, *Marital Purity*, p. 4.

9. Norman Himes, "Eugenic Thought in the American Birth Control Movement 100 Years Ago," *Eugenics* 2, no. 5 (May 1929): 3–8.

10. Benjamin Flower, "Wellsprings of Immorality," *Arena* 11, no. 1 (December 1894): 58–59.

11. Moses Harman, *The Right to Be Born Well* (Chicago: M. Harman, 1905), pamphlet.

12. Margaret Deland, "The Change in the Feminine Ideal," in *Atlantic Monthly*, March 1910. For other reflections of this idea, see Alice Stockham, "Controlled Parenthood—The Child," in *Omega*, no. 7, new series (April 1899); Kate Austin in *Lucifer* 4, no. 23.

13. Lillian Harman, *Regeneration of Society*, a speech before the Manhattan Liberal Club, March 31, 1898 (Chicago: Light Bearer Library, 1900), pamphlet.

14. *Woodhull and Claflin's Weekly* 1, no. 20 (October 1, 1870): 10.

15. Tennessee Claflin, *The Ethics of Sexual Equality*, a lecture delivered at the Academy of Music, New York City, March 29, 1872 (New York: Woodhull & Claflin, 1873), pamphlet; Victoria Claflin Woodhull, *Tried as by Fire: or, The True and the False Socially: An Oration* (New York: Woodhull & Claflin, 1874), pamphlet; Moses Hull, *The General Judgment* (Boston: author, 1875), pp. 32–33; Lillian Harman, *Regeneration of Society*.

16. For example: Mrs. P. B. Saur, *Maternity: A Book for Every Wife and Mother* (Chicago: L. P. Miller, 1891), p. 164; Eliza Barton Lyman, *The Coming Woman: or, The Royal Road to Physical Perfection* (Lansing, Michigan: W. S. George, 1880), pp. 207–208.

17. For explicit statements of this belief, see Charlotte Perkins Gilman, *Concerning Children* (Boston: Small, Maynard, 1900), pp. 9–16; and Helen Hamilton Gardener, "The Moral Responsibility of Woman in Heredity," a speech to World Congress of Representative Women, Chicago, 1893, in *Facts and Fictions of Life* (Boston: Arena Publications, 1895), a whole essay dedicated to refuting Weissman's theory that acquired characteristics are not transmissible; and Gardener, speech at National Purity Congress, Baltimore, 1895, in *Papers, Addresses, Portraits*, ed. Aaron M. Powell (New York: American Purity Alliance, 1896), pp. 101–102.

18. George Napheys, *The Physical Life of Woman: Advice to the Maiden, Wife and Mother* (Philadelphia: George MacLean, 1870), pp. 75–77.

19. For example: Saur, *Maternity*, p. 164; Lyman, *The Coming Woman*, pp. 206–10; Georgiana B. Kirby, *Transmission: or, Variation of Character through the Mother*, rev. ed. (New York: Fowler & Wells, 1889), pp. 11 ff.; James C. Jackson, *How to Beget and Rear Beautiful Children* (Dansville, N.Y.: Sanatorium Publications, 1884), passim; Jas. S. Cooley, "Prevention Versus Cure," serialized in *Laws of Health* 1, no. 4 (August 1878), passim.

20. Lyman, *The Coming Woman*, pp. 209–10; Alice Stockham, *Tokology: A Book For Every Woman* (New York: Fenno, 1883), p. 162; John H. Dye, *Painless Childbirth: or, Healthy Mothers and Healthy Children* (Silver Creek, N.Y.: The Local Printing House, 1882), p. 72; Joseph H. Greer, *True Womanhood: or, Woman's Book of Knowledge* (Chicago: Columbia Publications, 1902), pp. 206–207; Somerset, "The Unwelcome Child"; Hoffman, speech in *Report*; Martin Luther Holbrook, *Stirpiculture: or, The Improvement of Offspring through Wiser Generation* (New York: author, 1897), Chapter 2; Holbrook, *Marriage and Parentage and the Sanitary and Physiological Laws for the Production of Children of Finer Health and Greater Ability* (New York: M. L. Holbrook, 1882), p. 153; Holbrook, *Physical, Intellectual, and Moral Advantages of Chastity* (New York and London, 1894), passim; John Harvey Kellogg, *Plain Facts About Sexual Life* (Battle Creek, Mich.: Office of the Health Reformer, 1877), pp. 64–69.

21. Mary Gove Nichols, *Lectures on Anatomy and Physiology* (Boston: Saxon and Pierce, 1844), Chapter 1; Nellie Smith, *The Three Gifts of Life: A Girl's Responsibility for Race Progress* (New York: Dodd, Mead, 1913), pp. 98 ff.; Benjamin Grant Jefferis and J. L. Nichols, *Light on Dark Corners: A Complete Sexual Science & Guide to Purity* . . . (New York, 1894, reprinted 1919 as *Search Lights on Health*), p. 118.

22. Jefferis and Nichols, *Light on Dark Corners*, p. 118.

23. Andrew Sinclair, *Prohibition: Era of Excess* (Boston: Little, Brown, 1962), pp. 47–49.

24. See, for example, Frances Willard, speech in *Report*, International Council of Women, p. 111.

25. For example, Horatio Storer, *Why Not? A Book for Every Woman* (Boston: Lee and Shepard, 1868).

26. For example, Augustus K. Gardner, *Conjugal Sins* (New York: J. S. Redfield, 1870).

27. Lois Waisbrooker, in *Lucifer*, March 27, 1890, letter to the editor.

28. Hoffman, speech in *Report*, pp. 283–84.

29. Waisbrooker, letter in *Lucifer*. Others who explained that sex during pregnancy would cause defective children include Lucinda Chandler, "Marriage Reform," also in *Report*, International Council of Women, pp. 284–85; Stockham, *Tokology*, p. 150; Dye, *Painless Childbirth*, p. 72; Greer, *True Womanhood*, pp. 206–207. Still others merely cautioned generally that sexual

excess at any time would lead to defective offspring, such as Holbrook, *Advantages of Chastity*; J. B. Caldwell (editor of *Christian Life*), in *Familyculture* 1, no. 7 (September 1896); Eliza Bisbee Duffey, *The Relations of the Sexes* (New York: Estill & Co., 1876), passim.

30. Greer, *True Womanhood*, pp. 182–83.

31. Duffey, *Relations of the Sexes*, pp. 214–15.

32. Elizabeth Blackwell, letter to the Brussels International Congress Against the State Regulation of Vice, probably 1888, in Blackwell mss., Schlesinger Library; see also Duffey, *Relations of the Sexes*, pp. 203–207.

33. For one example, Ezra Heywood, *Cupid's Yokes: or, The Binding Forces of Conjugal Life* (Princeton, Mass.: Co-operative Publishing Co., 1876).

34. Blackwell, letter.

35. Clifford H. Scott, "Naturalistic Rationale for Women's Reform: Lester Frank Ward on the Evolution of Sexual Relations," *The Historian*, November 1970; Charlotte Perkins Gilman, *The Man-Made World: or, Our Androcentric Culture* (New York: Charlton, 1911), for example.

36. Charlotte Perkins Gilman, "How to Make Better Men," ms., n.d., 1890s, in Gilman mss., Folder 179, Schlesinger Library, Harvard University; Gilman, *The Man-Made World*, pp. 29–31; Gilman, *His Religion and Hers* (New York: Century, 1923), pp. 88–91; Gilman, "Sex and Race Progress," in Calverton and Schmalhausen, *Sex in Civilization* (New York: Macaulay, 1929), p. 112; editorial in *The Humanitarian*, ed. Woodhull and Claflin, no. 6 (1892), p. 88; Helen Hamilton Gardener, Introduction to *A Thoughtless Yes*, 9th ed. (Boston: Arena Publications, 1890).

37. For example: Dr. Rosalie Slaughter Morton of the American Society for Sanitary and Moral Prophylaxis, in *History of Woman Suffrage*, 5:224–25; the Rev. Mary Traffern Whitney, speech at National Purity Congress, *Papers*, ed. Powell, p. 107; Stockham, *Tokology*, pp. 154–55; Rachel Campbell, *The Prodigal Daughter: or, The Price of Virtue*, an essay read to the New England Free Love League, 1881 (Grass Valley, California, 1885), pamphlet, p. 10.

38. Lester Frank Ward, *Dynamic Sociology* (New York: Appleton, 1883), 1:633.

39. Gardener, "Moral Responsibility of Woman in Heredity," p. 163.

40. Gardener, speech at National Purity Congress, p. 104.

41. Whitney, speech at National Purity Congress, p. 107.

42. Harriot Stanton Blatch, "Voluntary Motherhood," in *Transactions*, National Council of Women, 1891, ed. Rachel Foster Avery (Philadelphia: J. B. Lippincott, 1891), pp. 282–83. See also Susan Anthony, "Social Purity," a speech of 1875, in Ida Husted Harper, *Life and Work of Susan Anthony* (Indianapolis, 1898), 2:1004–12.

43. From *The Next Revolution: or, Woman's Emancipation from Sex Slavery* (Valley Falls, Kansas: Lucifer Publishing Co. [1890]), p. 24, pamphlet, unsigned but probably by Moses Harman.

44. Moses Harman, "Our Drift Towards Imperialism," *American Journal of Eugenics* 2 (Fall 1908): 8–9.

45. Lillian Harman, *Regeneration of Society*.

46. Blatch, "Voluntary Motherhood," pp. 282–83.

47. For one clear exposition of sentimental crypto-feminism, see Gail Parker's Introduction to *The Oven Birds* (New York: Doubleday Anchor, 1972).

48. The exceptional rejections of this view, such as free-lover Mary Florence Johnson's recommendations that men as well as women should work in day-care centers, in *Lucifer*, November 8, 1906, merely emphasize by their scarcity how universal the view was.

49. For example, Julia Ward Howe, speech to the Association for the Advancement of Women, in 1896, in Florence Ward Howe Hall, ed., *Julia Ward Howe and the Woman Suffrage Movement* (Boston: Dana Estes, 1913).

50. Gilman, *Concerning Children*, pp. 261–65.

51. Willard, speech in *Report*, pp. 47–48. See also Alice Stockham, *Karezza: Ethics of Marriage* (Chicago: Stockham, 1898), pp. 49 ff.; Julia Ward Howe, "The Future of American Women," n.d., speech in *Julia Ward Howe and the Woman Suffrage Movement*, pp. 185–86.

52. Gilman, "Sex and Race Progress," pp. 111–12; Gilman, "Prize Children," *The Forerunner* 2, no. 7 (July 1911). See also Helen Gardener, speech at National Purity Congress.

53. Helen Gardener, *Pulpit, Pew and Cradle* (New York: Truth Seeker Library, 1891), p. 2.

54. Frederick Hinckley, *The New Life, Supposed Thoughts of a Young Man*, pamphlet no. 3, n.d., but probably 1897, p. 8.

55. Gardener, Introduction to *A Thoughtless Yes*, pp. vii–viii. See also Gardener, "Moral Responsibility of Woman in Heredity," pp. 161–63.

56. Duffey, *Relations of the Sexes*, Chapter 5.

57. Eliza Bisbee Duffey, *What Women Should Know* . . . (Philadelphia, 1873), p. 317. See also similar ideas in Gardener, "Moral Responsibility of Woman in Heredity," p. 161.

58. Gardener, *Pulpit, Pew and Cradle*, pp. 2–21; Saxon, speech in *Report*, International Council of Women, pp. 249–50; Willard, speech in *Report*, pp. 47–48.

59. *A Message to Girls*, National Purity Association pamphlet no. 2, n.d.; Saxon and Chandler speeches in *Report*; Whitney, speech at National Purity Council; Frances Willard, in *Familyculture* 1 (June 1896): 4; Greer, *True Womanhood*, Chapter 1; Ellen Martin Henrotin, "Psychology of Prostitution," unpublished typescript, n.d., p. 8, Henrotin mss., Schlesinger Library.

60. Duffey, *What Women Should Know*, p. 316; Elizabeth Boynton Harbert, vice-president of NWSA for Illinois, speech in *Report*, International Council of Women, p. 247.

61. For example, Julia Ward Howe Scrapbook, 5:117, Howe mss., Schlesinger Library.

62. Reply to E. A. Ross, "Western Civilization and the Birth-rate," in *American Journal of Sociology* 12, no. 5 (March 1907): 622–23.

63. Elizabeth Blackwell, Introduction to pamphlet by Francis William Newman (London: Moral Reform Union, 1889), in Blackwell mss., Schlesinger Library.

64. Moses Harman, "The Woman Question, Number VI," by "Penelope," in *The Next Revolution*, pp. 29–30.

65. Moses Harman, in *Lucifer*, May 11, 1905.

66. See Chapter 7.

67. Pascal K. Whelpton, "Geographic and Economic Differentials in Fertility," in Dublin, ed., *The American People*, special issue of *Annals of the American Academy of Political and Social Science* 188 (November 1936): 50–51.

Chapter 7. Race Suicide

1. Theodore Roosevelt, *Presidential Addresses and State Papers* (New York: Review of Reviews, 1910), 3:282–91.

2. For a compendium of journalistic expressions of these fears, see Arthur W. Calhoun, *A Social History of the American Family from Colonial Times to the Present* 3 (Cleveland: Arthur H. Clark, 1919), Chapter 11.

3. Nathan Allen, "The New England Family," *The New Englander* 145 (March 1882): 147.

4. Abbot Kinney, *The Conquest of Death* (New York, 1893), p. v.

5. For example, James Foster Scott, *The Sexual Instinct: Its Use and Dangers as Affecting Heredity and Morals* (New York: E. B. Treat, 1899); Joseph Spengler, "Notes on Abortion, Birth Control, and Medical and Sociological Interpretations of the Decline of the Birth Rate in Nineteenth Century America," in *Marriage Hygiene* (Bombay, India), November 1935; William Goodell, "The Dangers and the Duty of the Hour," *Transactions of the Medical and Chirurgical Faculty of the State of Maryland*, 83rd Annual Session, April 1881, pp. 71–87; John P. Reynolds, "The Limiting of Child-bearing Among the Married," *Transactions of the American Gynecological Society*, September 1890.

6. Francis A. Walker, "Immigration and Degradation," *Forum* 11, no. 6 (August 1891): 634–44.

7. Robert Hunter, *Poverty* ([1904] New York: Harper Torchbooks, 1965), ed. Peter d'A. Jones, pp. 305, 310–11.

8. Edward A. Ross, "Western Civilization and the Birth-rate," *American Journal of Sociology* 12, no. 5 (March 1907): 616. For other references, see Calhoun, *Social History.*

9. Edward M. East, *Mankind at the Crossroads* ([1923] New York: Scribners, 1928), p. 297.

10. Mark Haller, *Eugenics: Hereditarian Attitudes in American Thought* (New Brunswick, N.J.: Rutgers University Press, 1963), p. 79.

11. Charles Franklin Emerick, "College Women and Race Suicide," *Political Science Quarterly*, June 1909, p. 270.

12. "An Alumna," "Alumna's Children," *Popular Science Monthly*, May 1904, pp. 45–46. The use of pseudonyms was frequent in this controversy and suggests how fearful women were about supporting "race suicide."

13. Quoted in David Kennedy, *Birth Control in America* (New Haven, Conn.: Yale University Press, 1970), p. 44.

14. U. G. Weatherly, "How Does the Access of Women to Industrial Occupations React on the Family?" *American Journal of Sociology* 14, no. 6 (May 1909): 740–52; George J. Engelmann, "Education Not the Cause of Race Decline [rather false ambition is]," *Popular Science Monthly*, June 1903; Frederick A. Bushee, "The Declining Birth Rate and its Cause [women's employment]," *Popular Science Monthly*, August 1903; Henry T. Finck, "Are Womanly Women Doomed?" *Independent*, January 31, 1901, pp. 267–71; and Finck, "The Evolution of Sex in Mind," *Independent*, December 26, 1901, pp. 3059–64.

15. Arthur Macdonald, "Susceptibility to Disease and Physical Development in College Women," *Philadelphia Medical Journal*, April 20, 1901, p. 4; A. Lapthorn Smith, "Higher Education of Women and Race Suicide," *Popular Science Monthly*, March 1905, pp. 466–73; Edward L. Thorndike, "The Decrease in the Size of American Families," *Popular Science Monthly*, May 1903, pp. 64–70.

16. Engelmann, "Education Not Cause of Race Decline."

17. Roosevelt, Introduction to Mrs. John Van Vorst and Marie Van Vorst, *The Woman Who Toils* (New York: Doubleday, Page, 1903), p. vii.

18. Kinney, *Conquest of Death*, p. 13.

19. I am indebted for this perception to a fascinating article about race suicide in Australia (for it was indeed an international controversy), "Octavius Beale and the Ideology of the Birth-Rate: The Royal Commissions of 1904 and 1905," by Rosemary Pringle, *Refractory Girl* (Sydney), Winter 1973, p. 24.

20. Roosevelt, "The Greatest American Problem," *The Delineator*, June 1907, pp. 966–67.

21. Roosevelt, "Race Decadence," *Outlook*, September 13, 1927, p. 111; and "Birth Reform, from the Positive Not the Negative Side," in *The Works of Theodore Roosevelt*, National Edition, 19:156, 158.

22. William S. Rossiter, "The Pressure of Population," *Atlantic*, December 1911, p. 840.

23. Henry F. Pringle, *Theodore Roosevelt* (New York: Harcourt, Brace, 1913), p. 470.

24. Ibid., pp. 470–71.

25. From a letter to Cecil Arthur Spring Rice, in *The Letters of Theodore Roosevelt*, ed. Elting Morison (Cambridge, Mass.: Harvard University Press, 1951–54), 13:620–21; and in Stephen Gwynn, ed., *The Letters and Friendships of Sir Cecil Spring Rice* (Boston: Houghton Mifflin, 1929), 1:293. I am indebted to Donald K. Pickens, *Eugenics and the Progressives* (Nashville, Tenn.: Vanderbilt University Press, 1968), p. 124, for this reference.

26. Quoted in Pringle, *Theodore Roosevelt*, p. 471.

27. *A Compilation of the Messages and Speeches of Theodore Roosevelt 1901–1905*, ed. Alfred Henry Lewis, *Supplement to Messages and Papers of the Presidents* (Washington, D.C.: Bureau of National Literature and Art, 1906), p. 548.

28. Roosevelt, "Race Decadence," pp. 764–67.

29. *Compilation of Messages and Speeches of Roosevelt*, pp. 548, 576–81.

30. Aileen Kraditor, *Ideas of the Woman Suffrage Movement* (New York: Columbia University Press, 1965), Chapter 3.

31. McCulloch papers, Dillon mss., Schlesinger Library.

32. For a good summary of birth rates and family sizes, see Wilson H. Grabill, Clyde V. Kiser, and Pascal K. Whelpton, "Demographic Trends: Marriages, Birth and Death," in Michael Gordon, ed., *The American Family in Social-Historical Perspective* (New York: St. Martin's Press, 1973).

33. Jula Ward Howe, "Does the Big Decrease in the Birth Rate of Mass. Mean Race Suicide?" *Boston American*, September 3, 1905, in Howe Scrapbook, 5:117, Howe mss., Schlesinger Library.

34. Howe Scrapbook, 4, Howe mss.

35. Ida Husted Harper, "Small vs. Large Families," *Independent*, December 26, 1901, pp. 3055–59.

36. Elsie Clews Parsons, "Penalizing Marriage and Children," *Independent*, January 18, 1906, pp. 146–47.

37. Parsons, *The Family* (New York: Putnam, 1906), p. 351; see also Lydia K. Commander, *The American Idea* (New York: A. S. Barnes, 1907); Commander, "Has the Small Family Become an American Ideal?" *Independent*, April 14, 1904, pp. 836–40; and "Why Do Americans Prefer Small Families?" *Independent*, October 13, 1904, pp. 847–50.

38. Harper, "Small vs. Large Families."

39. For example, Anna Howard Shaw, address to National Suffrage Convention, Portland, Oregon, June 29, 1905, in *Woman's Journal*, July 15 and 22, 1905; Lady Florence Dixie, *President Roosevelt's Gospel of Doom*, pamphlet, reprinted from *Weekly Times and Echo* (London), April 18, 1903.

40. Martha Bensley, "Are Large Families Useless?" *Harper's Weekly*, April 15, 1905, pp. 534–36.

41. "An Alumna," "Alumna's Children."

42. For example, Helen La Reine Baker, in *National Woman's Daily* (St. Louis), December 29, 1909; Helen Campbell, "Why Race Suicide with Advancing Civilization? A Symposium," *Arena* 41 (February 1909): 192–94.

43. Ida Husted Harper, quoted in Kraditor, *Ideas of Woman Suffrage Movement*, pp. 117–18, from the *New York Sun*, February 22, 1903.

44. Anna Howard Shaw, quoted in Kraditor, *Ideas of Woman Suffrage Movement*.

45. For example, Peter E. Burrowes, "Woman and Her Masters," in *The Comrade* 3, no. 8 (May 1904): 173; Jonathan Mayo Crane, in *Lucifer*, no. 8 (March 28, 1907).

46. Susan B. Anthony, "Reply to President Roosevelt's Race Suicide Theory," *Socialist Woman* 2, no. 16 (September 1908): 6.

47. Charlotte Perkins Gilman, "Men's Babies," Gilman mss., Schlesinger Library. The paper is undated but probably written somewhat later, in consciousness of the Great War.

48. McCulloch papers.

49. Ellen Key, "Motherliness," *Atlantic* 110 (October 1912): 562–70.

50. Moses Harman, *Love in Freedom* (Chicago: Light Bearer Library, 1900), p. 42.

51. George Noyes Miller, *The Strike of a Sex* (London: W. H. Reynolds, 1891), pp. 61–63.

52. Harper, "Small vs. Large Families."

53. "Why I Have No Family," by "A Childless Wife," *Independent*, March 23, 1905, pp. 654–59. Yet she still wrote anonymously; indeed, I have found no signed article that discussed the issue from a personal standpoint.

54. Miscellaneous letters to the *Independent* in response to "Why I Have No Family"; for example, in the issue of April 13, 1905.

55. Ida Husted Harper, "Women Ought to Work," *Independent*, May 16, 1901, pp. 1123–27.

56. Kate O'Hare, *The Sorrows of Cupid* (St. Louis, Missouri: National Rip-Saw Publications, 1912), Chapter 13.

57. This view is corroborated by Mari Jo Buhle in her dissertation, "Women in the Socialist Party," University of Wisconsin, 1974.

58. *Universal Suffrage: Female Suffrage* (Philadelphia: J. B. Lippincott, 1867), pp. 103–104. I am indebted to Ellen Dubois for calling this reference to my attention.

59. Catherine Beecher, *Woman Suffrage and Woman's Profession* (Boston, 1871), pp. 3–4.

60. Daniel Scott Smith, "Family Limitation, Sexual Control and Domestic Feminism in Victorian America," *Feminist Studies* 1, no. 3–4 (Winter–Spring 1973–1974).

61. Commander, "Why Do Americans Prefer Small Families?"; Harper, "Women Ought to Work"; Commander, *The American Idea*; "Paterfamilias," "Race Suicide and Common Sense," *North American Review* 176, no. 6 (June 1903): 892–900; "Why I Have No Family"; "One of Them," "A Woman's Reason," *Independent* 62, no. 3044 (April 4, 1907): 780–84; Howe, in *Boston American*; John S. Billings, "The Diminishing Birth-Rate in the United States," *Forum* 15, no. 6 (June 1893): 467–77; the Rev. John Holmes, "Why Race-Suicide with Advancing Civilization?" *Arena* 41, no. 230 (February 1909): 189–96; Ross, "Western Civilization and the Birth-rate"; I. M. Rubinow, reply to Ross, both in *American Journal of Sociology* 12, no. 5 (March 1907), p. 629.

62. Commander, "Why Do Americans Prefer Small Families?"

63. Ibid.; "A Woman's Reason."

64. Joseph Ambrose and Olive Banks, *Feminism and Family Planning in Victorian England* (Liverpool: Liverpool University Press, 1964); and Joseph Ambrose Banks, *Prosperity and Parenthood: A Study of Family Planning Among the Victorian Middle Classes* (London: Routledge & Kegan Paul, 1954).

65. Robert Wiebe, *The Search for Order, 1877–1920* (New York: Hill and Wang, 1967), Chapters 5 and 6.

66. Emerick, "College Women and Race Suicide," pp. 278–80.

67. Wiebe, *Search for Order*, Chapters 5 and 6.

68. Emerick, "College Women and Race Suicide," p. 281.

69. "Paterfamilias," "Race Suicide and Common Sense," pp. 897–99.

70. *World's Work*, September 1908, pp. 10639–40.

71. *Harper's Weekly*, February 28, 1903, p. 349.

72. Ibid., June 6, 1903, p. 952.

73. Smith, "Family Limitation."

74. Charles Franklin Emerick, "Is the Diminishing Birth Rate Volitional?" *Popular Science Monthly* 78, no. 1 (January 1911): 71–80; Commander, *The American Idea*, Chapter 4.

75. Rubinow, in *American Journal of Sociology*, p. 629, for example.

76. For example, Billings, "Diminishing Birth-Rate."

77. Otey M. Scruggs, "The Economic and Racial Components of Jim Crow," *Key Issues in the Afro-American Experience*, ed. Huggins et al. (New York, 1971), 2:80–81. (I am indebted to Judith Stein for this reference.) Billings, "Diminishing Birth-Rate."

78. Grabill, Kiser, and Whelpton, "Demographic Trends," p. 386; Billings, "Diminishing Birth-Rate."

79. Spengler, "Notes on Abortion."

80. Roland Pressat, *Population* (Baltimore, Maryland: Penguin, 1971), pp 73–74; Joseph Spengler, *The Fecundity of Native and Foreign-Born Women in New England* (Washington, D.C.: Brookings Institution Pamphlet Series 2, no. 1 [1930]).

81. Jan Myrdal, "The Reshaping of Chinese Society," in *Contemporary China*, ed. Ruth Adams (New York: Pantheon, 1966), pp. 65–91, has an excellent discussion of this process.

82. Scott Nearing, "Race Suicide vs. Overpopulation," *Popular Science Monthly* 78, no. 1 (January 1911): 81–83.

83. Joseph Lorren in "Why Race-Suicide with Advancing Civilization? A Symposium," *Arena* 41 (February 1909): 194–95. Joseph Lorren was probably a pseudonym for Louis Brandeis.

84. Pearce Kintzing, letter to *Philadelphia Medical Journal*, reprinted in *Current Literature* 35, no. 2 (August 1903): 219–20.

85. From the point of view of the history of class relations in the United States, the race-suicide controversy is an example of how women of the upper classes did not share the safe class status of their husbands, but could be politically separated from them and condemned.

86. William Goodell, "The Dangers and the Duty of the Hour."

87. *Medico-Pharmaceutical Critic & Guide* 9, no. 2 (June 1907): 71.

Chapter 8. Continence or Indulgence: The Doctors and the "Sexual Revolution"

1. G. L. Austin, *Perils of American Women: or, A Doctor's Talk with Maiden, Wife, and Mother* (Boston: Lee and Shepard, 1883); [David Goodman Croly?], *The Truth About Love* (New York: David Wesley, 1872); P. C. Dunne and A. F. Derbois, *The Young Married Lady's Private Medical Guide*, 4th ed. (Boston: F. H. Doane, 1854); O. E. Herrick, "Abortion and Its Lessons," *Michigan Medical News*, January 10, 1882.

2. Norman Himes, *Medical History of Contraception* ([1936] New York: Gamut Press, 1963), p. 282.

3. Carroll Smith-Rosenberg and Charles Rosenberg, "The Female Animal: Medical and Biological Views of Woman and Her Role in Nineteenth-Century America," *Journal of American History*, September 1973; Smith-Rosenberg, "The Hysterical Woman: Sex Roles and Role Conflict in 19th-Century America," *Social Research*, Winter 1972; Barbara Ehrenreich and Deirdre English, *Witches, Midwives and Nurses* (New York: Feminist Press, 1973); Ehrenreich and English, *Female Disorders: Sick and Sickening Women in the 19th Century* (New York: Feminist Press, 1973); Ann Douglas Wood, "The Fashionable Diseases: Women's Complaints and Their Treatment in Nineteenth-Century America," *Journal of Interdisciplinary History*, Summer 1973.

4. H. S. Pomeroy, *The Ethics of Marriage* (New York: Funk & Wagnalls, 1888), p. 62.

5. Edward J. Ill, "The Rights of the Unborn—the Prevention of Conception," in *American Journal of Obstetrics and Diseases of Women and Children*, 1899, pp. 577–84.

6. Eliza Barton Lyman, *The Coming Woman: or, The Royal Road to Physical Perfection* (Lansing, Michigan: W. S. George, 1880), pp. 242–46. Others who gave such warnings were Horatio Robinson Storer, *Criminal Abortion: Its Nature, Its Evidence and Its Law* (Boston: Little, Brown, 1868); Webb J. Kelly, "One of the Abuses of Carbolic Acid," *Columbus Medical Journal*, 1883, pp. 433–36; Augustus Kinsley Gardner, *The Conjugal Relationships as Regards Personal Health and Hereditary Well-Being, Practically Treated* (Glasgow: Thomas D. Morison, 1905), pp. 84–109 passim; Frederick J. McCann, "Birth Control (Contraception)," *The Medical Press*, 1926, p. 359; for the same pattern among European doctors, see Alex Comfort, *The Anxiety Makers* (London: Nelson, 1967).

7. For example: Abbot Kinney, *The Conquest of Death* (New York, 1893); Horatio Robinson Storer, *Is It I? A Book for Every Woman* (Boston: Lee and Shepard, 1867); John Todd, *Serpents in the Doves' Nest* (Boston: Lee and Shepard, 1867).

8. Kinney, *Conquest of Death*.

9. Ill, "Rights of the Unborn."

10. Thomas E. McArdle, "The Physical Evils Arising from the Prevention of Conception," *American Journal of Obstetrics and Diseases of Women and Children*, 1888, pp. 934–39.

11. Kinney, *Conquest of Death*, pp. 93–94.

12. Ibid., p. 22. See also Irenaeus P. Davis, *Hygiene for Girls* (New York, 1883).

13. Kinney, *Conquest of Death*, pp. 65 ff., for example.

14. Ibid., p. 27.

15. Joseph F. Kett, *The Formation of the American Medical Profession: The Role of Institutions, 1780–1860* (New Haven: Yale University Press, 1968); Richard Harrison Shryock, *Medicine and Society in America: 1660–1860* (New York: New York University Press, 1960), pp. 143–51.

16. Kett, *American Medical Profession*, p. 108.

17. Ehrenreich and English, *Witches*, p. 24; for further corroboration of this interpretation, see Richard Harrison Shryock, *Medicine in America: Historical Essays* (Baltimore: Johns Hopkins Press, 1966), Chapter 5.

18. Shryock, *Medicine in America*, p. 116; Kett, *American Medical Profession*, pp. 117 ff.

19. Quoted in Kett, *American Medical Profession*, p. 117.

20. Quoted in ibid., p. 121.

21. Ibid., p. 119.

22. A. M. Mauriceau, *The Married Woman's Private Medical Companion* (New York, 1847), p. iii.

23. *New York Times*, August 23, 1871, p. 6.

24. Himes, *Medical History of Contraception*, pp. 262–63.

25. Ibid., p. 263.

26. Frederick Hollick, *The Marriage Guide: or, Natural History of Generation: A Private Instructor for Married Persons and Those About to Marry Both Male and Female* (New York: C. W. Strong, 1860), p. 4.

27. Ibid., pp. 336–39.

28. Ibid., pp. 215–18.

29. Edward Bliss Foote, *Medical Common Sense* (Philadelphia: Duane, 1859).

30. Edward Bliss Foote, *A Step Backward* (New York: Murray Hill, 1875), p. 7.

31. Ibid., p. 5.

32. Quoted in Adelaide Hechtlinger, *The Great Patent Medicine Era: or, Without Benefit of Doctor* (New York: Grosset & Dunlap, 1970), p. 108.

33. Quoted in Hechtlinger, pp. 110–11.

34. D. R. M. Bennett, *Anthony Comstock: His Career of Cruelty and Crime* (New York: author, 1878), pp. 1036 ff.

35. Foote, *A Step Backward*, p. 13.

36. Edward Bond Foote, *The Radical Remedy in Social Science; or, Borning Better Babies through Regulating Reproduction by Controlling Conception* (New York: Murray Hill, 1886), pp. 59–60.

37. Himes, *Medical History of Contraception*, p. 279.

38. *Medico-Pharmaceutical Critic & Guide* [hereinafter *C and G*] 8, no. 5 (May 1906).

39. Ibid. 11, no. 10 (October 1908): 355–56.

40. *Long Island Medical Journal* 2 (1908): 1–5.

41. John Foster Scott, *The Sexual Instinct* (New York: E. B. Treat, 1899), p. 34; for this general interpretation see also Smith-Rosenberg and Rosenberg, "The Female Animal."

42. This phenomenon was noticed by Ian Watt in *The Rise of the Novel* and described by Nancy Cott in an unpublished paper.

43. Gardner, *Conjugal Relationships*, p. 107.

44. Comfort, *Anxiety Makers*, Chapter 5.

45. For example: Adelyne More, *Uncontrolled Breeding* (New York: Critic and Guide Co., 1917), pp. 87–88, 98; and Max Hodann, *History of Modern Morals*, trans. Stella Browne (London: William Heinemann, 1937), passim.

46. *Journal AMA* 58, no. 23 (June 8, 1942).

47. *C and G* 3, no. 6 (June 1904): 189.

48. Ibid. 5, no. 8 (August 1905); and 12, no. 1 (January 1909).

49. For example, in ibid. 15, no. 10 (October 1912): 364–65.

50. Ibid. 10, no. 6 (December 1907): 157.

51. William J. Robinson, *Dr. Robinson and Saint Peter* (New York: Eugenics Publications, 1931), pp. 24–25.

52. *C and G* 8, no. 1 (January 1907): 2.

53. Edward Bliss Foote, *Reply to the Alphites* (New York: Murray Hill, 1882), pp. 5, 15, 18–19.

54. *C and G* 7, no. 1 (January 1906): 7.

55. Ibid. 8, no. 1 (January 1907).

56. Ibid. 14, no. 2 (February 1911): 43–45; and 14, no. 8 (August 1911): 283–84.

57. Ibid.

58. Ibid. 14, no. 8 (August 1911): 304–307.

59. Ibid. 14, no. 6 (June 1911): 201.

60. Ibid. 14, no. 10 (October 1911): 376.

61. For example: *Firebrand* (Portland, Oregon, 1895–1897); *Soundview* (Olalla, Washington, 1902–1908); *Free Society* (San Francisco, 1897–?).

62. *C and G* 14, no. 11 (November 1911): 403.

63. Ibid. 14, no. 10 (October 1911): 367.

64. Winfield S. Hall, *Developing into Manhood* (New York: Association Press, 1912), is one good example.

65. Max Joseph Exner, *The Physician's Answer* (New York: Association Press, 1913), p. 14.

66. *C and G* 14, no. 6 (June 1911): 201–206.

67. Hannah M. Stone, "The Vaginal Occlusive Pessary," in *The Practice of Contraception*, ed. Margaret Sanger and Hannah M. Stone (Baltimore: Williams & Wilkins, 1931), p. 4; see also Himes, *Medical History of Contraception*, p. 391.

68. Peter Cominos, "Late-Victorian Sexual Respectability and the Social System," *International Review of Social History* 7, nos. 1 and 2 (1963): 18–48, 216–50; Steven Marcus, *The Other Victorians* (London: Weidenfeld and Nicolson, 1966); Ben Barker-Benfield, "The Spermatic Economy," *Feminist Studies* 1, no. 1 (Summer 1972).

69. Charlotte Perkins Gilman, "Sex and Race Progress," for example, in Calverton and Schmalhausen, *Sex in Civilization* (New York: Macauley, 1929), pp. 114–20.

70. A.E.K., *Firebrand*, April 25, 1897. See also, for example, Lucy Parsons, September 27, 1896, and Shay Mayflower, October 25, 1896, in ibid.

71. Mrs. S. H. Pile, in *C and G* 15, no. 1 (January 1912): 26–29.

Chapter 9. Birth Control and Social Revolution

1. For fuller discussion of the whole question of Freud's influence and misinterpretation, see Russell Jacoby, *Social Amnesia* (Boston: Beacon, 1975) and Nathan Hale, *Freud and the Americans* (New York: Oxford University Press, 1971).

2. For corroboration see, for example, Frederick Lewis Allen, *Only Yesterday: An Informal History of the Nineteen-Twenties* (New York: Blue Ribbon Books, 1932), p. 98.

3. Edward Carpenter, *Love's Coming-of-Age* (New York: Modern Library, 1911), p. 37.

4. Ibid., p. 60.

5. For example: Havelock Ellis, *The Task of Social Hygiene* (London: Constable, 1912), pp. 63–65; and Ellen Key, *Love and Marriage* (New York: Putnam, 1911), pp. 227–28.

6. Havelock Ellis, "Leaves from a Diary," *Morals, Manners and Men* (London: Watts, 1939), p. 124.

7. For example: Anita Block, editorial, *New York Call*, October 22, 1916; *Boston Evening Record*, October 18, 1916.

8. James McGovern, "The American Woman's Pre-World War I Freedom in Manners," *Journal of American History*, September 1968, pp. 315–38, for example.

9. Floyd Dell, *Love in Greenwich Village* (New York: George H. Doran, 1926), pp. 18–20.

10. Josephine Herbst, "A Year of Disgrace," Herbst Papers, Beinecke Library, Yale. I am indebted to Elinor Langer for this reference.

11. V. F. Calverton, *The Bankruptcy of Marriage* (New York: Macauley, 1928), p. 11.

12. Samuel Schmalhausen, "The Sexual Revolution," in *Sex in Civilization*, ed. Calverton and Schmalhausen (New York: Macauley, 1929), p. 380.

13. Ben Lindsey, *The Revolt of Modern Youth* (New York: Boni & Liveright, 1925); William Trufant Foster, *The Social Emergency* (Boston: Houghton Mifflin, 1914), pp. 5–19.

14. Lewis M. Terman, *Psychological Factors in Marital Happiness* (New York: McGraw-Hill, 1938), p. 323; Gilbert Van Tassel Hamilton and Kenneth MacGowan, *What Is Wrong with Marriage* (New York: A. & C. Boni, 1929), pp. 244–47.

15. Daniel Scott Smith and Michael S. Hindus, "Premarital Pregnancy in America, 1640–1966: An Overview and Interpretation," paper presented at American Historical Association, New York City, December 1971.

16. Gilbert Van Tassel Hamilton, *A Research in Marriage* (New York: A. & C. Boni, 1929).

17. Terman, *Psychological Factors*, p. 321.

18. Ira L. Reiss, "Standards of Sexual Behavior," in Albert Ellis and Albert Abarbanel, *Encyclopedia of Sexual Behavior* (New York, 1961), 2:999, calculated from unpublished data from Institute for Sex Research, quoted in Daniel Scott Smith, "The Dating of the American Sexual Revolution," in Michael Gordon, ed., *The American Family in Social-Historical Perspective* (New York: St. Martin's Press, 1973), p. 329.

19. Katherine Bement Davis, *Factors in the Sex Life of Twenty-Two Hundred Women* (New York: Harper & Brothers, 1929), Chapters 10 and 11.

20. For one study of these close female relations, see Carroll Smith-Rosenberg, "The Female World of Love and Ritual," *Signs* (University of Chicago Press) 1, no. 1 (September 1975).

21. Floyd Dell, *Homecoming* (New York: Farrar & Rinehart, 1933), p. 288.

22. Caroline Ware, *Greenwich Village 1920–1930* (Boston: Houghton Mifflin, 1935), p. 258.

23. Personal interview, March 17, 1974.

24. Schmalhausen, "Sexual Revolution," p. 397.

25. Hutchins Hapgood, *A Victorian in the Modern World* (New York: Harcourt, Brace, 1939), p. 408.

26. Ibid., p. 354; Dodge Luhan, *Movers and Shakers* (New York: Harcourt, Brace, 1936), Chapter 10.

27. Max Eastman, *Enjoyment of Living* (New York: Harper & Brothers, 1948).

28. Floyd Dell, quoted in Gilman H. Ostrander, *American Civilization in the First Machine Age, 1890–1940* (New York: Harper & Row, 1970), pp. 24–25. This view of the class basis of the bohemians is shared by Malcolm Cowley in *Exile's Return* (New York: Viking, 1951), p. 58.

29. Hutchins Hapgood, quoted in Ostrander, p. 177.

30. Frederick Engels wrote: "It is a curious fact that with every great revolutionary movement the question of 'free love' comes into the foreground." This curious fact is well illustrated by Sheila Rowbotham's excellent discussion of the French, Russian, Chinese, Cuban, and Algerian revolutions in her *Women, Resistance and Revolution* (New York: Pantheon, 1972). See also E. J. Hobsbawm, *Revolutionaries* (New York: Pantheon, 1973), Chapter 22, "Revolution and Sex," pp. 216–19.

31. Dell, *Homecoming*, p. 287.

32. Stuart Ewen, "Advertising as a Way of Life," *Liberation*, January 1975, pp. 16–34. This article is an excerpt from Ewen's *Captains of Consciousness: Advertising and the Social Roots of the Consumer Culture* (New York: McGraw-Hill, 1976). My interpretation of the economic developments is based on Paul Baran and Paul Sweezy, *Monopoly Capital* (New York: Monthly Review, 1966) and Douglas Dowd, *The Twisted Dream* (Cambridge, Mass.: Winthrop, 1974).

33. Hapgood, *Victorian in the Modern World*, p. 395. See also Cowley, *Exiles Return*, Part 2, Chapters 2 and 3.

34. Calverton, *Bankruptcy of Marriage*, pp. 18–20.

35. Dell, *Homecoming*, p. 324.

36. Robert S. and Helen M. Lynd, *Middletown* (New York: Harcourt, Brace, 1929), pp. 241, 258, 263–69.

37. Foster, *Social Emergency*, p. 19. See also "Sex O'Clock in America," *Current Opinion*, August 1913.

38. Lynd, *Middletown*, pp. 266, 242.

39. Alba M. Edwards, *Comparative Occupation Statistics for the U.S., 1870–1940* (Washington: U.S. Bureau of the Census, 1943), Table 21.

40. Esther Packard, *A Study of Living Conditions of Self-Supporting Women in New York City* (New York: YWCA, 1915).

41. Ware, *Greenwich Village*, pp. 256–57.

42. Margery Davies, "The Feminization of the Clerical Labor Force," *Radical America*, July–August 1974, Table 2.

43. Ware, *Greenwich Village*, pp. 256–57.

44. John C. Burnham, "The Progressive Era Revolution in American Attitudes toward Sex," *Journal of American History*, March 1973, pp. 890–91.

45. T. A. Storey, *The Work of the U.S. Interdepartmental Social Hygiene Board* (New York: USISHB, 1920), p. 6.

46. Andrew Smith in Foster, *Social Emergency*, p. 33.

47. John C. Burnham, "The Social Evil Ordinance—A Social Experiment in Nineteenth Century St. Louis," *Bulletin of the Missouri Historical Society*, April 1971, pp. 203–17.

48. For examples: Lavinia Dock, *Hygiene and Morality* (New York: Putnam, 1910); American Social Hygiene Association, *Keeping Fit to Fight* (New York, 1918), p. 15.

49. Walter Franklin Robie, *Rational Sex Ethics for Men in the Army and Navy* (Boston: R. G. Badger, 1918), pp. 20–25.

50. *Keeping Fit to Fight*, p. 15.

51. Edith Houghton Hooker, "The Case Against Prophylaxis," *Journal of Social Hygiene* 5, no. 2 (April 1919): 163–84.

52. Davis, *Factors in Sex Life*, pp. 19–20.

53. Calverton, *Bankruptcy of Marriage*, pp. 13, 141.

54. Edward O. Sisson, "An Educational Emergency," *Atlantic Monthly*, July 1910, pp. 54–63; and Foster, *Social Emergency*, for example.

55. David A. Shannon, *The Socialist Party of America* (New York: Macmillan, 1955), p. 76; James Weinstein, *The Decline of Socialism in America* (New York: Monthly Review, 1967), p. 27.

56. Even suffragists acknowledged this support from the Socialist party. See, for example, Ida Husted Harper in *History of Woman Suffrage*, ed. Stanton, Anthony, Gage (New York, 1881–1922), 5:362.

57. Weinstein, *Decline of Socialism*, pp. 58–59; Caroline Lowe [General Correspondent, Woman's National Committee, Socialist Party], "Socialist Women Did Much in 1911," *Chicago Evening World*, February 23, 1912, p. 4.

58. Mrs. S. I. Jenson in *Socialist Woman*, September 1913; and Helen Unterman, in ibid., October 1913.

59. For example, Caroline Nelson, "Neo-Malthusianism," *International Socialist Review* 14, no. 4 (October 1913): 228. Nelson wrote for *Socialist Woman* on other topics.

60. Virginia Butterfield, *Parental Rights and Economic Wrongs* (Chicago: Stockham, 1906), p. 87.

61. For example, Theresa Malkiel, "The Lowest Paid Workers," *Socialist Woman*, September 1908; "Woman's Work and Pay," editorial, *Chicago Evening World* [a socialist paper], June 11, 1912, p. 8.

62. For example, Jonathan Mayo Crane, in *Lucifer*, March 28, 1907; Charlotte Perkins Gilman, "Men's Babies," Gilman mss., Schlesinger Library, Folder 176, n.d. but probably after 1914; Sam Atkinson, *Science and a Priest* (Seattle: Libertarian Press, [1910]).

63. Crane, in *Lucifer*; Helen Keller, in *New York Call*, November 26, 1915; Margaret Sanger, "Comstockery in America," *International Socialist Review* 16, no. 1 (July 1915): 46; Peter E. Burrowes, "Woman and Her Masters," *The Comrade* 13, no. 8 (May 1904): 172–74; Nelson, "Neo-Malthusianism."

64. William J. Robinson, "The Prevention of Conception," *The New Review* 3, no. 4 (April 1915): 196–99.

65. Adelyne More, *Uncontrolled Breeding or Fecundity versus Civilization* (New York: Critic and Guide Co., 1917), Chapters 7 and 8; Max Hodann, *History of Modern Morals*, trans. Stella Browne (London: William Heinemann, 1937), passim; William J. Robinson, "The Birth Strike," *International Socialist Review* 14, no. 7 (January 1914): 404; William English Walling, in *The Masses*, October 1913, p. 20.

66. For example, Winfield Scott Hall, *The Biology, Physiology and Sociology of Reproduction* ([1906] Chicago: Wynnewood, 1913).

67. For example: Dr. Edith Belle Lowry, *Herself: Talks with Women Concerning Themselves* (Chicago: Forbes, 1911); Ida Craddock, *Advice to a Bridegroom* (Chicago, 1909); *Helps to Happy Wedlock* (Philadelphia, 1896); *Letter to a Prospective Bride* (Philadelphia, 1897); *Right Marital Living* (Chicago, 1899); and *The Wedding Night* (Denver, 1900).

68. Diane Feelley, "Antoinette Konikow, Marxist and Feminist," *International Socialist Review*, January 1972, pp. 42–46; Birth Control League of Massachusetts mss., Schlesinger Library, passim.

69. June 1, 1913, and August 16, 1914, for example.

70. Robinson in *New York Call*, for example, August 11, 1912, June 8, 1913, June 15, 1913; Konikow in ibid., August 16, 1914.

71. *Mother Earth* 6 (April 1911): 2; Richard Drinnon, *Rebel in Paradise* (Boston: Beacon, 1961), pp. 166–68.

72. Drinnon, *Rebel in Paradise*, pp. 67, 166.

73. Hapgood, *Victorian in the Modern World*, p. 170.

74. This episode is described in James Reed's dissertation, "Birth Control and the Americans 1830–1970," Harvard, 1974. I am grateful to him for allowing me to read it.

75. Margaret Sanger, *Autobiography* (New York: W. W. Norton, 1938), pp. 80–83; *New York Call*, February 18, 1912; Reed, "Birth Control," pp. 37–38.

76. For example: *New York Call*, November 5, 19, 26; December 3 and 10, 1911.

77. *New York Call*, November 7 and 27; December 1, 8, 15, 22, and 29, 1912; January 12, 19, and 26, 1913.

78. *New York Call*, February 8, 1913.

79. Peter Fryer, *The Birth Controllers* (London: Secker & Warburg, 1965), p. 202.

80. William Haywood, *Bill Haywood's Book, Autobiography* (New York: International Publishers, 1929), p. 268.

81. Sanger, *Autobiography*, pp. 103–104; Sanger, *My Fight for Birth Control* (New York: Farrar & Rinehart, 1913), pp. 68–69, 72–75.

82. For example, in *Medico-Pharmaceutical Critic and Guide* 4, no. 6 (December 1904): 163–64.

83. Sanger, *Autobiography*, pp. 89–92.

84. Ibid., pp. 93–94.

85. Ibid., p. 96.

86. Elizabeth Gurley Flynn, *The Rebel Girl* (New York: International Publishers, 1973), p. 166.

87. If we lean toward diminishing Sanger's role in this movement, it is only to correct a historical record that has exaggerated her role. At the height of the movement, between 1915 and 1918, many leading political activists worked on birth control. For example, in New York most of the socialist suffrage leaders and a few nonsocialist suffragists joined in: Jessie Ashley, wealthy lawyer, former treasurer of the National American Woman Suffrage Association (NAWSA) and Socialist-party member; Clara Gruening Stillman and Martha Gruening; Mary Ware Dennett, a right-wing socialist and former secretary of NAWSA; Martha

Bensley Bruere, active in the Socialist party and the Women's Trade Union League (WTUL); Rose Pastor Stokes, an immigrant Jewish cigar maker now active in the Socialist party and married to a socialist millionaire railroad and mining magnate; Ida Rauh Eastman and Crystal Eastman, sisters-in-law and both socialist feminists; Elsie Clews Parsons, Barnard professor; of course Dr. William J. Robinson, who brought many others from his profession into the movement; Floyd Dell and Max Eastman and other male pro-suffragists. In San Francisco, Los Angeles, and Portland, Oregon, many IWW and Socialist-party leaders organized birth-control groups. In Michigan there was Agnes Inglis, a wealthy reformer. In Cleveland Sanger found and recruited Frederick Blossom, a skilled socialist administrator and money-raiser. There were also full-time organizers, traveling, speaking, and often distributing illegal birth-control literature: Emma Goldman, Ben Reitman, Elizabeth Gurley Flynn, Ella Reeve Bloor.

88. Letter in Himes mss., Countway Library, Harvard University Medical School, February 13, 1937. I am indebted to James Reed for this reference. I have corrected spelling and punctuation.

89. For example: Sanger to T. J. Meade, September 11, 1929, in Sanger Papers, Library of Congress [hereinafter given as Sanger, LC]; Sanger, *Autobiography*, passim; and *My Fight for Birth Control*, passim.

90. Emma Goldman, "Marriage and Love," in *Red Emma Speaks*, ed. Shulman (New York: Vintage, 1972); Goldman, *Living My Life* (Garden City, N.Y.: Garden City Pub., [1931] 1934), p. 556.

91. Mary Ware Dennett, *Birth Control Laws* (New York: F. H. Hitchcock, 1926), Appendix 4.

92. Eastman, *Enjoyment of Living*, pp. 423–24.

93. Alice Groff, "The Marriage Bed," *The Woman Rebel*, no. 5 (July 1914). Groff was also a contributor to Robinson's *Critic and Guide*.

94. Ibid., no. 6 (August 1914). See also Lily Gair Wilkinson, "Sisterhood," in ibid.; and editorial in the first issue, March 1914.

95. "Watchful Waiting," ibid., no. 3 (May 1914). A similar combination of ultrarevolutionary rhetoric and feminism reappeared in the women's liberation movement at the end of the 1960s.

96. Herbert Thorpe, "A Defense of Assassination," ibid., no. 5 (July 1914). See news stories about the suppression in *New York American*, August 27, 1914, and *New York Evening Globe*, August 25, 1914, clippings in Sanger, LC. Sanger disingenuously implied that the censorship was strictly directed against the journal's advocacy of birth control: see her *Autobiography*, pp. 110–11, and *My Fight for Birth Control*, pp. 86–87.

97. Sanger to Upton Sinclair, September 23, 1914, in Sinclair, *My Lifetime in Letters* (New York: Columbia University Press, 1960), pp. 148–49; Harold Hersey, "Margaret Sanger: The Biography of the Birth Control Pioneers," ms. in New York Public Library, pp. 122 ff.

98. Sanger, *Autobiography*, pp. 108–17.

99. Sanger, *My Fight for Birth Control*, p. 87; Sanger Diary, 1914, in Sanger, LC.

100. *Family Limitation*, 1914, in Sanger, LC.

101. Sanger, *Autobiography*, pp. 119–22; and *My Fight for Birth Control*, pp. 91 ff.

102. Sanger, letter to "Friend," printed, September 1914, Sanger, LC.

103. Sanger, *My Fight for Birth Control*, pp. 102–103.

104. Ibid.: Sanger, *Autobiography*, pp. 128 ff.

105. Sanger, *Happiness in Marriage* (New York: Brentano's, 1926), pp. 142–43. For other characteristic expressions of these sexual views by Sanger, see: Sanger to Edward Carpenter, April 13, 1918, in Carpenter Collection, Sheffield Public Library, Great Britain (I am indebted to Sheila Rowbotham for this letter); Sanger, "English Methods of Birth Control," pamphlet in Sanger, LC.

106. Sanger, *Woman and the New Race* (New York: Brentano's, 1920), pp. 239–40.

107. For example, Charles Schultz, Secretary, Oakland IWW, November 17, 1915; B. Greenberg, Devil's Lake, N.D., February 10, 1916; unsigned from Washington, D.C.,

August 23, 1915; and many other letters to Sanger; miscellaneous clippings; all in Sanger, LC.

108. Caroline Nelson, June 12, 1915, and Georgia Kotsch, January 18, 1916, to Sanger, in Sanger, LC.

109. For example, Alvin Heckethorn, Portland, Ore., September 9, 1914, Emma Goldman, December 16, 1915, and Caroline Nelson, June 12, 1915, to Sanger; all in Sanger, LC.

110. Elizabeth Gurley Flynn to Sanger, August 1915, in Sanger, LC.

111. Eugene Debs to Sanger, November 8, 1914 and December 16, 1914, in Sanger, LC.

112. Goldman to Sanger, from Columbus, Ohio, December 8, 1915, in Sanger, LC.

113. Various letters to Sanger, 1915, in Sanger, LC.

114. For example, March 16, 1915; April 17, 1915; December 11, 1915.

115. *New York Tribune*, May 21, 1915, p. 7, clipping in Sanger, LC. Speakers included Dr. Rosalie Slaughter Morton, professor at New York University; Dr. Emily Dunning Barringer, surgeon; Lavinia Dock, suffragist and secretary, International Council of Nurses; Dr. Lydia Allen DeVilbiss, formerly of the State Board of Health; Dr. Abraham Jacobi, president of the AMA; Dr. Ira Wile, member of the Board of Education.

116. The original call of formation of the NBCL listed Jessie Ashley, Otto Bobsien, Mary Ware Dennett, Martha Gruening, Bolton Hall, Charles Hallinan, Paul Kennaday, Helen Marot, James F. Morton, Lucy Sprague Mitchell, Lincoln Steffens, and Clara Gruening Stillman. This was published in *Survey*, April 1915, p. 5. The presence of socialist names on this list, such as Ashley and Morton, suggests that a few liberals led the organizational move—probably Dennett among them—and got the support of others who did not share equally in defining the policies of the new organization.

117. James Waldo Fawcett, ed., *Jailed for Birth Control: The Trial of William Sanger, September 10, 1915, Birth Control Review* Pamphlet (New York, 1917); Sanger, *My Fight for Birth Control*, pp. 119–21, and *Autobiography*, pp. 177–78.

118. Sanger, LC.

119. William to Margaret Sanger, September 1915, Sanger, LC. In response to the trial, many suffragists previously silent on birth control now spoke out in Sanger's defense, such as Carrie Chapman Catt, Bela Neuman Zilberman, Mrs. Norman De R. Whitehouse, and Catherine Waugh McCulloch, quoted in miscellaneous clippings from New York City newspapers, Sanger, Scrapbook no. 1, Sanger, LC.

120. James F. Morton, September 24, 1914; Bolton Hall, December 13, 1915; Max Eastman, January 11, 1916; and James Warbasse, December 7, 1915, all to Sanger, Sanger, LC.

121. Goldman, December 8, 1915 and December 16, 1915, and Alexander Berkman, December 18, 1915, to Sanger, Sanger, LC.

122. Warbasse to Sanger, December 7, 1915, Sanger, LC. See also Goldman's fury at Warbasse for his sexism, Goldman to Sanger, December 16, 1915, Sanger, LC.

123. Sanger, *My Fight for Birth Control*, pp. 132–34; clippings about the dinner in Sanger, LC.

124. *New York Times*, February 19, 1916.

125. Sanger, *My Fight for Birth Control*, pp. 144–49, and *Autobiography*, Chapter 16.

126. News item in *Survey*, October 21, 1916, pp. 60–61.

127. *St. Paul Dispatch*, June 12, 1916, in Sanger Scrapbook no. 3, Sanger, LC.

128. Inglis to Rose Pastor Stokes, June 2, 1916 and June 24, 1916, in Stokes mss., Tamiment Library, Tamiment, Pa.

129. Ella Westcott to Stokes, October 28, 1916, Stokes mss.

130. For example, H. P. Hough, from Fortress Monroe, Va., December 3, 1916; Joseph Rothman, Poughkeepsie, January 6, 1917; Carl Haessler, Urbana, Ill., May 25, 1916, all to Stokes, Stokes mss.; Robt. Peary, July 12, 1916, and B. Greenberg, Devil's Lake, N.D., February 10, 1916, to Sanger, all in Sanger, LC.

131. *Chicago Evening Journal*, April 25, 1916, in Sanger, LC; see also Sanger, *My Fight for Birth Control*, p. 145.

132. Flynn to Sanger in London, August 1915, Sanger, LC.

133. Flynn, *The Rebel Girl*, pp. 184–85.

134. Mrs. Elsie M. Humphries, Cincinnati, to Stokes, January 9, 1917, Stokes mss.

135. Mrs. W. R. Stevens, Swampscott, Mass., to Stokes, October 20, 1916, Stokes mss.

136. Margaret Sanger, ed., *Motherhood in Bondage* (New York: Brentano's, 1928), pp. 34, 281.

137. Mrs. K.A.B., to NBCL, n.d. (probably 1921), in Sanger, LC.

138. Letter to Sanger, February 1, 1916, in Sanger, LC.

139. Sanger, *My Fight for Birth Control*, p. 149.

140. Inglis to Stokes, June 2, 1916, Stokes mss.

141. *St. Paul Dispatch*, June 12, 1916, in Sanger Scrapbook no. 3, in Sanger, LC.

142. Sanger, *My Fight for Birth Control*, p. 144.

143. Sanger, *Autobiography*, p. 215.

144. Ibid., pp. 218–19.

145. Ibid., p. 220. Note that Sanger gives the figure as 488 in *My Fight for Birth Control*, p. 158.

146. Sanger, *Autobiography*, p. 234.

147. Ibid., for example, p. 231.

148. Ibid., p. 250.

149. Dennett, *Birth Control Laws*, Appendix 4; and Dennett, *Who's Obscene?* (New York: Vanguard Press, 1930), pp. 236–42.

150. *New York Evening Sun*, May 6, 1916, clipping in Sanger, LC; and F. M. Vreeland, "The Process of Reform with Especial Reference to Reform Groups in the Field of Population," Ph.D. dissertation, University of Michigan, 1929.

151. Jessie Ashley to Stokes, June 17, 1916, Stokes mss.

152. Rave statement, [1929], Alice Park mss., Stanford University. Carl Rave was not a representative longshoreman accidentally interested in birth control; he was married to Caroline Nelson, a birth-control activist. See Nominations for ABCL General National Committee, May 11, 1918, American Birth Control League Papers, Houghton Library, Harvard University [hereinafter given as ABCL].

153. Agnes Smedley to Sanger, November 1, 1918, in Sanger, LC.

154. Ibid.

155. Vreeland, "Process of Reform," pp. 274–75; Sanger, *Motherhood in Bondage*, p. 439.

156. Stokes mss.

157. Sanger, "The Unrecorded Battle," in Sanger, LC.

158. Nelson to Sanger, June 12, 1915, in Sanger, LC: I have corrected the spelling.

159. Nelson, "Neo-Malthusianism," p. 228.

160. Sanger, untitled speech, pp. 28–29, in Sanger, LC; letter from Parsons in *New Republic*, March 18, 1916, pp. 187–88.

161. Statement by Anna May Wood, January 31, 1917, in Sanger, LC.

162. Eliza Mosher, "A Protest Against the Teaching of Birth Control," *Medical Woman's Journal*, December 1925, p. 320.

163. Alice Park to Mary Ware Dennett, December 30, 1920, Park mss.

164. Dennett to Park, June 26, 1922, Park mss.

165. Carrie Chapman Catt to Sanger and Juliet Rublee, November 24, 1920, in Sanger, LC.

166. Charlotte Perkins Gilman, "Sex and Race Progress," in Calverton and Schmalhausen, *Sex in Civilization*, pp. 114–20.

167. Gilman, *His Religion and Hers: A Study of the Faith of Our Fathers and the Work of Our Mothers* (New York: Century, 1923), pp. 164–65.

168. David Kennedy, *Birth Control in America: The Career of Margaret Sanger* (New Haven: Yale University Press, 1970), p. 234. Gilman, "Progress Through Birth Control," *North American*

Review, December 1927, pp. 622–29; and "Divorce and Birth Control," *Outlook*, January 25, 1928.

169. Sanger, *Autobiography*, p. 93.

170. Konikow in *New York Call*, June 1, 1913.

171. Stokes, draft letter to Sanger, March 12, 1925, in Stokes mss.

172. Victor Berger, "Socialism and the Home," in *Vanguard*, August 1904, p. 8. This and other socialist opinions are quoted in Mari Jo Buhle's Ph.D. dissertation, "Women in the Socialist Party," University of Wisconsin, 1974, Chapter 9, p. 16.

173. Sanger Diary, April 8–9, 1919, in Sanger, LC.

174. Mrs. and Hermann S. Weissmann to Stokes, June 30, 1916, Stokes mss.

175. Letter in *New York Call*, December 19, 1912.

176. Nelson to Sanger, June 12, 1915, in Sanger, LC.

177. Copy of this letter, without signature, received February 6, 1925, in ABCL.

178. For example, in 1912 John Spargo devoted a great deal of his basic tract, *Applied Socialism*, to refuting any connection between socialist and free-love ideas or practice.

179. For example: Sanger to T. J. Meade, September 11, 1929; Meade to Sanger, September 19, 1929, in Sanger, LC.

180. For example, Floyd Dell, "Socialism and Feminism," *New Review*, June 1914, pp. 349–53.

181. Josephine Conger-Kaneko, "Socialism and the Sex War," *Progressive Woman*, August 1909, p. 9, for example.

Chapter 10. The Professionalization of Birth Control

1. Quoted in Clarence J. Karier, "Testing for Order and Control," in Clarence J. Karier, Paul Violas, and Josel Spring, eds., *Roots of Crisis: American Education in the Twentieth Century* (Chicago: Rand McNally, 1973), p. 122.

2. Henry Goddard, *Psychology of the Normal and Subnormal* (New York: Dodd, Mead, 1919), p. 234.

3. Karier, "Testing for Order and Control," p. 121.

4. C. Wright Mills, *White Collar* (New York: Oxford University Press, 1951), p. 113.

5. Quoted in Karier, "Testing for Order and Control," p. 122.

6. David Kennedy, *Birth Control in America: The Career of Margaret Sanger* (New Haven: Yale University Press, 1970), p. 169. My understanding of the role of the churches in the birth-control movement is generally indebted to Kennedy's excellent analysis.

7. For example: Charles F. Potter, "Why the Church Should Champion Birth Control," *Proceedings, Sixth International Neo-Malthusian and Birth Control Conference* (New York: ABCL, 1926), 4:18–19; Federal Council of the Churches of Christ, Committee on Marriage and the Home, *Moral Aspects of Birth Control* (New York, 1934), pamphlet.

8. Kennedy, *Birth Control in America*, p. 170.

9. For example: Father Francis J. Connell, "Birth Control: The Case for the Catholic," *Atlantic Monthly*, October 1939, p. 472; Father Gerald J. McMahon to Alice Hamilton, January 6, 1935, Hamilton mss., Schlesinger Library. Kennedy has a whole chapter on the church and birth control which discusses these issues thoroughly.

10. Alice Hamilton, "Poverty and Birth Control," ABCL pamphlet, [1927], Hamilton mss.

11. Sanger, "Original Speech," in Sanger, LC; Lawrence Lader, *The Margaret Sanger Story* (Garden City, N.Y.: Doubleday, 1955), p. 99. Lader's is an "official" biography.

12. William O'Neill, *Everyone Was Brave* (Chicago: Quadrangle, 1971), p. 251.

13. Quoted in *Birth Control Review* [hereinafter given as *BCR*], July–August 1932, p. 209.

14. Frederick Blossom to Rose Pastor Stokes, November 11, 1916, Stokes mss., Tamiment Library.

15. Henry Fruchter to Elizabeth Gurley Flynn, report on Blossom, September 16, 1922; Margaret Sanger to Flynn, November 3, 1922, both in Sanger, LC.

16. Margaret Sanger, *Autobiography* (New York: W. W. Norton, 1938), pp. 211–12, and *My Fight for Birth Control* (New York: Farrar & Rinehart, 1931), p. 110; Mary Ware Dennett, *Birth Control Laws* (New York: F. H. Hitchcock, 1926), p. 11.

17. Letter to members of NBCL from its Executive Committee, January 11, 1917, Stokes mss.; statement by Dennett, November 18, 1921, Sanger, LC.

18. Morris Fishbein, *Medical Follies* (New York: Boni & Liveright, 1925), p. 142.

19. Frederick McCann, Presidential Address to League of National Life, printed in *Medical Press and Circular*, November 3, 1926, p. 359.

20. For this and following quotations from Kosmak, see George Kosmak in *Bulletin, Lying-in Hospital of the City of New York*, August 1917, pp. 181–92. For similar views among other doctors, see, for example, Edward C. Podvin, "Birth Control," *New York Medical Journal*, February 10, 1917, pp. 258–60; C. Henry Davis, "Birth Control and Sterility," *Surgery, Gynecology and Obstetrics*, March 1923, pp. 435–39; B. S. Talmey, in *New York Medical Journal*, June 23, 1917, pp. 1187–91.

21. Robert L. Dickinson, "Hypertrophies of the Labia Minora and Their Significance," *American Gynecology* 1 (1902): 225–54, quoted in James Reed, "Birth Control and the Americans," Harvard dissertation, 1974.

22. Robert L. Dickinson, "Bicycling for Women from the Standpoint of the Gynecologist," *American Journal of Obstetrics* 31 (1895): 24–37, quoted in Reed thesis, pp. 51–52.

23. Robert L. Dickinson, "Marital Maladjustment: The Business of Preventive Gynecology," *Long Island Medical Journal* (1908): 1–5, quoted in Reed thesis, p. 58.

24. Kennedy, *Birth Control in America*, p. 179.

25. Dickinson to J. Bentley Squier, November 10, 1925, Dickinson mss., Countway Library, Harvard University Medical School.

26. Kennedy, *Birth Control in America*, p. 191.

27. Reed thesis, pp. 77–82; Kennedy, *Birth Control in America*, p. 190; Lader, *Margaret Sanger Story*, p. 216.

28. ABCL files, quoted in F. M. Vreeland, "The Process of Reform Groups in the Field of Population," Ph.D. dissertation, University of Michigan, 1929, p. 280.

29. Sanger to J. Noah Slee, February 22, 1925, Sanger, LC; see also ABCL Papers, Boxes 4, 5, 6, Houghton Library, Harvard University.

30. W. N. Wishard, Sr., "Contraception: Are Our County Societies Being Used for the American Birth Control League Propaganda?", *Journal of the Indiana Medical Association*, May 1929, pp. 187–89.

31. *Proceedings, Sixth International Birth Control Conference*, 3:19–30, 49–60.

32. Vreeland, "Process of Reform," p. 280.

33. Form letters in ABCL.

34. Kennedy, *Birth Control in America*, p. 196.

35. ABCL, *An Amendment to the Federal Law Dealing with Contraception*, pamphlet, n.d., in ABCL.

36. Mimeographed letter to VPL members from President Myra P. Gallert, December 2, 1925, Alice Park mss., Stanford University.

37. Dennett, *Birth Control Laws*, p. 88.

38. Antoinette Konikow, "The Doctor's Dilemma in Massachusetts," *BCR*, January 1931, pp. 21–22.

39. Kennedy, *Birth Control in America*, pp. 222–23.

40. Sanger to James Field, June 5, 1923, ABCL, Box 2; Sanger to Dennett, March 4, 1930 and unmailed draft of same February 25, 1930, in Sanger mss., Sophia Smith Collection, Smith

College [hereinafter given as Sanger, Smith]; see also *Journal of the American Medical Association* 85 (1925): 1153–54; and Sanger to Dennett, [1929], Park mss.

41. Cerise Carman Jack in *BCR*, April 1918, pp. 6–8.

42. Paul Blanshard, *Personal and Controversial* (Boston: Beacon, 1973), pp. 34–35.

43. *Boston Post*, July 25, 1916, quoted in Diane McCarrick Gieg, "The Birth Control League of Massachusetts," B.A. thesis, Simmons, 1973, p. 21; Cerise Carman Jack in *Boston American*, July 21, 1916, quoted in Gieg, "Birth Control League of Massachusetts," p. 21.

44. Richard Drinnon, *Rebel in Paradise* (Boston: Beacon, 1961), p. 141; *BCR*, February 1917, p. 10.

45. Jack to Blanche Ames Ames, June 17, 1917, Ames mss., Sophia Smith Collection, Smith College.

46. Jack to Charles Birtwell, June 17, 1917, Ames mss.

47. Jack to Blanche Ames Ames, January 7, 1918, Ames mss.

48. BCLM mss., Schlesinger Library.

49. See, for example, Konikow to Mrs. Edward East, January 20, 1929, and October 7, 1929, in Planned Parenthood League of Massachusetts mss., Sophia Smith Collection, Smith College.

50. From the opinion of C. R. Clapp, May 10, 1929, BCLM.

51. Konikow, "Doctor's Dilemma," p. 21.

52. Konikow to Blanche Ames Ames, March 29, 1931; VPL mimeographed letter, n.d.; both in BCLM.

53. Statements quoted by Gieg, "Birth Control League of Massachusetts," p. 77, from the *Boston Post*, February 19, 1931.

54. Dennett, *Birth Control Laws*, pp. 72–93.

55. There were six in New York, seven in Los Angeles, three in San Francisco, four in Alameda County in California, three in Chicago, and others in Baltimore, Detroit, Cleveland, Buffalo, Philadelphia, Denver, Atlanta, Minneapolis, Newark, Cincinnati, San Antonio, Charlottesville. See Lader, *Margaret Sanger Story*, p. 219; and Appendix B, pp. 358–59.

56. *Birth Control and Public Policy, Decision of Judge Harry M. Fisher of the Circuit Court of Cook County, November 1923*, pamphlet, Illinois Birth Control League, 1924.

57. Sanger was undoubtedly a difficult person who did not thrive on cooperative work. Her personal struggles within the birth-control movement are well described in Kennedy's *Birth Control in America*.

58. For example, see minutes of advisory council, Harlem Clinical Research Bureau, May 20, 1931, in Sanger, Smith.

59. Sanger to Dr. Clarence Gamble, February 4, 1940, in Sanger, Smith.

60. Conference program, Sanger, LC.

61. Letter to VPL from Gallert; for Sanger's justification of this exclusion, see, for example, Sanger to Prof. James Field, August 13, 1923, BCLM.

62. Caroline Nelson to Alice Park, February 3, 1930, Park mss.

63. J. Mayone Stycos, "Problems of Fertility Control in Under-developed Areas," in Stuart Mudd, ed., *The Population Crisis and the Use of World Resources* (Bloomington: Indiana University Press, 1964), p. 103.

64. Sanger, *Autobiography*, pp. 402–408.

65. For example, C. C. Little to Robert L. Dickinson, October 28, 1925, Sanger, LC.

66. Sanger, *Autobiography*, p. 374.

67. The best general secondary work on twentieth-century eugenics in the United States is Mark Haller, *Eugenics: Hereditarian Attitudes in American Thought* (New Brunswick, N.J.: Rutgers University Press, 1963); see also Leonard Ellman, "The American Eugenics Movement, 1905–1925," B.A. thesis, Harvard 1963, and Donald K. Pickens, *Eugenics and the Progressives* (Nashville: Vanderbilt University Press, 1968).

68. Mills, *White Collar*, pp. 129–34.

69. Jesse B. Sears, *Philanthropy in the History of American Higher Education* (Washington, D.C.: GPO, 1922), p. 55.

70. David Smith, *Who Rules the Universities?* (New York: Monthly Review, 1974), pp. 95–96, 100–101, 106.

71. For a sample textbook, see Michael F. Guyer, *Being Well-Born: An Introduction to Eugenics* (Indianapolis: Bobbs-Merrill, 1916).

72. Pickens, *Eugenics and the Progressives*, p. 51.

73. Ibid.

74. Haller, *Eugenics*, p. 174.

75. Karier, "Testing for Order and Control," pp. 115–16.

76. Paul Popenoe, *The Conservation of the Family* (Baltimore: Williams and Wilkins, 1926), pp. 129–30.

77. Guyer, *Being Well-Born*, pp. 296–98.

78. Lothrop Stoddard, *Revolt Against Civilization: The Menace of the Under Man* (New York: Scribners, 1922), p. 21.

79. Haller, *Eugenics*, pp. 55 ff. Eugenists were pushing immigration restriction as early as 1914; see, for example, articles by Stanley Gulick and Robert DeC. Ward, in *Proceedings, First National Conference on Race Betterment* (Race Betterment Foundation, 1914).

80. Fourth Report, Committee on Selective Immigration, American Eugenics Society, June 30, 1928, p. 16, in Anita Newcomb McGee mss., LC.

81. Paul Popenoe and Roswell Hill Johnson, *Applied Eugenics* ([1918] New York: Macmillan, 1925), pp. 294–97.

82. For example, the Virginia State Board of Health distributed a pamphlet among schoolchildren entitled, "Eugenics in Relation to the New Family and the Law on Racial Integrity," published 1924. It explained in eugenic terms the valiant and lonely effort of Virginia to preserve the race from the subversion planned by the nineteen states plus the District of Columbia which permitted miscegenation. It concluded, "Let us turn a deaf ear to those who would interpret Christian brotherhood to mean racial equality."

83. For more discussion of the politics of eugenics, see also John Higham, *Strangers in the Land: Patterns of American Nativism 1860–1925* (New York: Atheneum, 1965), Chapters 6 and 10.

84. For example: Eduard Bernstein, "Decline in the Birth-Rate, Nationality, and Civilization," and R. Manschke, "The Decline in the Birth-Rate," both in Eden and Cedar Paul, eds., *Population and Birth-Control* (New York: Critic and Guide, 1917); Frank Notestein, in *BCR*, April 1938; Haller, *Eugenics*, p. 79; Frank Lorimer, Ellen Winston, and Louise K. Kiser, *Foundations of American Population Policy* (New York: Harper & Brothers, 1940), pp. 12–15.

85. Lorimer, Winston, and Kiser, *American Population Policy*, p. 15.

86. See, for example, The National League for the Protection of the Family, *Annual Report for 1911* (Boston: Fort Hill Press, 1912).

87. For example, Scott and Nellie Nearing, *Woman and Social Progress* (New York: Macmillan, 1912), Chapter 1.

88. S. H. Halford, "Dysgenic Tendencies of Birth-Control and of the Feminist Movement," in Paul, *Population and Birth-Control*, p. 238.

89. Henry Bergen, in *BCR*, April–May 1920, pp. 5–6, 15–17. See also J. B. Eggen, "Rationalization and Eugenics," *Modern Quarterly*, May–July 1926; Eva Trew, "Sex Sterilization," *International Socialist Review*, May 1913, for similar socialist critiques.

90. Eden Paul, "Eugenics and Birth-Control," in Paul, *Population and Birth-Control*, p. 134.

91. *BCR*, April 1918, p. 13.

92. Bergen, in *BCR*.

93. Ludwig Quessel, "Race Suicide in the United States," in Paul, *Population and Birth-Control*, p. 118.

94. *Elizabeth Cady Stanton as Revealed in Her Letters, Diary and Reminiscences*, ed. Theodore Stanton

and Harriot Stanton Blatch (New York: Harper & Brothers, 1922), letter of December 20, 1865, to Martha Wright for an early example.

95. Aileen Kraditor, *Ideas of the Woman Suffrage Movement 1890–1920* (New York: Columbia University Press, 1965), Chapter 7.

96. "Why Not Birth Control in America?" *BCR*, May 1919, pp. 10–11.

97. Sanger, *Woman and the New Race* (New York: Brentano's, 1920), p. 34, for example.

98. Sanger, *The Pivot of Civilization* (New York: Brentano's, 1922), pp. 177–78.

99. *Stenographic Record of the Proceedings of the First American Birth Control Conference, 1921* (New York: ABCL, 1921), p. 24.

100. Oakland speech, "The Necessity for Birth Control," December 19, 1928, stenographic record in Sanger, LC.

101. "My Way to Peace," speech to New History Society, January 17, 1932, in Sanger, Smith.

102. Sanger, Oakland speech.

103. *Report, Fifth International Neo-Malthusian and Birth Control Conference*, ed. Raymond Pierpont (London: Heinemann, 1922).

104. Brochure in Sanger, Smith.

105. Paul Popenoe in *BCR*, March 1917, p. 6.

106. For example: Warren Thompson, "Race Suicide in the U.S.," *BCR*, series extending from August 1920 to March 1921: August 1920, pp. 9–10; September, pp. 9–10; October, pp. 10–11; January 1921, p. 16; February, pp. 9–12; March, pp. 11–13.

107. *BCR*, September 1923, pp. 219–20.

108. M. Winsor, *BCR*, September 1923, pp. 222–24.

109. *BCR*, October 1920, pp. 14–16.

110. "Unnatural Selection and Its Resulting Obligations," *BCR*, August 1926, pp. 244–57.

111. Quoted in Kennedy, *Birth Control in America*, p. 119, from an unpublished letter.

112. Vreeland, "Progress of Reform," p. 232.

113. East to Sanger, May 15, 1925, in ABCL.

114. National Committee on Federal Legislation for Birth Control, *Newsletter*, no. 9 (April 1932).

115. Vreeland, "Progress of Reform," pp. 376, 383–84.

116. Ibid., p. 297.

117. Tour schedules in Sanger, LC.

118. Sanger, *Autobiography*, pp. 385–86; for Sanger's polite version of this episode, see *My Fight for Birth Control*, p. 302.

119. For example: Lewis Terman and Edward Thorndike.

120. For example: Katherine Bement Davis, *Factors in the Sex Life of Twenty-Two Hundred Women* (New York: Harper & Brothers, 1929); Lewis Terman, *Psychological Factors in Marital Happiness* (New York: McGraw-Hill, 1938); Gilbert Van Tassel Hamilton, *A Research in Marriage* (New York: A. & C. Boni, 1929).

121. Kennedy, *Birth Control in America*, pp. 200–202.

122. Caroline Hadley Robinson, *Seventy Birth Control Clinics* (Baltimore: Williams and Wilkins, 1930), p. 44.

123. Kennedy, *Birth Control in America*, p. 200.

124. Edward East to Sanger, December 20, 1929; Sanger to East, December 31, 1929, in Sanger, Smith.

125. Robinson, *Seventy Birth Control Clinics*, Chapter 4.

126. Sanger, *Autobiography*, pp. 374–75.

127. Robinson, *Seventy Birth Control Clinics*, pp. 50–52.

128. For example, Sanger, *Autobiography*, p. 401; Sanger, *Motherhood in Bondage* (New York: Brentano's, 1928), passim.

129. Robinson, *Seventy Birth Control Clinics*, Chapter 5.

130. Haller, *Eugenics*, pp. 180 ff.; Pickens, *Eugenics and the Progressives*, Chapter 11.

131. For example, in *BCR*, 1938–1939, passim.

132. *Journal of Heredity* 24, no. 4 (April 1933): 143.

133. Henry Pratt Fairchild, speech in Planned Parenthood Federation of America Papers, Sophia Smith Collection, Smith College Library.

134. Vreeland, "Process of Reform," pp. 154 ff.

135. ABCL bylaws, n.d., in ABCL.

136. ABCL mss., passim.

137. *Birth Control Herald*, July 1922.

138. *The Prosecution of Mary Ware Dennett for Obscenity* (New York: ACLU, June 1929), pamphlet. A decision in Dennett's favor by a circuit court, in 1930 was an important free-speech precedent. Holding that the Comstock law was not intended to interfere with serious sex instruction, it was later cited in court decisions allowing the distribution of two contraception books by Marie Stopes and *Ulysses* by James Joyce. See *U.S.* v. *Dennett*, 39 F. 2d 564 (1930), cited by Kennedy, *Birth Control in America*, p. 244.

139. For example, Mary Ware Dennett to Alice Park, January 7, 1921 and June 26, 1922, Park mss.

140. Mary Ware Dennett, *The Sex Education of Children: A Book for Parents* (New York: Vanguard Press, 1931).

141. For example, Elizabeth Green to Anne Kennedy of ABCL, March 29, 1926, in ABCL.

142. For example, ABCL to Mrs. Edmonds, March 24, 1926, in ABCL.

143. For example, ABCL to board members, June 6, 1928, in ABCL.

144. The findings of this survey are presented in Vreeland, "Process of Reform," pp. 154 ff., and all the following information is taken from that source.

145. Sanger form letter and many responses are in ABCL.

146. This judgment is amply corroborated by a perusal of the ABCL papers.

147. Sarah Grimke signed her 1838 letters, an early statement of American feminism, with this *double entendre* on the word "bonds."

Chapter 11. The Depression

1. This interpretation is based on William Ryan, *Blaming the Victim* (New York: Random House, 1971), and C. Wright Mills, "The Professional Ideology of Social Pathologists," in *Power, Politics and People*, ed. Horowitz (New York: Ballantine, n.d.), pp. 525–52, orig. in *American Journal of Sociology* 49, no. 2 (September 1943).

2. Dorothy Dunbar Bromley, "Birth Control and the Depression," *Harper's*, October 1934, p. 563; James H. S. Bossard, letter to *New York Times*, January 25, 1935.

3. For example, *Time*, April 8, 1935, pp. 30–32; *Birth Control Review*, May 1935, pp. 2–3.

4. Margaret Sanger, "Is Race Suicide Possible?" *Collier's*, August 15, 1925, p. 25.

5. R. E. Baber and E. A. Ross, *Changes in the Size of American Families in One Generation*, University of Wisconsin Studies no. 10 (1924).

6. Dr. Lydia Allen DeVilbiss to Francis Bangs, ABCL president, April 26, 1935, in Planned Parenthood Federation of America Papers, Sophia Smith Collection, Smith College Library [hereinafter given as PPFA].

7. *BCR*, January 1933, p. 6.

8. *BCR*, May 1933, pp. 134–35.

9. *BCR*, June 1933, pp. 141–43.

10. Bossard, "The New Public Relief and Birth Control," address at American Conference on Birth Control and National Recovery, January 1934, in *BCR*, May 1934, p. 1.

11. *BCR*, February 1935, p. 1.

12. *BCR*, July–August 1932, p. 209.

13. Bromley, "Birth Control and the Depression," p. 564.

14. Paul Popenoe and Ellen Morton Williams, "Fecundity of Families Dependent on Public Charity," *American Journal of Sociology*, September 1934, p. 220. To obtain this "data" eugenist investigators actually subjected women on welfare to IQ tests at childbirth.

15. Edgar Sydenstricker and G. St. J. Perrott, "Sickness, Unemployment, and Differential Fertility," *Milbank Memorial Fund Quarterly*, April 1934, quoted in Norman Himes, "The Birth Rate of Families on Relief: A Summary of Recent Studies in the U.S.A.," *Marriage Hygiene* (Bombay, India), August 1935, p. 60.

16. Bossard, *Marriage and the Child* (Philadelphia: University of Pennsylvania, 1940), Chapter 8.

17. *New York Times*, August 24, 1932.

18. Osborn, "Birth Selection vs. Birth Control," *Forum and Century*, August 1932, pp. 79–83.

19. Editorial in *BCR*, October 1932, pp. 227–28.

20. David Loth, "Planned Parenthood," *Annals of the American Academy of Political and Social Science*, November 1950, p. 96.

21. *BCR*, 1930s, passim.

22. *BCR*, October 1932, p. 230.

23. Edgar Sydenstricker and Frank Notestein, "Differential Fertility According to Social Class," *Journal of the American Statistical Association*, March 1930, p. 25.

24. National Committee on Maternal Health, Round Table Discussion on Marriage and the Family, May 13, 1937, minutes, p. 4, in Himes mss., Countway Library, Harvard University Medical School.

25. *American Eugenics*, Proceedings of the Annual Meeting and Round Table Conferences of the American Eugenics Society, May 7, 1936, pamphlet, p. 46.

26. These alarms rested also on the fact that in the 1930s demographers finally became convinced that contraception was the major cause of the birth-rate decline. Raymond Pearl, for example, long a skeptic about the impact of contraception, was convinced by his own research that without contraception there would be no birth-rate differential at all. See his *Natural History of Population* (New York: Oxford University Press, 1939), Chapters 4 and 5.

27. *Omaha World-Herald*, quoted in *BCR*, May 1935, p. 3.

28. Bossard, "Marriage and the Child," Chapter 8.

29. Raymond Pearl, *Biology of Population Growth* (New York: Knopf, 1925), p. 167.

30. For example, Dr. Raymond Squier, comments at National Committee on Maternal Health, Round Table Discussion, p. 10.

31. T. R. Robie in ibid., p. 12.

32. Clarence Gamble, report on DeVilbiss method, 1937, in PPFA.

33. For example, DeVilbiss to Francis Bangs, June 30, 1934, PPFA.

34. For example, Bangs to DeVilbiss, July 6, 1934; Marguerite Benson, ABCL executive director, to DeVilbiss, June 21, 1935; both in PPFA.

35. Dennis Smith, "Techniques of Conception Control," in *Readings in Family Planning*, ed. Donald McCalister, Victor Thiessen, and Margaret McDermott (St. Louis: C. V. Mosby, 1973), p. 31.

36. For example, Dr. Regine K. Stix and Frank Notestein, *Controlled Fertility: An Evaluation of Clinic Service* (Baltimore: Williams & Wilkins, 1940), Chapter 9.

37. Ibid., pp. 91–92; Bessie L. Moses, *Contraception as a Therapeutic Measure* (Baltimore: Williams & Wilkins, 1936); Ruth A. Robishaw, "A Study of 4000 Patients Admitted for Contraceptive Advice and Treatment," *Journal of Obstetrics and Gynecology* 31, no. 3 (March 1936), pp. 426–34.

38. For a contemporary corroboration of this judgment, see Robert L. Dickinson and Lura Beam, *A Thousand Marriages* (Baltimore: Williams and Wilkins, 1932), p. 217.

39. For example, Pearl, *Natural History of Population*, Chapter 5.

40. *American Eugenics*, p. 40; see also Leon F. Whitney, *The Case for Sterilization* (New York: Frederick A. Stokes, 1934), p. 7.

41. For example: Margaret Sanger, "The Function of Sterilization," *BCR*, October 1926, p. 299; C. O. McCormick, "Eugenic Sterilization," *BCR*, October 1932, pp. 241–42.

42. J. H. Landman, *Human Sterilization* (New York: Macmillan, 1932), pp. 48–49.

43. Paul Popenoe, "Number of Persons Needing Sterilization," *Journal of Heredity*, 1928, pp. 405–10.

44. Landman, *Human Sterilization*, pp. 41–46. Who incurred this loss was not specified.

45. *BCR*, January 1939, p. 155.

46. Frederick S. Jaffe and Steven Polgar, "Family Planning and Public Policy: Is the 'Culture of Poverty' the New Cop-Out?", in McCalister, Thiessen, and McDermott, *Readings in Family Planning*, p. 169.

47. Caroline Hadley Robinson, *Seventy Birth Control Clinics* (Baltimore: Williams and Wilkins, 1930), pp. 91–94; Raymond Pearl, *Statistical Report on the Fifth Year's Operations of the Bureau for Contraceptive Advice* (Baltimore, 1933), pamphlet.

48. For example: Regine K. Stix, "Birth Control in a Midwestern City," *Milbank Memorial Fund Quarterly* 17, nos. 1, 2, and 4 (January, April, and October, 1939); Dorothy Dunbar Bromley, *Birth Control, Its Use and Misuse* (New York: Harper & Brothers, 1934), p. 4.

49. Lini Moerbeck Fuhr to Sanger, January 12, 1936, Sanger, LC.

50. For example, Robinson, *Seventy Birth Control Clinics*, p. 103.

51. Ibid., pp. 116–17.

52. *Time*, April 8, 1935, pp. 30–32; *BCR*, September 1935, p. 3.

53. *BCR*, January 1933, p. 144.

54. *BCR*, December 1935.

55. Frank Hankins, "Poverty and Birth Control," *BCR*, July–August 1932, p. 199.

56. Eleanor Dwight Jones, in *BCR*, January 1933, p. 6.

57. For example, C. C. Little, in *BCR*, 1934–1936, passim.

58. Sanger, "National Security and Birth Control," *Forum*, March 1935, pp. 139–41.

59. In his later life Dublin became an equally passionate exponent of the overpopulation theory which dominated the demography of the 1950s and 1960s. See his memoirs, Louis I. Dublin, *After Eighty Years* (Gainesville: University of Florida, 1966), pp. 140–41.

60. Arthur Schlesinger, Jr., *The Crisis of the Old Order, 1919–33* (Boston: Houghton Mifflin, 1956), pp. 425–26.

61. ABCL, 1934 Report, Sanger, LC.

62. "Survey of Policies of FERA Administrators," February 25, 1935, in Sanger, LC.

63. DeVilbiss to Bangs, March 25, 1935, PPFA.

64. Norman Himes, "Birth Control and Social Work," *Survey Midmonthly*, March 1939, pp. 74–75.

65. James Rorty, "Let Power Speak," *BCR*, May 1932, p. 136.

66. David Kennedy, *Birth Control in America: The Career of Margaret Sanger* (New Haven: Yale University Press, 1970), p. 269.

67. Report of the John Price Jones Corporation, September 15, 1930; and "Recommendations to the Joint Committee of ABCL and CRB," October 10, 1938; both in Sanger, LC.

68. Henry Pratt Fairchild, memo on his interview with Dr. Ray Lyman Wilbur, May 5, 1930, Sanger, Smith.

69. DeVilbiss to Bangs, March 25, 1935, PPFA.

70. Ironically, the combination of these two arguments overlooked the fact that the foremost proponent of the underpopulation theory, Louis Dublin, opposed most eugenic fears about the birth-rate differential, considering them racist, elitist, and unfounded. See, for example,

Dublin, "The Fallacious Propaganda for Birth Control," *Atlantic Monthly*, February 1926, pp. 189–93.

71. National Committee on Maternal Health, Round Table Discussion, pp. 4–5.

72. Dorothy Dunbar Bromley and Florence Haxton Britten, *Youth and Sex: A Study of 1300 College Students* (New York: Harper & Brothers, 1938), p. 13.

73. Elizabeth H. Garrett, "Birth Control's Business Baby," *New Republic*, January 17, 1934, p. 270.

74. Bromley and Britten, *Youth and Sex*, p. 13.

75. Bromley, "Birth Control and the Depression," p. 104.

76. Quoted in Norman Himes, *Medical History of Contraception* ([1936] New York: Gamut Press, 1963), p. 329.

77. *Health and Hygiene*, June 1935, p. 18; Bromley, "Birth Control and the Depression," p. 104.

78. Garrett, "Birth Control's Business Baby," p. 270.

79. Rachel Lynn Palmer and Sarah K. Greenberg, *Facts and Frauds in Woman's Hygiene* (New York: Vanguard Press, 1936), p. 168.

80. Ibid., pp. 250–51.

81. Report on Contraceptive Industry, prepared by Foote, Cone & Belding of Chicago, typescript, n.d., in PPFA.

82. Sanger, "National Security and Birth Control," p. 140.

83. Ibid.

84. Garrett, "Birth Control's Business Baby," p. 271.

85. Kennedy, *Birth Control in America*, p. 241.

86. *Ladies' Home Journal* poll, reported in Birth Control Clinical Research Bureau press release, February 17, 1938, Sanger, Smith.

87. The history of this case and Sanger's legislative work is well told in Kennedy, *Birth Control in America*, Chapter 8.

88. Unfortunately, very little research has been done on local community organizing during the Depression, and even less about women's activities. It is a difficult kind of research, involving reaching into local archives in many different places, but would be an amply rewarding undertaking.

89. *National Birth Control News* (published by National Committee for Federal Legislation on Birth Control), December–January 1936–1937, p. 14.

90. Lini Moerbeck Fuhr, typed report, mid-1930s, in Sanger, LC.

91. Lini Moerbeck Fuhr to Sanger, January 12, 1936, in Sanger, LC. Fuhr was especially impressed with this Paterson effort because she had worked in the mills there as a child. We have no documentation about the final outcome.

92. Quoted in *National Birth Control News*, March–April 1937, pp. 10–11.

93. Natalie Lamport, "Report on the Recreation Rooms and Settlement Birth Control Clinic," a branch of the Clinical Research Bureau at 84 First Street in New York City, Sanger, Smith. See also Stix and Notestein, *Controlled Fertility*. The percentage of Catholic women who attended clinics, as compared to non-Catholics, was never calculated and probably could not have been calculated accurately because of variables like the location of clinics.

94. *BCR*, December–January 1937–1938, p. 39.

95. *BCR*, May 1935, p. 3.

96. Himes, "Birth Control and Social Work," p. 75.

97. Hannah Stone in *BCR*, November 1932, p. 261; Eve Garrett, letter to *New York Times*, November 19, 1933, quoted in *BCR*, December 1933, p. 3.

98. "Birth Control—Questions and Answers," National Committee on Federal Legislation for Birth Control (NCFLBC) pamphlet, n.d.

99. Nadina R. Kavinoky, "A Program for Family Health," ABCL pamphlet.

100. Report of John Price Jones Corporation.

101. This was Sanger's claim; see, for example, her address at ABCL 18th Annual Meeting, January 19, 1939, p. 2, typescript in PPFA.

102. See, for example, documents concerning Sanger's formation of the Committee on Public Progress for Birth Control, established after the court victory, and its lobbying program, in Sanger, Smith.

103. Gretta Palmer, "Birth Control Goes Suave," *Today*, July 20, 1935, pp. 14–15. The Washington committee in the winter of 1934 included Mrs. J. Borden Harriman, Mrs. John F. Dryden, Mrs. Harold L. Ickes, Mrs. Mary Roberts Rinehart, Mrs. Frederic A. Delano, Mrs. Eugene Meyer, Mrs. Dean Acheson, and Mrs. Dwight Clark; sponsors elsewhere in the country included Mrs. E. Marshall Field, Mrs. Thomas W. Lamont, Miss Anne Morgan, Mrs. Narcissa Cox Vanderlip, Mrs. George Thomas Palmer, Mrs. Victor Du Pont, Mrs. George LeBoutillier, Mrs. Elizabeth Hooker, and Mrs. Thomas Hepburn.

104. Harry Hansen to Sanger, October 10, 1931, Sanger, LC.

105. Sanger to Hansen, October 13, 1931, Sanger, LC.

106. For example, Dorothy Dent to Sanger, April 30, 1932, Sanger, Smith; and many other personnel letters in these files at Smith.

107. Eleanor Dwight Jones, "A New Era in Social Service," *BCR*, July–August 1932, p. 209; and statement in *BCR*, January 1933, p. 6.

108. Statement of policy as approved by BCFA Executive Committee, September 16, 1941, in PPFA.

109. Loth, "Planned Parenthood," p. 96.

110. *BCR*, December 1938, p. 143.

111. Don Wharton, "Birth Control: The Case for the State," *Atlantic Monthly*, October 1939, p. 465.

112. DeVilbiss to Wood of ABCL, November 12, 1937; see also DeVilbiss to Moore of ABCL, July 26, 1937; both in PPFA.

113. For example, see Ellen H. Smith, chairman, board of directors, Virginia League for Planned Parenthood, to Marie S. Key, consultant on work with Negroes for PPFA, June 10, 1946; and Smith to D. Kenneth Rose, PPFA national director, June 10, 1946; both in PPFA. I have no information about the later history of segregation in the southern leagues.

114. For example, *Eugenics in Relation to the New Family and the Law on Racial Integrity*, 1924, and *The New Family and Race Improvement*, 1925, pamphlets of Virginia State Board of Health, Bureau of Vital Statistics, Widener Library, Harvard University.

115. W. A. Plecker, M.D., State Registrar of Vital Statistics, Virginia State Board of Health, to Mrs. Anne Kennedy, ABCL, February 10, 1926, in ABCL.

116. Wharton, "Birth Control," p. 467.

117. "Relief or Cure," leaflet of Mothers Health Clinic, n.d., PPFA.

118. Leaflet of Mothers Health Clubs, Inc., PPFA.

119. "Birth Control and the Negro," in Sanger, Smith. All further references to the project are from this proposal.

120. Sanger to Clarence Gamble, October 19, 1939, in Sanger, Smith.

121. Gamble memo, n.d., but probably November or December 1939, in Sanger, Smith.

122. Ibid.

123. Gamble to Sanger, January 25, 1940, in Sanger, Smith.

124. D. Kenneth Rose to Florence Rose, November 25, 1940, in Sanger, Smith.

125. Helen Countryman, "Conditions in Miami," typescript report, n.d. but undoubtedly late 1930s, in PPFA.

126. "Confidential Report of Governmental Projects in Cooperation with the Birth Control Clinical Research Bureau," n.d., unsigned, Sanger, Smith.

127. For example, Mildred Delp, R.N., "How Mrs. Joad Learned to Use a Doctor," *Medical Care* 4, no. 2 (n.d.): 115, in Sanger, Smith.

128. Pauline G. Shindler, "Tent Life in California," *BCR*, May 1932, p. 158.
129. For example, letter to Secretary of State from Dr. Adolphus Knopf, *BCR*, February 1933, pp. 50–51.
130. J. Enamorado Cuesta to editor, *BCR*, May 1932, p. 157.
131. *National Birth Control News*, May 1937, p. 3.
132. BCFA Information Service, May 1941, pp. 1 and 4.
133. "Birth Control Comes of Age," speech given at Mayflower Hotel, Washington, D.C., February 13, 1925, in Sanger, Smith.
134. Bossard, "Population and National Security," *BCR*, September 1935, p. 4.
135. Guy Burch, "Birth Control vs. Class Suicide," *Survey Graphic*, April 1932.

Chapter 12. Planned Parenthood

1. Lydia DeVilbiss to Dr. Eric Matsner, January 31, 1938, in PPFA.
2. Sanger to D. Kenneth Rose, August 20, 1946; Sanger to P. B. P. Huse, December 20, 1937; Summary of Recommendations to Joint Committee of ABCL and CRB, October 10, 1938, all in Sanger, Smith. Rose was later hired away from his public-relations firm to become PPFA national director.
3. Dr. Richard N. Pierson, speech at 1941 annual meeting, in PPFA.
4. Margaret Sanger, "National Security and Birth Control," *Forum* 93 (March 1935): 139–41.
5. Margaret Sanger, "Family Planning: A Radio Talk," CBS Broadcast, April 11, 1935, pamphlet, National Committee on Federal Legislation for Birth Control (NCFLBC).
6. Miscellaneous BCFA and PPFA leaflets and pamphlets in PPFA.
7. Woodbridge Morris to Rose, June 4, 1940, in PPFA.
8. For example, Eduard Lindeman, "The Responsibilities of Birth Control," *Atlantic Monthly*, July 1939, p. 23.
9. "Planned Parenthood . . . Its Contribution to Family, Community and Nation," PPFA pamphlet, n.d. (probably 1946), in PPFA.
10. Lindeman, "Responsibilities of Birth Control," p. 25.
11. For example, PPFA proposed policy statement, draft of April 6, 1943, in PPFA.
12. BCFA Executive Committee resolution October 29, 1940, in PPFA. This was not a new demand; the ABCL had called for a national birth-rate commission in 1928. Undated resolution, in ABCL.
13. Mimeographed form letter, March 22, 1943, in Sanger, Smith.
14. Unsigned memorandum, March 5, 1941, in Sanger, Smith.
15. "Planned Parenthood . . . Its Contribution," in PPFA.
16. "Planned Parenthood in Wartime," PPFA pamphlet, 1942, in PPFA.
17. Sanger, "National Security and Birth Control."
18. Sanger, speech at ABCL 18th Annual Meeting, in PPFA.
19. Rose, "War Psychology and Its Effect on the Birth Control Movement, Suggestions from Staff Members," memorandum to staff, June 7, 1940, in PPFA. See also memos from staff members to Rose on this subject.
20. L. Gill to Rose, [June 1, 1940], in PPFA.
21. "The Contribution of Birth Control to Preparedness," draft statement by C. M. Smith, June 11, 1940, in PPFA.
22. Kathryn Trent memorandum to Morris Lewis, May 19, 1941, in PPFA.

23. Helen K. Stevens memorandum to Rose, June 7, 1940; and Rose, "War Psychology"; both in PPFA.

24. Eugene Lyons, "The Stork Is the Bird of War," *Commentator*, February 1938, pp. 97–101.

25. For example, *Planned Parenthood and the War: A Statement of Policy*, leaflet, June 1942; "Contribution of Birth Control to Preparedness"; both in PPFA.

26. Sanger to P. B. P. Huse, January 2, 1940, in Sanger, Smith; see also Helen Keller to Margaret Sanger, August 5, 1944, and Sanger to Keller, August 24, 1944, in Sanger, Smith. Sanger was nevertheless strongly antifascist, and signed a message of support to a Soviet Women's Conference through the Communist-party-sponsored American Council on Soviet Relations, September 6, 1941, in Sanger, LC.

27. *Advanced Hygiene Protects Womanpower*, PPFA pamphlet, reprinted from *Modern Industry*, June, 1944, in PPFA.

28. *Employing the Married Woman Worker*, PPFA pamphlet, reprinted from publication of Alabama State Health Department, [1943], in PPFA.

29. Henry Pratt Fairchild, "Family Limitation and the War," *Annals of the American Academy of Political and Social Science* 229 (September 1943): 84.

30. BCFA national policies, May 10, 1940, and May 15, 1940, in PPFA.

31. *Planned Parenthood USA*, [1942], pamphlet of National Committee for Planned Parenthood of the BCFA, in PPFA.

32. Rose to Board of Directors, State Leagues, and so forth, July 6, 1940, "Birth Control's Opportunity to Strengthen Our Human Resources—Our Population," in PPFA.

33. Elmira Conrad to Rose, February 8, 1943, in PPFA.

34. *Birth Control Federation of American Information Service*, September–October 1940, p. 2.

35. PPFA Program Policies, adopted by Board of Directors, October 17, 1947, pp. 3–4, in PPFA. These pro-civil-rights policies may have been adopted in response to problems of racism within the PPFA or its affiliates. For example, in 1946 the chairman of the board of the Virginia League of Planned Parenthood refused a request of the PPFA's Negro Consultant to come to Virginia to present a special program on work with Negroes. Ellen Smith of the Virginia League wrote to the PPFA director: "I know you agree with the conservative approach we have had in Virginia which has brought such satisfactory results. I am sure that Mrs. Key [the Negro Consultant] understands that this had nothing to do with the racial problem, but is merely the continuation of our expressed policy since the League was organized." Doubtless Key and PPFA Director Rose suspected that Virginia's refusal did indeed have to do with the "racial problem" and may have struggled to overcome these prejudices as much as was possible within the structure of the PPFA. See Ellen H. Smith to Rose, June 10, 1946, and to Marie S. Key, same date, both in PPFA.

36. For example, Charles H. Garvin, "The Negro Doctor's Task," *Birth Control Review*, November 1932, p. 269.

37. For example, annual reports of Harlem Branch, Clinical Research Bureau, 1930–1932; Natalie Lamport, Report on the Recreation Rooms and Settlement Birth Control Clinic; both in Sanger, Smith.

38. Jessup memorandum to Rose, June 4, 1940, for example, in PPFA.

39. For example, "The Contribution of Birth Control to Preparedness," June 11, 1940; "Planned Parenthood in Relation to the War," memorandum to Board of Directors, State Leagues, October 5, 1942; both in PPFA.

40. Smith memorandum to Rose, June 3, 1940; "The Contribution of Birth Control to Preparedness"; both in PPFA.

41. BCFA memorandum on meeting with Captain Stephenson, October 22, 1941, in Sanger, Smith; Stephenson memorandum to Admiral McIntire, October 22, 1941, in PPFA.

42. For example, James H. S. Bossard, speech at National Conference of Social Work, quoted in BCFA press release, June 3, 1941, in PPFA.

43. William Fielding Ogburn, "Marriages, Births and Divorces," in *Annals of the American Academy of Political and Social Science* 229 (September 1943): 20–29.

44. "Birth Control, Ten Eventful Years," speech, probably delivered by Sanger in 1946, dated July 30, signed emc, in Sanger, Smith.

45. John F. Cuber, "Changing Courtship and Marriage Customs," in *Annals of the American Academy of Political and Social Science* 229 (September 1943): 30–38.

46. For example, Fairchild, "Family Limitation," p. 84. .

47. David Loth (PPFA public-relations director), "Planned Parenthood," in *Annals of the American Academy of Political and Social Science* 272 (November 1950): 97.

48. "Our Human Resources," report of the National Committee for Planned Parenthood Temporary Advisory Committee on Population Policy of the BCFA, March 1941, in PPFA.

49. "Birth Control's Opportunity to Strengthen Our Human Resources—Our Population," July 6, 1940, in PPFA.

50. Willard Waller, Sidney Goldstein, and Lawrence Frank, "The Family and National Defense," *Living* 3, no. 1 (February 1941): 1–3.

51. Pamphlet, PPFA.

52. For example, Stevens memorandum to Rose, June 7, 1940, in PPFA.

53. See, for example, Sheila Tobias and Lisa Anderson, *What Really Happened to Rosie the Riveter*, Mss. Modular Publications, no. 9 (1974).

54. Margaret Sanger, letter of June 17, 1942, in Sanger, LC.

55. Florence Rose to Sanger, [June 10, 1943], in Sanger, Smith.

56. BCFA memorandum to Sanger, July 30, 1940, in PPFA.

57. Sanger to Frank G. Boudreau, director, Milbank Memorial Fund, March 12, 1939, in Sanger, Smith.

58. This interpretation is my own, but it is based on an increasing number of studies of women's layoffs, their collective and individual struggles against them, compared to the myths that women expected and wished to return to full-time housewifery. See for example Tobias and Anderson, *What Really Happened to Rosie the Riveter.*

59. Betty Friedan, *The Feminine Mystique* ([1963] New York: Dell, 1970), p. 249.

60. Statement drafted by Janet Fowler Nelson, Ph.D., consultant on marriage and family-life education, accepted by PPFA Board March 20, 1947, in PPFA.

61. Numerous drafts of this manual and correspondence about it are in PPFA.

62. Ferdinand Lundberg and Marynia F. Farnham, M.D., *Modern Woman: The Lost Sex* (New York: Harper & Brothers, 1947), pp. 364–65.

63. Farnham, speech at Association for the Advancement of Psychotherapy Forum, April 28, 1943, in PPFA.

64. Note that the view that sexual continence was damaging for men and women was widespread at this time. For example, Mary Antoinette Cannon, professor of social work, Columbia University, *Outline for a Course in Planned Parenthood*, PPFA pamphlet, 1944–1945.

65. For example, Jes. H. Scull memorandum to Mrs. C. Damon, June 25, 1945, criticizing this policy, in PPFA.

66. For example: Karl Menninger, "Psychiatric Aspects of Contraception," PPFA reprint from *Bulletin of the Menninger Clinic*, January 1943; Harvie DeJ. Coghill, "Emotional Maladjustments from Unplanned Parenthood," speech at annual conference of Virginia League for Planned Parenthood, September 26, 1941; Adrian Holt Van der Veer, "The Unwanted Child," speech at annual meeting of Illinois League for Planned Parenthood, April 30, 1941; all in PPFA.

67. Farnham speech, p. 8.

68. Ibid., p. 9; see also Coghill, "Emotional Maladjustments," which offers an example of the prevalent view that resentful mothers "punish" their children.

69. Farnham speech, p. 15.

70. Clipping, April 1, 1947, in PPFA.

71. Cannon, *Outline for Course*, p. 15; see also Van der Veer, "Unwanted Child"; Menninger, "Psychiatric Aspects"; Coghill, "Emotional Maladjustments"; and Margaret Ribble, M.D., *The Rights of Infants* (New York: Columbia University Press, 1943), Chapter 1.

72. Rhoda J. Milliken, speech of January 22, 1947, in PPFA.

73. Loth, "Planned Parenthood," p. 97.

74. Personal interview with Dr. Regine Stix, Boston, Mass., May 5, 1975; Carl N. Degler, "What Ought to Be and What Was: Woman's Sexuality in the Nineteenth Century," *American Historical Review*, Winter 1974, pp. 1467–90.

75. Letter of June 14, 1916 in Stokes mss., Tamiment Library, NYU; many similar others in same collection.

76. HHH memorandum to Sanger, March 1924, in Sanger, LC.

77. Draft description of Marriage Advice Bureau, October 17, 1931, in Sanger, Smith.

78. Sanger to Bobby Walls of Tarrant, Ala., March 7, 1924, in Sanger, LC.

79. Sanger to Lydia Wentworth of Brookline, Mass., April 30, 1935, in Sanger, Smith.

80. Sanger to Ethelwyn Martz of Bloomfield, N.J., March 1, 1935, in Sanger, LC.

81. Sanger to Sam Voyner of Alberta, Canada, June 1, 1937, in Sanger, Smith.

82. Marie E. Kopp, *Birth Control in Practice: Analysis of Ten Thousand Case Histories of the Birth Control Clinical Research Bureau* (New York: McBride, 1934), pp. 101–103.

83. For example, see staff meeting minutes and case histories, February 1932 ff., in Sanger, Smith.

84. Robert Latou Dickinson, "Premarital Consultation," *Journal of the American Medical Association* 117 (November 15, 1941): 1687–92.

85. Case histories in Sanger, Smith.

86. For example: Klein memorandum to Rose, December 31, 1942; report of discussion at ABCL annual meeting, January 26, 1938, report dated February 21, 1938; both in PPFA.

87. C. C. Pierce report on conference with Dr. John Favill, February 16, 1943, in PPFA.

88. Numerous drafts and the final version of this statement are in PPFA, Box 41; all the following comments on the program are taken from this statement.

89. Report on BCFA Postgraduate Institute on Clinic Procedures held at Margaret Sanger Research Bureau, February 1940, in PPFA. Levine considered marriage counseling, premarital advice, sex education, and cancer detection all by-products of the birth-control movement.

90. Abraham and Hannah M. Stone, *Marital Maladjustments*, reprinted from *The Cyclopedia of Medicine, Surgery and Specialties* (Philadelphia: E. A. Davis, 1940), PPFA pamphlet, p. 821.

91. Ibid.

92. Transcripts of group-marriage-counseling sessions are in Sanger, Smith. See session of May 15, 1947.

93. Sanger, *Happiness in Marriage* (New York: Brentano's, 1926), pp. 60–63.

94. Ibid., pp. 99–100.

95. Ibid., passim.

96. Hannah and Abraham Stone, *A Marriage Manual* ([1935] New York: Simon and Schuster, 1939), pp. 203–204.

97. Abraham Stone and Lena Levine, "Group Therapy in Sexual Maladjustment," draft, n.d., in Sanger, Smith.

98. Ibid., p. 3.

99. Ibid.

100. Transcript of group session of February 6, 1947, p. 2.
101. Session of May 15, 1947.
102. Stone and Levine draft article, p. 7.
103. Session of March 13, 1947.
104. January 30, 1947.
105. April 24, 1947.
106. May 8, 1947, for example.
107. March 20, 1947.
108. December 26, 1946, for example.
109. For example: Helena Wright, *The Sex Factor in Marriage* (New York: Vanguard Press, 1931), p. 91; H. W. Long, *Sane Sex Life & Sane Sex Living* ([1919] New York: Eugenics Publications, 1937), Chapter 8; William J. Fielding, *Sex and the Love-Life* (Garden City, N.Y.: Blue Ribbon Books, 1927), Chapter 7.
110. Session of March 20, 1947; see also January 16, 1947, and November 7, 1946, for examples.
111. Wardell B. Pomeroy, *Dr. Kinsey and the Institute for Sex Research* (New York: Harper & Row, 1972), p. 169. Note that Kinsey and Stone were nevertheless warm acquaintances and that Stone gave Kinsey data from the birth-control clinic.
112. Stone and Stone, *Marital Maladjustments*, p. 827.
113. Session of December 5, 1946.
114. January 30, 1947, and December 12, 1946.
115. October 24, 1946.
116. December 26, 1946.
117. October 24, 1946, for example.
118. Stone and Stone, *Marital Maladjustments*, p. 824.
119. December 5, 1946.
120. February 27, 1947.
121. Entry of February 24, 1932. Sanger, Smith.
122. Entry of February 10, 1932, ibid.
123. Session of February 27, 1947.
124. Emily Mudd, "Counseling in Relation to the Clinic Patient," paper given to Clinic Session, BCFA Annual Meeting, January 30, 1942, mimeograph for press, in PPFA.
125. For example: Katherine Bement Davis, *Factors in the Sex Life of Twenty-Two Hundred Women* (New York: Harper & Brothers, 1929); Alfred C. Kinsey, Wardell B. Pomeroy, Clyde E. Martin, Paul H. Gebhard, *Sexual Behavior in the Human Female* (Philadelphia: W. B. Saunders, 1953).

Chapter 13. A Note on Population Control

1. Paul Ehrlich's *The Population Bomb* took its title from this pamphlet.
2. Population Policy Panel of the Hugh Moore Fund, *The Population Bomb*, pamphlet, 12th edition, 1965, p. 3.
3. FAO release 71/8, January 28, 1971.
4. For an excellent discussion of this phenomenon in China, see Jan Myrdal, "The Reshaping of Chinese Society," in *Contemporary China*, ed. Ruth Adams (New York: Pantheon, 1966), pp. 65–91.
5. This example cited by Hans Magnus Enzensberger in his excellent "Critique of Political Ecology," *New Left Review*, no. 84 (March–April 1974): 16.

6. Milbank Memorial Fund, *International Approaches to Problems of Underdeveloped Areas* (New York: Milbank, 1948), text of a roundtable conference of 1947.

7. This and all following information about the personnel and financing of the population-control groups are taken from the annual reports of these groups and from *Who's Who*. For a fuller discussion of eugenics/population-control unity, see my articles in *Radical America* 8, no. 4 (July–August 1974), and the *International Journal of Health Services* 5, no. 2 (Fall 1975).

8. Kingsley Davis, Clyde Kiser, Frank Notestein, Frank Lorimer, P. K. Whelpton, and Allan Guttmacher. Dudley Kirk, demographic director, and Warren Nelson, medical director, also came from eugenics work.

9. Guy Burch to Norman Himes, August 24, 1934, Himes mss., Countway Library, Harvard University Medical School.

10. Burch to Himes, June 30, 1930, and Burch letter in *Washington Post*, May 1, 1939, both in Himes mss.

11. Steve Weissman, "Why the Population Bomb Is a Rockefeller Baby," *Ramparts*, May 1970.

12. Miscellaneous papers, Dorothy Brush mss., Sophia Smith Collection, Smith College Library.

13. *New York Times*, May 11, 1969.

14. William Barclay, Joseph Enright, and Reid T. Reynolds, "The Social Context of U.S. Population Control Programs in the Third World," paper presented to the Population Association of America, April 17, 1970.

15. J. Mayone Stycos, "Latin American Family Planning in the 1970s," in Stycos, ed., *Clinics, Contraception, and Communication* (New York: Appleton-Century-Crofts, 1973), pp. 17–22.

16. For example: Kingsley Davis, "Population Policy: Will Current Programs Succeed?" *Science* 158, no. 3802 (November 10, 1967); Shirley Foster Hartley, *Population Quantity vs. Quality* (Englewood Cliffs, N.J.: Prentice-Hall, 1972), Chapter 11, "Possibilities: Family Planning or Population Control?"

17. *New York Times*, October 24, 1971.

18. The following generalizations about the use of incentive payments are taken from International Planned Parenthood Federation Working Paper no. 4, *Incentive Payments*, pamphlet, n.d., probably early 1970s. This report covered the seven countries listed, but there are undoubtedly others that also use incentive payments in their population-control programs.

19. Sharon Lieberman, "The Politics of Population Control," reporting statistics of 1974 HEW study, *Majority Report*, May 31, 1975, p. 14.

20. *Wall Street Journal*, August 7, 1971.

21. Some supporters of population control tried to claim that the conference had been a victory for them, on the grounds that the Plan was passed and that the conference took place without disruption. In this view they were trying to make the best of a bad situation. For example, Frederick Jaffe in "Bucharest: The Tests Are Yet to Come," *Family Planning Perspectives*, publication of the Planned Parenthood Federation of America, 6, no. 4 (Fall 1974), commented: "The principal thrust of the changes voted at Bucharest was to place relatively greater emphasis on economic and social development and international equity . . . and relatively less emphasis on efforts to reduce population growth. . . . There was sufficient opposition to the idea of population policy targets to delete the tentative language in the draft suggesting quantitative goals related to fertility decline."

22. Mahmood Mamdani, *The Myth of Population Control* (New York: Monthly Review, 1972).

23. For example, women are sometimes not informed of the irreversibility of the operation, or contraceptive methods are not offered as alternatives in encouraging terms. Consent forms for sterilization may be given to women just after abortions or childbirth. Cases of forced sterilization revealed in court testimony seem to represent just the tip of an iceberg. For example, judges in Pasadena and Santa Barbara have offered women charged with misdemeanors the choice of jail or sterilization. (Houston, Texas *Chronicle*, May 22, 1966; Santa Barbara *News Press*, July 13, 1965.) The Committee on Law and Family Planning of the American Bar Association recommended that "discouragement of further childbearing by welfare mothers be recognized as a deliberate goal in welfare programming. . . ." (*Harvard Law Review* 85, no. 8 [June 1971].) The states of California, Delaware, Georgia,

Illinois, Iowa, Louisiana, Maryland, Mississippi, North Carolina, and Virginia have considered laws in the last decade making it a felony to parent repeated "illegitimate" children and offering sterilization as an alternative to other punishment. ("The Return of Punitive Sterilization Proposals—Current Attacks on Illegitimacy and the AFDC Program," *Law and Society Review* 3, no. 1 [August 1968]: 87.) For a good journalistic view of the problem, see Claudia Dreifus, "Sterilizing the Poor," *The Progressive*, December 1975, pp. 13–19.

Index